Consumer Behaviour and Marketing Strategy

Consumer Behaviour and Marketing Strategy

J. PAUL PETER
University of Wisconsin, Madison

JERRY C. OLSON
Pennsylvania State University

KLAUS G. GRUNERT
The Aarhus School of Business

McGraw-Hill Publishing Company

London · Burr Ridge IL · New York · St Louis · San Francisco · Auckland Bogotá · Caracas · Lisbon Madrid · Mexico · Milan Montreal · New Delhi · Panama Paris · San Juan São Paulo · Singapore · Sydney · Tokyo Toronto

Published by
McGraw-Hill Publishing Company
Shoppenhangers Road,
Maidenhead,
Berkshire,
SL6 2QL,
England
Telephone 01628 23432
Facsimile 01628 770224

Further information on this and other McGraw-Hill titles is to be found at
http://www.mcgraw-hill.co.uk/textbooks/grunert

A catalogue record for this book is available from the British Library

ISBN 0 256 22529 X

Publisher: Alfred Waller
Desk Editor: Alastair Lindsay

Created for McGraw-Hill by the independent production company
Steven Gardiner Ltd TEL +44 (0)1223 364868 FAX +44 (0)1223 364875

McGraw-Hill

A Division of The **McGraw·Hill** *Companies*

1 2 3 4 5 IPM 2 1 0 9 8

Printed and bound in Malta by Interprint Ltd.

Contents in Brief

Contents

Preface

Consumer behaviour is a core topic in marketing curricula at universities and business schools around the world. In the vast majority of cases, teaching is based on North American textbooks. While many principles of consumer behaviour are probably universal and therefore applicable both in North America, Europe, and elsewhere, the use of North American textbooks outside North America bores students with examples they cannot relate to, presents with them views of culture and other social factors they cannot relate to, and presents consumer behaviour as a topic the academic basis of which stems almost exclusively from the United States. Most larger (France, Germany, United Kingdom) and a few smaller (Denmark, The Netherlands) European countries have their own national consumer behaviour texts, but there is a dearth of a truly European treatment.

This book is an adaptation of what I believe is presently the best consumer textbook in the world to the European context. *Consumer Behaviour and Marketing Strategy* by Peter and Olson has been around for some years and has been quite successful in Europe, even though it is a North American book. The reasons are probably many, but here are some I believe are particularly true in Europe. The Peter and Olson book retains a solid academic orientation even though it contains a wealth of examples and practical applications. It has an academically and pedagogically sound structure. It is probably the only textbook in the area which gives a balanced treatment of cognitive and behavioural approaches to the analysis of consumer behaviour.

In adapting the book to the European context, I have tried to retain all the strengths of the original version while adding a European flavour. Throughout the book, I have checked and mostly replaced examples, highlights, opening stories, and strategy-in-action cases. Throughout the book I have added references to European consumer behaviour research, and I have adapted the text to the different European marketing environment whenever appropriate. Apart from that, Sections 1 and 2 of the present book, containing the introductory chapters and the chapters on consumer affect and cognition, largely follow the original formula. In Section 3, which contains the treatment of behavioural approaches to the analysis of consumer behaviour, I have tried to integrate the distinctive European research done in this area (mainly in Germany and the United Kingdom), and to improve the linkage between Sections 2 and 3 of the book. This has resulted in a complete rewriting of Chapter 8, and some changes in the rest of the section. Section 4, dealing with environmental aspects, has undergone major changes mainly in Chapters 13 and 14 dealing with culture and subculture. Section 5, dealing with applications of consumer behaviour theory to marketing strategy, has been adapted to European conditions, and Chapter 21 has been written from scratch.

I owe considerable thanks to research assistants Helle Alsted Søndergaard and Rikke Gade Therkildsen for their help in finding and researching European examples, and to secretary Birgitte Steffensen for her work with processing text and illustrations. I also would like to thank the reviewers of the text for their constructive and encouraging comments. I will be most interested in reactions from users of the text both in Europe and elsewhere.

Klaus G. Grunert
The Aarhus School of Business
Aarhus, Denmark

Special thanks go to the reviewers who for this edition were:

Professor Fleming Hansen, Department of Marketing, Copenhagen Business School, Denmark
Professor Simon Knox, School of Management, Cranfield University, UK
I. C. M. van Kooten, Department of Marketing, Free University of Amsterdam, The Netherlands
Dr Lyndon Simkin, Warwick Business School, Warwick University, UK
Darrach Turley, DIT College of Marketing & Design, Ireland
Dr Gillian Wright, Management Centre, Bradford University, UK

A Perspective on Consumer Behaviour

Consumer Affect and Cognition

Consumer Environment

Consumer Behaviour

Introduction to Consumer Behaviour and Marketing Strategy

Staying Close to the Customers: Lessons from IKEA

In the 1990s, companies worldwide have increasingly realized that satisfying consumers with quality products and offering superior customer service is the foundation for success in the highly competitive, international business world.

Retailers, who are particularly close to customers must move especially fast to adapt to local peculiarities. One of the companies which has learnt this lesson the hard way is the Swedish furniture retailer IKEA in connection with their entry into the American market.

IKEA's formula is based on reinventing the furniture-retailing business. Traditionally, selling furniture was a fragmented affair, shared between department stores and small, family-owned shops. All sold expensive products for delivery up to two months after a customer's order. IKEA's approach trims costs to a minimum while still offering service. IKEA displays its enormous range of more than 10 000 products in cheap out-of-town outlets. It sells most of its furniture as knocked-down kits, for customers to take home and assemble themselves. An IKEA store, with its Scandinavian café, is supposed to be a complete shopping destination for value-conscious, car-borne consumers.

The company experienced much success in Western Europe with its vast out-of-town warehouse stores decked out in Sweden's blue and yellow colours, and in the mid-1980s the company headed for the highly competitive American retail market.

The company set up its first store in the USA in 1985, but by 1989 the American operation seemed to be in deep trouble. Why, then, did this successful and apparently flexible system hit problems in America?

Many people visited the American stores, looked at the furniture, and left empty-handed. Customers complained of long queues and constant nonavailability of stock. IKEA thought it could sell the same products in the same way in Houston as it could in Helsingborg. However, European products jarred with American tastes and sometimes physiques: Swedish beds were narrow and measured in centimetres – not in inches. IKEA did not sell the matching bedroom suites that Americans liked. Its kitchen cupboards were too narrow for the large dinner plates needed for pizza and its glasses were too small for a nation that piles them high with ice. IKEA realized that Americans were buying the firm's flower vases as glasses.

So IKEA's managers decided to adapt. Because Americans hate queuing, the firm installed new cash registers that increased the speed of throughput by 20 per cent, and altered store layout. IKEA now offers a more generous return policy in America than in Europe, and a next-day delivery service. The firm now sells king- and queen-sized beds, in inches, as part of complete suites. After noticing that customers were inspecting IKEA's bedroom chests and then walking away without buying, they worked out that because Americans use them to store sweaters in, they wanted the drawers in the chests to be an inch or two deeper. Sales of the chests immediately increased by 30–40 per cent. In all, IKEA has redefined around a fifth of its product range in America; its kitchen units are next on the list.

Source: 'Management Brief: Furnishing the World', © *The Economist*, London, 19 November 1994, pp. 83–84.

IKEA thought that its successful European strategy could be exported to the United States. They did not realize that customers on the US market were different. Put another way, they were not *market oriented*.

Market orientation has been defined as

> the organizationwide generation of market intelligence, pertaining to current and future customer needs, dissemination of the intelligence across departments, and organization-wide responsiveness to it.[1]

Market orientation has been shown to be a major factor in determining business success.[2] Companies who regularly generate information about their customers and use it as a basis for their organizational behaviour are doing consistently better than companies which do that to a lesser degree.

But who are a company's customers? For a company like IKEA, it is clear that their customers are consumers. But most companies manufacturing consumer goods do not sell directly to consumers. When asked about who their customers are, they would probably name retailers, wholesalers, agents, exporters, importers and other manufacturers – but not consumers.

Still, the consumer is the one who makes final decisions about whether a product or service is good or bad. Suppliers of raw material, manufacturers, retailers are all part of a *value chain* the purpose of which is to fulfil consumer needs. The price the consumer is willing to pay for a product or service is the limit of the earnings of all members in the value chain, as shown in Exhibit 1.1.

Successful companies have realized this and are market oriented not only with regard to their immediate customers, but also with regard to consumers. They continuously try to understand and analyse consumers as their final customers, and use this information, together with information about their immediate customers, to guide their organizational behaviour.

Many of the most successful companies in the world have become so by designing their entire organizations to serve consumers and stay close to them. These companies are committed to developing quality products and services and selling them at a price that gives consumers high value. In these companies, the marketing department and also design, engineering, production, human resources, finance, and other departments are focused on doing their jobs in ways that enhance the value of products to consumers. Some firms have found they can actually increase product quality and reduce costs at the same time, and they encourage employees throughout the company to seek ways to do so. Other firms first determine what consumers want and how much they are willing to pay for a product and then design, produce, and market the best-quality product possible for the price consumers are willing to pay. Exhibit 1.2 discusses four companies that owe their survival and success to focusing on consumers.

EXHIBIT 1.1

Consumers and the Value Chain

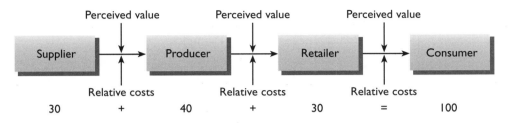

Companies are making changes to serve consumers better for three major reasons. First, the increasing international competition, and especially the dramatic success of Japanese companies, such as Toyota and Sony, that focus on providing consumers with value-laden products has spurred other companies to do so as well. During the 1960s and 1970s, many European and US companies could sell almost anything they produced. Consumers accepted the level of quality of goods and services produced as being as good as could be expected. However, increasing international competition has made consumers much more critical with regard to the value they get for their money. Many European and US companies had to redesign their organizations to serve consumers in order to survive and compete in world markets.

The second major reason for the shift to focusing on consumers is the dramatic increase in the quality of consumer and marketing research. In the past, companies often did not have detailed information on the actual purchasers and users of their products. While they did research to investigate new product concepts and to try to understand consumers, often this research was not continuous and did not identify the firm's actual customers. Today, it is possible for companies to know personally who their customers are and the effects on them of marketing strategy and changes in it. Both manufacturers and retailers can now carefully track consumer reactions to new products and services and evaluate marketing strategies better than ever before. Thus, companies are now better able to actually become market oriented. Highlight 1.1 offers several examples of databases developed by companies aiding them in performing these tasks.

A third reason for the increased emphasis on consumers is the development of consumer behaviour research. Both the number and sophistication of theories, concepts, and models to describe and understand consumer behaviour have grown dramatically in recent years. While there is no consensus on which theories or approaches are the best ones, marketers do have a greater variety of useful ideas for understanding consumers than they did in the past.

In sum, many successful companies have recognized the importance of consumers, and have sophisticated approaches and detailed data from which to develop organizational and marketing strategies. All of this should convince you that the consumer behaviour course you are about to take is an important part of your business education. In the remainder of this chapter, we will discuss the nature of consumer behaviour and the parties involved in studying and analysing it. We will also investigate some

EXHIBIT 1.2

Getting Close and Staying Close to Customers

 eading companies owe their success and profitability to designing the organization to stay close to customers. Below are a few examples.

Harley-Davidson

By the early 1980s, Japanese motorcycle manufacturers dominated the market. The Japanese bikes were more sophisticated, of better quality, and cheaper than Harelips. Harley-Davidson was days away from filing for bankruptcy by the end of 1985. However, it got refinanced and continued to work hard to improve the quality of its motorcycles through bettering the design, getting employees more committed to quality, working with dealers, and interacting continuously with consumers to get feedback on its products and ideas for improvements. By 1990, Harley-Davidson dominated the superheavyweight motorcycle market with a market share of over 62 per cent in the United States. Although Harley-Davidson has never dominated the superheavyweight motorcycle market in Europe the brand has also experienced a renaissance here where market share reached 10.9 per cent in 1995.

Dell Computers

In 1996, the American computer company Dell achieved the highest growth rate in Europe for personal business computers. Dell tailors the computers to their customers' personal demands, and sells and delivers directly to the customers. Their success is based on the flexibility achieved by producing to order; customers specify the computer they want and Dell manufactures them at their production plant in Ireland. Customer service includes an emergency agreement, where the customer is guaranteed delivery of a similar solution within three working days if they lose their computers and servers in, for example, a fire. Dell also runs ongoing customer panels with the aim of communicating to the company which of the new technologies they should include in their computers.

Nike

While there are many strong competitors in the sports shoe market, Nike is at the top. In 1996, sales jumped to $6.4 billion and profits reached $553 million worldwide. The company sells over 800 models for use in about 25 sports. In 1990, it developed three lines of basketball shoes, each expressing what Nike calls a different attitude. The Air Jordan is for consumers who want to follow in the footsteps of the Chicago Bulls superstar. The Flight is for players who value the lightest Nikes, while the Force incorporates the latest designs, such as a custom air bladder, for consumers who want a snug fit. The company updates its shoes at least every six months to tempt new customers to lace on new pairs before last year's wear out. By carefully segmenting the market, coming out with frequent innovations and style changes, and continually researching to develop the most effective and stylish athletic shoes, Nike offers quality products that consumers want.

Financial Supermarkets

Via loyalty cards leading British retailers have introduced a new way of competing for customers, giving the term financial supermarkets a whole new meaning. The British supermarket giant Tesco has introduced a Clubcard Plus which gives loyal customers discounts on their shopping. Additionally, customers with the new card get a 5 per cent interest on deposits, which is ten times more than many banks offer and as an extra service they can draw cash with the card in National Westminster Bank's cash dispensers throughout the country.

Sources: John Kekis, 'Business Rev Charges Harley after Long Slump', *Wisconsin State Journal*, 1 June 1991, p. 6B; Erik Calonius, 'Smart Moves by Quality Champs', *Fortune*, 1991, pp. 24–28; Jan Horsager, 'Skræddersyede PCere der øger markedsandele', *Børsen*, 30 September 1996, p. 6; Heidi Amsinck, 'Finansielle Supermarkeder på en ny måde', *Børsen*, 7 August 1996, p. 18.

relationships between consumer behaviour and marketing strategy and the value of this course for a successful career. While this text focuses on consumer behaviour and marketing strategy, it should be kept in mind that employees in every business function should be involved in serving consumers.

What Is Consumer Behaviour?

Consumer behaviour can be defined as 'the dynamic interaction of affect and cognition, behaviour, and environmental events by which human beings conduct the exchange aspects of their lives'.[3] There are at least three important ideas in this definition: (1) consumer behaviour is dynamic; (2) it involves interaction between affect and cognition, behaviour, and environmental events; and (3) it involves exchange.

Consumer Behaviour Is Dynamic

First, the definition emphasizes that consumer behaviour is dynamic. This means individual consumers, consumer groups, and society at large are constantly changing and evolving over time. This has important implications for the study of consumer behaviour as well as for developing marketing strategies. In terms of studying consumer behaviour, one implication is that generalizations about consumer behaviour are usually limited to specific periods of time, products, and individuals or groups. Thus, students of consumer behaviour must be careful not to overgeneralize theories and research findings.

In terms of developing marketing strategies, the dynamic nature of consumer behaviour implies that one should not expect the same marketing strategy to work all the time across all products, markets, and industries. While this may seem obvious, many companies have failed to recognize the need to adapt their strategies in different markets. For example, in the mid-1980s, Kellogg, a US food company, tried to launch its successful Nutragrain cereal into the UK market. It failed dismally. Kellogg had not spotted that British consumers lagged Americans in health consciousness. Kao, a Japanese producer of soaps and personal care products, assumed Europeans thought like the Japanese when it tried selling soaps and personal hygiene products as if they were functional items, rather than exotic and premium goods.

Further, a strategy that is successful at one point may fail miserably at another point. For example, Philips had no success in marketing their Laservision system (which used a laser beam to produce television pictures) as the successor to video cassette recorders. Customers regarded the new system as too complex a product, and the inability of the laser disc to record was seen as a deficiency in the eyes of many customers. In sum, it is the dynamic nature of consumer behaviour that makes marketing strategy development such an exciting, yet challenging, task.

HIGHLIGHT 1.1

Database Marketing

M any companies have developed extensive databases that allow them to target individual consumers. Here are a few of them.

Nestlé chose to launch a new pasta product through the post rather than through television. It is cheaper for them to develop a database of the right socioeconomic profile of pasta-eaters than it is to promote via television.

Unilever uses database marketing to target their loyal customers, trying to make loyalty last. In Sweden, they are creating a database with users of their Organics shampoo on the basis of participants in a recent competition. They have also sent out samples of a new Dove sensitive creme douche to target segments in order to create awareness.

Porsche has set up an integrated system where callers to a telephone service, asking questions about Porsche cars, spare parts or just general technical details, are registered in a central databank. Data on callers with the right sociodemographic and psychographic characteristics, those who could be potential customers, are then passed on to Porsche dealers for use in future marketing.

Esprit, a company which designs, manufactures and retails fashion clothes, uses its database to send out catalogues four to six times a year as an integrated part of direct marketing.

Sources: Nick Kochan, 'Smart Strategies for the 1990s', *Crossborder*, Winter 1994, p. 25; 'Flair versus Science', *The Economist*, 25 February 1995, p. 71; telephone interview with Elida Robert, Unilever; Karin Seitel, 'Lifestyle mit Dialogangebot', *Direkt Marketing*, 30, no. 10, 1994, pp. 6–9; Per Press, *Kæder i Dansk detailhandel*, Stockmann-Gruppen A/S, 1995, pp. 28–29.

Consumer Behaviour Involves Interactions

A second important point emphasized in the definition of consumer behaviour is that it involves interactions between affect and cognition, behaviour, and environmental events. This means that to understand consumers and develop superior marketing strategies, we must understand what they think (cognition) and feel (affect), what they do (behaviour), and the things and places (environmental events) that influence and are influenced by what consumers think, feel, and do. Whether we are evaluating a single consumer, a target market, or an entire society, analysis of all three elements is useful for understanding and developing marketing strategies.

Consumer Behaviour Involves Exchanges

A final point emphasized in the definition of consumer behaviour is that it involves exchanges between human beings. This makes the definition of consumer behaviour consistent with current definitions of marketing that also emphasize exchange. In fact, the role of marketing is to create exchanges with consumers by formulating and implementing marketing strategies.

Approaches to Consumer Behaviour Research

Two broad groups are interested in consumer behaviour – a basic research group and an action-oriented group. The basic research group is mainly composed of academic researchers interested in studying consumer behaviour as a way of developing a unique body of knowledge about this aspect of human behaviour. These researchers have backgrounds in anthropology, sociology, psychology, economics, and marketing, as well as other fields. The majority of published work on consumer behaviour is basic research, and this work forms the foundation of our text.

Because researchers dealing with consumer behaviour have different backgrounds, the way in which they analyse consumer behaviour, the topics they concentrate on, the kind of theories they develop, and the kind of research methods they employ differ as well. Some consumer research is very qualitative, with an emphasis on understanding a particular consumption event, a particular family's consumer behaviour, or the success of a particular brand based on the context in which these phenomena occur and on the history leading up to the occurrence of the phenomenon. Other consumer research concentrates on finding regularities in consumer behaviour that apply in a broad variety of contexts across time and space, such as the effect of personal involvement in a purchase, on information seeking behaviour or the effect of sales promotions on shopping behaviour in supermarkets.

Consumer research in the United States, which has been very influential in the international academic community, has for a long time concentrated on finding regularities in consumer behaviour and has only more recently begun to study single phenomena in more detail. European consumer research has always been more diverse and pluralistic, and both approaches have been applied.

It is important to realize that good consumer research involves both the understanding of single phenomena and of common regularities governing consumer behaviour. To come up with a good, general explanation of why consumers become brand loyal requires an understanding of a number of concrete cases of brand loyalty, or lack of the same, in some detail. We can then extract some common characteristics and try to formulate more general statements about the determinants of brand loyalty.

Uses of Consumer Research

As shown in Exhibit 1.3, the action-oriented group can be divided into three constituencies: (1) marketing organizations, (2) government and political organizations, and (3) consumers. Each of these is interested in consumer behaviour not just for the sake of knowledge, but for using this knowledge to influence the other constituencies. The first of these is the marketing organizations. These include not only what are conventionally thought of as business firms, but also other organizations such as hospitals, museums, law firms, and universities. Thus, marketing organizations include all groups that have a market offering and are seeking exchanges with consumers. While the primary focus of our text is on relationships between marketing strategy and consumers from the perspective of business firms, the ideas we present can also be applied to other marketing organizations, such as the Red Cross or your university.

The second group in Exhibit 1.3 comprises various government and political organizations. These include government organizations monitoring and regulating exchanges between marketing organizations and consumers, such as regulating advertising,

EXHIBIT 1.3

Relationships among Action-oriented Groups Interested in Consumer Behaviour

prescribing product labelling, and watching out for unfair business practices. Political constituencies include consumers, consumer associations, and special interest groups like antismoking leagues. These relationships are not the major concern of our text, but they are considered, particularly in Chapter 21.

The third group in Exhibit 1.3 includes both individual consumers and organizational buyers who exchange resources for various goods and services. Their interest in consumer behaviour is primarily to make exchanges that help them achieve their goals. Although the major concern of our text is with ultimate consumers, the logic presented here can be applied in organizational markets, and several examples of organizational buyer behaviour are discussed later in the text.

The Relationship between Consumer Behaviour and Marketing Strategy

From the viewpoint of marketing organizations, a **marketing strategy** is a plan designed to influence exchanges to achieve organizational objectives. Typically, a marketing strategy is intended to increase the probability or frequency of consumer behaviours, such as frequenting particular stores or purchasing particular products. This is accomplished by developing and presenting marketing mixes directed at selected target markets. A marketing mix consists of product, promotion, distribution, and pricing elements.

In Exhibit 1.4 we present some consumer behaviour issues involved in developing various aspects of marketing strategy. Issues such as these can be addressed through formal marketing research, informal discussions with consumers, or intuition and thinking about the relationships between consumer behaviour and marketing strategy.

Exhibit 1.4 shows that understanding consumers is a critical element in developing marketing strategies. Very few – if any – strategy decisions do not involve consideration of consumer behaviour. For example, analysis of the competition requires an

EXHIBIT 1.4

Examples of Consumer Issues Involved in Developing Marketing Strategy

Strategy Element	Consumer Issues
Segmentation	Which consumers are the prime prospects for our product?
	What consumer characteristics should we use to segment the market for our product?
Product	What products do consumers use now?
	What benefits do consumers want from this product?
Promotion	What promotion appeal would influence consumers to purchase and use our product?
	What advertising claims would be most effective for our product?
Pricing	How important is price to consumers in various target markets?
	What effects will a price change have on purchase behaviour?
Distribution	Where do consumers buy this product?
	Would a different distribution system change consumers' purchasing behaviour?

understanding of what consumers think and feel about competitive products, which consumers buy these products and why, and in what situations consumers purchase and use competitive products. In sum, the more you learn about consumers (and approaches to analysing them), the better your chances for developing successful marketing strategies. Highlight 1.2 offers some tips for developing marketing strategies.

Finally, it should be clear that marketing strategies, particularly as developed and implemented by successful corporations, exert a powerful force on consumers and society at large. We believe that marketing strategies not only adapt to consumers, but also change what consumers think and feel about themselves, about various market offerings, and about the appropriate situations for product purchase and use. This does not mean marketing is unethical or an inappropriate activity. However, the power of marketing and the ability of marketing research and consumer analysis to gain insight into consumer behaviour should not be discounted or misused.

Back to . . . IKEA

Regardless of whether you like IKEA's Scandinavian furniture style, it is clear that IKEA has succeeded in moving closer to the American customer. By altering store layout, installing new cash registers, offering a generous return policy and next-day delivery service, and redefining its product range to suit the tastes of its American customers IKEA has created a marketing strategy which has proven successful in the American market.

In terms of sales and profits, IKEA's American operation is finally booming. Since 1990 sales have tripled to $480 million and in 1992 the company finally made a profit in America. In October 1994 it opened its thirteenth American store and two more are under development. Apparently, IKEA has finally understood that profitable marketing strategies depend on staying close to the customers.

HIGHLIGHT 1.2

Tips for Being a Successful Marketer

 now Your Customers

Consumer goods companies are using high-tech techniques to find out who their customers are – and aren't. By linking that knowledge with data about ads they can fine-tune their marketing.

Make What They Want

In an age of diversity, products must be tailored to individual tastes. So where once there was just Stimorol chewing gum, there is now Stimorol sugar free and worldwide 30 variants of Stimorol, too.

Use Targeted and New Media

Companies aiming for micromarkets are advertising on TV and in magazines to reach special audiences.

Use Nonmedia

Marketers are sponsoring sports, festivals, and other events to reach local markets. In sports, golf, football, tennis, and sailing are popular. For example, in 1996 British Telecom sponsored an amateur round-the-world yacht race.

Reach Customers in the Store

Consumers make most buying decisions while they're shopping. So marketers are putting ads on supermarket loudspeakers, shopping trolleys, and in-store videos.

Sharpen Your Promotions

Price promotions are expensive and often harmful to a brand's image. Thanks to better data, some companies are using fewer, more effective promotions. One promising approach: Aiming promotions at a competitor's customers.

Work with Retailers

Consumer goods manufacturers must learn to 'micromarket' to the retail trade, too. Some link their computers to the retailers' computers, and some are tailoring their marketing and promotions to an individual retailer's needs.

Source: Adapted from Zachary Schiller, 'Stalking the New Consumer',
Business Week, 28 August 1989, p. 54.

Summary

In this chapter, we argued that consumer behaviour is an important topic in business education because achieving marketing objectives depends on knowing, serving, and influencing consumers. We discussed the nature of consumer behaviour and the various groups interested in the topic. We also discussed the relationships between consumer behaviour and marketing strategy. We hope that after reading this chapter you can now appreciate the relevance and importance of a consumer behaviour course for your business education. We also hope you will learn something about yourself by considering how the analytic framework and information in our text applies to you as a potential marketing manager, a consumer, and a human being.

Key Terms and Concepts

consumer behaviour   1
market orientation   4
marketing strategy   10

Review and Discussion Questions

1. Why is consumer behaviour an important course in business education?
2. Do you think marketing is a powerful force in society? Why or why not?
3. What is the role of consumer analysis in developing marketing strategies?
4. Offer three examples of situations in which a marketing strategy influenced your purchase behaviour. Why did each succeed over competitive strategies?
5. Using Exhibit 1.4 as a takeoff point, discuss other questions and decisions in marketing strategy that could be affected by your study of consumer behaviour.
6. Select a market segment of which you are not a member and, with other students in the class, discuss the kinds of information you would need to develop a strategy aimed at that segment.

Additional Reading

For more information on the market orientation concept and how it affects business performance, see:

Angelika Dreher, 'Marketing Orientation: How To Grasp The Phenomenon', in *Perspectives On Marketing Management*, vol. 4, ed. Michael J. Baker (Chichester: Wiley, 1994), pp. 149–170.

Bernard J. Jaworski and Ajay K. Kohli, 'Market Orientation: Antecedents and Consequences', *Journal of Marketing*, July 1993, pp. 53–79.

For insightful discussions of the role of consumers in developing marketing strategies, see:

George S. Day, *Market Driven Strategies: Processes for Creating Value* (New York: Free Press, 1990).

Al Ries and Jack Trout, *Bottom-Up Marketing* (New York: McGraw-Hill, 1989).

MARKETING STRATEGY IN ACTION
Toyota

f all the slogans kicked around Toyota, the key one is *kaizen*, which means 'continuous improvement' in Japanese. While many other companies strive for dramatic breakthrough, Toyota keeps doing lots of little things better and better. Consider the subcompact Tercel, the smallest Toyota sold in 1990. While this model contributes only modestly to profits, Toyota made the 1991 Tercel faster, roomier, and quieter than its predecessor – with less weight, equally good mileage, and, remarkably, the same competitive price for the basic four-door saloon car.

One consultant calls Toyota's strategy 'rapid inch-up': Take enough tiny steps and soon you outdistance the competition. By introducing six all-new vehicles within 14 months, Toyota grabbed a crushing 43 per cent share of car sales in Japan. In the United States it is pressing to move up from its number 4 position in the market; it is the number 3 carmaker in the world market. In Europe, Toyota's market shares range from less than 1 per cent in France, Italy, and Spain, where national carmakers are strong, to around 10 per cent in most of the Scandinavian countries, Ireland, and Greece. In the latter markets, Toyota is among the top two or three carmakers.

The company has the highest operating margins in the world car industry and is so rich it makes more money on financial investments than it does on operations. The company is simply tops in quality, production, and efficiency. From its factories pour a wide range of cars, built with unequalled precision. Toyota turns out luxury saloon cars with Mercedes-Benz-like quality using one-sixth the labour Mercedes does. The company originated just-in-time production and remains its leading practitioner. It has close relationships with its suppliers and rigid engineering specifications for the products it purchases.

Toyota pioneered quality circles, which involve workers in discussions of ways to improve their tasks and avoid what it calls the three D's: the dangerous, dirty, and demanding aspects of factory work. The company is investing a large amount of money to improve worker housing, add dining halls, and build new recreational facilities. On the assembly line, quality is not defined as zero defects, but as another Toyota slogan has it, 'building the very best and giving the customer what she or he wants'. Because each worker serves as the customer for the process just before hers, she becomes a quality control inspector. If a piece isn't installed properly when it reaches her, she won't accept it.

Toyota's engineering system allows it to take a new car design from concept to showroom in less than four years versus more than five years for US companies and seven years for Mercedes. This cuts costs, allows quicker correction of mistakes, and keeps Toyota better abreast of market trends. Gains from speed feed on themselves. Toyota can get its advanced engineering and design done sooner because, as one manager puts it, 'We are closer to the customer and thus have a shorter concept time'. New products are appointed to a chief engineer who has complete responsibility and authority for the product from design and manufacturing through marketing and has direct contacts with both dealers and consumers.

In Toyota's manufacturing system, parts and cars don't get built until orders come from dealers requesting them. In placing orders, dealers essentially reserve a portion of factory capacity. The system is so effective that rather than wait several months for a new car, the customer can get a built-to-order car in a week to 10 days.

Toyota is the best carmaker in the world because it stays close to its customers. 'We have learned that universal mass production is not enough', said the head of Toyota's Tokyo Design Centre. 'In the 21st century, you personalize things more to make them more reflective of individual needs.' The winners will be those who target narrow customer niches most successfully with specific models.

Discussion Questions
1. In what ways is Toyota's new-product development system designed to serve customers?
2. In what ways is Toyota's manufacturing system designed to serve customers?
3. How does Toyota personalize its cars and trucks to meet individual consumer needs?

Source: adapted from Alex Taylor III, 'Why Toyota Keeps Getting Better and Better and Better', *Fortune*, 19 November 1990, pp. 66–77. Also see William Spindle, Larry Armstrong, and James B. Treece, 'Toyota Retooled', *Business Week*, 4 April 1994, pp. 54–57. European market shares provided by Toyota Denmark.

A Framework for Consumer Analysis

Buying a Speciality Bed

Barbara Linton is 37, married, and the mother of two daughters, Joanne and Jenny, ages 7 and 9. They live in their own home in a London suburb.

One of her friends has had severe problems with her back, so much so that she hasn't been able to work for three months. The last few weeks Barbara has had a sore back herself, and the other day at work over lunch a group of colleagues discussed the problems of back aches. Barbara sits all day at her desk and is getting worried that this might be the reason for the soreness of her back, although they do have high-quality office chairs at work. She has been considering for some time what she might do in order to relieve her back apart from going to the gym once a week and taking long walks with their dog at the weekends.

Last week she saw a TV programme about the increasing occurrence of back aches among people of all ages. Apart from specialist doctors and physiotherapists the programme also included interviews with bed specialists arguing the importance of a proper mattress that is exactly matched to the individual's back. Barbara's uncle is a doctor and, although he is not a back specialist, she decides to ask him next time she sees him whether it might help her to buy a speciality bed.

One Saturday morning she can hardly get out of bed and decides to call on her uncle that same day. Her uncle tells her that as far as he can see there is nothing seriously wrong with her back, and that she may have strained it lifting something heavy. He also says that if she exercises regularly and sits properly at her desk she should be all right in the future. However, a good-quality bed may help relieve her back when she sleeps, and there is no harm in visiting one of the speciality bed shops.

The salesperson is very helpful and tells her all about the various types of bed. The main issue is to find the adequate texture or softness of the mattress which holds the spine in a straight horizontal position, since this is how the back is totally relaxed. In some mattresses the top springs are inter-changeable, which means Barbara can try a specific softness for some time before deciding on which mattress she prefers.

She purchases a semihard mattress and after a week with the new bed she feels much better, which, according to her uncle, may just have been the passing of time, and she also believes that she has done all that is possible to diminish the probability of her getting back problems in the future.

What factors are involved in the purchase made by Barbara Linton? Many theories, models, and concepts have been borrowed from other fields as well as developed by marketing researchers in attempts to understand consumer behaviour. In many cases, these ideas overlap and even compete with each other as useful descriptions of consumers. To date, no one approach is fully accepted; nor is it likely that a single, grand theory of consumer behaviour can be devised that all researchers would agree on.

However, in this chapter we present a *framework* for researching, analysing, and understanding consumers to help marketers develop more effective strategies. The framework is a general one that can be used to analyse any consumer behaviour issue facing marketers, from developing new products and services to improving strategies for existing products and services. The framework also provides the organizational structure for this book.

The chapter begins by introducing three elements that should be researched and analysed to develop effective marketing strategies. These are (1) consumer affect and cognition, (2) consumer overt behaviour, and (3) consumer environments. The special relationships among these and the role of consumer research and analysis in developing marketing strategies is then discussed. This is followed by a discussion of marketing strategy, the stimuli placed in the environment to influence consumers. The chapter concludes with a discussion of four levels of consumer analysis.

The Elements of Consumer Analysis

Exhibit 2.1 presents three elements of consumer analysis and the relationships among them. Each of the three elements is critical for developing a complete understanding of consumers and selecting strategies to influence them.

EXHIBIT 2.1

Three Elements of Consumer Analysis

Consumer Affect and Cognition

Consumer **affect** and **cognition** refer to two types of mental responses consumers have to stimuli and events in their environment. *Affect* refers to their feelings about stimuli and events, such as whether they like or dislike a product. *Cognition* refers to their thinking, such as beliefs about a particular product.

Affective responses can be favourable or unfavourable and vary in intensity. For instance, affect includes relatively intense *emotions*, such as love or anger; less strong *feeling states* such as satisfaction or frustration; moods such as boredom or relaxation, and milder overall *attitudes*, such as liking McDonald's chips or disliking Bic pens. Marketers typically develop strategies to create positive affect for their products and brands to increase the chances that consumers will buy them.

Cognition refers to the mental structures and processes involved in thinking, understanding, and interpreting stimuli and events. It includes the knowledge, meaning, and beliefs that consumers have developed from their experience and stored in their memories. It also includes the processes associated with paying attention to and understanding stimuli and events, remembering past events, forming evaluations, and making purchasing decisions and choices. While many aspects of cognition are conscious thinking processes, others are essentially automatic. Marketers often try to increase consumers' attention to products and their knowledge about them. For example, in order to increase consumers' knowledge and the chances that they will buy a Volvo, their ads often feature detailed information about the construction of the cars to make them safer.

Section 2 of this text offers a detailed treatment of consumer affect and cognition and explains the importance of understanding them for developing marketing strategies. Highlight 2.1 offers a sample of the types of questions Section 2 is designed to answer.

HIGHLIGHT 2.1

Some Basic Questions about Consumer Affect and Cognition

 lthough many competing theories and ideas about consumer affect and cognition have been proposed, no single theory completely describes the workings of the consumer's mind. However, carefully studying and thinking about the information in Section 2 of this text should help you develop informed answers to questions about affect and cognition such as the following:

1. How do consumers interpret information about marketing stimuli such as products, stores, and advertising?
2. How do consumers choose among alternative product classes, products, and brands?
3. How do consumers form evaluations of products and brands?
4. How does memory affect consumer decision making?
5. How do affect and cognition influence behaviour and environments?
6. How do behaviour and environments influence affect and cognition?
7. How do consumers interpret the benefits of marketing offerings?
8. Why are consumers more interested or involved in some products or brands than others?
9. How do marketing strategies influence consumers' affective and cognitive responses?
10. How do affective and cognitive responses influence each other?

Consumer Behaviour

In this text, **behaviour** refers to the physical actions of consumers that can be directly observed and measured by others. It is also called overt behaviour to distinguish it from mental activities, such as thinking, that cannot be observed directly. This means that a trip to Hennes & Mauritz involves behaviour; deciding whether to go there is not an overt behaviour because it cannot be observed by others. Examples of behaviours include shopping at stores, buying products, or using credit cards.

Behaviour is critical for marketing strategy because it is only through behaviour that sales can be made and profits earned. While many marketing strategies are designed to influence consumers' affect and cognition, these strategies must ultimately result in overt consumer behaviour for them to have value for the company. It is therefore critical for marketers to analyse, understand, and influence overt behaviour. This can be done in many ways including offering superior quality (Mercedes), lower prices (Woolworth's), greater convenience (IGLO frozen herbs), easier access (Coke is sold in millions of stores and vending machines), and better service ('no-excuse' programmes in SAS hotels). Marketers can also influence overt behaviour by offering products, stores, and brands that are trendier (Diesel clothing), sexier (Armani jeans), more popular (Heineken beer), and more prestigious (Mont Blanc pens) than competitive offering.

Section 3 of this text is devoted to a discussion of overt behaviour. Highlight 2.2 offers a sample of the types of questions Section 3 is designed to answer to aid in developing successful marketing strategies.

HIGHLIGHT 2.2

Some Basic Questions about Consumer Behaviours

 Many behaviour-influencing techniques are commonly used by marketing practitioners. Carefully studying and thinking about the information in Section 3 of this text should help you develop informed answers to questions about behaviour such as these:

1. How do behaviour approaches differ from affective and cognitive approaches to studying consumer behaviour?
2. What is classical conditioning, and how is it used by marketers to influence consumer behaviour?
3. What is operant conditioning, and how is it used by marketers to influence consumer behaviour?
4. What is vicarious learning, and how is it used by marketers to influence consumer behaviour?
5. What consumer behaviours are of interest to marketing management?
6. How much control does marketing have over consumers' behaviour?
7. How do affect and cognition, and environments affect behaviour?
8. How does behaviour influence affect and cognition, and environments?
9. How can behaviour theory be used by marketing managers?
10. Does the frequency and quality of consumer behaviour vary by individuals, products, and situations?

nvironmental psychology seeks to extend knowledge about the relationships between environmental stimuli and human behaviour. In consumer research, the major environmental factors examined have been concerned with the impact of various societal aspects. Carefully studying and thinking about the information in Section 4 of this text should help you develop informed answers to these questions about the environment:

1. In what physical environments do consumer behaviours occur?
2. How do environments affect consumers' affect and cognition and behaviour?
3. How do consumers' affect and cognition and behaviour affect the environment?
4. What effect does culture have on consumers?
5. What effect does subculture have on consumers?
6. What effect does social class have on consumers?
7. What effect do reference groups have on consumers?
8. What effect do families have on consumers?
9. In what ways do consumers influence each other concerning marketing offerings?
10. How powerful are interpersonal influences on consumer behaviour?

Consumer Environment

The consumer **environment** refers to everything external to consumers that influences what they think, feel, and do. It includes social stimuli that influence consumers, such as the actions of others in cultures, subcultures, social classes, reference groups, and families. It also includes other physical stimuli, such as stores, products, advertisements, and signs which can change consumers' thoughts, feelings, and actions.

The consumer environment is important for marketing strategy because it is the medium in which stimuli are placed to influence consumers. For example, marketers run commercials during TV programmes that their target markets watch in order to inform, persuade, and remind them to buy certain products and brands. Marketers can mail free samples, coupons, and catalogues, and use advertisements to get them into the consumers' environments. Stores are located close to populated areas to get them in the proximity of the consumers. Websites may also become part of a consumer's environment, but with the consumer as the driving force.

Section 4 of this text discusses the environment and its influence on consumers. Highlight 2.3 offers a sample of the types of questions Section 4 is designed to answer.

Relationships among Affect and Cognition, Behaviour, and the Environment

Each of the three elements in Exhibit 2.1 can be either a cause or an effect of a change in the other element. For example, a consumer might see an ad for a new laundry detergent that promises to wash clothes cleaner than OMO. This might change what the consumer thinks about the new brand and lead to a purchase of it. In this case, a change in the consumer's environment (the ad for the new detergent), led to a change in cognition (the consumer believed the new detergent was better) which led to a change in behaviour (the consumer bought the new brand).

A change in laundry detergent purchase and use could come about in other ways, however. For example, a consumer could receive a free sample of a new liquid detergent in the mail, try it out, like it and purchase it after that. In this case, a change in the consumer's environment (the free sample) led to a change in his or her behaviour (use and purchase) which led to a change in the individual's affect and cognition (liking the new brand).

Another possibility is that a consumer might be dissatisfied with his or her current brand of laundry detergent. On the consumer's next trip to the grocery, other brands are inspected, and one that promises to get white clothes whiter is selected. In this example, a change in affect and cognition (dissatisfaction) leads to a change in the consumer's environment (inspecting other brands) which leads to change in behaviour (purchase of a different brand).

While there are other ways changes could occur, these examples serve to illustrate our view of consumers. Namely, that not only do consumer processes involve a dynamic and interactive system, but they are also a *reciprocal system*.[1] A **reciprocal system** is one in which any of the elements could be either a cause or an effect of a change at any particular time. Affect and cognition could change consumers' behaviour and environments. Behaviour could change consumers' affect, cognitions, and environments. Environments can change consumers' affect, cognition, and behaviour. Exhibit 2.2 illustrates the reciprocal nature of the relationships.

There are five implications of viewing consumer processes as a reciprocal system involving affect and cognition, behaviour, and the environment. First, any comprehensive analyses of consumers must consider all three elements and the relationships of them. Descriptions of consumers in terms of only one or two of the elements are incomplete. For example, to assume that affect and cognition always cause the behaviour and to ignore the impact of the environment underestimates the dynamic nature of

---

EXHIBIT 2.2

What Affects What in Shopping Behaviour

---

1. Do consumer preferences for shops control where consumers go shopping? If so, affect and cognition influence behaviour.
2. Do consumer preferences and perceptions change which shops are opened and how shops are designed? If so, affect and cognition influence the environment.
3. Do consumer shopping behaviours influence consumer preferences for shopping at the same place again? If so, behaviour alters affect and cognition.
4. Do consumer shopping behaviours influence which shops remain and which are closed down? If so, behaviour influences the environment.
5. Does the availability of various shops influence consumer preferences for them? If so, the environment modifies affect and cognition.
6. Does the availability of various shops influence consumer shopping behaviour? If so, the environment influences behaviour.

EXHIBIT 2.3

The Role of Consumer Research and Analysis in Marketing Strategy

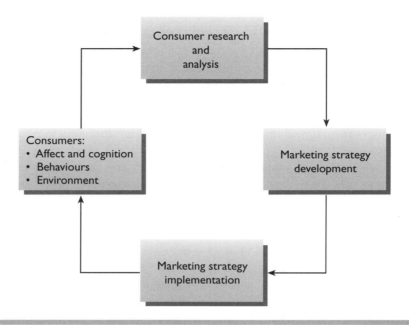

consumption processes. Similarly, to assume that the environment controls behaviour without consideration of affect and cognition also gives an incomplete description. The development of marketing strategies should include an analysis of all three elements, their relationships, and the direction of causal change at particular times.

Second, it is important to recognize that any of the three elements may be the starting point for consumer analysis. While we think that marketing strategists should start with an analysis of the specific overt behaviours consumers must perform to achieve marketing objectives, useful analyses could start with affect and cognition by researching what consumers think and feel about such things as the various brands of a product.

Alternatively, the analysis could start with consumers' environments by examining changes in their world that could change their affect, cognition, and behaviour. However, regardless of the starting point, all three elements and their relationships should be analysed.

Third, since this view is dynamic, it recognizes that consumers can continuously change. While some consumers may change little during a particular time period, others may frequently change their affect, cognition, behaviour, and environments. Keeping abreast of consumers therefore involves continuous research to detect changes that could influence marketing strategies.

Fourth, while our example focused on a single consumer, consumer analysis can be applied at several levels. It can be used to analyse not only a single consumer, but also a group of consumers that make up a target market, a larger group of consumers which make up all of the purchasers of a product in an industry, or for an entire society. Since marketing strategies can be applied at all of these levels this approach is useful for all types of marketing issue, as discussed at the end of the chapter.

Finally, this framework for analysing consumers highlights the importance of consumer research and analysis in developing marketing strategies. As shown in Exhibit 2.3, consumer research and analysis should be key activities for developing marketing strategies. Consumer research includes many types of study such as test marketing, advertising pretests, sales promotion effects, analysis of sales and market share data, pricing experiments, traffic and shopping patterns, brand attitude and intentions, and many others.

A logical sequence is to first research and analyse what consumers think, feel, and do relative to a company's offerings and those of competitors. In addition, an analysis of consumer environments is called for to see what factors are currently influencing them and what changes are occurring. Based on this research and analysis, a marketing strategy is developed which involves setting objectives, specifying an appropriate target market, and developing a marketing mix (product, promotion, price, place) to influence it. After the target market has been selected based on careful analysis of key differences in groups of consumers, marketing strategies involve placing stimuli in the environment that will hopefully become part of the target market's environment and ultimately influence its members' behaviours.

Consumer research and analysis should not end when a strategy has been implemented, however. Rather research should continue to investigate the effects of the strategy and whether it could be changed to be more effective. Thus, marketing strategy should involve a continuous process of researching and analysing consumers, developing strategies, implementing them, and continuously improving strategies.

Marketing Strategy

From a consumer analysis point of view, a **marketing strategy** is a set of stimuli placed in consumers' environments designed to influence their affect, cognition, and behaviour. These stimuli include such things as products, brands, packaging, advertisements, coupons, stores, credit cards, price tags, salespeople's communications, and in some cases sounds (music), smells (perfume), and other sensory cues.

Exhibit 2.4 presents our complete framework which we call the Wheel of Consumer Analysis. It is a wheel because it is constantly rotating with changes in consumers and changes in marketing strategy. Marketing strategy is treated as the hub of the wheel because it is a central marketing activity and is designed by marketing organizations to influence consumers.

Clearly, marketing strategies should not only be designed to influence consumers, but should also be influenced by them. For example, if research shows that consumers are disgusted (affect and cognition) with the advertisements for Armani jeans, the company may want to change its ads to better appeal to the market. If research shows that consumers in the target market do not shop (behaviour) in stores where a company's product is featured, then the distribution strategy may have to be changed. If research shows that consumers want to be able to get information from a company's homepage (environment) and none exists, the company may want to create one. Thus, marketing strategies should be developed, implemented, and changed based on consumer research and analysis.

EXHIBIT 2.4

The Wheel of Consumer Analysis

Section 5 of this text is devoted to a discussion of marketing strategy. While the entire text focuses on applying consumer analysis to marketing strategy issues, Section 5 focuses specifically on market segmentation and each of the elements of the marketing mix, product, promotion, price, and place (channels of distribution). Highlight 2.4 offers a sample of the types of questions Section 5 is designed to answer.

Levels of Consumer Analysis

As noted, consumer research and analysis can be conducted at several different levels. The Wheel of Consumer Analysis is a flexible tool that can aid in understanding different societies, industries, market segments, or individual consumers. It can be used fruitfully by both marketing strategists and public policy officials to understand the dynamics that shape each of these levels.

Societies

Changes in what a society believes and how its members behave can be analysed with the Wheel of Consumer Analysis. For example, many Western societies have experienced an increase in concern with health and fitness. How did this change occur? Surely consumers were always concerned with living long, happy lives. A growing body of medical research indicated people could be healthier and live longer if they ate properly and exercised regularly. This research may have changed attitudes of some consumers about their eating and exercise habits. As these consumers changed their attitudes and began adopting healthier lifestyles, many other consumers copied these beliefs and behaviour patterns. In addition, healthy, well-shaped people are considered

---

HIGHLIGHT 2.4

Some Basic Questions about Marketing Strategy and Consumers

 onsumers are the focal point in the development of successful marketing strategies. According to the principle of reciprocal determinism, marketing strategies both influence and are influenced by consumers' affect and cognition, behaviour, and environment. Carefully studying and thinking about the information in Section 5 of this text should help you develop informed answers to questions about marketing strategies such as the following:

1. What are some effective ways to segment markets?
2. How can products be effectively positioned?
3. What are the relationships between product strategies and consumers?
4. What are the relationships between promotion strategies and consumers?
5. What are the relationships between channels of distribution and consumers?
6. What are the relationships between pricing strategies and consumers?
7. What consumer variables affect the success of a marketing strategy?
8. How can a firm develop brand-loyal consumers?
9. What is the role of consumer satisfaction in developing successful market offerings?
10. What obligations do marketers have to consumers and society at large?

---

more attractive in our societies. This belief may have accelerated the health and fitness movement. Also, because a variety of health-related industries, such as health foods, exercise equipment, and sports apparel, developed and promoted correct eating and exercising regularly, consumers were more exposed to the idea and effects of an active lifestyle.

Of course, not everyone in society has changed his or her lifestyle, some who did have reverted to less healthful habits, and the latest indicators show that the health and fitness movement may have topped in at least some countries. However, the brief discussion here shows changes in the environment (medical research reports), cognition and affect (beliefs about how to live longer and more healthily), behaviour (eating healthful foods and exercising), and marketing strategies (development and promotion of health food, equipment, and apparel products) that interacted to create this change in societies in general. The Wheel of Consumer Analysis can account for these changes in our societies.

Industries

The Wheel of Consumer Analysis can be used to analyse the relationships of a company and its competitors with consumers in specific industries. For example, consider the effects of health concerns on the beer industry. Breweries across Europe have tried to take advantage of the health movement and have launched light or alcohol-free beers. The German Clausthaler brand, one of the first to produce an alcohol-free beer that actually tasted like beer, became a market leader by being the first to offer a product that was more consistent with a change occurring in society, and it also, through developing and marketing the product, helped accelerate the change. Thus, a change in consumer beliefs and behaviour concerning healthy drinking habits influenced a strategy to market an alcohol-free beer. In turn, this marketing strategy helped reinforce and spread the change in consumer beliefs and behaviours. The success of the product influenced competitors to also offer alcohol-free beers, further changing demand for this product category.

Market Segments

The Wheel of Consumer Analysis can be used to analyse groups of consumers who have some similarity in cognition, affect, behaviour, and environment. Successful firms in an industry usually divide the total market into segments and try to appeal most strongly to one or more of them. For example, the emphasis on health encouraged many consumers to become involved in sports. However, there were not always specific shoes designed to play each sport effectively. Today, consumers can find many varieties and styles of shoes for running, bicycling, football, tennis, basketball, squash, and other sports. These shoes vary in design, features, and price ranges to appeal to groups of consumers that are similar in some ways.

As another example, many households where both adults have full jobs find it increasingly difficult to find the time to prepare elaborate meals, especially on weekdays. This has resulted in a demand for more convenience-oriented food products, to which the food industry has responded.

Individual Consumers

Finally, the Wheel of Consumer Analysis can be used to analyse the consumption history, a single purchase, or some aspect of a purchase for a specific consumer. For example, to understand Barbara Linton's purchase of a speciality bed, we need to consider her cognition, affect, behaviour, and environment.

Back to . . . Buying a Speciality Bed

This case provides a simple description of the purchase of a speciality bed. We hope it is written in such a manner that you can easily understand the sequence of events. However, imagine how difficult it would be to try to describe these events by considering only cognitive and affective or behavioural or environmental factors.

Cognitive and affective factors, such as Barbara's concern for her sore back, her information processing and decision making to buy a speciality bed, and her feelings of greater security/that she has done something, are useful – but they could not explain what Barbara did and the environmental factors that influenced these thoughts and actions. Her overt behaviour, such as visiting her uncle and purchasing the bed, is also helpful – but it is incomplete for capturing the meaning of the behaviour and the contexts in which these actions occurred.

Environmental factors, such as the discussions at work, the programme on TV, the information from her uncle, the look and feel of the bed, the store, the salesperson, and the time lapses and place changes between the events described, are necessary for understanding the case – but are quite sterile when discussed independently of Barbara's cognitive, affective, and behavioural events.

Thus, even for a simple description

of a consumer purchase, all three elements – affect and cognition, behaviour, and environment – work together to provide efficient, useful knowledge of consumer behaviour. All three are also necessary for academic attempts to understand consumers and for managerial attempts to develop successful marketing strategies. Analysis of all three elements is superior to any one of two of the elements taken in isolation.

Summary

In this chapter, we presented our overall framework for the analysis of consumer behaviour. We also described a general approach to developing marketing strategies intended to influence consumers' affect and cognition, behaviour, and environments. We believe this framework can help you understand many of the complexities of consumer behaviour. However, other concepts related to consumer behaviour must be considered. Later in this text, we will present many of these concepts and discuss how they can be used to develop, select, and evaluate marketing strategies.

Key Terms and Concepts

affect   18
behaviour   19
cognition   18
environment   20
marketing strategy   23
reciprocal system   21

Review and Discussion Questions

1. Explain consumer affect and cognition, behaviour, and environment. Why do marketers need to consider all three in developing strategies?
2. Explain the relationship between consumer environments and marketing strategy.
3. Why must marketing strategies ultimately influence overt consumer behaviour in order to be successful?
4. What are the implications of viewing consumer processes as a reciprocal system?
5. Explain four levels at which consumer analysis is conducted. Offer one example of how consumer analysis could aid marketers at each level.
6. Offer three examples of how a change in a marketing strategy led to changes in your affect, cognition, behaviour, and environment.

Additional Reading

For further discussion of reciprocal systems as a way of analysing human behaviour, see:
Albert Bandura, *Social Learning Theory* (Englewood Cliffs, NJ: Prentice Hall, 1977).
Albert Bandura, 'Temporal Dynamics and Decomposition of Reciprocal Determinism: A Reply to Phillips and Orton', *Psychological Review*, April 1983, pp. 166–170.
Albert Bandura, 'Human Agency in Social Cognitive Theory', *American Psychologist*, September 1989, pp. 1175–1184.

D. C. Phillips and Rob Orton, 'The New Causal Principle of Cognitive Learning Theory: Perspectives on Bandura's Reciprocal Determinism', *Psychological Review*, April 1983, pp. 158–165.

For other comprehensive treatments of consumer behaviour theory with an emphasis on the European perspective, the following European texts may be of interest:

Bernard Dubois, *Comprendre le Consommateur* (Paris: Dalloz, 1990).

Robert East, *Consumer Behaviour* (London: Prentice Hall, 1997).

Gordon Foxall and Ronald Goldsmith, *Consumer Psychology for Marketing* (London: Routledge, 1994).

Flemming Hansen, *Forbrugeradfærd og -beslutning* (Copenhagen: Arnold Busck, 1987).

Werner Kroeber-Riel and Peter Weinberg, *Konsumentenverhalten*, 6th edn. (Munich: Vahlen, 1996).

MARKETING STRATEGY IN ACTION
The Body Shop

In 1976, Anita Roddick opened her first shop in a seaside town on the south coast of England – she called it The Body Shop. The philosophy was simple: to be an alternative to the established cosmetics industry, no glossy advertising, no wild promises, no products tested on animals, only minimal packaging and products which have minimal impact on the environment. The Body Shop would tell human stories about the skin care of the Polynesian woman or the foot care needs of the marathon runner, while the established cosmetics industry told stories of exclusive ingredients devised in the laboratory and patented. The Body Shop's philosophy has led to popular products such as Cocoa Butter Hand and Body Lotion, Peppermint Foot Lotion, and White Musk. Retail sales have grown at an average of 14 per cent the past three years and in 1995 reached £500 million. In 1996, there were almost 1400 Body Shops, mostly franchised, in 46 countries around the world.

Part of The Body Shop's success is due to the involvement in environmental, social, and ethical matters. It has a good record on the promotion of such issues to the public and this type of promotion is the main thrust of its PR campaigns – essentially the way it sells itself and its products to the public. The Body Shop does not use commercial advertising. It has nevertheless been highly successful in promoting itself through public relations, which has the advantage of greater credibility – advertising is to say you're good, PR is getting someone else to say it, as The Body Shop claims in its 1993 Annual Report.

The 1990s have shown a new trend for the cosmetics industry which draws closer to The Body Shop's point of view. There is a growing concern, led by consumer demand, for the environment, worker welfare, and animal protection, which today are the major debating points in the cosmetics industry. Animal testing, packaging, and the sourcing of materials have received special attention. The Body Shop has an image of natural products and sells itself and its products by claiming a high degree of social and ethical responsibility. It has attached a feel-good factor to cosmetic and personal care products which traditionally have carried a strong aura of self-indulgence. The Body Shop believes it has influenced significant changes within the cosmetics industry over the past 20 years. It has successfully sold skin care products without resorting to sex, glamour, and hype; it has led the call for an end to the practice of testing products and ingredients on animals; and it has spear-headed the whole notion of holistic beauty. The Body Shop's message to their customers is: 'Celebrate yourself and love your body'.

Discussion Questions

1. Based on the case information and your personal experience, list at least five things you know about The Body Shop. This list offers you some idea of your cognitions about this retail chain.

2. Based on the case information and your personal experience, list at least five things you like or dislike about The Body Shop. This list gives you some idea of your affect for this retail chain.

3. Based on your personal experience in buying cosmetics from The Body Shop (or a purchase in another cosmetics retailer if you haven't been to a Body Shop), list at least five behaviours you have performed in making the purchase. This list gives you some idea of the behaviours involved in purchasing from a cosmetics retailer.

4. Based on the case information and your personal experience, list at least five things The Body Shop has done in the environment to influence consumers to purchase their products. This list gives you some idea of how the environment influences cognition, affect, and behaviour.

5. Write a brief description of a purchase you have made from The Body Shop (or another cosmetics retailer if you haven't

been to a Body Shop). Did the purchase involve cognition, affect, behaviour, and the environment?

Sources: 'The Body Shop Controversy', *New Consumer Briefings*, October 1993–September 1994, www.arq.co.uk/ethicalbusiness/archive/bodyshop/index.htm; The Body Shop homepage on internet: www.the-body-shop.com.

Affect and Cognition and Marketing Strategy

Consumer Affect and Cognition

Consumer Environment

Consumer Behaviour

Introduction to Affect and Cognition

'Everyday' Affect and Cognition: The Peter Smith Story

s do millions of other consumers, Peter Smith makes a trip to a local supermarket for some major shopping one sunny Saturday morning. He has driven to the supermarket with his three-year-old daughter, Heather. As he walks through the front doors of the store, Peter enters one of the most complex information environments a consumer can face.

A supermarket is loaded with information. A supermarket may carry as many as 20 000 items. Large supermarkets offer many alternatives in each product category. For instance, one large store offers 18 brands of mustard in a variety of sizes. Moreover, most product packages contain lots of information. The average package of breakfast cereal, for example, contains some 250 individual pieces of information!

Despite this complexity, Peter (like most of us) feels no particular uneasiness or anxiety about grocery shopping. Neither is he particularly excited, for this is familiar territory. During the next hour or so, he will process a great deal of information. He will make numerous decisions during the time it takes to fill his shopping trolley. Most of his choices will be made easily and quickly, seemingly with little effort. Some choices, though, will involve noticeable cognition (thinking) and may require a few seconds. And a few of his choices may require substantial cognitive processing and several seconds, perhaps even minutes.

How does Peter Smith move through this complex informational environment so easily, buying dozens, perhaps hundreds, of products? The affective and cognitive processes that make this possible are the subject of this chapter.

This apparently simple, everyday example of shopping for groceries actually involves rather complex interactions between various aspects of the supermarket environment, marketing strategies, Peter Smith's behaviour, and his affective and cognitive systems. In this chapter, we begin our examination of the affect and cognition portion of the Wheel of Consumer Analysis. We will describe consumers' affective and cognitive systems, present a cognitive processing model of consumer decision making, and discuss the knowledge structures that consumers learn and store in memory. Our goal is to understand consumers' affective responses to their experiences, their cognitive interpretations of those experiences, and how these responses influence consumers' interpretations of new experiences and choice of behaviours to achieve their consumption goals.

Components of the Wheel of Consumer Analysis

In Chapter 2, you learned that consumer behaviour situations such as Peter Smith's grocery shopping trip can be analysed in terms of four elements – behaviour, environment, marketing strategies, and the internal factors of affect and cognition. We organized these four factors into a model called the Wheel of Consumer Analysis. Because these factors interact and influence each other in a continuous, reciprocal manner, no factor can be fully understood in isolation. Therefore, we begin our analysis of affect and cognition by first analysing Peter Smith's shopping trip in terms of the four elements in the wheel model.

Environment

What is the supermarket environment like? Well, on a Saturday morning, the market is likely to be busy, with many people *crowding* the aisles. The store is likely to be somewhat *noisy*. Because Peter is shopping with Heather, her chattering adds to the commotion. These social aspects of the environment will influence Peter's affect and cognition and his overt behaviour. The store *layout*, the *width* of the aisles, the special sale *signs* on the shelves, the product *displays* at the ends of the aisles and elsewhere in the store, the *lighting*, and other physical aspects of the supermarket environment may also have an effect. Other environmental factors, such as the *temperature*, background *music*, and the *wobbly wheel* on his shopping trolley may have important effects on Peter's affect, cognition, and behaviour.

Behaviour

What kinds of behaviour occur in this situation? Peter is engaged in a large number of behaviours, including *walking* down the aisles, *looking* at products on the shelves, *picking up* and examining packages, *talking* to Heather and a friend he meets in the store, *steering* the wobbly trolley, and so on. While many of these behaviours may not seem to be of much interest to a marketing manager, some behaviours have an important influence on Peter's affect and cognition and his eventual purchases. For example, unless Peter *walks* down the breakfast cereals aisle, he cannot notice and *buy* a package of Kellogg's All-Bran. Typically, marketers are most concerned about purchase behaviour. In the supermarket environment, this means *picking* up a package, *placing* it in the trolley, and *paying* for it at the checkout counter.

Marketing Strategies

Much of the in-store environment Peter experiences is a result of marketing strategy decisions made by the retailer and the manufacturers whose products are carried by the store. In fact, a grocery store is a very good place to observe marketing strategies in action. The huge number of products sold in such stores requires an equally large number of marketing strategies. For instance, a firm's *distribution strategy* (place products only in upmarket stores) determines whether that product is even available in a particular store. A variety of *pricing strategies* (reduced price on McVities Hobnobs biscuits) and *promotion strategies* (free samples of cheese) are evident in a supermarket environment. *Package designs* (resealable packaging) and specific product characteristics (low-calorie cold meats) are also marketing strategies. Finally, specific environmental details such as *point-of-purchase* displays (a stack of Tuborg six-packs near the store entrance) are important aspects of marketing strategy. All of these marketing strategies are environmental stimuli that are meant to influence consumers' affect and cognition and their behaviour.

Affect and Cognition

Peter's affective and cognitive systems were active in the supermarket environment. Indeed, consumers' affective and cognitive systems are active in every environment, but only some of this internal activity is conscious, while a great deal of activity may occur without much awareness. For instance, Peter may *feel a bit angry* about getting a trolley with a wobbly wheel. He also *pays attention* to certain aspects of the store environment and ignores other parts. Some products catch his attention while others do not. He *interprets* a large amount of information in the store environment – from aisle signs to brand names to price tags. In addition, he *evaluates* some of the products in terms of meeting his needs and those of his family. He *remembers* what products he still has on hand at home and what he has run out of and needs to replace. He *makes choices* from among some of the thousands of products available in the store. In addition, he *makes decisions* about other specific behaviours. Should he go down aisle 3 or skip it this week? Should he stock up on peeled tomatoes or buy just one tin? Should he give Heather a sweet for being good? Should he take the wobbly trolley back and get another one? Should he pay with cash or by credit card? Should he get paper or plastic bags?

In sum, Peter's grocery purchasing behaviour on this particular Saturday morning is a complex function of his social and physical environment, the marketing strategies intended to influence him, his own behaviour, and the processes of his affective and cognitive systems. Each factor interacts with and reciprocally influences the others.

About 45 minutes after entering the supermarket, Peter emerges with five bags of groceries containing 48 different products. Given our analysis of his shopping trip, we might be somewhat surprised to find that he has a smile on his face and does not feel at all tired. How did Peter's affective and cognitive systems accomplish so much so quickly, with such apparent ease? How do we all perform similar cognitive feats while shopping?

Affect and Cognition as Psychological Responses

Affect and cognition are rather different types of psychological responses consumers can have in situations such as grocery shopping. **Affect** refers to feeling responses, while **cognition** consists of mental (thinking) responses. Consumers can have both affective and cognitive responses to any element in the Wheel of Consumer Analysis – the environment, behaviours, or even other affective and cognitive responses. Affect and cognition are produced by the affective and cognitive systems, respectively. Although the two systems are distinct, they are richly interconnected, and each system can influence and be influenced by the other.[1]

In distinguishing affect from cognition, you can think of affect as something people *are* or something people *feel* (I *am* angry; Linda *is* in a good mood; Thomas *feels* bored).[2] Because people experience affect in their bodies, affect seems to be a part of the person at the time they experience it. In contrast, people *have* cognitions, thoughts, or beliefs (your mother *believes* light mayonnaise is not fattening; Susanne *knows* where the grocery store is; you *think* your sweater is stylish). As mental states, cognitions are not usually felt in the body.

Types of Affective Response

People can experience four broad types of affective response: emotions, specific feelings, moods, and evaluations. Exhibit 3.1 identifies these affective responses and gives some examples of each type. Each type of affect can involve positive or negative responses. Feelings, for example, can be favourable (Jane was satisfied with her T-shirt) or unfavourable (John was disgusted with the service he got). Moods can be positive (relaxed) or negative (sad).

The four types of affect differ in the level of bodily arousal or the intensity with which they are experienced.[3] The stronger affective responses, including emotions such as fear or anger, may involve physiological responses (that are felt in the body) such as increased heart rate or blood pressure, perspiration, dry mouth, tears, rushes of adrenaline, or butterflies in the stomach. Specific feelings involve somewhat less intense physiological reactions (Jennifer was sad when she sold her old guitar). Moods, which involve lower levels of felt intensity, are rather diffuse affective states (Robert was bored by the long shopping trip).[4] Finally, evaluations of products or other concepts (I like Colgate toothpaste) often are rather weak affective responses accompanied by low levels of arousal (sometimes, one hardly feels anything at all).

EXHIBIT 3.1

Types of Affective Response

Type of Affective Response	Level of Physiological Arousal	Intensity or Strength of Feeling	Examples of Positive and Negative Affect
Emotions	Higher arousal and activation	Stronger	• Joy, love
			• Fear, guilt, anger
Specific feelings	↑	↑	• Warmth, appreciation, satisfaction
Moods			• Disgust, sadness
			• Alert, relaxed, calm
			• Blue, listless, bored
Evaluations			• Like, good, favourable
	↓	↓	• Dislike, bad, unfavourable
	Lower arousal and activation	Weaker	

The Affective System

Affective responses are produced by the affective system. Although researchers are still studying how the affective system operates, they generally agree on six basic characteristics.[5] One important property is that the affective system is *largely reactive*. That is, the affective system cannot plan, make decisions, or purposefully try to achieve some goal. Rather, a person's affective system usually responds immediately and automatically to significant aspects of the environment. An obvious example is colour. Most people immediately have a positive affective response when they see a favourite colour on a car or an item of clothing (see Highlight 3.1).

A related characteristic of the affective system is that people have *little direct control* over their affective responses. For instance, if you are insulted by a rude salesperson, your affective system might immediately and automatically produce feelings of frustration or anger. However, people can have indirect control over their affective feelings

---

HIGHLIGHT 3.1

Automatic Affective Responses to Colour

All living creatures have certain innate responses to the environment, and the response to colour is one of them. One of the first things people react to in evaluating an object (a product or building) is its colour. Your affective response to colour can influence other emotions and feelings, as well as your cognitions and behaviours. Colours can attract or distract you; colours can make you feel good or bad; colours can draw you towards other people or repel you; colours can make you want to eat more or less.

A person's affective response to colour involves automatic reactions of the eye, optic neurones, parts of the brain, and various glands. Consider people's responses to red. When the eye sees primary red, the pituitary gland (embedded in the brain) is stimulated to send out a chemical signal to the adrenal medullae (located above the kidneys), which secrete epinephrine or adrenaline that activates and arouses the body. People's emotions such as anger or fear are enhanced by this automatic reaction to red; this is why danger signs are usually red. Affective feelings of excitement are generated by red. Thus, cosmetics such as lipstick and rouge are based on red. In the presence of red, people also tend to eat more, which is why red is a popular colour for restaurants.

People's affective systems have similar automatic reactions to other colours. For instance, a particular shade of vivid pink causes the brain to secrete norepinephrine, a chemical that inhibits the production of epinephrine. Thus, pink is a useful colour for places where angry people must be confronted (a principal's office, certain areas of a prison, or the complaints centre in a department store).

Yellow is the fastest colour for the eye to see because the electrochemical reactions that produce vision work fastest in response to yellow stimulation. Thus yellow is an excellent colour to command attention (Post-it notes are a good example). Placing a yellow car in the car showroom will attract more attention from passing motorists. Although many people think of yellow as cheerful and sunny, the yellow kitchen they often request may increase anxiety and loss of temper.

Source: Adapted from Carlton Wagner, 'Colour Cues', *Marketing Insights*, Spring 1990, pp. 42–46.

by changing their behaviour that is triggering the affect or moving to another environment. For instance, you might complain about the rude salesperson to the manager, which could reduce the negative affect you felt and create a new feeling of satisfaction. As another example, consumers who have negative affective reactions to a crowded clothing shop (feelings of discomfort, frustration, or even anger) might leave the store to shop in a less crowded environment, which stimulates more positive affective feelings.[6]

A third feature of the affective system is that affective responses are *felt physically* in the body. Consider the butterflies in the stomach associated with the excitement of making an important purchase, such as a new car or a house. These physical reactions can be powerful feelings for the people experiencing them. People's body movements often reflect their affective states (they smile when happy, frown when disturbed, clench fists in anger, sit up straight in anticipation, or slouch in boredom) and communicate their emotional states to other people. Thus, competent salespeople read the body language of their prospects and adapt their sales presentations accordingly.

Fourth, the affective system can *respond to virtually any type of stimulus*. For instance, consumers can have an evaluative response to a physical object (I *love* my Technics stereo system) or a social situation (I *disliked* talking to the salesperson in the electronics store). People's affective systems can also respond to their own behaviours (I *enjoy* playing my stereo system). Finally, consumers' affective systems can respond to thoughts produced by their cognitive systems (I *like* to think about stereo systems).

Fifth, most affective responses are *learned*. Only a few basic affective responses, such as preferences for sweet tastes or negative reactions to loud, sudden noises, seem to be innate. Consumers learn some of their affective responses (evaluations or feelings) through classical conditioning processes (this topic is discussed later in the text). Consumers also acquire many affective responses through early socialization experiences as young children. Because affective responses are learned, they may vary widely across different cultures, subcultures, or other social groups. Thus, people's affective systems are likely to respond in rather different ways to the same stimulus.

Sixth, affective states can be *measured* and are actually measured in the context of consumer research, both applied and academic. There are mainly two ways in which this can be done. One way is to ask consumers to describe their affective states, usually by some kind of questionnaire device like a set of scales.[7] Another way is to measure the physiological states known to be associated with affective states. The most popular way of doing this is to measure consumers' skin resistance: electrodes are applied to the body to measure how skin resistance changes when a consumer is exposed to potentially arousing stimuli.[8] Both methods are complementary: measuring physiological states like skin resistance tells something about the degree of arousal and hence about the intensity of affective states, but not about the kind or direction of the affective states – a high degree of arousal, as indicated by low skin resistance, can mean both a very positive or a very negative affective response. Questionnaire-based methods are suitable to indicate the kind and direction of affective states, but may be influenced by problems of social desirability.

What Is Cognition?

Human beings have evolved a highly sophisticated cognitive system that performs the higher mental processes of understanding, evaluating, planning, deciding, and thinking:[9]

- Understanding – Interpreting, or determining the meaning of specific aspects of one's environment.
- Evaluating – Judging whether an aspect of the environment, or one's own behaviour, is good or bad, positive or negative, favourable or unfavourable.
- Planning – Determining how to solve a problem or reach a goal.
- Deciding – Comparing alternative solutions to a problem in terms of their relevant characteristics and selecting the best alternative.
- Thinking – The cognitive activity that occurs during all of these processes.

In this book, we use the term *cognition* broadly to refer to all these mental processes, as well as the thoughts and meanings produced by the cognitive system.

A major function of people's cognitive systems is to interpret, make sense of, and understand significant aspects of their personal experience. To do so, the cognitive system creates symbolic, subjective meanings that represent our personal interpretations of the stimuli we encounter; for instance, Peter Smith made many cognitive interpretations during his shopping trip. Our cognitive systems are capable of interpreting virtually any aspect of the environment (that is one of the early Beatles' tunes). We can also interpret our behaviour (why did I buy that CD?) and our own affective states (do I really like this sweater?). Cognitive interpretations can include the deeper, symbolic meanings of products and behaviours (see Highlight 3.2). Finally, people can interpret the meaning of their own cognitions or beliefs (what does it mean that Daell's department store has 'low prices everyday'?). Exhibit 3.2 lists some of the interpretations consumers' cognitive systems can create.

EXHIBIT 3.2

Types of Meaning Created by the Cognitive System

Cognitive interpretations of physical stimuli
This sweater is made of lambswool.
This car gets 12 kilometres per litre.

Cognitive interpretations of social stimuli
The salesperson was helpful.
My friends think Pepe's Pizza is the best.

Cognitive interpretations of affective responses
I love Magnum (ice cream).
I feel guilty about not sending Mum a birthday card.
I feel mildly excited and interested in a new store.

Cognitive interpretations of symbolic meanings
This car is sexy.
This style of dress is appropriate for older women.
Wearing a Rolex watch means you are successful.

Cognitive interpretations of sensations
Colours on a box of breakfast cereal.
Sound of a soft-drink can being opened and poured.
Sweet taste of chocolate chip cookies.
Smell of your favourite cologne.
Feel of your favourite pair of jeans.

Cognitive interpretations of behaviours
I drink a lot of Jolly Cola.
How to pay with a credit card.

HIGHLIGHT 3.2

Symbolic Meaning of Food

ost marketers recognize that the consumption of many products depends on their symbolic meanings as well as their functional utility. In fact, the symbolic qualities of products and services can be the key determinants of product evaluation and purchase. Take food, for example.

Some foods symbolize age and sex differences. Milk and soft mushy foods are appropriate for babies or the elderly. Hamburgers are a youth food, especially appropriate for teenagers, whereas foods such as steak or lamb are appropriate for more sophisticated adults. Red meat is typically considered a male food, whereas vegetarian dishes are considered female food.

Foods are often symbols of a culture. Many people associate the United States with hamburgers, England with steak-and-kidney-pie, Belgium with chips, Denmark with red sausages, and Germany with sauerkraut – even though the citizens in those countries would regard this as gross simplification and possibly even as an unjust characterization.

Certain foods are symbols of social status, although what exactly gives status may differ between countries. Champagne and caviar connote status in most countries, whereas drinking wine connotes status only in Northern Europe.

Eating outside the home also connotes symbolic meaning. For instance, eating outdoors (in the garden, at the beach) symbolizes freedom from conventions, a return to nature, and a return to more primitive ways of cooking (open fire) and eating (with one's fingers). The symbolic meaning of going out to eat in a restaurant depends very much on the type of restaurant. Fast-food restaurants symbolize youth and unpretentious values. Going to 'nice' restaurants involves rituals of dressing up and having 'good' manners that help create special, festive meanings and contribute to the symbolic meanings of the experience.

The method of food preparation also has symbolic meanings. Very elaborate cooking procedures signify the rarefied, sophisticated tastes of people who can appreciate such fare. Raw foods tend to symbolize primitive, animal meanings. However, a few foods that are served uncooked have higher status meanings – caviar, sushi (raw fish and rice), steak tartar (raw ground beef) – perhaps because they symbolize mature, refined, aesthetic tastes.

Sources: Claude Fischler, *Lhomnivore*, Paris: Odile Jacob, 1986; Sidney J. Levy, 'Interpreting Consumer Mythology: A Structural Approach to Consumer Behaviour', *Journal of Marketing*, Summer 1981, pp. 49–61; Mary Douglas, *Food as a System of Communication* (London: Routledge & Kegan Paul), 1982; Michael R. Solomon, 'The Role of Products as Social Stimuli: A Symbolic Interactionism Perspective', *Journal of Consumer Research*, December 1983, pp. 319–329.

A second function of our cognitive systems is to process (think about) these interpretations or meanings in carrying out cognitive tasks such as identifying goals and objectives, developing and evaluating alternative courses of action to meet those goals, choosing a course of action, and carrying out the behaviours. The amount and intensity of cognitive processing varies widely across situations, products, and consumers. Consumers are not always engaged in extensive cognitive activity. In fact, many behaviours and purchase decisions probably involve minimal cognitive processing.

Relationship between Affect and Cognition

The relationship between affect and cognition remains an issue in psychology.[10] Several researchers consider the affective and cognitive systems to be (at least somewhat) independent.[11] Others argue that affect is largely influenced by the cognitive system.[12] Still others argue that affect is the dominant system. We believe that some degree of independence is plausible because the affective and cognitive systems appear to involve different parts of the brain. However, the affective and cognitive areas are richly connected by neural pathways, so we must recognize that each system can influence the other.

For understanding consumers, it is more useful to emphasize the interaction between the affective and cognitive systems than to argue about which system is more important or dominant. Exhibit 3.3 presents a simple model to illustrate how the two systems are related. Note that each system can respond independently to aspects of the environment, and each system can respond to the output of the other system. For instance, the affective responses (emotions, feelings, or moods) produced by the affective system in reaction to stimuli in the environment can be interpreted by the cognitive system (I wonder why I am so happy; I don't like the insurance agent because she is too serious). These cognitive interpretations, in turn, might be used to make decisions (I won't buy insurance from this person). We also know that consumers' affective reactions to the environment can influence their cognition during decision making. For instance, if you go grocery shopping when you are in a good mood, you are likely to spend more money than if you are in a bad mood. The affect associated with being in a good mood influences cognitive processes during shopping so that you are more likely to think about the favourable qualities of things to buy. As another example, your cognitive

EXHIBIT 3.3

The Relationship between the Affective and Cognitive Systems

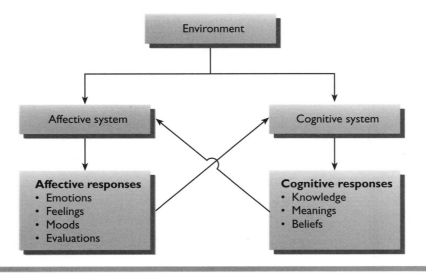

interpretation of a TV commercial can be influenced by your affective reactions to the preceding programme material.[13]

In contrast, consumers' cognitive interpretations of information in the environment can trigger affective reactions (Oh, is that a Volvo 850 Turbo? I like it). We know that people's affective systems can be influenced by their cognitive interpretations of their experiences in a situation.[14] For instance, if you interpret a salesperson's behaviour as pushy, you will probably have a negative evaluation of the salesperson. On the other hand, you will probably have a favourable affective response if you interpret the salesperson's behaviour as helpful.

A good example for the interaction of affective and cognitive processes in a consumer behaviour context is the consumption of food.[15] Many people eat to get rid of a bad mood, for example by indulging in chocolate when they are sad, or they try to prolong a good mood by celebrating something with a good meal. The affective state is related to a behavioural response by means of cognitive processes which retrieve from memory coping strategies which have worked well in the past.

Marketing Implications

Both affect and cognition are important for understanding consumer behaviour. Consider, for instance, the cognitive and affective components of brand image.[16] A brand image includes knowledge and beliefs (cognitions) about brand attributes, the consequences of brand use, and appropriate consumption situations, as well as evaluations, feelings, and emotions (affective responses) associated with the brand. Marketers need to understand both affective and cognitive responses to marketing strategies such as product design, advertisement, and store layout. For some marketing purposes, consumers' affective responses are more important; in other cases, cognition is key.

Haagen-Dazs uses sexual innuendo to emphasize the sensuous qualities of its ice cream, Courtesy: Haagen-Dazs; agency: Bartle Bogle Hegarty, London: Rooney Carruthers; copywriter: Larry Barker; photographer: Barry Lategan.

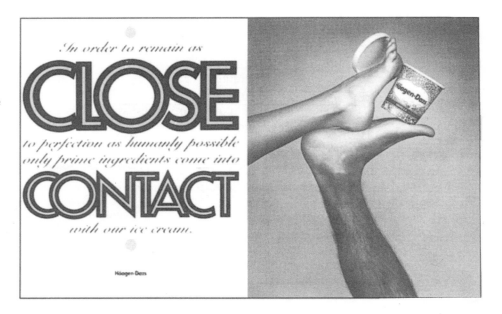

Affective responses are especially important for so-called *feeling* products.[17] These include certain foods (sweets, snacks, pizza), beverages (soft drinks, beer, wine), greetings cards, perfume, skin care products, and sports cars. For instance, consider consumers' affective responses to ice cream. For most people, eating ice cream is a highly sensory experience, and they associate the product with affective feelings of happiness, fun, and excitement, even sensual pleasure. For example, Haagen-Dazs, the UK-owned maker of superpremium ice cream noted for its high butterfat content and intense flavours, promotes people's affective, sensual reactions to ice cream in its European advertising.[18] One British ad portrayed a seminude couple feeding ice cream to each other. The product was very successful in England, France, and Germany, where sales grew from £1 million to £20 million in just two years.

As another example, consumers' initial affective responses to the smell of a perfume may be critical to its purchase. To introduce its Spellbound perfume, Estée Lauder inserted scented strips in magazines such as *Elle, Cosmopolitan*, and *Vogue*.[19] But once the product is bought, consumers' affective responses to the fragrance are also influenced by their cognitive interpretations of how other people in the social environment react to the scent. Perfume advertising may try to portray both affective and cognitive responses. For example, Estée Lauder's ads for Spellbound portrayed attractive models gazing intently into each others' eyes. Apparently, it hoped to communicate the affective and cognitive meanings associated with romance, sensuality, and sexual attraction. (Highlight 3.3 discusses the affective and cognitive aspects of romance.) In the remainder of this chapter, we consider the cognitive system and the knowledge it creates.

HIGHLIGHT 3.3

The Return of Romance

T he concept of romance gained favour in Western society during the 1990s, as people sought a refuge from the pressures of work and economic crisis. Wedding advertisements in *Bride's* magazine portrayed much more romantic settings. Sales of romance novels were strong. The rising interest in old-fashioned furniture and decorations is seen as a nostalgic return to a more romantic time.

Romance is difficult to define, but it surely involves affective states, including emotions, feelings, and moods. Romance is about relationships, fantasy, imagery, nostalgia, and tradition. The affective responses associated with romantic love are quite different from those associated with explicit sexual stimuli. For instance, Calvin Klein first introduced the perfume Obsession and portrayed naked, interlocked bodies in the advertising to create an image of casual but intense sexuality. Klein used completely different advertising imagery to promote the perfume called Eternity, introduced in most European countries in the mid-1990s. Here the advertising theme was romance, commitment and the cycle of life, and the goal was to elicit different types of affective responses – romantic emotions and moods, feelings of commitment, and close relationships.

Source: Adapted from Lea Bayers Rapp, 'The Return of Romance',
Marketing Insights, June 1989, pp. 31–39

Cognitive Processes in Consumer Decision Making

The most important aspect of consumer behaviour for marketers to understand is how consumers make decisions. Consumers make decisions about many types of behaviour:

- What product or brand should I buy?
- Where should I shop?
- Which TV programmes should I watch tonight?
- Should I pay for this purchase with cash or a credit card?
- How much money should I borrow?
- Should I read this ad carefully?
- Which friend should I consult?
- Which salesperson should I buy from?

Consumers use information to make such decisions. From a consumer perspective, most aspects of the environment are potential information. In a supermarket, for instance, marketing strategies such as a price tag, sale signs in a store window, or a tasting demonstration of a new product provide information to consumers. In addition, people's internal affective responses and their own behaviours constitute information that can be interpreted by their cognitive systems. If this information is to influence consumers' decisions, it must be *processed* (taken in, interpreted, and used) by their cognitive systems. To explain how the cognitive system processes information, researchers have developed **information-processing models**.[20] These models identify a sequence of cognitive processes in which each process transforms or modifies information and passes it on to the next process, where additional operations take place.[21] The decisions that underlie many human actions can be understood in terms of these cognitive processes.

Reduced to its essence, consumer decision making involves three important cognitive processes. (1) Consumers must *interpret* relevant information in the environment to create personal meanings or knowledge. (2) Consumers must combine or *integrate* this knowledge to evaluate products or possible actions and to choose among alternative behaviours. (3) Consumers must *retrieve product knowledge from memory* to use in integration and interpretation processes. All three cognitive processes are involved in any decision-making situation.

A Model of Consumer Decision Making

Exhibit 3.4 presents a model of consumer decision making that highlights these three features of interpretation, integration, and product knowledge in memory. We provide an overview of this decision-making model here, and in subsequent chapters we discuss each element of the model in more detail.

Consumers must interpret or make sense of information in the environment around them. In the process, they create new knowledge, meanings, and beliefs about the environment and their place in it. **Interpretation processes** require exposure to information and involve two related cognitive processes – attention and comprehension. *Attention* governs how consumers select which information to interpret and which information to ignore. *Comprehension* refers to how consumers determine the subjective meanings of information and thus create personal knowledge and beliefs. We discuss exposure, attention, and comprehension processes in Chapter 5.

EXHIBIT 3.4

A Cognitive-Processing Model of Consumer Decision Making

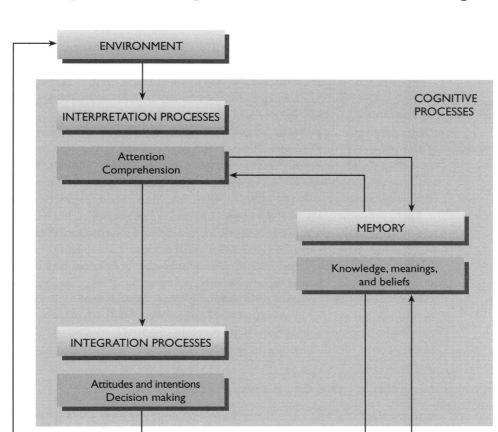

In this book, we use the terms **knowledge**, **meanings**, and **beliefs** interchangeably to refer to the various types of personal or subjective interpretations of information produced by interpretation processes. Exhibit 3.4 shows that knowledge, meanings, and beliefs may be stored in memory and later retrieved from memory (activated) and used in integration processes.[22] Later in the chapter, we discuss how consumers may organize these meanings and beliefs into *knowledge structures*.

Integration processes concern how consumers combine different types of knowledge (1) to form overall evaluations of products, other objects, and behaviours, and (2) to make choices among alternative behaviours, such as a purchase. In the first instance, consumers combine knowledge and affective feelings about a product or a brand to form an overall evaluation or a *brand attitude* (I like Mövenpick chocolate ice cream, or Wrangler jeans are not as good as Levi's). We discuss attitudes and intentions in Chapter 6. Consumers also engage in integration processes when they combine knowledge and affective responses to choose a behaviour (Should I shop at Marks & Spencers or Woolworths?). When consumers choose among different purchase behaviours, they form an *intention* or *plan* to buy (I intend to buy a new Bic pen this afternoon). Integration processes are also used to make choices among other behaviours besides purchase. For instance, a consumer might integrate knowledge in deciding when to go on a shopping trip, whether to pay with a cheque or a credit card, or whether to recommend a film to a friend.

Product knowledge and involvement concern the various types of knowledge, meanings, and beliefs that are stored in consumers' memories. For example, consumers may have product knowledge about the characteristics or attributes of a brand of athletic shoe (gel inserts in the heel), the outcomes of using the brand (I can run faster), or the ability of the brand to satisfy important objectives (I will be fit). Product knowledge that is retrieved from memory has the potential to influence interpretation and integration processes. For example, consumers need a certain amount of knowledge about nutrition to interpret and understand the many health claims made by food companies. *Product involvement* refers to consumers' knowledge about the personal relevance of the product in one's life (nutrition information is important to my health goals). People's level of involvement with health issues will influence how much effort they exert in interpreting a nutritional message. We discuss product knowledge and involvement in Chapter 4.

In summary, Exhibit 3.4 shows that consumer decision making involves the two cognitive processes of interpretation and integration, which are influenced by product knowledge, meanings, and beliefs in memory. In Chapter 7, we discuss how all of these factors operate together in consumer decision making.

More Characteristics of the Cognitive System

Several aspects of the cognitive system influence decision making by consumers. **Activation**, for instance, refers to the process by which product knowledge is retrieved from memory for use in interpreting and integrating information. Activation of knowledge in memory is often automatic in that little or no conscious effort is involved.[23] Consumers typically experience activated knowledge as thoughts that 'just come to mind'. Daydreaming is a good example of activation – various bits of knowledge or meanings surface as a person's mind drifts from one thought to another. Activation also operates when consumers intentionally try to recall certain bits of knowledge such as the location of a particular shop in the shopping centre, the salesperson's name, or the price of that black sweater. People sometimes try to remember such knowledge by giving themselves cues that might activate the desired knowledge (Let's see, I think her name begins with a 'B').

The product knowledge in consumers' memories can be activated in various ways. The most common way is by exposure to objects or events in the environment. Seeing something, such as the distinctive BMW grille, can activate various meanings (you might think about sportiness or that this is an affluent person's car). Because marketers control certain aspects of the environment, they have some influence on consumers' cognition. People's internal, affective states can also activate knowledge. For instance, positive knowledge and beliefs tend to be activated when a person is in a good mood, while more negative meanings are activated when the same person is in an unpleasant

HIGHLIGHT 3.4

Increasing Automatic Cognitive Processing – Learning to Drive a Car

P ractised subjects can do what seems impossible to both the novice and the theorist. People can achieve dramatic improvements in skills with practice. For instance, consider your experience in learning to drive a car. When you first learned to drive, you probably couldn't drive and talk at the same time. The task of driving seemed difficult and was probably physically and mentally tiring. Today, if you are a skilled driver, you can probably drive in moderate traffic, listen to music on the radio, and carry on a casual conversation with a friend. Could you have done this when you first started driving? Probably then you kept the radio off. If anyone tried to talk to you, you ignored them or told them to shut up. Of course, even today you will probably stop talking if something unfamiliar occurs such as an emergency situation on the road up ahead. At least, we hope you do!

Learning to drive a car illustrates how cognitive processes (and associated behaviours) become increasingly automatic as they are learned through practice. However, even highly automatic skills such as eating seem to require some cognitive capacity. Perhaps you like to munch on something while you study. You might snack on crisps or eat an apple while you read this chapter. But if you come upon a difficult passage that requires deeper thought, you will probably stop chewing, or your hand with the crisps may pause in mid-air, while you interpret the meaning of what you are reading.

mood. Finally, product knowledge in memory can be activated because it is linked to other activated meanings. Because meanings are associated in memory, activation of one meaning concept may trigger related concepts and activate those meanings as well. Consumers have little control over this process of **spreading activation**, which occurs unconsciously and automatically.[24] For instance, seeing a magazine ad for Haribo wine gum bears might activate first the Haribo name and then related knowledge and meanings such as cute, soft and tasty, and kids love them. Through spreading activation, various aspects of one's knowledge in memory can spring to mind during decision making.

Another important characteristic of the human cognitive system is its **limited capacity**. People can consciously consider only a small amount of knowledge at one time.[25] This suggests that the interpretation and integration processes during consumer decision making are fairly simple. For instance, it is unlikely that consumers can consider more than a few characteristics of a brand in forming an attitude or intention to buy the brand. At the same time, we know people are able to handle rather complex tasks such as going to a restaurant because cognitive processes tend to become more *automatic* with experience. That is, over time, cognitive processes gradually require less capacity and conscious control (less thinking is necessary).[26] Grocery shopping, for instance, is routine and cognitively easy for most consumers because many of the interpretation and integration processes involved in choosing food products have become automatic. Highlight 3.4 describes a common example of how **automatic processing** develops.

Marketing Implications

The simple model of consumer decision making just presented has many implications. Because the next several chapters cover this model in detail, only a few examples are given here.

Obviously, it is important for marketers to understand how consumers interpret their marketing strategies. For instance, marketers might have a sale on a brand that is overstocked, but consumers might interpret the price decrease as indicating that product quality has dropped. Marketers are also highly interested in the knowledge, meanings, and beliefs that consumers have for their products, brands, stores, and so on.

The integration processes involved in forming brand attitudes (Do I like this brand?) and purchase intentions (Should I buy this brand?) are critically important for understanding consumer behaviour. Marketers need to know what types of product knowledge are used in integration processes and what knowledge is ignored. Due to the limited capacity of the cognitive system, marketers should expect that consumers integrate only small amounts of knowledge when choosing brands to buy or stores to patronise.

Activation of product knowledge has many implications for marketing. For instance, the choice of a brand name can be highly important for the success of the product because of the various meanings the brand name can activate from consumers' memories. Jaguar is a good name for a sports car because it activates such meanings as

---

HIGHLIGHT 3.5

Automatic Activation of Meanings from Memory

A *wareness of Activation*. It is difficult to become aware of our own activation processes. You would have to pay special attention to what happens when you are exposed to an object, for instance, because most activation tends to be automatic and very rapid. Normally, we are not conscious of the activation process that retrieves stored information from memory. The meanings just 'come to mind'.

'The Family Circus' copyright © by Bil Keane.
Reprinted with special permission of King Features Syndicate.

speed, agility, exotic, rare, beautiful, powerful, and graceful.[27] Another implication is that marketers need to pay attention to differences between consumers because the same stimulus may activate different knowledge in different consumers. The cartoon in Highlight 3.5 illustrates this point.

Knowledge Stored in Memory

Exhibit 3.4 shows that consumers' knowledge in memory influences the cognitive processes involved in decision making. We will discuss consumers' product knowledge and involvement in the next chapter. In this section, we describe two broad types of knowledge that consumers create, and we discuss how this knowledge is organized in memory. We also discuss the cognitive learning processes by which consumers acquire knowledge.

Types of Knowledge

The human cognitive system can interpret virtually any type of information and thereby create knowledge, meanings, and beliefs.[28] Broadly speaking, people have two types of knowledge: (1) general knowledge about their environment and behaviours, and (2) procedural knowledge about how to do things.[29]

General knowledge concerns people's interpretations of relevant information in their environments. For instance, consumers create general knowledge about product categories (compact disks, fast-food restaurants), stores (Marks & Spencer, Debenham, Alders), particular behaviours (shopping at centres, eating ice cream, talking to sales-people), other people (one's best friend, the cute assistant at the local shop, the professor of this course), and even themselves (I am shy, intelligent, and honest).

General knowledge is stored in memory as *propositions* that link or connect two concepts:

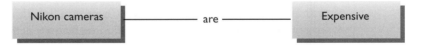

Most propositions are based on some personally relevant connection between the two concepts. For instance, your knowledge that a favourite clothing shop is having a sale creates the simple proposition:

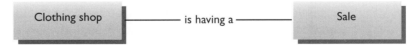

The connections or links in propositions are the key to understanding meaning. Knowledge exists when a meaning concept in memory is linked to another concept via a proposition. Essentially, knowledge or meaning is defined by the connections between concepts.

Consumers' general knowledge is either episodic or semantic.[30] **Episodic knowledge** concerns the specific events that have happened in a person's life. For instance, 'Yesterday I bought a Snickers candy bar from the vending machine' or 'My last credit-card bill had another mistake' are examples of episodic knowledge. Consumers also have **semantic knowledge** about objects and events in the environment. For instance, the personal meanings and beliefs you have about Snickers candy bars – the peanuts, caramel, and calories it contains; the wrapper design; the aroma or taste – are part of your semantic knowledge. When activated from memory, the episodic and semantic components of general knowledge can have important influence on consumers' decision making and overt behaviours.

Consumers also have **procedural knowledge** about how to do things.[31] Procedural knowledge is stored in memory as a production. A *production* is a special type of 'if . . . , then . . . ' proposition that links a concept or event with an appropriate behaviour.

Other examples of productions include 'If the phone rings when you are busy, don't answer it', or 'If a salesperson presses you for a quick decision, say no and leave'.

Over a lifetime of experience, consumers acquire a great deal of procedural knowledge, much of which is highly specific to particular situations. When activated from memory, these productions directly and automatically influence a person's overt behaviour. For instance, Susanne has a production: 'If the price of clothing is reduced by 50 per cent or more, I will consider buying it.' If this procedural knowledge is activated when Susanne sees a half-price sign in the jeans section, she will stop and decide if she needs a new pair of jeans.

Like general knowledge, people's procedural knowledge is relevant for many everyday situations. Consider the procedural knowledge consumers need to operate high-tech equipment such as computers, videocameras and VCRs, stereo receivers, and televisions. Many consumers feel such products have become too complex and difficult to operate.[32] For instance, a recent survey found that only 3 per cent of total TV viewing time is spent watching programmes that have been recorded in advance. Apparently, many people do not have the appropriate procedural knowledge to use the timed recording feature on their VCRs. In recognition that relatively few consumers want and use all the features on their high-tech equipment, some manufacturers are simplifying their products to reduce the procedural knowledge necessary to use them. For example, Philips, the giant Dutch electronics firm, has developed a group of easy-to-use clock radios called 'Easy Line'.[33]

Both general knowledge and procedural knowledge have important influences on consumers' behaviours. Consider the grocery shopping situation described at the beginning of this chapter. Various aspects of Peter Smith's general and procedural knowledge were activated as he moved through the grocery store environment. This knowledge affected his interpretation and integration processes as he made numerous shopping decisions.

Structures of Knowledge

Consumers' general and procedural knowledge is organized to form structures of knowledge in memory. Our cognitive systems create **associative networks** that organize and link many types of knowledge together.[34] Exhibit 3.5 presents an associative network of knowledge for Nike trainers.[35] In this knowledge structure, the Nike concept is connected to various types of general knowledge including episodic

EXHIBIT 3.5

An Associative Network of Knowledge

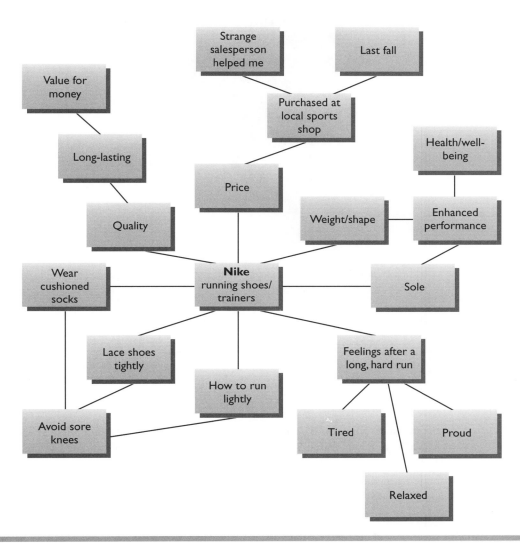

knowledge about past events (shopping at the local sports shop) and semantic knowledge about the features of Nike shoes (their shape, weight, and sole). Also included is knowledge of affective responses (memory of one's feelings after a hard run) and the interpretations of those affective feelings (relaxed and proud). This structure of Nike knowledge also contains productions (how to run lightly, wear cushioned socks) and related semantic knowledge about the consequences of these behaviours (avoid sore knees).

Parts of this knowledge structure might be activated in certain circumstances. For example, some knowledge could be activated by exposure to an athlete wearing Nike shoes on TV or noticing the Nike swoosh symbol on a billboard ad. Other knowledge

As the market for sports shoes matured, Nike introduced many different types of shoe, requiring consumers to form more complex knowledge structures. Courtesy: Nike, Inc.

Lightweight hiking shoe? Or very strong ant? WELL, BOTH REALLY. THE CALDERA IS VERY LIGHT, ESPECIALLY FOR SUCH A DURABLE OUTDOOR SHOE. STILL, YOU'VE GOT TO GIVE THAT ANT A LOT OF CREDIT. THE CALDERA BY NIKE. CARRY A PAIR HOME TODAY.

associated with Nike could be activated by experiencing the pleasant affective feelings of satisfaction and relaxation after a hard workout. Finally, some meanings associated with Nike could be activated through spreading activation as 'activation energy' spreads from one meaning concept in the network to related meanings. Whatever Nike knowledge is activated during decision making has the potential to influence consumers' interpretation and integration processes at that time.

Types of Knowledge Structures

People have two types of knowledge structures – schemas and scripts. Each is an associative network of linked meanings, but **schemas** contain mostly episodic and semantic general knowledge, while **scripts** are organized networks of production knowledge. Both schemas and scripts can be activated in decision-making situations, and they can influence cognitive processes. The structure of knowledge in Exhibit 3.5 is a schema that represents one consumer's general knowledge about Nike running shoes. Marketers are highly interested in understanding consumers' schemas about brands, stores, and product categories.

When consumers experience common situations such as eating in a restaurant, they learn what behaviours are appropriate in that situation. This knowledge may be organized as a sequence of if . . . , then . . . productions called a *script*.[36] Following is an example of a simple script:

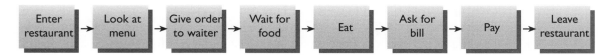

Marketing Implications

To understand consumers' behaviour, marketers need to know what product knowledge consumers have acquired and stored in memory. For instance, marketers may wish to determine how consumers organize a product category into product forms (Do consumers see freeze-dried and instant coffee as separate product forms?). Marketers might want to know the contents of consumers' product schemas (associative networks of general knowledge) or shopping scripts (associative networks of procedural knowledge). In addition, marketers might need to know what types of knowledge are likely to be activated by particular marketing strategies. This could require a detailed analysis of the meanings that are activated when consumers are exposed to a particular colour of a car or a certain typeface for a print ad. In the next chapter, we will examine consumers' product knowledge and involvement.

Cognitive Learning

How do consumers learn the general and procedural knowledge in their schema and script structures? In this text, we distinguish between two broad types of learning – behavioural and cognitive learning. Behavioural learning is discussed in Section 3, and cognitive learning is discussed here.

Cognitive learning occurs when people interpret information in the environment and create new knowledge or meaning. Often these new meanings modify their existing knowledge structures in memory. Basically, consumers come into contact with information about products and services in three ways. Consumers can learn about products or services through *direct personal use experience*. Marketers use a variety of strategies such as in-store trial and free samples to give consumers a direct use experience. Car dealers encourage consumers to drive the car around the block. Clothing shops provide fitting rooms for customers to try on garments, and mirrors to evaluate their appearance. Ice-cream parlours offer free taste samples, and bedding retailers nearly always set up beds so customers can lie down and experience the feel of a mattress before buying.

Cognitive learning can also occur through consumers' vicarious product experience. That is, consumers can acquire knowledge indirectly by observing others using the product. Most vicarious observation probably occurs accidentally when consumers notice other people using a product or service. Marketers can create vicarious product experience for consumers through marketing strategies such as using in-store demonstrations or paying sports stars to wear certain clothes or shoes. Brands with higher market shares have an advantage over less popular brands because consumers are more likely to observe other people using a best-selling brand. Finally, much cognitive learning occurs when consumers *interpret product-related information* from the mass media (news stories, advertising, consumer magazines, etc.) or from personal sources (friends and family).

Interpreting information about products and services can result in three types or levels of cognitive learning – accretion, tuning, and restructuring.[37] Exhibit 3.6 illustrates how these three types of cognitive learning can create and modify associative networks of knowledge. Marketers may develop strategies to influence each type of cognitive learning.

Accretion

Most cognitive learning probably occurs by **accretion**. As consumers interpret information about products and services, they add new knowledge, meaning, and beliefs to their existing knowledge structures. Consumers who learn that Nike shoes have good cushioning will add that knowledge to what they already know, e.g. Nike shoes are expensive (see Exhibit 3.6). Much learning research has focused on how people form declarative knowledge through accretion learning. However, more complex types of cognitive learning that involve changes to the *structure* of the associative knowledge network can also occur.

Tuning

As consumers gain experience with a product, knowledge structures tend to become larger and more complex through accretion processes. At some point, consumers may adjust their knowledge structures to make them more accurate and more generalizable. Most knowledge structures undergo minor changes in meaning as consumers continue to process information from the environment. As shown in Exhibit 3.6, **tuning** can occur when parts of a knowledge structure are combined and given a new overall meaning. For instance, several characteristics of a Nike shoe (lacing pattern, insole, reinforced heel) might be interpreted to mean 'good support'.

Restructuring

Restructuring involves revising the entire associative network of knowledge, which might involve creating entirely new meaning structures and/or reorganizing an old knowledge structure. Accretion, and sometimes tuning, can occur without much cognitive effort. In contrast, restructuring usually involves extensive cognitive effort and substantial thinking and reasoning processes. Therefore, restructuring tends to be rare, occurring only when existing knowledge structures become excessively large and cumbersome (and possibly inaccurate). As illustrated in Exhibit 3.6, this may have happened in the athletic shoe market with the proliferation of specialized shoe models and styles introduced in the 1980s.

Sometimes the introduction of a new product that is quite different from current products can force consumers to restructure their existing product knowledge to accommodate the new product. For instance, many consumers had to restructure their knowledge about cooking techniques when they began using microwave ovens. Changes in consumers' values can also precipitate a restructuring of consumers' product knowledge. For instance, the increasingly strong environmental values of the late 1980s may have led some consumers to restructure their knowledge about disposable nappies and aerosol containers.

EXHIBIT 3.6

Three Types of Cognitive Learning

Type of cognitive learning

Changes in knowledge structure

Accretion
Consumer begins to acquire knowledge, meanings, and beliefs about Nike shoes. Over time, more and more pieces of knowledge will be linked to the Nike shoes concept.

Tuning
More structure is added to the knowledge accumulated by grouping pieces of knowledge into larger units, e.g. several product characteristics may be grouped into the overall category good support.

Restructuring
As more and more knowledge accumulates, consumers may restructure their knowledge. For example, separate knowledge structures may evolve for different types of Nike shoes.

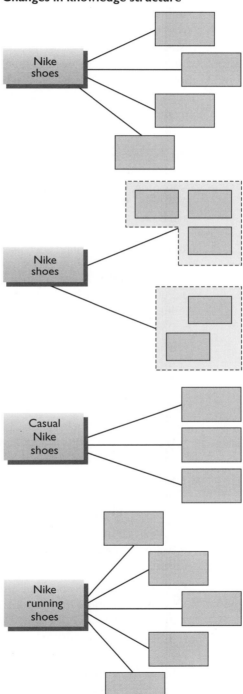

Many marketing strategies are aimed at accretion learning. Marketers often present simple informational claims about their products (Zendium toothpaste contains calcium) and hope that consumers will accurately interpret the information and add this knowledge to their knowledge structures. In other cases, marketers may try to stimulate consumers to tune their knowledge structures (you need special Nike shoes for 'cross training'). On rare occasions, marketers may wish to encourage consumers to restructure their knowledge (actually, beef is just as wholesome as chicken).

In sum, marketers need to monitor consumers' knowledge structures and manage that knowledge. Marketers need to consider what types of meanings they want consumers to form and provide the appropriate information for consumers to process. The next chapter presents several ideas for analysing consumers' product knowledge.

**Back to . . .
Peter Smith**

To summarize what we have covered in this chapter and to review the cognitive processing model, let's return to our friend Peter Smith doing his weekly grocery shopping. Consider what happened as Peter walked down the breakfast cereal aisle. We have divided this purchase occasion into smaller, discrete events and related each one to the appropriate part of our cognitive-processing model. As you work through this example, consider how the various pieces and parts of the model fit together to help explain each event. (You may want to refer to Exhibit 3.4.)

Environmental/Behavioural Event	*Cognitive and Affective Processes*
• Peter noticed a bright orange shelf tag with an arrow and the words 'Unadvertised Special'.	Exposure to information and initial attention; slightly positive affective response
• The sign reminded him that the supply of breakfast cereal at home was getting low.	Activation of stored knowledge
• He looked at the package more closely.	More attention
• He saw that the product was a Kellogg's cereal, All-Bran.	Simple comprehension – interaction with stored knowledge
• He thought to himself that he likes most Kellogg's cereals and that his wife likes fibre-rich cereal.	Activation of additional stored knowledge about affective states
• He picked up a package and read 'With 3 essential B-vitamins and iron'.	Comprehension – interaction with activated knowledge
• As he turned the package around, he noticed more nutritional information. This reminded him of things he knows about nutrition.	Attention and more activated knowledge
• Peter quickly noticed that All-Bran has between 10 to 35 per cent RDA of important vitamins and minerals.	Attention and comprehension; interaction with activated knowledge

He understood what most of this nutritional information meant.	
• Based on this information, Peter was favourably disposed towards All-Bran.	Integration and attitude formation with mildly positive affect
• He then looked at the price on the shelf: £1.78 for 500 g.	Attention and comprehension
• Peter considered all this information and decided to buy a package to see whether his wife would like it.	Integration processes: form an intention to buy
• He tossed a package of Bran into the grocery trolley and continued shopping.	Choice behaviour
• When Peter got to the checkout counter, he paid for the All-Bran and the other products.	Purchase behaviour

Summary

This chapter has presented a number of concepts and ideas that will be used in later chapters. In particular, we introduced the important internal factors of affect and cognition and the affective and cognitive systems. We identified four types of affective responses ranging from emotions to specific feelings to moods to evaluations. We also described the cognitive system and the various types of meanings it constructs. We emphasized that these two systems are highly interrelated and the respective outputs of each can elicit responses from the other. We believe this interactive view is the most useful for understanding consumer behaviour.

Next we presented a model of the cognitive processes involved in consumer decision making. The model has three basic components – knowledge (also called meanings and beliefs) in memory – and two broad cognitive processes: interpretation and integration. An important feature of this model is the close reciprocal interaction between knowledge structures and the cognitive processes that both create and use this knowledge.

We discussed the content and organization of knowledge as associative networks or knowledge structures. We described how meaning concepts are linked together to form propositions and productions that represent general knowledge (episodic and semantic knowledge) and procedural knowledge (how to perform behaviours). Then we described two types of knowledge structures – schemas and scripts – that contain general and procedural knowledge, respectively. Schemas and scripts can be activated to guide cognitive processes and influence overt behaviours.

Key Terms and Concepts

accretion   **54**
activation   **46**
affect   **35**
associative network   **50**

Review and Discussion Questions

1. Describe the four broad types of affective responses that are produced by the affective system, and give an example of each.
2. What is a cognition? Give an example that illustrates the distinction between information (stimuli) and cognition that represents the information.
3. How are the cognitive and affective systems different? How are they interrelated?
4. Consider a product such as an automobile or a perfume. Describe at least three types of meanings that consumers might construct to represent various aspects of the product. Discuss how marketers might try to influence each meaning.
5. Describe three types of consumer decisions marketers might be interested in. What are the three main cognitive processes involved in consumer decision making?
6. For each type of knowledge activation process give an example from personal experience that is related to marketer influence and one that is not marketing related.
7. Compare and contrast general and procedural knowledge. Are they related?
8. Give an example of how exposure to a marketing strategy could cause spreading activation within a consumer's associative network of product knowledge.
9. Using a recent purchase as an example, develop a list of (*a*) influence factors; (*b*) reciprocal interactions; (*c*) affective responses; and (*d*) cognitive responses.
10. Describe how each of the cognitive processes in the model of consumer decision making (Exhibit 3.4) was present in your purchase situation (Question 9).

Additional Reading

For a discussion of the relationship between affect and cognition, see:

Rik G. M. Pieters and W. Fred Van Raaij, 'Functions and Management of Affect: Applications to Economic Behaviour', *Journal of Economic Psychology*, 9, 1988, pp. 251–282.

Many examples of affect related to consumer behaviour are provided in:

Christian Derbaix and Michel T. Pham, 'Affective reactions to consumption situations: A pilot investigation', *Journal of Economic Psychology*, 12, 1991, pp. 325–355.

For a general discussion of the information-processing approach to cognition, see:

Klaus G. Grunert, 'Cognition and Economic Psychology', in *Essays in Economic Psychology*, eds. Hermann Brandstätter and Werner Güth (Berlin: Springer, 1994), pp. 91–108.

For a review of information-processing research in consumer behaviour, see:

James R. Bettman and Mita Sujan, 'Research in Consumer Information Processing', in *Review of Marketing, 1987*, ed. Michael J. Houston (Chicago: American Marketing Association, 1988), pp. 197–235.

For discussions of how information-processing theory can be used to understand consumers and develop marketing strategies, see:

Alice M. Tybout, Bobby J. Calder, and Brian Sternthal, 'Using Information Processing Theory to Design Marketing Strategies', *Journal of Marketing Research*, February 1981.

For a readable discussion of some of the problems with the early information-processing models and suggestions for how they can be improved, see:

Klaus G. Grunert, 'Research in Consumer Behaviour: Beyond Attitudes and Decision Making', *European Research*, August 1988, pp. 172–183.

For an analysis of procedural knowledge and scripts (of salespeople, not consumers), see:

Thomas W. Leigh and Patrick F. McGraw, 'Mapping the Procedural Knowledge of Industrial Sales Personnel: A Script-Theoretic Investigation', *Journal of Marketing*, January 1989, pp. 16–34.

For an analysis of how consumers' knowledge structures change as they acquire more experience and expertise, see:

Joseph Alba and J. Wesley Hutchinson. 'Dimensions of Consumer Expertise', *Journal of Consumer Research*, March 1987, pp. 411–454.

For a discussion of five types of emotional experiences, see:

Robert A. Westbrook and Richard L. Oliver. 'The Dimensionality of Consumption Emotion Patterns and Consumer Satisfaction', *Journal of Consumer Research*, June 1991, pp. 84–91.

MARKETING STRATEGY IN ACTION
Giorgio Armani

 hen Melrose Plant, the Former Earl of Caverness, tries to infiltrate the Holdsworth family under the guise of a librarian in Martha Grime's mystery novel *The Old Contemptibles*, he has to find some clothes which will hide his noble origin. He finally settles for an Armani suit, because it is the least formal of all his clothing, and tears the label out. The ploy does not work out: 'Nice suit you have – Armani, isn't it?' he is asked. He concludes that you can take the label out of a suit, but you cannot take the Armani out.

Born in northern Italy in 1934, the young Armani had thought of becoming a doctor before he turned to fashion. Starting on the shop floor, he soon became assistant designer with Cerruti, then went freelance. Giorgio Armani first made his name with his elegant, sexy men's suits. In 1974, after many years' experience in all facets of fashion, Armani launched his own womenswear, with an unconventional emphasis on unstructured ease and masculine shapes. It was his pattern mixes that attracted the initial attention; plaid shirts over other shirts in coordinating plaid and pants, and classic raglan coats over kangaroo-pocket sweaters.

'At the age of 38, on Corso Venezia in Milan, in two rooms which we furnished with the money from the sale of our Volkswagen, we began', he recalled. 'I wanted women to be able to wear jackets, like men, without losing anything of their feminine allure. My "teachers" were the creators of the costumes for American films in the 1930s, not to mention Coco Chanel. What I had in mind was that elegant, understated air of the thirties and forties . . . . Traditional clothing depressed me. Even suits tailored to order made me feel old before my time. When I began to design, men all dressed in the same way. American industry called the shots, with its technicians scattered all over the world . . . all impeccably equal, equally impeccable. The Mao syndrome. Everyone wore the same uniform, a bit wider here, a bit more tapered there, but the substance was always the same. You couldn't tell them apart. They had no defects. But I liked defects. I wanted to personalize the jacket, to make it more closely attuned to its wearer. How? By removing the structure. Making it into a sort of second skin.'

Armani kept making what had become the ultimate power suits for men, but more than that, he changed the way women dressed. He made the supple neutral-toned tailored jacket a business uniform, the pantsuit a way to look chic anywhere, and his own name a by-word for sleek, exquisite tailoring and taste. And in the 1990s, he succeeded with drop-dead glamour, dressing stars for the Oscar night and transforming the way Hollywood looked. Armani made movie stars fashion icons once again. Understated elegance pervades all Giorgio Armani clothes, and has made him one of the world's most critically acclaimed and commercially successful designers.

Armani designed for a thinking audience, and his underlying aesthetic sense enabled him to eliminate the superfluous and to emphasize comfort in his clothes.

He likes to explain his thinking about style and design by reference to three golden rules; eliminate the superfluous, emphasize the comfortable, and acknowledge the elegance of the uncomplicated. It is a simple philosophy perhaps, but it is also one which has revolutionized the fashion of the last 15 years, literally changing the way men and women dress the world over. From his very first collections, Giorgio Armani created clothes which abandoned rigid conventional tailoring and were, as one writer put it, 'ostentatious only in their rich comfort'. Also notable for their use of multi-textured fabrics. Armani's unique clothes found ready buyers from the outset and their appeal has never faded. In particular the designer's legendary unstructured jacket soon became, and remains, a fashion classic. Today there are more than 2000 stores worldwide selling Armani collections, and the Armani label comprises everything from perfumes and lingerie to shoes and umbrellas. This international fashion empire, with Giorgio Armani as its sole head, has estimated annual sales of more than $1.7 billion.

Today the centre of Armani's empire is to be found at 11 Via Borgonuovo, an elegant Milanese palazzo built in the seventeenth century. Behind its façade are not only Giorgio Armani's own spacious apartments, but also the design studios where everything from perfumes to ties are created, and the theatre where each season's shows are presented.

Giorgio Armani himself is a fit and tanned man with bright blue eyes. His usual outfit comprises a plain navy pullover and grey or navy trousers. He admits to being a workaholic and to being 'extremely demanding', and his attention to every detail – not only to the design of his clothes, but also to the fittings of the shops which sell them and to each and every Armani advertisement – is well known. Meanwhile the Armani organization goes from strength to strength.

Back in 1982 Giorgio Armani became the first fashion designer to appear on the cover of *Time* magazine since Christian Dior and he won prestigious awards throughout the world, among them the Grand Ufficiale Dell'Ordine Al Merito, Italy's highest government award.

Despite such acclaim, he remains a shy and retiring man. Whenever possible he avoids the limelight, preferring instead to be at work in his studio on the designs which will bear the Armani name: designs which eliminate the superfluous, emphasize the comfortable and acknowledge the elegance of the uncomplicated . . .

His approach to creativity is distinctive, seen as it is through a prism which balances the social changes in the world and the evolution of consumer tastes and needs. As he views it, his designs are often influenced by what his audience inspires. 'Drastically imposing a fashion – whatever it may be – would mean having no respect for the consumer. As far as I am concerned, I do just the opposite: if I catch sight of a man or woman on the street dressed in a way that strikes me as uniquely elegant, I might interpret it for my collections. The goal I seek is to have people refine their style through my clothing without having them become victims of fashion.'

Discussion Questions

1. What types of affective responses to the Armani name might be created by consumers' affective systems? How might the cognitive system interpret these responses?

2. What types of cognition (knowledge) do Armani customers have about Giorgio Armani and Armani?

3. How might consumers' affective and cognitive responses influence their decision making and contribute to Giorgio Armani's success?

4. How are consumers' scripts relevant for the marketing of Armani products?

Source: Adapted from Lynda Stretton, *The Fashion Page*, www.glitter.com/designers/Giorgio Armani.

Consumers' Product Knowledge and Involvement

Fish for the Family

Many people believe that Danes eat a lot of fish. Given the many kilometres of coastline, that seems like a natural conclusion. As a matter of fact, however, fish consumption in Denmark is considerably lower than in neighbouring countries like Sweden and Norway. Apart from the traditional marinated herring and the equally traditional fried plaice, Danes do not eat much fish. In particular, consumption of fresh fish (as opposed to tinned or frozen fish) is low.

Why is that? Public authorities have untiringly proclaimed how healthy it is to eat fish. Also, consumer focus groups have indicated that most people actually have a quite positive attitude towards fish. They realize that it is healthy to eat it, and many consumers actually say that they enjoy the taste of it, and they regard both health and taste as important ingredients for a good family life. Why don't they eat more of it, then?

When analysing what consumers thought about buying and preparing fresh fish, it turned out that a major barrier was that fresh fish was perceived as difficult to get hold of, difficult to prepare, and difficult to eat. Danish supermarkets do not carry it, because the usual cooling counters used for meat do not have the right temperature for fish, and consumers had to go to a fishmonger's to buy it fresh. Consumers did not have recipes and thought that its preparation was complicated and time-consuming. Both aspects meant that additional time had to be spent on shopping and cooking, time which many consumers would rather spend with their families. Consumers also think that fresh fish has many bones, which makes for a disagreeable eating experience, especially for children.

One company, Thorfisk, listened to the voice of the consumer and developed a product concept to encourage consumers to eat fresh fish. They equipped some of the supermarkets with special cooling counters which had the right temperature for storing it, thus making it easier for the supermarkets to carry it. They offered a variety of fish, all cut into fillets or other serving-size portions, and all of them guaranteed boneless. They were packaged in attractive blue, plastic packaging, raising associations to freshness and the sea, instead of the dull white ones usually used in cooling counters. Each package contained a recipe that was easy and convenient to use, but which at the same time was sophisticated enough to avoid the impression of fast food. The concept was so successful that other supermarket chains actively pushed for establishing a similar product line.[1]

This case illustrates the importance of product attributes in marketing strategy and the need for marketers to understand what consumers think about product attributes and related concepts. In this chapter, we examine consumers' product knowledge and involvement, two important concepts in the affect and cognition part of the Wheel of Consumer Analysis model. We begin by discussing four levels of product-related knowledge. Then we discuss consumers' knowledge about product attributes, benefits, and values. We show how these three types of meaning can be linked to form a simple associative network of knowledge called a *means–end chain*. Next, we examine the important concept of consumers' interest or involvement in products and other aspects of their environments. The means–end model is used to help explain consumers' feelings of involvement. We conclude the chapter by discussing how means–end chains can be used to analyse consumers' relationships with products and brands and how marketing strategies can influence consumers' product involvement.

Levels of Product Knowledge

Consumers have different **levels of product knowledge**, which they can use to interpret new information and make purchase choices.[2] Levels of knowledge are formed when people acquire separate meaning concepts (*accretion*) and combine them into larger, more abstract categories of knowledge (*tuning*).[3] For instance, you might combine knowledge about the braking, acceleration, and cornering ability of a car to form a more inclusive concept that you call *handling*. Your knowledge of handling is at a higher, more abstract level because it includes these less abstract meanings.[4] Another example is the various types of bicycle that make up the overall bike category – racing, mountain, road, and city bikes. Each of these meaning categories can be separated into more specific knowledge categories (different types of road or mountain bikes). Thus, a person's knowledge about bikes, mountain bikes, and types of mountain bike may form a hierarchical structure of bicycle knowledge at different levels.[5]

No single level of knowledge captures all the possible meanings of an object, event, or behaviour. Each level of meaning is useful for certain purposes, but not all purposes. Meanings at different levels of abstraction are related hierarchically in that more abstract meanings subsume (incorporate or include) meanings at lower levels. Thus, 'responsiveness' for a tennis racquet subsumes the materials of its construction, the head shape, the type of strings, and so on. We use the concept of *levels of meaning* throughout the text to help us understand consumers' product knowledge. A useful distinction of different levels of product knowledge is a distinction into knowledge at the levels of the product class, product forms, brands, and models. Exhibit 4.1 gives examples of each level of product knowledge.

Marketers are very interested in consumers' *brand* knowledge. A brand, in most cases, is a product or a series of products carrying a brand name identifying the manufacturer of the product. In other cases, a brand can be a product carrying a name identifying not the manufacturer, but the retailer selling the product. Most marketing strategies for consumer goods are brand oriented in that they are intended to make consumers aware of a brand, teach them about a brand, and influence them to buy that brand. Most marketing research focuses on consumers' knowledge and beliefs about brands. Likewise, much of our discussion in this text will concern consumers' brand knowledge.

For some products, consumers can have knowledge about models, a more concrete level of product knowledge than brands. A *model* is a specific example of a brand that

EXHIBIT 4.1

Levels of Product Knowledge

More Abstract ←			→ Less Abstract
Product Class	Product Form	Brand	Model/Features
Coffee	Ground	Jacob's	500-gram package
	Instant	Nescafé	125-gram jar
Cars	Sports car	Mazda	MX 3 with sun roof
	Off roader	Suzuki	Vitara with V6 engine
Pens	Ball point	Bic	NKr 5 model, regular tip
	Fountain pen	Waterman	Thin tip, ink converter
Beer	Lager	Heineken	6-pack cans
	Stout	Guinness	0.33 l bottles

has one or more unique product features or attributes (Exhibit 4.1 gives several examples). For instance, Nikon 35 mm cameras are available in several different models; Coca-Cola comes in light, caffeine-free, cherry-flavoured, and other versions; and Haagen-Dazs ice cream is sold in various flavours. The 325, 528, and 740 models of BMW cars vary in size, price, and exterior design and in distinctive features and options such as fancy wheels, automatic transmission, leather seats, and so on.

Going in a more abstract direction from the brand and model levels of knowledge, a *product form* is a broader category that includes several brands that are similar in some important way. Often, the basis for a product-form category is a physical characteristic that the brands share. For instance, freeze-dried, instant, ground, and whole-bean coffee are defined by their physical form. In some cases, certain product forms become so well established in the consumers' minds that marketers can treat them as separate markets. Light soft drinks, sports cars, fast-food hamburger restaurants, and laptop computers are examples.

The *product class* is the broadest and most inclusive level of product knowledge and may include several product forms (and many brands and models within those categories). Coffee, cars, and soft drinks are examples. Concepts at the product class level may have relatively few characteristics in common (the various product forms of coffee are made from coffee beans). Marketing strategies to promote the entire product class can be effective for promoting brands with a high market share. For example, Estrella might promote consumption of salty crisp snacks (a product class that includes various types of potato and flavoured crisps). Because the company controls as much as a 45 per cent market share in Scandinavia, any increase in overall consumption of the product class is likely to benefit Estrella just as much as its competitors.

Because consumers are likely to make separate purchase decisions at each level of knowledge, marketers need to understand how consumers organize their product knowledge in terms of these different levels.[6] For instance, a consumer might make a choice between alternative product classes (Should I buy a television or a stereo?), ifferent product forms (Should I purchase a large-screen TV or a portable one?), rious brands (Should I buy a Philips or a Sony TV?), and alternative models (Should I oose a 27-inch TV with stereo speakers or a 32-inch set with surround sound?). In ʰ, all levels of product knowledge are relevant to the marketing manager, with the ᵈ level of particular importance.

ʰuct Knowledge

guish three types of product knowledge – knowledge about the attributes ʰstics of products, the positive consequences or benefits of using products, lues the product helps consumers satisfy or achieve (see Exhibit 4.2). ʰave thought about and analysed these three types or levels of consumers' ᵒwledge, when developing marketing strategies.

s of Attributes

ʰ example demonstrates, marketers have many strategic options for product ʰstics or attributes. Within the limits imposed by production capabilities and ᵗ resources, marketing managers can add new attributes to a product (the fish ᵗᵉ ᵒmplete with a recipe), remove old attributes (the fish has no bones), or modify existing attributes (the fish is packaged in a blue container instead of the common white one). Marketers can change brand attributes in an attempt to make their products more appealing to consumers. Highlight 4.1 describes a successful change of product attributes.

HIGHLIGHT 4.1
What's in a Handle?

T he old Pyrex measuring cup made by Corning Glass Works was a kitchen classic in the US and in many other countries. The glass cup with its familiar attributes – a simple volume gauge printed in red on one side, the pouring lip, and the nice big handle – was found in as many as 80 per cent of American households. Even though the bulky handle made the three sizes (1-, 2-, and 4-cup) difficult to stack, no one complained. In fact, the cups had not changed much since they had been introduced some 50 years before. Why should marketers change the attributes of a product this successful?

The idea for changing the attributes of the Pyrex measuring cup came about by accident when the handle on a test product sagged during heating. This gave designers the idea of an 'open' handle that was attached to the cup only at one end. Besides being cheaper to produce, this handle would make the cups stackable and therefore more convenient to store in a cupboard. Corning also added a second new attribute, making the cup a bit deeper so that foods could be heated in microwave ovens without boiling over. However, the designers kept the familiar red measuring gauge on the side. What was the result of making these simple changes in the attributes of this product? Sales increased 150 per cent.

Source: Toni Mack, 'What's in a Handle?' *Forbes*, 25 January 1988, p. 87.
Reprinted by permission of *Forbes* Magazine. © Forbes Inc., 1988.

Perhaps because they are so interested in the physical characteristics of their products, marketers sometimes act as if consumers think about products and brands as *bundles of attributes*. Even the simplest products have several attributes (pencils have varying lead densities, softness of erasers, shapes, and colours). Of course, complex products, such as cars and stereo receivers, have a great many attributes. From a cognitive processing perspective, however, we might wonder if consumers really have knowledge in memory about all of these attributes, and whether consumers actually activate and use this knowledge when deciding which products and brands to buy. Marketers need to know which product attributes are most important to consumers, what those attributes mean to consumers, and how consumers use this knowledge in cognitive processes such as comprehension and decision making.

Consumers can have knowledge about different types of product attributes.[7] Consumers' knowledge about **concrete attributes** represents tangible, physical characteristics of a product such as the type of fibre in a blanket or the front-seat legroom in a car.[8] Knowledge about **abstract attributes** represents intangible, subjective characteristics of a product such as the quality or warmth of a blanket or the stylishness or comfort of a car. In addition, consumers' attribute knowledge may also contain affective evaluations of each attribute (I don't like the itchiness of wool blankets; I love strawberry ice cream).

Products as Bundles of Benefits

Marketers also recognize that consumers often think about products and brands in terms of their consequences, not their attributes.[9] *Consequences* are the outcomes that happen when the product is purchased and used or consumed. For instance, a stereo system might be very loud, require assembly or repairs, or make the user feel proud. A face cream might cause an allergic reaction or cost too much. Other consumers might think the buyer is either hip or foolish for buying a certain brand of jeans or trainers.

Consumers can have knowledge about two types of product consequences – functional and psychosocial. **Functional consequences** are tangible outcomes of using a product that consumers experience rather directly. For instance, functional consequences include the immediate physiological outcomes of product use (eating a Big Mac satisfies your hunger; drinking a Pepsi quenches your thirst). Functional consequences also include the physical, tangible performance outcomes of using or consuming a product – a hair dryer dries your hair quickly, a car gets a certain number of kilometres per litre, a toaster toasts bread evenly, and an ink pen writes smoothly without skipping.

Psychosocial consequences refer to the psychological and social outcomes of product use. *Psychological consequences* of product use are internal, personal outcomes, such as how the product makes you feel. For instance, using L'Oréal shampoo might make you feel more attractive, wearing Benetton sportswear might make you feel more stylish, and eating a Magnum ice cream might make you feel happy. Consumers may also have knowledge about the *social consequences* of product use (my friends will like/respect/envy me if I buy a Sony stereo system; my mother will think I am a clever shopper if I buy this jacket in a sale).

People's affective and cognitive systems interpret these consequences of product use and form knowledge and beliefs about these functional and psychosocial consequences in memory. People's affective systems may result in a consumer feeling negative affect (dissatisfaction) if a product needs repairs soon after being bought. Or a consumer might experience positive feelings of pride and self-esteem if other people comment favourably on a new sweater. At a later time, both affective and cognitive knowledge may be activated from memory and used in other interpretation or integration processes.

Consumers can think about the positive and negative consequences of product use as possible benefits or potential risks. **Benefits** are the desirable consequences consumers seek when buying and using products and brands (I want a car with fast acceleration; I want a car with good fuel economy). Consumers can have both cognitive knowledge about benefits and affective responses to benefits. Cognitive knowledge includes propositions linking the product to desired functional and psychosocial consequences (I want my stereo system to have excellent sound reproduction; if I wear that suit, people will notice me). Affective reactions to benefits include positive affective responses associated with the desired consequence (I feel good when people notice me).

Consumers often think about products and brands as *bundles of benefits*[10] rather than bundles of attributes (see Exhibit 4.2). Therefore, marketers can divide consumers

EXHIBIT 4.2

Types of Product Knowledge

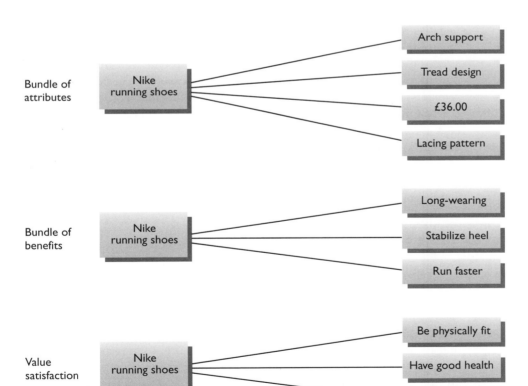

into subgroups or market segments according to their *◌* consequences, a process called *benefit segmentation.*[11] For of toothpaste are seeking appearance benefits (whiter *◌* interested in health benefits (preventing tooth decay).

Perceived risks concern the undesirable consequences that c◌◌◌ avoid when they buy and use products. A variety of negative consequences might occur. Some consumers worry about the *physical risks* of product consumption (side effects of a cold remedy, injury on a bicycle, electric shock from a hair dryer). Other types of unpleasant consequences include *financial risk* (finding out the warranty doesn't cover fixing your microwave oven; buying new athletic shoes and finding them in a sale the next day), *functional risk* (an aspirin product doesn't get rid of headaches very well; a motor oil additive doesn't really reduce engine wear), and *psychosocial risk* (my friends might think these sunglasses look weird on me; I won't feel confident wearing this suit). In sum, perceived risk includes consumers' knowledge or beliefs about unfavourable consequences, including the negative affective responses associated with these unpleasant consequences (unfavourable evaluations, bad feelings, and negative emotions).

The amount of perceived risk a consumer experiences is influenced by two things: (1) the degree of unpleasantness of the negative consequences and (2) the likelihood that these negative consequences will occur. In cases where consumers do not know about the potential for negative consequences (a side effect of a health remedy, a safety defect in a car), perceived risk will be low. In other cases, consumers may have unrealistic perceptions of product risks because they overestimate the likelihood of negative physical consequences. Highlight 4.2 describes some marketplace problems created by consumers' misperceptions of risk.

Because consumers are unlikely to purchase products with high perceived risk, marketers try to manage consumers' perceptions of the negative consequences of product purchase and use. Most mail-order companies try to reduce consumers' perceptions of financial and performance risk by offering an unconditional, money-back-if-not-satisfied guarantee. A different marketing strategy is to intentionally activate knowledge about product risk in order to show how using a particular brand avoids the negative consequences. For instance, Volvo had advertising campaigns in the 1970s emphasizing the risks of driving, while emphasizing the additional safety features of Volvo cars.[12]

Products as Value Satisfiers

Consumers also have knowledge about the personal, symbolic values that products and brands help them to satisfy or achieve (Exhibit 4.2). **Values** are people's broad life goals (I want to be successful; I need security). Values also involve the affect associated with such goals and needs (the feelings and emotions that accompany success). Recognizing when a value has been satisfied or a basic life goal has been achieved is an internal event that is rather intangible and subjective (I feel secure; I am respected by others; I am successful). In contrast, functional and psychosocial consequences are more tangible, and it is more obvious when they occur (people noticed when I wore that silk shirt).

There are many ways in which values can be classified.[13] One useful scheme identifies two types or levels of values – instrumental and terminal.[14] **Instrumental values** are preferred modes of conduct. They are ways of behaving (having a good time,

HIGHLIGHT 4.2

The Perception and Reality of Risk

M any consumers seem to believe consumer products should involve no risk and that attaining zero risk is possible. Yet, as we reduce significant risks in our environments, consumers seem to become ever more anxious about the imagined hazards of modern life. People are confused about perceived risks of products, partly because several of the major 'hazards' of recent years turned out to be false alarms or were greatly exaggerated. An example is what occurred in 1990, when Perrier mineral water was discovered to contain minute amounts of benzene, a known carcinogen. The benzene was a natural ingredient in the carbon dioxide gas that bubbles up in the springs in France. The benzene was usually removed by filters, but an employee had not changed the filter frequently enough.

Before the actual cause of the contamination was established the company's divisions in France, the United Kingdom and North America had sent out conflicting messages, which confused the public and resulted in unintentional damage to the company's reputation. All divisions recalled millions of bottles, but while the UK division admitted they did not initially know the cause of the problem, the French and North American division immediately announced that the problem was in the bottling line – which was not true. Perrier clearly benefited from the media coverage of its global recall, but failure to come forward from the beginning with a clear policy may have cost the company some credibility. Despite the immediate scare Perrier quickly regained market leadership; a full month after its return it had regained almost half its previous market share.

One problem in risk assessment is that our technologies for measuring tiny quantities of harmful compounds in products outstrip our ability to make reasonable judgements about what to do about it. The amount of benzene detected in Perrier was 19 parts per billion. Fifteen years earlier, that level of benzene concentration could not have been detected.

Did this make Perrier dangerous? It all depends on your perceptions of and tolerance for very small risks. The actual risks of developing cancer from drinking Perrier were extremely small. One expert estimated the additional cancer risk from drinking one litre of the 'contaminated' Perrier every day for 70 years as somewhere between 1 in 100 000 and 1 in 10 million. This means that if every European drank one litre of Perrier a day every day of his or her life, the additional number of cancer deaths might be 300 or so per year. Of course, virtually no one consumes that much mineral water. Yet in the emotional climate of 1990, Perrier believed it had to throw away ECU29 million worth of an essentially harmless product.

Source: Warren T. Brookes, 'The Wasteful Pursuit of Zero Risk,' *Forbes*, 30 April 1990, pp. 161–172. Reprinted by permission of *Forbes* Magazine. © Forbes Inc., 1990; Gary Kurtzbard and George J. Siomkos, 'Crafting a Damage Control Plan: Lessons from Perrier', *Journal of Business Strategy*, 13(2), 1992, pp. 39–43; D. Butler, 'Perrier's painful period', *Management Today*, August 1990, pp. 72–73.

acting independently, showing self-reliance). **Terminal values**, on the other hand, are preferred states of being or broad psychological states (happy, at peace, successful). Both instrumental and terminal values (goals or needs) represent the broadest and most personal consequences people are trying to achieve in their lives. Exhibit 4.3 gives a categorization of values that has been shown to be almost universal, i.e. which can be used to characterize people all over the world.[15]

EXHIBIT 4.3

Instrumental and Terminal Values

Value Domain	Instrumental Values (Preferred Modes of Behaviour)	Terminal Values (Preferred End States of Being)
Self-direction	Choosing own goals Curious Independent	Creativity Freedom Self-respect
Stimulation	Daring	A varied life An exciting life
Hedonism	Enjoying life	Pleasure
Achievement	Ambitious Successful Capable Influential Intelligent	
Power	Preserving my public image	Authority Wealth Social power Social recognition
Security	Clean Healthy	Social order Family security National security Reciprocation of favours Sense of belonging
Conformity	Obedient Honouring parents and elders	Self-discipline Politeness
Tradition	Humble Devout Accepting my portion in life Moderate	Respect for tradition
Spirituality		A spiritual life Meaning in life Inner harmony Detachment
Benevolence	Helpful Loyal Forgiving Honest Responsible	True friendship Mature love
Universalism	Broad-minded Protecting the environment	Social justice Equality A world at peace A world of beauty Unity with nature Wisdom

Source: Adapted from Shalom H. Schwartz, 'Universals in the Content and Structure of Values: Theoretical Advances and Empirical Tests in 20 Countries', in *Advances in Experimental Social Psychology*, ed. Mark P. Zanna (San Diego, CA: Academic Press, 1992), pp. 1–65.

Certain values – called *core values* – are a central aspect of people's self-concept – their knowledge about themselves. These core values are the key elements in a *self-schema* – an associative network of interrelated knowledge about oneself.[16] Besides values, self-schemas include knowledge of important life events (episodic memories), knowledge of one's own behaviour, and beliefs and feelings about one's body (body image).[17] Consumers' core values have a major influence on their cognitive processes and choice behaviours; therefore, they are of particular interest to marketers. For instance, the growing core value of protecting the environment has created many new marketing opportunities (for example for improved packaging made from bio-degradable, or reusable materials).

Because they represent important consequences that are personally relevant, values often are associated with strong affective responses. Satisfying a value usually elicits a positive affect (happiness, joy, satisfaction), while blocking a value produces a negative affect (frustration, anger, disappointment). For many people, buying their first car satisfies the values of independence and freedom, and generates positive affective feelings of pride and satisfaction. On the other hand, your value of security is not satisfied if your new bicycle lock is broken by a thief, which could create a substantial negative affect (anger, frustration, fear).

In summary, consumers can have product knowledge about product attributes, consequences of product use, and personal values. Most marketing research focuses on one type of product knowledge – usually attributes or consequences, where the usual focus is on benefits rather than on risks. Values are examined less frequently. The problem is that studying only one type of knowledge gives marketers an incomplete understanding of consumers' product knowledge. They miss the connections between attributes, consequences, and values.

Means–End Chains of Product Knowledge

Consumers can combine the three types of product knowledge to form a simple associative network called a means–end chain.[18] A **means–end chain** is a knowledge structure that links consumers' knowledge about product attributes with their knowledge about consequences and values.[19]

The means–end perspective suggests that consumers think about product attributes subjectively in terms of personal consequences. (What is this attribute good for? What does this attribute do for me?) In other words, consumers see most product attributes as a *means to some end*. The end could be a consequence (a benefit or a risk) or a more abstract value.

A common representation of a means–end chain has four levels:[20]

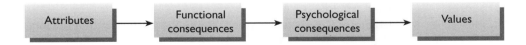

Exhibit 4.4 presents definitions of the four levels in the means–end chain and gives examples of each level. Sometimes the distinctions between the four levels can be a bit fuzzy. For instance, you might be uncertain whether 'being with friends' is a psycho-social consequence or a value. Fortunately, marketers don't have to worry about making such fine distinctions when using the means–end chain model to develop

EXHIBIT 4.4

A Means–End Chain Model of Consumers' Product Knowledge

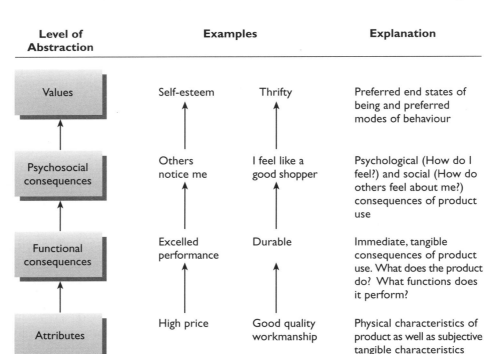

Level of Abstraction	Examples		Explanation
Values	Self-esteem	Thrifty	Preferred end states of being and preferred modes of behaviour
Psychosocial consequences	Others notice me	I feel like a good shopper	Psychological (How do I feel?) and social (How do others feel about me?) consequences of product use
Functional consequences	Excelled performance	Durable	Immediate, tangible consequences of product use. What does the product do? What functions does it perform?
Attributes	High price	Good quality workmanship	Physical characteristics of product as well as subjective tangible characteristics

marketing strategies. The main point of the means–end chain model is that consumers think in terms of personal consequences. They create means–end knowledge structures that link tangible product attributes to functional and psychosocial consequences and in turn to more abstract and personal values and goals.

Because means–end chains contain consumers' personally relevant meanings for products and brands, they are unique to each consumer's background and personal interests. Thus, different consumers are likely to have different means–end chains for the same product or brand, although there usually are some similarities. And we should not be surprised to find that consumers' product meanings can be quite different from those of a marketing manager.

To summarize, the means–end chain model proposes that the meaning of a product attribute is given by its perceived consequences.[21] Consider two physical attributes Gillette designed into its popular Sensor razor – a spring suspension system and a lubricating strip. These product attributes probably don't mean much to most consumers until they use the product and experience its consequences or else learn about them from advertising or other consumers. Gillette's advertising was designed to communicate key product benefits hoping that consumers might form the following means–end chains:

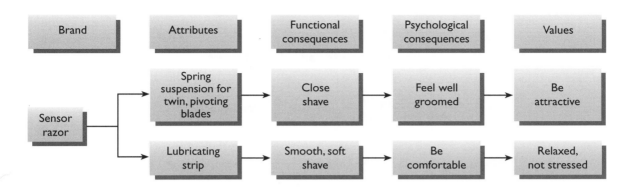

Examples of Means–End Chains

Exhibit 4.5 presents several means–end chains that represent one consumer's product knowledge about a product class (hair spray), a product form (low fat cheese), and a brand (Adidas running shoes). This figure illustrates four important points about means–end chains. First, actual means–end chains vary considerably in the meanings they contain. Second, not every means–end chain leads to a value. In fact, the end of a means–end chain can be a consequence at any level of abstraction – from a functional consequence (This toothpaste will give me fresh breath) to a psychosocial consequence (My friends will like being close to me) to an instrumental value (I will be clean) to a terminal value (I will be happy). In cases where product attributes have no connections to consequences, consumers do not know what the attribute is good for, and it will probably have little effect on their behaviour. Third, some of the means–end chains in Exhibit 4.5 are incomplete, with 'missing' levels of meanings. This illustrates that the actual product knowledge in consumers' means–end chains does not necessarily contain each of the four levels of product meaning shown in the idealized means–end chain model. Finally, although not shown in Exhibit 4.5, some product attributes may have multiple means–end chains, which can be conflicting. That is, some attributes can lead to both positive and negative ends. For example, consider the means–end chains that may be associated with price. For a fairly expensive product such as a watch, higher prices may have both positive and negative consequences (perceived benefits and risks). Consumers may find it difficult to make purchase decisions that involve such conflicting meanings:

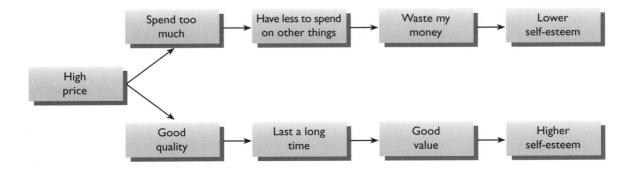

EXHIBIT 4.5

Examples of Means–End Chains

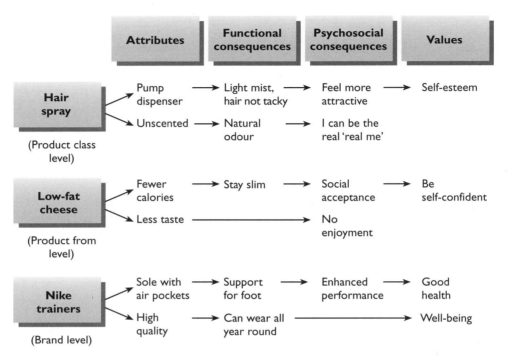

Source: The Nike example is from Susan Baker, 'Extending Means–end Theory Through an
Investigation of the Consumer Benefit/Price Sensitivity Relationship in Two Markets',
PhD dissertation (Cranfield University, 1996). The other examples are by the authors.

Measuring Means–End Chains

Various interview methods have been developed for measuring means–end chains. They all involve two basic steps. First, the researcher must identify or elicit the product attributes that are most important to each consumer when he or she makes a purchase decision. Exhibit 4.6 describes four ways of identifying the most relevant attributes.[22] The second step is an interview process called *laddering*, intended to reveal how the consumer links product attributes to more abstract consequences and values.[23] For each important attribute, the researcher asks the consumer a series of questions in the format of 'Why is that important to you?' Exhibit 4.7 shows an example of a laddering interview. The example is an excerpt from a one-to-one, personal interview. However, laddering can also be done by self-administered questionnaires or computer-aided interviewing, and quantitative approaches, allowing data collection with large samples, have been tried as well. [24]

By identifying the connections between product attributes, consequences, and values in the consumers' means–end chains, laddering helps managers understand what

EXHIBIT 4.6

Identifying Key Attributes Considered by Consumers

‡itation

IER: 'Please tell me what characteristics you usually consider when
which brand of ball-point pen to buy.'

R: 'Let's see. I think about the price, the colour of the ink, the fineness of
? pen feels in my hand.'

e are several brands of running shoes. Assume that you are thinking of
nning shoes. I want you to sort these brands into groups so that the shoes
ke in some way important to you and are different from the shoes in the

l brands of running shoes. I want you to sort them into groups using any

:ribe what each pile means to you. Why are these brands together? How are
1t from those other shoes?'

these shoes are all high-tech and expensive. These are cheaper and have
's. And these brands are in between.'

e are three brands of running shoes. Assume that you were thinking of
.nning shoes. In what important way are two of these similar and different
? there any other ways?'

1m. Well, these two shoes have special construction features to keep your
id. This one doesn't. And these two have a staggered lacing system, while
itional lacing pattern.'

'e I have four frozen ready-meals. Please rank them according to how likely
l choose them as dinner for your family tomorrow. As you rank them, please
or your ranking.'

)ne contains fish, and I don't like fish, so that one would come last. This one
dish, not really suitable for a weekday. That leaves these two, they are both
; one takes only 15 minutes to prepare; I would rank this one first.'

:t attributes mean to the consumer. Based on these consumer insights from the
–end chains, marketing managers can develop more effective marketing
ies.

ations

c advantage of means–end chain models is that they provide a deeper under-
1g of consumers' product knowledge than methods focusing only on attributes or

benefits.[25] For instance, consider the following means–end chain for Ariel laundry detergent:

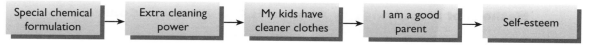

This hypothetical consumer interprets the chemical attributes of Ariel (e.g. special molecules) in terms of the more abstract attribute 'cleaning power'. Cleaning power, in turn, is seen as providing the functional benefit of 'cleaner clothes for the children', which is seen as helping achieve the instrumental value of 'being a good parent', which finally leads to the terminal value of 'feeling good about myself' or 'self-esteem'.

By identifying the sequence of connections between product-related meanings at different levels of abstraction, marketers can see more clearly what consumers really mean when they mention an attribute or a consequence such as 'cleaning power'. Means–end chain analyses also identify the basic ends (values and goals) consumers are seeking when they buy and use certain products and brands, and this gives insight into consumers' purchase motivations. Finally, means–end chains reflect the consumer–product relationship – that is, they show how consumers relate product attributes to important aspects of their self-concepts. In sum, the more complete understanding of consumers' product knowledge provided by means–end analysis helps marketers devise more effective advertising, pricing, distribution, and product strategies.

EXHIBIT 4.7

An Example of a Laddering Interview

RESEARCHER: 'You said that a shoe's lacing pattern is important to you in deciding what brand to buy. Why is that?'

CONSUMER: 'A staggered lacing pattern makes the shoe fit more snugly on my foot.' [**physical attribute and functional consequence**]

RESEARCHER: 'Why is it important that the shoe fits more snugly on your foot?'

CONSUMER: 'Because it gives me better support.' [**functional consequence**]

RESEARCHER: 'Why is better support important to you?'

Consumer: 'So I can run without worrying about injuring my feet.' [**psychosocial consequence**]

RESEARCHER: 'Why is it important for you not to worry while running?'

CONSUMER: 'So I can relax and enjoy the run.' [**psychosocial consequence**]

RESEARCHER: 'Why is it important that you can relax and enjoy your run?'

CONSUMER: 'Because it gets rid of tension I have built up at work.' [**psychosocial consequence**]

RESEARCHER: 'Why is it important for you to get rid of tension from work?'

CONSUMER: 'So when I go back to work in the afternoon, I can perform better.' [**instrumental value–high performance**]

RESEARCHER: 'Why is it important that you perform better?'

CONSUMER: 'I feel better about myself.' [**terminal value–self-esteem**]

RESEARCHER: 'Why is it important that you feel better about yourself?'

CONSUMER: 'It just is!' [**the end!**]

' do consumers seem to care about some products and brands and not others? Why
consumers sometimes highly motivated to seek information about products, or to
and use products in certain situations, while other consumers seem to have no
rest? These questions concern consumers' involvement, a key concept for under-
ding consumer behaviour.[26]

ivolvement refers to consumers' perceptions of importance or personal relevance
in object, event, or activity.[27] Consumers who perceive that a product has personally
vant consequences are said to be involved in the product and to have a personal
tionship with it. Involvement in a product or brand has both cognitive and affective
ects.[28] Cognitively, involvement includes means–end knowledge about important
sequences created by using the product (this CD would be fun to play at parties).
olvement also includes affect such as product evaluations (I like the taste of Magnum
cream). If product involvement is high, people may experience stronger affective
onses such as emotions and strong feelings (I really love my BMW). Although
rketers often treat consumers' product involvement as either high or low, involve-
it actually can vary from low levels (little or no perceived relevance) to moderate
ne perceived relevance) to high levels (great perceived relevance).

nvolvement is a motivational state that energizes and directs consumers' cognitive
cesses and behaviours as they make decisions.[29] For instance, consumers who are
olved in cameras are motivated to work harder at choosing which brand to buy. They
ght spend more time and effort shopping for cameras (visiting more shops, talking to
re salespeople). They might interpret more product information in the environment
d more ads and brochures). And they might spend more time and effort in
grating this product information to evaluate brands and make a purchase choice.

ome researchers have used the term *felt involvement* to emphasize that involvement
psychological state that is experienced by consumers only at certain times and on
tain occasions.[30] Consumers do not continually experience feelings of involvement,
n for important products such as a car, a home, or special hobby equipment. Rather,
ple feel involved in such products only on certain occasions when means–end
owledge about the personal relevance of products is activated. As circumstances
nge, that means–end knowledge is no longer activated, and people's feelings of
olvement fade away (until another time).

ement

rketers are interested in understanding consumers' involvement in products and
nds. But people may also be involved in other types of *physical objects* such as
ertisements. During the 1990s, many Danes became involved in a series of ads for
ash, a local soft drink brand, that portrayed two well-known comedians in an
-fashioned grocery shop; one as the grocer and the other as the customer who has
ble pronouncing and therefore buying a 'Squash'. Consumers may be involved in
er *people* – friends, relatives, lovers, perhaps even salespeople. People can also become
olved in certain *environments* (their home or back garden, amusement parks, a lake,
he seashore). Some of these may be marketing environments – a clothing shop that
consumer especially likes, a shopping mall, or a favourite restaurant. Finally, people
y be involved in specific *activities* or *behaviours* such as playing tennis, working, wind-

surfing, or reading. Some consumers become involved in *marketing-related activities* such as shopping for new clothes, finding the cheapest price in town, or haggling with vendors at flea markets.

It is important that marketers clearly identify the focus of consumers' involvement. Marketers need to know exactly what it is that consumers consider to be personally relevant: a product or brand, an object, a behaviour, an event, a situation, an environment, or several or all of these together. Since marketers are mostly interested in consumers' involvement in products and brands, this is our main focus in this chapter. In principle, however, marketers can analyse consumers' involvement in virtually anything.

The Means–End Basis for Involvement

Means–end chains can help marketers understand consumers' product involvement because they show how knowledge about product attributes is related to knowledge about self.[31]

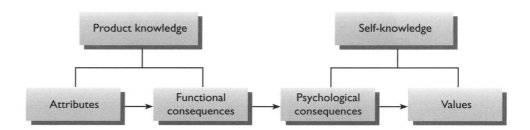

The level of product involvement a consumer experiences during decision making is determined by the type of means–end knowledge activated in the situation.[32] A consumer's level of involvement or self-relevance depends on two aspects of the means–end chains that are activated: (1) the importance or self-relevance of the ends and (2) the strength of connections between the product knowledge level and the self-knowledge level. Consumers who believe that product attributes are strongly linked to important end goals or values will feel higher levels of involvement in the product. In contrast, consumers who believe that the product attributes lead only to functional consequences, or that product attributes are only weakly linked to important values, will experience lower levels of product involvement. Consumers who believe that product attributes are not associated with any relevant consequences will experience little or no involvement in the product. We suspect that in the typical purchase decision, most consumers experience low to moderate levels of involvement for most products and brands.[33]

The affective system is likely to respond to the means–end knowledge that is activated in a decision situation.[34] This affect could vary from weak evaluations with little arousal (if relatively unimportant consequences are linked to the product) to highly charged affect such as emotions and strong feelings (when core values are related to the product).

ncing Involvement

hibit 4.8 shows that a person's level of involvement is influenced by two sources
self-relevance – intrinsic and situational.[35] Each source can activate or generate
eans–end chains linking product attribute knowledge to personally relevant
nsequences and values.

Intrinsic self-relevance is based on consumers' means–end knowledge stored
memory.[36] Consumers acquire this means–end knowledge through their past
periences with a product. As they use a product (or observe others using it),
nsumers learn that certain product attributes have consequences that help achieve
portant goals and values. For example, a consumer may learn that various attributes
a stereo system (surround sound, remote control, programmability) have favourable

EXHIBIT 4.8

A Basic Model of Consumer Product Involvement

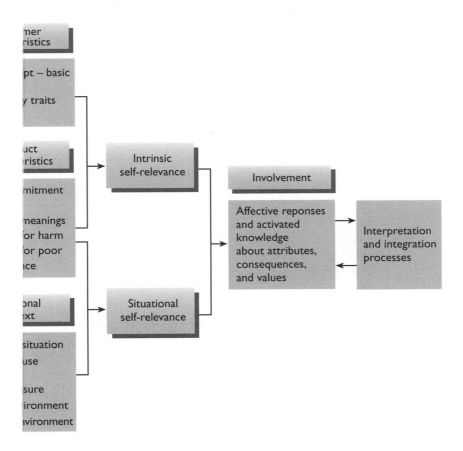

Adapted from Richard L. Celsi and Jerry C. Olson, 'The Role of Involvement in Attention
rehension Processes', *Journal of Consumer Research*, September 1988, pp. 210–224; and
Peter H. Bloch and Marsha L. Richins, 'A Theoretical Model for the Study of Product
Importance Perceptions', *Journal of Marketing*, Summer 1983, pp. 69–81.

and unfavourable consequences (impress my friends, I can be comfortable and relaxed, too much trouble to use). Because this means–end knowledge is stored in memory, it is a potential *intrinsic* source of involvement. If this knowledge is activated in a decision situation, the consumer will experience feelings of personal relevance or involvement.

Exhibit 4.8 shows that intrinsic self-relevance is a function of both consumer and product characteristics, as is all means–end knowledge. Key consumer characteristics include people's values and life goals. Relevant product characteristics are the product attributes and the associated functional consequences (benefits and perceived risks). Perceived risks are important elements in product involvement, because consumers tend to feel more involved in products that might have negative consequences. Other product factors that may influence intrinsic sources of involvement include social visibility[37] (do people know you own the product?) and time commitment (buying a refrigerator is involving because you are committed to your choice for a long time).

Situational self-relevance is determined by aspects of the immediate physical and social environment that activate important consequences and values, thus making products and brands seem self-relevant. For instance, a '50% Off' sign on fishing rods might activate self-relevant thoughts in a person interested in fishing (I can get a good deal on a new rod). Because many environmental factors change over time, situational self-relevance usually involves temporary means–end linkages between a product and important consequences or values. These connections between the product and personal consequences may disappear when the situation changes. For example, the person's involvement in buying this particular fishing rod might last only as long as the sale continues.

Aspects of the social environment can create situational self-relevance. For instance, shopping with others can make some consumers more self-conscious than shopping alone (I want to impress my friends with my sense of style, I shop carefully when accompanied by my friend the famous consumer researcher). A chance observation in the physical environment, such as noticing a window display in a clothing store, might activate means–end knowledge about consequences that become associated with the clothing in the display (that sweater would be nice to wear to the party next week). More general aspects of the physical environment can also influence situational self-relevance. The high temperatures on a summer's day can make certain consequences more personally relevant and desirable (I need to take a break, cool off, or relax). In turn, this makes buying an ice-cream cone or going to an air-conditioned cinema more relevant and involving.

Exhibit 4.8 shows that consumers' overall level of involvement is always determined by a combination of intrinsic and situational self-relevance. Although intrinsic factors have the highest influence on involvement in some cases, situational sources of involvement can have a major influence in many circumstances. Consider the common situation when a consumer's intrinsic self-relevance for a product is low (the product is not very important). For instance, most people do not consider kitchen sinks as having much self-relevance. But if yours became blocked, the negative consequences of not being able to use it were highly self-relevant. This means–end knowledge (which was activated only when your kitchen sink became blocked) is a situational source of self-relevance when trying to find somebody to clear the sink. You are likely to feel this involvement and motivation only for the time it takes to solve the problem.

This example shows that marketers need to understand the focus of consumers' involvement and the *sources* that create it. Even though most consumers are not personally involved in mundane products such as kitchen sinks, they can experience a temporary involvement. Having to clear a blocked kitchen sink (a situational source of involvement) makes people think about particular consequences (paying money, find a plumber, waiting for the plumber to come, dirt and inconvenience involved, creating stress and hassle) that are important to them. The situation also might activate knowledge that is important during decision making (reliability of the plumber, prices of plumbers previously used) but is not relevant later, when the sink has been repaired.

This is not an isolated or rare example. Situational self-relevance always combines with consumers' intrinsic self-relevance to create the level of involvement they actually experience during decision making. This means that consumers usually experience some level of involvement when making purchase choices, even for relatively unimportant products. Even though personal sources of involvement are low for many everyday consumer products (soap, bread, socks), situational sources are likely to influence the level of involvement consumers feel. This suggests that marketers can influence consumers' product involvement by manipulating aspects of the environment that might function as sources of situational self-relevance.

Implications

The means–end approach to product knowledge and involvement can help marketers understand the critical consumer–product relationship and develop more effective marketing strategies. A basic goal of many marketing strategies is to enhance consumers' product involvement by connecting products and services to consumers' goals and values.

ing the Key Reasons for Purchase

Marketers can use means–end analyses to identify the key attributes and consequences underlying a product purchase decision and to understand the meaning of those concepts to consumers.

A good example is the growth of the market for alcohol-free beer, which came as a surprise to many. Why have consumers become interested in a beer without alcohol? Means–end analysis shows that there are several quite distinct reasons as to why the attribute is personally relevant for consumers. For some consumers, no alcohol means more self-control, leading to better socializing at parties and hence to more self-esteem. For others, no alcohol means you are allowed to drive, which means mobility, which means freedom. For still others, no alcohol means you can have beer for lunch and still work well afterwards, leading to both enjoyment and achievement. Finally, it can also be associated with health-related or beauty-related consequences. While all these means–end chains add personal relevance to the attribute 'no alcohol' of a beer, they may otherwise call for different marketing strategies in terms of how the beer should taste, should be packaged, advertised, and so on.

ing the Consumer–Product Relationship

One of the most important concepts in this book concerns consumers' relationships with products and brands. For instance, many people feel highly involved in their cars, often treating them like pets (stroking, petting, grooming). For some consumers, the product–self relationship reflects a passionate level of intrinsic self-relevance. Such people love their cars and may engage in ritual forms of 'worship', such as weekend cleaning and waxing. Marketers need to understand the cognitive and affective aspects of these consumer–product relationships. [38] For instance, teenagers who are hooked on cars may link the general attributes of cars to important self-relevant consequences (self-respect, envy of peers, freedom). A key task to marketing management is to manage the customer–product relationship. [39] Marketing strategies should be designed to create and maintain meaningful consumer–product relationships and modify those means–end relationships that are not optimal.

If marketers can understand the consumer–product relationship, they may be able to segment the market in terms of consumers' intrinsic self-relevance. For instance, some consumers may have positive means–end knowledge about a product category, while others may have favourable beliefs and feelings for a brand. Still other consumers may have favourable means–end knowledge about both the product category and a brand. Highlight 4.3 gives examples of the varying levels of brand loyalty in different product categories in the US market.

Researchers have identified four market segments with different levels of intrinsic self-relevance for a product category and brand. [40] Those with the strongest feelings are brand loyalists and routine brand buyers.

- *Brand loyalists* have strong affective ties to one favourite brand that they buy regularly. In addition, they perceive the product category in general to provide personally relevant consequences. Their intrinsic self-relevance includes positive means–end knowledge about both the brand and the product category and leads them to experience high levels of involvement during decision making. They strive to buy the 'best' brand for their needs. For instance, consumers often have strong brand loyalty for sports equipment such as tennis racquets or athletic shoes.
- *Routine brand buyers* have low intrinsic self-relevance for the product category, but they do have a favourite brand that they buy regularly (low brand switching). For the most part, their intrinsic self-relevance with a brand is not based on knowledge about the means–end consequences of product attributes. Instead, these consumers are interested in other types of consequences associated with regular brand purchase (it's easier to buy Heineken each time I need beer). These beliefs can lead to consistent purchase, but these consumers are not so interested in getting the 'best' brand; a satisfactory one will do.

The other two segments have weaker levels of intrinsic self-relevance for a particular brand. Information seekers and brand switchers do not have especially positive means–end knowledge about a single, favourite brand.

- *Information seekers* have positive means–end knowledge about the product category, but no particular brand stands out as superior (you may be 'into' skis, but you know that many ski brands are good choices). These consumers use a lot of information to find a 'good' brand. Over time, they tend to buy a variety of brands in the product category.
- *Brand switchers* have low intrinsic self-relevance for both the brand and the product category. They do not see that the brand or the product category provides important consequences, and they have no interest in buying 'the best'. They have no special relationship with either the product category or specific brands. Such consumers

HIGHLIGHT 4.3

Consumers' Relationships with Brands

l loyalty among consumers is a highly desirable goal for most marketers. Although
ıd loyalty seems to have eroded considerably over the past 30 years due to
eased brand competition and extensive sales promotions (coupons and price
ıctions), it is not dead. As the diagram below shows, a survey of some 2000
the United States found wide variations in brand loyalty across product classes
laimed to buy mostly the same brand).

thful or Fickle?
rcentage of users of these products who are loyal to one brand

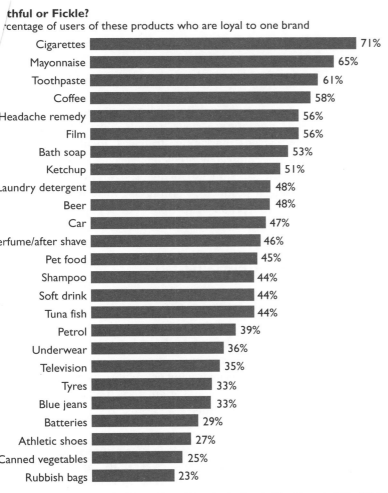

Product	Percentage
Cigarettes	71%
Mayonnaise	65%
Toothpaste	61%
Coffee	58%
Headache remedy	56%
Film	56%
Bath soap	53%
Ketchup	51%
Laundry detergent	48%
Beer	48%
Car	47%
Perfume/after shave	46%
Pet food	45%
Shampoo	44%
Soft drink	44%
Tuna fish	44%
Petrol	39%
Underwear	36%
Television	35%
Tyres	33%
Blue jeans	33%
Batteries	29%
Athletic shoes	27%
Canned vegetables	25%
Rubbish bags	23%

Source: Ronald Alsop, 'Brand Loyalty Is Rarely Blind Loyalty', *The Wall Street Journal*,
19 October 1989, pp. B1, B8.

tend to respond to environmental factors such as price deals or c
promotions that act as situational sources of involvement.

In sum, different marketing strategies are necessary to address the
product knowledge, intrinsic self-relevance, and involvement of con
four market segments.

Influencing Intrinsic Self-Relevance

If marketers can understand the means–end knowledge that make
intrinsic self-relevance, they are able better to design product attributes
will connect with important consequences and values.[41] A good e
convenience-added fresh fish products mentioned at the beginning
Marketers can also try to strengthen consumers' intrinsic self-releva
brand. Mazda once asked owners of Mazda cars to send in pictures of
their cars, and some of these pictures were included in magazine ads.
might have activated and strengthened the intrinsic self-relevance of M
their cars.

In the short run, it is difficult to modify consumers' intrinsic self
product or brand. Over longer periods, though, consumers' means–end
be influenced by various marketing strategies, including advertisin
of this process is not completely predictable because many factors be
strategy can modify consumers' means–end knowledge. For insta
experience of using a product or brand can have a strong impact
knowledge. If the actual product experience doesn't measure up to the i
advertising, consumers are not likely to form the desired means–end m

Influencing Situational Self-Relevance

Marketers use many strategies to create, modify, or maintain consun
self-relevance, usually with the goal of encouraging purchase. Semia
sales on summer or winter clothing are situational factors that may t
consumers' involvement in buying such products. Likewise, premiums
or small toys in cereal boxes or sweets packages may temporarily inc
involvement in a brand. Special pricing or credit strategies ('buy now, s
year') may function as situational influences that create a tempor
involvement in buying the product.

**Back to . . .
Fish for
the family**

Understanding consumers' product knowledge and consumer–product relationships requires marketers to examine the meanings by which consumers represent product attributes and link those to higher-ordered meanings, such as the psychosocial consequences and values in consumers' self-schemas.

A reason for Thorfisk's success,

mentioned in the opening
that they understood
attributes link to cons
values. They understood
consumers means–end
regard to fresh fish lea
conflict: on the one hand,
the naturalness, the lov
and the high content of
vitamins lead to desirable

in terms of taste and health, which are positively related to the family's quality of life. On the other hand, the fact that fresh fish has to be bought at a fishmonger's, and that it is perceived as difficult to prepare, lead to the consequence that more time is consumed shopping and cooking, which otherwise could have been spent with the family, thus detracting from the family's quality of life. The product design emphasized the desirable attributes of freshness and naturalness by the way it was packaged and cooled. At the same time, the undesirable attributes were diminished by cutting the fish into ready-to-serve pieces, distributing it via supermarkets, and adding convenient, quick, tasty recipes.

The means–end perspective is also useful for understanding consumers' intrinsic self-relevance for products and brands. Consumers differ widely in their involvement in food. For some it is a necessary ingredient for survival, while others are highly involved. Thorfisk products probably appeal to consumers with a moderate degree of involvement – involved enough to have those means–end chains which relate the attributes of fresh fish to positive consequences, but not so involved that they would take enjoyment in the time it takes to go to a specialist shop and then to follow a complicated recipe.

Summary

In this chapter, you learned about consumers' affective and cognitive responses to products. Consumers don't buy products to get attributes; rather, they think about products in terms of their desirable or undesirable consequences – benefits or perceived risks. By relating product attributes to their own personal and self-relevant consequences, values, goals, and needs, consumers form hierarchical knowledge structures called means–end chains. The attributes of some products are strongly linked to important ends (consequences and values), whereas other products are only weakly associated with self-relevant consequences. These are sometimes called high and low involvement products, respectively. Consumers experience involvement as cognitive perceptions of importance and interest and affective feelings of arousal. Their feelings of involvement are determined by intrinsic self-relevance – the means–end knowledge stored in memory. In addition, situational factors in the environment also influence the content of activated means–end chains and thereby affect the involvement consumers experience when choosing which products and brands to buy.

Key Terms and Concepts

Review and Discussion Questions

1. Select a product category and identify examples of product forms, brands, and models. Describe some of the attribute, consequence, and value meanings for each of these levels.
2. Analyse the possible meanings of toothpaste or deodorant in terms of positive (perceived benefits) and negative (perceived risks) consequences of use. Why are both types of meaning important?
3. Relate the fundamental assumptions underlying means–end chains to your own assessment of the managerial usefulness of means–end chains.
4. Define the concept of involvement and illustrate it by discussing products that, for you, would fall at various levels along an involvement continuum.
5. Consider the difference between consequences of possession and consequences of consumption as the basis for intrinsic self-relevance. What products are relevant to you for these two reasons? How does that change your purchasing behaviour?
6. Do you agree that most products have low to moderate levels of intrinsic self-relevance for most consumers? Why or why not?
7. Prepare one or two means–end chains for your choice of a major or an emphasis in marketing as part of your degree programme. Label the attributes, consequences, and values that you identify.
8. Using the concept of means–end chains, discuss why different people might shop for athletic shoes at department stores, speciality athletic footwear shops, and discount stores. Why might the same consumer shop at these places on different occasions?
9. Discuss how a marketer of casual clothing for men and women can use consumers' product knowledge (means–end chains) and involvement to understand the consumer–product relationship.
10. Identify three ways that marketers can influence consumers' situational self-relevance, and discuss how this will affect consumers' overall level of involvement. For what types of products are these strategies most suitable?

Additional Reading

For a discussion of how young children form product categories, see:
Deborah Roedder-John and Mita Sujan, 'Age Differences in Product Categorization', *Journal of Consumer Research*, March 1990, pp. 452–460.

For a discussion of the influences of knowledge structures on categorization, see:
Mita Sujan and James R. Bettman, 'The Effects of Brand Positioning Strategies on Consumers' Brand and Category Perceptions: Some Insights from Schema Research', *Journal of Marketing Research*, November 1989, pp. 454–467.

For examples of using means–end chains to understand consumers' meanings for a product attribute, see:

Jonathan Gutman and Scott D. Alden, 'Adolescents' Cognitive Structures of Retail Stores and Fashion Consumption: A Means–End Chain Analysis of Quality', in *Perceived Quality: How Consumers View Stores and Merchandise*, ed. Jacob Jacoby and Jerry C. Olson (Lexington, MA: Lexington Books), 1985, pp. 99–114.

Pierre Valette-Florence and Bernard Rapacchi, 'A Cross-Cultural Means–End Chain Analysis of Perfume Purchases', in *Proceedings of the Third Symposium on Cross-Cultural Consumer and Business Studies*, ed. Nicholas E. Synodinos, Charles E. Keown, Klaus G. Grunert, T. E. Muller, and Julie H. Yu (Honolulu, HI: University of Hawaii, 1990), pp. 161–172.

For a discussion of how consumers use products to define and establish a self-concept or self-schema, see:

Russell W. Belk, 'Possessions and the Extended Self', *Journal of Consumer Research*, September 1988, pp. 139–168.

For a discussion of aspects of involvement and how it affects information processing, see:

Gilles Laurent and Jean-Noël Kapferer, 'Measuring Consumer Involvement Profiles', *Journal of Marketing Research*, no. 1, 1985, pp. 41–53.

For interesting examples of how involved some consumers can become with a simple product like blue jeans, see:

Michael R. Solomon, 'Deep-Seated Materialism: The Case of Levi's 501 Jeans', in *Advances in Consumer Research*, vol. 13, ed. Richard J. Lutz (Ann Arbor, MI: Association for Consumer Research, 1986), pp. 619–622.

MARKETING STRATEGY IN ACTION

Nike

y the mid-1980s, the signs were becoming clear – after years of mystique and spectacular growth, jogging was puffing into middle age. In 1984, for instance, both unit and money sales of running shoes decreased significantly. Nike, the market leader, lost half their market share of athletic shoes between 1983 and 1987, a market it had dominated just a few years earlier. What happened?

Nike had become successful as a manufacturer of technically sophisticated shoes for the serious runner. Unfortunately, the market for running shoes had peaked. The running shoe market was saturated, as nearly everyone who wanted to run had tried it.

Part of the reason was demographic. During the late 1970s and early 1980s, the large baby boomers group filled the primary market for running gear – ages 25 to 40. But in the middle to late 1980s, fewer people were entering this age group, thus decreasing overall demand. As the older members of this group pushed toward 40, lacing up the old shoes for another five-mile run began to seem less adventurous and fun than it had at age 24.

Also, the running shoe market had become highly segmented by the mid-1980s – a sure sign of a mature market. This meant marketers had to pay even closer attention to consumers' needs, goals, and values in order to produce product variations for smaller groups of consumers. And, finally, the industry had begun to engage in sporadic price cutting as companies fought to maintain their market share. Another reason for the drop in running concerns consumers' ideas about health. Running develops the legs and cardiovascular system, but little else. Many runners had begun to notice that the rest of their bodies needed conditioning, too. Athletically oriented people became increasingly interested in total fitness.

All these changes meant fewer people were taking up running, and the millions of joggers who were still on the run were doing fewer laps.

This translated into fewer replacement shoes sold by Nike, Converse, Adidas, Asics, and all the others. As the biggest manufacturer in the business, Nike had the most to lose.

From one perspective, makers of running shoes had enjoyed a long run, especially in the sports equipment market, which is often dominated by short-lived fads. Consider tennis, for example. Sales of tennis racquets peaked in 1976. Despite technological innovations and space-age materials such as kevlar, boron, and graphite, the industry sold only one-third the amount in 1984. Instead, the big boom in 1984 and 1985 was aerobics gear and home gym equipment.

Some commentators believe Nike did not react quickly enough to these fundamental changes in the consumer markets. One company that did capitalize on these changes was Reebok International. Its sales more than tripled between 1984 and 1985, with profits increasing sixfold. According to Reebok President Paul Fireman: 'We go out to consumers and find out what they want. Other companies don't seem to do that.'

It seems that what many consumers wanted in the mid-1980s was fashion. Perhaps this would have been evident by simple observation of consumers' product-use behaviours. It is estimated that between 70 and 80 per cent of the shoes designed for basketball and aerobic exercise are actually used for street wear instead of the sports they were intended for. These products must have been satisfying some fashion needs or ends.

So when Reebok introduced its first soft-leather Freestyle aerobic shoes in the mid 1980s, the brilliant colours and soft leather made them an overnight sensation. In a way, Reebok actually expanded the overall market for athletic shoes, because it attracted women customers from more traditional shoe manufacturers and got them to spend more money on athletic shoes. People began to think of this product class as something more than 'just trainers'. Reebok's spectacular popularity continued, and by 1986 Nike had lost the top spot to Reebok.

In response to these changes in consumers, Nike expanded its product line beyond running shoes in the mid-1980s. It began to produce shoes for the aerobic market and other speciality sports activities. Nike introduced a line of walking shoes to appeal to a submarket that had emerged rapidly in the mid-1980s, perhaps as ageing baby boomers found running too stressful on their joints.

By the early 1990s, Nike had regained the lead in the trainers race with Reebok. One out of every five trainers sold in Europe bore the Nike swoosh symbol. But now the company faced another challenge. After gaining several hundred per cent between 1982 and 1990, Nike hit a sales plateau. Total trainers sales in 1992 had levelled off, the bloom was off the trainer market . . . again. What happened?

Basically, consumers' meanings and involvement in trainers changed. Athletic trainers had acquired some powerful symbolic meanings in the 1970s and 1980s, that drove sales up nearly every year. Fitness and performance were important values to the serious athlete. But for the 70 per cent of consumers who did not use the shoes for the designated sport, trainers signified rebellion, informality, practicality and fun. Nike managers recognized that their trainers embodied key values held by consumers and tried to link Nike shoes to those values.

In a way, the solution to the earlier problem became part of the problem in 1992–93. For most consumers, trainers were more fashion than function. Then the fashion changed. Jaded by the heavy commercialization in the trainer market, many teens and young adults were fed up with paying as much as DM200 to DM250 for high-end trainers. These consumers were into the grunge look, influenced by music groups such as Nirvana and Pearl Jam. They took up heavy work boots from Doc Martens, hiking boots from Raichle, Technica and Hi-Tech, and rugged shoes and boots from Timberland. Combined with plaid flannel shirts tied at the waist, several layers of T-shirts, and torn jeans, these clunky boots completed the look of grunge fashion much better than a pair of hi-tech trainers.

In response to these changes in consumer knowledge and involvement, Nike created an Outdoor Division to sell hiking-oriented trainers such as the Air Mowabb, sports sandals, and new models of hiking boots that directly competed against Timberland. Some Nike advertising also took on a cynical tone to appeal to these Generation X consumers. Of course, there was still a demand for athletic trainers. So, Nike continued to develop new models while also reducing prices on some of its more expensive models.

Discussion Questions

1. Apparently there are two market segments of consumers for many product forms of athletic shoes – those who use the shoes to engage in the designated athletic activity and those who primarily use the shoes for casual wear and seldom engage in the dathletic activity.
   - Discuss the differences between these two segments in means–end chains and especially end goals, needs, and values for running, aerobics, or tennis shoes.
   - Draw means–end chains to illustrate your ideas about how these two segments differ.
   - What types of special difficulty does a marketer face in promoting its products to two market segments of consumers who use the product in very different ways?

2. Many manufacturers of athletic shoes promote so-called technological advances such as the 'Air Sole' or the 'Energy Wave'. How do consumers make sense of such attributes? Which types of attribute are likely to have a major impact on their purchasing behaviour?

3. As the market for athletic shoes has become more segmented, marketers have produced shoes for very specialized purposes. Why? Discuss the special types of means–end chains held by people who buy athletic shoes for very special purposes (walking, tennis, aerobics, etc.). Analyse the source of consumers' involvement in these products – intrinsic or situational self-relevance. How can these analyses help explain the consumer–product relationship and help marketers develop more effective marketing strategies?

4. Analyse the changes that have occurred over

time in consumers' product–self relationships for running shoes (or some other type of athletic shoe). Consider changes in consumers' affective responses and their product knowledge, as well as their overt behaviours and general environmental factors. How could Nike have kept better track of these changes so that its marketing strategies would have been more effective in the mid-1980s?

Sources: Marcy Magiera, 'Nike Plans Rebound with Fashion Shoe', *Advertising Age*, 25 January 1988, p. 1; Patrick McGeehan, 'Wave Action: Converse Goes Toe-to-Toe with Nike High-Performance', *Advertising Age*, 22 February 1988, p. 76; Joseph Periera, 'Footwear Fad Makes Nike, Reebok Run for Their Money', *The Wall Street Journal*, 24 June 1993, pp. B1 & B5; Richard Phalon, 'Out of Breath', *Forbes Magazine*, 22 October 1984, pp. 39–40; Richard Stengel, 'America's Rubber Soul', *Business Week*, 20 January 1992, p. 53; Gary Strauss and Martha T. Moore, 'New Fashions Slam-Dunk Sneakers', *USA Today*, 24 June 1993, pp. B1 & B2; Lois Therrien and Amy Borrus, 'Reeboks: How Far Can a Fad Run?' *Business Week*, 24 February 1986, pp. 89–90; Dori Jones Yang and Michael Oneal, Charles Hoots, and Robert Neff, 'Can Nike Just Do It?' *Business Week*, 18 April 1994, pp. 86–90.

CHAPTER 5

Attention and Comprehension

Is Anybody Watching?

How can marketers know if their ads are reaching the public they are paying to reach? Researchers have been trying to measure viewer exposure and attention to TV commercials since at least 1952, when a water commissioner in Ohio in the United States noticed that huge drops in the city's water pressure (due to thousands flushing toilets) coincided with commercial breaks in the then most popular entertainment show.

Audience measurement had become a bit more sophisticated by the mid-1980s. A. C. Nielsen measured TV audiences using a 20-year-old method. They attached electronic meters to the TV sets of a sample of households. The meters measured whether the set was on, which channel was selected, and how long the set was tuned to that channel. But the meters could not tell which, if any, family members watched the programme (and presumably the commercials). So Nielsen supplemented the meter data with another, larger sample of households that recorded which programmes each family member watched. The diaries were supposed to be filled in each week and mailed in monthly.

This procedure had obvious problems. For one, the diary data did not reveal whether the purported viewer(s) actually paid attention to the programme or the commercials. In addition, the television environment had become so complex that filling out diaries describing the TV watching behaviour of an entire family was extremely difficult. Many homes received multiple TV channels via cable and had multiple TV sets. Adding further complexity were VCRs, which can record shows for later viewing, and remote controls, which made switching between channels easy. Little wonder that few advertisers had much faith in the accuracy of people's diaries. Who could remember which family member watched which programme when? A new system was needed that could provide more accurate measures of exposure and attention to television advertising.

Enter UK-based AGB Research, the top ratings company in Europe, with a new idea – a people meter. This remote-controlled device had eight buttons that signalled a small monitor box wired to the set. Each family member was assigned a number to push each time he or she started and stopped watching TV. The data were recorded electronically and passed automatically over telephone lines each night to the company, where they were analysed and given to broadcasters the next day. Under this competitive threat, the A. C. Nielsen Company quickly developed its own version of a people meter and is now using it in 24 countries around the world. People meters were an advance, but even they could not tell if anyone was actually paying attention to the advertising. Research showed that many people did not. One resourceful researcher mounted a small camera on the sets in about 20 British households to periodically take pictures of the room. He found that approximately equal numbers of viewers were paying close attention, some attention, and no attention at all. The last group included consumers who were sleeping, reading, or kissing instead of watching the commercials.

An even more sophisticated system was tested by R. D. Percy & Company, which combined a people meter with a heat sensor that could determine if anyone was in the room. If a viewer left the room and forgot to indicate that on the people meter, the system would ask if anyone was there. If no response was forthcoming, it would record that the set played to an empty room. This system produced separate ratings for the programme and for the com-

mercials. Of course, we would expect that most commercial ratings would be lower than the show's rating.

By the mid-1990s, the so-called passive people meter was still on the horizon, and questions remained about whether people would allow such 'seeing' devices into their homes (and bedrooms).

Sources: Brian Dumaine, 'Who's Gypping Whom in TV Ads?' *Fortune*, 6 July 1987, pp. 78–79; Dennis Kneale, 'Using High-Tech Tools to Measure Audience', *The Wall Street Journal*, 25 April 1988, p. 21; Jeffery A. Tachtenberg, 'Anybody Home Out There?' *Forbes*, 19 May 1986, pp. 169–170; Jeffery A. Tachtenberg, 'Diary of a Failure', *Forbes*, 19 September 1988, pp. 168–170; Howard Scholssberg, 'Case of Missing TV Viewers', *Marketing News*, 17 September 1990, pp. 1, 7; and Lynn G. Coleman, 'People Meter Rerun', *Marketing News*, 2 September 1991, pp. 1, 44.

This example illustrates the importance to marketers of understanding consumers' exposure to marketing information as well as their attention to and comprehension of that information. The example also illustrates the difficulty in measuring consumers' exposure and attention to TV programmes and commercials, given multiple TV sets in households, 10 to 50 channels of TV programming, and remote controls that make frequent channel changing easy. Other forms of marketing information, like newspaper ads, billboards, or direct mail, are not easy to deal with either. The Wheel of Consumer Analysis (see Exhibit 2.4) provides an overall perspective for understanding exposure, attention, and comprehension. Consumers' everyday environment contains a great deal of information, large parts of which are created through marketing strategies. For example, marketers modify consumers' environments by creating advertisements and placing them in the media. For the advertisements to be effective, consumers must be exposed to them. Exposure often occurs through consumers' own behaviours – they turn on the TV and switch to a favourite programme, they buy a newspaper, they choose to walk along a certain street and become exposed to a billboard. Once exposed, consumers must attend to and comprehend the advertisements (affective responses and cognitive interpretations).

In this chapter, we continue our examination of the affect and cognition portion of the Wheel of Consumer Analysis. We will consider the interpretation process, a key cognitive process in our general model of consumers' cognition shown in Exhibit 3.4. First we examine how consumers become exposed to marketing information. Then we discuss attention processes by which consumers select certain information in the environment to be interpreted. Finally, we examine the comprehension processes by which consumers construct meanings to represent this information, organize them into knowledge structures, and store them in memory. We emphasize the reciprocal inter-actions between attention and comprehension and the knowledge, meanings, and beliefs in memory. Throughout the chapter, we discuss the implications of these interpretation processes for developing marketing strategy.

Although we discuss attention and comprehension separately, the boundary between the two processes is not very distinct. Rather, attention shades off into comprehension.[1] As interrelated processes of interpretation, attention and comprehension serve the same basic function of the cognitive system – to construct personal, subjective interpretations or meanings that make sense of the environment and one's behaviours. This knowledge can then be used in subsequent interpretation and integration pro-cesses to guide consumers' behaviours and help them get along in their environment.

Before beginning our analyses, we briefly review four important aspects of the cognitive system that influence how consumers interpret information.

- Interpretation involves interaction between knowledge in memory and information from the environment. The incoming environmental information activates relevant knowledge in memory, which could be either schema or script knowledge structures.
- The activated knowledge influences how consumers attend to information and comprehend its meaning.
- Because their cognitive systems have a limited capacity, consumers can consciously attend to and comprehend only small amounts of information at a time.[2]
- Much attention and comprehension processing occurs quickly and automatically with little or no conscious awareness.[3] For instance, simple interpretations, such as recognizing a familiar product, occur automatically and virtually instantly upon exposure, without any conscious awareness of comprehension. Automatic pro-cessing has the obvious advantage of keeping our limited cognitive capacity free from unfamiliar interpretation tasks that do require conscious thought.

Exposure to Information

Although not a part of cognition in a strict sense, **exposure** to information is critically important for consumers' interpretation processes. Consumers are exposed to infor-mation in the environment, including marketing strategies, primarily through their own behaviours. We can distinguish between two types of exposure to marketing information: purposive or **intentional exposure** and random or **accidental exposure**.

Consumers are exposed to some marketing information due to their own intentional, goal-directed *search behaviour*. Consumers search for relevant marketing information to help solve a purchasing problem. Before buying a camera, for instance, a consumer might read product evaluations of 35 mm cameras in consumer or photography magazines. Another consumer might ask a friend or a salesperson for advice about which brand of earphones to buy for her Walkman radio.

Most investigations of consumer search behaviour have found that levels of inten-tional exposure to marketing information are rather low. Often, consumers visit only one or two retail stores and consult very few salespeople and external sources of information.[4] This limited search may be surprising until you realize that most consumers already have substantial product-related knowledge, meanings, and beliefs stored in their memories. If they feel confident in their existing knowledge, or if they feel little involvement in the decision (low self-relevance), consumers have little motivation to engage in extensive search for information.

Marketing information is everywhere in the consumer-oriented environments of most industrialized countries. In most countries, advertisements for products and services are found in magazines and newspapers, on radio and TV, and on bus placards and bus-stop shelters – and they are increasing. Between the 1970s and 1980s, the total number of ads doubled; and by the late 1990s that number is expected to double again.[5] Billboards and signs promoting products, services, and retail stores are found along roads in many countries. Stores contain a great deal of marketing information, including signs, point-of-purchase displays, and advertisements, in addition to information on packages. Consumers also receive product information from friends and relatives, from salespeople, and occasionally even from strangers.

Typically, consumers are not exposed to these types of marketing information through intentional search behaviour. Instead, most exposures are random or semi-random events that occur as consumers move through their environments and 'accidentally' come into contact with marketing information. For instance, browsing ('just looking') in shops is a common source of accidental exposure to marketing information.[6] Consumers may discover new products, sales promotions, or new retail outlets when browsing. Some retailers design their shop environments to encourage browsing and maximize the amount of time consumers spend in it, which increases the likelihood they will be exposed to products and make a purchase.

Consumers are seldom intentionally seeking information about products or services when they watch television, yet they may be accidentally exposed to commercials during an evening of TV watching at home. Since consumers probably don't feel very involved in most of the products promoted in these ads, their attention and comprehension processes are probably not extensive. Even so, increased levels of accidental exposure can have a powerful effect on behaviours. For example, during the Persian Gulf War in early 1991 viewership of CNN skyrocketed to almost twice previous levels (exposure was up as much as 20 times in some periods).[7] Advertisers on CNN received large increases in accidental exposure to their ads, which also increased their business.

Selective Exposure to Information

As the amount of marketing information in the environment increases, consumers become more adept at avoiding exposure (some consumers intentionally avoid reading product test reports or talking with salespeople). Or consumers do not maintain accidental exposure to marketing information (some people automatically throw away most junk mail unopened). Such behaviours result in **selective exposure** to marketing information. Consider the problem marketers are having with consumers' exposure to TV commercials.

Current technology enables consumers to control what ads they see on TV more easily than ever before. Thanks to remote controls for TV sets, viewers can turn off the sound or 'dial hop' from one station to another during a commercial break. Consumers who have videocassette recorders can fast-forward past commercials on taped programmes. In advertising circles, these practices are known as *zapping* and *zipping*, respectively. European studies have shown that in homes with remote controls, the zapping (tune-out) factor can be up to 20–25 per cent of viewers during an average commercial break. There is evidence that zapping increases, as the use of remote

The food industry has developed and marketed new products to respond to consumers' demand for faster food preparation.
Courtesy: Knorr.

The colour red in this ad is likely to generate affective arousal.
Courtesy: Saatchi & Saatchi, Milan.

Packaging often includes a great deal of product information that consumers may process.
Courtesy: Kellogg's UK Ltd.

Some manufacturers promote their products by emphasizing the lack of certain attributes.
Courtesy: Jordan Cereals Ltd and Osprey Park Ltd.

controls becomes more widespread. By mid-1995, 87 per cent of all TV homes in western Europe had remote control. According to a Nielsen survey, 50 per cent of VCR owners zip through the commercials, and 25 per cent omit the commercials when recording programmes.[8] Advertisers, who pay media rates based on a full audience, are worried they do not get their money's worth. One of their strategies to combat zapping is to develop commercials that are so interesting and exciting that they won't be zapped. For instance, one study found that Pepsi ads featuring Michael Jackson were zapped by only 1–2 per cent of the audience.[9]

Marketing Implications

Because of the crucial importance of exposure, marketers should develop specific strategies to enhance the probability that consumers will be exposed to their information and products. There are three ways to do this: facilitate intentional exposure, maximize accidental exposure, and maintain exposure.

In cases where consumers' exposure to marketing information is the result of intentional search, marketers should *facilitate intentional exposure* by making appropriate marketing information available when and where the consumers need it. For instance, to increase sales, some IT retailers train their salespeople to answer consumers' technical questions on the spot so that they don't have to wait while the salesperson looks up the answer. Consumers' search for information should be made as easy as possible. This requires that marketers anticipate consumers' needs for information and devise strategies to meet them. That may involve such simple things as providing telephone numbers on packaging and in ads, making sure there is enough capacity for answering phone calls and receiving faxes, and training those people who are the first contact with the motivated potential customer in such a way that they appear as competent partners instead of underpaid and ill-motivated telephone clerks.[10]

Whenever intentional exposure is rare, it becomes decisive that marketers try to place their information in environmental settings that *maximize accidental exposure* to the appropriate target groups of consumers. Certain types of retail outlets such as convenience stores and fast-food restaurants should be placed in locations where accidental exposure is high. High-traffic locations such as local locations, shopping centres, and busy intersections are prime spots. Prestige brand outlets also tend to cluster in certain areas where they believe their customers are. Bang & Olufsen, a prestigious Danish brand of hi-fi equipment known for unique design and a systems approach, has developed a prime site concept, where it uses shops located in the most prestigious shopping areas in European capitals as a major medium of market communication.

Most media strategies are intended to maximize accidental exposure to a firm's advertisements. Media planners must carefully select a mix of media (magazines, billboards, radio, and TV programming) that maximizes the chances the target segment will be exposed to the company's ads. Solving this very complex problem is crucial to the success of the company's communication strategy because the ads have no impact if no one sees them. Besides inserting ads in the traditional media, companies attempt to increase accidental exposure by placing ads inside taxicabs, in sports stadiums, and on boats, buses, and airships. Another marketing strategy involves placing advertisements (for noncompeting products) on grocery store shopping trolleys. A big advantage of shopping trolley ads is the much lower cost compared to the price of TV ads. Advocates also claim this 'reminder advertising' reaches consumers at the critical point when they make a purchase choice (an estimated 65–80 per cent of brand buying decisions occur in the supermarket).

A long-standing strategy to increase accidental exposure to a brand is to get it into films, but many companies are trying to get their brands into TV shows for even greater exposure.[11] Sometimes actors mention brand names on TV. Typically, these exposures are not paid for; they are just part of the new realism in television. For instance, on the show 'Thirtysomething', Hope announced she was going out to buy some Junior Mints. It is illegal for marketers to pay to have a product placed on TV unless the payment is disclosed, but it is OK to provide products free to be used as props. For instance, two recent films *Mission: Impossible* and *Independence Day* show Apple Macintosh computers in various scenes. Also the James Bond films have always been popular for high-prestige products. Marketers may hire a company that specializes in placing products in films and on TV hoping to expose their brand to millions of viewers.

A company's distribution strategy plays the key role in creating accidental exposure to products. Distribution is to products such as beer, cigarettes, chewing gum, and crisps what location is to fast-food restaurants – it's nearly everything. Obviously, if the product is not on the grocery store shelves, at the checkout counter, or in the vending machine, the consumer cannot be exposed at the point of purchase, and sales will suffer.

Maximum exposure at the retail level is not desirable for all products, though. For instance, Burberry all-weather coats (with the distinctive plaid lining) or Bang & Olufsen stereo components are sold only in a few exclusive, high-quality stores. Exposure is controlled by using a highly selective distribution strategy. In sum, one of the most important functions of a company's distribution strategy is to create the *appropriate level of exposure* to the product.

Other marketing strategies are intended to *maintain exposure* once it has begun. Television advertisements, for instance, must generate enough attention and interest so that the consumer will maintain exposure for 30 seconds rather than zap the ad, turn to a magazine, or leave the room to go to the kitchen. Shops must be designed to encourage customers to linger and be exposed to the products. For example, IKEA, the Swedish furniture retailer, encourages browsing by providing lots of real-life furniture settings in its huge stores.[12] It also provides baby-sitting, restaurants, and snack bars that serve Swedish specialities at low prices. A key goal is to maximize the amount of time consumers spend in the store, which maintains their exposure to the products and increases the likelihood they will make a purchase.

Attention Processes

Once consumers are exposed to marketing information, whether accidentally or through their own intentional behaviours, the interpretation processes of attention and comprehension begin. In this section, we discuss attention, levels of attention, and factors affecting attention, and we describe several marketing strategies that can influence consumers' attention.

What does it mean for a consumer to attend to a marketing stimulus such as a newspaper ad, a display in a store, or a salesperson's sales pitch? First, **attention** implies selectivity.[13] Attending to certain information involves *selecting* it from a large set of information and ignoring other information. Consider the cognitive processes of shoppers in a crowded, noisy department store. They must selectively attend to conversations with salespeople, attend to certain products and brands, read labels and signs, and so on. At the same time, they must ignore other stimuli in the environment. Selective attention is highly influenced by the goals that are activated in a situation.

Attention also connotes awareness and consciousness. To attend to a stimulus usually means being *conscious* of it. Attention also suggests intensity and arousal.[14] Consumers must be somewhat *alert* and *aroused* to consciously attend to something, and their level of alertness influences how intensively they process the information. If you have ever tried to study when you were very tired, you know about the importance of arousal. If your level of arousal is very low, you might drift off to sleep while trying to read a text chapter (not this one, we hope!). When arousal is low, attention and comprehension suffer.

Variations in Attention

Attention processes vary along a continuum from a highly automatic, unconscious level called **preconscious attention** to a controlled, conscious level called **focal attention**.[15] As a consumer's interpretation processes shift from preconscious attention towards focal attention, greater cognitive capacity is needed, and the consumer gradually becomes more conscious of selecting and paying attention to a stimulus. At a focal level, attention is largely controlled by the consumer, who decides which stimuli to attend to and comprehend based on what goals are activated. As attention processes reach focal levels, comprehension begins to involve sense-making processes for constructing meaning. Exhibit 5.1 summarizes these differences in levels of attention.

As an example of these levels of attention, consider the shopping trolley ads described earlier. How well do they work? ACTMEDIA, a dominant company in the industry, claims trolley ads increased sales of advertised brands by an average of 8 per cent, but other research found rather low levels of attention to them.[16] For instance, one study interviewed shoppers in stores with the trolley ads. Only about 60 per cent of these

EXHIBIT 5.1

Levels of Attention

Preconscious attention	Focal attention
• Uses activated knowledge from long-term memory	• Uses activated knowledge from long-term memory
• No conscious awareness	• Conscious awareness
• Automatic process	• Controlled process
• Uses little or no cognitive capacity	• Uses some cognitive capacity
• Presupposes that concepts attended to are familiar and well-learned	• Is more likely for concepts of high importance or involvement, or for concepts which are unfamiliar and/or unusual

shoppers were aware of ever having seen any trolley ads. Apparently the other 40 per cent of shoppers did not attend to the ads beyond a preconscious level, even though they were exposed to them (they had the opportunity to see them). In addition, only 13 per cent of the interviewed shoppers were aware of seeing any ads on that particular shopping occasion. Presumably these consumers processed the ads at relatively low levels of focal attention that produced some memory that an ad had been seen, but not enough to make the consumers aware of the brand. Only 7 per cent of the interviewed shoppers could name any brands advertised on their trolleys. Only these few consumers processed the ads at a sufficiently high level of focal attention to comprehend the brand names of the advertised brands and create a strong memory for them. In sum, these results question the effectiveness of shopping trolley ads. In the crowded information environment of the supermarket, most consumers do not pay much attention to ads, even those on their grocery trolleys.

Most researchers assume that consumers' cognitive systems respond to all stimuli that receive some level of attention, whether preconscious or focal. The affective system also responds to attended stimuli. Affective responses can range from simple evaluations (good/bad) to strong feelings (disgust) to emotions (joy or anger). As interpretation processes move towards focal levels of attention, affective responses usually become more intense, and consumers become more conscious of their affective states.

Factors Influencing Attention

Many factors can influence consumers' attention to marketing information. In this section, we discuss three particularly important influences – consumers' *general affective state*, consumers' *involvement* in the information, and the *prominence* of the information in the environment. We also discuss how marketers can try to influence consumers' attention to marketing information by influencing their involvement and by making the information more prominent.

Affective States

Consumers' affective arousal can influence their attention processes. As discussed earlier, low arousal reduces the amount and intensity of attention. In contrast, a state of high affective arousal is thought to narrow consumers' focus of attention and make attention more selective, even though this type of overarousal seems to be rare in a consumer behaviour context.[17] Some affective states that are responses to specific stimuli or situations are considered part of involvement. These are discussed in the next section. Other affective states like moods are diffuse and general and are not related to any particular stimulus. These affective states can also influence attention. For instance, consumers who are in a bad (or good) mood are more likely to notice negative (or positive) aspects of their environment.[18] Another example concerns whether consumers' general affective responses to happy and sad TV programmes influence their cognitive reactions to the TV commercials shown on those programmes.[19]

Involvement

The level of involvement felt by a consumer is determined by the means–end chains activated from memory and related affective responses and arousal. Involvement is a motivational state that guides the selection of stimuli for focal attention and comprehension.[20] For instance, consumers who experience high involvement because of an intense need (Joe desperately needs a new pair of shoes for a wedding in two days) tend to focus their attention on marketing stimuli that are relevant to their needs.

A consumer's involvement is determined by a combination of situational and intrinsic self-relevance. Thus, people who find photography to be intrinsically self-relevant are more likely to notice and attend to ads for photo products. Or the involvement generated by actively considering the purchase of a new refrigerator influences consumers to notice and attend to ads and sales announcements for refrigerators. On occasion, marketing strategies (contests, sales, price deals) can create a temporary state of involvement that influences consumers' attention to stimuli in that situation.

Often, marketers can take advantage of situational sources of self-relevance. One popular way of doing this is to place advertisements into specialized magazines. An advertisement for kitchen tools placed in a gourmet magazine will be exposed to people when they are in the process of thinking about or even preparing meals, when they are situationally involved in kitchen tools. Billboards for hotels placed in airports confront people travelling, situationally involved in hotels and other travel needs.

Environmental Prominence

The stimuli associated with marketing strategies can also influence consumers' attention. However, not every marketing stimulus is equally likely to activate relevant knowledge structures, receive attention, and be comprehended. In general, the most prominent marketing stimuli are most likely to attract attention; hence, marketers usually try to make their stimuli prominent features in the environment. For instance, to capture consumers' attention, some radio and TV commercials are slightly louder than the surrounding programme material, and the smells of baking products are emitted from bakeries onto pavements. Highlight 5.1 describes how large amounts of advertising can influence attention and brand awareness.

Marketing Implications

Marketers have developed many strategies to gain (or maintain) consumers' attention to their marketing information. Basically these strategies involve increasing consumers' involvement in the marketing information and/or making the marketing information more prominent in the environment. Influencing involvement requires attention to intrinsic and situational self-relevance.

Intrinsic Self-Relevance

In the short run, marketers have little ability to control consumers' intrinsic self-relevance for a product. Therefore, the usual strategy is to deal with consumers' existing intrinsic self-relevance (the relationship between a product and the consumer's self-concept). First marketers must identify through research (or guess) the product consequences and values that consumers consider most self-relevant. Then marketers design strategies that will activate those meanings and link them to the product. The involvement thus produced should motivate consumers to attend to this information and interpret it further.

HIGHLIGHT 5.1

Attention and Brand Awareness

 hat is Avia International Ltd?
  a. A small Italian commuter airline
  b. An up-and-coming courier service
  c. A map exporter specializing in exotic locations
  d. None of the above

If you answered 'none of the above', you might be among the 4 per cent who know that Avia (ah-VEE-ah) makes sneakers and sports apparel. According to a company vice president, Avia has a big problem: 'There's a whole segment of people who are not buying our shoes because they don't know who we are'. In contrast, Nike and Reebok are known by more than 70 per cent of consumers.

The power of a well-known brand name, supported by strong advertising, is so great (and long-lasting) that 20 of the top 25 leading brands in 1990 were also among the top 25 in 1923. But companies are finding it increasingly difficult to attract the customer's attention and create brand awareness because of the clutter of new products, brands, and advertising in the environment. Thus, approximately 90 per cent of new products are pulled from the market within two or three years of their introduction. Most of them failed for lack of name recognition – consumers were just not aware of them.

The risks of creating a new brand are so great that many companies are developing so-called line extensions. Rather than developing a new brand name, marketers are applying their existing, well-known brand name to new products. Red Bounty (with dark chocolate), Coca-Cola Light, and Ariel Colour are but a few well-known examples.

Building name recognition can be very difficult and very expensive, especially for small companies. Market leaders often command budgets up to 10 times greater than smaller companies. For instance, Nike and Reebok spend about $100 million each year on European media-advertising and sponsoring, compared to Avia's total of $10 million. Coca-Cola and Pepsi-Cola can afford to spend hundreds of millions of dollars on extensive advertising campaigns. For instance, Coca-Cola spent about $350 million on marketing connected with the Olympic games in 1996. However, this was less than 10 per cent of its total sales, while other smaller competitors may spend upward of 40 per cent of total revenues on advertising and promotions.

Other small companies that cannot afford large advertising budgets have used creative marketing strategies to gain exposure for their brands and attract consumers' attention. For example, Nevica, a British manufacturer of high-quality ski clothing, lacked the funds to saturate the ad pages of skiing magazines. So it offered freelance photographers free ski gear and a fee for every picture of a Nevica-clad skier that got published in a magazine. Nevica clothes were frequently pictured in the magazines, which increased brand awareness.

Sources: William M. Bulkeley, 'It Needn't Always Cost a Bundle to Get Consumers to Notice Unknown Brands', *The Wall Street Journal*, 14 February 1991, pp. B1, B4; Joseph Pereira, 'Name of the Game: Brand Awareness', *The Wall Street Journal*, 14 February 1991, pp. B1, B4; Vibeke Hjortlund, 'Coca-Cola tørster efter volumen', *Børsen*, 7 August 1996, p. 19.

For instance, many marketers of antiperspirants have emphasized qualities such as 'stops odour' and 'stops wetness' – rational and fairly tangible functional consequences of using the product. The marketers of Sure deodorant (Rexona in some European countries), however, identified two more self-relevant and emotionally motivating consequences of using their product – social confidence and avoiding embarrassment. They communicated these psychosocial consequences in an ad campaign, 'Raise your hand if you're Sure', that showed coatless consumers in social situations raising their arms and not being embarrassed by damp spots on their clothing. In a similar example, the marketers of Vaseline Intensive Care lotion in the UK and Spanish markets identified a consequence that represented the key meaning of many consumers' intrinsic self-relevance with the hand-lotion product category: while other brands discussed their greaseless formula, Vaseline marketers promoted skin restoration. They communicated the implied psychosocial consequence of 'looking younger' in ads showing dried-up leaves before and after being rejuvenated with Intensive Care lotion.[21]

Situational Self-Relevance

All marketing strategies involve creating or modifying aspects of consumers' environments. Some of these environmental stimuli may act as situational sources of self-relevance (a temporary association between a product and important self-relevant consequences). Situational self-relevance generates higher levels of involvement and motivation to attend to marketing information.[22] Consider consumers who receive a brochure in the mail describing a £500 000 sweepstakes contest sponsored by a magazine publisher. This marketing information might generate affective feelings of excitement and perceptions of interest and personal relevance with the details of the contest. The resulting involvement could motivate consumers to maintain exposure and focus their attention on the marketing offer for magazine subscriptions that accompanies the sweepstake's announcement.

Factors Affecting Environmental Prominence

Marketers attempt to influence the prominence of their marketing information by designing bright, colourful, or unusual packages; by developing novel advertising executions; or by setting unique prices (having a sale on small items, all priced at NLG1). Because they must attract the attention of consumers hurrying by the newsstand, magazine covers often feature photos known to have high attention value – pictures of celebrities, babies, or dogs, or pictures using that old standby, sex (attractive, seductively clothed or unclothed models).

Vivid pictorial images can attract consumers' attention and help focus it on the product,[23] although there may also be a risk of distraction, such as when car maker Citroën used pictures of a nude Claudia Schiffer to advertise its newest model. Window displays in retail stores attract the attention (and subsequent interest) of consumers who happen to pass by. Tiffany's, the famous New York jeweller, once used a window display showing construction of a giant doll, four times larger than the figures who were working on it. The doll had nothing to do with jewellery; it was intended to attract the attention of shoppers during the Christmas season.[24] Many shops use creative lighting to emphasize selected merchandise and thus attract and focus consumers' attention on their products. Mirrors are used in clothing shops and hair salons to focus consumers' attention on their appearance.

Novel or *unusual stimuli* that don't fit with the consumers' expectations may be 'selected' for additional attention (and comprehension processing to figure out what they are). For instance, a British ad agency created a dramatic stimulus to attract attention to the staying qualities of an adhesive called Araldite. The product was used to attach a car to a billboard along a major road into London. The caption read, 'It also sticks handles to teapots'.[25]

Even a novel placement of a print ad on a page can influence consumers' attention.[26] For instance, Sisley, a manufacturer and retailer of trendy clothing owned by Benetton, has run its print ads in an upside-down position as the back pages of magazines like *Elle*. Other marketers have experimented with ads placed sideways, in the centre of a page surrounded by editorial content, or spanning the top half of two adjacent pages.

Marketers must be careful in using novel and unusual stimuli, however, for two reasons. First, if an ad does not clearly communicate what it is about, consumers may choose not to pay attention to it at all, because they do not want to allocate cognitive effort to something that may turn out to be irrelevant.[27] Second, if novel and unusual stimuli are used over long periods, the prominence due to novelty wears off and fails to attract extra attention. For instance, placing a black-and-white ad in a magazine where all the other ads are in colour will capture consumers' attention only as long as there are few other black-and-white ads.

The strategy of trying to capture consumers' attention by making stimuli more prominent sometimes backfires. When many marketers are trying very hard to gain attention, consumers may tune most of the stimuli out, giving little thought to any of them. This happens especially on mature markets, and as a result all producers in the market may end up spending large amounts on advertising, none of which really moves their market shares – but nobody dares to cut down on advertising, because the individual supplier would be better off doing so only when everybody else follows suit.[28]

Comprehension

Comprehension refers to the interpretation processes by which consumers understand or make sense of their own behaviours and relevant aspects of their environment. In this section, we discuss the comprehension process, variations in comprehension, and the factors that influence comprehension. We conclude by discussing implications for developing marketing strategy.

During comprehension, consumers construct meanings and form knowledge structures that represent salient concepts, objects, behaviours, and events. When consumers' attention is focused on specific environmental stimuli, relevant knowledge structures (schemas and scripts) may be activated from long-term memory. This knowledge provides a framework that guides and directs comprehension processing. Thus, the environmental stimuli are interpreted in terms of one's 'old' knowledge activated from memory.[29] Through cognitive learning processes (accretion or tuning, sometimes restructuring) these newly constructed meanings are incorporated into existing knowledge structures in memory. Then, in future comprehension episodes, these modified knowledge structures might be activated to influence the interpretation of new information; the reciprocal process continues.

Variations in Comprehension

As shown in Exhibit 5.2, consumers' comprehension processes can vary in four important ways: (1) comprehension may be automatic or controlled, (2) it may produce more concrete or abstract meanings, (3) it may produce few or many meanings, and (4) it may create weaker or stronger memories.

Automatic Processing

Like attention, simple comprehension processes tend to be *automatic*.[30] For instance, most consumers around the world who see a can of Coca-Cola immediately comprehend what it stands for. We can think of the direct recognition of familiar products as a simple comprehension process in that exposure to a familiar stimulus automatically activates its relevant meanings from memory – perhaps its name and other associated knowledge. Thus, the person 'recognizes' the stimulus.

In contrast, comprehending less familiar stimuli usually requires more conscious thought and control. Because consumers do not have well-developed knowledge structures for unfamiliar objects and events, they may have to consciously construct the meanings of such information (or ignore it). Exposure to completely unfamiliar stimuli is likely to activate knowledge structures that are only partially relevant at best. In such cases, comprehension is likely to be highly conscious and controlled and require substantial cognitive capacity. Interpretations may be difficult and uncertain.

EXHIBIT 5.2

Variations in Comprehension

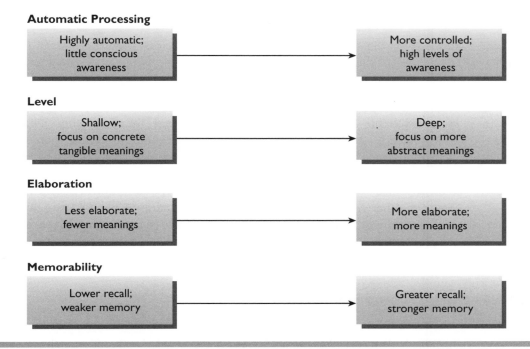

Level

The specific meanings that consumers construct to represent products and other marketing information in their environment depend on the **level of comprehension** that occurs during interpretation.[31] Comprehension can vary along a continuum from 'shallow' to 'deep'.[32] *Shallow comprehension* produces meanings at a concrete, tangible level. For example, a consumer could interpret a product in terms of its concrete product attributes (these running shoes are black, size 10, and made of leather and nylon).

In contrast, *deep comprehension* produces more abstract meanings that represent less tangible, more subjective, and more symbolic concepts. For instance, deep comprehension of product information might create meanings about the functional consequences of product use ('I can run faster in these shoes') or the psychosocial and value consequences ('I feel confident when I wear these shoes'). From a means–end perspective, deeper comprehension processes generate product-related meanings that are more self-relevant, whereas shallow comprehension processes tend to produce meanings about concrete product attributes.

Elaboration

Comprehension processes also vary in their extensiveness or **elaboration**.[33] The degree of elaboration during comprehension determines the amount of knowledge or the number of meanings produced as well as the complexity of the interconnections between those meanings.[34] *Less elaborate* (simpler) *comprehension* produces relatively few meanings and requires little cognitive effort, conscious control, and cognitive capacity. *More elaborate comprehension* requires greater cognitive capacity, effort, and control of the thought processes. More elaborate comprehension produces a greater number of meanings that tend to be organized as more complex knowledge structures (schemas or scripts).

Memorability

Both the level and elaboration of comprehension processes influence consumers' ability to remember the meanings created during comprehension.[35] Deeper comprehension processes create more abstract, more self-relevant meanings that tend to be remembered better (higher levels of recall and recognition) than the more concrete meanings created by shallow comprehension processes. More elaborate comprehension processes create greater numbers of meanings that tend to be interconnected in knowledge structures. Memory is enhanced because the activation of one meaning can spread to other connected meanings and bring them to conscious awareness.[36] In sum, marketing strategies that stimulate consumers to engage in deeper, more elaborate comprehension processes tend to produce meanings and knowledge that consumers remember better.

Inferences During Comprehension

When consumers engage in deep, elaborate comprehension processes they create inferences. **Inferences** are knowledge or beliefs that are not based on explicit information in the environment.[37] That is, inferences are interpretations that always go beyond the information given. For instance, some consumers might infer that a product is of good quality because it is advertised heavily on TV.[38]

Inferences play a large role in the construction of means–end chains.[39] By making inferences during comprehension, consumers can link meanings about the physical attributes of a product with more abstract meanings about its functional consequences and perhaps the psychosocial and value consequences of product use.

Inferences are heavily influenced by consumers' existing knowledge in memory.[40] If activated during comprehension, relevant knowledge provides a basis for forming inferences. For instance, consumers who believe that more expensive brands of chocolates are higher in quality than cheaper brands are likely to infer that Anthon Berg chocolates are high quality when they learn that the chocolates cost up to DKK100 per 300 g.[41] As another example, incomplete or missing product information sometimes prompts consumers to form inferences to 'fill in the blanks', based on their schemas of knowledge acquired from past experience.[42] For instance, consumers who are highly knowledgeable about clothing styles may be able to infer the country of origin and even the designer of a coat or dress merely by noticing a few details.

Consumers often use tangible, concrete product attributes as *cues* in making inferences about more abstract attributes, consequences, and values.[43] In highly familiar situations, these inferences may be made automatically without much conscious awareness. For instance, some consumers draw inferences about the cleaning power of a powdered laundry detergent from the colour of the granules: blue and white seem to connote cleanliness. Or consumers could base inferences about product quality from physical characteristics of the package: the colour, shape, and material of perfume bottles are important cues to quality inferences. As another example, Unilever sells its premium-priced ice cream, Magnum, wrapped in gold foil, a packaging cue that implies quality to many consumers.

Marketers sometimes try to stimulate consumers to form inferences during comprehension. For example, Kellogg's once used an advertising strategy for All-Bran with the headline, 'At last, some news about cancer you can live with'. The ads repeated the National Cancer Institute's recommendation for increasing levels of fibre in the diet and then stated 'no cereal has more fibre' than All-Bran. Apparently, Kellogg's hoped consumers would make the inference that the product attribute of high fibre leads to the desirable consequence of reduced risk of cancer. Most consumers probably then formed additional inferences that reduced risk of cancer helps to achieve the universal values of long life, health, and happiness. For most consumers, such self-relevant consequences probably elicited favourable affective responses.

Factors Influencing Comprehension

Many factors affect the depth and elaboration of comprehension that occurs when consumers interpret marketing information.[44] In this section, we examine three important influences – consumers' existing knowledge in memory, their involvement at the time of exposure, and various aspects of the environment during exposure.

Knowledge in Memory

Consumers' *ability to comprehend* marketing information is largely determined by their existing knowledge in memory. The particular knowledge, meanings, and beliefs that are activated in a given comprehension situation determine the level of comprehension that will occur and the comprehended meanings that are produced. Marketing researchers often discuss consumers' knowledge in terms of **expertise** or familiarity.[45] *Expert consumers* are quite familiar with a product category, product forms, and specific brands. They tend to possess substantial amounts of declarative and procedural knowledge organized in schemas and scripts. When parts of this knowledge are activated, these expert consumers are able to comprehend marketing information at relatively deep, elaborate levels.[46]

In contrast, *novice consumers* have little prior experience or familiarity with the product or brand. They tend to have poorly organized knowledge structures containing relatively few, typically shallow meanings and beliefs. When parts of these knowledge structures are activated during exposure to marketing information, novices are able to comprehend the information only at shallow and nonelaborate levels that produce relatively few concrete meanings. Novices find it difficult, if not impossible, to comprehend at a deep, elaborate level. To do so, they would have to increase their knowledge to the level of an expert.

Marketers need to understand the existing knowledge structures of their target audience in order to develop effective marketing strategies that consumers can comprehend. For instance, a manufacturer of bug killers knows that most consumers have limited technical knowledge about how insecticides work. Instead of technical information, 'the customer wants to see action'.[47] The company's formulation for bug spray allows consumers to immediately comprehend that the product works effectively. It attacks cockroaches' central nervous systems and drives them into a frenzy out onto the kitchen floor, where they race around in circles before they die.

Involvement

Consumers' involvement at the time of exposure has a major influence on their *motivation to comprehend* marketing information.[48] Consumers with high intrinsic self-relevance for certain products associate those products with personally relevant consequences and values that are central to their self-concept. The involvement experienced when such self-relevant knowledge structures are activated motivates these consumers to process the information in a more conscious, intensive, and controlled manner. For instance, consumers who feel highly involved tend to form deeper, more abstract meanings for the marketing information, creating more elaborate knowledge structures. In contrast, consumers who experience low levels of involvement when exposed to marketing information tend to find the information uninteresting and irrelevant. Because of their low motivation to interpret the information, their attention probably will be low and they are likely to produce few meanings (low elaboration) at a relatively shallow, concrete level. Their comprehension processes might produce only a simple identification response (this is a pair of socks).

Exposure Environment

Various aspects of the exposure situation or environment can affect consumers' *opportunity to comprehend* marketing information. These include factors such as time pressure, consumers' affective states (a good or bad mood), and distractions (noisy, pushing crowds). For instance, consumers who are in a hurry and under a lot of time pressure don't have much opportunity to process marketing information even though they may be motivated to do so (high involvement).[49] In this situational environment, they are likely to engage in relatively shallow and nonelaborate comprehension processes.

Marketers can consider these environmental factors when designing their marketing strategies. Some retailers, for instance, have created a relaxed, slow-paced environment that encourages people to slow down and thoroughly comprehend the information marketers make available.

Marketing Implications

To develop effective marketing strategies, marketers need to understand consumers' comprehension processes in order to design marketing information that will be interpreted appropriately. This requires a consideration of the characteristics of the target consumers and the environment in which consumers are exposed to the information.[50]

Knowledge and Involvement

To encourage appropriate comprehension processing, marketers should design their messages to fit consumers' ability and motivation to comprehend (their knowledge structures and involvement). For instance, marketers of high-involvement products such as luxury cars usually want consumers to form self-relevant meanings about their products. Many print ads for Saab, BMW, or Mercedes-Benz contain a great deal of information describing technical attributes and functional aspects of the cars. To comprehend this information at a deep, elaborate level, consumers must have fairly sophisticated knowledge about cars and sufficient involvement to motivate extensive comprehension processes.

For other types of products, however, marketers may not want consumers to engage in extensive comprehension processes. Sometimes marketers are interested in creating only simple, nonelaborate meanings about their product. For example, simple products (perfume or beer) are promoted largely through *image advertising*, which is not meant to be comprehended deeply or elaborately.[51] Consider the typical advertising for cigarettes or soft drinks. Often these ads contain virtually no written information beyond a brief slogan such as 'Try the West' or 'Coke Is It'. Most consumers probably comprehend such information in a nonelaborate way that produces an overall image and perhaps a general affective reaction, but not detailed means–end chains.[52] Other ads, such as billboards, are reminders mainly intended to activate the brand name and keep it at a high level of 'top-of-mind' awareness. In such cases, comprehension might be limited to simple brand recognition.

Remembering

Memory and consumers' ability to recall meanings are important to marketers because consumers often do not make purchase decisions at the time of exposure, attention, and comprehension. Marketers usually want consumers to remember certain key meanings associated with their marketing strategy. Marketers hope consumers will remember the brand name and main attributes and benefits (main copy points) conveyed in their ads. Retailers want consumers to remember their name and location, the types of merchandise they carry, and the dates of the big sale. Despite the millions spent each year on advertising and other marketing strategies, much marketing information is not remembered well. For instance, few advertising slogans are accurately recalled from memory. And, even though some people can remember a slogan, many of them cannot associate it with the right brand name.[53] A UK study on memory of print ads showed that recognition levels for whole ads were around 25 per cent after 24 hours, while recognition for the logo and the company names was nearly zero.[54]

Miscomprehension of Marketing Information

Research shows that a substantial amount of marketing (and other) information is miscomprehended in that consumers form inaccurate, confused, or inappropriate interpretations. In fact, most (perhaps all) marketing information is probably miscomprehended by at least some consumers.[55] The type of miscomprehension can vary from confusion over similar brand names (see Highlight 5.2) to misinterpreting a product claim by forming an inaccurate means–end chain. It has been estimated that people may miscomprehend an average of 20–25 per cent of the many different types of information they encounter, including ads, news reports, and so on.[56]

Although unethical marketers may intentionally create deceptive or misleading information that will be miscomprehended by consumers, most professional ones work hard to create marketing information that is understood correctly. For those who don't, most countries have an authority that can remove deceptive marketing information and force a company to correct the false beliefs it creates. For instance, in 1996, the Advertising Standards Authority in the United Kingdom sent a protest to MD Foods, a Danish dairy, concerning the marketing of Pact margarine. The ASA opposed the exaggerated use of health characteristics in the campaign for Pact, a margarine with omega 3 sebacic/polyunsaturates.

Exposure Environment

Many aspects of the environment in which exposure to marketing information occurs can influence consumers' comprehension processes. For instance, the type of store can affect how consumers comprehend the product and brands sold there. Thus, for some customers, a brand of jeans purchased in 'high-image stores' like the House of Fraser ones may have a more positive set of meanings than the same brand bought at bhs or C&A. Characteristics, such as size, exterior design, or interior decoration can activate networks of meanings that influence consumers' comprehension of the meanings of products and brands displayed there.

HIGHLIGHT 5.2
Confusing Brand Names

arketers guard their brand names jealously. Establishing a brand name in consumers' minds (making it familiar and meaningful) usually requires a large financial investment. When another manufacturer uses the same brand name or a similar one, companies believe their hard work and creative marketing strategy are being stolen. Lawsuits often result.

For example, McDonald's constantly has around 200 cases worldwide involving infringement of their trademark – which they usually win. However, in a recent case in Denmark, the Supreme Court ruled against the multinational chain. In 1994, McDonald's filed a trademark infringement suit against Allan Pedersen for using the letters 'Mc' in the name for his hot-dog stand, which he calls McAllan. McDonald's claimed that his use of the 'Mc' letters will water down the 39 trademarks the chain has registered in Denmark. Allan Pedersen on the other hand claimed that the hot-dog stand, where consumers eat their hot dog, outside, from a piece of paper, cannot be mistaken for McDonald's and that if he had wished to exploit the company's well-known trademark he would have imitated both product line and the golden M which is the distinctive mark for McDonald's. The company is very surprised about the verdict, which is contrary to prior legal usage, and fears that it may form a precedent in the other Nordic countries which have similar trademark legislation.

Source: Tea Hviid Møller, 'Højesteret tygger på Mc-strid', *Morgenavisen Jyllands-Posten*, 4 December 1996, p. 5; Tea Hviid Møller and Thomas Qvortrup, 'Big Mac blev den Lille', 'McDonald's i evig strid', *Morgenavisen Jyllands-Posten*, 5 December 1996, p. 4. Photograph courtesy: © Nordfoto

Another aspect of the exposure environment concerns the actual content and format of the marketing information.[57] Some information may be confusing, unclear, and hard to comprehend. For instance, the huge amounts of nutritional information on food product labels and in advertising claims can be difficult for many consumers to comprehend in a meaningful way.[58]

**Back to . . .
Is Anybody
Watching?**

The opening vignette described some of the difficulties in measuring the audience for television advertising. The sophisticated people-meter technology described attempts to measure *exposure* to television programmes and commercials. However, the people meter does not provide good measures of consumers' *attention* to the ads. Taking pictures every two seconds of people in their living rooms does indicate their attention, but obviously isn't practical on a large scale. Finally, the task of measuring consumers' *comprehension* of advertising in a natural viewing environment is even more difficult.

Because of the difficulties in studying consumers' interpretation processes in the real world, most measures of attention and comprehension are produced in small-scale research studies, often using only a few consumers (50–150). Many of these studies are conducted in highly artificial viewing contexts such

as a theatre setting, where several ads are shown to a group of consumers. Although exposure does not occur in a natural way, marketers can measure the *amount of attention* consumers give to a marketing stimulus and/or the *level and elaboration of comprehension*. Such research can provide useful information to marketers about the relative likelihood of success of alternative marketing strategies. In these artificial settings, marketers can learn which package design or ad layout attracts the most attention, what inferences consumers make about different price increases, what types of meanings are elicited by different brand names, or how deeply and elaborately consumers comprehend alternative television commercials. By understanding consumers' interpretation processes, marketers are better able to design effective new marketing strategies and modify existing ones.

Summary

In this chapter, we discussed the behavioural process of *exposure*, by which consumers come into contact with marketing information. We also discussed the interrelated cognitive processes of *attention*, by which consumers select some of this marketing information for further processing, and *comprehension*, by which consumers interpret the meaning of this information.

Exposure to marketing information can occur by accident or as a result of an intentional search for information. Once exposure has occurred, the interpretation processes of attention and comprehension begin. For unfamiliar marketing information, these processes are likely to require some conscious thought. However, as consumers become more experienced in interpreting marketing stimuli, attention and comprehension processes require less cognitive capacity and conscious control and become more automatic. Attention varies from preconscious, automatic levels to focal levels where the comprehension begins. Comprehension varies in the depth of meanings produced (from concrete product attributes to abstract consequences and values) and in elaboration (few or many interrelated meanings). Both factors influence the memorability of the meanings created.

Attention and comprehension are strongly influenced by two internal factors – the knowledge structures activated in the exposure situation and the level of consumers' involvement. These factors respectively influence consumers' ability and motivation to interpret the information.

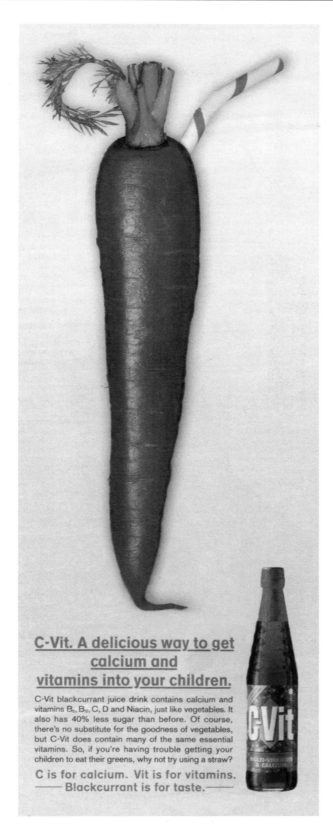

C-Vit. A delicious way to get calcium and vitamins into your children.

C-Vit blackcurrant juice drink contains calcium and vitamins B$_6$, B$_{12}$, C, D and Niacin, just like vegetables. It also has 40% less sugar than before. Of course, there's no substitute for the goodness of vegetables, but C-Vit does contain many of the same essential vitamins. So, if you're having trouble getting your children to eat their greens, why not try using a straw?

C is for calcium. Vit is for vitamins.
—— **Blackcurrant is for taste.** ——

Marketers try to associate the attributes of their product with values that are important to consumers — here, good health.
Courtesy: SmithKline Beecham and Ogilvy and Mather.

This ad promotes the functional and psychosocial consequences of using the product.
Courtesy: Clarins UK Ltd.

This ad communicates a means—end chain to mothers: tried and trusted formula ⟹ lowers temperature, soothes pain ⟹ mother and baby can sleep ⟹ peace of mind.
Courtesy: Seven Seas Ltd

Left side

White side

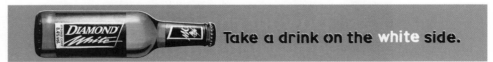

Vivid, unusual images give this ad increased environmental prominence.
Courtesy: Matthew Clark Brands Limited.

In sum, designing and implementing successful marketing strategies – whether price, product, promotion, or distribution strategies – require that marketers consider three issues associated with these three processes:

1. How can I *maximize* and/or *maintain exposure* of the target segment of consumers to my marketing information?
2. How can I *capture and maintain the attention* of the target consumers?
3. How can I *influence* the target consumers to *comprehend* my marketing information *at the appropriate level of depth and elaboration?*

Key Terms and Concepts

accidental exposure   93
attention   96
comprehension   104
elaboration   104
expertise   106
exposure   93
focal attention   97
inferences   104
intentional exposure   93
level of comprehension   104
preconscious attention   97
selective exposure   94

Review and Discussion Questions

1. Describe the differences between accidental and intentional exposure to marketing information. Identify a product for which each type of exposure is most common and discuss implications for developing effective marketing strategies.
2. Give an example of automatic attention and contrast it with an example of controlled attention. What implications does this distinction have for marketing strategy?
3. Give an example of automatic comprehension and contrast it with an example of controlled comprehension. What implications does this distinction have for marketing strategy?
4. Discuss the different types of knowledge and meanings that 'shallow and deep' comprehension processes create. Can you relate these differences to different segments of consumers for the same product?
5. Review the differences in the knowledge and meanings that are produced by more and less elaborate comprehension processes. Should marketing activities encourage or discourage elaboration of knowledge and meaning?
6. Describe how consumers' existing knowledge structures and their level of involvement might affect (*a*) attention to and (*b*) comprehension of marketing communications regarding prices of branded products.
7. List some factors that could affect the inferences formed during comprehension of ads for packaged foods and for medical services. Give examples of marketing strategies you would recommend to influence the inferences that consumers form.

8. Consider an example of a marketing strategy you think might result in some consumer miscomprehension. Describe why this miscomprehension occurs. What could marketers (or public policymakers) do to reduce the chances of miscomprehension?

9. Discuss how interpretation processes (attention and comprehension) affect consumers' ability to recall marketing information. Illustrate your points with marketing examples.

10. Identify a recent brand extension and discuss how exposure, attention, and comprehension processes can influence the effectiveness of that brand extension.

Additional Reading

For a discussion of how various factors affect interpretation processes, see:

Deborah J. MacInnis, Christine Moorman, and Bernard J. Jaworski, 'Enhancing and Measuring Consumers' Motivation, Opportunity, and Ability to Process Brand Information from Ads', *Journal of Marketing*, October 1991, pp. 32–53.

For a discussion of consumers' intentional search for information, see:

James W. Harvey, 'Correlates of Search Patterns for an Innovation', in *Advances in Consumer Research*, vol. 13, ed. Richard J. Lutz (Provo, UT: Association for Consumer Research, 1986), pp. 414–418.

Merrie Brucks, 'The Effects of Product Class Knowledge on Information Search Behaviour', *Journal of Consumer Research*, June 1985, pp. 1–16.

For a discussion of automatic processes in attention and comprehension, see:

Klaus G. Grunert, 'Automatic and Strategic Processes in Advertising Effects', *Journal of Marketing*, no. 4, 1996, pp. 88–101.

For a discussion of elaboration in comprehension of advertising, see:

Kenneth R. Lord and Robert E. Burnkrant, 'Television Program Elaboration Effects on Commercial Processing', in *Advances in Consumer Research*, vol. 15, ed. Michael J. Houston (Provo, UT: Association for Consumer Research, 1988), pp. 213–218.

For a discussion of how involvement affects attention and comprehension processes, see:

Laura M. Buchholz and Robert E. Smith, 'The Role of Consumer Involvement in Determining Cognitive Response to Broadcast Advertising', *Journal of Advertising*, 20, 1991, pp. 4–17.

For a discussion of how consumers react to brand extensions, see:

David A. Aaker and Kevin Lane Keller, 'Consumer Evaluations of Brand Extensions', *Journal of Marketing*, no. 1, 1990, pp. 27–41.

For a discussion of measuring miscomprehension of marketing information, see:

Klaus G. Grunert and Konrad Dedler, 'Misleading Advertising: In Search of a Measurement Methodology', *Journal of Public Policy & Marketing*, 1985, pp. 153–165.

MARKETING STRATEGY IN ACTION
DeWalt Power Tools

In 1985, managers at Black & Decker faced a difficult problem concerning the brand name on their products. In 1984, the company had purchased General Electric's small appliance business (toasters, irons, electric tin openers, and so on) for $300 million. The General Electric name had a very positive image and was highly familiar to consumers, but Black & Decker management was obligated under the purchase agreement to remove the GE brand name from all the appliances. They decided to switch all the brand names to 'Black & Decker'. This was a risky decision with a high potential for consumer confusion and uncertainty.

Management decided to market each appliance as if it was a new Black & Decker product, making no mention of the GE name. They made simple alterations to some products, such as changing the colour, and thoroughly redesigned other appliances. They also doubled the warranty to two years. Despite new product introductions and heavy counterpromotions by key competitors such as Sunbeam, Rival, and Hamilton Beach, Black & Decker successfully managed the name change. Five years later, most consumers were familiar with the Black & Decker brand name for small appliances and had a good opinion of the brand. In fact, Black & Decker had one of the strongest brand names in the United States, ranked seventh behind such brands as Coca-Cola and Kodak, and ahead of powerhouse names such as Levi's and Hershey's.

Then, in 1991, managers at Black & Decker again faced a difficult brand-name decision. This time the product category was power tools, a key product line and the major source of Black & Decker's positive image. Black & Decker's power tools had tremendous name recognition and brand equity with the do-it-yourself home-owner, and they dominated the consumer market for small power tools. But many professional builders (contractors, carpenters, construction workers) saw those tools as amateurish, and Black & Decker sold only about 10 per cent of the heavy-duty tools preferred by these customers. The professional segment, worth about $400 million a year in the United States, was dominated by Makita, a Japanese company.

Black & Decker did manufacture a line of tools directed at the professional market. Also named 'Black & Decker', these heavier duty products were charcoal-grey, in contrast to the black tools in the consumer line. The professional line was sold through many of the same channels as the consumer products, and the two lines often appeared on the same shelves at mass retailers such as Home Depot and Lowes. The problem was that many builders did not perceive the grey tools to be 'good enough or tough enough'. Black & Decker managers wondered if the professional line was sufficiently distinct from the consumer line. They considered creating a new line of power tools targeted directly at the professional building market using the brand name DeWalt (DeWalt was a 65-year-old maker of high-quality power saws that Black & Decker had acquired back in 1960).

A number of questions faced Black & Decker managers in 1991 as they considered how to market power tools to the professional market. Should Black & Decker give up one of the best brand names in America and use the DeWalt brand name for their line of professional tools? How could they expose target customers to the new line and get their attention? How could they make the DeWalt tools distinctive and different from the consumer line of Black & Decker tools? How could they communicate the key features of the DeWalt line so consumers would comprehend them correctly?

Discussion Questions

1. Discuss the pros and cons of switching from the Black & Decker name to the DeWalt name. What would you recommend Black & Decker managers do to help make this decision?

2. Describe some typical situations in which consumers would be exposed (accidentally or intentionally) to information about the

DeWalt line of tools. What implications would the type of exposure have for Black & Decker's marketing of the DeWalt brand name?

3. What types of product and brand knowledge do target customers have that would be relevant for understanding how they would comprehend the DeWalt brand name? How could Black & Decker managers find out?

4. To what extent do you think Black & Decker should identify DeWalt tools with Black & Decker? Should Black & Decker mention that DeWalt is owned by (manufactured by or serviced by) Black & Decker?

5. Discuss possible strategic actions Black & Decker might adopt for marketing the DeWalt brand to the target customer. Consider product attributes, warranty, price, distribution channels, and packaging. For each possible action, consider the impact on consumers' exposure and attention (how would consumers learn about this?) and comprehension (what level of comprehension and elaboration would you expect?).

Sources: Bill Saporito, 'Ganging Up on Black & Decker', *Fortune*, 23 December 1985, pp. 63–72; Patricia Sellers, 'New Selling Tool: The Acura Concept', *Fortune*, 24 February 1992, pp. 88–89; and Jonathan Friedland, 'Shoppers Talk, Black & Decker Listens, Profits', *The Wall Street Journal*, 9 January 1995, pp. B1, B6.

CHAPTER 6

Attitudes and Intentions

**Can Jaguar
Turn Around
Owners'
Attitudes,
Again?**

In the early 1980s, Jaguar was in desperate shape. Sales were falling, product quality was terrible, and owners had increasingly negative attitudes towards the company, the car, and the dealers. Then, almost at the last minute, Jaguar pulled itself back from the brink of disaster.

The problem with Jaguar was not that the cars were boring or unattractive; to the contrary, few automobile makes had such passionate customers. But in the early 1980s, these passions were mostly negative. Owners (and many nonowners, too) had unfavourable beliefs about product quality and reliability. Jokes about Jaguar abounded, such as 'Jaguar will soon begin selling its cars in pairs, so you can have one to drive while the other is in the service shop'. Unfortunately, the beliefs and attitudes of Jaguar owners accurately reflected reality – the car and the dealers had serious problems.

Finally, Jaguar management, factory workers, and dealers undertook drastic measures to improve production quality and dealer service. Then the company boldly doubled the warranty to two years. Customers' beliefs and attitudes began to change, and sales increased dramatically. To learn how owners felt about their cars, Jaguar management began to track consumers' attitudes towards the car, its dealers, and the company. A research company was hired to interview several hundred buyers each month and track these customers by measuring their attitudes and beliefs after 1, 8, and 18 months.

The early results showed that consumers believed the cars were improved, but attitudes towards dealer service were still poor. So Jaguar terminated about 20 per cent of its worst dealers. That, combined with the continued improvements in product quality and service, produced the single biggest jump in favourable consumer attitudes ever recorded. Of course, not every Jaguar owner had entirely positive beliefs and attitudes, but the turnaround in consumer attitudes towards Jaguar had succeeded.

In the early 1990s, a severe sales decline hit luxury cars in general and Jaguar in particular. Consumer attitudes again were negative. Jaguar continued to suffer from a lower quality image relative to other luxury cars, even though they had reduced defects by 80 per cent. Managers produced ads emphasizing the emotional relationship between consumers and the Jaguar cars. To stimulate sluggish sales, managers slashed the price of the XJS model by over 18 per cent while also changing from a V-12 to a six-cylinder engine. Sales did improve in 1993 and 1994, but attitude problems remained. It was time for another turnaround in consumer attitudes.

Sources: Michael H. Dale, 'How We Rebuilt Jaguar in the US', *Fortune*, 28 April 1986, pp. 110–119; Krystal Miller, 'Jaguar Pulls in Its Car-Pricing Claws', *The Wall Street Journal*, 14 October 1992, pp. B1, B8; Valerie Reitman and Oscar Suris, 'Can the Very British Jaguar Be Made in Japan?' *The* *Wall Street Journal*, 9 December 1994, p. B1; and Neal Templin, 'Old Look May Be Key to Jaguar's Future' *The Wall Street Journal*, 1 April 1994, pp. B1, B8.

This example illustrates the concept of consumers' attitudes, one of the most important concepts in the study of consumer behaviour. Each year marketing managers like those at Jaguar spend considerable funds researching consumers' attitudes towards products and brands, and then spend even more funds trying to influence those attitudes through advertisements, sales promotions, and other types of persuasion. By influencing consumers' attitudes, marketers hope to influence their purchase behaviours. In this chapter, we examine two types of attitudes – attitudes towards objects and attitudes towards behaviours. We begin by defining the concept of attitude and discussing how people's salient beliefs cause attitudes. Then we consider the information integration process by which attitudes towards objects are formed. Next, we discuss the information integration process that forms attitudes towards actions and influences people's intentions to perform behaviours. Finally, we discuss the imperfect relationship between behavioural intentions and actual behaviours. Throughout, we identify implications of these concepts and processes for developing marketing strategies.

What is an Attitude?

Attitude has been a key concept in psychology for more than a century, and at least 100 definitions and 500 measures of attitude have been proposed.[1] Although the dominant approach to attitudes has changed over the years (see Highlight 6.1), nearly all definitions of attitude have one thing in common: they refer to people's evaluations.[2] We define **attitude** as a *person's overall evaluation of a concept*.[3]

As you learned in Chapter 3, **evaluations** are *affective responses* at relatively low levels of intensity and arousal (refer to Exhibit 3.1). There are various approaches to explaining how such evaluations are formed. One approach is called *attitudinal conditioning*,[4] and explains attitude formation by the way in which evaluations are transferred between stimuli if these stimuli have been paired frequently. We will discuss this approach in more detail in Chapter 9. In this chapter, however, we treat attitudes as evaluations created by the cognitive system. The cognitive processing model of consumer decision making (refer to Exhibit 3.4) shows that an overall evaluation is formed when consumers integrate (combine) knowledge, meanings, or beliefs about the attitude object. The goal of this **integration process** is to analyse the *personal relevance* of the concept and determine whether it is favourable or unfavourable: 'What does this concept have to do with me? Is this a good or bad thing for me? Do I like or dislike this object?' We assume consumers form attitudes towards every concept they interpret in terms of its personal relevance. Highlight 6.2 discusses consumer attitudes towards a popular product.

As shown in Exhibit 3.4, the evaluations produced by the attitude formation process may be stored in memory. Once an attitude has been formed and stored in memory, consumers do not have to engage in another integration process to construct another attitude when they need to evaluate the concept again. Instead, the existing attitude can be activated from memory and used as a basis for interpreting new information. Because

HIGHLIGHT 6.1

A Brief History of the Study of Attitude

 ttitude has been called the most distinctive and indispensable concept in contemporary social psychology. And it is one of the most important concepts marketers use to understand consumers. Over the years, researchers have tried a variety of approaches to studying attitudes in an attempt to provide a more complete understanding of behaviour.

The attitude concept goes back as far as 1907, when the American social psychologist Thomas used it to describe a mental state which directs behaviour concerning a class of objects. In the following decades, research on attitude developed mainly along two lines. One line (exemplified by researchers like Allport and Triandis) was concerned mainly with describing various aspects of this mental state and how it relates to behaviour. This line of research defined attitude as a learned disposition to react consistently positively or negatively towards an attitude object. As the definition shows, an attitude was thought to consist of three components: a *cognitive component* (it is learned), an *affective component* (it has to do with positive and negative evaluations), and a *behavioural component* (it directs reactions to objects). The other line (exemplified by researchers like Thurstone and Likert) tried to develop instruments to measure attitudes, and they tended to concentrate on only one of the three components, namely the *evaluative component*.

Today, most researchers agree that the one-dimensional concept of attitude, which defines attitude as a person's favourable or unfavourable feelings towards an object, is most useful. Attitude can then be explained by beliefs about the attitude object, i.e. the cognitive structure with regard to the attitude object, and attitude can be used to explain or predict behaviour towards that object. This is the perspective we take in this book.

HIGHLIGHT 6.2

Attitudes Towards Off-Roaders

n the 1980s, consumers fell in love with four-wheel drive vehicles such as the Mitsubishi Pajero, Nissan Pathfinder, Suzuki Vitara, and Jeep Grand Cherokee. Led by baby boomers, many consumers began buying such cars instead of the more conventional ones. Most of the cars of this type sold in Europe are Japanese or American, with the exception of the upmarket Range Rover. Only very late did European car builders like Ford, Opel or Mercedes-Benz react to a development which turned out to be more of a trend than a fad.

Changes in consumer attitudes and values have brought this trend about. Most buyers want to have these cars because they think they are fun to own and drive, even though they only rarely have need for the four-wheel drive facility. According to a Ford dealer, 'Social acceptance of off-roaders is on a par with the luxury car, and for the yuppie-type individual, it's even more accepted'. The vehicles are easy to like. Once spartan, the current models can be fitted with all the luxurious goodies once reserved for top-of-the-range cars, including leather trim, plush carpeting, and CD players. To many younger buyers, the cars have greater appeal than conventional luxury cars. Some carmakers hope that affluent baby boomers will eventually want luxury cars along with off-roaders, but they will have to keep close tabs on changing consumer attitudes.

activated attitudes can influence consumers' judgements, taste tests are usually conducted blind (tasters are not told what brands they are tasting). Finally, the activated attitude can be integrated with other knowledge in decision making (we discuss how attitudes are used in decision processes in the next chapter).[5] This avoids activating brand attitudes that could bias the taste judgements.

Whether a given attitude will affect interpretation or integration processes depends on its **accessibility** in memory or its *probability of activation*.[6] Among the many factors that can influence the accessibility of attitudes are salience or importance (more self-relevant attitudes are more easily activated), frequency of prior activation (attitudes that are activated more often are more accessible), and the strength of the association between a concept and its attitude (puppies tend to activate positive attitudes; zebras usually do not activate an attitude).[7] Marketers sometimes use cues to 'prime' (activate) an attitude that is relevant to their strategy – consider the cute babies in ads for Dunlet softener.[8]

Attitudes can be measured simply and directly by asking consumers to evaluate the concept of interest. For instance, marketing researchers might ask consumers to indicate their attitudes toward Mars chocolate bar on three evaluative scales:

Mars chocolate bar

Extremely Unfavourable	-3	-2	-1	0	$+1$	$+2$	$+3$	Extremely Favourable
Dislike Very Much	-3	-2	-1	0	$+1$	$+2$	$+3$	Like Very Much
Very Bad	-3	-2	-1	0	$+1$	$+2$	$+3$	Very Good

Consumers' overall attitudes towards Mars chocolate bar (A_o) are indicated by the average of their ratings across the three evaluative scales. Attitudes can vary from negative (ratings of -3, -2, -1) through neutral (a rating of 0) to positive (ratings of $+1$, $+2$, $+3$). Attitudes are not necessarily intense or extreme. On the contrary, many consumers have essentially neutral evaluations (neither favourable nor unfavourable) towards relatively unimportant, noninvolving concepts. A neutral evaluation is still an attitude, however, although probably a weakly held one.

Attitudes Towards What?

Consumers' attitudes are always towards some concept. We are interested in two broad types of concept – objects and behaviours. Consumers can have *attitudes towards various physical and social objects* (A_o) including products, brands, models, stores, and people (salesperson at the camera shop), as well as aspects of marketing strategy (a rebate from Volkswagen; an ad for Stimorol chewing gum). Consumers also can have attitudes towards imaginary objects such as concepts and ideas (market economy, a fair level of taxation). Also, consumers can have *attitudes towards their own behaviours or actions* (A_{act}) including their past actions (why did I buy that sweater?) and future behaviours (shopping locally tomorrow afternoon).

Consumers can have distinct attitudes to many variations of the same general concept. Exhibit 6.1 shows several attitude concepts that vary in their *levels of specificity*, even though all concepts are in the same product domain. For instance, a person may have a moderately positive attitude towards men's clothing in general, but a distinctly negative attitude towards formal men's clothing. Still, the same person may have a moderately positive attitude towards the Boss brand, or even have a positive attitude towards wearing a Boss suit at his brother's wedding.

EXHIBIT 6.1

Variations in Level of Specificity of Attitude Concept

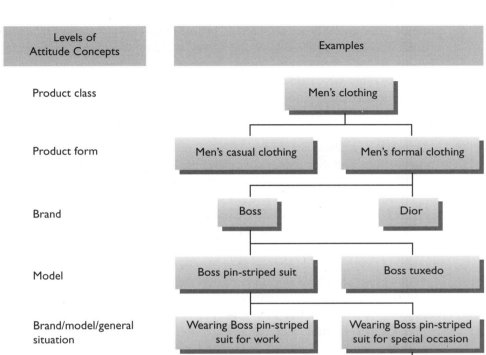

Note that some attitude concepts are defined in terms of a particular behavioural and situational context (wearing a Boss suit at the brother's wedding), whereas other concepts are more general (Boss formal men's wear). Consumers could have different attitudes towards these concepts, and the attitudes might not be consistent with each other. While somebody may have an unfavourable attitude towards wearing Boss formal attire at work (he'd rather wear more casual clothes), he may have a somewhat favourable attitude towards wearing it for special occasions. Note that although the same Boss 'object' is present in each of these concepts, the attitude towards Boss is different in the two situations.[9] Because consumers are likely to have different attitudes towards different attitude concepts, marketers must identify precisely the attitude concept at the level of specificity most relevant to the marketing problem of interest.

Marketing Implications

Marketers are highly interested in market share, a measure of purchasing behaviour indicating the proportion of total sales in a product category (or product form) received by a brand. But marketers also need to attend to consumers' brand attitudes.

Brand attitude is a critically important aspect of brand equity. Brand equity concerns the *value* of the brand to the marketer and to the consumer.[10] From the marketer's perspective, brand equity implies greater profits, more cash flow, and greater market share.[11] From a consumer perspective, **brand equity** involves a strong, *positive brand attitude* (favourable evaluation of the brand) based on favourable *meanings and beliefs* that are *accessible* in memory (easily activated).[12] These three factors create a strong, favourable *consumer–brand relationship*, a very important asset for a company and the basis for brand equity.

Basically, marketers can get brand equity in three ways: they can build it, borrow it, or buy it.[13]

Companies can *build brand equity* by ensuring the brand actually does deliver positive consequences, and that it does so consistently over time. Brand equity is strongest in cases where consumers cannot evaluate the quality of a product before actually buying it,[14] because in this case the consumer will be interested in reducing the risk associated with the purchase. A well-established brand name communicates the brand's history in delivering consistent quality, and consumers are willing to pay for the reassurance this gives. Consider the considerable brand equity built up over time by brands like Ajax household cleaner, Heineken beer, Mercedes-Benz cars, and Esprit clothing.

Companies can *borrow brand equity* by extending a positive brand name to other products. For example, a line of children's toys now bears the name of the Lego brand, famous fashion houses like Dior, Lagerfeld, and Boss have extended their brand to perfume and cosmetics, and Camel cigarettes operates a travel agency. Consumer researchers are busy trying to determine if and how brand equity is transferred by brand-name extensions.[15] Some research shows the success of a brand extension depends on the key meanings consumers associate with a brand name and whether those meanings are consistent or appropriate for the other product.[16]

Finally, a company can *buy brand equity* by purchasing brands that already have equity. For instance, the mergers and leveraged buyouts of the 1980s were partially motivated by the desire to buy brands with strong equity. Thus, when Philip Morris bought Kraft, they acquired the equity of all the acquired brands.

Because many marketing strategies are intended to influence consumers' attitudes towards a brand, marketers can use measures of consumers' attitudes to indicate the success of those strategies. For instance, many companies regularly conduct large-scale attitude surveys, called *tracking studies*, to monitor consumers' brand attitudes over time. When these studies identify changes in consumer attitudes, marketers can adjust their marketing strategies, as Jaguar did in the opening example.

Attitudes Towards Objects

In this section, we examine the information integration process by which consumers form **attitudes towards objects (A_o)**, including products or brands. As shown in Exhibit 3.4, during the integration process, consumers combine some of their knowledge, meanings, and beliefs about a product or brand to form an overall evaluation.

These considered beliefs may be formed by interpretation processes or activated from memory.

Salient Beliefs

Through their varied experiences, consumers acquire many beliefs about products, brands, and other objects in their environments. As an example, Exhibit 6.2 presents some of the beliefs one consumer has about Colgate toothpaste. These beliefs constitute an associative network of linked meanings stored in memory. Because people's cognitive capacity is limited, only a few of these beliefs can be activated and consciously considered at once. The *activated beliefs* (highlighted in Exhibit 6.2) are called **salient beliefs**. Only the salient beliefs about an object (those that are activated at a particular time and in a specific context) cause or create a person's attitude towards that object.[17] Thus, one key to understanding consumers' attitudes is to identify and understand the underlying set of salient beliefs.

In principle, consumers can have salient beliefs about any type and level of meaning associated with a product. For instance, consumers with complete means–end chains of product knowledge could activate beliefs about the product's attributes, its functional consequences, or the values achieved through using it. In addition, beliefs about other types of product-related meanings such as country of origin could be activated.[18]

EXHIBIT 6.2

Relationship between Salient Beliefs about an Object and Attitude towards the Object

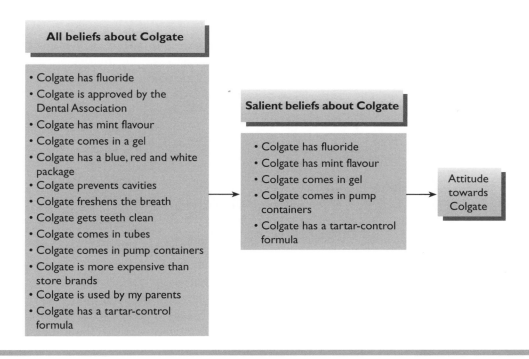

Salient beliefs could include tactile, olfactory, and visual images, as well as cognitive representations of the emotions and moods associated with using the product. If activated, any of these beliefs could influence a consumer's attitude towards a product.

Many factors influence which beliefs about an object will be activated in a situation and thus become salient determinants of A_o. They include prominent stimuli in the immediate environment (point-of-purchase displays, advertisements, package information), recent events, consumers' moods and emotional states, and consumers' values and goals activated in the situation.[19] For instance, noticing a price-reduction sign for bath soap may make price beliefs salient and therefore influential on A_o.

Marketers may find that consumers' salient beliefs vary over time or situations for some products. That is, different sets of salient beliefs about a product may be activated in different situations or at different times.[20] For instance, consumers who have just returned from the dentist are more likely to activate beliefs about tooth decay and cavities when thinking about which brand of toothpaste to buy. Variations in the set of salient beliefs over time and situations can produce changes in consumer attitudes depending on the situation, context, time, consumer's mood, and so forth. Consumers have more stable attitudes towards objects that have a stable set of salient beliefs. Normally, though, the amount of variation in salient beliefs and attitudes is not great for most objects.

The Multiattribute Attitude Model

A great deal of marketing research has focused on developing models for predicting the attitudes produced by this integration process. These are called **multiattribute attitude models** because they focus on consumers' beliefs about multiple product or brand attributes.[21] Of these, Martin Fishbein's model has been most influential in marketing.

The key proposition in Fishbein's theory is that *the evaluations of salient beliefs cause overall attitude*. Simply stated, people tend to like objects that are associated with 'good' characteristics and dislike objects they believe have 'bad' attributes. In Fishbein's multiattribute model, overall attitude towards an object is a function of two factors: the *strengths* of the salient beliefs associated with the object and the *evaluations* of those beliefs.[22] Formally, the model proposes that:

$$A_o = \sum_{i=1}^{n} b_i e_i$$

where
   A_o = Attitude towards the object
   b_i = The strength of the belief that the object has attribute i
   e_i = The evaluation of attribute i
   n = The number of salient beliefs about the object

This multiattribute attitude model accounts for the integration process by which product knowledge (the evaluations and strengths of salient beliefs) is combined to form an overall evaluation or attitude. The model, however, does not claim that consumers actually add up the products of belief strength and evaluation when forming attitudes towards objects. Rather, this and similar models attempt to predict the attitude produced by the integration process. The actual integration process may be by conscious reasoning or by automatic processing.[23] In this book, we consider the multiattribute model to be a useful tool for investigating attitude formation and predicting attitudes.

Exhibit 6.3 illustrates how the major components of the Fishbein attitude model are combined to form attitudes towards two brands of soft drinks.[24] This consumer has salient beliefs about three attributes for each brand. These beliefs vary in content, strength, and evaluation. The Fishbein model predicts that this consumer has a more favourable attitude towards 7UP than towards Pepsi.

Belief strength (b_i) is the perceived probability of association between an object and its relevant attributes. Belief strength is measured by having consumers rate this probability of association for each of their salient beliefs, for example as shown here:

'How likely is it that 7UP has no caffeine?'
Extremely Unlikely   −3   −2   −1   0   +1   +2   +3   Extremely Likely

'How likely is it that 7UP is made from all natural ingredients?'
Extremely Unlikely   −3   −2   −1   0   +1   +2   +3   Extremely Likely

Consumers who are quite certain that 7UP has no caffeine would indicate a very strong belief strength, perhaps −3. Consumers who have only a moderately strong belief that 7UP is made from only natural ingredients might rate their belief strength as +1.

The strength of consumers' product or brand beliefs is affected by their past experience with the object. Beliefs about product attributes or consequences tend to be

EXHIBIT 6.3

An Example of the Multiattribute Attitude Model

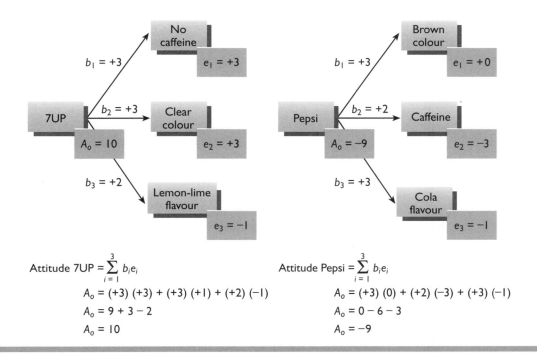

Attitude 7UP $= \sum\limits_{i=1}^{3} b_i e_i$

$A_o = (+3)\,(+3) + (+3)\,(+1) + (+2)\,(-1)$

$A_o = 9 + 3 - 2$

$A_o = 10$

Attitude Pepsi $= \sum\limits_{i=1}^{3} b_i e_i$

$A_o = (+3)\,(0) + (+2)\,(-3) + (+3)\,(-1)$

$A_o = 0 - 6 - 3$

$A_o = -9$

stronger when based on actual use of the product. Beliefs that were formed indirectly from mass advertising or conversations with a salesperson tend to be weaker. For instance, consumers are more likely to form a strong belief that '7UP tastes good' if they actually drink a 7UP and experience its taste directly than if they read a product claim in an advertisement. Because they are stronger (and more likely to be activated), beliefs based on direct experience tend to have a greater impact on A_o.[25] Marketers therefore try to induce potential customers to actually use their product. They may distribute free samples; sell small, less expensive trial sizes; offer money-off coupons; or have a no-obligation trial policy.

Fishbein argued that the typical number of salient beliefs about an attitude object is not likely to exceed seven to nine.[26] Given consumers' limited capacities for interpreting and integrating information, we might expect even fewer salient beliefs for many objects. In fact, when consumers have limited knowledge about low-involvement products, their brand attitudes might be based on very few salient beliefs, perhaps only one or two. In contrast, their attitudes towards products or brands that are more self-relevant might be based on more salient beliefs. Associated with each salient belief is a **belief evaluation (e_i)** that reflects how favourably the consumer perceives that attribute. Marketers can measure the e_i component by having consumers indicate their evaluation of (favourability towards) each salient belief, as shown below.

'7UP has no caffeine'

Very Bad   −3   −2   −1   0   +1   +2   +3   Very Good

'7UP has all natural ingredients'

Very Bad   −3   −2   −1   0   +1   +2   +3   Very Good

As shown in Exhibit 6.3, a strong belief that a product has a very desirable attribute will contribute positive to attitude. The same holds when the consumer thinks that it is very improbable that a product has an undesirable attribute. Negative contributions to attitude will result when the consumer believes it to be probable that a product has an undesirable attribute, or when the consumer thinks it is improbable that the product has a desirable attribute.

As you learned in Chapter 4, beliefs may be linked to form means–end chains of product knowledge. Exhibit 6.4 presents means–end chains for three attributes of 7UP. Note that the evaluation of each product attribute is ultimately derived from the evaluation of the end consequence in its means–end chain. As shown in Exhibit 6.4, the evaluation of the end 'flows down' the means–end chain to determine the evaluations of the less abstract consequences and attributes.[27] For instance, a person who positively evaluates the end 'relaxation', an instrumental value, would tend to positively evaluate the functional consequence 'I'm not jittery'. In turn, the product attribute 'no caffeine', which is perceived to lead to relaxation and not being jittery, would have a positive evaluation. These evaluations would then influence the overall attitude, A_o, towards 7UP.

Consumers' evaluations of salient attributes are not necessarily fixed over time or constant across different situations.[28] For instance, consumers may change their minds about how good or bad an attribute is as they learn more about its higher-order consequences. Situational factors can also change the e_i components. In a different situation, some consumers may want to be stimulated (when getting up in the morning or working late at night to finish a project). If so, the now-negative evaluation of the

EXHIBIT 6.4

The Means–End Chain Basis for Attribute Evaluations

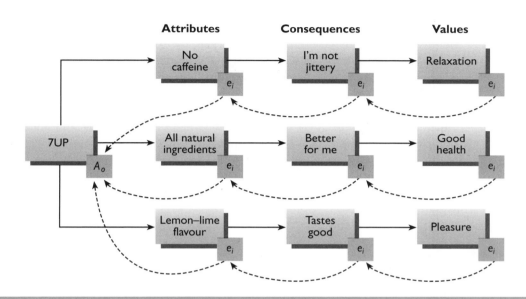

end value 'relaxation' would flow down the means–end chain and create a *negative* evaluation of the 'no caffeine' attribute – which, in turn, would contribute to a less positive overall attitude towards 7UP (for that situation). In this situation, the consumer might have a more positive attitude towards Pepsi, which does contain caffeine. This is yet another example of how the physical and social environment can influence consumers' affect and cognitions.

Marketing Implications

Marketers have been using multiattribute models to explore consumer behaviour since the late 1960s. These models became popular because they have an intuitive appeal to researchers and managers, and are relatively easy to use in research.[29] Not all of these models accurately reflect the basic Fishbein model, but most are adaptations of it. We will discuss a few of the many applications of these models below.

Understanding Your Customers

The multiattribute attitude model is useful for identifying which attributes are the most important (or most salient) to consumers. Often, one finds that different attributes are important to different consumers. For example, when buying food products, some consumers emphasize 'rational' attributes like health, freshness, and naturalness, while others emphasize hedonistic attributes like taste and novelty, and still others find it most important that the food is convenient, i.e. fast and easy to prepare. Depending on which attributes are important, this will call for different marketing strategies in terms of product development, advertising, and distribution.[30]

Diagnosis of Marketing Strategies

Although multiattribute models were developed to predict overall attitudes, marketers often use them to diagnose marketing strategies. By examining the salient beliefs that underlie attitudes towards various brands, marketers can learn how their strategies are performing and make adjustments to improve their effectiveness. For instance, in the suddenly value-conscious 1990s, marketers found that many consumers were more concerned with the quality and value of products relative to their prices.[31] It became fashionable once again to get a bargain, spend one's money wisely, and not overpay for quality. Many companies adjusted their strategies in light of these beliefs. Even Mercedes-Benz, the maker of high-quality cars who earlier wouldn't have dreamt about naming price as a benefit, started emphasizing value for money in its advertisements, claiming that the high price for the car is more than justified by its high quality and long lifetime.

Understanding Situational Influences

Marketers also can use the multiattribute attitude model to examine the influence of situations. The relative salience of beliefs about certain product attributes may be greatly influenced by the situations in which the product is used. Situations vary in many ways, including time of day, consumer mood, environmental setting, weather, and hundreds of other variables. These situational characteristics affect which beliefs are activated from memory and influence attitudes towards the brands that might be purchased for use in those situations. For instance, one study of vegetable oil found that when the oil is to be used for preparing salad dressings, it was important to consumers that it was made of pure and natural raw materials. When the oil was to be used for frying, it was more important that it was inexpensive. In both cases consumers wanted the product to be healthy and to have a good taste.[32]

Attitude-Change Strategies

The multiattribute model is a useful guide for devising strategies to change consumers' attitudes. Basically, a marketer has four possible **attitude-change strategies**: (1) add a new salient belief about the attitude object – ideally, one with a positive e_i; (2) increase the strength of an existing positive belief; (3) improve the evaluation of a strongly held belief; or (4) make an existing favourable belief more salient.

Adding a new salient belief to the existing beliefs that consumers have about a product or brand is probably the most common attitude-change strategy.[33] This strategy may require physical changes in the product. Haribo, a successful German manufacturer of sweets (primarily wine gums and licorice) has its marketing strength in the effective and continuous introduction of new tastes and shapes. Haribo avoids children getting bored with their products by launching 20–30 new products every year. Haribo keeps track of the newest trends among children, by reading youth magazines and looking at cartoons, and has successfully introduced new products such as dinosaur wine gums, ice-tea and coke–licorice flavours.[34]

Marketers may also try to change attitudes by *changing the strength of already salient beliefs.*[35] They can attempt to increase the strength of beliefs about positive attributes and consequences; or they can decrease the strength of beliefs about negative attributes and consequences. SAS, the Scandinavian airline, was traditionally reputed as an airline with a good record of on-time departures – a belief evaluated very positively by travellers. In the mid-1990s, however, this belief had weakened considerably. SAS reacted by rescheduling flights so that there was more time on the ground between flights, having more mechanics on duty, allocating more manpower to de-icing and a number of other measures to increase on-time performance. They then started a campaign informing customers about these measures, trying to strengthen the belief that SAS was a punctual airline.

Also, marketers can try to change consumers' attitudes by *changing the evaluative aspect of an existing, strongly held belief* about a salient attribute. This requires constructing a new means–end chain by linking a more positive, higher ordered consequence to that attribute. Consider how evaluations of beliefs about food attributes have changed as their means–end meanings have changed.[36] Fat in food has come to be evaluated very negatively, because consumers associate it with negative health consequences. This creates a problem for producers of meat, because a certain amount of intramuscular fat (marbling) is actually necessary for the meat to be tender and tasty. Meat manufacturers may therefore be forced to educate consumers in the positive effects of (moderate amounts of) fat in meat, thus changing consumers' means–end chains about fat and thereby their evaluations of this attribute.[37]

The final strategy for changing consumers' attitudes is to *make an existing favourable belief more salient,* usually by convincing consumers that the attribute is more self-relevant than it seemed. This strategy is similar to the previous one in that it attempts to link the attribute to valued consequences and values. Creating such means–end chains increases both the salience of consumers' beliefs about the attribute as well as the evaluations (e_i) of those beliefs. For example, the marketing strategies of sun-care lotion manufacturers emphasize the perceived risks of not using lotions with a sunscreen attribute.[38] By linking the sunscreen attribute to important ends such as avoiding skin cancer and premature wrinkling, they sought to make the sunscreen attribute more salient (more self-relevant) to consumers. Such means–end chains should make sunscreen beliefs more likely to be activated and considered during decision making.

Attitudes Towards Behaviour

Consumers' attitudes have been studied intensively, but marketers tend to be more concerned about consumers' overt *behaviour*, especially their purchase behaviour. Thus, it is not surprising that a great deal of research has tried to establish the relationship between attitudes and behaviour.[39] Based on the idea of consistency, you might expect attitudes towards an object (A_o) to be related to behaviours towards the object. For instance, 'most market researchers believe, and operate under the assumption, that the more favourable a person's attitude towards a given product (or brand), the more likely the person is to buy or use that product (or brand)'.[40]

Thus, returning to the opening example of Chapter 4, a marketing researcher might measure the consumers' attitudes to fresh fish and use this to predict whether each person will purchase fresh fish (at the fishmonger's) within the next month. If this approach seems reasonable, you may be surprised to learn that consumers' attitudes towards objects are seldom good predictors of their specific behaviours regarding those objects. In fact, with a few notable exceptions, most research has found rather weak relationships between A_o and *specific* individual behaviours.[41]

One of the problems with relating A_o to individual behaviours is illustrated in Exhibit 6.5, which presents the relationships among a consumer's beliefs, attitude, and behaviours concerning a particular object – fresh fish. First, note that Ann, our consumer, has an *overall attitude* towards fresh fish (in her case, a favourable A_o), which is based on her salient beliefs about fresh fish. Second, note that Ann *can engage in many different behaviours regarding fresh fish*. For instance, she might see a new recipe with fresh fish, go to the fishmonger's on Wednesday afternoon and buy some filleted plaice or recommend the new recipe/the fishmonger to a friend. However, none of these specific behaviours is necessarily consistent with or strongly related to her overall A_o, although some of them might be.

This does not mean that consumers' attitudes are irrelevant to their behaviours. As shown in Exhibit 6.5, Ann's overall attitude (A_o) is related to the overall pattern of her behaviours (all of her behaviours regarding fresh fish taken together). However, it is not possible to predict with accuracy any specific behaviour based on a person's overall attitude towards the object of behaviour.

Although this proposition may seem strange, there are many examples of its validity. Consider that many consumers probably have positive attitudes towards Porsche cars, Rolex watches, and vacation homes, but most do not buy these products. Because favourable attitudes towards these products can be expressed in many different behaviours, it is difficult to predict which specific behaviour will be performed. Consider three consumers who have generally favourable attitudes towards Porsches, but do not own one. One consumer may read ads and test reports about Porsches. Another consumer may go to showrooms to look at Porsches. A third consumer may just day-

EXHIBIT 6.5

Relationships Among Beliefs, Attitude, and Behaviours Regarding a Specific Object

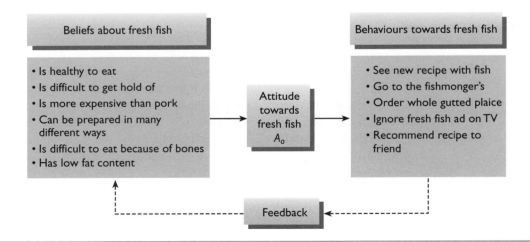

dream about owning a Porsche. In sum, having a generally favourable (or unfavourable) attitude towards a product does not mean the consumer will perform every possible favourable (or unfavourable) behaviour regarding that product. Marketers need a model that identifies the attitudinal factors that influence specific behaviours; such a model is provided by Ajzen's theory of planned behaviour.[42]

The Theory of Planned Behaviour

Ajzen's theory and its predecessor, Fishbein's theory of reasoned action,[43] recognizes that people's attitudes towards an object may not be strongly or systematically related to their specific behaviours. Rather, the immediate determinant of whether consumers will engage in a particular behaviour is their *intention* to engage in that behaviour. Fishbein and Ajzen modified and extended the multiattribute attitude model to relate consumers' beliefs and attitudes to their behavioural intentions. The entire model is presented in Exhibit 6.6.

EXHIBIT 6.6

The Theory of Planned Behaviour

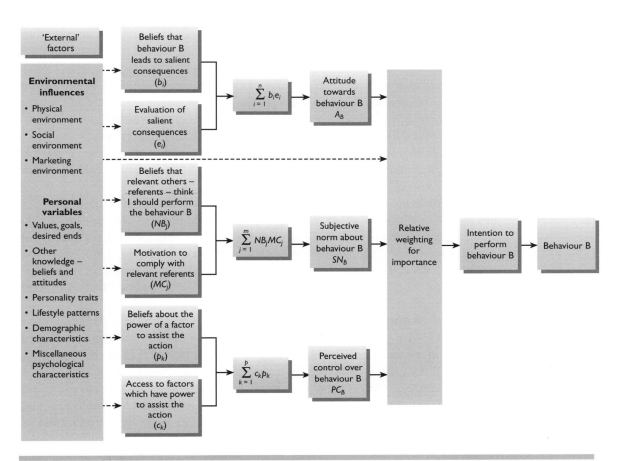

The model is called a **theory of planned behaviour** because it assumes consumers *consciously consider* the consequences of the alternative behaviours under consideration and choose the one that leads to the most desirable consequences and that seems realistic to carry out. The outcome of this reasoned choice process is an intention to engage in the selected behaviour. This behavioural intention is the single best predictor of actual behaviour. In sum, the theory of planned behaviour proposes that any reasonably complex behaviour which is at least partly under *volitional* control (such as buying a pair of shoes) is determined by the person's intention to perform that behaviour. The theory of planned behaviour is not relevant for extremely simple or *involuntary* behaviours such as automatic eye blinking, turning your head at the sound of the telephone, or sneezing.

Formally, the theory of planned behaviour can be presented as follows:

$$B \approx BI = A_{act}(w_1) + SN(w_2) + PC(w_3)$$

where

$$
\begin{aligned}
B \;&=\; \text{a specific behaviour} \\
BI \;&=\; \text{consumer's intention to engage in that behaviour} \\
A_{act} \;&=\; \text{consumer's attitude towards engaging in that behaviour} \\
SN \;&=\; \text{subjective norm regarding whether other people want the consumer} \\
&\quad\; \text{to engage in that behaviour} \\
PC \;&=\; \text{perceived control over the behaviour} \\
w_1, w_2, w_3 \;&=\; \text{weights that reflect the relative influence of the } A_{act},\, SN,\, \text{and } PC \\
&\quad\; \text{components on } BI
\end{aligned}
$$

According to this theory, people tend to perform behaviours that are evaluated favourably, that are popular with other people, and which they feel confident they can perform. They tend to refrain from behaviours that are regarded unfavourably, that are unpopular with others, and/or which they do not think they can perform.

In this section, we describe and discuss each component of the theory of planned behaviour, beginning with behaviour.[44] Note that all the components of the model are defined in terms of a specific behaviour, B.

Behaviours are specific actions directed at some target object (driving to the store, buying a swimsuit, looking for a lost pen). Behaviours always occur in a situational context or environment and at a particular time (at home right now, in the grocery shop this afternoon, or at an unspecified location in your town next week).[45] Marketers need to be clear about these aspects of the behaviour of interest because the components of the theory of planned behaviour must be defined and measured in terms of these specific features.

Basically, a **behavioural intention (BI)** is a proposition connecting self and a future action: 'I intend to go shopping this Saturday'. One can think of an intention as a *plan* to engage in a specified behaviour in order to reach a goal.[46] Behavioural intentions are created through a choice/decision process in which beliefs about two types of consequences (A_{act} and SN) and about capabilities to perform the behaviour (PC) are considered and integrated to evaluate alternative behaviours and select among them. Behavioural intentions vary in strength, which can be measured by having consumers rate the probability that they will perform the behaviour of interest, as shown below:

'All things considered, how likely are you to shop at Safeway's this week or next?'
Extremely Unlikely   1   2   3   4   5   6   7   Extremely Likely

As shown in Exhibit 6.6, the strengths and evaluations of a consumer's salient beliefs about the *functional consequences* of an action are combined to form an **attitude towards the behaviour or action (A_{act})**. A_{act} reflects the consumer's overall evaluation of performing the behaviour. Marketers measure the strengths and evaluations of the salient beliefs about the consequences of a behaviour in the same way that they measure beliefs about product attributes. Highlight 6.3 discusses how the consequences of visiting a website influence attitudes and intentions to return.

A_{act} is quite different from A_o. Although both attitudes are based on an underlying set of salient beliefs, the beliefs are about rather different concepts. For instance, consider the following salient beliefs about 'Opel Corsa' (an object) and 'buying a new Opel Corsa this year' (a specific action involving the object).

Opel Corsa (A_o)	Buying a new Opel Corsa this year (A_{act})
Moderately priced (+)	Gives me a mode of transportation (+)
Ordinary (−)	Will put me in financial difficulty (−)
Well built (+)	Will lead to high upkeep costs (−)
Dependable (+)	Will lose value rapidly (−)
Easily serviced (+)	Will lead to low insurance rates (+)

Note that these salient beliefs have quite different evaluations. Thus, we should not be surprised to find that some consumers like Opel Corsa in general (A_o), but have negative attitudes towards buying one this year (A_{act}).

It is possible for marketing strategies to have a differential impact on A_o and A_{act}. For instance, one study found that information about the shop where a new product was sold affected consumers' attitudes towards purchasing the product (A_{act}), but did not influence their attitudes towards the product itself (A_o).[47] Marketers therefore must be careful to determine whether they are concerned with consumers' attitudes towards the object in general or some action regarding the object (such as buying it). Only attitudes towards behaviours are likely to be strongly related to specific behavioural intentions.

In addition, marketers must carefully identify the level of specificity most appropriate for the marketing problem. Attitudes at one level of specificity are not always consistently related to attitudes at other levels. For instance, Rick and Linda very much like to go shopping (a general behaviour), yet they dislike shopping on Saturdays when the streets and shops are crowded (a more specific behaviour).

The **subjective or social norm** (SN) component reflects consumers' perceptions of what they think other people want them to do. Consumers' salient *normative beliefs* (NB_j) regarding 'doing what other people want me to do' and their motivation to comply with the expectations of these other people (MC_j) are combined ($\sum_{j=1}^{m} NB_j MC_j$) to form SN. Along with A_{act}, and PC, SN affects consumers' behavioural intentions (*BI*).

Measuring the strength of normative beliefs is similar to the belief–strength measures discussed earlier.

'Members of my family are in favour of me shopping at Safeway's'
Extremely Unlikely   −3   −2   −1   0   +1   +2   +3   Extremely Likely

---

HIGHLIGHT 6.3

Attitudes and Intentions Towards Websites on the Internet

M arketers and web designers need to know which features of a website create positive attitudes towards returning to the site and which features create negative attitudes. In 1997, a research firm called SurveySite interviewed visitors to 87 web sites in different categories, including news, entertainment, travel, and health. SurveySite placed a feedback icon in each site for two weeks. Visitors who clicked on the icon could take an on-line survey in which they rated various dimensions of the site and evaluated their experience. Participants were also asked if they intended to make a repeat visit to the site.

SurveySite identified about 40 factors that could potentially influence intentions to make a repeat visit. They condensed these to 12 factors in two broad categories – design feature of the website and emotional experiences during the visit. The most influential factor in determining a repeat visit was 'good content' … content that is relevant or interesting to the participant. Other factors related to good content include the quality of the layout, the ease of getting information, and the uniqueness of the site.

The second most important factor in people's intentions to return to the site was whether they enjoyed their first visit (positive affective reactions). Enjoyment could be due to various factors, such as the novelty of the experience, interesting design features, or the sheer fun of the visit. According to the respondents, the overall quality of the graphics was not an important consideration in influencing their intentions to return. And, sites that were 'like all the rest' did not receive high attitude and intention scores.

Source: Marshall Rice, 'What Makes Users Revisit a Web Site?',
Marketing News, 17 March 1997, p. 12.

Motivation to comply is measured by asking consumers to rate how much they want to conform to other people's desires.

'Generally, how much do you want to do what your family wants you to?'
Not At All   1   2   3   4   5   6   7   Very Much

The **perceived control** (PC) component reflects to what extent the consumer believes that he or she is actually able to perform the behaviour. Shopping at Safeway's presupposes that there is a Safeway outlet in the neighbourhood, that consumers know where it is, and that there is a means of transportation to get there and to bring the groceries home after shopping. If some of these preconditions are not met, consumers may not form an intention of shopping there, even though both they and their families have a positive attitude. The power (p_k) of a factor to assist the action, weighted with the degree to which the consumer believes he or she has access to that factor (c_k) are combined ($\sum_{k=1}^{n} c_k p_k$) to form PC.

Again, measuring the strength of control beliefs can be done in a fairly similar way as the other beliefs. The power of a factor can be measured like this:

'Shopping at Safeway's is easier for me when I have a car'
Extremely Unlikely   1   2   3   4   5   6   7   Extremely Likely

and the access to the factor like this:

'If I want to, I can easily go by car when going shopping this or next week'
Extremely Unlikely   1   2   3   4   5   6   7   Extremely Likely

The theory of planned behaviour proposes that A_{act}, SN, and PC combine to affect behavioural intentions (BI) and that their relative influence varies from situation to situation. During the information integration process that creates BI, A_{act}, SN, and PC may be weighted differently (see Exhibit 6.6).[48] Some behaviours are primarily affected by the SN factor. For instance, intentions to wear a certain style of clothing to a party or to work are likely to be influenced more strongly by SN and the normative beliefs regarding conformity than beliefs about the general consequences of wearing those clothes (A_{act}).[49] For other behaviours, normative influences are minimal, and consumers' intentions are largely determined by A_{act}. For instance, consumers' intentions to purchase headache remedies are more likely to be affected by their salient beliefs about the functional consequences of using the product and the resulting attitude towards buying it than by what other people expect them to do. For still other behaviours, the perceived control component will be decisive. Many people have positive attitudes (A_{act}) towards stopping smoking, eating less fat, or exercising more, and also expect others to evaluate such behaviour favourably (SN). However, they do not think they have access to the necessary resources (PC) – will-power, availability of low-fat food, time to go the gym – to actually perform the behaviour.

Marketing Implications

The situational context in which behaviour occurs can have powerful influences on consumers' behavioural intentions. Consider a consumer named Jean, a 26-year-old assistant brand manager for Master Foods in Belgium. Last week, Jean had to decide whether to buy Stella Artois or Duvel beer in two different situations. In the first situation, Jean was planning to drink a few beers at home over the weekend while watching TV. In the other context, he was having a beer after work in a plush bar with a group of his coworkers. The different sets of product-related and social beliefs activated in the two situations created different A_{act} and SN components. In the private at-home situation, Jean's product beliefs and A_{act} had the dominant effect on his intentions (he bought the basic Stella Artois beer). In the highly social bar situation, his normative beliefs and SN had the greater impact on his intentions (he bought the expensive and strong Duvel beer). In neither situation did he buy his actual favourite, traditional Kriek, because it was not available in neither the supermarket where he shopped nor the bar where he went with his colleagues.

To develop effective strategies, it is important to determine which of the A_{act}, SN and PC components has the major influence on behavioural intentions (and thus on behaviour). If the primary reason for a behaviour (shopping, searching for information, buying a particular brand) is normative (you think others want you to), marketers need to emphasize that the relevant normative influences (friends, family, coworkers) are in favour of the behaviour. Often this is done by portraying social influence situations in advertising. If intentions are largely influenced by A_{act} factors, the marketing strategy should attempt to create a set of salient beliefs about the positive consequences of the behaviour, perhaps by demonstrating those outcomes in an advertisement. If intentions are largely influenced by perceived control, marketing has to find out which barriers consumers perceive to deter them from the behaviour, and then try to remove these barriers – for example by making products more easily available, or less time-consuming to use. In sum, the theory of planned behaviour identifies the types of cognitive and affective factors that underlie a consumer's intention to perform a specific behaviour.

Although intentions determine most voluntary behaviours, measures of consumers' intentions may not be perfect indicators of the actual intentions that determine the behaviour. In the following section, we discuss the problems of using intention measures to predict actual behaviours.

Intentions and Behaviours

Predicting consumers' future behaviours, especially their purchase behaviour (sales, to marketers), is a critically important aspect of forecasting and marketing planning. According to the theory of planned behaviour, predicting consumers' purchase behaviours is a matter of measuring their intentions to buy just before they make a purchase. In almost all cases, however, this would be impractical. When planning strategies, marketers need predictions of consumers' purchase and use behaviours weeks, months, or sometimes years in advance.

Unfortunately, predictions of specific behaviours based on intentions measured well before the behaviour occurs may not be very accurate. For instance, one survey found that only about 60 per cent of people who intended to buy a car actually did so within a year.[50] And of those who claimed they did not intend to buy a car, 17 per cent ended up buying one. Similar examples could be cited for other product categories (many with even worse accuracy). This does not mean the theory of planned behaviour is wrong in identifying intentions as an immediate influence on behaviour. Rather, failures to predict the behaviour of interest often lie with *how* and *when* intentions are measured.

To accurately predict behaviours, marketers should measure consumers' intentions at the same level of abstraction and specificity as the action, target, and time components of the behaviour. Situation context also should be specified when it is important.

Exhibit 6.7 lists several factors that can weaken the relationship between measured behavioural intentions and the observed behaviours of interest. In situations where few of these factors operate, measured intentions should predict behaviour quite well.

In a broad sense, *time* is the major factor that reduces the predictive accuracy of measured intentions. Intentions, like other cognitive factors, can and do change over time. The longer the intervening time period, the more unanticipated circumstances (such as exposure to the marketing strategies of competitive companies) can occur and change consumers' original purchase intentions.[51] Thus, marketers must expect lower levels of predictive accuracy when intentions are measured long before the behaviour occurs. However, unanticipated events can also occur during very short periods. An appliance manufacturer once asked consumers entering an appliance shop what brand they intended to buy. Of those who specified a brand, only 20 per cent came out with it.[52] Apparently, events occurred in the shop to change these consumers' beliefs, attitudes, intentions, and behaviour.

Certain behaviours cannot be accurately predicted from beliefs, attitudes, and intentions.[53] Obvious examples include nonvoluntary behaviours such as sneezing or getting sick. It is also difficult to predict purchase behaviours when the alternatives

EXHIBIT 6.7

Factors That Reduce or Weaken the Relationship between Measured Behavioural Intentions and Observed Behaviour

Factor	Examples
Intervening time	As the time between measurement of intentions and observation of behaviour increases, more factors can occur that act to modify or change the original intention so that it no longer corresponds to the observed behaviour.
Different levels of specificity	The measured intention should be specified at the same level as the observed behaviour, otherwise the relationship between them will be weakened. Suppose we measured John's intentions to wear jeans to work (in general). But we observed his behaviour on a day he was receiving visitors and didn't think jeans were appropriate in that specific situation.
Unforeseen environmental event	Jan fully intended to buy Tuborg beer this afternoon, but the shop was sold out. Jan could not carry out the original intention and had to form a new intention on the spot to buy Carlsberg beer.
Unforeseen situational context	Sometimes the situational context the consumer had in mind when the intentions were measured was different from the situation at the time of behaviour. In general, Peter has a negative intention to buy wine in cartons. However, when he had to prepare a punch calling for eight bottles of wine, Peter formed a positive intention to buy the inexpensive wine.
Stability of intentions	Some intentions are quite stable. They are based on a well-developed structure of salient beliefs for A_{act} and PC. Other intentions are not stable, as they are founded on only a few weakly held beliefs that may easily be changed.
New information	Consumers may receive new information about the salient consequences of their behaviour, which leads to changes in their beliefs and attitudes towards the act and/or in the subjective norm, or they may get new information which changes their perceived control. These changes, in turn, change the intention. The original intention is no longer relevant to the behaviour and does not predict the eventual behaviour accurately.

(brands) are very similar and the person has positive attitudes towards several of them. Finally, behaviours about which consumers have little knowledge and low levels of involvement are virtually impossible to predict because consumers have very few beliefs in memory on which to base attitudes and intentions. In such cases, consumers' measured intentions were probably created to answer the marketing researcher's question; such intentions are likely to be unstable and poor predictors of eventual, actual behaviour. In sum, before relying on measures of attitude and intentions to predict future behaviour, marketers need to determine whether consumers can be expected to have well-formed beliefs, attitudes, and intentions towards those behaviours.

Back to . . .
Jaguar

The Jaguar example illustrates how consumer attitudes can be used to help develop and evaluate marketing strategies. Measures of beliefs and attitudes can also be used to gauge the success of marketing strategies in solving a problem. Measures of A_o (attitudes towards Jaguar) and the related salient beliefs can identify problem areas needing attention. For instance, the negative consumer attitudes and the underlying beliefs, especially about poor product quality, shoddy dealer service, and outdated styling, suggested actions the company could take to increase the favourability of consumers' attitudes towards Jaguar cars.

In 1989, the Ford Motor Company purchased Jaguar for $2.5 billion and incurred losses estimated at $1.2 billion over the next four years. A key strategy was the redesign of the boxy XJ6 (the model that accounted for 80 per cent of Jaguar sales). Ford spent $300 million to create a more curvaceous Jaguar that arrived on the scene in late 1994. In addition, Ford considered expanding the Jaguar line by introducing a new, cheaper entry model (for under $50 000), perhaps built by Ford or Mazda. However, Ford was concerned that the typical customer's positive attitudes towards Jaguar might be damaged if the new car was partly built by Ford or Mazda. 'You don't want to do anything that detracts from that Jaguar image', said one consultant. 'The name just strikes a note of passion.'

It is important to recognize that this example deals primarily with A_o. To predict purchase behaviours of consumers (Jaguar owners or potential owners), the company should measure consumers' A_{act}, SN, and PC concerning buying a Jaguar, as well as their behavioural intentions to do so.

Summary

We began this chapter by defining attitude as a consumer's overall evaluation of an object. We discussed how attitude objects varied in levels of abstraction and specificity. We then discussed consumers' attitudes toward objects, A_o, and described Fishbein's multiattribute model of how salient beliefs create A_o. We also discussed the theory of planned behaviour, which identifies consumers' attitudes toward performing behaviours (A_{act}), social influences (SN), and perceived control (PC) as the basis for behavioural intentions (BI). Finally, we considered the problems of using measures of behavioural intentions to predict actual behaviours. Throughout, we discussed implications for marketers. In this chapter, we identified consumers' activated knowledge, in the form of beliefs, as the basic factor underlying their attitudes, subjective norms, perceived control, and intentions – and ultimately their behaviours. Moreover, we showed that these activated salient beliefs and the resulting attitudes and intentions are sensitive to situational factors in the environment, including marketing strategies. This provides another example of how cognition, environment, and behaviour interact in a continuous, reciprocal process to create new behaviours, new cognitions (beliefs, attitudes, and intentions), and new environments.

Key Terms and Concepts

accessibility   118
attitude   116
attitude-change strategies   126
attitude towards the behaviour or action (A_{act})   131
attitudes towards objects (A_o)   120
behavioural intention (*BI*)   130
behaviours   130
belief evaluation (e_i)   124
belief strength (b_i)   123
brand equity   120
evaluations   116
integration process   116
multiattribute attitude models   122
perceived control   132
salient beliefs   121
subjective or social norm   137
theory of planned behaviour   130

Review and Discussion Questions

1. Define attitude and identify the two main ways that consumers can acquire attitudes.
2. How are salient beliefs different from other beliefs? How can marketers attempt to influence belief salience?
3. Discuss the integration process of forming an attitude according to Fishbein's multiattribute attitude model.
4. Consider a product category in which you make regular purchases (such as soft drinks or clothing). How have your belief strengths and evaluations and brand attitudes changed over time?
5. Using an example, describe the key differences between A_o and A_{act}. Under what circumstances would marketers be most interested in each type of attitude?
6. Describe the theory of planned behaviour and discuss the three main factors that are integrated to form a behavioural intention. Describe one marketing strategy implication for each factor.
7. Use the example of Jaguar to distinguish between the multiattribute attitude model and the theory of planned behaviour. How could each model contribute to the development of a more effective marketing strategy for Jaguar?
8. Discuss the problems in measuring behavioural intentions to (*a*) buy a new car; (*b*) buy a soft drink from a vending machine; and (*c*) save £250 per month towards the eventual purchase of a house. What factors could occur in each situation to make the measured intentions a poor predictor of actual behaviour?
9. How could marketers improve their predictions of behaviours in the situations described in Question 8? Consider improvements in measurements as well as alternate research or forecasting techniques.

10. Negative attitudes present a special challenge for marketing strategy. Consider how what you know about attitudes and intentions could help you to address consumers who have a brand relationship described as 'Don't like our brand and buy a competitor's brand'.

Additional Reading

For a thorough review of alternative approaches to attitudes, including a discussion of measuring attitudes and intentions, see:

Richard E. Petty and John T. Cacioppo, *Attitudes and Persuasion: Classic and Contemporary Approaches* (Dubuque, I.A.: William C. Brown, 1981).

For a discussion of more recent developments see:

Richard P. Bagozzi, 'The Rebirth of Attitude Research in Marketing', *Journal of the Market Research Society*, 30, no. 2, 1988, pp. 163–195.

For a discussion of conscious and unconscious processes of attitude formation, see:

Chris Janiszewski, 'Preconscious Processing Effects: The Independence of Attitude Formation and Conscious Thought', *Journal of Consumer Research*, September 1988, pp. 199–209.

For a practical application of multiattribute attitude models, see:

George E. Belch and Michael A. Belch. 'The Application of an Expectancy-Value Operational-ization of Functional Theory to Examine Attitudes of Boycotters and Nonboycotters of a Consumer Product', in *Advances in Consumer Research*, vol. 14, ed. M. Wallendorf and P. Anderson (Provo, UT: Association for Consumer Research, 1987), pp. 232–236.

For a discussion of the difficulties in relating attitude to behaviour, see:

R. Brannon, 'Attitudes and the Prediction of Behavior', in *Social Psychology*, ed. Bernard Seidenberg and Alvin Snadowsky (New York, NY: Free Press, 1976), pp. 145–198.

For an application of the theory of planned behaviour in a marketing context, see:

Robert East, 'Investment Decisions and the Theory of Planned Behaviour', *Journal of Economic Psychology*, 14, no. 2, 1993, pp. 337–375.

For a discussion of the limits of analysing attitudes in consumer behaviour, see:

Gordon Foxall, 'Evidence for Attitudinal-Behavioural Consistency: Implications for Consumer Research Paradigms', *Journal of Economic Psychology*, 5, no. 1, 1984, pp. 71–92.

MARKETING STRATEGY IN ACTION
The Dualit Toaster

You've got a small family manufacturing business. You've got customers on an ever-increasing waiting list, you can dictate terms to buyers, you are coining in a healthy profit. And without any advertising mega-bucks you have managed to create one of the most stylish premium products to grace the wedding lists of urbane trendies the world over. A tall tale? No: welcome to the shiny, happy – and very real – world of upmarket chrome toaster and kettle company Dualit.

The story goes like this. The company was started in 1944 by Swiss engineer Max Gort-Barten. Gort-Barten liked to invent things and before production of the familiar chrome toaster began, Gort-Barten had a string of inventions to his name. For example, he designed a parabolic infra-red heater which allowed heat direction to be manipulated. However, manufacturing in the postwar era often meant resources were scarce, and despite Mrs Gort-Barten's scouring the nation's Woolworth's for more ceramic tubes the Dual Light heater was laid to rest.

The toaster was its replacement. In a plastic and bakelite era the shiny metal toaster was instantly heralded as an innovation and adopted by postwar Londoners who wanted to take breakfast in style.

However, when major players such as Kenwood began to enter the market with mass manufactured kitchen goods, Gort-Barten struggled to compete and looked instead to exploit a gap in the commercial catering market.

He developed the first commercial toaster – a huge six-slot beast – and the rest, as they say, is history.

Although there was a certain amount of consumer appeal in the early days, it was nothing like the phenomenal success Dualit toasters enjoyed in the 1980s. In the designer decade, when expensive gadgetry was hip, no self-respecting kitchen was complete without the oversized, premium-priced, chrome toaster that wore its label on the outside. But whereas many brands disappeared along with padded shoulders, the Dualit toaster has survived and prospered well into the 1990s – the company enjoyed its 20–25 per cent year-on-year sales growth even through the recession.

Sean O'Flynn, creative director with brand development consultants Grey, attributes Dualit's enduring appeal to the fact that, while its chrome industrial form-follows-function style worked in the eighties, it now fits perfectly with the current fashion for romantic nostalgia and all things traditional. 'It fits in with the return to the unfitted kitchen, with Belfast sinks and Le Creuset cookware, and the original Kenwood food processors. It also fits the desire for robustness and reliability which make people treat it like they do a VW or Harley-Davidson motorcycle – like a genuine article which stands the test of time', he says.

Michael Howard, a Retail Planning Association designer and Dualit owner, shares this passion. 'It's butch and attractive and it looks like it can do the job. It looks industrial and hard-wearing especially next to other more feeble toasters. The fact it is expensive helps.'

Of course Leslie Gort-Barten (Max's son, now the managing director) is well aware of this. When the company introduced one of its kettles to one shop, the shop actually requested that another £15 be added to the price. 'People want to spend more money', he says. 'Buying a Dualit demonstrates that they can pay £50 or £60 for a kettle. It's all part of what you could call an illusion, except the products really are worth the money.' He would say that of course, but when he begins to explain that every toaster is hand-assembled by workers on a piecework rate, the average worker turning out around 15 toasters a day, and that Dualit is the only retail toaster still made in Europe, you find yourself thinking £120 for a toaster is not too much money. The fact we are only talking about a breakfast staple has become beside the point.

'The big manufacturers produce what we make in a month in a week using automated methods', Gort-Barten explains. 'We employ a small but efficient staff and deliberately maintain the 'Handmade in England' stance as opposed to "robotbuilt in China" in order to sustain the appeal we have built up.' Not to mention the profit. With only 70 employees Dualit turns over around £9 million a year, some 55 per cent of which derives from exports to 34 countries around the world. There is no consumer or retailer advertising whatsoever, and this makes it all the more impressive that Dualit products have such a solid brand awareness and fashionable image. Gort-Barten attributes this to the fact that the product is good and the retail environment right.

'We pick our distributors and monitor how they perform and who they sell to. We pick our retailers at the top end of the market, so in the UK we are stocked in Selfridges, John Lewis, Bentalls, Libertys, Heals, The Conran Shop. We have a limited capacity, and so people have to wait for toasters and that also is part of the attraction. Customers are on allocations irrespective of what they order. That again is part of the uniqueness of the product.'

So with no advertising and limited availability – factors which for other products would lead to dwindling demand – how does Gort-Barten keep customers coming back?

The answer is by line extension and new product development. A range of coloured toasters are now selling well, a breadbin has just been launched at a trade show in Germany, two new kettles are in the pipeline and a new toaster is about to enter design stage and should be on the shelves in two years. 'And', says Gort-Barten, 'the best part is that all these add-ons don't reduce sales of the original range and base models, so bring about a genuine increase in revenue.'

But exactly how far can you go with a toaster? And with the fashion for innovation and new product development, doesn't Gort-Barten feel pressure to innovate for innovation's sake?

'I have read that the Dualit toaster was the product of the eighties, but that's not true. It is a product of the eighties and the nineties because, forget the design, it still makes toast well and will carry on making toast well for 20 years. We're not talking about jazzy products with limited lifespan It is sold and keeps going . . . . Yes, the design does play a part and we do bring in designers to look at how we can continually tweak and improve it, but the basic guts of the toaster hasn't changed. It's not fashion; it is basically an extremely good toaster.'

Inevitably there have been attempts to emulate the Dualit style which is why the company invested heavily in trademarking. But, in fact, Gort-Barten says the copycats just enhance the real thing. 'It has tended to do us a favour because people can see how light and insubstantial the others are next to ours.' As Andy Knowles at JKR says, 'The Dualit toaster is a very tactile, solid, authentic piece of European engineering. It is a perfectly designed thing, not clichéd, not marketed – it looks like it does because it's designed to work. It is made by people who take pride in it against the rampant commercialism of other manufacturers.'

Or, as Leslie Gort-Barten more succinctly puts it, 'You can have all the hype you want, but if the toaster's no good it's not going to sell. And it is a good toaster.'

Discussion Questions

1. Try to explain the positive attitude many people seem to have to the Dualit toaster. Which beliefs do you think are most salient?

2. Why do you think attitude to Dualit became more positive in the 1980s? Which type of attitude change do you think has taken place – in terms of beliefs, their strengths and their evaluations?

3. Do you think the positive attitude towards the Dualit toaster will extend to other Dualit products?

4. Do you think subjective norm and perceived control play any role in determining behavioural intention towards buying a Dualit toaster?

Source: Adapted with the kind permission of Nicky Wnek, 'The Breakfast Business', *Marketing Business*, November 1996, pp. 18–21.

Consumer Decision Making

Buying a Set of Dishes

In mid-September Barbara decided to host a dinner party for 10 people on 17 October. She immediately called and invited all the guests. But now she had a problem: She didn't have enough dishes to serve 10 people. Actually Barbara had two sets of dishes – Wedgwood stoneware and Lenox china – but several pieces of the stoneware had broken over the years, and she had only seven place settings of the china. Barbara decided she had to buy some new dishes. Given her budget restrictions, Barbara decided to replace the missing pieces of stoneware because she thought the stoneware would be less expensive than the china.

That Friday Barbara called several department stores, only to discover that none of them had her pattern in stock. In fact, they said it would take from two to six months to get the dishes, and that Wedgwood would probably discontinue the pattern soon. Barbara decided to order the stoneware and borrow dishes for the party. First, though, she would check with her husband.

Barbara's husband was not very enthusiastic. He thought replacing the stoneware might be more expensive than buying a complete set of new dishes, especially with the sales at the department stores; and he noted that a six-month wait was also a high cost. Besides, their old stoneware was chipped and scratched. But Barbara argued that at the sale prices, it might be better to replace the missing stoneware or to add three place settings to the china. Barbara developed a complex plan to take all of these factors into consideration. She decided that if finishing her set of china cost £100 or less than the stoneware replacements, she would buy three place settings of china. If a new set of stoneware cost £50 or less than replacing the missing stoneware, she would buy the new set of stoneware dishes. But if these two alternative actions were more expensive, she would order the replacement pieces for her Wedgwood stoneware.

When she called stores to check sale prices, Barbara learned that the sales offered 25 per cent off all dishes in stock. She also learned that one store was selling a service for eight of Chinese porcelain for £60. At that price, she could buy two sets (a service for 16) for less than any of her other options would cost. She decided to buy the Chinese porcelain if she liked it.

On Saturday morning Barbara's mother-in-law called, and Barbara reviewed the situation with her. Barbara's mother-in-law said to forget the Chinese porcelain because it is too fragile – either bone china or stoneware is much stronger. She also told Barbara about a factory outlet that had a large inventory and very low prices, but she had forgotten the name. Barbara decided to go back to her previous plan, but to check out the factory outlet, too.

Barbara began to visit department stores. She learned from one salesperson that porcelain and bone china are equally strong, and both are stronger than stoneware. She also discovered that ordering the replacement Wedgwood would cost several hundred pounds and could take up to 12 months. Barbara saw an Imari stoneware pattern she liked that was on sale and within her budget. She decided to check with the factory outlet to see whether it had the Imari pattern because she might be able to save a lot of money buying at the outlet. If the price was low enough, it might be worth the extra effort in driving there.

Barbara found the number of the outlet and called it. She learned it did not have the Imari pattern in stock, and an order would take two months. However, it did have many other patterns. Although the outlet could not quote prices over the phone, Barbara was told that many people drive a considerable distance to shop there. Now Barbara was in a quandary. She could probably save a considerable amount of money by going to the outlet, but it was a long drive and she couldn't go until the weekend. But by then the department store might be sold out of the Imari pattern she liked. And there was a chance that she wouldn't find anything she liked at the outlet. However, the outlet did have a large inventory, so she probably would find an acceptable pattern. Barbara decided to check out the Chinese porcelain and buy it if she liked it. Otherwise, she would drive to the outlet at the weekend and buy something.

On Wednesday Barbara went to the department store to examine the Chinese porcelain. Although it was pretty, it came only in a delicate flower pattern, which she did not like. She decided to drive to the outlet right away. If it didn't have anything she liked, she could go back to the department store and buy the Imari pattern.

Barbara drove 45 minutes to the outlet. It had a huge inventory at much lower prices than the department store. However, none of the stoneware had the Oriental pattern she wanted. So she telephoned the department store to see whether it still had the Imari pattern. It did, but it didn't have 10 place settings left. Perhaps this disappointment led Barbara to ask once again if the outlet had the Imari pattern. She was surprised to find that it did have the pattern in stock, and even better, it was on sale for 25 per cent off the already low price. Unfortunately, the dishes were at the warehouse and couldn't be picked up for 7 to 10 days. Barbara was pleased to find a complete set of the dishes she liked best at an acceptable price. Her only worry was that the dinner party was exactly 10 days away. She decided to order the Imari dishes and take the chance that they would be there on time. (They were . . . and the dinner party was a great success.)

Source: Adapted from Barbara Hayes-Roth, 'Opportunism in Consumer Behavior', in *Advances in Consumer Research*, Vol. 9, ed. Andrew A. Mitchell, Ann Arbor, MI: Association for Consumer Research, 1982, pp. 132–135.

This example describes a complex purchase process that involved making several decisions. A **decision** involves a choice 'between two or more alternative actions [or behaviours]'.[1] *Decisions always require choices between different behaviours.* For instance, after examining the products in a vending machine, Joe chose a Snickers chocolate bar instead of a KitKat. His choice was between the alternative actions of *buying Snickers* versus *buying KitKat*. Monica is trying to decide whether to see a particular film. Her choice is really between the set of behaviours involved in *attending the film* versus the behaviours involved in *staying at home* (or going bowling, or whatever behavioural alternatives she was considering). In sum, even though marketers often refer to choices between objects (products, brands, or shops), consumers are actually choosing between alternative *behaviours* that concern those objects.

Marketers are particularly interested in consumers' *purchase behaviours*, especially their choices of which brands to buy. Given the marketing orientation of this text, we emphasize consumers' purchase choices ('Should I buy Calvin Klein or Diesel jeans?'). It must be recognized, however, that consumers also make many decisions about non-purchase behaviours. Sometimes these nonpurchase choices can influence consumers' purchase decisions (deciding to go for a walk or watch TV may expose consumers to marketing information about products). Sometimes these other behaviours are the targets of marketing strategies – 'Come down to our shop this afternoon for free coffee and biscuits'. Our analyses of purchase decisions can be generalized to these non-purchase choices.

As shown in our model of consumer decision making in Exhibit 3.4, consumer decision making is based on the knowledge, meanings, and beliefs activated from memory and the attention and comprehension processes involved in interpreting new information in the environment.[2] The key process in **consumer decision making**, however, is the *integration process* by which knowledge is combined to *evaluate* two or more alternative behaviours and *select* one.[3] The outcome of this integration process is a **choice**, represented cognitively as a *behavioural intention* (*BI*). As you learned in the previous chapter, a behavioural intention is a plan (sometimes called a decision plan) to engage in some behaviour.

We assume all voluntary behaviours are based on the intentions produced when consumers consciously choose from among alternative actions. Thus, decision-making processes occur even for impulsive purchases. This does not mean, however, that a conscious decision-making process necessarily occurs each time a purchase behaviour is performed.[4] Some voluntary behaviours become habitual. They are based on intentions stored in memory that were formed by a past decision-making process. When activated, these previously formed intentions or decision plans automatically influence behaviour; additional decision-making processes may not be necessary. Finally, some behaviours are not voluntary and are affected largely by environmental factors. For instance, product displays and aisle placements dictate how consumers move through stores. Decision making is not relevant in such cases.

In this chapter we view consumer decision making as a problem-solving process. We begin with a general discussion of this perspective. Then we identify and describe the key elements in a problem-solving approach. Next we discuss the problem-solving processes involved in purchase decisions. We identify three levels of problem-solving effort and describe several influences on problem-solving activities. We conclude by identifying several implications of consumer problem solving for marketing strategy.

Decision Making as Problem Solving

In treating consumer decision making as problem solving, we assume consumers have goals (desired consequences or values in a means–end chain) that they seek to achieve or satisfy. A consumer perceives a 'problem' because the desired consequences have not been attained ('I am hungry'; 'I need a reliable car;' 'I want to lose weight'.). Consumers make decisions about which behaviours to perform to achieve their goals and thus 'solve the problem'. In this sense, then, *consumer decision making is a goal-directed, problem-solving process.*

As the opening example illustrates, consumer problem solving is actually a continuous flow of reciprocal interactions among environmental factors, cognitive and affective processes, and behavioural actions. Researchers can divide this stream into separate stages and subprocesses to simplify analysis and facilitate understanding. Exhibit 7.1 presents a generic model of **problem solving** that identifies five basic stages or processes. The first stage involves *problem recognition*. In the opening example, Barbara's plan to host a dinner party made her aware of a problem – she needed a set of dishes for 10 people. The next stage of the problem-solving process involves *searching for alternative solutions*.[5] (Barbara called and visited stores, talked to salespeople, and discussed the purchase with her mother-in-law.) At the next stage, *alternatives are evaluated* and the most desirable action is *chosen*. (Barbara evaluated dishes as she found them during her search. In the end, she decided – formed a behavioural intention – to buy the Imari pattern at the factory outlet.) In the next stage, *purchase*, the choice/intention is carried out. (Barbara ordered the dishes and then returned a few days later to pay for them and pick them up.) Finally, the purchased product is *used*, and the consumer may *reevaluate* the wisdom of the decision. (Apparently Barbara was quite satisfied with the dishes and with her problem-solving process.)

EXHIBIT 7.1

A Generic Model of Consumer Problem Solving

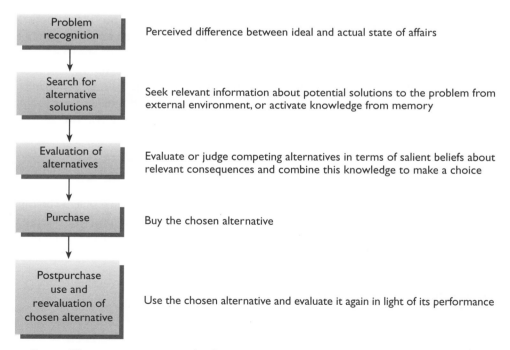

Source: There are many sources for this general model. See James Engel and Roger D. Blackwell, *Consumer Behavior*, 4th edn. (Hinsdale, IL: Dryden Press, 1982).

This basic model identifies several important activities involved in problem solving, beginning with problem recognition, which activates the initial motivation to engage in problem solving. Other activities include searching for information relevant to the problem, evaluating alternative actions, and choosing an action. However, for several reasons, the generic model often provides an imperfect account of actual problem-solving processes such as those in the opening example. One reason is that *actual consumer problem solving seldom proceeds in the linear sequence* portrayed in the generic model. For instance, Barbara evaluated alternative dishes as soon as she found them; she did not wait until all alternatives had been found.

Second, as emphasized in our Wheel of Consumer Analysis (refer to Exhibit 2.4), *actual problem-solving processes involve multiple, reciprocal interactions among consumers' cognitive processes, their behaviours, and aspects of the physical and social environment.*[6] Reciprocal interactions occurred throughout Barbara's problem-solving process. For instance, her cognitions (beliefs) changed as a function of environmental factors her behaviours led her to: First her mother-in-law said Chinese porcelain is fragile, but later a salesperson said it is quite robust. These complex interactions are not easily handled by the generic model.

Third, *most problem-solving processes actually involve multiple problems and multiple decisions.* Consider the number of separate decisions Barbara made during the two weeks of her problem-solving process: Should I go to the department store? Should I drive to the factory outlet? When should I go? Should I get the Chinese porcelain? Actual problem-solving processes usually involve several choices that produce multiple behavioural intentions. Each intention is a step in an overall decision plan. A decision plan, in turn, produces a sequence of purposive behaviours that consumers perform to achieve their desired consequences, values, and goals (go to the department store, find the dishes section, look at Chinese porcelain). The generic model implies that consumer problem solving involves one decision, typically brand choice, which is seldom the case.

Our cognitive process model of consumer decision making, shown in Exhibit 3.4, is flexible enough to account for the nonlinear flow; for the reciprocal interactions among behaviours, environments, and cognitions; and for the multiple decisions that occur in actual consumer problem-solving episodes. Moreover, it can help us understand how consumers process information during the important problem-solving stages of problem recognition, search for information, and evaluation of alternatives. Before using this model to analyse actual consumer decisions, however, we must discuss several elements of problem solving.

Elements of Problem Solving

In this section we describe three basic elements of problem solving: problem representation, integration processes, and decision plans. Later we discuss how they operate in consumer decision making.

Problem Representation

When faced with a choice, consumers must interpret or represent various aspects of the decision problem. This **problem representation** may include (1) an end goal, (2) a set of subgoals organized into a goal hierarchy, (3) relevant product knowledge, and (4) a set of simple rules or heuristics by which consumers search for, evaluate, and integrate this knowledge to make a choice. A problem representation serves as a *decision frame* – a perspective or frame of reference through which the decision maker views the problem and the alternatives to be evaluated.[7]

Often consumers' initial problem representations are not clear or well developed (Barbara's wasn't). Neither are they fixed. In fact, the components of a problem representation often change during the decision-making process, as was true in the opening example. Marketers sometimes try to influence how consumers represent or frame a purchase choice.[8] For instance, consumers might be portrayed in advertisements as representing and then trying to solve a purchase problem in a particular way. Salespeople also try to influence consumers' problem representations by suggesting end goals (buy life insurance to insure a happy retirement), imparting product knowledge (this special flash eliminates red eyes in the pictures), or suggesting choice rules (the more expensive coat is of a higher quality).

The basic consequences, needs, or values that consumers want to achieve or satisfy are called **end goals**. They provide the focus for the entire problem-solving process. Some end goals represent more concrete, tangible consequences; other end goals are more abstract. For instance, a purchase decision to replace a bulb for a flashlight probably involves the simple end goal of obtaining a bulb that lights up – a simple functional consequence. Other product choices involve more abstract end goals such as desired psychosocial consequences of a product – some consumers want to serve a wine that indicates their good taste to their guests. Finally, end goals such as instrumental and terminal values are even more abstract and general – consumers might choose a car that makes them happy or enhances their self-esteem. End goals also vary in evaluation. Some consumer decisions are oriented towards positive, desirable end goals, while others are focused on negative end goals – aversive consequences the consumer wishes to avoid.

Some end goals (e.g. being happy) are so general and broad that they cannot be directly acted on by consumers. For instance, most consumers cannot specify the decision plan of specific actions that will yield the best brand of calculator or avoid a 'lemon' of a car. When consumers try to solve problems involving abstract end goals, they break down the general goal into several more specific subgoals. The end goal and its subgoals are a **goal hierarchy**. Forming a goal hierarchy is analogous to decomposing a complex problem into a series of simpler subproblems, each of which can be dealt with separately. For instance, buying a new car requires at least one trip to a showroom, creating the subproblems of which dealer(s) to visit and when to go shopping. Usually the consumer can solve the overall problem by solving the simpler subproblems in order.

Consumers' **relevant knowledge** in memory about the choice domain is an important element in problem solving.[9] Some knowledge may be acquired by interpreting information encountered in the environment during the problem-solving process. For instance, in the opening example, Barbara learned a lot about porcelain, factory locations, and price ranges for dishes. Other relevant knowledge may be activated from memory for use in integration processes.[10] The relevance of knowledge is determined by its means–end linkages to the currently active end goal. Parts of the activated knowledge may be combined in the integration processes by which consumers evaluate alternative behaviours (form A_{act}) and choose among them (form BI). Two types of knowledge are particularly important in problem solving – choice alternatives and choice criteria.

The alternative behaviours that consumers consider in the problem-solving process are called **choice alternatives**. For purchase decisions, the choice alternatives are the different product classes, product forms, brands, or models the consumer considers buying. For other types of decisions, the choice alternatives might be different shops to visit, times of the day or week to go shopping, or methods of payment (cash or credit card). Given their limited time, energy, and cognitive capacity, consumers seldom consider every possible choice alternative. Usually, only a subset of all possible alternatives – called the **consideration set** – is evaluated.

Exhibit 7.2 illustrates how a manageable consideration set of brands can be constructed during the problem-solving process.[11] Some of the brands in the consideration set may be activated directly from memory; this group is called the **evoked set**.[12] For highly familiar decisions, consumers may not consider any brands beyond those in the evoked set. If consumers are confident they already know the important choice alternatives, they are not likely to search for additional ones. In other decisions, choice alternatives may be found through intentional search activities such as reading consumer magazines, talking to knowledgeable friends, or finding brands while shopping.[13] Finally, consumers may learn of still other choice alternatives through accidental exposure to information in the environment, such as overhearing a conversation about a new brand, new store, or sale. In the opening case, Barbara learned about the factory outlet from her mother-in-law, essentially by accident. However the choice alternatives are generated, consumers form a consideration set of possible purchase options to be evaluated in the decision-making process.

To be successful, a brand must be included in the consideration sets of at least some

EXHIBIT 7.2

Forming a Consideration Set of Brand Choice Alternatives

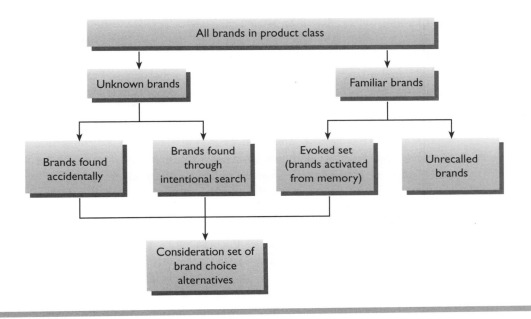

consumers. Marketers therefore develop strategies to increase the likelihood that a brand will be activated from consumers' memories and included in their evoked sets of choice alternatives. The activation potential of a brand, sometimes called its *top-of-mind awareness*, is influenced by many factors. One is the amount of past purchase and use experience consumers have had with the brand. Consumers are much more likely to think of (activate) brands that they have used before. For this reason, popular brands with higher market shares have a distinct advantage. Because they are used by more consumers, these brands are more likely to be activated from memory and included in more consumers' consideration sets.[14] This increases the brands' probability of purchase, which, in turn, increases their activation potential, and so on. In contrast, unfamiliar and low-market-share brands are at a disadvantage because they are much less likely to be included in consumers' evoked sets and thereby be considered as choice alternatives.

One marketing strategy to increase the activation potential of a brand is the repetitive and costly advertising campaigns devised by marketers of cigarettes, beer, soft drinks, and toothpaste (among others).[15] The heavy expenditures may be worth while because brands with high top-of-mind awareness are more likely to be included in the evoked set of choice alternatives that come to mind during problem-solving processes.

A company's distribution strategy can influence whether a brand is in consumers' consideration sets. Consider food products, for which an estimated 65 per cent of decisions are made in the shop. A key marketing strategy for such products is making sure the product is always on the shelf. This enhances the likelihood that consumers will encounter the brand at the time of the decision, which increases its chances of entering consumers' consideration sets, and thus the probability of purchase.

Package design can influence both the consideration set and the final choice. Package design can catch the consumer's attention and increase the probability of considering the product further. Packaging can also communicate important information such as ingredients, the product's ease-of-use, and overall value which may be integrated in the consumer's decision-process.

As we described in Chapter 6, consumers' evaluations of the choice alternatives in the consideration set are based on their beliefs about the consequences of buying those products or brands. The specific consequences that are used to evaluate and choose among choice alternatives are called **choice criteria**. Virtually any type of product-related consequence can become a choice criterion in a brand-choice decision, including salient beliefs about functional consequences (product performance), psychosocial consequences (admiration of friends), or value consequences (a sense of achievement or self-esteem).[16] Consumers probably have beliefs stored in memory about some of the relevant consequences of at least some of the choice alternatives in the consideration set. If additional knowledge is desired, consumers may form the sub-goal of obtaining information about those choice alternatives. Achieving this subgoal may require intentional search behaviours such as visiting shops, reading consumer magazines, or talking with knowledgeable friends. Information search may be motivated by consumers' uncertainty about appropriate choice criteria and/or choice alternatives.[17] In the opening case, Barbara engaged in a substantial amount of intentional search to identify possible choice alternatives and form beliefs about appropriate choice criteria.

The probability that product knowledge is activated and used in the evaluation process is highly influenced by the means–end relevance of that knowledge to the goal

A simple ad to increase top-of-mind awareness and get the brand into consumers' evoked sets.
Courtesy: DuPont.

or subgoal being considered.[18] Consumers try to use choice criteria which will be predictive of the consequences and values they try to achieve by buying the product.[19] Finding such choice criteria is not always easy for consumers. When buying fruits and vegetables consumers are interested in, among other things, taste, but since the taste cannot be ascertained before the purchase (unless free samples are offered) consumers may have to rely on uncertain criteria like the shape or colour of the product. When buying cleaning products, consumers will be interested in cleaning power, but most consumers will be unable to infer cleaning power from the chemical ingredients of the product, even when these are listed on the packaging. Instead, they may use the smell or the consistency of the product as criteria. Consumers who are knowledgeable about wine may use vintage year and area of origin as choice criteria, because they know what these mean in terms of taste and quality, but less knowledgeable consumers may have to refer to simpler criteria like price and shape of the bottle in order to infer the same desired consequences. In short, even though consumers may have the same goals with a purchase, the criteria they actually use may differ depending on how knowledgeable they are about the product category. Highlight 7.1 shows some more examples of this, and how they are related to marketing solutions.[20]

As we discussed in earlier chapters, marketers often place prominent stimuli in the immediate decision environment to activate certain choice criteria from consumers' memories. For instance, special price tags activate beliefs about price consequences (saving money). Prominent labels on food packages, such as 'sugar-free' or 'low fat', enhance the likelihood that the consequences associated with those attributes (good

Attribute Usage and Inferential Belief Formation

 uch of what consumers regard as desirable consequences of a product is difficult to evaluate at the time of purchase. The taste and tenderness of a steak, the durability of an appliance, the cleaning power of a household cleaner can be evaluated only after the purchase. Consumers therefore have to find attributes which they think allow them to predict these desired consequences with some certainty. That can lead to quite surprising forms of problem solving.

- A manufacturer of household cleaners found out that consumers use the consistency of the liquid cleaner to predict cleaning power: a thick liquid was associated with more cleaning power than a thin one. Based on this finding, the manufacturer changed the consistency of the cleaner.

- A shop sold women's stockings from two identical piles. On one pile, the stockings had an orange scent, on the other pile, there was no scent. Shoppers selected predominantly the scented stockings. When asked why, they said the stockings were of better quality and would have a longer lifetime.

- When buying meat, consumers use visible fat as an indicator of quality. The less fat, the better the taste and the tenderness of the meat is believed to be. Actually, research shows that intramuscular fat has a positive impact on taste and tenderness, not a negative one. This creates a problem for meat producers who both want to please consumers in the shop and assure that the meat will be tender and tasty when prepared.

- Many consumers associate the country of origin of a product with certain quality beliefs. Japanese cars are reliable, French wine is good and expensive, Italian clothes are fashionable. The beliefs can also be negative – Italian cars rust, Dutch vegetables lack taste. Often marketers have to make conscious decisions on whether to emphasize or deemphasize the origin of a product.

health) will be used as choice criteria. Finally, salespeople often emphasize certain product benefits in their sales pitches, which increases the likelihood that beliefs about those consequences will be used as choice criteria.

Not every activated belief about product or brand consequences is necessarily used as a choice criterion. Only *discriminant consequences* – consequences that are perceived to differ across choice alternatives – can be used as choice criteria.[21] Beliefs about common or very similar consequences of the choice alternatives do not discriminate between alternative actions. To present an obvious example, if all drinks available at a reception contain alcohol, then the consequences of alcohol (intoxication) cannot be used as a choice criterion for deciding which drink to consume. However, if a different set of choice alternatives (both alcoholic and nonalcoholic drinks) is being considered, alcohol content might be a choice criterion. This is an important point. The choice criteria that are relevant (activated) for a decision depend, in part, on the particular set of choice alternatives under consideration.[22]

Consumers' choice criteria also vary in evaluation. Some choice criteria are perceived as positive, desirable consequences and elicit positive affective responses. Other choice criteria, such as price, may be thought about in negative terms as unpleasant consequences or perceived risks to be avoided.[23] To avoid rejection, marketers may try to reduce perceived risk by assuring consumers of product quality or by offering warranties and guarantees.[24] Choice alternatives perceived to have negative consequences tend to be rejected unless they also have several positive consequences. For example, many people have a negative choice criterion for food products – fat content. The popularity of this choice criterion was influenced by basic changes in societal values about health, and food producers have responded to it by launching lines of products which are low in fat. However, for some products such as cheese, consumers associate low fat not only with positive health consequences, but also with negative taste consequences. Consumers who perceive that a choice involves both positive and negative consequences may be motivated to search for information to resolve the conflict between the benefits and risks of the decision.[25]

Integration Processes

The integration processes involved in problem solving perform two essential tasks: the choice alternatives must be evaluated in terms of the choice criteria, and then one of the alternatives must be chosen.[26] Two types of integration procedures have been proposed to account for these evaluation and choice processes: formal integration strategies and simpler procedures called *heuristics*.

Exhibit 7.3 presents several formal models of the integration processes involved in evaluating and choosing among choice alternatives. The key distinction is between compensatory and noncompensatory strategies.

Compensatory integration processes combine all the salient beliefs about the consequences of the choice alternatives to form an overall evaluation or attitude (A_{act}) towards each behavioural alternative. The multiattribute attitude model ($A_{act} = \Sigma b_i e_i$) is a compensatory model, so-called because a negative consequence (expensive) can be compensated for or balanced by a positive consequence (high status). Compensatory models seem to describe human information integration quite well, even in cases where people actually believe that their information processing proceeds in a different way.[27] Also, although the multiattribute attitude model accounts for how the choice alternatives are evaluated, it does not specify how the consumer chooses which behaviour to perform. Most marketers assume consumers select the alternative with the most positive A_{act}. Other *choice rules* are possible, however. For instance, consumers might choose the first alternative they find with a positive A_{act}.

Several types of **noncompensatory integration processes** are also described in Exhibit 7.3.[28] They are noncompensatory because the salient beliefs about the positive and negative consequences of the choice alternatives do not balance or compensate for each other. For example, applying the *conjunctive* choice rule requires that an alternative be rejected if any one of its consequences does not surpass a minimum threshold level of acceptability. Thus, Erik might reject a particular model of Reebok aerobic shoes if it had one negative consequence (too expensive), even though it had several other positive consequences (good support, comfortable, stylish colours). As another example, applying a *lexicographic* integration strategy might require a consideration of only one choice criterion, which makes a compensatory process impossible. Tina might evaluate a pair of dress shoes favourably and buy them because they were superior to the other alternatives on the most important consequence (the colour matched her outfit exactly), while other, even unfavourable consequences were not considered (not durable and slightly uncomfortable).

EXHIBIT 7.3

Formal Models of Information Integration Processes in Choice

Compensatory processes	
Multiattribute model	A perceived weakness or negative evaluation on one criterion can be compensated for by a positive evaluation on another criterion. Separate evaluations for each choice criterion are combined (added or averaged) to form an overall evaluation of each alternative. Then the highest-rated alternative is chosen.
Noncompensatory processes	
Conjunctive	Consumer establishes a minimum acceptable level for each choice criterion. Accept an alternative only if every criterion equals or exceeds the minimum cutoff level.
Disjunctive	Consumer establishes acceptable standards for each criterion. A product is acceptable if it exceeds the minimum level on at least one criterion.
Lexicographic	Consumer ranks choice criteria from most to least important. Choose the best alternative on the most important criterion. If tie occurs, select best alternative on second most important criterion, and so on.
Elimination by aspects	Consumer establishes minimum cutoffs for each choice criterion. Select one criterion and eliminate all alternatives that do not exceed until one alternative remains. Choose it.
Combination processes	Mix of compensatory and noncompensatory processes, combined or 'constructed' on the spot to adapt to environmental factors.

Source: Adapted from James R. Bettman, *An Information Processing Theory of Consumer Choice,* © 1979, Addison-Wesley Publishing Co., Inc. Reading, MA. Reprinted with permission of the publisher.

Research suggests consumers do not seem to follow any single rule or strategy in evaluating and choosing from among alternatives.[29] Many problem-solving tasks do not involve a single choice to which a single integration rule could be applied. Instead, consumers make multiple choices in most purchase situations (choices of information sources to examine, shops to visit, product forms or brands to buy, methods of payment). Each choice is a separate subproblem that requires separate integration processes.

Rather than a single integration strategy, consumers are likely to use a combination of processes in many problem-solving situations.[30] A noncompensatory strategy might be used to quickly reduce the choice alternatives to a manageable number by rejecting those that lack one or two key criteria (a conjunctive strategy). For example, Boris might reject all vacation destinations which do not have a beach. Then the remaining alternatives in his consideration set could be evaluated on several choice criteria (price, weather, type of hotel, night life) using a more strenuous compensatory strategy. Various methodologies have been developed to find out which integration strategy consumers use in a given situation – for example think-aloud protocols, or providing consumers with an array of attribute information (called an *information display board*) and watching how they proceed using information to arrive at a decision.[31]

Another issue is whether consumers have complete integration rules stored in memory ready to be activated and applied to the relevant product beliefs. In many cases, it seems that consumers rather build up integration processes in such a way that they invoke a series of simple, flexible rules and combine them to an integration process tailored to the specific situation at hand.[32] These simple integration 'rules' are called *heuristics*.

Basically, **heuristics** are simple 'if . . . , then . . .' productions that connect an event with an appropriate action. Because they are applied to only a few bits and pieces of knowledge at a time, heuristics are highly adaptive to specific environmental situations and are not likely to exceed cognitive capacity limits.[33] Heuristics may be stored in memory like miniature scripts that are applied fairly automatically to information encountered in the environment. Or they may be constructed on the spot in response to the immediate environment.

Exhibit 7.4 presents examples of three types of heuristics that are particularly important in problem solving. *Search heuristics* are simple procedures for seeking information relevant to a goal. Some consumers have a simple search rule for buying any small durable product such as a radio or a kitchen appliance – read the product tests in a consumer magazine. *Evaluation heuristics* are procedures for evaluating and weighting beliefs in terms of the current goal being addressed in the problem-solving process. Dieting consumers may have a heuristic that identifies the most important choice criteria for food – few calories and the resulting consequence of losing weight. *Choice heuristics* are simple procedures for comparing evaluations of alternative actions in order to choose one. A simple choice heuristic is to select the alternative you bought last time if it was satisfactory, or to choose the cheapest available alternative.[34]

Decision Plans

The process of identifying, evaluating, and choosing among alternatives during problem solving produces a **decision plan** made up of one or more behavioural intentions. Decision plans vary in their specificity and complexity.[35] Specific decision plans concern intentions to perform particular behaviours in highly defined situations: 'This afternoon John intends to go to Nextman to buy a blue cotton sweater to go with his new slacks'. Other decision plans involve rather general intentions: 'Pia intends to shop for a new car some time soon'. Some decision plans contain a simple intention to perform a single behaviour: 'Andreas intends to buy a large tube of Zendium toothpaste'. In contrast, more complex decision plans involve a set of intentions to perform a series of behaviours: 'Sabine intends to go to the department stores, browse through their sportswear departments, and look for a lightweight jacket'.

Having a decision plan increases the likelihood that the intended behaviours will be performed. However, as we discussed in Chapter 6, behavioural intentions are not always carried out. For instance, a purchase intention may be blocked or modified if environmental circumstances make it difficult for the decision plan to be accomplished.

EXHIBIT 7.4

Examples of Consumer Heuristics

Search heuristics	Examples
• Store selection	If you are buying stereo equipment, always go to Sam's Hi-Fi.
• Sources of information	If you want to know which alternatives are worth searching for, read the test reports in a consumer magazine.
• Source of credibility	If a magazine accepts advertisements from the tested products, don't believe its product tests.

Evaluation heuristics	Examples
• Key criteria	If comparing processed foods, examine sodium content.
• Negative criteria	If a salient consequence is negative (high sodium content), give this choice criterion extra weight in the integration process.
• Significant differences	If alternatives are similar on a salient consequence (all low sodium), ignore that choice criterion.

Choice heuristics	Examples
For familiar, frequently purchased products:	**If choosing among familiar products . . .**
• Works best	Choose the product that you think works best—that provides the best level of performance on the most relevant functional consequences.
• Affect referral	Choose the alternative you like the best (select the alternative with most favourable attitude).
• Bought last	Select the alternative you used last, if it was satisfactory.
• Important person	Choose the alternative that some 'important' person (spouse, child, friend) likes.
• Price-based rule	Buy the least expensive alternative (or buy the most expensive, depending on your beliefs about the relationship of price to product quality).
• Promotional rule	Choose an alternative for which you have a coupon or that you can get at a price reduction (seasonal sale, promotional rebate, special price reduction).
For new, unfamiliar products:	**If choosing among unfamiliar products . . .**
• Wait and see	Don't buy any software until someone you know has used it for at least a month and recommends it. Don't buy a new car (computer, etc.) until the second model year.
• Expert consultant	Find an expert or more knowledgeable person, have them evaluate the alternatives in terms of your goals, then buy the alternative the expert selects.

Perhaps the problem-solving process will recycle, and a new decision plan might be developed: 'Andreas found that the store was sold out of large tubes of Zendium, so he decided to buy two medium-sized tubes'. Sometimes unanticipated events identify additional choice alternatives or change consumers' beliefs about appropriate choice criteria; this could lead to a revised decision plan: 'While reading the paper, Sabine learned that Kaufhof was having a 25 per-cent-off sale on lightweight jackets, so she decided to shop there first'.

Problem-Solving Processes in Purchase Decisions

The amount of cognitive and behavioural effort consumers put into their problem-solving processes is highly variable. Problem-solving effort varies from virtually none (a decision plan is activated from memory and is carried out automatically) to very extensive. For convenience, marketers have divided this continuum into three levels of problem-solving activity: extensive, limited, and routine or habitual.[36]

Relatively few consumer choice problems require **extensive decision making**. Extensive decision making usually involves a substantial amount of search behaviour required to identify choice alternatives and learn the appropriate choice criteria with which to evaluate them. Extensive decision making also involves multiple-choice decisions and substantial cognitive and behavioural effort. Finally, it is likely to take rather long periods – such as Barbara's decision to buy new dishes in the opening example or purchasing your first stereo system.

Many consumers' choice problems require **limited decision making**. The amount of problem-solving effort in limited decision making ranges from low to moderate. Compared to extensive decision making, limited decision making involves less search for information. Fewer choice alternatives are considered, and less integration processing is required. Choices involving limited decision making usually are carried out fairly quickly, with moderate levels of cognitive and behavioural effort.

For still other problems, consumers' choice behaviour is habitual or routine. **Routinized choice behaviour** – such as buying another Pepsi from the vending machine down the hall or purchasing a package of gum at the checkout counter – occurs relatively automatically with little or no apparent cognitive processing. Compared to the other levels, routinized choice behaviour requires very little cognitive capacity or conscious control. Basically, a previously learned decision plan is activated from memory and is carried out relatively automatically to produce the purchase behaviour.

The amount of effort consumers exert in problem solving tends to decrease over time as they learn more about a product and gain experience in making decisions. With repeated decisions, product and brand knowledge becomes organized into means–end structures and becomes more clearly related to consumers' goals. Consumers also learn new productions and heuristics, which become organized into scripts or decision plans

---

EXHIBIT 7.4

Source: Reprinted from Wayne D. Hoyer, 'An Examination of Consumer Decision Making for a Common Repeat Purchase Product', *Journal of Consumer Research*, December 1984, pp. 822–829, by permission of the University of Chicago Press, © 1984 by the Universityof Chicago.

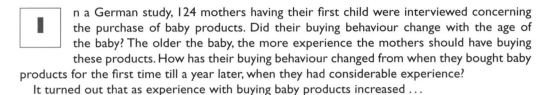

HIGHLIGHT 7.2

Developing Habits of Buying Baby Products

In a German study, 124 mothers having their first child were interviewed concerning the purchase of baby products. Did their buying behaviour change with the age of the baby? The older the baby, the more experience the mothers should have buying these products. How has their buying behaviour changed from when they bought baby products for the first time till a year later, when they had considerable experience?

It turned out that as experience with buying baby products increased . . .

- the number of information sources used and the frequency of use declined – at the beginning, the mothers asked doctors and other mothers, read information on packages, etc., whereas later on they used considerably less information;
- information search was directed more at attributes like price and size of package, whereas at the beginning it was directed mostly at aspects of the physical product;
- 'polarized' brand attitudes developed – at the beginning, the mothers hardly knew the brands and had no clearly positive or negative attitudes towards them, but after a year they had developed such attitudes;
- larger quantities were bought, indicating that they regarded the purchase as less risky than at the beginning.

The shopping behaviour of these women thus changed quite a lot as they accumulated knowledge and experience about these products. At the beginning, it resembled complex decision making, but after a year it resembled routinized choice behaviour.

Source: Adapted from Klaus Peter Kaas, 'Consumer Habit Forming, Information Acquisition, and Buying Behaviour', *Journal of Business Research*, March 1982, pp. 3–15.

stored in memory.[37] When activated, these heuristics and decision scripts automatically affect purchase-related behaviours. Running down to the bakery for a loaf of bread or stopping to fill up the car's tank at a favourite petrol station are well-developed decision plans that require little cognitive effort. In summary, consumers develop increasingly routinized, automatic problem-solving processes as they gain experience making various purchase decisions (see Highlight 7.2).

Influences on Consumers' Problem-Solving Activities

The level of consumers' problem-solving effort in making brand purchase decisions is influenced by environmental factors as well as by the cognitive (knowledge) and affective responses activated during the problem-solving process. We discuss three aspects of this activated knowledge and affect that have direct effects on problem solving: (1) consumers' goals; (2) their knowledge about choice alternatives and choice criteria, as well as heuristics for using this knowledge; and (3) their level of involvement. Following the discussion of these affective and cognitive factors, we examine several environmental influences on consumer problem solving.

EXHIBIT 7.5

Types of Purchase End Goals and Related Problem-Solving Processes

Dominant End Goal	Basic Purchase Motivation	Examples
Optimize satisfaction	Seek maximum positive consequences	Buy dinner at the best restaurant in town
Prevention	Avoid potential unpleasant consequences	Buy rust-proofing for a new car
Resolve conflict	Seek satisfactory balance of positive and negative consequences	Buy a moderately expensive car of very good quality
Escape	Reduce or escape from current aversive circumstances	Buy a shampoo to get rid of dandruff
Maintenance (satisfice)	Maintain satisfaction of basic need with minimal effort	Buy bread at the nearest bakery

Source: Adapted from Geraldine Fennell, 'Motivation Research Revisited', *Journal of Advertising Research*, June 1975, pp. 23–28; and J. Paul Peter and Lawrence X. Tarpey, Sr., 'A Comparative Analysis of Three Consumer Decision Strategies', *Journal of Consumer Research*, June 1975, pp. 29–37.

Effects of End Goals

The particular end goals consumers are striving to achieve have a powerful effect on the problem-solving process. Exhibit 7.5 presents five broad end goals that lead to quite different problem-solving processes. For instance, consumers who have an *optimizing* end goal are likely to expend substantial effort searching for the best possible alternative. In contrast, consumers with a *satisfaction/maintenance* end goal are likely to engage in minimal search behaviour. In yet other decisions, consumers may have conflicting end goals that must be resolved in the problem-solving process.

In general, marketers have relatively little direct influence over consumers' abstract end goals, such as basic values. However, marketers can try to influence less abstract end goals, such as desired functional or psychosocial consequences, through promotional strategies. Perhaps the major implication for marketers is to identify the dominant goals in consumers' problem representations and design product and promotion strategies that link product attributes to those goals.[38]

Effects of Goal Hierarchies

Consumers' goal hierarchies for a problem have a powerful influence on problem-solving processes. If consumers have a well-defined goal hierarchy stored in memory, it may be activated and the associated decision plan carried out automatically.[39] Even if a complete decision plan is not available, a general goal hierarchy provides a useful structure for developing an effective decision plan without a great deal of problem-solving effort. In contrast, consumers who have very little past experience will not have well-developed goal hierarchies. Their problem solving is likely to proceed haltingly, by trial and error. Consider first-time buyers of relatively important products such as stereos, sports equipment, cars, and houses. These consumers must construct a goal hierarchy (a series of subgoals that seem related to the end goal) and develop a decision plan to achieve each subgoal (as Barbara had to do in the opening example). In these types of decisions, marketers are likely to find confused or frustrated consumers who use general 'strategies' such as wandering around various stores in a mall, hoping to accidentally run into something that will satisfy their end goal. Highlight 7.3 discusses the related behaviour of browsing.

Effects of Involvement and Knowledge

Consumers' problem-solving processes are greatly affected by the amount of product knowledge they have acquired through their past experiences and by their level of involvement with the product and/or the choice process. People who are expert in an area find it easier to structure a problem and to understand what the relevant alternatives and attributes are; they will therefore search for different types of information than the novices, who first have to acquire information which helps them structure the problem.[40] Consumers' involvement with the product or decision affects their motivation to engage in the problem-solving process.[41] Exhibit 7.6 summarizes how different combinations of product knowledge and involvement influence specific elements of consumers' problem representations and the overall problem-solving process.[42] Marketers should determine the levels of knowledge and involvement of their target customers and develop strategies consistent with the types of problem solving described in Exhibit 7.6. One problem they should be especially aware of is the problem of information overload. Consumers with limited knowledge can become overwhelmed by the information available, and revert to more simple decision heuristics, making it more improbable that the information supplied by the marketer will actually be used.[43]

Environmental Effects

Environmental factors can affect consumer decision making by interrupting or disrupting the ongoing flow of the problem-solving process. Four types of disruptive events, or **interrupts**, have been identified.[44] First, interrupts can occur when *unexpected information* (inconsistent with established knowledge structures) is encountered in the environment. For instance, carrying out a decision plan or script may be interrupted when you unexpectedly find that aspects of the physical or social environment have changed – a department store has been remodelled and departments have been moved around, a rejected brand now has a new attribute, or your friends now favour a different night spot. These environmental interrupts may cause the consumer to take conscious control of the problem-solving process, identify a new end goal, develop a new goal hierarchy, and construct a different decision plan.

Second, *prominent environmental stimuli* can interrupt a problem-solving process. Many marketing strategies are intended to interrupt consumers' ongoing problem

HIGHLIGHT 7.3

Browsing as Search and Entertainment

Sometimes consumers browse as a vague search plan. But frequently, browsing consumers have no specific decision plan in mind. They are shopping for other reasons – recreation, stimulation from store environments, social contact, escape from home or work, or even exercise. In other words, some consumers get satisfaction from shopping/browsing apart from solving a purchase problem. Browsing thus can be both a form of leisure and a problem-solving strategy.

One reason for browsing without a specific decision plan in mind is that the consumer feels involved in a particular product class or form and likes to associate with it. Consumers who are very interested in music may enjoy browsing in record shops. Some consumers are involved in a particular store or set of stores in a mall or a shopping area in town. Perhaps the atmosphere of these stores is exciting and stimulating, and this provides part of the attraction. In sum, browsing can and usually does serve multiple goals, needs, and values for different consumers.

Retail stores need to pay attention to browsers because they can have a major impact on the success of the store. The retailer may have a serious problem if browsers crowd the store and keep serious customers away. Discouraging browsers is relatively easy – just have a salesperson follow the browser around the store asking if he or she can be helped. Some clothing stores seem to do this effectively. But driving browsers away can be risky. Many browsers become buyers later. If a particular store creates a negative reaction, the browser may make a purchase in a different store.

Some retailers seem to have trouble dealing with browsers. Consider auto dealers. Many people feel uncomfortable going into auto showrooms to browse, partly because of the aggressive salespeople who descend upon them. One strategy has been to set up regional auto shows in the shopping mall, where consumers feel more comfortable browsing without having to deal with an enthusiastic salesperson. Another retailing strategy is to develop a store environment that stimulates impulse buying. In-store promotions, displays, and special signs can help convert a browser to a buyer.

Finally, browsers seem likely to relay information to other consumers. Thus, browsers are doubly important. Not only might they buy something themselves, but they are more likely to spread word-of-mouth information to less well-informed consumers.

Source: Peter H. Bloch and Marsha L. Richins, 'Shopping without Purchase: An Investigation of Consumer Browsing Behavior', in *Advances in Consumer Research*, vol. 10, eds. Richard P. Bagozzi and Alice M. Tybout (Ann Arbor, MI: Association for Consumer Research, 1983), pp. 389–393.

solving. For instance, a large in-store display for Hobnob biscuits, 'as advertised' shelf tags, or the announcement of a sales promotion ('Attention Tesco shoppers. Today we are offering . . . ') may interrupt an ongoing problem-solving process as well as activate new knowledge or goals from memory.

Third, *affective states* such as moods (feeling bored) and physiological events (feeling hungry, sleepy, or thirsty) can interrupt an ongoing problem-solving process.[45] For instance, feeling tired during a shopping trip might activate new goals and start a different problem-solving process (find a comfortable place to sit down and have a cup of coffee). Getting into a bad mood can terminate a problem-solving process.

EXHIBIT 7.6

Effects of Involvement and Product Knowledge on Consumers' Problem-Solving Processes

Levels of Involvement and Product Knowledge

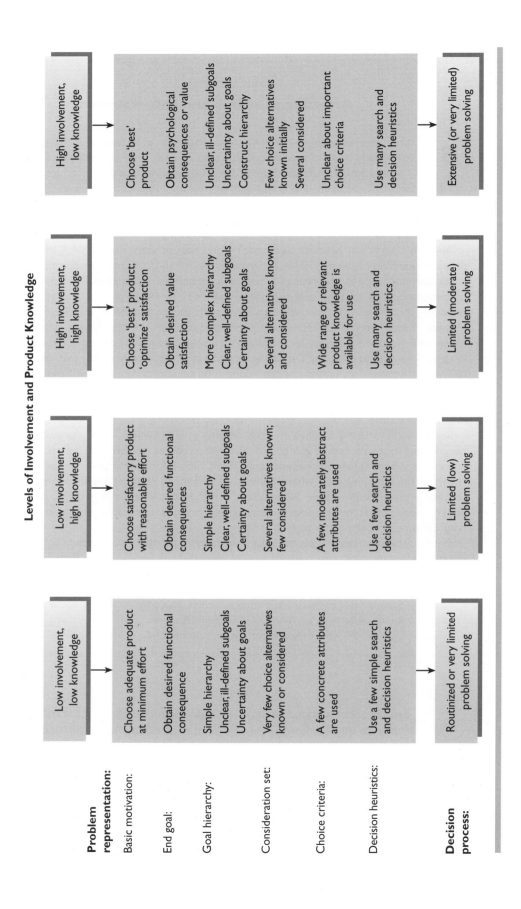

Problem representation:	Low involvement, low knowledge	Low involvement, high knowledge	High involvement, high knowledge	High involvement, low knowledge
Basic motivation:	Choose adequate product at minimum effort	Choose satisfactory product with reasonable effort	Choose 'best' product; 'optimize' satisfaction	Choose 'best' product
End goal:	Obtain desired functional consequence	Obtain desired functional consequences	Obtain desired value satisfaction	Obtain psychological consequences or value
Goal hierarchy:	Simple hierarchy Unclear, ill-defined subgoals Uncertainty about goals	Simple hierarchy Clear, well-defined subgoals Certainty about goals	More complex hierarchy Clear, well-defined subgoals Certainty about goals	Unclear, ill-defined subgoals Uncertainty about goals Construct hierarchy
Consideration set:	Very few choice alternatives known or considered	Several alternatives known; few considered	Several alternatives known and considered	Few choice alternatives known initially Several considered
Choice criteria:	A few concrete attributes are used	A few, moderately abstract attributes are used	Wide range of relevant product knowledge is available for use	Unclear about important choice criteria
Decision heuristics:	Use a few simple search and decision heuristics	Use a few search and decision heuristics	Use many search and decision heuristics	Use many search and decision heuristics
Decision process:	Routinized or very limited problem solving	Limited (low) problem solving	Limited (moderate) problem solving	Extensive (or very limited) problem solving

Fourth, *conflicts* that arise during the course of purchase decision making can interrupt the problem-solving process. *Goal conflict* occurs when consumers recognize the presence of incompatible goals.[46] Goal conflict may occur when consumers discover that alternatives cannot be found to satisfy incompatible goals. For instance, Susan may experience an *approach–approach conflict* in choosing between a new camera and a new stereo receiver because each product leads to a desirable goal (creativity and relaxation, respectively), but neither product can satisfy both goals. *Avoidance–avoidance conflicts* occur when consumers choose between two alternatives with different negative consequences. For instance, Sam is trying to decide whether to buy a new suit. He doesn't want to be embarrassed by his old suit, but he doesn't want to spend money on a new one, either. Finally, *approach–avoidance conflicts* occur when consumers consider both the positive and negative consequences of a purchase or action. For instance, Paul is trying to decide about a new personal cassette player that is on sale at a very low price (positive outcome), but he is afraid the quality may be low (negative outcome).

Fifth, the effects of *interrupts* on consumers' problem-solving processes depend on how consumers interpret (comprehend) the interrupting event. In general, consumers tend to resume an interrupted problem-solving task, especially if it is important or involving.[47] In other cases, however, an interrupting event can change the problem-solving process. For instance, an interrupt might activate new end goals that require a new problem-solving process. Interrupt events (such as learning about a new product attribute) might activate knowledge structures that suggest new decision criteria. In other cases, a choice heuristic might be activated by the interrupt (a friend recommends a brand, and you decide to take her advice). Finally, an especially strong interrupt, such as losing your job, might block the current problem-solving process (choosing a new car), and the process might not resume again. In sum, the effects of interrupts depend on how they are interpreted by the consumer. For instance, is your hunger severe enough to stop shopping for a new suit, or can you skip lunch today? Does this new brand of styling mousse seem worth trying, or should you ignore it? Do you care that your friend thinks these shoes are ridiculous?

Implications for Marketing Strategy

To develop effective marketing strategies, marketers need to know the type of problem-solving processes their customers use to make purchase decisions. As shown in Exhibit 7.6, these processes can vary widely. Marketers that target several consumer segments, each with different problem-solving processes, may have to develop multiple strategies to influence the different decision outcomes. In the following sections we consider some general implications for marketing strategies for routinized choice behaviour and limited and extensive decision making.

Routinized Choice Behaviour

Much consumer choice behaviour is routinized. When consumers think they know all they need to know about a product category, they are not motivated to search for new information. Their choice behaviour is based on a learned decision plan stored in memory. In such cases, the appropriate market strategy depends on the strength of the brand's position in the market.

Marketers of established brands with substantial market shares must maintain their brand in the evoked sets of a significant segment of consumers. Because consumers in this situation engage in little or no search, marketers have minimal opportunities to interject their brand into consumers' consideration sets during problem solving. Thus, it is important that a brand be included in the choice alternatives activated at the beginning of the problem-solving process. In general, the more automatic the choice behaviour becomes, the more difficult it is for marketers to interrupt and influence the choice.

Marketers of new brands or brands with a low market share must somehow interrupt consumers' automatic problem-solving processes. They may develop strategies of producing prominent environmental stimuli such as large or unusual store displays, create strong package graphics that stand out on the shelf, give away free samples, or run sales promotions (buy one, get one free).[48] Such strategies are intended to catch consumers' attention and interrupt their routine choice behaviour. The goal is to jolt consumers into a more conscious and controlled level of limited decision making that includes the new brand in the consideration set.

Finally, marketers of leading brands such as Snickers bars, Heineken beer, and IBM computers may *want* consumers to follow a routine choice process. Because these brands already have a high market share, they are in the evoked sets of many buyers. It is important for these marketers to avoid marketing-related environmental interrupts such as stockouts, which could jolt consumers into a limited decision-making process and lead them to try a competitor's brand. One critical aspect of the overall marketing strategy for such brands is an efficient distribution system to keep the brands fully stocked and available (in a prominent shelf/display position) whenever consumers are in a choice situation. Manufacturers of many snack products have developed a superb distribution system partly for this reason. Marketers of industrial products attempt to make their buyers' decision-making processes more routine by computerizing and automating the order process.

Limited Decision Making

Most consumer decisions involve limited problem-solving effort. Because most consumers already have a lot of information about the product from previous experiences, the basic marketing strategy here is to make additional pieces of information available to consumers when and where they need them.

Advertisements to increase top-of-mind awareness may help get a brand into the evoked set of choice alternatives at the beginning of the decision process. This is important because most consumers are not likely to search extensively for other alternatives. Moreover, it is critical that the brand is perceived to possess the few key choice criteria used in the evaluation process. Advertisements that capture the attention of the consumer and communicate favourable beliefs about salient attributes and consequences of the brand may be able to create that knowledge. Finally, because consumers are giving some conscious thought to the decision, successful interrupts are not as difficult as they are with routinized problem solving. Marketers may try to design a store environment that stimulates impulsive purchases, a type of limited decision making.[49] Highlight 7.4 describes another way of creating a marketing environment suitable for limited decision making.

HIGHLIGHT 7.4

Problem Solving on the Internet

Shopping for food products usually involves running up and down the supermarket aisles and waiting for ages along with everyone else in the long queues at the counter. Fortunately, multimedia has come up with an alternative to this situation by introducing on-line shopping via the Internet. Here consumers can choose the products they wish to purchase, while sitting in front of their computer in the cosiness of their own home. After having chosen the store where buyers want to shop they stroll through the supermarket with their virtual trolley, clicking the products they wish to buy, and at the end of the trip they see the trolley filled with the products they have chosen. Payment takes place either when the goods are picked up or delivered. These virtual Internet stores are open 24 hours a day, all week and shopping can therefore take place whenever it suits the family. The typical Internet user is still a 30–40 year old male, of above average intelligence and income, but the target segments for food shopping on the Internet are primarily working singles and working mothers. As young people become more familiar with the Internet this group is expected to start taking advantage of these kinds of services.

Sources: Bernd Homann, 'Online-Shopping Einkauf per Mausklick', *Lebensmittel Praxis*, no. 23, 1996, pp. 20–26; Arndt Striegler, 'In Vollem Gange', *Lebensmittel Praxis*, no. 23, 1996, p. 28.

Extensive Decision Making

Compared to more common routinized choices and limited decision making, relatively few consumer decisions involve extensive problem solving. However, when consumers do engage in extensive decision making, marketers must recognize and satisfy their special needs for information. In extensive decision-making situations where their knowledge is low, consumers need information about everything – including which end goals are important, how to organize goal hierarchies, which choice alternatives are relevant, what choice criteria are appropriate, and so on. Marketers should strive to make the necessary information available in a format and at a level that consumers can understand and use in the problem-solving process.[50]

Because consumers intentionally seek product information during extensive decision making, interrupting their problem-solving processes with a brand promotion is relatively easy. Informational displays at the point of purchase – for instance, displays of mattresses that are cut apart to show construction details – or presentations by sales-people can be effective sources of information. Complex sales materials such as brochures and product specifications may be effective, along with high-information advertisements. Consumers in extensive problem-solving situations will attend to relevant information, and they are motivated to comprehend it. Marketers may take advantage of the information receptivity of consumers by offering free samples, coupons, or easy trial (take it home and try it for a couple of days) to help consumers gain knowledge about their brand.

**Back to . . .
Buying a
Set of Dishes**

In this chapter, we examined a number of concepts that can help us understand Barbara's problem-solving process. Her decision to buy dishes involved fairly extensive problem-solving activities, including a substantial amount of search behaviour and quite a bit of cognitive activity in evaluating alternative actions. As you review her decisions, note that her choice alternatives and choice criteria were greatly influenced by the information she came across in the environment because she had relatively little knowledge about dishes stored in memory. Her goal hierarchy and decision plan were constructed through trial and error during the problem-solving process. This example shows the importance of the continuous, reciprocal interactions among affect and cognition, behaviour, environment, and marketing strategy. Many limited decision-making processes are also like this, although less complex. In contrast, habitual choice behaviour involves little or no problem solving. Because the decisions were made in the past and stored in memory, purchase behaviours are generated automatically when the decision plan is activated. Thus, environmental factors have less chance to interrupt and influence the purchase process.

Summary

In this chapter, we examined consumers' decision-making processes as they choose between alternative behaviours. Our primary focus was on purchase choices of products and brands. We treated decision making as a problem-solving process in which consumers' cognitive representations of the problem are a key to understanding the process. Problem representation involves end goals, a goal hierarchy, activated product knowledge, and choice rules and heuristics. For many consumer decisions, the problem representation involves several interrelated subproblems, each with its own set of subgoals, organized as a goal hierarchy. Consumers use simple decision rules, called heuristics, for finding, evaluating, and integrating beliefs about the alternatives relevant for each subgoal in a goal hierarchy. The entire set of decisions produces a series of behavioural intentions or a decision plan.

We also saw that consumers' problem-solving processes vary widely. Some purchase choices require very extensive problem-solving efforts, while other purchases are made virtually automatically in a highly routinized manner. Many purchases involve limited decision making that falls somewhere between these two extremes. We described how consumers' end goals, goal hierarchies, product knowledge, and involvement affect the problem-solving process. And we discussed how various aspects of the decision environment affect the problem-solving process. We concluded by drawing implications of these concepts for marketing strategy.

Key Terms and Concepts

choice   143
choice alternatives   147
choice criteria   148
compensatory integration processes   151
consideration set   147
consumer decision making   143

Review and Discussion Questions

1. Give two examples to illustrate the idea that decision choices are always between alternative behaviours.
2. Describe the problem-solving approach to consumer decision making, and discuss why it is a useful perspective.
3. Identify three ways that choice alternatives can enter the consideration set. Describe a marketing strategy that could be used to get your brand into consumers' consideration sets for each situation. Why do products or brands not in the consideration set have a low probability of being purchased?
4. Describe the components of a problem representation. Give an example of how marketers can influence consumers' problem representations?
5. Give an example of how two different 'frames' for the same purchase decision could lead to different problem-solving processes. Can you relate these differences to consumer-product relationships discussed earlier?
6. Think of a purchase decision from your own experience in which you had a well-developed goal hierarchy. Describe how that affected your problem-solving processes. Then select a decision in which you did not have a well-developed goal hierarchy and describe how it affected your problem-solving processes.
7. Assume the role of a product manager (product management team) for a product about which target consumers have a fairly high level of product knowledge. Consider how each of the formal integration processes would result in different responses to your product and how you could adjust marketing strategy to deal with these differences.
8. Give at least two examples of how a marketing manager could use the various types of interrupts discussed in this chapter to increase the likelihood of purchase of his or her product.
9. Discuss how consumers' involvement and their activated product knowledge affect the problem-solving processes during purchase decisions for products like new automobiles, an oil change, cold remedies, and health insurance.
10. Relate the examples of decision heuristics shown in Exhibit 7.4 to the concept of involvement. When are these heuristics likely to be useful to the consumer? Under what conditions might they be dysfunctional?

Additional Reading

For a discussion of consumer decision making, see:

Michael Ursic, 'Consumer Decision Making – Fact or Fiction? Comment', *Journal of Consumer Research*, December 1980, pp. 331–333.

Richard W. Olshavsky and Donald H. Granbois, 'Rejoinder', *Journal of Consumer Research*, December 1980, pp. 333–334.

For a discussion of the problem-solving process, see:

Anthony Cox, Donald Granbois, and John Summers, 'Planning, Search, Certainty and Satisfaction among Durables Buyers: A Longitudinal Study', in *Advances in Consumer Research*, vol. 10, eds. Richard P. Bagozzi and Alice T. Tybout (Ann Arbor, MI: Association for Consumer Research), 1983, pp. 394–399.

For a discussion of the usefulness of the compensatory model to describe decision making, see:

Robyn M. Dawes and Bernard Corrigan, 'Linear models in decision making', *Psychological Bulletin*, 2, 1974, pp. 95–106.

For a discussion of factors influencing the use of noncompensatory models, see:

Hillel J. Einhorn, 'Use of Nonlinear, Noncompensatory Models as a Function of Task and Amount of Information', *Organizational Behavior and Human Performance*, 6, 1971, pp. 1–27.

For an interesting study on the effect of involvement on decision making, see:

Banwari Mittal and Myung-Soo Lee, 'A Causal Model of Consumer Involvement', *Journal of Economic Psychology*, 3, 1989, pp. 363–389.

An example of a study looking at how knowledge affects decision making can be found in:

Fred Selnes and Sigurd V. Trøye, 'Buying Expertise, Information Search, and Problem Solving', *Journal of Economic Psychology*, 3, 1989, pp. 411–428.

For a discussion of how decision plans are modified during decision making, see:

Easwar S. Iyer and Sucheta S. Ahlawat. 'Deviations from a Shopping Plan: When and Why Do Consumers Not Buy Items as Planned', in *Advances in Consumer Research*, vol. 14, eds. Melanie Wallendorf and Paul Anderson (Provo, UT: Association for Consumer Research, 1987), pp. 246–250.

For an early, but still eminently readable discussion of inferential beliefs in consumer decision making, see:

Donald F. Cox, 'The Sorting Rule Model of the Consumer Product Evaluation Process', in *Risk Taking and Information Handling in Consumer Behaviour*, ed. Donald F. Cox (Boston, MA: Graduate School of Business Administration, Harvard University, 1967), pp. 324–369.

And for an interesting concrete example:

Klaus G. Grunert, 'What's in a Steak? A Cross-Cultural Study on the Quality Perception of Beef', *Food Quality and Preference*, 3, 1997, pp. 157–174.

A good discussion of the use of country-of-origin as an inferential cue can be found in:

Johny K. Johansson, 'Determinants and Effects of the Use of "Made In" Labels', *International Marketing Review*, 1, 1989, pp. 47–58.

For a discussion of how to measure the cognitive processes that occur during decision making, see:

Gabriel Biehal and Dipankar Chakravarti, 'The Effects of Concurrent Verbalization on Choice Processing', *Journal of Marketing Research*, February 1989, pp. 84–96.

For a discussion of how consumers make choices among very different choice alternatives, see:

Michael D. Johnson, 'The Differential Processing of Product Category and Noncomparable Choice Alternatives', *Journal of Consumer Research*, December 1989, pp. 300–309.

MARKETING STRATEGY IN ACTION

Free-Range Pigs in The Netherlands

T he rearing of free-range pigs has recently emerged as a new phenomenon in various European food markets. It is often seen as an 'ethical' alternative, concerning animal welfare, to industrialized pig production. It is very visible in the landscape and has been an interesting subject for the mass media.

Free-range pork deviates from regular pork by process characteristics which cannot be controlled by the consumer. There are no measurement methods developed yet which can tell whether a pig carcass originated from a free range or a conventionally raised pig. And even if a method did exist, it would probably be too expensive or too impractical for the consumers to use.

In 1983, the most important Dutch organizations concerned with the environment, animal protection, and consumer interests, along with the organizations for free-range pig farmers and alternative butchers, laid down rules for free-range pig production. They also started the ISC, Internationale Scharrelvlees Controlé (International Free-Range-Meat Control) in 1985. The establishment of this control system was influenced by a free-range egg scandal in The Netherlands. Up to 25 per cent of the eggs sold under a 'free-range' label had turned out to be eggs produced in the traditional intensive way, i.e. by battery hens. This scandal made the Dutch consumers very sceptical towards free-range products, including pork. Therefore, the ISC had to establish a much more foolproof control system

In the period from 1985 to 1988, free-range pig farmers and butchers were perceived as 'alternative' by the established slaughterhouses, meat-processing companies and supermarkets ('people with windmills in their backyard'). Farmers and butchers were divided into two groups at that time: 'serious' and 'nonserious'. The 'alternative' image was caused by the rather large group of nonserious farmers and butchers and the technical problems of producing free-range pigs whose meat would meet the normal standard for pork. In those days, the sale of free-range pork was limited, and the main reason for the survival of its production was the free advertising due to lots of interviews in the mass media (and thus a limited investment in creating a customer base). The basic message was more room for pigs in the pigsties and access to outdoor areas, allowing the pigs to act according to their natural behaviour, and control of veterinary treatment including the use of drugs, feedstuff requirements, demands about when to separate the piglets from the sow, and so on. It helped build up an image of being alternative and independent of the existing meat industry.

The main problem in this period was the generally bad quality of the free-range pork. The meat was, for example, too fat. This quality problem was caused by 'nonserious' farmers and butchers and by the technical problems mentioned above. The ISC rules were not made to provide for good eating quality. It was only a system which was established to secure the free-range process characteristics. The 'alternative' image was dominant during this period. The quality, measured as mean and variance of, for example, fat content and other product standards, was below that of meat from conventionally raised pigs.

The image of free-range pig meat changed dramatically in 1987–88, when Albert Heijn, the biggest supermarket chain in The Netherlands, showed interest in pigs produced in an animal-friendly way. In 1993, 150 pig farmers supplying 60 000 free-range pigs, 150 butchers, 450 supermarket outlets, 7 or 8 slaughterhouses and 7 or 8 meat processing plants were affiliated to the ISC, indicating the considerable volume of the production, manufacturing, and distribution the organization was monitoring eight years after it was started.

Albert Heijn's involvement in the development of free-range pork products corresponded with the company's policy of 'wide choice' and Albert

Heijn's focus on alternative food products. Free-range pork gives consumers with a critical attitude towards regular pork an option. That consumers do not need to buy this kind of meat at a special butcher's shop also creates an image of being comprehensive.

The profile of the typical free-range pork consumer – 'high social class, high income, a high level of education, and a good job' – is attractive to Albert Heijn, because of its strategy of a high-quality image instead of a discount concept relying on low prices. The typical consumer buying free-range pork is assumed to be part of the core consumer group of Albert Heijn, and, in addition, because of the above-average income level, an attractive consumer group at that. Free-range pork consumers have been characterized as consumers who on the one hand are not willing to turn vegetarian, but on the other hand reject the way pigs are usually raised. If Albert Heijn did not sell this type of meat, some of their customers would go to a *scharrelslager* (free-range meat butcher) to buy it, rather than not buy meat or buy some other kind of meat.

According to Mr Louwman, Assortment Manager for fresh meat and poultry, free-range pork has been one out of the two most important new products in the fresh meat market in Albert Heijn during the last five years.

Discussion Questions

1. Compare evaluative criteria and dominant overall end goals between buyers of regular pork and buyers of free-range pork.
2. How does the fact that 'free range' is a process characteristic influence problem-solving? Which inferential belief formation processes would you expect for regular and occasional buyers of free-range pork?
3. Do you think the ISC control mark and the Albert Heijn store name is part of the problem representation when buying free-range pork? How and why?
4. What heuristics might consumers develop to simplify their problem-solving processes for buying free-range pork?
5. Which interrupt mechanisms could sellers of free-range pork use to break the purchasing habits of buyers of conventional pork?

Source: Based on Kristian Philipsen and Esben Sloth Andersen, 'Free-Range Pigs: The Innovation and Control of a New Credence Good', MAPP working paper no. 33, Aarhus: The Aarhus School of Business, 1998.

Behaviour and Marketing Strategy

Consumer Affect and Cognition

Consumer Environment

Consumer Behaviour

Introduction to Behaviour

What Were These Marketers Trying to Do?

atusan Kids, a line of hair care products aimed at children, encourages children to peel the bar code off the product bottles and paste them on a piece of paper. Five bar codes can be exchanged for a smart children's backpack.

Brioche Pasquier, a French industrial baking company producing brioches and croissants, sponsors a first league basketball team, Pitch Cholet Basket, which leads the French league; 20 sports tournaments at schools are sponsored every year, and 1100 teams are provided with T-shirts.[1]

The Shell petrol company has been issuing customer charge cards which can be used at Shell stations around Europe. For purchases made with the card, cash rebates were awarded to the customer. The company also sold a high-quality book of European road maps for as little as DM12/DKK50/£6. The maps also indicated where Shell filling stations could be found across Europe.

Stimorol chewing gum, which has become the market leader on the growing Russian market for chewing gum, is airing nationwide commercials in Russia five or six times per day. It sponsors the Russian football league, now called the Stimorol league, and the Stimorol brand name is on the players' clothing, the tickets, score boards, and programmes, and commercials are inserted into the television transmissions of the football matches. Stimorol has also sponsored the Russian ice hockey team and the weather forecast on TV; rock concerts and disco evenings at Moscow university have been arranged.[2]

What were these marketers trying to do? In this and the next three chapters, we will be dealing with behaviour. That may sound strange at first, because in the previous chapters also we were dealing with consumer behaviour – more specifically, we were dealing with how consumer behaviour can be explained by consumers' cognitive and affective processes. In this and the next chapters, we will be dealing with behaviour from a different point of view. We will introduce you to analysing consumer behaviour from what is called a *behavioural perspective*. The behavioural perspective is a good complement to the cognitive view of explaining consumer behaviour, which you were exposed to in the previous chapters. More specifically, it turns out to be useful in cases where there is a strong relation between marketing stimuli and consumer action, as in the opening examples. In addition, it turns out to be useful in explaining consumer behaviour in low involvement situations.

In this chapter, we will introduce the behavioural perspective and how it differs from the cognitive perspective applied in the previous chapters. We will briefly review the major theories within the behavioural perspective and their main application in the marketing area. We also comment on how the cognitive and the behavioural approach supplement each other.

In the subsequent chapters, we elaborate on these aspects. In Chapter 9, classical and operant conditioning are explained and illustrated with a variety of marketing examples. In Chapter 10, we then turn to vicarious learning and its value for marketing. These two chapters provide an overview of the major approaches employed from the behavioural perspective. In Chapter 11, the last chapter of this section, we develop a model of overt consumer behaviour and a management model for systematically influencing these behaviours.

Cognitive versus Behavioural Approaches

Remember the model of consumer decision making in Exhibit 3.4. The model quite obviously aimed at explaining consumer behaviour, and how it is influenced by what happens in the outside world – informational input from advertising, friends, family, media, etc., and the consumer's own experience with products and services. In trying to explain how the input from the outside world affects behaviour, we invoked things like interpretation processes, integration processes, memory, knowledge, beliefs, attitudes . . . . All these have one thing in common: they are not observable. We cannot 'see' a consumer's attitude or belief structure. We have to infer it by means of questionnaires or other devices. In a way, we can say that attitudes, beliefs, and all the concepts we have discussed in the previous chapters do not really exist. They are *constructs* – that means concepts which researchers have invented because they believe it makes it easier to explain something, in our case consumer behaviour.

Whether it makes sense to use constructs, that means concepts which cannot be observed, to explain behaviour, is an issue that has been debated heavily in psychology over the years. Today, most psychologists would probably agree that the use of constructs is unavoidable. But a few decades ago many of them were of the opinion that serious analysis of human behaviour is only possible if we avoid the use of unobservable constructs. If we want to explain human behaviour, which is observable, we have to do that by relating it to other factors that are observable, namely characteristics of the environment in which the behaviour occurs. Thus, one attempts to relate behaviour directly to input from the environment, without all the constructs in Exhibit 3.4. This school of psychology came to be known as *behaviourism*.

Today, we usually talk about cognitive versus behavioural approaches to the understanding of human behaviour. **Cognitive approaches** emphasize constructs dealing with mental structures and processes, like those we have discussed in the preceding chapters. **Behavioural approaches** emphasize direct links between characteristics of the environment and behaviour. Both approaches are accepted ways of analysing human behaviour, including consumer behaviour, and it is widely acknowledged that they supplement each other.

Positions and Assumptions

Even though the two approaches complement each other, it is helpful to recognize that they build on different basic assumptions, both on the nature of human behaviour and on the way human behaviour is to be researched. Exhibit 8.1

EXHIBIT 8.1

A Comparison of Positions and Assumptions

Positions and Assumptions	Behavioural Approach	Cognitive Approach
Emphasis in explanation	Observable behaviour, manifest determinants	Mental constructs
Role of the environment	Predominant controlling variable	One influence among others
Role of cognitive factors	Merely mediators	Predominant controlling variables
View of freedom	All behaviour is controlled by environmental factors	Humans are autonomous, independent centres of action

summarizes some main differences in assumptions about the nature of human behaviour.

One major difference is the view on the ultimate causes of behaviour. If we disregard mental constructs and concentrate on how the environment affects behaviour, as we do from the behavioural perspective, we assume that the environment is the ultimate cause of human behaviour. From the cognitive perspective, one also acknowledges that the environment affects behaviour, but the human individual has some degrees of freedom on how that occurs. More specifically, cognitivists assume that human beings select, interpret, store, and use information from the environment in such a way that the information helps them in behaving in a goal-directed way. And even though the way consumers form goals and values is also assumed to be influenced by the environment, cognitivists usually maintain that human beings have some degree of autonomy in shaping their goals. So, in the final analysis, the difference in basic assumptions is about the question whether human beings have a free will.

It should be noted that this is a philosophical question that will never be finally answered by either a yes or a no. Neither cognitivists nor behavioural researchers will ever be able to explain human behaviour completely. But in some cases, like those in the opening section, consumers seem to be strongly dominated by external stimuli, and their behaviour can be analysed from a behavioural perspective. In other cases, consumers have lots of freedom to decide and form opinions, and such behaviour will be more difficult to explain from a behavioural perspective. We can imagine a person browsing at a flea market. Will this consumer buy something, and if yes, what? There are lots of degrees of freedom, in which stands to look at, which products to take up and handle, which ones to consider, how to negotiate the price, and perhaps finally buy. This type of consumer behaviour is more easily analysed as an extended problem-solving behaviour, in the way discussed in the previous chapter. But imagine a person at the same flea market, who has been instructed by a friend to look for old Märklin toy trains from before 1940. Predicting this person's behaviour from environmental cues in the flea market will be considerably easier, compared with the first example. It will be amenable to behavioural analysis.

Research Approaches

The differences in emphasis on mental constructs versus observable factors necessarily affect the type of research being conducted. Since mental constructs are not observable and have to be inferred, research from the cognitive perspective relies heavily on verbal data – the kind of data produced by questionnaires, interviews, and surveys, because it is believed that these data are useful for inferring mental constructs. Even when cognitivists are concerned with explaining actual behaviour, the data they gather often are not observations of real behaviour, but verbal accounts of behaviour, for example when a respondent in a survey has to indicate how many times he or she has been eating out in the preceding month. Since behavioural researchers are concentrating on observable phenomena, they prefer to rely on observing the behaviour itself, and on observing cues in the environment which are related to the behaviour.

Concentrating on observable behaviour and how it is related to observable cues in the environment is easiest when both behaviour and environment are simple and closely related to each other. Much of the current knowledge from the behavioural perspective originally stems from animal research. Such research can be done in laboratories, where the environment can be controlled. For example, when animals are rewarded with food for performing specific behaviours, one can study how the pattern of rewards is related to the degree of learning or unlearning of the behaviour.

Can results obtained in the animal laboratory be generalized to human behaviour? Intuitively, many people would say yes. It is easy to find parallels. For example, if one varies the effort a rat has to expend to obtain food – which can be done by varying the number of times the animal has to press a lever – we find that the amount of food consumed is inversely related to the effort necessary to get a unit of food.[3] This is basically the same way consumers are assumed to react to price in economic theory – the more a product draws on a scarce resource (which in the human case is money instead of physical effort), the less the consumer is expected to demand that product. Many of the basic relationships between price and demand in economic theory can be reproduced in the animal laboratory. Exhibit 8.2 shows an example of the type of demand curve derived from animal experiments.

From basic price-based economic behaviour it is easy to generalize to marketing. The marketing mix, that means the totality of the physical product, the shopping experience, the packaging, the advertising, can be interpreted as a reward to the consumer buying the product. The size and structure of the reward will be related to the consumers' learning or unlearning of the behaviour to buy the product. If we understand these relationships, we should be able to design marketing parameters in such a way that we maximize consumer purchases.

But as soon as we move from animal to human behaviour, we usually have to move out of the laboratory, and that makes things more complicated. Humans do not live in controlled environments, and the number of cues in the environment which potentially can influence human behaviour is, in most cases, indefinite. Some laboratory research on consumer behaviour has been done with human subjects, which we will present later. But most behavioural analysis of consumer behaviour has to rely on an interpretation of real-world consumer behaviour from a behavioural perspective, instead of

EXHIBIT 8.2

The Economic Behaviour of Animals

T he chart shows results from an experiment with male albino Sprague–Dawley derived rats, 90–120 days old. The rats could obtain food pellets by pressing a lever a specified number of times. The number of times the lever was to be pressed before the food was delivered was varied as follows: 1, 15, 45, 90, 180, and 360. The chart relates the number of food pellets demanded per day as a function of the 'price', as measured by the number of times the lever had to be pressed.

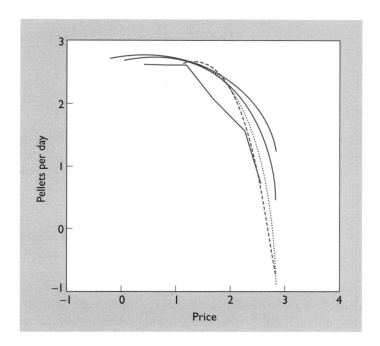

Source: With kind permission from Kluwer Academic Publishers. Steven R. Hursh, Thomas G. Raslear, Richard Bauman, and Harold Black, 'The Quantitative Analysis of Economic Behaviour With Laboratory Animals', in *Understanding Economic Behaviour*, eds. Klaus G. Grunert and Folke Ölander (Dordrecht: Kluwer Academic Publishers, 1989), pp. 393–407.

strictly controlled laboratory experiments. That means that results from laboratory experiments, both animal and human, are taken as hypotheses which then can guide our interpretation of real-world phenomena.[4]

Open and Closed Settings

A laboratory with a limited number of environmental cues and a limited number of possibilities on how to behave can be called a **closed setting**. A consumer shopping in a supermarket with thousands of options on what to do operates in an **open setting**.

Generalizing behavioural principles from the laboratory to the real consumer world will be easier, the more closed the setting is in which the consumer operates.

The opening examples were examples of relatively closed settings. Consumers operate in closed settings when they have relatively few options on how to behave, and/or when the environment clearly favours some behaviours over others. When I am running out of petrol and I see a sign saying that there will be a service station 5 kilometres from here and the next one will not be until after an additional 200 kilometres, I will most probably fill up now. The alternative behaviour would involve all kinds of hassles. Note how marketers have shaped the environment bringing this behaviour about: without the sign, the behaviour would not have occurred.

Generally, from the behavioural perspective, if marketers want to increase the likelihood of the purchase of a product, they may want to increase the closedness of the setting in such a way that it favours the behaviour of buying their own product. This can be done in many ways, but the most common ones are advertising and sales promotion. We will come back to that after the following section, where we introduce the basic theoretical concepts used in the behavioural approach.

Mechanisms of Behavioural Explanation

The basic mechanisms of behavioural explanation can be expressed by the 'three-term contingency' (see Exhibit 8.3). The **three-term contingency** consists of the behaviour to be explained, a stimulus in the environment causing the behaviour, and a reward or punishment following the behaviour. The reward or punishment will have an impact on the probability of repeating the behaviour, that means on whether the behaviour will be learned or unlearned.

The relationships in the three-term contingency are explained by the processes of classical and operant conditioning. We will only briefly introduce these terms here and come back to them in Chapter 9.

Classical conditioning deals with how one learns to react in a specific way to a stimulus in the environment. The example you probably have heard about is Pavlov's dog. When dogs smell food, they start to salivate. Salivation is an innate behavioural response to a stimulus in the environment (food). Russian psychologist Pavlov rang a bell every time he served food to his dog. Over time, the dog came to associate the bell with the reaction to the food – that means, the dog started to salivate when the bell rang, even when there was no food. Because of the repeated pairing of bell and food, the bell became a discriminative stimulus in the dog's environment, i.e. it led to a certain behaviour.

EXHIBIT 8.3

The Three-Term Contingency Model

Many discriminative stimuli in the consumer environment are marketer-created. The motorway sign indicating the service station is a **discriminative stimulus**, because consumers have experienced that it is usually paired with an actual service station. Brand names can be discriminative stimuli when they have been paired with a positive experience or advertising a sufficient number of times. Elements of a store layout can become discriminative stimuli when they become associated with, for example, a good fresh-meat counter or a supersales section of the shop.

Operant conditioning is concerned not with the causes, but with the results of the behaviour. If a behaviour leads to positive results, it will be reinforced, i.e. the likelihood of the behaviour being performed again will increase. If the behaviour leads to negative consequences, the likelihood of performing the behaviour again will decrease. If marketers want consumers to 'learn' buying their products, they should make sure that their purchases are rewarded. Of course, a good product is a reward in itself, but in cases of low-involvement products marketers may add additional rewards, like small gifts, rebates, or sweepstakes. Rewards are also important as to whether a discriminative stimulus remains a discriminative stimulus over time. When a brand name functions as a discriminative stimulus and leads to buying the product, and the experience in using the product is rewarding, the consumer will tend to buy the product again, i.e. the brand name keeps being a discriminative stimulus. But when the quality is lousy, the behaviour is being punished and the brand loses its discriminatory power. When drivers repeatedly follow signs to filling stations and find that the filling stations do not exist, such signs will lose their ability to direct behaviour.

Operant conditioning is thus concerned with how rewards and punishments of a behaviour affect future repetition of that behaviour. Both classical and operant conditioning will be dealt with in detail in Chapter 9. In the following two sections, we will provide some more detailed examples of how marketers try to influence consumer behaviour in a way which is compatible with behavioural principles.

Applications of Behavioural Principles in Marketing

All types of consumer behaviour can be analysed from a behavioural perspective. However, most of the discussion has concentrated on two marketing techniques: **Advertising** and **sales promotion**.

Advertising

In the previous chapters, we have discussed advertising by the way in which it relates to cognitive processes and cognitive structures. We looked at it with regard to how it shapes and changes beliefs and knowledge in consumer memory, which then, in turn, influences consumer behaviour by way of integration processes. We introduced the means–end framework as a useful tool to describe the kinds of beliefs advertising can create in consumer memory.

However, for quite an amount of advertising it is difficult to see which kinds of beliefs it can possibly create in the consumer mind. Much advertising hardly contains information about the product. Some advertising shows the product in a context which is pleasant, but has nothing to do with the product itself – a bottle of gin standing on a beach, a vacuum cleaner held by a bikini-clad girl. Other advertising does not even show the product, but only displays the brand name in a pleasant context. Ads for perfume often show attractive people in sensual or sexual poses, ads for cigarettes have been using everything from lonely cowboys or powerful workers to abstract paintings, and advertising for clothing sometimes shows people without clothes. Finally, some forms of advertising show the brand name and nothing else. This goes notably for advertising in sports arenas, but also for some forms of billboard advertising, advertising on public transport, and in cinemas. All of these forms of advertising have in common that it is difficult to see how they could possibly contribute to the formation of consumers' means–end chains, which, from the cognitive perspective taken in the previous chapters, is a prerequisite for them to result in consumer motivation to buy the product advertised.

Of course some of this advertising may be useless, and the fact that it exists only goes to show that advertisers often lack an understanding of how it works. However, we may also view advertising from the behavioural perspective, and try to see whether some of it could possibly make sense from this perspective.

From the behavioural perspective, advertising has an effect when it contributes to the shaping of a discriminative stimulus, or when it rewards consumer behaviour.

The most common function of advertising, at least from the behavioural perspective, is probably the shaping of a discriminative stimulus. Advertising tries to make the product or the brand advertised a discriminative stimulus, so that when the consumer is confronted with the product or brand in a shopping environment the likelihood of a purchase will be increased. This can be achieved in various ways, and feeding the consumer with information about the product is only one way. Another way may simply be creating familiarity with the product or with the brand. In many shopping situations consumers exhibit a low degree of involvement, and none of the many brands on the shelf in the supermarket elicit a specific response – typical examples of that can be buying mineral water, kitchen paper, toilet tissue, breakfast cereal, canned tomatoes, or frozen rolls. In that situation, when one of the brands is more familiar than the others, this brand will be a more discriminative stimulus than the others. Therefore we find lots of advertising creating nothing but brand familiarity for low-involvement products.[5]

Another way of increasing the discriminatory power of a product or brand by advertising is to pair the product or brand with something else which consumers regard as positive – nice music, a pleasant landscape, sexy girls, a famous pop star. Over time, consumers may come to associate these positive elements with the product, and, even though this says nothing about the product itself or the self-relevant consequences it will have for the consumer, it may contribute to increasing the discriminatory power of the product stimulus in a low-involvement situation.[6]

Various advertising media differ in the extent to which they are able to carry out this function of making a brand or product a more discriminative stimulus, as opposed to creating beliefs in the consumer's mind. Media which appeal to more than one of the senses, notably TV commercials and cinema advertising, are best suited for pairing a product or brand name with positive stimuli, and are at the same time less suited for conveying actual product information, i.e. the type of information which helps consumers build means–end chains, unless the product benefits are themselves of an emotional nature. With print media it is the other way round: print ads and brochures are well-suited to convey product information, mainly because they can convey larger amounts of information, and the consumer him- or herself can decide on the speed of information intake, but they are less suited for the type of affective setting which can

HIGHLIGHT 8.1

A Smell of Sales

R etailers have been experimenting with exploiting one of the human senses which is not usually a target of market communication: smell.

Smell-emitting devices have been placed in the neighbourhood of products where smell is believed to be important. An outlet of the Danish Bilka chain had smell emitters for Bamseline cloth softener and for Mentos pastilles posted near those products. Compared to another store with no smell-emitters, it seems that sales of pastilles increased because of the smell, whereas smell of the cloth softener was unaffected.

Interviews with customers showed that they were not aware of the smell. The retail chain has therefore decided not to use this kind of sales promotion device in the future – for ethical reasons.

Source: Niels H. Carstensen, 'En duft af ekstrasalg', *Morgenavisen Jyllands-Posten*,
3 September 1996, p. 3.

increase the discriminatory power of a low-involvement brand or product. Billboards and other forms of outdoor advertising are best when promoting the familiarity of brand names and in this way increase the brand's discriminatory power. Another way of creating discriminative stimuli in a shopping environment is discussed in Highlight 8.1.

When advertising contributes to making a product or brand a more discriminative stimulus, it will increase the likelihood of this stimulus causing behaviour. The behaviour marketers mainly have in mind is, of course, a purchase. However, other behaviours may be relevant: inducing consumers to request more information about the product, ordering a brochure, asking for a free sample.

Marketers usually hope that advertising will result in a behaviour, but advertising can also be a way of rewarding behaviour. It is a well-known phenomenon that consumers who have just made a major purchase such as a car like to look at advertisements for the product they have bought.[7] The reason for this is that consumers may feel uncertain about whether they have made the correct decision, and therefore appreciate information which supports that decision. Advertising which emphasizes how good a product they have bought fulfils that function. We can say that advertising in this way rewards their behaviour, and therefore increases the likelihood of the behaviour occurring again. Some marketers design market communication especially for that purpose. For example, it is common for the instructions that come with a new car, a major household appliance, or an expensive piece of clothing to start with congratulating the consumer on the choice made.

Sales Promotion

Another area of consumer research that has recognized the value of a behavioural approach is **sales promotion**. Leading experts define sales promotion as 'an action-focused marketing event whose purpose is to have a direct impact on the behaviour of a firm's customers.'[8] Two points are noteworthy in this definition.

First, the firm's customers may be channel members, such as retailers, in which case the promotion is called a **trade promotion**. Trade promotions, such as advertising or display allowances, are used by companies to push products through the channel to consumers. Alternatively, the firm's customers may be final consumers, in which case the promotions are called **consumer promotions**. Consumer promotions, such as free samples, price reductions, and special offers, are used by manufacturers and retailers to persuade consumers to purchase products and visit retail outlets.

Second, the emphasis on affecting the behaviour of customers clearly positions this definition with the behavioural approach taken in this section of our text. Many consumer promotions contain little information designed to change consumer cognitions about the product. Rather, most consumer promotions are designed to influence the probability of purchase or other desired behaviours without necessarily changing prepurchase consumer attitudes about a brand. If the promotion is for a new brand, purchase and use may lead to favourable postpurchase attitudes and future purchases. If purchase is for an existing brand, consumers with a neutral or slightly positive attitude may use the promotion to reduce purchase risk and try it. For consumers who already purchase a brand, a promotion may be an added incentive to remain loyal.

There are many types of consumer promotions. The list below covers the majority of them, but it should be noted that regulations of sales promotions vary across Europe, and what may be useful in one country may be outlawed in another.[9]

1. *Sampling.* Consumers are offered regular or trial sizes of the product either free or at a nominal price. For example, samples of a new type of kitchen paper may be distributed to households to make them try the product and experience the difference to the existing products.
2. *Price deals.* Consumers are given discounts from the product's regular price. Supermarkets regularly offer discounts on various types of convenience products.
3. *Bonus packs.* Bonus packs consist of additional amounts of the product that a company gives to buyers of the product. This has frequently been used with products like shampoo, toothpaste, and salad dressing.
4. *Rebates and refunds.* Consumers are given reimbursements for purchasing products. For example, many petrol filling stations give rebates to drivers who pay with the company's charge card.
5. *Sweepstakes and contests.* Consumers are offered chances to win cash and/or prizes through either chance selection or games of skill. For example, department stores promoting products from a particular country may offer a contest with a trip to that country as the main prize.
6. *Premiums.* A premium is a reward or gift that comes from purchasing a product. For example, many cosmetics companies offer small complimentary handbags with the purchase of skin care products.

These basic types of consumer promotions are often used in combination to increase the probability of desired behaviours. For example, a department store may have a week promoting products from the United Kingdom. That may include price deals on UK clothing, a contest with a trip to London for two as the main prize, free samples of

UK food, and household article premiums for those buying large pieces of UK furniture – all with the aim of promoting the desired consumer behaviour of visiting the department store.

Consumer promotions can be used to influence behaviour in a variety of ways. Most are designed to increase the probability that consumers will purchase a particular brand or combination of products. However, a firm may hope to achieve any of a number of subgoals when running a promotion. The primary goal may be to get consumers to try a new product. For example, A/S Hatting Bageri, a Danish manufacturer of frozen bread, included a free sample of their new frozen bagel product in every package of frozen breakfast rolls. A second subgoal of consumer promotions is to obtain a brand switch. Consumer promotions may obtain brand switches by making the purchase of a brand more attractive than purchasing the usual brand at full price. A final goal of consumer promotions is to develop brand loyalty. Because some consumers tend to purchase products based on price deals, frequent deals on particular brands may keep them relatively loyal in terms of purchasing the firm's brands.

A number of consumer promotions are designed not only to influence purchase of a brand, but also to influence the number or size of units purchased. Promotions of the type 'buy two – get one free' are of that type. Such promotions are being used with various products, including groceries, cosmetics, and clothing. Such promotions may increase the amount of a company's product that consumers purchase and may increase brand loyalty. However, consumers who are already loyal to particular brands may simply stock up on them during a promotion and wait until the next promotion to purchase again. Some consumers prefer to purchase products only when they can get a deal on them.

Consumer promotions can also be used to influence the time at which consumers purchase. Services such as airlines and telephone companies offer special rates to encourage consumers to use them at specific times and dates to even out demand. Most clothing stores have special sales twice a year to clear their winter or summer stock. Restaurants which serve expensive dinners in the evening may have favourably-priced business lunches during the day.

There is little question that promotions influence consumer behaviour. However, which promotion tools are generally most effective for achieving particular behavioural changes is not fully understood. One American study compared four consumer promotion tools – coupons, rebates, sweepstakes, and premiums – for their impact on various consumer purchase behaviours.[10] These behaviours included purchasing a product consumers said they didn't need, purchasing a product they had never tried before, purchasing a different brand than they regularly used, purchasing more than usual, purchasing sooner than usual, and purchasing later than usual. In general, it was found that coupons were the most effective promotions at changing these various behaviours. Over 70 per cent of the consumers reported that they purchased a product they had never tried before because of a coupon, and more than 75 per cent said that they purchased a different brand than they regularly use because of a coupon. Rebates and premiums were both shown to be effective in changing consumer behaviour in this study, but less so than coupons. The study found that the greater the rebate, the greater effort consumers would expend to obtain it. Finally, while some consumers also reported that sweepstakes influenced them, such promotions were the least effective overall. The study also found that changes in behaviour varied by the type of product and characteristics of the consumers. For example, for products such as shampoo, coffee, batteries, toothpaste, and personal appliances, promotions could persuade the majority of consumers to try a different brand. However, for products such as alcoholic beverages, cars, motor oil, pet food, and floor coverings, consumers reported that promotions would not persuade them to switch brands. In terms of consumer characteristics, consumers who are more affluent, educated, and older are more likely to participate in consumer promotions, according to this study.

In sum, promotions can change consumer behaviour, although there are many contingencies that can influence their effectiveness. Consistent with the behavioural approach, it seems likely that the greater the reward, the less effort required to obtain the reward, and the sooner the reward is obtained after the behaviour, the more likely the promotion will be influential.

The Complementarity of Behavioural and Cognitive Approaches

Behavioural and cognitive approaches are alternative ways of analysing human behaviour. As we have shown, they build on different assumptions about some basics of human nature. Both behavioural and cognitive researchers claim that every aspect of human behaviour can be explained by their approach. Thus, the advertising and sales promotion effects discussed in this chapter can be explained by a cognitive approach as well, although it may seem like stretching the cognitive approach a bit. The fact that sheer brand familiarity can affect a purchase decision could be explained by consumers having formed a belief that the brand is well known, which they associate with the abstract attribute that it is probably of decent quality, which, in turn, leads to the consequence that they can buy the product and have peace of mind. Having done this many times, consumers then will form a heuristic of buying familiar brands, as discussed in Chapter 7. That free toys in a package of cereal increase the probability of buying can be explained by consumers forming a belief that this brand has free toys, which the kids like, which leads to more happiness in the family. Again, over time, a heuristic may be formed.

What about the other way round – can behavioural approaches explain complex consumer behaviour, like Barbara's purchase of a set of dishes in Chapter 7? Behavioural researchers would say yes, and argue that Barbara's behaviour can be explained by the discriminative stimuli in her environment (including her mother-in-law, the department store, the factory outlet) and her own learning history, which has resulted in the fact that she has inferred rules about which behaviour leads to which consequences (driving to a factory outlet probably carries a reward in the form of lower prices, but a punishment in the form of time use).

From the marketing perspective, we are less interested in the basic philosophical issues about free human will versus environmental determination. We are interested in having theoretical tools which will guide us in designing good marketing strategy. From that perspective, it is easy to see that cognitive and behavioural approaches complement each other. Two dimensions seem to be related to the relative usefulness of the two approaches. One we have named above: open versus closed settings. The fewer the factors potentially influencing consumer behaviour in a particular situation, and the fewer the alternative behaviours open to the consumer, the more closed the setting and

EXHIBIT 8.4

Four Types of Consumer Behaviour

Involvement	Setting	
	Open	**Closed**
High	Cognitive/affective dominance	Cognitively mediated environmental dominance
Low	No dominance	Environmental dominance

the more useful will a behavioural approach be. The more complex the situation, with many behavioural options, the more difficult will it be to explain consumer behaviour by a behavioural approach. The other dimension is involvement. The more involved a consumer is in a purchase, the more conscious problem-solving will usually take place, and the more difficult it will be to explain consumer behaviour based on three-term contingencies. But the less involved, the more direct a relationship we will observe between discriminative stimuli, behaviour, and rewards.

Exhibit 8.4 shows four categories of consumer behaviour, depending on whether the setting is more open or more closed, and depending on whether the degree of involvement is high or low. In an open setting with high involvement, such as Barbara buying a set of dishes, we will find it rather difficult to explain consumer behaviour by behavioural approaches, and have to resort to cognitive and affective factors for explanation. We can call this a situation of *cognitive/affective dominance*. In the case of low involvement and a closed setting, like a consumer choosing one among three available brands of chewing gum from a shelf, the environment will have a strong, rather direct impact on behaviour, making it amenable to analysis by a behavioural approach. We can call this a situation of *environmental dominance*. Then we have two intermediate cases. When the setting is closed, but involvement is high, like deciding whether to fill up the car with petrol or risk being stranded on the motorway, the environment will have a strong impact on behaviour, and the consumer will be very aware of the alternative consequences of the various courses of action, making such a situation equally amenable to an analysis by a cognitive or a behavioural approach. We can call it *cognitively mediated environmental dominance*. Finally, in an open setting with low involvement, like selecting one's way through and sampling brochures at a consumer fair, behaviour will be rather erratic, almost random, making it difficult to analyse by both cognitive and behavioural approaches. We can call this a situation of *no dominance*.

**Back to . . .
What Were
These
Marketers
Trying
to Do?**

What were these marketers trying to do? Clearly, they were trying to influence consumer behaviour. Their attempts can be analysed from the behavioural perspective.

Both Natusan and Shell were trying to change the consequences of the behaviour. Natusan tried to keep families buying their line of Kids products by rewarding them with a free backpack after a certain number of purchases. Shell rewards loyal customers, i.e. those who use the Shell charge card, with a cash rebate. In both cases, the aim is almost certainly to increase the probability of repeat purchases.

Brioche Pasquier and Stimorol were trying to make their brand name a more discriminative stimulus. Products like chewing gum are not usually planned purchases, they are bought when the consumer confronts the shelf of products. A brand name to which the consumer has been exposed many times will appear more familiar, which increases its discriminatory power. In addition, both the Stimorol and the Brioche Pasquier brand names were placed in the context of sports events which potential customers may regard as interesting and stimulating, and part of that interest and stimulation may be carried over to the brand name, making it even more discriminatory on the shelf.

Shell was also trying to provide discriminative stimuli, albeit in a different way. By providing cheap roadmaps with Shell filling stations indicated, Shell is providing stimuli that drivers can use when they have to fill up in unfamiliar surroundings.

All four examples are products with relatively low degrees of consumer involvement. The Shell and the Stimorol examples also refer to relatively closed settings, with clearly defined behavioural alternatives and not too many discriminative stimuli.

Summary

This chapter introduced the behavioural approach to analysing consumer behaviour. In the behavioural approach, consumer behaviour is analysed in terms of how the consumer reacts to stimuli in the environment, and how this behaviour is rewarded or punished. The behavioural approach is different from the cognitive approach, discussed in earlier chapters. It builds on different assumptions about human behaviour and also uses different research methods. However, both approaches complement each other when analysing consumer behaviour to derive marketing strategy. Examples from advertising and sales promotion were presented to show the usefulness of the behavioural approach.

Key Terms and Concepts

advertising and **sponsoring**   179
behavioural approach   174
cognitive approach   174
consumer promotion   182
discriminative stimulus   179
open and closed settings   177
sales promotion   181
three-term contingency   178
trade promotion   182

Review and Discussion Questions

1. Why have behavioural and cognitive approaches not been fully integrated in psychology or consumer research?
2. Explain how behavioural and cognitive approaches differ in their views of consumer research.
3. Give examples of purchase decisions where you believe a behavioural view would be appropriate in terms of consumer knowledge needed by the marketing manager.
4. In what kinds of purchase decisions would understanding of consumer cognitive processes be superior to a behavioural view for the marketing manager?
5. Offer three examples of situations where you have attempted to modify someone else's behaviour or where someone else has attempted to modify your behaviour.
6. Consider a specific situation, such as dinner at a restaurant. Offer both cognitive and behavioural views of the script you might observe.
7. Presume that you wish to change the response of restaurant patrons. Suggest strategies based on a cognitive view and based on a behavioural view.

Additional Reading

For a general discussion of the application of the behavioural approach to consumer behaviour, see:

Gordon R. Foxall, 'Scientific Progress in Consumer Psychology: The Contribution of a Behavioural Analysis of Choice', *Journal of Economic Psychology*, 9, no. 3, 1986, pp. 292–314.

Gordon R. Foxall, 'The Consumer Situation: An Integrative Model for Research in Marketing', *Journal of Marketing Management*, 13, no. 3, 1992, pp. 383–404.

For examples of the analysis of economic behaviour in animals and a comparison with human behaviour, see:

Stephen E. G. Lea, 'The Psychology and Economics of Demand', *Psychological Bulletin*, 1978, pp. 441–466.

For discussions and research on advertising and sales promotion which can be interpreted from a behavioural perspective, see:

Leland Campbell and William D. Diamond, 'Framing and Sales Promotions: The Characteristics of a "Good Deal" ', *Journal of Consumer Marketing*, Fall 1990, pp. 25–31.

Klaus Deimel, 'Erinnerungswirkungen der Sportwerbung', *Marketing-ZFP*, issue 1, 1993, pp. 5–14.

Ellen R. Foxman, Ratriya S. Tansuhaj, and John K. Wong, 'Evaluating Cross-National Sales Promotion Strategy: An Audit Approach', *International Marketing Review*, no. 4, 1988, pp. 7–15.

Sunil Gupta, 'Impact of Sales Promotions on When, What, and How Much to Buy', *Journal of Marketing Research*, November 1988, pp. 342–355.

Arnold Hermanns and Michael Püttmann, 'Internationales Musik-Sponsoring – Grundlagen und Fallbeispiele aus der Pop-Musik', *Jahrbuch der Absatz- und Verbrauchsforschung*, no. 3, 1989, pp. 277–291.

Aradhna Krishna, Imran S. Currim and Robert W. Shoemaker, 'Consumer Perceptions of Promotional Activity', *Journal of Marketing*, April 1991, pp. 4–16.

Scott A. Neslin and Robert W. Shoemaker, 'An Alternative Explanation for Lower Repeat Rates after Promotion Purchases', *Journal of Marketing Research*, May 1989, pp. 205–213.

For examples of empirical research designed to achieve behavioural changes, see:

William Gaidis and James Cross, 'Behaviour Modification as a Framework for Sales Promotion Management', *Journal of Consumer Marketing*, Spring 1987, pp. 65–74.

Jeannet H. van Houwelingen and W. Fred van Raaij, 'The Effects of Goal-Setting and Daily Electronic Feedback on In-Home Energy Use', *Journal of Consumer Research*, June 1989, pp. 98–105.

Richard A. Winnett, John F. Moore, Jana L. Wagner, Lee A. Hite, Michael Leahy, Tamara E. Neubauer, Janet L. Walberg, W. Bruce Walker, David Lombard, E. Scott Geller, and Laurie L. Mundy, 'Altering Shoppers' Supermarket Purchases to Fit Nutritional Guidelines: An Interactive Information System', *Journal of Applied Behaviour Analysis*, Spring 1991, pp. 95–105.

For an attempt to integrate behavioural and cognitive approaches in explaining consumer behaviour, see:

Günther Wiswede, 'Eine Lerntheorie des Konsumentenverhaltens', *Die Betriebswirtschaft*, 45, no. 5, 1985, pp. 544–557.

MARKETING STRATEGY IN ACTION
Mölnlycke

S CA Mölnlycke is the Swedish producer of the well-known Libero nappies, Libresse sanitary towels, and o.b. Fleur tampons. In Scandinavia, the company holds an approximate market share of 50 per cent. When it comes to marketing, SCA Mölnlycke prefers to reach its customers with more selective tools than just TV advertising. The company places emphasis on more qualified and personal advice, and favours information to and dialogue with its customers. This attitude is reflected in the marketing strategy of their Libero nappies in Scandinavia.

The health care system is used to get in touch with the target group. For 27 years, SCA Mölnlycke has published a booklet called *Pregnancy and Birth – The Newborn Baby*, which the midwife gives the parents-to-be the first time they attend an antenatal clinic. The booklet contains factual, nonpromotional information about pregnancy, birth, and the time immediately afterwards.

As one mother-to-be expressed it: 'When you are pregnant, you are so curious about what is happening to your body, the physical and psychological reactions, etc. You really enjoy reading about it to find out whether your reactions are normal. The booklet from SCA Mölnlycke contains the necessary information written in an easily digestible form.'

Not until halfway through the book does the reader encounter any promotion for the company's products. Even then, SCA Mölnlycke stresses that it doesn't want to intrude on the reader with its information. Therefore the pages with product information have been sealed. It is then up to the reader to decide whether she or he wants to skip this section or to cut open the pages and read about the products. By showing this lack of importunity, SCA Mölnlycke hopes to obtain an image of credibility.

An enthusiastic expectant mother said: 'Before reading the booklet, I didn't know that SCA Mölnlycke was the producer of Libero. Because the booklet is totally objective and very serious, I didn't realize until I saw the company

and product information that this was in fact promotion material. I don't mind though, because it is made in a very sober-minded and informative way.'

In the booklet, SCA Mölnlycke offers membership of the Libero Baby Club, which sends samples, gifts, and information circulars to the parents for as long as the baby uses nappies. To become a member, the mother must fill out a card attached to the book and return it to SCA Mölnlycke. By joining the club, the parents receive samples of Libero nappies, a bib, a baby mobile, and for the mother a cassette with exercises for the bottom of the pelvis and samples of Libresse sanitary towels. By far the greater part of the mothers-to-be respond to the offer.

The sample package arrives around the time of the birth, and SCA Mölnlycke encloses a letter with good advice to the new parents combined with information on Libero's Newborn nappies. It explains how the nappies are designed specifically to meet the characteristics of the newborn baby.

In the letter, SCA Mölnlycke further informs the customer that after having bought a pack of Libero nappies, she or he can cut out a small coupon and send it to the company. In return, the customer gets another booklet about becoming a family or simply a refund of DKK20. Besides that, SCA Mölnlycke offers a nursing bra and breast pads at favourable prices. Finally, there are some questions to be answered about the customer's satisfaction with the product and probability of repurchase.

If it is the customer's second child, the information material is adjusted to the different situation, addressing the relationship between the parents and their first and now older child. By returning the coupon, the customer receives either a rattle or the booklet *I Also Want to Be a Baby* for the elder child.

From the database of Libero Baby Club members, the company has addresses of their target group, which form the basis of later direct mail and analyses of consumer satisfaction. Every now and then, SCA Mölnlycke informs its customers that the average baby will now need to advance to a larger Libero nappy category. Every letter contains both an offer, in form of toys or a book, which is available in return for a coupon cut out from a pack of nappies, and some questions to be answered concerning satisfaction with Mölnlycke products.

The satisfaction expressed by the customer determines how the communication between SCA Mölnlycke and the customer will continue. If the customer expresses dissatisfaction, the company will respond by advising on what could be the reason for the unsatisfactory product performance. If the answer is positive, the communication will continue at regular intervals, until the child reaches the age of two and a half and usually stops using nappies.

Discussion Questions

1. Which (sub)goals do you think SCA Mölnlycke had in mind when designing this promotion strategy?

2. Interpret SCA Mölnlycke's promotional strategy (*a*) from a cognitive perspective, (*b*) from a behavioural perspective.

3. Generate ideas about how SCA Mölnlycke could exploit the effects from the nappies promotion by transferring it to other product types, e.g. Libresse sanitary towels.

Source: SCA Mölnlycke

Classical and Operant Conditioning

Frequent Flyer Programmes

 ll major airlines have introduced frequent flyer programmes to increase customer loyalty. The basic principle is simple and always the same: once you have joined the frequent flyer programme of a particular airline, you earn miles or points every time you fly with that airline. The number of miles or points depends on the distance flown and the level of service (economy, business, first) paid for. Miles/points can then be redeemed for free tickets and other rewards.

The details of the programmes differ considerably between airlines, however. Some airlines award miles only for full-fare tickets. Most airlines have temporary special offers where you would get double the amount of miles on particular routes, for example in connection with opening new routes. The free tickets for which the miles can be exchanged may be restricted with regard to possible dates and possible classes of service. While free tickets are the major reward, numerous others are available. Most airlines offer free hotel rooms and free car rentals, but Lufthansa also offers to hire a top German chef to prepare meals for your next party, SAS offers trips on a vintage steamer through the Swedish Göta canal, and Sabena offered to exchange miles for diamonds.

Most airlines also use miles accumulated to distinguish classes of customers – often they distinguish between a basic level, a silver level, and a gold level. Silver and gold members are offered additional service benefits, like free lounge access in airports, priority on waiting lists, and hot lines in case of emergency.

Frequent flyer programmes favour larger airlines, because a larger route network increases chances for the frequent traveller to accumulate the number of miles necessary for an award. Smaller airlines have therefore launched combined frequent flyer programmes to compensate for this. Thus, Sabena, Austrian Airlines, and Swissair have a joint frequent flyer programme.

Can consumer behaviour theory explain why or to what extent frequent flyer programmes are effective in securing more business to airlines? As we started to explain in the previous chapter, the answer is yes. In this chapter, we look in more detail into the basic processes of classical and operant conditioning, which are the two major theoretical tools within the behavioural approach. In the first major section, the process of *classical conditioning* is described and illustrated. In the second section, *operant conditioning* is explained, some successful applications are presented, and examples from marketing practice are given.[1] We treat these two conditioning processes as conceptually distinct, although they overlap in a number of areas.[2]

Classical Conditioning

In Chapter 8, we mentioned Pavlov's experiments in which he conditioned a dog to salivate at the sound of a bell. Pavlov's research provided the basis for classical conditioning.

In general, **classical conditioning** can be defined as a process by which a previously neutral stimulus (the bell in Pavlov's experiment), by being paired with an unconditioned stimulus (dog food, meat powder), comes to elicit a response (salivation) very similar to the response originally elicited by the unconditioned stimulus. This process is depicted in Exhibit 9.1, and two points should be noted.

First, classical conditioning can be accomplished not only with unconditioned stimuli, but also with previously conditioned stimuli. For example, most of us are previously conditioned to the sound of a doorbell ringing, and will look up almost automatically on hearing it. This previously conditioned stimulus has been used at the beginning of Avon TV commercials to attract consumers' attention to the ad itself as well as to Avon's services.

Second, and most important for consumer behaviour and marketing strategy, emotions appear to follow the principles of classical conditioning.[3] For example, when a new product for which people have neutral feelings is repeatedly advertised during exciting sports events (such as the Wimbledon tennis cup), it is possible for the product to eventually generate excitement on its own solely through the repeated pairings with the exciting events. Similarly, an unknown political candidate may come to elicit patriotic feelings in voters simply by having patriotic music constantly playing in the background of his or her political commercials. Many firms currently use stimuli in commercials and ads that are designed to generate emotions (see also Highlight 9.1).

Because it can account for many of the responses that environmental stimuli elicit from individuals, classical conditioning has important implications for marketing and consumer behaviour. Through it a particular stimulus can come to evoke positive,

EXHIBIT 9.1

The Process of Classical Conditioning

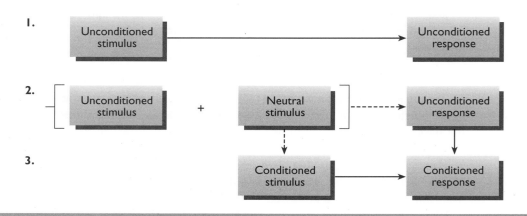

HIGHLIGHT 9.1

Emotional Conditioning of Hoba Soap

T he HOBA experiment was the first to show the effects of emotional conditioning in a consumer context. The experiment started by finding fictitious brand names which were emotionally neutral. Both physiological measures (electrodermal reaction) and verbal scales showed that the name HOBA had no emotional significance for the respondents.

The respondents were then asked to view various films. Before the actual film started, they were shown a number of slide advertisements, including some for HOBA soap. The slides advertising HOBA were of four types: they included either strong or weak emotional pictures, and they included or did not include substantial information on the product. The emotional pictures were motives related to eroticism, social happiness, and vacations.

Each respondent viewed nine films, at intervals of a day or more, and saw 30 HOBA ads, plus numerous other (distracter) ads. Each respondent saw only one of the four types of HOBA ads. After viewing all movies and ads, the effects of emotional conditioning were measured by both physiological measures and verbal scales.

The results clearly showed that those respondents who were exposed to the strong emotional stimuli now attributed a number of emotional characteristics to HOBA soap. These included happy, exciting, and sensual. This effect was independent of whether the ads also included substantial information about the product.

Source: Adapted from Werner Kroeber-Riel and Peter Weinberg, *Konsumentenverhalten*, 6th edn. (Munich: Vahlen, 1996), pp. 133–135.

negative, or neutral feelings. Consequently, classical conditioning can influence an individual to work to obtain, to avoid, or to be indifferent to a wide variety of products and services.

Consider product-related stimuli. External stimuli that elicit positive emotions can be paired with the product so that the product itself elicits a positive effect. Behaviour may then be triggered that brings the potential consumer into closer contact with the product. 'Closer contact' refers to a general relationship between a person's behaviour and a given stimulus (e.g., a product). For example, if a product elicits positive affect, an individual exposed to it is more apt to behave positively towards it than if negative emotions are elicited. Attending behaviour is also apt to be a function of classically conditioned affect. Stimuli that elicit stronger emotional responses (either positive or negative) are, at least over a considerable range, apt to receive more attention from an individual than stimuli that are affectively neutral. To the degree that attending behaviour is necessary for product purchase or other product-related behaviour, classical conditioning influences whether consumers come into contact with products.

Similarly, stimuli may produce certain general emotional responses, such as relaxation, excitement, nostalgia, or some other emotion likely to increase the probability of a desired behaviour (such as product purchase). Radio and TV ads often use famous broadcasters whose voices have been paired for years with popular TV shows of exciting sports events. These voices may elicit familiarity and excitement as a result of

EXHIBIT 9.2

Some Marketing Tactics Consistent with Classical Conditioning Principles

Unconditioned or Previously Conditioned Stimulus	Unconditioned or Previously Conditioned Response	Example
Exciting event	Excitement, attention	Product advertised during sports event
Popular music	Relaxation, positive mood	Background music in commercials, in retail stores
Familiar voices	Relaxation, feeling of security	Well-known TV hosts narrating commercials
Sexy voices, bodies	Excitement, arousal	Many advertisements, for example perfume and clothing ads
Familiar social cues	Feelings of friendship and love	Many advertisements, for example cleaning products, insurance

this frequent pairing. Repeated pairings of the voices with the advertised product can result in feelings of familiarity and excitement associated with the product.

Music, sexy voices and bodies, and other stimuli are used in similar ways. For example, magazine ads for Calvin Klein's Obsession perfume featured a naked woman being kissed by three men. Such stimuli may influence behaviour without conditioning simply by drawing attention to the ad. Of course, the attention-generating properties of the stimulus itself are apt to have developed through previous conditioning that occurs 'naturally' in society.

The use of telephones ringing or sirens in the background of radio and TV ads and the presence of famous celebrities are common examples of how stimuli that are irrelevant to the content of an ad or the function of the product are used to increase attention paid to the ad itself. For example, Steffi Graf was featured in a series of commercials for a pasta product. In this context, one of the major resources that organizations use to market their products is made available through previous classical conditioning of members of society.

Stimuli at or near the point of purchase also serve the goals of marketers through the stimuli's ability to elicit behaviours. Christmas music in a toy department is a good example. Although no data are available to support the point, we suspect that carols are useful in eliciting the emotions labelled the 'Christmas spirit'. Once these feelings have been elicited, we suspect (and retailers seem to share our suspicions) that people are more apt to purchase a gift for a loved one. In other words, Christmas carols are useful in generating emotions that are compatible with purchasing gifts. Exhibit 9.2 summarizes many of these examples.

There are several generalizations concerning classical conditioning as a marketing tool. First, the concept of classical conditioning directs attention to the presentation of stimuli that, due to previous conditioning, elicit certain feelings in the potential consumer. Sometimes (as with Christmas music) these stimuli trigger emotions that are apt to increase the probability of certain desired behaviours (or reduce the probability of undesired responses). Second, in many cases, marketers may find it useful to actually condition responses to stimuli. When promoting political candidates, for example, it may be desirable to repeatedly pair the candidate with the national flag to condition the feelings elicited by the flag to the candidate. After a while, the candidate alone may stimulate the same feelings in voters as the flag does. In fact, research on classical conditioning, as well as advertising research, supports the idea that repetition increases the strength of the association between stimuli.[4]

Consumer Research on Classical Conditioning

Several studies in the marketing/consumer behaviour literature demonstrate classical conditioning effects. A well-known study by Gorn investigated the effects of the music used in advertising on consumer choices.[5] The first study identified one musical selection that was liked and one that was disliked by consumers. It also identified two colours of pens that had neutral evaluations (light blue and beige). This created four conditions: (1) liked music, light blue pen; (2) liked music, beige pen; (3) disliked music, light blue pen; (4) disliked music, beige pen. After looking at an ad for one of the pens while hearing a tape of one of the types of music, subjects were allowed to select and keep one of the pens.

If classical conditioning were occurring, then subjects should select the advertised pen when it was paired with the liked music. Similarly, they should select the other pen when the advertised pen was paired with the disliked music. Exhibit 9.3 shows the results of this experiment. Clearly, the vast majority of subjects appear to have been influenced by the pairing of the unconditioned stimulus (liked and disliked music) with the neutral stimulus (light blue and beige pens) resulting in predicted choice behaviours (pen selection).

EXHIBIT 9.3

Liked versus Disliked Music and Pen Choices

	Pen Choice	
	Advertised Pen (%)	Nonadvertised Pen (%)
Liked music	79	21
Disliked music	30	70

Source: Adapted from Gerald J. Gorn, 'The Effects of Music in Advertising on Choice Behaviour: A Classical Conditioning Approach', *Journal of Marketing*, 46, Winter 1982, pp. 94–101.

EXHIBIT 9.4

Information versus Music and Pen Choices

	Decision-Making Situation (%)	Nondecision-Making Situation (%)
Advertised with information	71	29
Advertised with music	37	63

Source: Adapted from Gerald J. Gorn, 'The Effects of Music in Advertising on Choice Behaviour: A Classical Conditioning Approach', *Journal of Marketing*, 46, Winter 1982, pp. 94–101.

A second experiment by Gorn compared pen selections after exposure to advertisements that contained either product information or music. Subjects were either in a decision-making or a nondecision-making situation. It was hypothesized that product information would influence pen choice in the decision-making situation, but that music would influence pen choice in the nondecision-making situation. Exhibit 9.4 presents the results of this experiment. Clearly, the majority of subjects appear to be classically conditioned in the nondecision-making situation, but less so in the decision-making one. These differences might be explained in terms of involvement – the nondecision-making task may be less involving for subjects. This is in line with our discussion of the relative usefulness of cognitive and behavioural approaches under different circumstances in the previous chapter. It has been noted that:

> Consumer involvement is low when the products have only minor quality differences from one another . . . . This is especially the case in saturated markets with mature products. It is exactly in these markets that product differentiation by means of emotional conditioning is the preferred strategy of influencing consumers.[6]

Because a variety of markets meets these conditions, classical conditioning should be a useful strategy for low-involvement purchases. It is commonly used in advertising and in-store promotion, although it may be used by marketing practitioners only on an intuitive basis. Further research in this area could be useful not only for marketing practitioners, but also for understanding conditioning effects on information processing, attitude formation and change, and, most importantly, overt consumer behaviour.[7]

Operant Conditioning

Operant conditioning differs from classical conditioning in at least two important ways. First, whereas classical conditioning is concerned with involuntary responses, operant conditioning deals with behaviours that are usually assumed to be under the conscious control of the individual. Second, while classically conditioned behaviours are *elicited* by stimuli that occur *before* the response, operant behaviours are emitted because of consequences that occur *after* the behaviour.

In any given situation, at any given time, there is a certain probability that an individual will emit a particular behaviour. If all of the possible behaviours are arranged in descending order of probability of occurrence, the result is a **response hierarchy**. Operant conditioning has occurred when the probability that an individual will emit a behaviour is altered by changing the events or consequences that follow that behaviour.

Some events or consequences increase the frequency with which a given behaviour is likely to be repeated. For example, if a reward, such as a price reduction, a free sample, or a generous smile, is given at the time of purchase, it may increase the probability that a shopper will purchase in the same store in the future. In this case, because the reward increases the probability of the behaviour being repeated, it is called **positive reinforcement**. Positive reinforcement is probably the most common type of consequence used by marketers to influence consumer behaviour. In general, the greater the reward, and the sooner it is received after the behaviour, the more likely it is that the behaviour will be reinforced and consumers will perform similar behaviours in the future. For example, a free full-size pack of Clinique night cream with the purchase of Clinique cosmetics would be likely to increase the probability of purchasing Clinique again, more than would a free sample of a Clinique refreshment towel. Similarly, free gifts at the time of purchase would probably be more effective than vouchers which have to be mailed in order to receive the gift.

The frequency of consumer behaviour can also be increased by removing aversive stimuli. This is called **negative reinforcement**. For example, if a consumer, through purchasing a product, gets a salesperson to quit pressuring him or her, the consumer may be negatively reinforced. That is, by performing the behaviour of purchasing, the aversive stimuli (the actions of the pushy salesperson) are removed. In the future, when confronted with pushy salespeople, operant conditioning would predict the consumer would be more likely to purchase again.

Operant conditioning principles can be used to explain the decrease in the probability of a response. If the environment is arranged so that a particular response results in neutral consequences, over a period of time that response will diminish in frequency. This process is referred to as **extinction**. For a period Kellogg's included 'video pictures' of well-known European soccer stars in its packages of breakfast cereal, prompting many children to beg their mothers to buy more of the product. The begging continued for some time after the video pictures were discontinued, but when the children repeatedly experienced that the expected reward was not forthcoming, this behaviour was gradually unlearned.

If a response is followed by a noxious or aversive event, the frequency of the response is also likely to decrease. The term **punishment** is usually used to describe this process.[8] For example, suppose you went to a clothing shop and the salespeople were rude to you. Wouldn't this decrease the chances of your going back there? Punishment is often confused with negative reinforcement, but they are distinctly different concepts. Exhibit 9.5 presents a summary of the four methods of operant conditioning.

There are a number of other important ideas about operant conditioning. We discuss three – reinforcement schedules, shaping, and discriminative stimuli – that have major implications for designing marketing strategies to influence consumers' behaviour.

Reinforcement Schedules

A number of different **reinforcement schedules** can be employed. For example, it is possible to arrange conditions so that a positive reinforcer is administered after every

EXHIBIT 9.5

Operant Conditioning Methods

Operation Performed after Behaviour	Name	Effect
Presents positive consequences	Positive reinforcement	Increases the probability of behaviour
Removes aversive consequences	Negative reinforcement	Increases the probability of behaviour
Neutral consequences occur	Extinction	Decreases the probability of behaviour
Presents aversive consequences	Punishment	Decreases the probability of behaviour

desired behaviour. This is called a **continuous schedule**. Marketers usually try to keep the quality of their products and services constant so that they will be continuously reinforcing every time they are purchased, but this is difficult. Services, especially where the quality provided is dependent on many situational factors, often have problems in maintaining stable levels of quality. For example, services such as airlines may not be able to control contingencies such as bad weather; overbooked, cancelled, and late flights; and unfriendly employees, which can make flights not reinforcing. Sporting events, because they may be boring or the home team may get beaten, may not be continuously reinforcing for some consumers.

Conditions can also be arranged so that every 2nd, 3rd, or 10th time the behaviour is performed, it is reinforced. This is called a **fixed ratio schedule**. Highlight 9.2 gives a number of examples of the use of a fixed ratio schedule to increase purchases.

Similarly, it is possible to have a reinforcer follow a desired behaviour *on an average* of, say, one-half, one-third, or one-quarter of the time the behaviour occurs, but not necessarily every second, third, or fourth time. This is called a **variable ratio schedule**. The various state lotteries are examples of prizes being awarded on variable ratio schedules.

The variable ratio schedules are of particular interest because they produce high rates of behaviour that are reasonably resistant to extinction. Gambling devices are good examples. Slot machines are very effective in producing high rates of response, even under conditions that often result in substantial financial losses. This property of the ratio schedule is particularly important for marketers because it suggests that a great deal of desired behaviour can be developed and maintained with relatively small, infrequent rewards. Giving free samples when buying cosmetics and toiletries may be an example of this – sometimes there are no samples, sometimes there are one or two, and sometimes there are many. The effect on behaviour obtained in this way may not be much weaker than when the consumer received many free samples every time he or she shopped.

Numerous other examples of the use of the variable ratio schedule can be found in

HIGHLIGHT 9.2

Using Fixed Ratio Schedules in Marketing

A pizza chain offers a free pizza after every ten pizzas bought – each pizza purchase has to be stamped in a customer's card.

A restaurant offering a Sunday brunch for families with children offers a club membership to the children. For every visit, they get a stamp in their membership card. After five visits they get a present, after ten visits they and their parents get a free brunch.

A cosmetics chain has a customer loyalty programme where purchases of a certain amount result in a free item.

A children's clothing shop has a customer loyalty programme where purchases of a certain amount result in a cash rebate.

marketing practices. In addition to state lotteries, common examples include sweepstakes and contests, in which individuals must behave in a certain way to be eligible for a prize.

Shaping

Another operant conditioning concept that has important implications for marketing and consumer behaviour is shaping. Shaping is important because – given consumers' existing response hierarchies – the probability that they will make a particular desired response may be very small. In general, **shaping** involves a process of arranging conditions that change the probabilities of certain behaviours *not as ends in themselves, but to increase the probabilities of other behaviours*. Usually shaping involves the positive reinforcement of successive approximations of the desired behaviour or of behaviours that must be performed before the desired response can be emitted.

Many firms employ marketing activities that are roughly analogous to shaping. For example, loss leaders and other special deals are used to reward individuals for coming to a store. Once customers are in the store, the probability that they will make other desired responses (such as purchasing full-priced items) is much greater than when they are not in the store. Shopping centres or car dealers that hold carnivals in their parking lots may be viewed as attempting to shape behaviour because consumers are more likely to come in and purchase when they are already in the parking lot than when they are at home. Similarly, free trial periods may be employed to make it more likely that the user will have contact with the product so that he or she can experience the product's reinforcing properties. Real estate companies that offer free trips to look over resort properties are employing a shaping tactic, as are casinos that offer gamblers free trips. In both cases, moving people to the place of purchase or place of gambling increases the probability of these behaviours being performed.

Shaping is not confined to a one-step process, but can be used to influence several stages in a purchase sequence. For example, suppose a car dealer wants to shape a car purchase. Free coffee and biscuits are offered to anyone who comes to the dealership.

A free car wash is offered to any licensed driver who will test-drive a car. A package of extras at no additional price is offered to anyone who purchases a car. This example demonstrates not only how operant principles can be used in a multistep process, but also how they can be used in a high involvement purchase situation.

Discriminative Stimuli

It is important to distinguish between the reinforcement and discriminative functions played by stimuli in the operant model. In our treatment of classical conditioning, we noted that a stimulus can act as a reinforcer or can function to trigger certain emotions or other behaviours. So far in this section, the focus has been on the reinforcing function. However, the *mere presence or absence of certain stimuli* can serve to change the probabilities of behaviour. These are called **discriminative stimuli**.

Discriminative stimuli are often said to 'set the occasion' for behaviours. This means discriminative stimuli can be presented before a behaviour and can influence whether the behaviour occurs. For example, suppose a filling station runs an ad offering a free car wash with any purchase of petrol over a certain amount. This offer may increase the probability of purchasing petrol from that filling station. However, the offer itself is not a reinforcer because it is offered before the behaviour. Rather, the offer is a discriminative stimulus.

As we already noted in the previous chapter, many marketing stimuli are discriminative. Store signs ('50 per cent off sale') and store logos (the distinctive 'H&M' of Hennes and Mauritz) or distinctive brand marks (the Mercedes star, the Lacoste crocodile) are examples of discriminative stimuli. Previous experience has perhaps taught consumers that purchase behaviour will be rewarded when the distinctive symbol is present, and will not be rewarded when the symbol is absent. For example, many consumers purchase Ralph Lauren shirts that have the embroidered polo player symbol displayed on them and avoid other Ralph Lauren apparel that does not have that symbol. A number of competitors have tried to copy the polo player symbol because of its power as a discriminative stimulus. Clearly, much of marketing strategy involves developing effective discriminative stimuli that increase certain behaviours, as well as selecting appropriate reinforcers. Exhibit 9.6 summarizes a number of marketing tactics consistent with operant conditioning principles.

Consumer Research on Operant Conditioning

While considerable research has employed operant conditioning procedures in consumer-related contexts, most of it is not reported in the traditional literature on marketing or consumer behaviour. One study investigated the effects of positive reinforcement on jewellery store customers.[9] In this study, jewellery store charge-account customers were divided into three groups. One group received a telephone call thanking them for being customers; a second group received a telephone call thanking them and informing them of a special sale; the third group was a control group and received no telephone calls. This study reported a 27 per cent increase in sales during the test month over the same month of the previous year. This figure was considered impressive because year-to-date sales were down 25 per cent. Seventy per cent of the increase came from the 'thank-you only' group; the remaining 30 per cent of the increase came from the 'thank-you and sale-notification' group. Purchases made by

EXHIBIT 9.6
Some Marketing Tactics Consistent with Operant Conditioning Principles

A. Continuous Reinforcement

Desired Behaviour	Reward Given Following Behaviour
Product purchase	Rebates, trading stamps
Store visits	Discounts, door prizes

B. Partial Reinforcement

Desired Behaviour	Reward Given Following Behaviour
Product purchase	Prize for every second, third, etc. purchase
	Prize to some fraction of people who purchase
Store patronage	Cash or free meal after ten purchases

C. Shaping

Approximation of Response	Consequence Following Approximation	Final Response Desired
Opening a charge account	Prizes, etc. for opening account	Expenditure of funds
Trip to point of purchase	Loss leaders, entertainment, or event at the shopping location	Purchase of products
Entry into store	Door prize	Purchase of products
Product trial	Free product and/or some bonus for using	Purchase of products

D. Discriminative Stimuli

Desired Behaviour	Reward Signal	Examples
Entry into store	Store signs	50 per cent off sale
	Store logos	H&M sign
Brand purchase	Distinctive brand marks	Lacoste crocodile, Ralph Lauren polo player

customers in the control group were unchanged. The authors suggested that positive reinforcement resulted in sustained increases in purchases for every month but one in the remainder of the year.

As we have noted, extensive treatment of operant conditioning in marketing and social marketing contexts exists outside of the traditional marketing and consumer behaviour literature. Most of this research deals with changing such behaviours as energy conservation, smoking, littering, charitable contributions, and other socially relevant actions.

One interesting example of the use of this technology by a profit-oriented firm concerns the use of punishment by charging phone customers for local directory assistance.[10] Directory assistance is an expensive, labour-intensive service. This study reported the effects of levying extra charges for local directory-assistance calls for more than three calls in a given period. Long-distance directory-assistance calls were not charged. Local directory-assistance calls dropped dramatically through the use of a response–cost punishment. The fact that long-distance directory assistance did not change supports the conclusion that the response cost and not some other factor led to the change in phone customers' behaviour. Other types of punishment include voiding car warranties if owners do not perform required maintenance.

Conditioning from a Cognitive Perspective

As we pointed out earlier, behavioural and cognitive approaches do supplement each other, and to some extent the same phenomena can be rephrased in both approaches. It is not particularly difficult to rephrase operant conditioning in terms of cognitive learning. When a certain behaviour is continuously rewarded, like the repeated purchase of a product with good quality, then from the cognitive perspective we would say that the consumer will form beliefs associating the product with the good quality, and the strength of these beliefs will increase over time. This, in turn, will result in the consumer forming an increasingly positive attitude towards the product, which will affect future purchases positively. Both approaches thus can deal with the same phenomena, but the emphasis is different. In the cognitive approach, we concentrate on the type of beliefs consumers form and how they affect future purchases. In the behavioural approach, we concentrate on the strength and frequency of rewards and punishments and their effect on overt behaviour.

Classical conditioning can also be explained cognitively, as we briefly mentioned in the last chapter. A product repeatedly paired with an emotional stimulus such as a sexy lady will, from the cognitive perspective, make the consumer learn an association between the product and the emotional stimulus. When confronted with the product on the shelf, the consumer will retrieve that association and may use it together with other information in his or her decision making.

Back to . . . Frequent Flyer Programmes

Frequent flyer programmes can be interpreted in terms of operant conditioning principles. They are systems of rewards aimed at influencing the behaviour of air travellers.

The core of frequent flyer programmes approximates a fixed ratio reinforcement schedule, because the availability of the reward is predictable based on the number of miles accumulated, even though some of the programmes are so complicated that making that prediction will be difficult for the traveller, and the programme may rather resemble a variable ratio schedule. Also, some of the major rewards such as exotic trips, cruises, or diamonds require so many miles that for most travellers they resemble a potential prize in a sweepstake.

For its élite customers, where main-taining loyalty is especially important, airlines combine the fixed ratio reinforcement schedule with continuous reinforcement in terms of improved levels of service.

The behaviour airlines want to shape is, of course, travel on its planes. However, the target of behaviour modification may be more specific. Airlines may want to encourage travel on particular routes or at particular times, and discourage travel on other routes or at other times. The schedule of point rewards used is one of the instruments (along with price) which airlines use to achieve this.

Frequent flyer programmes have become a major competitive tool for airlines and seem to be efficient in creating increased customer loyalty.

Summary

This chapter has provided an overview of classical and operant conditioning processes and has illustrated their use in marketing practice. The study of these processes in conjunction with cognitive approaches can increase the effectiveness of marketing strategies as well as our understanding of consumer behaviour.

Key Terms and Concepts

classical conditioning   192
continuous schedule   198
discriminative stimuli   200
extinction   197
fixed ratio schedule   198
negative reinforcement   197
operant conditioning   196
positive reinforcement   197
punishment   197
reinforcement schedules   197
response hierarchy   197
shaping   199
variable ratio schedule   198

Review and Discussion Questions

1. Describe classical conditioning and identify three responses in your own behaviours that are the result of classical conditioning.
2. Under what conditions would the use of classical conditioning be likely to produce positive results as part of marketing strategy?
3. What are the major differences between classical and operant conditioning?
4. Describe operant conditioning and identify three responses in your own behaviours that are the result of operant conditioning.
5. Review each of the four types of manipulations of consequences that can be used to change the probabilities of a behaviour under operant conditioning. Give marketing examples for each.
6. Why are variable ratio reinforcement schedules of greater interest to marketing managers than other types of reinforcement schedules?
7. Define shaping and tell why it is an essential part of many marketing conditioning strategies.
8. Pick an example of advertising which includes positive emotional stimuli and explain its possible effects (*a*) from a conditioning perspective, (*b*) from a cognitive perspective.

Additional Reading

For several consumer behaviour works dealing with issues in conditioning, see:

Gerold Behrens, 'Kommunikative Beeinflussung durch Emotionale Werbeinhalte', in *Marktorientierte Unternehmensführung*, eds. Josef Mazanec and Fritz Scheuch (Vienna: Fachverlag an der Wirtschaftsuniversität Wien, 1984), pp. 687–705.

Gordon R. Foxall, *Consumer Psychology in Behavioural Perspective*, London: Routledge, 1990.

Gordon R. Foxall, 'Radical Behaviorism and Consumer Research: Theoretical Promise and Empirical Problems', *International Journal of Research in Marketing*, 4, 1987, pp. 111–129.

Gordon R. Foxall, 'Theoretical Progress in Consumer Psychology: The Contribution of a Behavioral Analysis of Choice', *Journal of Economic Psychology*, 7, 1986, pp. 393–414.

Gordon R. Foxall, 'The Behavioral Perspective Model of Purchase and Consumption: From Consumer Theory to Marketing Practice', *Journal of the Academy of Marketing Science*, Spring 1992, pp. 189–198.

U. E. Ghazizadeh, *Werbewirkungen Durch Emotionale Konditionierung*, Frankfurt: Lang, 1987.

Barbara E. Kahn, Manohar U. Kalwani and Donald G. Morrison, 'Measuring Variety-Seeking and Reinforcement Behaviours Using Panel Data', *Journal of Marketing Research*, May 1986, pp. 89–100.

Harold H. Kassarjian, 'Presidential Address, 1977: Anthropomorphism and Parsimony', in *Advances in Consumer Research*, vol. 5, ed. H. Keith Hunt, Chicago: Association for Consumer Research, 1978, pp. xiii–xiv.

Werner Kroeber-Riel, 'Emotional Product Differentiation by Classical Conditioning', in *Advances in Consumer Research*, vol. 11, ed. Thomas C. Kinnear (Provo, UT: Association for Consumer Research, 1984), pp. 538–543.

Michael L. Rothschild and William C. Gaidis, 'Behavioral Learning Theory: Its Relevance to Marketing and Promotions', *Journal of Marketing*, Spring 1981, pp. 70–78.

For an excellent summary of recent developments in behaviour modification, see:

Alan E. Kazdin, *Behaviour Modification in Applied Settings*, 4th edn. (Pacific Grove, CA: Brooks/Cole Publishing, 1989).

MARKETING STRATEGY IN ACTION
Europe's Largest Shopping Centre

It used to be Germany's biggest steel mill. Now Europe's largest shopping centre, CentrO, has been opened in Oberhausen, in Germany's industrial Ruhr district. It opened at a time when German retailing otherwise was not doing particularly well, and was said to be in its worst crisis in the history of the Federal Republic. But British Edwin D. Healey, the main power behind CentrO, was taking this as a challenge rather than a problem. His aim was no less than creating the ultimate shopping experience.

The CentrO consists of long, airy shopping galleries with pleasant music and lots of eating places. The total shopping front of the more than 200 shops amounts to about 3 kilometres, and includes several international brands and retailers for whom this is their first venture into the German market. There is a leisure park with attractions for the whole family, a hall for concerts, theatre, and sports events, which can seat 10 000, a restaurant lane facing a water canal with ethnic restaurants ranging from the Japanese to the Bavarian, a cinema with nine screens, several service facilities like a post office, and a direct rapid transit link to the main station.

There are also more than 10 000 free parking lots.

About 15 million people are assumed to be able to reach the centre within less than an hour's travelling time, and about 100 000 consumers are expected per day. Other activities are going on near the centre. New office facilities and 600 apartments for private use are being built. Filling stations, a marina, a hotel, a kindergarten, and a church will contribute, so that the area will also be lively outside shopping hours.

Discussion Questions
1. Which marketing tactics that are compatible with conditioning principles are being applied in the CentrO?
2. Considering operant conditioning concepts, such as positive reinforcement, variable ratio schedules, and shaping, offer at least five recommendations for CentrO to attract shoppers.

Source: Adapted from Kent Olsen, 'Europas største indkøbscenter', *Morgenavisen Jyllands-Posten*, 2 January 1997, p. 6.

Vicarious Learning

Karl Takes a Bus

 arl lives in Odense, Denmark. In that city, he is a frequent user of the public bus system. He is used to entering the bus at the rear and paying the driver at the front when leaving the bus. When he is in Copenhagen he knows that he has to enter the bus at the front and pay the driver upon entering, and leave the bus through the rear door. He also visited Aarhus, where he found out that he had to enter the bus at the rear and leave in the front, and that tickets had to be purchased from a vending machine at the rear of the bus.

Recently, Karl went on a trip to Hamburg in Germany. Hamburg has an efficient public transport system, and upon arrival at the main station he wanted to take the underground and bus to visit friends, who live in a suburb. However, obtaining tickets for doing so turned out to be a daunting experience.

He discovered that tickets had to be purchased from a vending machine before entering the train or bus, and he also found such a vending machine. But he was bewildered by the array of tickets that could be bought, and the quantity of buttons needed to inform the machine about the required ticket. It seemed that the price of the ticket varied with the distance travelled, where distance was computed according to a complicated zonal system displayed on the vending machine. There was not only a choice between single and multiple-ride tickets, in addition there were tickets that could be used only after 9 o'clock in the morning, there were short-ride tickets, family tickets, day tickets, and three-day tickets. In addition to bus and underground, the tickets also seemed to be valid on trains, but not on all trains. Sometimes there was a choice between first and second class, at other times there was not. And it seemed that some tickets had to be stamped in the train/bus or at the station, whereas others were valid as they came out of the vending machine.

Karl pressed a number of buttons and found a slot where he could insert a bank note. He noted with satisfaction that the machine returned change. He received a ticket, which he stamped, just to be on the safe side. He thought he had done his best, but he certainly hoped that he would not run into a ticket inspector on his way to visit his friends.

Just how do consumers learn to act in complex environments such as Karl had to face when travelling in Hamburg? This chapter is concerned with vicarious learning or modelling influences on consumer behaviour. While vicarious learning has been used successfully in psychological work for many years, it has only received modest attention in published consumer and marketing research. Nonetheless, there is a variety of

EXHIBIT 10.1

The Modelling Process

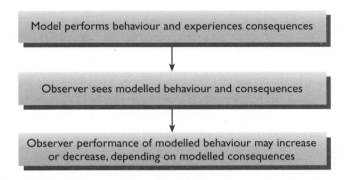

examples of its use in marketing strategy. In fact, we discuss several real-world marketing examples and suggest that vicarious learning offers a useful approach to develop marketing strategy and consumer education programmes. We use the terms *vicarious learning*, *modelling*, *observational learning*, and *imitative learning* interchangeably in this chapter, although other writers sometimes draw distinctions between these terms.

Vicarious learning is a deceptively simple idea. Basically, it refers to people changing their behaviour because they observed the behaviour of others and its consequences. In general, people tend to imitate the behaviour of others when they see that it leads to positive consequences, and they avoid performing the behaviour of others when they see that it leads to negative consequences. While vicarious learning was developed as part of the behavioural approach, a number of attempts have been made to describe the cognitive processes by which it works. We will briefly review these cognitive accounts at the end of the chapter.

We begin our discussion of vicarious learning by focusing on its most common form, called **overt modelling**. Overt modelling requires that consumers actually observe the model in person; examples include a salesperson demonstrating a product (*live modelling*) or television commercials or in-store videotapes (*symbolic modelling*).

The modelling process is depicted in Exhibit 10.1. As an example, many commercials for cosmetics and grooming aids show the model using the product and then being complimented or sought after by a member of the opposite sex. Commercials for hair-care products may show a woman with dull, drab hair (and an equivalent social life) being admired and dated by a handsome, well-dressed man after she uses the products advertised. Thus, the modelled behaviour (use of the product) is shown to have reinforcing consequences (attention from men).

Uses of Modelling

There are three major uses of modelling in marketing. First, modelling can be used to help observers *acquire one or more new response patterns* that did not previously exist in their behavioural repertoires. Second, modelling can be used to *decrease or inhibit undesired behaviours*. Third, there is *response facilitation*, whereby the behaviour of others 'serves merely as discriminative stimuli for the observer in facilitating the occurrence of previously learned responses'.[1]

Developing New Responses

Modelling can be used to develop new responses that were not previously in the consumer's behavioural repertoire. Consider, for example, the videocassette machines used in a variety of department and other stores to demonstrate use of a product. The method has been used for everything from demonstrating the use of chain saws, to the appropriate use of cooking ingredients or the application of fertilizer in the garden. New behaviours are also frequently modelled in television commercials. For example, many commercials for Lego building blocks have demonstrated to children (and parents) the many ways in which the blocks can be combined in building. When liquid detergents were new, commercials demonstrated how to use them in the washing machine. When marketers found that one of the reasons why consumers did not eat more fish was that they thought it was difficult and time-consuming to prepare, campaigns were launched featuring television commercials demonstrating fast and easy recipes using fish (such campaigns have been used in various countries, including Denmark and the United Kingdom).

These examples offer several generalizations about the use of modelling to develop new consumer behaviours.[2] First, modelling can be used to develop behaviours that enable potential consumers to use products appropriately. Demonstrating ways to use a product may make purchase more probable, particularly if the models appear to experience positive consequences from using the product. Moreover, repurchase, or influencing one's friends, may become more probable if the consumer has learned to use the product appropriately by watching someone else.

Second, models may be helpful in developing the desired purchasing behaviours. Suppose, for example, a firm has a product that is technically superior to those of the firm's competitors. It may be important to teach potential consumers to ask questions about such technical advantages at the point of purchase. Advertisements could show individuals doing just this or behaving in other ways that appear to give the product a differential advantage.

Third, it is often necessary (particularly at early stages in the purchase process) to find ways to increase the degree to which potential customers attend to information in ads and other messages about a product. This can be facilitated by applying findings from recent research on factors that influence the attention observers pay to models. For example, attending behaviour is influenced by such factors as the characteristics of the observers, the characteristics of the model, and the characteristics of the modelling cues themselves. These are discussed in more detail later in the chapter.

Advertising practitioners seem to be sensitive to these factors. Many ads reflect their creators' accurate awareness of salient characteristics of the target audience, of the models in the ad, and of the behaviours exhibited by the model. Many ads show the models receiving positive social or other reinforcement from the purchase or use of the product. Finally, modelling can also be beneficial for consumers because it can help them to develop effective behaviours in the marketplace and to avoid costly errors resulting from poor product purchases or inappropriate uses of the product.

Inhibiting Undesired Responses

Modelling can also be used to decrease the probability of undesired behaviours. Because of the ethical and practical problems involved in using punishment to affect consumer behaviour, we have given little attention to ways of reducing the frequency of undesired responses. Such problems are far less prevalent when aversive consequences are administered to models rather than to actual consumers, however. Thus, vicarious learning may be one of the few approaches that can be used to reduce the frequency of unwanted elements in the behavioural repertoire of a potential or present consumer.

It is well known from the modelling literature that, under appropriate conditions, observers who see a model experience aversive outcomes following a particular act will reduce their tendency to exhibit that behaviour. Similarly, vicarious learning can employ extinction to reduce the frequency of behaviour.

Consider the following examples. Advertising for a plastic household wrapping film has shown the consequences of using a cheap, low-quality product, which results in the wrap tearing. Ads for a travel agency have shown frustrated travellers entering a dirty, uncomfortable hotel, because they did not use a travel agency for their booking. Shampoo commercials show people initially being found attractive by members of the opposite sex, but then being rejected when the models scratch their heads, indicating they may have dandruff. Following the use of the advertised product, the model is shown being happily greeted by an attractive member of the opposite sex.

A common use of this type of modelling is in public service advertising. Many behaviours considered socially undesirable can be modelled and shown to have aversive consequences. These behaviours include smoking, driving drunk, using drugs, wasting energy, and causing pollution.

Response Facilitation

In addition to developing new behaviours and inhibiting undesired ones, modelling can be used to facilitate the occurrence of desired behaviours that are currently in the consumer's repertoire. Modelling has been used extensively in advertising not only to illustrate the uses of a product, but also to show what types of people use it and in what settings. Because many of these uses involve behaviours already in the observer's response hierarchy, the model's function is merely to *facilitate these responses* by depicting positive consequences for using the product appropriately. For example, ads for a cold remedy show adult cold sufferers using the product before going to bed and then sleeping comfortably. This technique also appears frequently in advertising for high-status products. Such ads do not demonstrate any new behaviours, but show the positive consequences of using the product. A series of ads for Campari, associating this drink with festive and/or sentimental occasions, is a good example.

It is also possible to influence emotional behaviour through a vicarious learning approach. Bandura noted that many emotional behaviours can be acquired through observations of others as well as through direct classical conditioning:

> Vicarious emotional conditioning results from observing others experience positive or negative emotional effects in conjunction with particular stimulus events. Both direct and vicarious conditioning processes are governed by the same basic principles of associative learning, but they differ in the force of the emotional arousal. In the direct prototype, the learner himself is the recipient of pain- or pleasure-producing stimulation, whereas in

EXHIBIT 10.2

Some Applications of Modelling Principles in Marketing

Modelling Employed	Desired Response
Instructor, expert, salesperson using product (in ads or at point of purchase)	Use product in correct, technically competent way
Models in ads asking questions at point of purchase	Ask questions at point of purchase that highlight product advantages
Models in ads receiving positive reinforcement for product purchase or use	Try product; increase product purchase and use
Models in ads receiving no reinforcement or receiving punishment for performing undesired behaviours	Extinction or decrease of undesired behaviours
Individual or group (similar to target) using product in novel, enjoyable way	Use product in new ways

Source: Reprinted from Walter R. Nord and J. Paul Peter, 'A Behaviour Modification Perspective on Marketing', *Journal of Marketing*, 44, 1980, p. 43.

vicarious forms somebody else experiences the reinforcing stimulation and his affective expressions, in turn, serve as the arousal stimuli for the observer.[3]

To the degree that positive emotions towards a product are desired, vicarious emotional conditioning may also be useful for the design of effective advertisements. Exhibit 10.2 offers a summary of some applications of modelling principles in marketing.

Covert and Verbal Modelling

Up to this point, we have been discussing the most commonly studied and used type of vicarious learning, overt modelling. Two other types of modelling should be mentioned: covert and verbal modelling.

Covert Modelling

In **covert modelling**, no actual behaviours or consequences are shown or demonstrated. Rather, subjects are told to imagine observing a model behaving in various situations and receiving particular consequences.[4] For example, covert modelling could be used in radio commercials as follows. The commercial could tell listeners to imagine that Theo Dehuize, a burly construction worker, just got off work. It's July, it's hot, and Theo has just worked for eight hours pouring concrete. He's driving home; he's tired and thirsty. His mouth is parched and his throat is dry. Imagine how good a cold glass of Heineken is going to taste!

Covert modelling has received less research attention than overt modelling, but a review of the literature suggests the following generalizations:

1. Covert modelling can be as effective as overt modelling in modifying behaviour.
2. The parameters that affect overt modelling should have similar effects on covert modelling.
3. Covert modelling can be tested and shown to be effective.
4. Covert modelling can be made more effective if alternative consequences of the model's behaviour are described.[5]

While we are aware of no consumer or marketing research on covert modelling, we believe it is a potentially useful marketing tool and should be investigated.

Verbal Modelling

In **verbal modelling**, behaviours are not demonstrated, and people are not asked to imagine a model performing a behaviour. Instead, people are *told* how others similar to themselves behaved in a particular situation. This procedure thus sets a social norm that may influence behaviour. One study, for example, investigated the effects of verbal modelling on contributions to charity.[6] People were contacted door-to-door for donations to a charity. One condition in the experiment manipulated the percentage of households the collector said had already contributed to the drive: 'More than (three-quarters/one-quarter) of the households that I've contacted in this area have contributed so far'. People who were told that three-quarters of their neighbours had contributed usually donated more. Verbal modelling also outperformed several other strategies, such as the amount people were told others had given, social responsibility arguments, and arguments for helping less fortunate people. It was concluded that verbal modelling was an effective means of eliciting behaviour.

Again, as with covert modelling, little is known about verbal modelling in other consumer behaviour contexts. However, the procedure is quite convenient to administer because actual models need not be present.

Verbal modelling is easily employed in personal selling situations. For example, salespeople sometimes inform potential buyers that people like themselves have purchased a particular product, brand, or model. This may be an effective tactic, but it would be unethical for the salesperson to lie or to use the tactic to induce customers to buy only the most expensive products.

Exhibit 10.3 summarizes overt, covert, and verbal modelling and suggests appropriate media in which these types of modelling could be used. Investigations of the effectiveness of these procedures using different media and approaches could add considerable insight into effective modelling processes and development of marketing strategies.

Why Does Modelling Work?

In this section we investigate two related issues. First, we discuss some of the factors that affect how well a particular modelling attempt works. Second, we examine several explanations of why modelling is effective. The fact that there is no consensus on the cognitive processes that mediate modelling influences suggests the need for further enquiry into this area.

EXHIBIT 10.3

A Comparison of Three Types of Modelling

Type	Description	Example	Useful Media
Overt modelling (live and symbolic)	Consumer observes modelled behaviour and consequences	Commercial demonstrating use of liquid detergent	Television, personal selling, in-store video machines
Covert modelling	Consumer is told to imagine a model (or self) performing behaviour and consequences	Airline or travel agency commercial during cold, northern winter inviting consumers to 'Imagine you're on the warm sunny beaches of the Seychelles'	Radio, personal selling, possibly print advertising
Verbal modelling	Consumer is given a description of how others similar to him-herself (or aspirational groups) behave in purchase/ use situation	Charity collector reporting on gift-giving behaviour of neighbours	Personal selling, radio, direct mail, possibly other print advertising

Factors Influencing Modelling Effectiveness

There is no question that watching a model perform a behaviour often increases the likelihood that the observer will also perform the behaviour. It is well established in the psychological literature that, in many situations, modelling is effective in changing behaviour, as illustrated in Highlight 10.1. However, certain factors have been found to increase the likelihood that vicarious learning will occur. These factors can be divided into three groups: (1) model and modelled behaviour characteristics, (2) observer characteristics, and (3) characteristics of modelled consequences.

Model and Modelled Behaviour Characteristics

Several personal characteristics of observed models influence the probability that an observer will imitate the modelled behaviour.[7] Models who are found to be attractive may be sought out, while less attractive models may be ignored. Models who are perceived to be credible and successful exert greater influence than those who are not. In addition, high-status and competent models are more influential in determining modelling success.

HIGHLIGHT 10.1

Modelling Effects in Apes and Humans

Until recently, many zoos in the US always removed newborn primates from their mothers and families. But when these primates grew up, they made lousy parents, sometimes beating and fatally injuring their own babies. Researchers determined the social isolation was the leading cause of the abuse, and they had to alter the primates' environment if the animals were to thrive. They made sure biological mothers reared infants in more spacious group settings, exposed them to play with infants and peers, and introduced older mothers to help with the caretaking. They found that inexperienced and even abusive mothers, once given examples of good mothering (modelling) and a chance to play with infants, became competent parents. Today, as few as 2 per cent of primate mothers abuse or neglect their babies, compared to about 75 per cent in the 1970s.

A similar programme was tested for human mothers by researchers at the University of Rochester in the United States. Nurses developed friendships with new mothers by regularly visiting them in their homes. The nurses showed new mothers how to play and talk to a child, much as the older primates had modelled mothering skills. Attempts were made to get new mothers jobs and obtain benefits to reduce tension in the home. In the end, only 4 per cent of the low-income teen mothers who received the nurse visits neglected or abused their children compared with 19 per cent of those mothers who did not receive the visits. The nurses also succeeded in teaching parents who had been abused as children how to trust in their abilities as nurturing parents.

One important difference was found between the effects of modelling on abusive humans and animals, however. The animals apparently learned much more quickly. Just two days of contact with newborn infants made primate females more likely to hug and feed their own infants. By contrast, the only programmes effective for humans required intensive, long-lasting intervention. Apparently, in some cases, humans could become more human by modelling the behaviour of primates.

Source: Based on Art Levine, 'The Biological Roots of Good Mothering', *US News & World Report*, 25 February 1991, p. 61. Copyright, 25 February 1991, *US News & World Report*.

Observers are also influenced by the manner in which the modelled behaviour is performed. If the sequence of the modelled behaviour is detailed very carefully and vividly, modelling effects tend to increase. The rate of learning also depends on the salience and complexity of the modelled behaviours. Interestingly, models who display a bit of apprehension and difficulty and yet complete the task are more effective than models displaying no struggle or difficulty. A reason for this has been suggested by Manz and Sims:

> It appears that an observer can identify more with a model who struggles and overcomes the difficulties of a threatening task than a model who apparently has no problem. A model who is seen as possessing substantially greater abilities may not be considered a reasonable reference point for the observer. However, experts who display little difficulty in completing a task (e.g. professional athletes) may serve as ideals to be emulated in nonthreatening situations.[8]

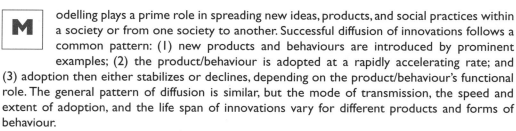

Diffusion of Innovations: A Modelling Process?

Modelling plays a prime role in spreading new ideas, products, and social practices within a society or from one society to another. Successful diffusion of innovations follows a common pattern: (1) new products and behaviours are introduced by prominent examples; (2) the product/behaviour is adopted at a rapidly accelerating rate; and (3) adoption then either stabilizes or declines, depending on the product/behaviour's functional role. The general pattern of diffusion is similar, but the mode of transmission, the speed and extent of adoption, and the life span of innovations vary for different products and forms of behaviour.

Modelling affects adoption of innovations in several different ways. It instructs people in new styles of behaviour through social, pictorial, or verbal displays. Some observers are initially reluctant to buy new products or embark on new undertakings that involve risks until they see the advantages gained by earlier adopters. Modelled benefits accelerate diffusion by weakening the restraints of more cautious, later adopters. As acceptance spreads, the new gains further social support. Models not only exemplify and legitimize innovations, they also serve as advocates for products by encouraging others to adopt them.

Source: Adapted from *Albert Bandura, Social Learning Theory* (Englewood Cliffs, NJ: Prentice Hall, 1977), pp. 50–51.

Another factor that influences the effectiveness of models is the perceived similarity of the model to the observer. This finding supports the common practices of using models similar to people in the target market in commercials and of attempts to increase similarities between customers and salespeople when hiring and assigning sales personnel. Many advertisers take advantage of these characteristics in developing commercials. These characteristics may also influence whether modelling aids in the diffusion of new products, an issue discussed in Highlight 10.2.

Characteristics of Observers

Any number of individual difference variables in observers could be expected to mediate successful modelling. For example, individual differences in cognitive processing as well as in physical ability to perform a modelled behaviour may affect the process. In covert modelling, people apparently differ in their ability to imagine modelled behaviour.[9] Bandura suggests that in many cases observers who are dependent, lack confidence and self-esteem, and have been frequently rewarded for imitative behaviour are especially prone to adopt the behaviour of successful models.[10] However, perceptive and confident people readily emulate idealized models who demonstrate highly useful behaviours.

Perhaps most important is the value the observer places on the consequences of the modelled behaviour. For example, if consumers value the social approval obtained by a model in a Polycolor (hair colouring) commercial, they are more likely to purchase and use the product.

Characteristics of Modelled Consequences

Just as operant conditioning places importance on the consequences of behaviour, so does vicarious learning. Of course, in vicarious learning, the observer does not experience the consequences directly. Thus, a major advantage of vicarious learning for consumers is that they can learn effective purchase and use behaviour while avoiding negative consequences.

Research has demonstrated that positively reinforcing a model's behaviour is a key factor in facilitating vicarious learning. In terms of consumer behaviour, much fruitful research could be done on identifying appropriate reinforcers for various types of products. Currently, however, little is known about what types of positive consequences would be most effective to model. Similarly, for modelling applications that seek to decrease undesired behaviours, the most effective types of negative consequences to model in commercials are unknown. While it has been demonstrated that modelling is useful in deterring smoking,[11] reducing drinking,[12] reducing uncooperative behaviour of children,[13] and reducing energy consumption,[14] many other areas of consumer behaviour are unexplored.

Theories of Modelling

As we noted earlier, there is no question in the psychological literature that modelling is an effective procedure. As with many phenomena, however, there is considerable disagreement about why it works. From a behavioural perspective, operant conditioners view modelling as a discriminative stimulus that may change the probability of the modelled behaviour. Of course, operant conditioners do not attempt to describe the cognitive processes required for successful modelling. However, several limited attempts have been made to describe these processes, which we discuss next.

One cognitive theory that has been suggested as an explanation for modelling is **expectancy theory**,[15] which is closely related to the theory of planned behaviour which we discussed in Chapter 6. It is suggested that models influence observer behaviour by influencing expectations. These expectations are of two types: self-efficacy and outcome expectations. *Self-efficacy expectations* deal with the observers' convictions that they can successfully perform the behaviour that produces the outcome. In other words, after seeing a model perform the behaviour, observers' confidence in their own ability increases. For example, the confidence young children have in their ability to use money to make a purchase may increase when they see other children buying their own toys. Self-efficacy expectations are closely related to the perceived control component in the theory of planned behaviour.

Outcome expectations refer to observers' assessments of whether they will receive the same consequences the model receives. In other words, modelling provides information that helps observers form expectations about the outcomes of performing the modelled behaviour. For example, if a child sees a peer being complimented for using money correctly, it may increase the child's expectation of receiving a compliment for performing this behaviour well. Outcome expectations are quite similar to the beliefs about consequences of a behaviour assumed to determine the attitude towards the behaviour in the theory of planned behaviour.

Another cognitive approach towards describing modelling effects uses the concept of **category accessibility**.[16] This suggests that the process of viewing a model's

EXHIBIT 10.4

A Social Learning Description of the Modelling Process

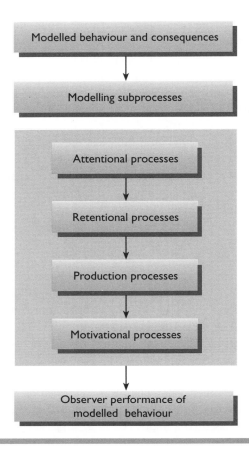

behaviour involves the activation of an interpretative schema. Once the schema is activated, the information in it becomes more accessible for subsequent use. If the schema incorporates (or is closely related to) information that helps specify behaviour, that information becomes more accessible as well, thus making it more likely to influence overt behaviour. Modelled consequences are considered less important with this approach than with others.

The most detailed and best-documented account of modelling is provided by Albert Bandura in his **social learning theory**.[17] This approach recognizes four subprocesses that intervene in modelling. These four, shown in Exhibit 10.4, include attentional, retention, production, and motivational subprocesses. We briefly describe each of these before concluding the chapter.

Attentional processes refer to the ways in which observers attend to and extract information about the major features of the modelled behaviour. The characteristics of the model and the modelled behaviour, as described earlier, affect this process, as do other attention-getting tactics such as the use of novelty and contrast.

Retention processes refer to the representation of observed models and behaviour in memory. Observers cannot be influenced much by modelled behaviour if they do not remember it. Retention processes include both visual and verbal representation systems. Visual imagery is particularly important in early periods of human development; most of the cognitive processes that regulate behaviour are thought to be verbal.

The third process, *production*, involves converting symbolic representations into appropriate behaviour. A modelled behaviour is reproduced by organizing responses in accordance with the modelled pattern. This process requires cognitive organization of the response, initiating the response, monitoring performance, and refinement on the basis of feedback.

Finally, *motivational process* refers to the factors by which consequences of modelled behaviours are judged to be rewarding or unrewarding. If consumers value the outcomes of modelled behaviour, they are more likely to perform the behaviour. External reinforcers, vicarious reinforcers, and self-reinforcers can increase the probability of modelled responses.

Back to . . . Karl Takes a Bus

For public transport authorities, teaching their customers how to obtain the right tickets is a major task. Usually, symbolic modelling is used, by combining a number of verbal and graphic stimuli. Often, for example the various phases one has to go through for buying a ticket are illustrated on the vending machine. Many providers of public transport also use brochures and flyers for the purpose. Still, to a large extent most consumers seem to learn by observing the behaviour of others. Consumers unfamiliar with the system step back at the vending machine and observe what others do. In families and work groups, people demonstrate to each other what to do in order to both get a 'right' (that means, valid) ticket and also to exploit the various special offers the providers have.

While providers of public transport make effective use of various operant conditioning techniques – for example, they ensure (largely) legal behaviour by having controls following a variable ratio schedule, and they try to even out demand over time by giving time-specific rebates – it seems that they make only limited use of modelling techniques. The use of live overt modelling, for example by using video-tapes at main stations, could help people like Karl finding their way in unknown territory.

Summary

This chapter provided an overview of vicarious learning or modelling processes that can be used to develop new responses, inhibit undesired responses, and facilitate previously learned responses. Several factors that increase the effectiveness of modelling were also discussed, as were some theories of how modelling works. While a consensus has not been reached on why it works, it is well established that modelling is an effective procedure. Modelling is currently employed in marketing, yet there is little research on the topic in the traditional marketing or consumer behaviour literature. This area represents an opportunity for increasing the effectiveness of current marketing strategies and for integrating affect and cognition, behaviour, and the environment.

Key Terms and Concepts

Review and Discussion Questions

1. Describe the steps necessary for behaviour change in the modelling process.
2. What are the three major uses of modelling in marketing strategy?
3. Why might a marketing organization use symbolic rather than live overt modelling? Give examples to illustrate your points.
4. How are covert and verbal modelling different from overt modelling? How are they similar?
5. Give examples, not already discussed in the text, in which you have observed marketing strategies that use each of the types of modelling.
6. In what situations would you recommend that a marketing manager use vicarious learning in advertisements?
7. How could modelling be used to facilitate the introduction of the newest models of lightweight portable personal computers?
8. Explain the process of vicarious learning from both behavioural and cognitive perspectives. Which view is more useful for the marketing manager?

Additional Reading

For an advanced treatment of vicarious learning, see:

Albert Bandura, *Social Foundations of Thought and Action: A Social Cognitive Theory* (Englewood Cliffs, NJ: Prentice Hall, 1986), Chap. 2.

For an early work examining various views of modelling, see:

Albert Bandura, *Psychological Modelling: Conflicting Theories* (Chicago, IL: Aldine Publishing, 1971).

For recent empirical research employing modelling, see:

Thomas G. Haring, Craig H. Kennedy, Mary J. Adams, and Valerie Pitts-Conway, 'Teaching Generalization of Purchasing Skills across Community Settings to Autistic Youth Using Video-tape Modelling', *Journal of Applied Behaviour Analysis*, Spring 1987, pp. 89–96.

D. Krebs, 'Gewaltdarstellungen im Fernsehen und die Einstellungen zu aggressiven Handlungen bei 12–15 jährigen Kindern', *Zeitschrift für Sozialpsychologie*, 1981, pp. 281–302.

Richard A. Winett, Kathryn D. Kramer, William B. Walker, Steven W. Malone, and M. K. Lane, 'Modifying Food Purchases in Supermarkets with Modeling, Feedback, and Goal-Setting Procedures', *Journal of Applied Behavior Analysis*, Spring 1988, pp. 73–80.

MARKETING STRATEGY IN ACTION
Alcopops

Early in the summer of 1995 a new phenomenon, which had already had great success in Australia, appeared on the UK market; namely alcoholic lemonade or 'alcopops' as they are popularly called. Alcopops are fruit or soft-drink-flavoured drinks containing pure alcohol. Typically the alcopops contain around 5 per cent ABV.

Bass Beers was the first to launch an alcoholic lemonade, Hooper's Hooch, in the UK market, and, shortly after, cult Australian alcoholic lemonade, Two Dogs, was introduced by the UK licensee Merrydown. By the end of 1996, numerous brands had been launched into the sector: Vault, Lemonhead, and Orangehead by Carlsberg-Tetley, Sub Zero by Scottish Courage, Diamond Zest by Taunton and Mrs Pucker's by Maison Caurette just to mention the most prominent brands.

Sales were fuelled by an extraordinarily warm summer, and, besides that, boredom with beer seemed to be a major factor. A year after the alcopops craze started, the UK market was estimated to be worth £250 million a year and maybe even £500 million. Most people considered it a fad which would pass as quickly as it had started, but it seemed to meet an untapped need.

Alcopops are aimed at the 18–24-year-olds and thereby the younger consumers automatically follow, as they typically imitate the older teenagers. When introducing the product, the primary consumers were the experimenters in the alcohol and nonalcohol sector. Alcopops are meant as a refreshing alternative to beer on a beer-drinking occasion – particularly for young females who don't like the taste of beer.

Being alcoholic beverages, the age of the target group is a major obstacle for the breweries, as the code of conduct is to avoid marketing appealing to under-18s. This includes the use of characters or imagery, as well as antisocial shapes and names which suggest aggression, violence, danger, and sexual success.

Though insistently denied by the producers, the drinks are marketed with an ill-concealed appeal to the teen culture. This is obvious both in the taste, packaging, and formulation of the products. The packaging of Hooper's Hooch, which is the UK market leader with an estimated market share of 70 per cent, features a 'wicked' lemon cartoon character. The product is kept in synthetic acid colours, popular with the young and likely to appeal particularly to the 'aficionados' of ecstasy. The concept is 'fun' with the language kept in an aggressive and antisocial tone, which appeals to the growing antiestablishment tendencies among young people.

The first six months after the product launch, Bass Beers held back from advertising, following the conviction that 'You can't force it down people's throats; drinkers will want to discover it themselves', as one Bass brand manager expressed it. Bass Beers tested this theory with the success story Caffrey's Irish Ale, which received no advertising during its first year.

The advantage for the producer of alcopops, as opposed to producers of long drinks served in a glass, is that when drinking from the bottle, the customer handles the brand name which thereby markets itself. The producer primarily has to ensure that the product is available: Alcopops are sold both in the on and the off trades with a distribution of approximately 55:45 respectively. The on trade has led the category, which is another advantage for the producer, as the empty bottles typically remain on the tables offering others the opportunity to pick them up, examine them, and discover them for themselves. For the off trade, the opportunity lies in recruiting users who have acquired the taste in the on trade. (Below the line support is crucial.)

Hooper's Hooch has been effectively marketed without the use of heavy advertising, with word-of-mouth and press releases as the most important factors. The product has received huge tabloid attention for encouraging underage drinking, due to complaints from antialcohol pressure groups. One can only wonder whether Bass Beers deliberately asked for controversy, by promoting Hooper's Hooch in a poster ad campaign with the provocative slogan 'One taste and you're hooched' with its clear association to addiction.

Eventually Hooper's Hooch poster ads featuring the lemon cartoon character were banned by the Advertising Standards Authority. It ruled the character 'was likely to appeal to people under 18 in a way that would encourage them to drink alcohol'. Bass has promised not to repeat poster ads featuring the cartoon lemon. Furthermore, it will have to check all future ads with the ASA.

Carlsberg-Tetley was the first to launch a broadcast campaign, pushing its Lemonhead brand in anarchic radio and cinema ads. Other producers have followed, and some have announced plans to start heavy advertising on TV – the most powerful media. Time will show whether this will fuel the consumption of alcopops or whether the interest in the product will fade away.

Discussion Questions

1. What role do you think modelling has played in the diffusion of this innovation?
2. How would you design the marketing strategy of an alcopop, taking the restrictions of marketing of alcohol to underaged consumer into account?
3. If you were to design a commercial for Hooper's Hooch to be used for an in-store videotape demonstration, how would you design the commercial to take advantage of your knowledge of modelling?

Sources: Tony Scouller, 'A Short History of Alcopops', *Admap*, March 1997, pp. 44–46; David Benady, 'Soft Targets', *Marketing Week*, 19 January 1996, pp. 28–29; Ros Snowdon, 'Hooch to hit on young drinkers', *Marketing*, June 1995, p. 3.

Analysing Consumer Behaviour

Shopping at Jack & Jones

P eter and Susan were using their lunch break to run a few errands in the city centre. Peter wanted to pick up a prescription from the pharmacy, and Susan wanted to buy cigarettes and some magazines at the newsagent. On their way to the pedestrian precinct, they chatted about the recent snowfall and how much they had enjoyed Christmas and New Year, although both agreed that they were glad the holidays were over. It was nice to get back to a more normal routine without all the hassle of shopping for Christmas gifts and buying food and drink for festive dinners.

While Peter went to the pharmacy, Susan went to the newsagent. Looking at the magazine rack, she pulled out copies of *Vogue* and *Elle*. She asked for a pack of Benson & Hedges, and pulled a bank note from her wallet to pay for the purchases.

When they met again in the street, Peter suggested that they should take a few minutes to look into the Jack & Jones shop, two blocks away. 'I like the sweater which is in the window. Perhaps I could try it on; I really need a new sweater. And maybe they already have end-of-season sales.'

'That would be fine with me', replied Susan. 'I could look for a new pair of trousers. I don't have to be back at work until two.'

Peter tried the sweater on and liked it. He decided to purchase it and saw another which he also liked, and which was already marked down at 30 per cent off. The other sweater was a teal-coloured wool cardigan. Peter was a little reluctant to purchase the second one because, even when marked down, it was more expensive and wasn't much different from a green sweater he had received for Christmas, but he decided to purchase it, too. After all, he deserved it.

Susan found a pair of sand-coloured trousers and was trying them on. She looked doubtfully at herself in a mirror and had almost decided not to buy them when Peter saw her. 'You look great', Peter said. 'They have character and style. You should buy them.' Susan looked at him hesitantly. A salesperson came by and reassured her that she looked great. Reluctantly she decided to buy them.

After agreeing that the trousers and sweaters were good buys, Peter and Susan went to the cash desk in the centre of the store. The salesperson checked the price tags and scanned them into the till. 'That will be £165 all together', the salesperson said, and Peter handed him his Access card. While the salesperson ran the card through the machine and waited for the response, Susan admired the sweaters which Peter had bought. The salesperson gave Peter the credit card slip for signature, bagged the items bought, put the receipt into the bag and wished them good luck with their purchases.

On their way back to work, they discussed how nice it was to buy some new clothes, and decided that they would do some more shopping next Saturday.

As you are now well aware, a typical everyday shopping sequence like this trip to Jack & Jones can be analysed in various ways. It can be analysed with an emphasis on the cognitive and affective processes in the minds of Peter and Susan which lead to the behaviour observed. Or it can be analysed with an emphasis on Peter and Susan's overt behaviour.

In this chapter, we present a general model of consumer behaviour which concentrates on overt behaviour. We begin by contrasting it with the more common models concentrating on cognitive and affective processes. We then discuss the model in detail and look at ways in which the model components can be measured. Finally, we discuss applications of the model from the perspective of marketing strategy.

A Sequential Model of Consumer Behaviour

Exhibit 11.1 shows a number of common models of the consumer purchasing or adoption process. In these models, a single behavioural act, namely the purchase of a product, is related to a sequence of cognitive/affective processes. In some of the models, the purchase is viewed as a result of several steps of cognitive/affective processing. This is also called the *classical hierarchy of effects*, and it is usually applied to purchases in which the consumer has a high degree of involvement. In other models, the purchase is assumed to trigger cognitive/affective processes, like the development of product knowledge and of preference. These models are usually used to analyse purchases with a low level of involvement.

While the models in Exhibit 11.1 are valuable, adoption or purchase can also be analysed as a *sequence of behaviours*. Doing this will sharpen our attention to a purchase not usually being an isolated act, but just one step in a sequence of related behaviours. From this perspective, marketing managers usually want to increase the frequency of these behaviours, and they design strategies and tactics for doing so. While strategies and tactics to change affective and cognitive processes, such as attention or attitude, may be useful intermediate steps, they must ultimately change behaviour to be profitable for marketers.

Exhibit 11.2 offers a model of a behaviour sequence that occurs in the purchase of many consumer goods. Before discussing each of these stages, several qualifications should be noted. First, while we suggest this is a logical sequence, many other combinations of behaviour are also commonly performed by consumers. For example, an unplanned (impulse) purchase of Mars chocolate bars could start at the store contact stage. Not every purchase follows the sequence shown in Exhibit 11.2, and not every purchase requires that all of these behaviours be performed. However, the model is useful for categorizing a variety of marketing strategies in terms of the behaviours they are designed to influence.

Second, the model in Exhibit 11.2 is intended to illustrate only one type of behaviour sequence for retail purchases; similar models could be developed for other types of purchases, such as mail-order, phone, or Internet exchanges. Further, the sequences

EXHIBIT 11.1

Cognitive/Affective Models of the Adoption/Purchase Process

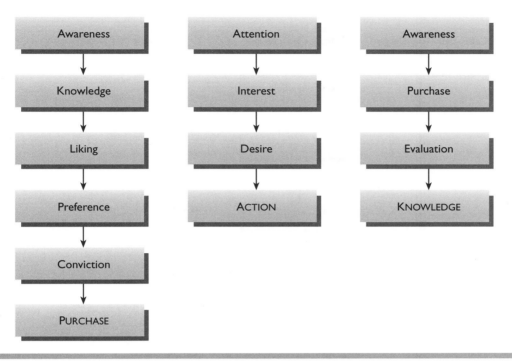

involved in other behaviours of interest to consumer analysis, such as voting, medical care, banking, or consumer education, could also be modelled in much the same way. We believe that any attempt to influence behaviour should include an analysis of the behaviour sequence that is necessary or desired.

Third, the time it takes for a consumer to perform these behaviours depends on a variety of factors. Different products, consumers, and situations may affect not only the total time to complete the process, but also the time lags between stages. For example, an avid water-skier purchasing a speedboat will probably spend more time per stage, and more time will elapse between stages, than a consumer purchasing a Swatch watch.

Fourth, members of the channel of distribution usually vary in their emphasis on encouraging particular behaviours. Retailers may be more concerned with increasing store contact than with purchase of a particular brand; manufacturers are less concerned with the particular store patronized, but attempt to increase brand purchase; credit-card companies may be less concerned with particular store or product contacts so long as their credit card is accepted and used. However, while emphasis may vary, all three of these behaviours are common for a retail exchange, and all three organizations can benefit from the others' efforts.

Finally, the seven categories of the consumer behaviour chain in Exhibit 11.2 deserve comment. While we believe these are logical and useful categories of behaviour, other

EXHIBIT 11.2

A Common Behaviour Sequence for a Retail Consumer-Goods Purchase

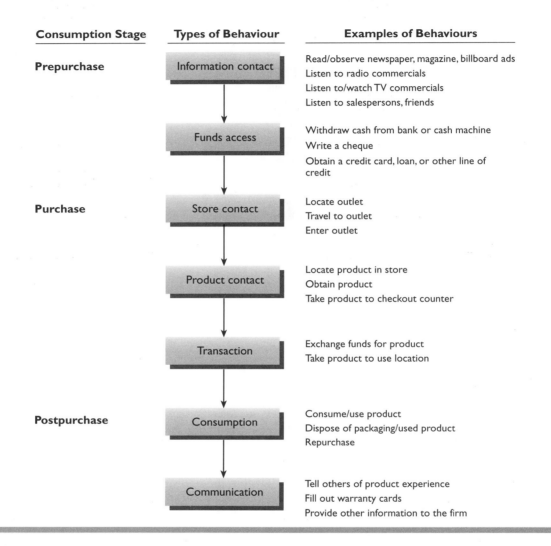

Consumption Stage	Types of Behaviour	Examples of Behaviours
Prepurchase	Information contact	Read/observe newspaper, magazine, billboard ads Listen to radio commercials Listen to/watch TV commercials Listen to salespersons, friends
	Funds access	Withdraw cash from bank or cash machine Write a cheque Obtain a credit card, loan, or other line of credit
Purchase	Store contact	Locate outlet Travel to outlet Enter outlet
	Product contact	Locate product in store Obtain product Take product to checkout counter
	Transaction	Exchange funds for product Take product to use location
Postpurchase	Consumption	Consume/use product Dispose of packaging/used product Repurchase
	Communication	Tell others of product experience Fill out warranty cards Provide other information to the firm

labels or breakdowns could also be useful. For instance, this behaviour chain could be carefully broken down into individual actions of each muscle in the consumer's body, and research could be conducted at that level. However, given the lack of knowledge concerning overt consumer behaviour, the levels in Exhibit 11.2 are a useful starting point. With these qualifications, we now turn to a discussion of each type of behaviour and some marketing strategies currently employed to increase the probability of one or more of them.

Information Contact

A common early stage in the purchase sequence, called **information contact**, occurs when consumers come into contact with information, either intentionally or accidentally, about products, stores, or brands. This stage includes behaviours such as reading or observing newspaper, magazine, and billboard ads; listening to radio commercials; watching TV commercials; and talking to salespeople and friends. At this point, the practical problem for marketers is to increase the probability that consumers will observe and attend to the information and that this will increase the probability of other behaviours. In finding ways of doing so, the cognitive techniques discussed in Chapter 5 are useful.

Not only do marketers seek to provide consumers with information, but consumers also search for information about products, brands, stores, and prices.[1] Marketing managers for brands with low market shares usually want to increase overall search behaviour because it may increase the probability of switching to the firm's brand. High market-share brands may try to discourage external search behaviours because the behaviour may result in a shift to another brand.

The extent of a consumer's search depends on many factors, such as those listed in Exhibit 11.3. In general, empirical research has shown that:

1. Consumers tend to engage in more search when purchasing higher-priced, more visible, and more complex products, i.e. products that intrinsically create greater perceived risk.[2]
2. Search is also influenced by individual factors such as the perceived benefits of search (e.g. enjoyment, self-confidence, role), demographic aspects, and product knowledge already possessed.[3]
3. Search efforts tend to be further influenced by factors in the marketplace (such as availability of information and the difficulty in processing and understanding it) and by situational factors (such as time pressure impinging on the shopper).[4]

From a public policy standpoint, information search is encouraged to develop more knowledgeable consumers.[5] However, there are differences in the effort required by consumers to obtain information from different sources – and in the believability of the information. For example, Exhibit 11.4 illustrates five common sources of information and rates them on these two dimensions.

This classification suggests that internal sources (stored experiences) and personal sources (friends and relatives) are commonly used because they are easiest to access and most believable. Marketing sources (advertising) would also be commonly used because they are readily available. However, marketing sources are not as believable because advertisers have something to gain from the transaction. Finally, public sources (consumer magazines and other impartial studies) and experiential sources (personally examining or testing the product) are less likely to be used, because more effort is required to obtain information from these sources. However, research has shown that there usually exists a minority of consumers using these kinds of sources, and their existence has a watchdog function on the marketplace.[6]

Information search could also be broken down into a sequence of basic behaviours. However, the main marketing task is to increase the probability that the target market comes into contact with product, brand, or store information and pays attention to it.

Numerous marketing strategies are directed at bringing about these attentive

EXHIBIT 11.3

Some Determinants of the Extent of Consumers' Information Search

Market Environment
Number of alternatives
Complexity of alternatives
Marketing mix of alternatives
Stability of alternatives on the market (new alternatives)
Information available

Situational Variables
Time pressure
Social pressure (family, peers, boss)
Financial pressure
Organizational procedures
Physical and mental condition
Ease of access to information sources

Potential Payoff/Product Importance
Price
Social visibility
Perceived risk
Differences among alternatives
Number of crucial attributes
Status of decision-making activity (in family, organization, society)

Knowledge and Experience
Stored knowledge
Rate of product use
Previous information
Previous choices (number and identity)
Satisfaction

Individual Differences
Training
Approach to problem solving (compulsiveness, open-mindedness, preplanning, innovativeness)
Approach to search (enjoyment of shopping, sources of information, etc.)
Involvement
Demographics (age, income, education, marital status, household size, social class, occupation)
Personality/lifestyle variables (self-confidence, etc.)

Conflict andConflict-Resolution Strategies

Source: Reprinted from 'Individual Differences in Search Behaviour for a Nondurable', William L. Moore and Donald R. Lehmann, *Journal of Consumer Research*, December 1990, pp. 296–307, by permission of the University of Chicago Press, © 1990 by the University of Chicago. For a summary of empirical research on these and other search determinants, see Sharon E. Beatty and Scott M. Smith, 'External Search Effort: An Investigation across Several Product Categories', *Journal of Consumer Research*, June 1987, pp. 83–95.

EXHIBIT 11.4

A Comparison of Information Sources

Source	Effort Required	Believability
Internal (stored experiences in memory)	Low	High
Personal (friends, relatives)	Low	High
Marketing (advertising)	Low	Low
Public (consumer magazine, other studies)	High	High
Experiential (examining or testing product)	High	High

HIGHLIGHT 11.1

Encouraging Information Contact for Magazine Subscriptions

I ncluding subscription cards in magazines is a useful marketing tactic because the cards are available while the magazine is being read and enjoyed. These cards make it convenient for readers of the magazine (the likely target market for future issues) to renew a subscription or start a new one.

Traditionally, magazine marketers have bound subscription cards to the magazines. One drawback to such 'bind-in' cards is that readers often simply ignore them. Because the cards are bound to the issue, readers leaf through the entire magazine without giving the card (or the idea of starting or renewing a subscription) any consideration.

An alternative method of including subscription cards in magazines is to place them between the pages, unbound. These are called 'blow-in' cards. When magazines are being read or carried, blow-in cards frequently fall out. Consumers usually pick up the cards and examine them for at least a moment. In other words, the probability of information contact is increased when blow-in rather than bind-in cards are used. It is not surprising, then, that blow-in cards are more effective than bind-in cards at generating subscription renewals.

behaviours. For example, media scheduling, message content and layout, colour and humour in advertising, and repetition all involve presenting stimuli to increase the probability that potential consumers will attend to relevant cues, as we also discussed in Chapter 5. In addition, *fear appeals* are used to bring about attentive behaviours and to vicariously stimulate emotions by exposing the observers to possible aversive consequences of certain conditions (inadequate insurance, faulty tyres and batteries, the absence of smoke alarms).

Strategies such as contests and prizes bring about attentive behaviour and promise rewards for engaging in certain actions that bring the consumer into closer contact with the product or point of purchase. Finally, ads that show models receiving positive reinforcement in the form of social approval and satisfaction for purchasing a product provide stimuli that can move the consumer closer to purchase by stimulating the 'buying mood'. Highlight 11.1 discusses a strategy for encouraging information contact for magazine subscriptions.

Funds Access

Current views of marketing emphasize exchange as the key concept for understanding the field. While time and effort costs are involved, money is the primary medium of consumer exchanges. The consumer must access this medium in one form or another before an exchange can occur, engaging in what is known as **funds access**. The primary marketing issues at this stage are (1) the methods used by consumers to pay for particular purchases and (2) the marketing strategies to increase the probability that consumers can access funds for purchase.

Consumers can pay for a product offering in a variety of ways. These include cash in pocket; bank withdrawal of cash; writing a cheque; using credit cards such as Visa, Eurocard, and American Express; opening a store charge account; using debit cards; and drawing on other lines of credit, such as bank loans. Another issue concerns the effort exerted by the consumer to obtain the actual funds that are spent or used to repay loans. Funds obtained from tax refunds, stock sales and dividends, gambling winnings, awards, or regular salaries may be valued differently by the consumer and spent in different ways. Some retailers encourage the purchase of big-ticket items by offering interest-free loans for a few months while consumers recover from the expenses incurred during their summer vacation or the Christmas period.

A variety of other strategies can increase the probability that consumers can access funds for purchases. For example, department stores like Innovation in Belgium or Magasin du Nord in Denmark may offer a small gift to anyone who fills out an application for the store's own credit card. The probability of purchasing at these stores is increased when a consumer has a credit card, because cash may not always be available. Other strategies include locating cash machines in shopping districts, instituting liberal credit terms, and accepting a variety of credit cards. Deferred payment plans and layaway plans that allow the consumer additional time to raise the required funds help stores avoid lost sales. Gift certificates are also used to presell merchandise and to provide some consumers with another source of funds that is restricted to particular purchases.

Store Contact

Although catalogue, telephone-order and Internet purchases are important, most consumer goods purchases are still made in retail stores. Thus, a major task of retailers is to get consumers into the store where purchase can occur. **Store contact** includes (1) locating the outlet, (2) travelling to the outlet, and (3) entering the outlet.

The nature of the consumers in their roles as shoppers affects the probability of store contact. Some consumers may enjoy shopping and spend many hours looking in stores. To others, shopping may be drudgery. Some shoppers may be primarily price oriented and favour particular low-price outlets. Others may seek a high level of service or unique products and stores that express their individuality. These differences are important dimensions of designing market segmentation strategies for stores.

Many strategies are designed to increase the probability of store contact. For example, consider the methods used to increase the probability that shoppers will be able to locate a particular outlet. Selecting central locations in local high-traffic areas has been successful for retailers selling quality clothing, travel, or cosmetics, whereas selecting out-of-town locations with ample parking space has been successful for retailers selling

---

HIGHLIGHT 11.2

Bang & Olufsen's Prime Site Concept

 ang & Olufsen is known among hi-fi enthusiasts for good technology and unusual design. In addition, the company promotes the systems concept, where TV, video, radio, CD and other home entertainment equipment is designed as a joint system with common access to, e.g. loudspeakers, and all parts can be centrally controlled by one common remote control. The remote control can even be used to switch on and off the lights in the house.

Bang & Olufsen has decided to emphasize store contact as a means for promoting the sales of its products. The company has developed the prime site concept, where shops carrying only Bang & Olufsen products are established in the best shopping districts of major European cities. In this way, many potential buyers become exposed to the product, and there is no interference from competing products within the store.

In order to further promote this strategy, the company has decided to cut down the number of common (multibrand) dealers by 25 per cent, or 700 dealers, and at the same time increase the number of B&O-only shops from 165 to 420 by the year 2000. In 1995–96, the B&O-only shops accounted for only 6 per cent of all sales outlets, but for 35 per cent of sales.

Source: Adapted from Jesper Olesen, 'B&O vil åbne 255 nye butikker',
Morgenavisen Jyllands-Posten, Erhverv & Økonomi, 22 March 1997, p. 2.

---

household goods, discount clothing, electrical appliances, and do-it-yourself housing supplies.

For retailers, it is a major advantage to locate in areas where there are many shops, such as local shopping districts or shopping malls. This increases consumers' ability to find the outlet and generates additional shopping traffic due to the presence of the other stores. *Yellow Pages*, newspaper, and other ads frequently include maps and information numbers to aid shoppers in locating an outlet.

Other tactics are used to get potential customers to the vicinity of stores, shopping districts, and malls. For example, carnivals in pedestrian streets or parking lots, free fashion shows or other entertainment, and visits by celebrities such as Santa Claus, the Easter Bunny, and Sesame Street characters are used to shape behaviour. In shopping centres, directories and information booths help shoppers find particular stores.

Finally, tactics are used to get the potential customer physically into the store. Frequently advertised sales, sale signs in store windows, loss leaders, sounds (such as popular music), and smells (such as freshly-baked pastry) are commonly employed. A variety of other in-store issues are discussed later in the text, particularly in Chapter 20. Highlight 11.2 shows an example where store contact is a central element in marketing strategy.

Product Contact

While a major concern of retailers is increasing and maintaining selective store patronage, manufacturers are primarily concerned with selective demand-purchase of their particular brands and models. Many of the methods employed to accomplish such **product contact** involve **push strategies** such as trade discounts, advertising subsidies, and other incentives to enhance the selling effort of retailers. For example, offering retailers a free case of Ariel liquid detergent for every 10 cases purchased can be a powerful incentive for retailers to feature liquid Ariel in newspaper ads, put it in prominent displays, and even sell it at a lower price while maintaining or increasing profit margins. Many approaches also involve **pull strategies**, such as sweepstakes, where consumers have to obtain entry forms when buying the product.

Once potential buyers are in the store, the type of behaviour necessary for a purchase to occur will depend on whether the store is primarily self-service or primarily sales-person service. In a self-service store, three behaviours are usually necessary for a purchase to occur: (1) locate the product or brand in the store, (2) physically obtain the product or brand, and (3) take the product or brand to the checkout.

Products must be easily located. Store directories, end-of-aisle and other displays, in-store signs, information booths, and helpful store personnel all encourage consumers to move into visual contact with products. While consumers are in the store, their visual contact with the many other available products increases the probability of purchase.

Physically coming into contact with a product provides an extremely important source of stimuli and possible consequences that influence whether a purchase will occur. Attractive, eye-catching packaging and other aspects of product appearance influence the stimuli attended to by the consumer. Trying the product in the store can also affect purchase probabilities.

The behaviour of sales personnel can also affect the contingencies at the point of purchase. Sales personnel can positively reinforce certain behaviours, extinguish or punish others, influence the stimuli attended to, and model appropriate product usage. Even negative reinforcement can be employed. For example, consider salespeople who are overly aggressive and use high-pressure tactics. One way for consumers to remove the aversive treatment is to purchase the product – and some consumers do this rather than walk away. Thus the consumer is negatively reinforced to purchase; and the probability of this response would probably be increased in similar situations in the future. However, the consumer may feel that the visit to the particular shop has been punished, and may therefore shop somewhere else in the future.

Salespeople can also change the contingencies for purchasing versus not purchasing. Consumers shopping for furniture often state their intention to 'go home and think it over'. Once the potential buyer leaves the store, the probability of a sale is reduced. Sales-people can offer a discount if the product is bought right away rather than some time in the future, or they can offer to deliver the furniture on a trial basis, so that the consumer can see whether it fits into the house – which usually tends to increase the likelihood of purchase.

A number of tactics are used to get potential buyers to the payment location. For example, payment counters are commonly placed next to the exit. Also, salespeople frequently escort the buyer to the payment counter.

Transaction

In a macro sense, *facilitating exchanges* is viewed as the primary objective of marketing. In a micro sense, this involves **transactions** in which consumers' funds are exchanged for products and services. Many marketing strategies involve removing obstacles to transactions. The credit methods discussed earlier are examples. So is the use of express checkout lanes and electronic scanners to decrease the time consumers must queue. (Some consumers will leave stores without making a purchase if checkout queues are too long.) Credit-card companies offer prompt purchase approvals to decrease the chances a sale will be missed because of a long wait. American Express, for example, spends $300 million to $400 million annually to ensure prompt service for its 15 million customers. From its Phoenix computer centre, the company approves 250 000 credit-card transactions a day from all over the world in an average of five seconds or less.[7]

Because the behaviour of store personnel has long been recognized as an important influence on purchase, personnel are often trained to be friendly and efficient. McDonald's personnel frequently offer prompts in an attempt to increase the total amount of purchase. Regardless of the food order, prompts for additional food are offered: 'Would you like some chips with that?' or 'How about a McDonald's doughnut?' Because these are very low-cost tactics, few incremental sales are required to make them profitable.

The positive reinforcers involved are critical elements in obtaining transactions. Tactics such as rebates, friendly treatment, and compliments by store personnel may increase the probability of purchase and repurchase. The reinforcing properties of the product or service itself are also important. These may involve both functional and psychosocial benefits.

Consumption

While **consumption** and use would seem to be very simple behaviours to delineate, they are not because of the vast differences in the natures of various products and services. For example, compare typical behaviours involved in the purchase of non-durables such as crisps and beer versus a durable such as a car. The crisps and beer are likely to be consumed rather quickly and the packaging disposed of. Certain strategies can increase the probability that consumption will be rather quick, such as seats in a restaurant that are comfortable for only a short time. As a result, current customers do not take up space for too long that could be used for new customers. Various marketing strategies may be used to encourage proper disposal of packaging, such as provision of recycle containers in central locations.[8]

A car purchase usually involves several years of consumption or use. In addition, periodic service is required, and additional complementary products such as petrol must be purchased. Finally, a car may be disposed of in several ways (selling it, junking it, or trading it in for another model).

Many products are not consumed as such, but serve as input to a home production process. Most food items are not eaten as they are, but serve as ingredients in preparing meals. Home and building supplies are used in redecorating houses. Gardening supplies and equipment are used to create a beautiful and relaxing setting for the house. Cosmetics are used to create beauty and well-being.

The use to which the product is put will have considerable influence on how the purchase of the product is reinforced. A steak of good quality, when kept too long over the fire, will not taste good, resulting in consumers feeling punished and decreasing the probability of repeat purchase. Therefore marketers have an interest in that products are used in the best possible way, and may use various tactics, including the modelling approaches described in the last chapter, to assure this.

Communication

A final set of behaviours that marketers attempt to increase involves **communication**. Marketers want consumers to communicate with two basic audiences. They want consumers to (1) provide the company with marketing information and (2) tell other potential consumers about the product and encourage them to purchase it. Consumers can communicate with the company or other consumers about products, brands, or stores at any time, not just at the end of the purchase sequence. We place this behaviour here because consumers who have purchased and used a product are likely to be more knowledgeable about it and more influential in telling other consumers about it.

From Consumers to Marketers

Marketers typically want at least three types of information from consumers. First, they want *information about the consumer* to investigate the quality of their marketing strategy and the success of market segmentation. Warranty cards are commonly used for this. These cards often ask about consumer demographics, what magazines consumers read, where they obtained information about the product, where they purchased it, and what competing brands they own or have tried. Subtle threats that the warranty will be cancelled if the card is not filled out and returned promptly are sometimes employed to encourage this behaviour.

A second type of information sought from consumers is the *names of other potential buyers* of the product. Some firms and organizations offer awards if the names of several potential buyers are given, and a larger award if any of the prospects actually makes a purchase. Finally, marketers seek information about consumers' satisfaction with the product, especially *causes of complaint*.[9] Telephone hotlines, where consumers can phone when they have problems or want to complain, can be employed for this.

From Consumers to Consumers

Marketers also want consumers to tell their friends and others about the product. A product that is effective and performs well may encourage this behaviour. However, other tactics can also encourage it. Tupperware parties have long been used to take advantage of the fact that consumers respond favourably to information from their friends and to create an environment in which purchase is heavily encouraged. This approach has been so successful that, over the first 25 years of its existence, Tupperware doubled its sales and earnings every five years.

Newly opened bars and restaurants frequently offer customers free drinks or starters to encourage them not only to return, but also to tell others about the place and to bring their friends. Word-of-mouth communication is the primary way such establishments become popular. A German mail-order house for tea and coffee credits DM5 to any customer who gets a friend to ask for their catalogue. Such tactics increase not only communication, but also other behaviours in the purchase sequence. Finally, consumers often learn purchase and use behaviours through vicarious learning processes.

Measuring Behaviours

The preceding part of this chapter outlined a common behaviour sequence for retail purchases. A number of examples of current marketing strategies were categorized according to the factors in this model. In order to make models like this usable in devising, implementing, and controlling marketing strategies, it is necessary to measure the frequency of the various behaviours. This is what we deal with in the present section.

There are many ways to measure various consumer behaviours; Exhibit 11.5 provides some examples. These measurement methods are commonly employed in

EXHIBIT 11.5

Examples of Methods Used to Measure Consumption Behaviours

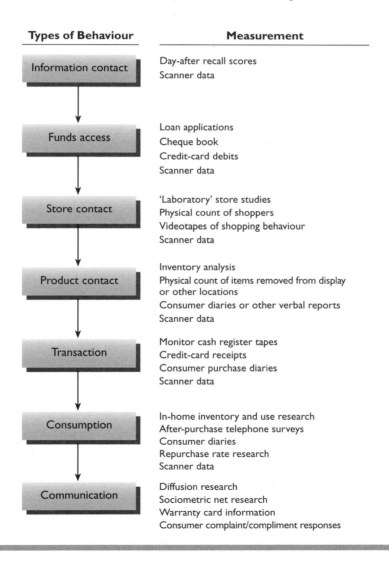

Types of Behaviour	Measurement
Information contact	Day-after recall scores Scanner data
Funds access	Loan applications Cheque book Credit-card debits Scanner data
Store contact	'Laboratory' store studies Physical count of shoppers Videotapes of shopping behaviour Scanner data
Product contact	Inventory analysis Physical count of items removed from display or other locations Consumer diaries or other verbal reports Scanner data
Transaction	Monitor cash register tapes Credit-card receipts Consumer purchase diaries Scanner data
Consumption	In-home inventory and use research After-purchase telephone surveys Consumer diaries Repurchase rate research Scanner data
Communication	Diffusion research Sociometric net research Warranty card information Consumer complaint/compliment responses

current marketing research, although they are not always used sequentially to assess every behaviour stage.

Scanner data obtained from store cashiers in supermarkets and other shops is becoming a popular method to monitor elements of the purchase sequence.[10] Scanner data can also be combined with household-related data; a method that is getting increasingly popular in many countries. Consumers are recruited into panels. Panel members provide information about the size of their families, their income, their marital status, ownership of appliances, what types of newspapers and magazines they read, who does most of the shopping, etc. Cognitive/affective variables like brand preferences, brand awareness, life style elements, and so on, may also be measured. Panel members receive machine-readable identification cards that they present to the cashier when they pay for products. The household-related data can then be combined with data on the products actually purchased.

A number of behaviours in the purchase sequence can be monitored and influenced using scanner methods. For example, information contact can be influenced because media habits of households are monitored, and commercials can be changed until contact occurs. Funds access can be monitored on the cash register tape by recording prices and the method of payment. Because every purchase in the store is recorded, store contact, product contact, and transaction information are available, as well as the dates and times of these behaviours. As such, the effectiveness of various sales promotions and other marketing strategies on specific consumer behaviours can be determined. Successful promotions can be offered again to encourage store and brand loyalty. Since the time between purchases can be determined, information is also available on consumption and usage rates.

Overall, our discussion is intended to demonstrate that consumer behaviours can be measured quite well using current technology. However, as with any element of marketing strategy, the costs and benefits of extended research on consumer behaviours must be carefully analysed. While there are substantial benefits, many firms have to use less costly methods. Even simpler, less expensive methods – such as analysis of advertising expenditures and shipping orders in various markets – may provide useful information about consumer behaviour.

Influencing Consumer Behaviour

When a model of a sequence of consumer behaviours has been established and measured, it becomes possible to specify, implement, and control strategies for influencing these behaviours. In so doing, we can now draw on insights from both the cognitive/affective and the behavioural approach to analysing consumer behaviour.

Consumer-Behaviour Influence Strategies

Exhibit 11.6 presents a strategic model of how marketers can attempt to influence overt consumer behaviours. First, marketers can obtain information on consumers' affect, cognition, and behaviour relative to the product, service, shop, brand or model of concern. Based on this information and managerial judgement, various marketing mix stimuli can be designed or changed and implemented by placing them in the environment. These stimuli include such things as products, brand marks, packaging, advertisements and commercials, price tags, coupons, shop signs and logos, and many

EXHIBIT 11.6

A General Model of Approaches to Influencing Overt Consumer Behaviour

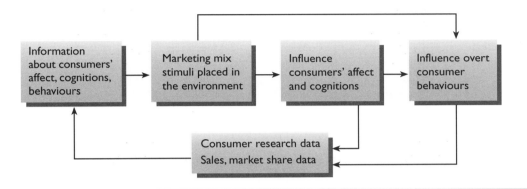

others. These stimuli are designed to influence consumers in one or more ways. Often they are designed to influence consumers' affect and cognition in positive ways to increase the changes of overt behaviour. In other cases, they are designed to influence behaviour directly without an analysis of affective and cognitive responses. Measuring changes in consumers' affect, cognition and behaviours results in feedback in the form of consumer research data, as well as sales and market share information. These help marketers evaluate the success of the strategy and provide new input into the strategy development process. Based on this information, the process continues as marketing mix stimuli are reworked to further influence consumers.

Exhibit 11.7 presents four strategies designed to influence overt consumer behaviour. For affective strategies, marketing mix elements are designed to influence consumers' affective responses in order to influence overt consumer behaviour. For example, for many years Michelin tyre ads have featured a cute baby sitting in a floating tyre to generate warm feelings and attention to the importance of safe tyres when driving with children.

In the second, marketing mix elements are designed to influence consumers' cognitions in order to influence consumer behaviours. Fashion mail-order catalogues include extensive product information to help consumers decide whether particular garments are right for them.

In the third, marketing mix elements are designed to influence consumers' overt behaviours directly. This does not mean that consumers do not think about or feel anything when they experience antecedents or consequences of their behaviours. However, it does suggest that in some cases, information processing is rather automatic and that little conscious information processing is going on. Many consumer behaviours are habitual and involve little decision making. Many marketing strategies are designed to influence these behaviours without a complete analysis of affect and cognitions, such as coupons and other sales promotion tactics. We can analyse these by employing tools from the behavioural approach.

EXHIBIT 11.7

Strategies Designed to Influence Overt Consumer Behaviours

Type of Strategy	Description of Strategy	Strategic Focus	Sample Strategies	Ultimate Objective of Strategy
Affective	Strategies designed to influence consumers' affective responses	Consumers' emotions, moods, feelings, evaluations	Classically conditioning emotions to products	Influence overt consumer behaviour
Cognitive	Strategies designed to influence consumers' cognitive responses	Consumers' knowledge, meanings, beliefs	Providing information highlighting competitive advantages	Influence overt consumer behaviour
Behavioural	Strategies designed to influence consumers' behavioural responses	Consumers' overt behaviours	Positive reinforcement; modelling desired behaviours	Influence overt consumer behaviour
Combined	Strategies designed to influence multiple consumer responses	More than one of the above	Information about product benefits with emotional tie-ins and rebates	Influence overt consumer behaviour

Finally, as is common in practice, various marketing mix stimuli are used to influence some combination of consumers' affect, cognition, and behaviours in order to influence other consumer behaviours. For example, a Fætter BR ad featured a colour picture of a Little Tikes Playhouse with two cute kids enjoying it, a product description, age around 1.5 to 4, 'assembly required', and a sale price of DKR609. This ad was trying to influence affect from the cute kids enjoying the playhouse, cognition in terms of product and price information, and the behaviours of store contact, product contact, transaction, and consumption.

In sum, marketing strategies are designed ultimately to influence consumer behaviour. These strategies should be designed with a precise understanding of the behaviours they are designed to influence, as well as whether affect and cognition are also to be influenced in important ways.

We can break down the process of influencing consumer behaviour into several elements: identifying the behaviour to be influenced, analysing factors affecting the behaviour, and developing and applying a behaviour change strategy.

Identifying Behaviour to be Influenced

Each behaviour in the purchase/consumption sequence is dependent on many factors. In some cases – such as the promotion of a clearly superior product – information contact may be sufficient to drive the entire behaviour chain and result in the successful performance of all of the required behaviours. Even a simple comment about a product by a trusted friend may result in all the required behaviours. In many cases, however, initial consumer behaviours are performed with sufficient frequency and quality to lead to other behaviours – but the other behaviours do not occur. For example, consumers may go to retail stores where the product is carried and may even come into visual contact with the product, but not purchase it. In other cases, information contact may not occur, and thus no additional behaviours are performed. A sound way of determining the behaviour to be influenced is therefore to find the earliest behaviour in the sequence that is not being performed – or is not being performed appropriately or frequently enough to lead to the next behaviour. For example, consumer research could indicate the following:

1. Information contact – 90 per cent of the target market has been exposed to two commercials per week in their homes for the past month. Unaided recall scores are 40 per cent; 30 per cent indicate they like the features of our product.
2. Funds access – 87 per cent of the target market purchases a competitive brand at the same price as ours; 67 per cent pay with credit cards.
3. Store contact – 96 per cent of the target market shops at least once per week in stores in which our brand is carried; 40 per cent come into the physical vicinity of our product once per week.
4. Product contact – 30 per cent of the target market comes into visual contact with our product; 14 per cent pick up the product and inspect it; 2 per cent take our product with them.
5. Transaction – slightly less than 2 per cent pay for our product; a few replace it on the shelf.
6. Consumption – most purchasers use the product for the first time within two weeks of purchase.
7. Communication – no indication of significant communication with other consumers; 60 per cent of warranty cards are returned in three weeks.

Which behaviour should be the target in this example? It appears that consumers' information contact, funds access, and store contact are all exceptionally good. Even some phases of product contact are good, but few consumers actually take the product with them. Thus, we might conclude the behaviour to be influenced is product contact. Potential ways to deal with the problem behaviour are discussed next.

Analysing Factors Affecting the Behaviour

Once the behaviour to be influenced is identified, possible factors affecting the behaviour must be identified. From a behavioural perspective, we say that the contingencies or relationships between the behaviour and the environment must be analysed. Among

EXHIBIT 11.8

Primary Relationships between Consumer Behaviours and Marketing Mix Elements

Consumer Behaviours	Elements			
	Product	Price	Promotion	Place
Information contact			X	
Funds access		X		
Store contact				X
Product contact	X			X
Transaction	X	X	X	X
Consumption	X			
Communication	X	X	X	X

the major contingencies are the efforts of competition and their success in maintaining or changing consumer behaviour. Many successful firms attempt to interfere with new-product test marketing (or other marketing efforts) of their competitors to avoid losing market share and to confound competitors' research results. Other contingencies that require analysis are the target market and the marketing mix elements, particularly those elements most closely related to the problem behaviour. Exhibit 11.8 suggests the major marketing mix elements associated with particular consumer behaviours. While each element requires analysis, Exhibit 11.8 suggests useful starting points.

While some behaviour modifiers may focus only on behaviour–environment interactions, the assessment of affective and cognitive variables is equally important and gives valuable information. For example, many new products fail because consumers do not perceive a difference in the new product. Thus, research on consumer perceptions and attitudes can be very useful for investigating the problem and analysing contingencies.

Returning to the example in which product contact is the problem, analysis of the contingencies might begin with a comparison of our product and package with those of successful competitors. We could interview consumers to investigate their perceptions of and attitudes towards our product. We might directly investigate other contingencies such as competitive differences in packaging, labelling, instructions for use, colours, and price markings.

Developing and Applying Behaviour Change Strategy

Once the behaviour to be influenced is delineated and the contingencies surrounding it have been analysed, a **behaviour change strategy** is developed and applied. Such strategies can be classified into the general behaviour influence strategies shown in Exhibit 11.7.

Returning to our example, suppose the analysis reveals an important difference between our product and those of successful competitors. Their packaging gives

Den lille detalje...

- kan gøre
den store forskel

Du skal have reflekser på bilen og på cyklen. Ifølge loven. Men dit barn behøver ikke selv at have reflekser på. LEGO® Kids Wear gør noget ved dette og har 3M reflekser på alt det nye overtøj, som du kan finde i vores butik.

® LEGO er et registreret varemærke

LEGO
KIDS WEAR
APPROVED BY CHILDREN

Shop logo

Lego Kids Wear borrowed the positive brand equity associated with Lego toys in promoting their line of children's clothing. Courtesy: KA-BOO-KI A/S.

Bare fordi din mor ka' li' det kan det godt drikkes

Bergsø 4

Foreningen af Danske Kaffeimportører minder om, at kaffe nydes sort, stærk og varm som bare...

Kaffe. Råt og usødet

This ad tries to change the subjective norm component of behavioural intention formation based on the finding that some young people may not want to drink coffee because their mothers like coffee.
Courtesy: Dansk Kaffeinformation and Bergsø 4.

DER MITSUBISHI SPACE RUNNER

Wenn Ihre Garage zu klein für sieben verschiedene Autos ist, empfiehlt Mitsubishi den hier:

als **Kinderwagen** läßt er den hier aufrecht mitfahren

Fahrer- und Beifahrer-Airbag

als **Sportwagen** können bei entfernter Rückbank 2 davon mitfahren

als **Geschäftswagen** ist er komfortabel und variabel

als **Familienauto** hat er Platz für 5

Abb.: Space Runner Colours

Space Runner modellabhängig auch mit Schiebedach oder Klimaanlage

keine **Limousine** ohne Servolenkung

als **Einkaufswagen** hat er eine große Ladeklappe und die Schiebetür

als **Reisebus** faßt er viel Gepäck

3 Jahre Garantie bis 100.000 km

Space Runner schon ab DM 31.590,–*

Der Space Runner. Das mobile Multitalent.

0% Anzahlung, ab 1,99% effektiver Jahreszins für alle Modelle. Ein Angebot der MKG Kreditbank GmbH.

*Unverbindliche Preisempfehlung der MMC Auto Deutschland GmbH, 65468 Trebur, ab Importlager zzgl. Überführungskosten.
Mehr von Mitsubishi: http://www.mitsubishi-motors.de

MITSUBISHI MOTORS

This ad attempts to create a positive attitude to the product by forming beliefs about product attributes and consequences.
Courtesy: MMC Auto Deutschland GmbH and Asatsu Deutschland GmbH.

" 'Do you know,' I said, 'you can spend 4 years of your life washing up?'

'No wonder it feels like we never see each other', he shouted from the kitchen.

Then, I gave him the good news about our new Candy dishwasher.

'It's got a High Performance **System** that doubles the water pressure inside to shift all those really stubborn leftovers. And a self cleaning filter that traps all the bits as they go round.'

(I thought he'd appreciate the last point as he fished a piece of soggy onion from the plug hole.)

'Apparently', I went on, 'the water's injected straight into the system, so we get a quieter, better wash. Especially if we use those Finish tablets they recommend.'

'And the best thing is, it arrives tomorrow.'

'You don't waste much time', he said, hanging his rubber gloves over the sink to dry. 'Darling', I replied, 'that's the whole idea.'

I've chosen. It's Candy."

CANDY RECOMMEND FINISH

Candy Domestic Appliances Ltd, New Chester Road, Bromborough, Wirral, Merseyside L62 3PE. Tel: 0151 334 2781. Quote dept XXXXX.

This ad links choice criteria for buying a dishwasher to consumers' goals and values.
Courtesy: Candy Domestic Appliances Ltd.

detailed assembly and use instructions, whereas our package instructions are rather sketchy. We might decide to improve the instructions and also to add pictures of models appropriately assembling and using the product. We could also include a toll-free number consumers can call for additional information or help. This is an example of a combined strategy, that contains elements of providing information, highlighting advantages, and making use of modelling to further learning.

Measuring Behaviour Change

After implementing the strategy, the target behaviour must be measured to determine whether the problem has been solved. If the behaviour has not changed sufficiently, we must reanalyse the contingencies and develop a new strategy.

How much behaviour has to change for the strategy to be successful depends on the marketing objectives, the particular behaviour, and the situation. For example, if after implementing the strategy, only 3 per cent (instead of 2 per cent) of those who inspect the product actually purchase it, this would probably not be considered a successful strategy – and may not even cover the cost of the toll-free number.

If the majority of those who inspect the product now purchase it, however, we might conclude we have successfully solved the behaviour problem. In some cases, a very small amount of behaviour change may be sufficient for a strategy to be successful. For example, Procter & Gamble increased its market share for Crest toothpaste from 35 per cent to 41 per cent by updating the formula, adding a gel version, and sharply increasing advertising and promotion. While a change in toothpaste market share of 6 per cent may not sound impressive, it translated into additional sales of $42 million!

Maintaining Behaviour

Up to this point, our main focus has been on developing behaviour. If the new strategy is successful in developing a sufficient amount of behaviour, we must consider methods of maintaining that behaviour. Because much consumer behaviour is habitual, maintaining behaviour is usually much easier and less expensive than developing it. In fact, one of the major reasons new-product introductions are so expensive is the promotional cost of developing initial purchase behaviour.

Often when positive reinforcers are used, their frequency and amount can be decreased without a loss in behaviour performance. If continuous schedules of reinforcement were initially employed, it may be possible to switch to ratio schedules and still maintain behaviour.

Different organizations may be primarily concerned with maintaining different behaviours in the purchase-consumption chain. Credit-card companies want to maintain card usage or loyalty across a variety of purchase situations; retailers want to maintain store contact or store loyalty; manufacturers want to maintain product contact or brand loyalty. From a behaviour viewpoint, these actions are controlled by contingencies in the environment, and loyalty is the degree to which the behaviours are repeated.

Many scholars are critical of viewing loyalty as repeat behaviour. They argue that repeating a behaviour can be due to vastly different reasons. It can be due to a firm belief that the product is superior and the best product to fulfil personal needs. But repeat behaviour can also be due to some kind of inertia, where a consumer keeps on buying a product because of laziness, because involvement is low and continuing to buy the same product is the easiest way to make a choice. In the first case the consumer can be expected to be very loyal in the future, in the second case external circumstances – like the introduction of a new brand – could easily disrupt the sequence of repeat behaviours.[11] By combining the analysis of behaviours with an analysis of the cognitive/affective antecedents of the behaviour, we would be able to distinguish these cases.

In addition to changing and then maintaining the behaviour that was formerly a problem, we must also investigate whether the remaining behaviours are now being performed appropriately and frequently enough to achieve our objectives. If not, we identify the new problem behaviour that is blocking the behaviour chain – the next one in the sequence that is not being performed appropriately.

Back to . . . Shopping at Jack & Jones

This case discusses a simple shopping trip and mentions a variety of behaviours. Although the story does not detail every behaviour, such as the ones necessary to get to the central shopping district, there is sufficient information to understand what occurred. Let's examine Peter's and Susan's actions in terms of the types of behaviours discussed in the chapter and evaluate the value of the behavioural sequence model.

Event	Type of Behaviour
Susan goes to tobacco shop	Store contact
Susan enters tobacco shop	Store contact
Susan locates magazines and picks two	Product contact
Susan asks for cigarettes	Product contact
Susan takes bank note from wallet	Funds access
Susan exchanges money for products	Transaction
Peter suggests going to J&J store	Communication
Susan and Peter go to and enter J&J store	Store contact
Peter locates and tries on sweaters	Product contact
Susan tries on trousers	Product contact
Peter and Susan discuss trousers	Communication
Peter takes out Access card	Funds access
Peter and Susan discuss sweaters	Communication
Peter exchanges funds for products	Transaction
Peter and Susan take products home	Transaction

From this brief description we get a good idea of what behaviours were performed and consider some marketing strategies to increase desired behaviours. For example, Susan almost did not buy the trousers because she did not like the way they looked on her. Thus, the behavioural sequence model helps explain behaviours, isolate them into manageable parts, and allow the analysis of tactics and strategies to increase desired behaviours.

A second point discussed in the chapter is also illustrated in this case. Consumer behaviours do not always follow the exact sequence laid out in Exhibit 11.2. For example, communication can occur at any stage in the process. Also, more than one product is often purchased on a single shopping trip, which can lead to differences from the exact sequence laid out in Exhibit 11.2. However, the general model, the categories of behaviour listed, and the level of analysis seem useful for understanding the behaviours.

A third point concerns the limitations of the behaviour approach for understanding consumer behaviour and developing marketing strategies. For one thing, the analysis has not considered what Peter and Susan were thinking and feeling during this shopping episode. For example, we certainly know more about Peter from the descriptions of what he remembered, what he decided, his reluctance to purchase, his feeling that he deserved the other sweater, and that he felt good about the purchases. In addition, a more detailed description of the major environmental stimuli would allow a deeper understanding of the shopping episode. Thus, while studying overt behaviour can provide valuable insights for designing effective marketing strategies, it is also necessary to study consumers' cognitions and affect as well as environmental factors.

Summary

This chapter developed a model (Exhibit 11.2) which outlines the purchase process as a sequence of behaviours that included information contact, funds access, store contact, product contact, transaction, consumption, and communication. We then discussed measuring such a sequence of behaviours, and how the data obtained can be made the point of departure for the development of strategies for influencing behaviour. While the chapter emphasized relationships between behaviour and the environment, a number of attempts were made to demonstrate that the analysis of cognitive and affective variables and the behavioural approach are useful supplements in trying to influence overt consumer behaviour.

Key Terms and Concepts

behaviour change strategy   **238**
communication   **232**
consumption   **231**
funds access   **228**
information contact   **225**
product contact   **230**
pull strategies   **230**
push strategies   **230**
scanner data   **234**
store contact   **228**
transactions   **230**

Review and Discussion Questions

1. Describe the differences between cognitive models of the adoption/purchase process and the behaviour sequence presented in Exhibit 11.2.
2. What advantages and disadvantages do you see in the use of the behaviour sequence model for marketing researchers and for marketing managers?
3. Use the behaviour sequence model to describe recent purchases of a product and of a service.

4. Consider the challenges presented by the information search stage of the behaviour sequence for each of the following: (*a*) a leading brand, (*b*) a new brand, and (*c*) an existing low-share brand.

5. Give some examples of marketing strategies aimed at addressing the funds access problems of university students.

6. Visit several local supermarkets and note evidence you observe of push and pull strategies used to increase product contact for grocery items.

7. List at least three examples of situations in which marketing efforts have been instrumental in changing your consumption or disposal behaviour for products you have purchased.

8. Assume the role of a marketing manager for each of the purchases you described in response to Question 3. Which behaviours would you want to change? Suggest behaviour change strategies you might recommend.

Additional Reading

For further discussion of the search component of information contact, see:

Merrie Brucks, 'Search Monitor: An Approach for Computer-Controlled Experiments Involving Consumer Information Search', *Journal of Consumer Research*, June 1988, pp. 117–121.

Hans-Georg Gemünden, 'Perceived Risk and Information Search. A Systematic Meta-Analysis of the Empirical Evidence', *International Journal of Research in Marketing*, 3, no. 2, 1985, pp. 79–100.

Julie L. Ozanne, Merrie Brucks, and Dhruv Grewal, 'A Study of Information Search Behaviour during the Categorization of New Products', *Journal of Consumer Research*, March 1992, pp. 452–463.

Fred Selnes and Sigurd V. Trøye 'Buying Expertise, Information Search, and Problem Solving', *Journal of Economic Psychology*, no. 3, 1989, pp. 411–428.

Joel E. Urbany, Peter R. Dickson and William L. Wilkie, 'Buyer Uncertainty and Information Search', *Journal of Consumer Research*, September 1989, pp. 208–215.

For a discussion of the importance of communication after the purchase, see:

Dick A. Francken, 'Postpurchase consumer evaluations, complaint actions and repurchase behaviour', *Journal of Economic Psychology*, 1983, pp. 273–290.

For further discussion of a behaviour approach to analysing consumer behaviour, see:

Gordon Foxall, *Consumer Psychology in Behavioural Perspective* (London: Routledge, 1990).

MARKETING STRATEGY IN ACTION
Bras Direct

Buying women's lingerie is a delicate matter. It is an intimate product, it is a product with enormous differentiation, and with high symbolic value. And it is bought by both sexes. Women, when buying lingerie for themselves, may want to do so in quiet surroundings and without being disturbed by men. But men are also frequent buyers. They buy women's lingerie as gifts for wives, girlfriends, and lovers. In a way they buy gifts for themselves as well. But it has also been observed that men are hesitant to enter lingerie shops, which they regard as an essentially female domain in which they feel insecure.

UK-based Bras Direct is a company selling women's lingerie on the Internet. They offer bras, bodies, briefs, and other items of lingerie from twelve major European brands. Each item is presented by a picture, which is expandable by clicking on it, and by a verbal description. Shopping can be assisted by a 'virtual shopping assistant', who will make a suggestion of suitable items based on customer specifications. The suggestions are based on the type of product desired (bras, bodies, briefs, suspenders, etc.), on usage occasion, and on price sensitivity. Choices in terms of price sensitivity include best price, value for money, just got paid, and money no object. Usage occasions include everyday, sportive use, special occasion, and naughty nights.

In order to make shopping easier, a measuring guide to finding the right size is included. Items can be added to a shopping basket by mouse-clicking, indicating size and colour wanted. The order has to be finalized by confirming the shopping basket, giving details of delivery address and credit-card payment, and specifying special wishes in terms of packaging, for example, gold-foil wrapping. Orders sent are confirmed by e-mail. The first order over £50 qualifies for membership in a Bras Direct Loyalty Club, which gives 20 per cent rebate on future orders. Items may be returned for refunds or exchange after trying on.

How is the Bras Direct web site handling Internet users who are just browsing for nice pictures? Actually, it is encouraging this kind of contact with potential customers. It has pictures of both male and female models that can be downloaded as Windows wallpaper, and a selection of pictures of its products which can be downloaded as a screen saver. It even has a contest where users can vote for their favourite model among those displaying Bras Direct products on the web site.

This seems to lead to a lot of browsing. Of 90 000 casual visitors in the first two weeks of operation on the Internet, only 12 actually bought items.

Discussion Questions

1. Develop and describe a sequence of behaviours characterizing the Internet shopper for Bras Direct. How does this sequence differ from a retail purchase of a lingerie product?
2. Which behaviours do you believe to be critical for the success of the company?
3. What are some marketing tactics Bras Direct could use to increase the probability of the behaviours you have identified as critical?

Source: http://www.brasdirect.co.uk

Introduction to the Environment

Shopping with Small Children

Marketing to young children is big business in the 1990s. The children of the baby boomers of the sixties are now having children of their own which has led to a surge in the sales of children's clothes. In the United Kingdom in the first half of the 1990s, children's wear spending grew by 5 per cent, and in the second half, growth is likely to be about 8 per cent. Children's wear is subsequently the only area of the clothing industry predicted to show substantial growth over the next five years.

The growing market in the children's wear industry has, however, attracted a lot of new players, which has brought along sharpened competition and intensified the struggle for market shares. One of the parameters used to attract customers is in-store facilities.

The dominant UK children's wear chain, Mothercare, was one of the first to design its stores with both children's and parents' interests in mind. Baby changing rooms comply with the needs that parents of new-born babies have. The Mummy's Room is decorated like a nursery and offers feeding facilities to prepare the baby's bottle, as well as comfortable surroundings where the mother can breast-feed undisturbed. Men are not allowed in the Mummy's Room, but a Parent Room offers similar facilities in order that fathers also may change and feed their babies. In every shop, toilet facilities are found both for the grown-up and the child with a normal-sized toilet next to a miniature children's toilet. Furthermore, spacious lifts combined with wide aisles and lots of space between the racks enable parents to get around with their prams.

Marion is a heavy user of the facilities at Mothercare as it allows her to continue her extensive recreational shopping activities. When she and her husband go shopping, they typically arrange it in such a way that he takes care of the shopping which he can deal with alone while she breast-feeds the baby. She does realize, though, that she is not the only one who benefits from this, because once she is in the shop she often gets tempted by a cute baby dress which she absolutely must buy.

Knowing how disturbing a factor a bored child can be in a shopping situation, the children's wear retailers also make an effort to create an enjoyable in-store environment for children. Thus, Mothercare shops have 'fun' elements, including talking trees and singing clocks or sounding automatic cars in which children can take a ride for 30p. Also, the store decoration is targeted to children with different themes like, for example, Hans & Gretchen and Noah's Ark covering the walls.

From customer research, Adams, another British retailer of children's clothing, found that children didn't like shopping and even less to try on clothes. To overcome this obstacle, Adams created a fitting room, which looked like a playroom with toys and games, and kites dangling from the ceiling. Furthermore, a schoolroom theme for the stores was designed. The design included wooden floors and red doors, blackboards and desks, and fittings at child height. Traditional toys and games such as snakes and ladders, skipping ropes and hopscotch are also featured.

As Sally, mother of six year-old Thomas, sighed: 'It can be quite a nightmare to go shopping with my son, so I am really grateful when the shops succeed in catching his attention by means of toys or imaginative store decoration. I even have it in mind when I decide on where to shop.'

Sources: 'Chainstores lead clothing race', *Marketing Week*, 3 May 3 1996. 'Neil Buckley describes how concept retailing is used to increase sales and motivate staff', *Financial Times*, 15 September 1995.

This example describes some aspects of the physical and social environment that can influence people's behaviours, cognitions, and affective responses. In this chapter, we provide an overview of these environmental influences. Our goal is to present a framework for thinking about environmental influences on consumers that is useful for creating effective marketing strategies.

We begin by discussing several ways of thinking about the environment. Next we identify three environments – the social, physical, and marketing environments – and we review the key dimensions of each. Then we discuss the related concept of situations and show how marketers can analyse environmental factors in terms of situations. We conclude the chapter by discussing five marketing-related situations – information acquisition, shopping, purchasing, consumption, and disposition situations.

The Environment

The **environment** refers to all the physical and social characteristics of a consumer's external world, including physical objects (products and stores), spatial relationships (location of stores and products in stores), and the social behaviour of other people (who is around and what they are doing). As part of the Wheel of Consumer Analysis (see Exhibit 2.4), the environment can influence consumers' affective and cognitive responses and their behaviour. For instance, consumers' cognitive and affective systems respond to a new shopping environment by interpreting features of this environment and deciding what behaviours to perform to accomplish shopping goals.

Marketers are especially interested in the interpreted environment, sometimes called the *functional* (or *perceived*) *environment*, because this is what influences consumers' actions.[1] Because each consumer has a unique set of knowledge, meanings, and beliefs, the perceived or functional environment for each consumer will be somewhat different. However, marketers are seldom interested in the idiosyncratic perceptions of individual consumers; they need to understand the interpretations of the environment shared by groups of consumers. Marketers therefore attempt to identify target market segments of consumers who share common cultural backgrounds and have similar interpretations. In Europe, cultural differences among nations result in the fact that the way in which shopping environments and other consumption-related stimuli are interpreted often differs considerably between countries.[2] As a result, the various European countries are often treated as segments in cross-national marketing. However, at least in some areas,

HIGHLIGHT 12.1

Taking Refuge Under the Sun

The Costa del Sol in southern Spain has become a refuge for elderly people from northern Europe. A considerable number of people collect their savings after retirement, buy a house in Spain, and move south. They are attracted mainly by the climate – 325 days of sun per year contrast very favourably with the weather at home, and the dry and warm climate is good for a number of age-related diseases such as rheumatism. People who were earlier sent to southern Spain for treatment, found how well they were in the warm climate, and decide to move there permanently.

There are also other attractions. The cost of living is lower than in northern Europe, which makes the pension and savings go further. There are lots of things to do. Many people play golf or engage in various kinds of arts. And the various nationalities have gathered in certain areas where they can live according to their own cultural norms, without having to adapt to the host country's culture or even learn its language. The Costa del Sol is far enough south for the climate to be warm, without being so far south that cultural differences become so considerable that adaptation is required.

Various types of company have specialized in filling these people's needs. This goes for real estate agents, airlines, and travel agents. Real estate agents advertise in these people's home countries, and then offer charter tours to check out the premises. Airlines and travel agents care for the need to combine low-cost fares with flexibility and long-term ticketing.

Only a few people actually relinquish their citizenship and become Spaniards. Most even continue to pay taxes at home, because they have more trust in the social security system at home than in the Spanish one, should the need to use it arise.

Source: Based on material supplied by Don Quijote Rejser, Copenhagen.

there are signs that pan-European segments are developing, and this opens up new possibilities for international consumer marketing.[3]

The environment can be analysed at two levels – macro and micro. Marketers need to determine which level of environmental analysis is relevant for a marketing problem and design their research and marketing strategies accordingly. The *macro environment* includes large-scale, general environmental factors such as the climate, economic conditions, political system, and general landscape (seashore, mountains, farmland). These macro environmental factors have a general influence on behaviour, as when the state of the economy influences aggregate purchases of homes, cars, and shares. Highlight 12.1 gives a specific example of how the macro environment affects consumer behaviour.

The *micro environment* refers to the more tangible physical and social aspects of someone's immediate surroundings – the dirty floor in a store, a talkative salesperson, the hot weather today, or the people in your family or household. Such small-scale factors can have a direct influence on consumers' specific behaviours and affective and cognitive responses. For instance, people tend not to linger in dirty, crowded stores; consumers may be unwilling to go shopping during a heatwave unless there is evening shopping; you get frustrated and angry in a slow-moving checkout queue when you want to get home to prepare dinner.[4]

Aspects of the Environment

As noted in Chapter 2, the environment has two aspects or dimensions – the social and physical. Through their marketing programmes (building a new store), managers have direct control over certain aspects of the social and physical environments, but marketers have little or no control over large parts of them. Both the controllable and uncontrollable aspects of the social and physical environment can influence consumers' overt behaviours as well as their affective and cognitive responses.

The Social Environment

Broadly defined, the social environment includes all social interactions between and among people. Consumers can interact with other people either directly (you might discuss sports equipment or clothes with a friend, talk to a salesperson) or vicariously (you watch your father negotiate a car price, observe the clothing other people are wearing). People can learn from both types of social interactions, direct and vicarious.

It is useful to distinguish between macro and micro levels of the social environment. The **macro social environment** refers to the indirect and vicarious social interactions among very large groups of people. Researchers have studied three macro social environments – culture, subculture, and social class – that have broad and powerful influences on the values, beliefs, attitudes, emotions, and behaviours of individual consumers in those groups. For instance, a marketer might find that consumers in different subcultures or social classes have quite different means–end chains concerning a product, which indicates they are likely to respond differently to marketing strategies. Such differences make macro social environments useful for market segmentation.

The **micro social environment** includes face-to-face social interactions among smaller groups of people such as families and reference groups. These direct social interactions can have strong influences on consumers' knowledge and feelings about products, stores, or ads and on their consumption behaviour. For instance, people learn acceptable and appropriate behaviours and acquire many of their values, beliefs, and attitudes through direct social interaction with their families and reference groups. The influence of families, moreover, can continue for years as some adult consumers purchase the same brands, the same stores, and shop in the same way their parents once did.

Families and reference groups are influenced by the macro social environments of culture, subculture, and social class. Exhibit 12.1 illustrates the flow of social influence from the macro environments of culture, subculture, and social class to the micro social environments of reference groups and family and then on to the individual consumer. We discuss these social influences at length in Chapters 13, 14, and 15.

In discussing the relationships in Exhibit 12.1, it should be noted that the distinction between culture, subculture, and social class can be quite blurred. We readily talk about a British culture or a German culture, but talking about a Scottish culture or a Bavarian culture sounds right, too, even though strictly, when the former is a culture, the latter should be a subculture. Social class can be distinguished within or across cultures and subcultures, and sometimes a social class develops its own subculture. Generally, social class as a marketing concept has become less useful in Europe over the past decades, because rises in the general level of income and education have blurred many of the

EXHIBIT 12.1

The Social Environment and Consumer Behaviour

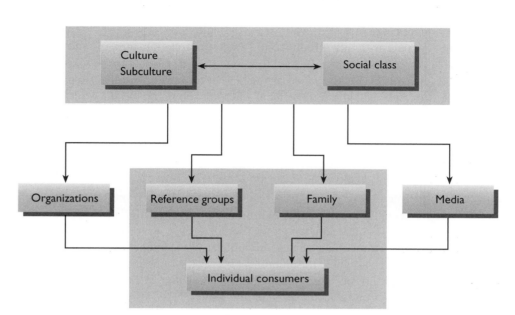

differences traditionally associated with consumption behaviour of social classes. Marketers have therefore turned to an increasing degree to the concepts of culture and subculture for understanding the macro environment.

Exhibit 12.1 also identifies social entities involved in transferring meanings, values, and behaviour norms from the macro social environment to individual consumers. These include media such as TV programmes, newspapers, magazines, films and videos, literature, and music as well as other organizations such as religious and educational institutions, police and the courts, and government. Organizations also include business firms that develop marketing strategies to influence individual customers.

The Physical Environment

The **physical environment** includes all the nonhuman, physical aspects of the field in which consumer behaviour occurs.[5] Virtually any aspect of the physical environment can affect consumer behaviour. The physical environment can be divided into spatial and nonspatial elements. Spatial elements include physical objects of all types (including product and brands) as well as countries, cities, stores, and interior design. Nonspatial elements include factors such as temperature, humidity, illumination, noise level, and time. Marketers need to understand how aspects of the physical environment influence consumers' affect and cognitions and behaviours.

Time has a great effect on consumer behaviour.[6] For instance, behaviours are influenced by the time of day (stores tend to be more crowded during the lunch or early evening hours), the day of the week (Mondays often are slow days for restaurants), the day of the month (sales may drop off just before the last of the month and pick up again after the first), and the season of the year (during the pre-Christmas holiday season, people's shopping behaviours are quite different from those at other times of the year).

The time of the year is related to weather. Many firms have recognized that weather influences consumer behaviour (see Highlight 12.1). Obviously, earmuffs, gloves, and heavy coats are winter products, and most suntan lotion, air fans, and bathing suits are sold during the summer. Beyond that, one should suspect that people's shopping mood depends on the weather. Cold or rainy weather may encourage shopping in shopping centres, but will discourage local outdoor shopping. Bright and friendly weather may encourage outdoor shopping, unless it becomes too warm, when shops with air-conditioning will have an advantage as consumers drop in just to cool off. While research on the relationships between weather and consumer behaviour is in its early stages, the weather is an important influence on affect (such as moods), cognitions, and purchase behaviour.[7]

The time of the year is also related to light. Dark winter days create a different shopping environment to that on bright summer days. Marketers exploit the dark days by creating illuminations aimed at shaping a cosy atmosphere, whereas they exploit long, sunny summer days by encouraging strolling in open shopping environments. In northern Europe, where the differences between winter and summer daylight hours are especially pronounced, marketers face the challenge of having to create quite distinct shopping environments for summer and winter.

Marketing Implications

Every marketing strategy created by a marketing manager involves changing some aspect of the social and physical environment. For example, aspects of the physical environment are changed by promotion strategies (a magazine ad, a billboard on the side of the road), product strategies (a new squeeze bottle for Colgate toothpaste, a styling change in the Ford Escort), pricing strategies (a sale sign in a window, a price tag on a sweater), and distribution strategies (the location of a department store, a product display in a store).

Other marketing strategies modify aspects of the social environment. For instance, Lexus trains its car salespeople to be less aggressive and pushy with customers. A health club encourages members to invite a friend for a free workout. Norsk Hydro filling stations have an attendant coming to your car to wash your windscreen.

These environmental factors are created through marketing strategies and are designed to influence consumer affect, cognition, and behaviour. In this sense, marketers can be seen as environmental managers.[8]

Situations

Because a huge number of elements make up the social and physical environment, marketers may find it difficult to identify the most important environmental influences on consumers' affect, cognitions, and behaviours. It can be easier to analyse the influences of the environment in the context of specific *situations*.[9] A situation is neither the tangible physical environment (a checkout counter, a storefront, your living room, the temperature today, a landscape) nor the objective features of the social environment (the number of people in a store, the time of day).[10] A situation is constructed or defined by a person who is acting in an environment for some purpose. A situation occurs over a period of time that can be very short (buying a drink from a vending machine), somewhat longer (eating lunch), or quite protracted (buying a house). The person's goals define the situation's beginning (goal activation or problem recognition), middle (working to achieve the goal), and end (achieving the goal). Thus, a **situation** is a sequence of *goal-directed behaviours, along with affective and cognitive responses and the various environments in which they occur.* For instance, going downtown to look for a new CD is a shopping situation, whereas having lunch with your best friend is a consumption situation. This view of situations as a series of goal-directed interactions between the environment, affect and cognitions, and behaviour is consistent with the Wheel of Consumer Analysis.

Situations vary in complexity. Some situations take place within a single physical and social environment and involve simple goals, relatively few behaviours, and few affective and cognitive responses. Examples of relatively simple consumption-related situations include buying a stamp at the post office, bargaining with a salesperson over the price of a stereo system, or discussing a spring break trip with your friends over dinner. Other consumer situations are more complex. Complex situations may take place in several physical and social environments, involve multiple (perhaps conflicting) goals, and require many different behaviours and cognitive and affective responses. Shopping for a new winter coat in several shops is an example of a more complex situation.

Many consumer-related situations are common and *recurring*. For instance, many consumers frequently buy petrol for their cars, watch TV in the evening, shop for new clothes, rent videos, and go to grocery stores. As their experiences accumulate over time, consumers form clear goals, develop consistent problem representations for these recurring situations, and learn appropriate behaviours. Thereafter, when the problem situation occurs again, appropriate knowledge schemas and scripts may be activated from memory to influence consumers' behavioural, affective, and cognitive responses in that environment/situation. To the extent that people tend to form approximately the same interpretations for common consumer-related situations, their behaviours will also tend to be similar. When this occurs, marketers can develop marketing strategies that should affect consumers in a target segment in similar ways.

In contrast, consumers may not have clear goals or relevant knowledge when faced with new or unfamiliar situations. They may have to consciously interpret and integrate information to determine their goals, identify salient environmental factors, and choose appropriate behaviours. Marketers should develop strategies to help consumers cope with unfamiliar situations. For instance, life insurance salespeople are trained to help consumers define their goals (higher education for children, retirement plans, pay off mortgage) and identify key environmental considerations (current savings, children's ages, time to retirement), so that they can demonstrate the self-relevance of life insurance.

Analysing Situations

A powerful approach to understanding environmental influences is to analyse the situations in which the consumer experiences the environment. Marketers should understand the physical and social environments in terms of the perspectives of the consumers who experience them.[11] To analyse a situation, marketers should first determine their target customers' major goals that define the situation.[12] Then they should identify the key aspects of the social and physical environments in those situations, including marketing strategies that might affect the consumer. Finally, marketers should attempt to understand consumers' affective, cognitive, and behavioural responses to these environmental characteristics.[13]

Marketers can learn about personal consumption situations by asking consumers to describe the major occasions when they consume the product. A study conducted by one of the authors provides an example of such an analysis. People who were regular consumers of Danish pastries were interviewed and asked to describe the major situations when they ate a Danish pastry. It turned out that several different situations could be discerned:

1. Hungry during shopping trip.
    Environment: hectic; many other people around.
    Goal: satisfy hunger and get energy.
    Affect/cognition: feeling hungry, stressed, and tense.
    Behaviour: buy Danish pastry from in-store bakery in supermarket.
2. Afternoon coffee with guests.
    Environment: quiet; social; at home.
    Goal: be a good host, offer something everybody likes.
    Affect/cognition: feel apprehensive for guests' well-being.
    Behaviour: serve Danish pastry together with other types of cake.
3. Breakfast at home.
    Environment: at home in the morning, somewhat hectic, kids are getting ready for school.
    Goal: Get some energy for the day fast and efficiently.
    Affect/cognition: feed family something it likes, be ready in time for school/work.
    Behaviour: serve Danish pastry for breakfast.

These three consumption situations occurred in three different environments, and each situation involved somewhat different affective and cognitive states (goals) and behaviours. The frequency with which these situations occur may also depend on culture and subculture. The situations may require different marketing strategies in terms of product, distribution, pricing, and communication.[14] The first situation requires a dense distribution in the shopping district so that the product is available when the consumer becomes hungry, and it must be convenient to eat while on the move. The second situation requires high product quality and particularly good visual appearance of the product, which may be distributed through bakeries and speciality stores. The third situation requires a product perceived as nutritious and healthy, and which can be stored at home and easily warmed before serving. Highlight 12.2 shows another example of the interaction of situation and shopping/consumption environment.

Generic Consumer Situations

We can characterize consumer behaviour by a sequence of typical situations. Actually, we have already done that in Chapter 11, although the emphasis was a little different. In Exhibit 11.2 we presented a sequence of behaviours to analyse overt consumer behaviour. Each of the stages in Exhibit 11.2 can be regarded as a situation, which we

This ad uses a classical conditioning approach by evoking positive emotions and linking them to the brand. Courtesy: Chanel Ltd.

This promotion tries to induce the desired behaviour by promising a reward in terms of a price reduction. Courtesy: *The Economist*.

The picture evokes fresh, unspoiled, pure meaning that may become classically conditioned to the brand. Courtesy: Walkers Shortbread Ltd; agency: Cox, Landy & Partners.

Modelling the type of people who use a product.
Courtesy: Burberrys, London.

HIGHLIGHT 12.2
The Business Lunch

In most people's perception, eating out at a gourmet restaurant is an evening affair. They put on different, more festive clothes than those they wear at work. They would like to take their time – to such an extent that customers become offended when the courses are served too quickly one after another. Many people do a fair amount of drinking – an aperitif first, then some wine with the meal, and a brandy to go with the coffee. This, too, is something they wouldn't usually do during the day, at least not when they are supposed to return to work afterwards.

As a result, most gourmet restaurants only open in the evening. Those who are open for lunch usually have very little business during lunch hours.

Still, because all the facilities are there and have to be financed, restaurant owners have thought about how to attract lunch business. An analysis of the lunch-eating situation can give hints on how the menus would have to be adapted. First of all, people eating lunch are mostly short of time. Second, most of them go back to work after the meal. Third, if they go out at all instead of eating in a canteen there is a special reason for doing so – for example, they want to entertain visitors, have a quiet talk with a colleague away from the noise of the canteen, or reward themselves with a meal better than the usual standard.

Some gourmet restaurants offer business lunches which try to cater for these needs and adapt to the situation. Business lunches tend to be lighter and cheaper than the evening meals offered in the same restaurant. A wider variety of wines is offered by the glass instead of by the bottle. Sometimes an extended range of nonalcoholic drinks is offered. The menu is shorter, thus speeding up decision making, and fixed menus may be served with a promise of completing the whole meal within a prespecified time. At the same time, the high quality of the food itself, the upmarket surroundings, and the good waiter service is upheld, contributing to the goals of relaxation, reward, and entertaining guests.

can characterize not only by the behaviour occurring and the reinforcement schedules associated with them, as we did in Chapter 11, but also by the environment in which they occur, the goals the consumer pursues with the behaviour, the cognitions and affective reactions associated with the behaviour.

For example, the **information acquisition situation** includes the environments where consumers acquire information relevant to a problem-solving goal such as a brand or store choice. An information acquisition situation may contain social factors (word-of-mouth communications from friends, persuasion attempts by a salesperson) and physical stimuli (prominent signs in a shop, labels on the product package) that can influence consumers' affect, cognitions, and behaviours. Marketers have considerable control over many aspects of consumers' information environment, especially the advertising, sales promotion, and personal selling elements of the promotion mix.

The purchasing situation includes the physical, spatial, and social characteristics of places where consumers shop for products and services. Shopping behaviour can occur in a variety of environments, such as in boutiques, department and discount stores, local pedestrian-only retail areas, at home (via catalogues or television home-shopping programmes), at flea markets, at auctions, and so on. In retail environments alone, a huge number of physical factors – including store design and layout, lighting and

HIGHLIGHT 12.3

Mobile Shopping Environments

t might seem quite paradoxical that a cold-climate country like Denmark is one of the relatively largest ice-cream-consuming nations in the EU. There is, however, a perfectly valid explanation: due to the winter time's lack of fresh fruit, which is the prevalent Mediterranean dessert, the Danes have adopted the habit of eating ice cream for dessert.

Hjem-Is is a company which has profited from this eating habit. Having developed a unique concept, Hjem-Is has conquered a considerable market share of 12 per cent in the highly competitive ice-cream market in Denmark. The core of the concept is that the shopping environment is moved to the consumer.

Hjem-Is is a franchising concept with centrally owned production where each vendor independently owns a refrigerated van. Everyday the vendor goes to the storehouses located strategically around the country and buys the ice cream to be delivered to the private households. Each 'iceman' has a geographically defined sales area split into certain routes, which he or she visits on an announced day – typically every fortnight. Almost every housing estate in the country gets frequent visits from the Hjem-Is vendors.

The characteristic blue refrigerated vans with the Hjem-Is logo, as well as the unmistakable bell attached to each van which enthusiastically announces the arrival of the Hjem-Is van, makes it easy to spot the Hjem-Is vendors. The concept is so deeply rooted in the Danish everyday life that practically everybody – child or grown-up – knows the sound of the Hjem-Is bell.

Brochures are distributed before the visit so that the customers at their leisure can decide and plan on which ice cream to buy the next time the van comes around. The vendors also benefit from the fact that ice cream is an impulse purchase which consumers might not want to travel far to get, but which they are willing to purchase when it is brought right to their home.

Source: Svend Hollensen and Marcus J. Schmidt, *Scener fra dansk erhvervsliv: Casebaseret lærebog i markedsanalyse og markedsføringsplanlægning* (Copenhagen, Nyt Nordisk Forlag Arnold Busck, 1988).

display fixtures, colours, the overall size of the store, and miscellaneous other factors (such as temperature and noise level) – may affect consumers' behaviour (the time spent in the shop) and their cognitions and affective states (moods or feelings of involvement with shopping). In addition, the shopping environment includes social factors such as how many salespeople and checkout personnel are in the shop, how shop personnel act towards customers, the presence of friends and relatives accompanying the consumers, the crowding, and the types of other people found there. All these aspects of the shopping environment can influence consumers' behaviours, cognitions, and affective responses.[15] Highlight 12.3 gives an example of a special type of shopping environment.

Likewise, the **consumption situation** includes the social and physical factors present in the environments where consumers actually use or consume the products and services they have bought. Obviously, consumption behaviours (and related cognitive and affective processes such as enjoyment, satisfaction, or frustration) are most relevant in such situations.[16] Consider how clean, tidy, appropriately lighted, and attractively decorated consumption environments in restaurants, pubs and bars, night-clubs and discos can enhance consumers' enjoyment of the services purchased. In many service businesses, such as hairstylists, dentists and doctors, and hotels and restaurants, marketers have total control over the consumption environment because consumption of the products and services occurs on the premises of the seller. For products such as appliances, clothing, cars, and furniture, marketers have almost no direct control over the consumption environment. These products are taken from the retail environment and consumed elsewhere (usually in consumers' homes). Moreover, for many of these products, the consumption situation involves multiple consumption behaviours over long periods (most people own and use a car or a microwave oven for several years). In some cases, the consumption environment might change during the useful life of the product, and this could affect consumption-related cognitive and affective responses (satisfaction) and behaviours (repairs and service). Perhaps the best marketers can do is to monitor consumers' satisfaction levels and behaviours in these consumption situations over the lifetime of the product.

Marketing Implications

Marketers need to identify the key social and physical environmental features of the situations in which their products are bought and consumed. They also need to understand consumers' affective, cognitive, and behavioural responses to these environmental factors. For example, some aspects of these environments may block behaviours crucial to the marketing success of the firm's product. Marketing strategies can be developed that modify the environment to stimulate, facilitate, and reinforce the desired behaviours, as we have discussed in Chapter 11.

Back to . . . Shopping with Small Children

Shopping with small children is a special type of shopping situation, and what Mothercare and similar retailers of children's wear have done is to create shopping environments adapted to that situation. Mothers have various goals when shopping with small children – to get the shopping done, to keep the child quiet and happy, to avoid annoying other people in the environment, to be able to change nappies or feed the child when necessary. Most of these goals are difficult to fulfil in most shopping environments. By adapting the environment to the special needs of this particular group of consumers, Mothercare has been able to obtain a leading edge in the UK market for children's clothing.

Summary

This chapter presented an overview of environmental influences on consumer behaviour. Two basic types of environments were identified: social, and physical. The social environment includes the effects on consumer behaviour of culture, subculture, social class, reference group, and family. The physical environment includes the effects of both spatial and nonspatial factors.

We also discussed the important concept of situations, which involves the continuous interaction over time of consumers' affective and cognitive responses and behaviours with one or more environmental settings.

A basic premise of the chapter was that marketing strategies must not only be adapted to changing environmental conditions but also play an important role in creating the environment.

Key Terms and Concepts

consumption situation   256
environment   248
information acquisition situation   255
macro social environment   250
micro social environment   250
physical environment   251
shopping situation
situation   253

Review and Discussion Questions

1. Define the functional or perceived environment using examples of cosmetics shops to illustrate your point.
2. How does the concept of marketing segmentation relate to the functional environment?
3. Consider the distinction between macro and micro environments for grocery shopping. Which of these is more important for marketing strategy?
4. Contrast the two approaches marketers can take to analysing environmental effects – considering the direct effects of specific environmental factors versus considering environmental factors in the context of situations. Under what circumstances might each of these two approaches be most appropriate?
5. Use the situation of shopping for a personal cassette player to describe the relationships between the physical and social environments. Point out those aspects that marketers could control.
6. What is a situation? Use examples from your own recent purchases to show how situations differ from environments.
7. Are environmental factors more important influences for new or recurring situations? Why?
8. Use the Wheel of Consumer Analysis to describe how affect and cognition and behaviours interact with environmental factors in a textbook purchase situation.
9. How can marketers use situational analysis to segment markets? Identify some product categories where the approach could be used to the advantage of the marketing organization.

Additional Reading

For a readable text on environmental psychology, see:
Amos Rappaport, *The Meaning of the Built Environment* (Beverly Hills, CA: Sage Publications, 1982).

For a discussion of the meaning of 'situations', see:
Joseph A. Cote Jr., 'The Person by Situation Interaction Myth: Implications for the Definition

of Situations', in *Advances in Consumer Research*, vol. 13, ed. Richard J. Lutz (Provo, UT: Association for Consumer Research, 1986), pp. 37–41.

For a discussion of the relationship between consumer affective and cognitive states and shopping environments, see:

Andrea Gröppel, 'Evolution of Retail Categories – An Explanation from Consumers' Point Of View', in *European Advances in Consumer Research*, vol. 2, ed. Flemming Hansen (Provo, UT: Association for Consumer Research, 1995), pp. 237–245.

Christian Derbaix and Michel T. Pham, 'Affective Reactions to Consumption Situations: A Pilot Study', *Journal of Economic Psychology*, June 1991, pp. 325–356.

For a discussion of the role of time as an aspect of the environment, see:

Gabriele Morello, 'The Time Dimension in Marketing', *Irish Marketing Review*, no. 1, 1989, pp. 11–20.

For an interesting discussion of the information/shopping/purchasing environment at a flea market, see:

John F. Sherry Jr., 'A Sociocultural Analysis of a Midwestern Flea Market', *Journal of Consumer Research*, June 1990, pp. 13–30.

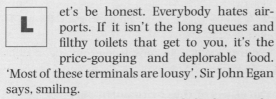

MARKETING STRATEGY IN ACTION
Airport Shopping

Let's be honest. Everybody hates airports. If it isn't the long queues and filthy toilets that get to you, it's the price-gouging and deplorable food. 'Most of these terminals are lousy', Sir John Egan says, smiling.

Sir John loves airports – and the lousier the better. As chief executive of Britain's BAA plc, he has built one of Europe's best-performing companies by taking over humdrum airports in Britain and the US and turning them around.

Now more than ever, the governments that run airports are in the mood to sell. With a severe shortage of airport capacity and steep government deficits, hundreds of airports around the world, from Mexico to Argentina to Russia, are hitting the block. Analysts expect tens of billions of dollars to change hands over the next decade in airport-related deals – many of them led by BAA and its radical ideas about how airports should be managed.

Marie Benton embodies one radical idea: upscale airport shopping. A BAA personal shopper based at London's Heathrow Airport, Ms Benton helps the rich and famous shop duty-free. She has watched Sharon Stone buy Hermes scarves, Richard Gere price expensive cameras, and an unnamed Texas oil man fork over $20 000 for loose diamonds for his wife. 'These are people who live very busy lives', says the impeccably dressed Ms Benton, gliding over the faux marble floor in Heathrow's Terminal Four. 'And there aren't many places they can find everything they want in one place.'

Once a lethargic government bureaucracy, BAA has more than trebled its pretax profits since privatization, to £418 million ($650 million) last year from £122 million in 1987. In addition to owning Heathrow and the smaller Gatwick airport outside London and five others in Britain, BAA runs airport operations in Indianapolis and Pittsburgh in the United States. And its shares have been London Stock Exchange stars, surging to a high of 555 pence this year from just over 100 pence immediately after privatization.

All around the world, airports are in trouble. Terminals are congested, passengers are grumpy, and airlines are starting to panic about increasing gridlock. While the number of airline passengers is expected to more than quadruple in the next decade – to five billion nearly equal to the world's current population – airports have failed miserably to keep pace.

The problem is mostly money. With local and national budgets stretched and basic services such as education underfunded, many governments simply don't have the money to improve airports. So, airports have been neglected. The alternative to huge government outlays is privatization. But until BAA came along, with its airport-as-shopping-mall glitz, few private companies have been able to make airports fly as a business. Now, BAA executives testify before US congressional committees about the benefits of privatization and are taking their show on the road elsewhere. BAA is bidding to run airports in the US, Australia, Europe, and South Africa.

Not surprisingly, other private companies are becoming interested, too. Financier George Soros has teamed up with a Lockheed Martin Corp. unit to bid for the Australian airports, and General Motors Corp.'s Hughes Electronics division is gunning for deals elsewhere. Even airports are getting into the game; in Europe, Amsterdam's airport is a part-owner of Vienna's recently privatized airport.

However, the success of BAA has not been without its critics. Despite the focus on upmarket stores, they say Heathrow – the first big airport to fall into private hands – remains a mess. 'The place is a permanent building site', says Peter Morrell, a professor at Britain's Cranfield University who has studied BAA. 'The cynical view is that BAA lets the passengers deal with the headaches and the airlines deal with the problems. For the business passenger making a short trip to Paris, they have to go through a great maze of shopping to get there.' And, while attention and cash are lavished on the departures hall – where people mill around and spend money –

the arrivals hall, where they don't, is crowded and dingy.

Nevertheless, nobody pines for the preprivatization days, when a government agency, the British Airports Authority, lorded over some wretched airports. Since the authority was founded in the 1960s, it was the only one of Britain's state-owned companies to make money since its inception – mainly by robbing its customers blind. At Heathrow – passengers once called it Thiefrow – people parking a car for 15 minutes had to pay for two hours and passengers wanting a quick cup of tea had to buy a full pot.

Sir John's first move when he arrived at BAA was to persuade his employees that the high-price strategy wasn't working. 'People confused capitalism with stealing', he says. 'My system was to explain to our employees that stealing from the customer was a bad thing.'

The changed system worked. BAA's retailing revenue, which was £213 million in 1989, now exceeds £556 million a year and makes up 44 per cent of the group's £1.3 billion in total revenue. The rest comes from property rentals and landing and traffic fees. Though BAA runs nearly all the operations at its airport – from fire-fighting and security to baggage handling – analysts now follow the company as a retail stock rather than a transportation stock.

Through its outlets, BAA sells more Rolex watches than anywhere else in the United Kingdom and controls 20 per cent of the British perfume market. Every year, about 10 million people pass through each terminal at Heathrow and Gatwick, about as many as a big regional mall in the United States. Run by retailing specialists – experts in narrow product areas such as perfumes, shoes or whisky – BAA has mastered the minutiae of airport retailing. It knows, for instance, that at 6:30 am, Heathrow is full of British passengers on their way to the Continent, while at 3 pm, it is full of Japanese heading home.

For Bally Shoes International Ltd, the upmarket Swiss retailer, that is important information: Bally managers continuously rotate the shoes they display to highlight national preferences as well as the fact that people from different countries have different-sized feet. The result: Bally sells more shoes per square metre at Heathrow than at any other outlet in the world.

'What you've got here is a high-profile, high-calibre [customer]', says Aliza Reger, whose family-owned lingerie shop plans to open an outlet in Heathrow that will be its first outside its highbrow base in London's Knightsbridge. 'We expect to have a lot of men buying guilt gifts.'

Surveys show that the average international passenger spends about $71 at BAA's airports, by far the highest amount in the world and about three times the outlay at New York's La Guardia. To be sure, the numbers are skewed by a few big spenders. Last year, one passenger spent £8500 on a magnum of Chateau Margaux at Heathrow, while a Japanese restaurateur shelled out £10000 for a 60-year-old bottle of Scotch whisky – one of only 12 such bottles in the world.

Although no other company has BAA's breadth, other airports are catching on. In Frankfurt, government airport officials have stolen a few ideas from the privatization handbook: passengers can drop off dry cleaning, get a haircut, even catch a pornographic movie. In Amsterdam, the vice of choice is gambling, in the world's biggest airport casino.

Back in Britain, BAA is pressing ahead. It plans to open soon a Planet Hollywood restaurant at Gatwick, and Sir John says he even is considering a theme park.

'When I first came here, a lot of people thought I was wasting my time,' he says. 'They don't say that as much any more.'

Discussion Questions

1. Compare and contrast the purchase situations of shopping in an airport versus shopping locally. Discuss the reciprocal interactions between environment, behaviour, and cognitive and affective responses. What long-term effects do you think airport shopping will have on consumers' shopping behaviour? What can competing local shopping outlets do in response?

2. What macro environmental factors might affect airport shopping behaviours (both decrease and increase)? Consider their impacts on different market segments. What marketing implications does your analysis have for companies like BAA?

3. Analyse the information acquisition, purchasing, and consumption environments of airports you have seen. What recommendations do you have for changing these environments to increase sales?

Source: Adapted by permission of Kyle Pope, 'Airport Privatization Begins to Take Off', *The Wall Street Journal Europe*, 24 September 1996, p.1, 5. © 1996 Dow Jones & Company, Inc. All rights reserved worldwide.

Cultural and Cross-Cultural Influences

**The Birth
of the
Consumer
Society**

odern consumption cultures are a rather recent historical development. According to one analysis, the birth of the consumer society occurred in England during the 18th century when several important events occurred. For one thing, the new mass production technologies developed during England's Industrial Revolution allowed companies to produce large quantites of standardized goods at relatively low prices. A cultural revolution occurred about the same time, without which the Industrial Revolution would not have been successful.

During the 18th century, England was gradually transformed from a largely agrarian society into a more urban society. When people moved into towns, their culture changed dramatically. They developed new values, performed different types of work, and developed new lifestyles. Many people developed an increased desire for material goods, stimulated partly by new marketing strategies such as advertising. Increasingly, ordinary citizens (not just the wealthy) became concerned with the symbolic meanings of goods and felt it necessary to buy products that were fashionable and up-to-date. Owning such objects helped satisfy the new cultural need for status

distinctions that had become more relevant in the relatively anonymous urban societies where few people knew each other or their family backgrounds. Thus, people began to see consumption as an acceptable way to acquire important social meanings. Finally, more people had disposable income and were willing to spend it to achieve those values.

These cultural changes, combined with industry's rapidly developing ability to mass-produce products of reasonable quality at low prices, created a dramatic increase in consumption in 18th-century England. Essentially, the same events occurred in France and the United States during the 19th century, and the modern consumer society was born there, too.

Sources: Adapted from Grant McCracken, 'The Making of Modern Consumption', in *Culture and Consumption* (Bloomington, IN: University of Indiana Press, 1988); and Janeen A. Costa, 'Toward an Understanding of Social and World Systematic Processes in the Spread of Consumer Culture: An Anthropological Case Study', in *Advances in Consumer Research*, vol. 17, eds. Marvin E. Goldberg, Gerald Gorn and Richard W. Pollay (Provo, UT: Association for Consumer Research, 1991), pp. 826–832.

This brief summary of the complex events at the beginning of the modern consumption society points to the importance of culture in understanding consumer behaviour. To develop effective strategies, marketers need to identify important aspects of culture and understand how they affect consumers. In this chapter we examine the topic of culture and consider its influence on consumers' affect, cognitions, and behaviours. We discuss the importance of cultural differences and the implications of cultural analysis for developing marketing strategies. Then we present a model of the cultural process that shows how cultural meaning is transferred to products by marketing strategies and how consumers then acquire those meanings.

What Is Culture?

As the broadest aspect of the macro-social environment, culture has a pervasive influence on consumers. Yet, despite increasing research attention, culture remains difficult for marketers to understand. Dozens of definitions have confused researchers about what 'culture' is or how culture works to influence consumers.[1] Fortunately, recent theoretical developments help clarify the concept of culture and how it affects people.[2] We treat **culture** as *the meanings that are shared by (most) people in a social group*. In a broad sense, cultural meanings include common affective reactions, typical cognitions (beliefs), and characteristic patterns of behaviour. Each society establishes its own vision of the world and constitutes or constructs that cultural world by creating and using meanings to represent important cultural distinctions. For example, Highlight 13.1 presents some of the meanings of the Christmas holiday shared by people in different cultures.

Marketers should consider several issues when analysing culture. First, cultural meaning can be analysed at different levels. Often, culture is analysed at the macro level of an entire society or country (Canada, France, Poland, Kenya, or Australia). However, cross-cultural differences do not always coincide with national borders. This is obvious in many countries where cultural differences among internal social groups are as great as between separate nations. Consider Belgium (with two language cultures – Flemish and French), Canada (two language cultures – English and French), and Switzerland (with German, French, and Italian-speaking regions). Also national borders do not always demarcate clear cross-cultural differences. For instance, the people in southern Austria and northern Italy, or northern France and southern Belgium, have many things in common.

In addition to these distinctions at the macro level, marketers can also analyse the cultural meanings of subcultures (immigrants, the elderly, people who live in Bavaria) or social classes. We discuss subcultures and social class in Chapter 14. Marketers can even analyse the shared cultural meanings of smaller groups such as a reference group (people who live on the same dormitory floor, members of a street gang, or a group of coworkers) or family (people in one's nuclear or extended family). We discuss reference groups and family influences in Chapter 15.

A second issue, the concept of shared or common meaning, is critical to understanding culture. In Section 2 we examined psychological meaning – the personal, mental representations of objects, events, and behaviours stored in the memories of individual consumers. In this chapter we consider **cultural meaning** at a macro social level. *A meaning is cultural if many (most) people in a social group share the same basic meaning.* These cultural meanings are somewhat fuzzy in that all people in a social group are not likely to have exactly the same meaning for any object or activity (what is an old person, an environmentally safe product, or a good bargain?) Fortunately, meanings only have to be 'close enough' to be treated as shared or common.

Christmas Buying Around the World

 witch flies on a broomstick to drop Christmas gifts down Italian chimneys; a kindly old Father Christmas brings gifts on a sleigh drawn by reindeer to Scandinavian homes; a camel does the hauling in southern Syria; and the honourable porter's name is Santa-san in Japan. Although the exact method of delivery varies, shoppers around the world buy presents in large quantities every holiday season.

Each year, eager shoppers record huge purchases during the Christmas holiday season. Most department stores record about one-third of their annual sales during this period. Toy vendors from London to Madrid to Los Angeles expect to do about 50 per cent of their yearly business in these three months.

Shopping for and giving presents at Christmas time has become a worldwide phenomenon. Even in Japan, where less than 1 per cent of the population is Christian, Yuletide is widely celebrated with artfully packaged gifts and late-hour partying. Germany's lively outdoor Christmas markets sell sausages, sweets, and holiday gifts. Shoppers in Rome's oval-shaped plaza Piazza Navona are bathed in light from stalls selling items like books, toys, records, candy, and video games while being entertained by street musicians and magicians.

Holiday decorations, especially lights, are popular everywhere. For instance, Christmas trees decorate plazas around the globe. In Scandinavia, candles glow from every window to brighten the darkness that arrives by mid-afternoon. The Strøget, Copenhagen's large pedestrian-only shopping district, is illuminated by thousands of coloured lights and stars. The Via Condotti, Rome's pedestrian-only shopping area, is decorated with hundreds of red poinsettias, called 'Christmas stars' in Italian.

For many, the winter weather in the northern hemisphere heightens the holiday mood. But cold weather and lights in the early darkness are not prerequisites for Christmas spirit. South of the equator, the holiday falls in the middle of summer. So when enthusiastic shoppers in Australia and Rio get too hot, they just head for the beach to cool off.

There are differences, of course, between the consumers in various cultures, subcultures, and social classes. Marketers need to identify these factors and understand how they are related to purchasing and consumption behaviour. However, there are also similarities between cultures. One example is the generosity and good spirit of the Christmas season. Holiday spending and gift giving seem to be fairly universal in most societies with a well-developed consumption ethic. The details, of course, often differ. The weather (cold and snowy or hot, humid, and rainy), the most desirable gifts (fur coats in northern Europe, ice-cream makers in Brazil), the particular details of the holiday rituals (who brings the gifts), and the religious symbolic meanings may vary considerably.

But the core meaning of the holiday, captured by Charles Dickens in *A Christmas Carol*, seems fairly universal. 'Christmas', Dickens wrote, 'is the only time I know of, in the long calendar year, when men and women seem by one consent to open their shut-up hearts freely.' And, we might note, they open their wallets, too.

Source: Adapted from Jaclyn Fierman, 'Christmas Shopping around the World', *Fortune*, 21 December 1987, pp. 92–100.

Third, cultural meanings are created by people. Anthropologists often say cultural meanings are constructed or negotiated by people in a group through their social interactions. The *construction of cultural meaning* is more obvious at the level of smaller groups (consider the social meanings of clothing fads among students – which look is in this semester?) At the macro societal level, cultural institutions such as government, religious and educational organizations, and business firms are also involved in constructing cultural meaning.

A final issue is that social groups differ in the amount of freedom people have to adopt and use certain cultural meanings. European and North American societies afford people a great deal of freedom to select cultural meanings and use them to create a desired self-identity. In many other societies (China, India, Saudi Arabia), people have less freedom to do so.

In the following sections we discuss two useful perspectives for understanding cultural meaning. Marketers can examine the *content* of a culture, and marketers can treat culture as a *process*.[3]

The Content of Culture

The usual approach in marketing is to analyse culture in terms of its major attributes or its content.[4] Marketers typically focus on identifying the dominant values of a society, but culture is more than values.[5] The **content of culture** includes the beliefs, attitudes, goals, and values held by most people in a society, as well as the meanings of characteristic behaviours, rules, customs, and norms that most people follow. The content of culture also includes meanings of the significant aspects of the social and physical environment, including the major social institutions in a society (political parties, religions, chambers of commerce) and the typical physical objects (products, tools, buildings) used by people in a society. The goal of cultural analysis is to understand the cultural meanings of these concepts from the point of view of the consumers who create and use them.

The content of culture can be related to the affective and cognitive responses consumers have to consumption-related stimuli in their environment. For example, many Europeans have basically similar responses to a 50 per cent-off sale – it results in interest and excitement, and in thoughts about the quality of the items on sale, how one possibly could get hold of them, and whether one could afford to buy. Likewise, accidentally breaking a vase in a store results in anxiety or guilt and in thoughts about either escaping from the situation or recompensing the store-owner for the damage. Beyond these basic similarities, however, considerable cultural differences may occur. Consumers in Sweden are overfed with sales promotions in supermarkets and may be reluctant to buy when something is not on sale, whereas consumers in Germany have few sales promotions and may be suspicious when something actually is on sale. For other stimuli, there may not even be basic similarities in consumers' reactions in different cultures. The national flag on a product may create feelings of warmth and belonging in Danes and lead to associations of social gatherings and partying, but will not lead to similar reactions in a German consumer. The European Union symbol with golden stars on a blue background will be met with dominantly negative feelings in Norway and dominantly positive feelings in Italy.

Also people's reactions to advertising tend to be culturally specific.[6] The British tend to be embarrassed by a direct sell; their ads are noted for self-deprecating humour. In contrast, the French rarely use humour but prefer stylish and rather indirect appeals, which foreigners may find surrealistic. For example, the best French ad in 1991 showed a lion and a tawny-haired woman crawling up opposite sides of a mountain; at the peak the woman outroars the lion for a bottle of Perrier. Most Japanese consumers prefer ads in which affective mood and emotional tone are emphasized over facts. Although some Japanese ads travel well to other cultures, many are not understood outside Japan.[7]

When people's affective and cognitive reactions to consumption-related stimuli are culturally dependent, it follows that their consumption-related behaviours also have cultural meanings. Bargaining about prices of certain items is acceptable in some cultures but inadmissible in others. Conspicuous consumption demonstrating your wealth is seen as a sign of achievement in some countries and as signs of bad taste in others. Being successful is associated with expensive clothing, a large car, or a fancy house in many cultures, but any of these may be the primary indicator in any given culture.

Finally, consumption objects themselves, as part of the social environment, have often considerable cultural meaning. For instance, for many consumers objects such as wedding rings and new cars have cultural meaning. The Volkswagen beetle meant universal mobility and freedom for all to the postwar Germans. Grøn Tuborg beer symbolizes socializing, sense of belonging, and fun in life to the Danes.

Measuring the Content of Culture

Measuring the content of culture is actually a tricky matter. The reason is that a researcher from one culture trying to understand another culture will use his or her own culture as a frame of reference and may thus misinterpret the other culture. The problem will be compounded when the other culture also uses another language, and understanding the other culture therefore involves problems of translation. These problems are widely recognized among people doing cross-cultural research, but marketing managers analysing their markets are not necessarily aware of the problems involved.

Typical consumer research techniques such as surveys, focus groups, and laddering can and have been employed in order to understand culture content. In addition, special techniques like content analysis and ethnographic fieldwork have been invoked.

Surveys, Focus Groups, and Laddering

These classic consumer research techniques all involve eliciting information from consumers based on standardized or semi-standardized instruments, and the content of culture must then be inferred based on the answers obtained. There are two basic approaches in employing such instruments, which are sometimes labelled as 'emic' and 'etic'.[8] *Emic* research emphasizes the uniqueness of each culture and therefore calls for the use of instruments which are adapted to the culture to be investigated. This involves not only using the culture-specific language, but also trying to use those terms and concepts which are particular to that culture in naming and describing consumer-related phenomena. As a consequence of that, results from emic research allow insight into a particular culture, but cannot be used for comparisons across cultures. *Etic* research, on the other hand, concentrates on those aspects of cultures which are comparable, and therefore tries to employ terms and concepts which will be common across the cultures to be investigated. Etic research can therefore be used for comparing cultures.[9]

In analysing the content of cultures, it is important to have a clear stand on whether the purpose of the analysis is etic or emic. Emic research requires considerable adaptation of the methods used to the culture to be investigated. Etic research requires that the methods used are cross-culturally valid. The problem is that the same word may have somewhat different meanings in different cultures, and not being aware of this may result in misinterpretations of the results. This may apply even to simple concepts like asking consumers whether they live in a 'big city' – which may have quite different meanings dependent on the distribution of city sizes in a given country.

Surveys have been widely used to measure consumer values and compare them across cultures. One popular approach is the Rokeach Value Survey in which consumers rank order 36 general values in terms of their importance. Kahle's List of Values asks consumers to rank order nine person-oriented values. The Schwartz Value Survey measures how people evaluate the importance of 10 value domains.[10]

Research of this type, comparing values across cultures, has an etic approach, the instruments used should therefore be tested for cross-cultural validity. Testing for cross-cultural validity of a survey instrument means investigating whether the various parts or items of a questionnaire are being interpreted in similar ways by consumers in the various cultures.[11] The major instrument which researchers have used in investigating cross-cultural validity is to look at whether the internal relationships among the data obtained are the same or at least similar across the various cultures.[12] This can be done by applying factor analysis to the data and look for whether comparable factor structures emerge from the analysis, but other approaches have been used as well. An example of this will be presented later when we look at the Schwartz Value Survey in more detail.[13]

Less structured techniques like focus groups and laddering have the advantage that they provide richer (more redundant) information, which reduces the danger of misinterpretation in a cross-cultural context somewhat. Exhibit 13.1 shows an example of cross-cultural differences in product perception as measured by the laddering study.[14]

Content Analysis

Content analysis deals with the manifest content of documents. It usually involves collecting a sample of documents, like advertisements or newspaper articles, and analysing them for the occurrence of particular content elements – such as the occurrence of endorsers in ads, whether the product is shown in the ad, or the number of product claims made. The results can be analysed quantitatively, or can be restricted to qualitative interpretation.[15]

In analysing culture, it is assumed that cultural content is mirrored in the kinds of documents which a culture produces. For instance, consumer researchers have scrutinized comic books, consumer magazines, popular novels, and print advertisements to gain insight into the dominant values in a culture and how they change over time.[16] Highlight 13.2 shows an example of how content analysis was used to infer value changes in three countries based on consumer product test magazines.

Marketers use **ethnographic studies** (adapted from anthropology) to study culture.[17] These studies involve detailed and prolonged observation of consumers' emotional responses, cognitions, and behaviours during their ordinary daily lives. Based on this rich and detailed data, researchers interpret or infer the values and key meanings of the culture. Unlike anthropologists who might live in the studied society for months or years, consumer researchers tend to make their observations more quickly. To this end, they use a multitude of methods, including direct observations, interviews, and video and audio recordings. For example, to study cultural differences in how people use food products, researchers would interview consumers in their homes, observe how they cook meals and how they eat, take pictures of the cooking and eating process, and later reinterview the same consumers while showing them the pictures.

Human Values and How They Differ Between Cultures

Shalom Schwartz from the Hebrew University in Jerusalem has done considerable research on **human values** and their differences and commonalities across cultures.[18] He has devised a questionnaire instrument, the Schwartz Value Survey, which has been demonstrated to have cross-cultural validity across a large number of countries and cultures. His research indicates that cultures can be characterized by seven types of values: conservatism, intellectual autonomy, affective autonomy, hierarchy, mastery, egalitarian commitment, and harmony (see Exhibit 13.2).

Conservatism concerns values emphasizing maintenance of the status quo, propriety, and avoidance of actions or inclinations of individuals that might disturb the traditional order. Cultures emphasizing conservatism are concerned with security, conformity, and tradition. They are typically cultures where the fate of the individual is seen as not distinct from that of the group of society at large.

Intellectual and affective autonomy concern values which are in contrast to conservatism – values which are important in societies that view the person as autonomous entitled to pursue his or her own interests. It includes values like enjoying life, being curious, broad-minded, and creative.

Hierarchy deals with values indicating a preference for power, wealth, and authority, as well as being humble facing people being endowed with these characteristics. Hierarchy is related to conservatism.

Mastery emphasizes active mastery of the social environment through self-assertion – active efforts to modify one's surroundings and getting ahead of other people. It includes values like being ambitious, daring, and successful.

Egalitarian commitment deals with values which are quite opposite to mastery and hierarchy – values concerned with voluntarily promoting the welfare of others, which can complement values emphasizing the intellectual and affective autonomy of people. This includes values like social justice, equality, freedom, being helpful, honest, and responsible.

Harmony, finally, is related to egalitarian commitment, and opposite to mastery – these values promote being in harmony with nature, not dominating it. Protecting the environment is one important value here.

As the description of the six value types indicates, they are related to each other in particular ways, and these relationships are spelled out in Exhibit 13.2. Value types

EXHIBIT 13.1

Cultural Meanings of Beef

 hat are the cultural meanings of beef? The following diagrams summarize results from laddering interviews carried out with consumers in Finland and the United Kingdom. There are considerable differences. The Finnish respondents emphasize children and family. They focused on the food itself, the way it should be prepared, the extent to which it is appropriate for an everyday meal, and whether the children like it or not. The latter supports the achievement of providing the children with good and healthy food habits. In general the Finnish respondents appear to be very much guided by the well-being of the children and the family. In contrast, the British respondents' approach to cooking is a very pragmatic one. There is a tendency to dislike cooking, and therefore it becomes important that the preparation should be quick and easy. Economic issues such as price, money saving, and avoidance of wasting food are very much in focus. More hedonistic aspects like taste, variation, and excitement are also sought, but guidance by higher-order personal values is weak.

Source: Adapted from Richard Shepherd, Hely Tuorila and Klaus G. Grunert,
'The Development of Models for Understanding and Predicting Consumer Food Choice'
(Reading: Institute of Food Research, 1996).

adjacent to each other in Exhibit 13.2 are related, i.e. cultures high on one of them will also tend to be high on the other, while value types opposite to each other in the figure are contrasts, and cultures high on the one will be low on the other. Thus, cultures emphasizing mastery will also tend to emphasize hierarchy and will deemphasize harmony and egalitarian commitment. Cultures emphasizing conservatism will also emphasize harmony, and deemphasize affective and intellectual autonomy.

Exhibit 13.3 shows scores for the seven value types from 38 samples covering a wide range of cultures. School teachers, who are assumed to be good indicators of the values prevalent in a particular culture, were used in all the samples. Most west European countries score relatively highly on affective and intellectual autonomy, but also on egalitarian commitment. Asian countries tend to score high on mastery and hierarchy.

Even though these value types are highly abstract, they can be related to consumer behaviour. It has been shown that consumers who score high on the values related to egalitarian commitment and harmony are more prone to buy products which are positioned as friendly to the environment, like ecological food.[19] Ongoing research indicates that consumers scoring high on affective and intellectual autonomy tend to emphasize novelty and taste when buying food products, while deemphasizing health and price.[20] Exhibit 13.4 shows some more possible relationships between the six basic value types and consumer behaviour.

EXHIBIT 13.1 (cont.)

Cut-off = 7   **Finland (n = 30)**

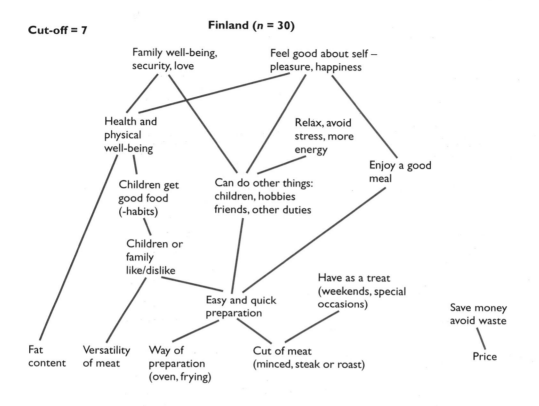

Cut-off = 7   **England (n = 30)**

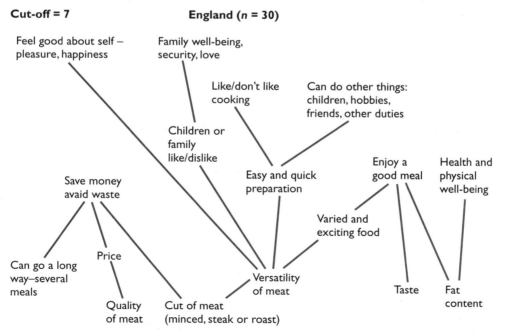

EXHIBIT 13.2

The Schwartz Value Types

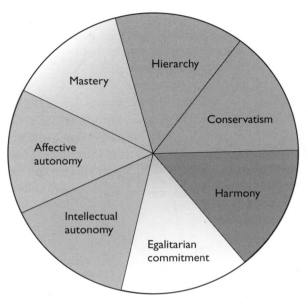

Source: Adapted from Shalom H. Schwartz, 'Beyond Individualism/Collectivism: New Cultural Dimensions of Values', in *Individualism and Collectivism*, eds. Uichol Kim, Harry C. Triandis, Cigdem Kagitcibasi, Sang-Chin Choi, and Gene Yoon (Thousand Oaks, CA: Sage, 1994), pp. 85–119. Reprinted by permission of Sage Publications, Inc.

Culture as a Process

Understanding the content of culture is useful for designing effective marketing strategies, but we can also think about culture as a *process*. Exhibit 13.5 presents a model of the cultural process in a highly developed consumer society.[21] The model shows that cultural meaning is present in three locations – in the social and physical environment, in products and services, and in individual consumers. The **cultural process** describes *how this cultural meaning is moved about or transferred between these locations* by the actions of organizations (business, government, religion, education) and by individuals in the society. There are two ways that meaning is transferred in a consumption-oriented society. First, marketing strategies are designed to move cultural meanings from the physical and social environment into products and services in an attempt to make them attractive to consumers. Second, consumers actively seek to acquire these cultural meanings in products in order to establish a desirable personal identity or self-concept.

Moving Cultural Meanings into Products

Advertising has been the most closely studied method of transferring cultural meaning from the physical and social environment into products.[22] From a cultural process

EXHIBIT 13.3

Mean Importance of Culture-Level Value Dimensions in 38 Cultures

Conservatism		Affective Autonomy		Intellectual Autonomy	
Israel – Druze	4.51	France	4.41	Switzerland (Fr)	5.33
Malaysia	4.46	Switzerland (Fr)	4.24	France	5.15
Bulgaria – Turks	4.43	East Germany	4.16	Slovenia	5.03
Singapore	4.38	West Germany	4.03	Spain	4.90
Estonia – Rural	4.37	Denmark	4.01	West Germany	4.75
Isr – Christ Arab	4.36	New Zealand	3.98	Japan	4.68
Isr – Muslim Arab	4.33	Spain	3.97	Finland	4.62
Taiwan	4.31	Greece	3.96	Italy	4.60
Poland	4.31	Zimbabwe	3.85	Denmark	4.58
Slovakia	4.28	Slovenia	3.76	Guangzhou (PRC)	4.58
Slovenia	4.27	United States	3.65	East Germany	4 47
Turkey	4.27	Thailand	3.62	Hungary	4.44
Estonia – Urban	4.26	Israel – Jews	3.62	The Netherlands	4.44
Thailand	4.22	Portugal	3.54	New Zealand	4.36
Zimbabwe	4.21	Japan	3.54	Israel – Jews	4.31
Shanghai (PRC)	4.10	The Netherlands	3.51	[China (comb)	4.27]
Israel – Jews	4.08	Finland	3.51	Shanghai (PRC)	4.25
Hebei (PRC)	4.07	Australia	3.50	United States	4.20
Australia	4.06	Hebei (PRC)	3.46	Mexico	4.20
Hong Kong	4.04	Guangzhou (PRC)	3.45	Brazil	4.13
Mexico	4.03	Hungary	3.34	Portugal	4.12
Hungary	3.97	[China (comb)	3.32]	Australia	4.12
[China (comb)	3.97]	Brazil	3.30	Turkey	4.12
Brazil	3.97	Isr – Muslim Arab	3.27	Greece	4.09
United States	3.90	Isr – Christ Arab	3.27	Poland	4.09
Japan	3.87	Turkey	3.25	Hong Kong	4.08
Finland	3.84	Mexico	3.23	Thailand	4.08
Italy	3.82	Taiwan	3.21	Malaysia	4.07
Portugal	3.76	Malaysia	3.16	Israel – Druze	4.07
Guangzhou (PRC)	3.75	Israel – Druze	3.16	Isr – Muslim Arab	4.07
New Zealand	3.73	Bulgaria – Turks	3.13	Slovakia	4.03
Greece	3.68	Poland	3.13	Hebei (PRC)	4.01
The Netherlands	3.68	Hong Kong	3.11	Taiwan	3.93
Denmark	3.64	Shanghai (PRC)	3.09	Estonia – Urban	3.93
East Germany	3.50	Estonia – Urban	3.08	Zimbabwe	3.82
West Germany	3.42	Singapore	3.04	Isr – Christ Arab	3.80
Spain	3.42	Estonia – Rural	3.03	Bulgaria – Turks	3.78
France	3.35	Italy	2.95	Estonia – Rural	3.69
Switzerland (Fr)	3.25	Slovakia	2.76	Singapore	3.68

EXHIBIT 13.3 (cont.)

Hierarchy		Mastery		Egalitarian Commitment	
Hebei (PRC)	3.98	Guangzhou (PRC)	4.84	Portugal	5.62
Guangzhou (PRC)	3.78	Hebei (PRC)	4.76	Italy	5.57
[China (comb)	3.70]	[China (comb)	4.73]	Spain	5.55
Shanghai (PRC)	3.36	Zimbabwe	4.62	Denmark	5.52
Thailand	3.32	Shanghai (PRC)	4.57	France	5.45
Turkey	3.30	Greece	4.53	The Netherlands	5.39
Isr – Muslim Arab	3.17	Malaysia	4.34	West Germany	5.37
Zimbabwe	3.14	United States	4.34	Greece	5.35
Bulgaria – Turks	3.07	Mexico	4.34	East Germany	5.29
Isr – Christ Arab	2.93	Japan	4.27	Finland	5.26
Japan	2.86	Portugal	4.25	Switzerland (Fr)	5.19
Taiwan	2.85	New Zealand	4.23	New Zealand	5.15
Israel – Druze	2.83	Isr – Muslim Arab	4.22	Turkey	5.12
Hong Kong	2.83	Isr – Christ Arab	4.21	United States	5.03
Singapore	2.75	Hong Kong	4.18	Estonia – Rural	5.02
East Germany	2.69	Switzerland (Fr)	4.18	Mexico	4.99
Israel – Jews	2.69	Israel – Druze	4.16	Slovakia	4.98
Brazil	2.64	Brazil	4.16	Australia	4.98
Poland	2.53	East Germany	4.16	Estonia – Urban	4.96
Malaysia	2.43	Spain	4.11	Brazil	4.92
Hungary	2.42	Taiwan	4.11	Isr – Muslim Arab	4.88
United States	2.39	Slovakia	4.09	Isr – Christ Arab	4.88
New Zealand	2.38	Australia	4.09	Hungary	4.87
Australia	2.36	Italy	4.08	Israel – Druze	4.86
Mexico	2.35	West Germany	4.07	Hong Kong	4.85
West Germany	2.27	Israel – Jews	4.06	Bulgaria – Turks	4.83
The Netherlands	2.26	Bulgaria – Turks	4.04	Poland	4.82
Switzerland (Fr)	2.20	Poland	4.00	Singapore	4.79
Estonia – Rural	2.18	Thailand	3.99	Israel – Jews	4.78
France	2.16	The Netherlands	3.98	Japan	4.69
Slovakia	2.11	Denmark	3.97	Taiwan	4.68
Portugal	2.08	Hungary	3.96	Malaysia	4.66
Spain	2.03	Singapore	3.93	Shanghai (PRC)	4.65
Finland	2.03	Turkey	3.90	[China (comb)	4.49]
Greece	2.01	France	3.89	Zimbabwe	4.48
Estonia – Urban	2.00	Slovenia	3.76	Hebei (PRC)	4.46
Denmark	1.86	Estonia – Urban	3.73	Slovenia	4.36
Slovenia	1.76	Estonia – Rural	3.64	Guangzhou (PRC)	4.35
Italy	1.69	Finland	3.63	Thailand	4.34

EXHIBIT 13.3 *(cont.)*

Harmony

Italy	4.80	France	4.31	Guangzhou (PRC)	3.83
Slovenia	4.72	Portugal	4.29	Singapore	3.72
Mexico	4.67	Turkey	4.26	Hebei (PRC)	3.71
Estonia – Urban	4.65	Taiwan	4.17	[China (comb)	3.71]
Finland	4.54	Denmark	4.16	United States	3.70
Estonia – Rural	4.53	Poland	4.10	Shanghai (PRC)	3.63
Spain	4.53	East Germany	4.08	Israel – Druze	3.50
Hungary	4.51	Japan	4.07	Malaysia	3.50
Switzerland (Fr)	4.50	Australia	4.05	Zimbabwe	3.42
West Germany	4.42	Brazil	4.02	Hong Kong	3.34
Slovakia	4.40	New Zealand	3.99	Isr – Christ Arab	3.28
Greece	4.39	The Netherlands	3.98	Isr – Muslim Arab	3.05
Bulgaria – Turks	4.32	Thailand	3.93	Israel – Jews	3.01

Source: Shalom H. Schwartz, 'Beyond Individualism/Collectivism: New Cultural Dimensions of Values', in *Individualism and Collectivism*, eds. Uichol Kim, Harry C. Triandis, Cigdem Kagitcibasi, Sang-Chin Choi, and Gene Yoon (Thousand Oaks, CA: Sage, 1994), pp. 85–119. Reprinted by permission of Sage Publications, Inc.

EXHIBIT 13.4

Value Dimensions and Relevance to Consumer Behaviour

Value Dimension	Relevance to Consumer Behaviour
Conservatism	Stimulates interest in products which are traditional, which are used by others in the same social group, and which contribute to orderliness and cleanliness.
Affective autonomy	Stimulates interest in products which make life enjoyable, exciting, and varied.
Intellectual autonomy	Stimulates interest in products which further consumers' creativity, and contribute to leisure activities.
Hierarchy	Stimulates interest in products which communicate status and power.
Mastery	Stimulates desire for new products, for products provide increased control of life.
Egalitarian commitment	Stimulates interest in social aspects of products, stimulates patronage of smaller competitors.
Harmony	Stimulates interest in environmental aspects of products, of products which emphasize naturalness and being close to nature.

HIGHLIGHT 13.2

Value Changes in Consumer Product Test Magazines

In many countries, consumer magazines perform and publish comparative product tests – such as the *test* magazine in Germany, *Which?* in the United Kingdom, and *test achat* in Belgium. Analysing the content of these magazines, and the type of products being tested, is a possible source of insight into consumer values in these countries, at least when one assumes that consumers' values are mirrored in the type of content consumer magazines will publish.

One study analysed how the type of products being tested changed in the three consumer magazines mentioned over the period 1966 to 1986. Products were categorized into three groups:

1. Basic products refer to basic necessities in everyday life – food, cleaning products, heating, and health care.
2. Supplementary products make life easier and may have social significance – household appliances, cars, furniture, textiles, cosmetics, radios, and TV sets.
3. Stimulating products are products used for leisure activities, where the activity is the primary objective and not the possession as such – photo equipment, do-it-yourself products, gardening equipment.

The results, shown below, indicate that the number of stimulating products, relative to the number of supplementary products, has been rising in Germany and Belgium over the time analysed, while this trend cannot be found in the United Kingdom. At the same time, the number of supplementary products tested relative to the number of basic products has risen in the United Kingdom, a trend which cannot be found in Germany and Belgium.

Do you think these results say anything about differences in consumer values between these countries, or about differences in value changes? Why or why not? If yes, what are the differences?

Source: Adapted from Suzanne C. Grunert and Klaus G. Grunert,
'Product Testing Organizations as a Source of Information on Consumer Values and Needs:
A Three-Country Example', *Journal of International Consumer Marketing*, 4, 1989, pp. 29–39.

perspective, advertising can be seen as a funnel through which cultural meaning is poured into consumer goods.[23] Essentially, advertisers must decide what cultural meanings they want their products to have, and then create ads that communicate those cultural meanings, often using symbols (whether words or images) to stand for the desired cultural meanings.[24]

A *symbol* is something (a word, an image, or an object) that stands for or signifies something else (the desired cultural meaning). For instance, to communicate cool, refreshing meanings, Carlsberg shows a person emerging from crystal-clear water in an ad for mineral water. The naked bodies shown in Calvin Klein's ads for Obsession perfume connote obvious meanings about the product. Horses in Marlboro and off-roaders in Camel advertising are supposed to be symbols of freedom and independence. Café chairs and open spaces are used to symbolize elegance in advertising for Campari or Martini. Highlight 13.3 describes another cultural symbol used in advertising.

HIGHLIGHT 13.2 (*cont.*)

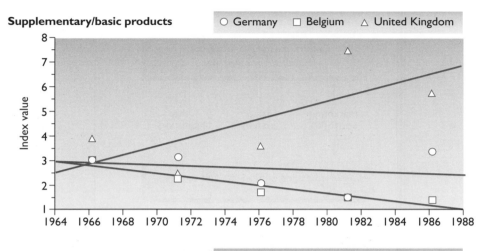

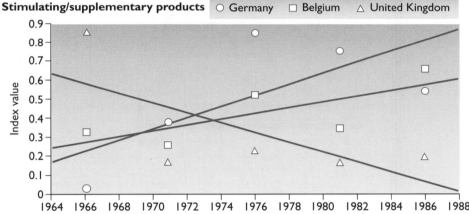

Although advertising may be the most obvious marketing mechanism for moving meanings into products, other aspects of marketing strategy are involved as well. Consider pricing strategies. Discount stores such as Aldi and Netto use low prices to establish the meaning of their stores. For many consumers, high prices have desirable cultural meanings that can be transferred to certain products (Mercedes-Benz cars, Rolex watches, Chivas Regal Scotch, Armani suits) to create a luxurious, high-status, high-quality image.

The product itself conveys considerable symbolic meaning. Many German car manufacturers like Mercedes-Benz and BMW design attributes of their cars to communicate perfection and reliability. This is mirrored, among other things, in the design of control panels, the steering wheel, and devices to adjust seats. Other manufacturers, like Italian Alfa Romeo, use the same details to communicate sportiveness and daring.

EXHIBIT 13.5

A Model of the Cultural Process

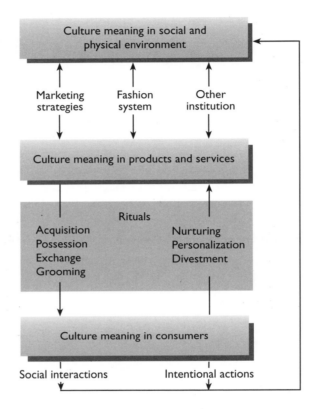

Source: Adapted from Grant McCracken, 'Culture and Consumption: A Theoretical Account of the Structure and Movement of the Cultural Meaning of Consumer Goods', *Journal of Consumer Research*, June 1986, pp. 71–84.

Other factors besides marketing strategies can influence the transfer of meaning from the cultural world into products.[25] For instance, journalists who report the results of product tests of cars, stereo systems, or ski equipment are moving meaning into the products. The so-called fashion system, including designers, reporters, opinion leaders, and celebrities, transfers fashion-related meanings into clothing, cooking, and home furnishing products.[26] Food and wine journalists contribute to some products achieving a status of exclusivity.

Moving Meanings from Products into Consumers

The cultural process model identifies rituals as ways of moving meanings from the product to the consumer. **Rituals** are *symbolic actions performed by consumers to create, affirm, evoke, or revise certain cultural meanings.*[27] For instance, the consumption rituals

HIGHLIGHT 13.3

The Cultural Meanings in Products and Brands –
'The Jolly Green Giant'

 eople are often unaware of the cultural origins of everyday objects in their environments, even though they may sense the fundamental meaning of these objects.
Consider the Jolly Green Giant, the symbol of the Green Giant Company, a vegetable
cannery, which is part of the UK Grand Metropolitan group. The Giant is clad entirely
in green leaves.

What is the cultural meaning of the Jolly Green Giant? Is the Jolly Green Giant only an easy-
to-remember brand symbol or something more? From a cultural perspective, the Jolly Green
Giant can be seen as a 20th-century manifestation of ancient European fertility symbols that
represented the spirit of vegetation.

Figures clothed in leaves have deep cultural meanings that date back hundreds of years. Fraser
described many of these symbolic figures in his masterwork, *The Golden Bough*. In many early
European cultures, people celebrated the rites of spring by honouring the spirits of sacred trees
or plants. By the 19th century, this ritual had become personalized in that a person from each
rural community was dressed in leaves or flowers. For instance, the Gypsies of Transylvania and
Romania had Green George, a boy 'covered from top to toe in green leaves and blossoms'. In
Bavaria (southern Germany), the leaf person was Quack; in England, it was Jack in the Green; in
Switzerland, it was the Whitsuntide Lout. Other popular names for the fertility symbol were the
Leaf King, the Grass King, the May King, and the Queen of May.

Even as recently as 100 years ago, fertility figures representing the spirit of vegetation could
be found in many parts of eastern Europe, Germany, and England. Although the details of the
costume and the ritual varied from place to place, the overall concept and the representation
of the central figure were consistent. A youthful person was dressed with leaves and other
vegetation. Sometimes the person was symbolically dunked into a pond or stream. Thus were the
spirits of fertility and water honoured, and the community was assured continued supplies of
water and forage.

Clearly, these fertility figures are similar to the Jolly Green Giant. Is this just a coincidence,
or does the obvious symbolism of such a figure still convey compelling meanings to the
sophisticated citizens of the modern world?

Source: Adapted from Tom E. Sullenberger, 'Ajax Meets the Jolly Green Giant: Some Observations on the
Use of Folklore and Myth in American Mass Marketing', *Journal of American Folklore*, 87, 1974, pp. 53–65.

performed at weddings are related to the cultural meaning of marriage: customs like
sharing the wedding cake, breaking dishes on the evening before the wedding, receiving
gifts for the shared household, and unwrapping and admiring them together.

Not all rituals are formal ceremonies such as a special dinner, a graduation, or a
wedding. Rather, many rituals are common aspects of everyday life, although people
usually do not recognize their behaviour as ritualistic. Consumer researchers have
begun to investigate the role of rituals in consumer behaviour.[28] We discuss five
consumption-related rituals involved in the movement of meaning between product
and consumer – the actions associated with acquisition, possession, exchange,
grooming, and divestment.

Acquisition Rituals

Some of the cultural meanings in products are transferred to consumers through the simple *acquisition rituals* of purchasing the product. For instance, there are widely accepted rituals for the purchase of wine in a restaurant: when the waiter has shown the guest the bottle, he uncorks the bottle, pours a little bit, and the customer then thoughtfully looks at the glass, sniffs, finally tastes it, and usually nods to the waiter indicating that everything is in order. These rituals contribute to the meaning of wine as a product of class and a product of quality variation, as well as to the expertise of the customer who has to accept or reject the product. As another example, collectors who are interested in possessing scarce or unique products (antiques, stamps or coins, and so on) may perform special search rituals when they go out on the hunt.

The *bargaining rituals* involved in negotiating the price of a car, stereo system, or some object at a garage sale can help transfer important meanings to the buyer (I got a good deal). Consider how an avid plate collector in his early 60s describes the meanings conveyed by bidding rituals at an auction or a flea market.[29]

> There's no Alcoholics Anonymous for collectors. You just get bit by the bug and that's it. The beauty and craftsmanship of some of these things are amazing. They were made by people who cared. There's nothing like getting a hold of them for yourself. Especially if you get it for a song and you sing it yourself. It's not just getting a great deal, it's knowing that you've got a great deal that makes for the thrill. It's even better if you have to bid against someone for it.

In sum, the acquisition rituals performed in obtaining products (purchase, search, bargaining, bidding) can help move meanings to the buyer.

Possession Rituals

Possession rituals help consumers acquire the meanings in products. For instance, the new owners of a house (or apartment) might invite friends and relatives to a house-warming party to admire their dwelling and formally establish its meanings. Many consumers perform similar ritualistic displays of a new purchase (a car, clothing, stereo system) to show off their new possession, solicit the admiration of their friends, and gain reassurance that they made a good purchase.

Other possession rituals involve moving personal meaning from the customer into the product. For instance, *product nurturing rituals* put personal meaning into the product (washing your car each Saturday; organizing your record or CD collection; tuning your bicycle; working in your garden).[30] Later, these meanings can be moved back to the consumer, where they are experienced and enjoyed as satisfaction or pride. These possession rituals help create strong, involving relationships between products and consumers.

Personalizing rituals serve a similar function. Many people who buy a used car or a previously owned house perform ritualistic actions to remove meanings left over from the previous owner and move new meanings of their own into the product. For instance, consumers will purchase special accessories for their new or used car to personalize it (new floor mats, a better radio, different wheels and/or tyres, custom stripes). Repainting, wallpapering, or installing carpeting are rituals that personalize a house to 'make it your own'.

Exchange Rituals

Certain meanings can be transferred to consumers through *exchange rituals* such as giving gifts.[31] For instance, giving wine or flowers to your host or hostess on arriving at a formal dinner party is a ritual that transfers cultural meanings (thanks, graciousness, generosity).

People often select gifts for anniversaries, birthdays, or special holidays such as Christmas that contain special cultural meanings to be transferred to the receiver. For instance, giving a nice watch to a high school graduate might be intended to convey cultural meanings of achievement, adult status, or independence. Parents often give gifts to their children that are intended to transfer very particular cultural meanings (a puppy represents responsibility; a bike represents freedom; a computer conveys the importance of learning and mastery).

Grooming Rituals

Certain cultural meanings are perishable in that they tend to fade over time. For instance, personal care products such as shampoo, mouthwash, and deodorants and beauty products (cosmetics, skin care) contain a variety of cultural meanings (attractive, sexy, confident, influence over others). But when transferred to consumers through use, these meanings are not permanent. Such meanings must be continually renewed by drawing them out of a product each time it is used. *Grooming rituals* involve particular ways of using personal care and beauty products that coax these cultural meanings out of the product and transfer them to the consumer. Many people engage in rather elaborate grooming rituals to obtain these meanings.

Divestment Rituals

Consumers perform *divestment rituals* to remove meaning from products. Certain products (items of clothing, a house, a car or motorcycle, a favourite piece of sports equipment) can contain considerable amounts of personal meaning. These meanings may be the basis for a strong customer–product relationship. For instance, products can acquire such personal meaning through long periods of use or because they symbolize important meanings (a chair might be a family heirloom).

Often consumers believe that some of these personal meanings must be removed before such products can be sold or even thrown away. Thus, for instance, consumers may wash or dry clean a favourite item of clothing that they plan to give away or donate to charity to remove some of the personal meanings in the product. Consumers might remove certain highly personal parts of a house (a special chandelier), car (a special radio), or motorcycle (a custom seat) before selling it.

In certain cases the personal meaning in the product is so great the consumer cannot part with the object. Academics hang on to their desks at which they have written both their Master's thesis and their PhD dissertation. People hang on to their wedding dresses, suits they wore for an exam, or shoes they wore when they fell in love. If divestment rituals are unable to remove these meanings, consumers may keep such objects forever or at least until the personal meanings have faded and become less intense.

Marketing Implications

Managing Cultural Meaning

The cultural process model suggests a basic marketing task is to manage the cultural meaning of the brand or product.[32] The shared cultural meanings of a brand are a large part of its economic value or its *brand equity*.[33] Managing brand meanings requires that marketers identify the brand meanings shared by consumers and monitor changes in those meanings. Means–end analysis is useful for this purpose. Marketing strategies might be directed at maintaining positive brand meanings or creating new meanings. These strategies would have to select appropriate meanings from the cultural environment and move or transfer them into products and brands.

Although marketers usually think cultural meanings are fixed or static and are not affected much by a company's actions, marketing strategies do influence the overall cultural environment. A conspicuous example is the proliferation of marketing stimuli in the physical environment (signs, billboards, ads, shops, advertisements). Less obvious is how the huge volume of marketing strategies affects our social environment and the shared meanings of modern life.[34]

Using Celebrity Endorsers in Ads

A popular advertising strategy for moving cultural meanings into products and brands is to have celebrities endorse the product.[35] From a cultural perspective, celebrities are cultural objects with specific cultural meanings. In developing an effective celebrity endorsement strategy, marketers must be careful to select a celebrity who has appropriate meanings consistent with the overall marketing strategy (the intended meanings) for the product.[36] For example, some actor celebrities such as Arnold Schwarzenegger have relatively clear meanings, based largely on the types of roles they usually play. Musicians may have distinctive cultural images based on their records, live performances, and video appearances, which enhances their appeal as celebrity spokespersons. Sometimes the cultural meanings of a celebrity spokesperson are related to their credibility and expertise concerning the product, as when sports celebrities endorse sports equipment and apparel or when supermodel Naomi Campbell endorses Hennes & Mauritz clothes. Of course, the perceived expertise of the celebrity must be related to the product – German tennis star Steffi Graf endorsing a brand of noodles will not add credibility to the quality of the product, even though she is certainly well known and may communicate cultural meanings of success and achievement.

Developing Marketing Strategies in Different Cultural Environments

Cross-cultural differences provide difficult challenges for international marketers.[37] Even when cultural differences have been identified and understood, how should marketers react to them? The traditional view of international marketing is that each local culture should be carefully researched for important differences from the domestic market. Differences in consumer needs, wants, preferences, attitudes, and values, as well as in shopping, purchasing, and consumption behaviours, should be carefully examined. The marketing strategy should then be tailored to fit the specific values and behaviours of the culture.

This is actually widely practised. Manufacturers of electric equipment like AEG, for example, have to modify their appliances because electric outlets and voltages vary in different parts of the world. Philip Morris had to alter its ads for Marlboro cigarettes in the United Kingdom because the government believed British children are so impressed with American cowboys they might be moved to take up smoking. Nestlé modifies the taste of its Nescafé coffee and the promotions for it in various countries to accommodate the different preferences in each nation.[38] The percentage of fruit juice contained in Fanta varies depending on the country it is sold in.

However, there are also voices arguing against adaptation to local differences and calling for a **global marketing** approach. One of its major advocates has been Theodore Levitt of the Harvard Business School.[39] Levitt argues that because of increased world travel and worldwide telecommunication capabilities, consumers across the world think and shop increasingly alike. Tastes, preferences, and motivations of people in various cultures are becoming more homogeneous. Also, he argues, once we look beyond concrete product attributes, the things consumers are really interested in are quite similar around the world – while consumers may differ in their preferences for the size of knobs of a washing machine, they share the basic interest in not having to wash by hand, i.e. an alleviation of life's burdens. When marketers realize that, they can market the same product worldwide, realize economies of scale, and be successful by having lower priced products helping more people to an easier life.

Levitt's arguments have caused considerable discussion over the years.[40] One of the counterarguments is that even the most frequently cited examples of global marketing, like the McDonald's fast food chain, actually adapt their products to local preferences, even though these adaptations may be minor. A more theoretical argument is that consumers around the world are interested not only in an alleviation from life's burdens, but also in an increase in its pleasures – and this is where cultural differences are likely to become more prominent.

The more moderate version of the global marketing argument points at two ways in which marketers can profit from common approaches in various markets. First, certain segments of consumers may be comparable across cultural boundaries. This seems to be especially true for the high end of many markets. These segments (and not the whole market) may then be addressed by a global marketing approach. Second, usually some marketing parameters may be standardized across cultures, while others may not. Even though the product may be the same, advertising may have to be adapted to local tastes and regulations. For example the British-based Land Rover brand, which includes the Defender, Discovery, and Range Rover cars, has been trying to position its brand in a pan-European way, emphasizing the brand values of individualism, authenticity, freedom, adventure, guts, and supremacy.[41] This is possible because the segment to which these cars appeal seem to be comparable in various countries. Other products, such as food, are more culturally sensitive. MD Foods introduced its functional food Gaio – a yoghurt-type product supposed to have a positive health effect on blood pressure – in Denmark with success, but experienced considerable difficulties in launching the same product in Sweden and the United Kingdom. In both countries, the product had to be withdrawn after considerable losses.[42]

**Back to . . .
The Birth
of the
Consumer
Society**

The opening example described several changes in the culture of 18th-century England, which led to the birth of a consumer society. One fundamental change occurred as many people moved from rural areas to larger and more anonymous urban communities. Such a cultural change can influence various cultural meanings in a continuous, reciprocal process much like that of the Wheel of Consumer Analysis. For instance, the new city dwellers were concerned about their social class status. These changes in values led to new beliefs and attitudes about products that could communicate social distinctions, which led to changes in purchase behaviour. As more people bought these status products, the social environment changed for all consumers, leading to further changes in values and meanings, and so on.

Other cultural changes occurred as people's shopping and purchasing behaviours became more frequent, even daily, rather than only on the weekly market day. The shopping environment also changed in that people could buy things in various shops rather than from pedlars or street hawkers. The evolving consumption culture was also influenced by marketing strategies (especially advertising and forms of social influence such as opinion leaders).

Finally, mass consumption increased as more people had significant discretionary income. Many people who previously had been unable to buy much (low purchasing power) or were unwilling to do so (they didn't see the need or value of making fashion-oriented purchases) now became increasingly interested in consumption. These people had developed new cultural needs, values, and goals that could be satisfied rather easily through consumption. Gradually, goods of all types became infused with symbolic meaning, and people began to buy and use goods as a way to acquire these important meanings.

Many scholars who have identified social competition and people's need for status differentiation as largely responsible for the consumer revolution write as if they do not approve of people seeking to satisfy such 'unimportant' and 'trivial' values.[43] Although status distinction was (and still is) an important end state for most people, other cultural meanings were also desired.[44] The cultural process of meaning transfer is a natural process people use to obtain important meanings. The cultural process model is not evidence of people's inherent irrationality, nor is it applicable only to 'manipulative' marketing strategies. All known cultures imbue certain objects with special meaning, and people obtain and use those objects to gain those important cultural meanings. One difference is that people in modern consumer societies often purchase objects (products and services) to obtain cultural meaning.

Similar cultural changes occurred later in America, France, and elsewhere as those societies also developed consumption-oriented cultures. The same events are occurring right now around the world, including societies in Asia, South America, Africa, and eastern Europe. A big difference, though, is that cultural changes spread much more rapidly today because of modern communications and more sophisticated and effective marketing strategies.

Summary

In this chapter we examined the influence of culture and cross-cultural factors on consumers' affective responses and cognitions, behaviours, and the physical and social environment. We defined culture as the meanings shared by people in a society (or in a social group), and we discussed how marketers can study the content of culture. We identified several important values and lifestyle trends in various cultures, and we drew some implications for marketing strategies. We presented a model of the cultural process by which cultural meaning is moved between different locations – especially from the environment to products and on from products to consumers. Then we examined the influence of cross-cultural differences on consumers. Finally, we discussed how marketers might use this knowledge to develop effective international marketing strategies.

Key Terms and Concepts

content of culture   266
cross-cultural differences   282
cultural meaning   264
cultural process   272
culture   264
ethnographic studies   269
global marketing   283
human values   269
rituals   278

Review and Discussion Questions

1. Define culture and contrast two approaches to cultural analysis: the content of the culture versus the cultural process.
2. Identify a major change in cultural values that seems to be occurring in your society. Discuss its likely effects on consumers' affect, cognitions, and behaviours and on the social and physical environment.
3. Select a product of your choice and discuss two implications of your analysis in Question 2 for developing marketing strategies for that product.
4. Briefly describe one example of a price, product, and distribution strategy that moves cultural meaning into the product.
5. Select a print ad and analyse it as a mechanism for moving cultural meaning into the product.
6. Choose a popular celebrity endorser and analyse the meanings being transferred to the product endorsed.
7. Select a public holiday other than Christmas – for example, Easter or mid-summer. Discuss the major cultural values reflected in this holiday celebration.
8. Think about what you do when getting ready to go out. Try to identify some grooming rituals you perform that involve certain products. Try to discover how you use some particular product (blow-dryers, perfume, or after-shave, shampoo). What implications might this have for marketing this product?

9. Describe how possession rituals can transfer meaning from products to consumers.
10. Describe a personal experience in which you performed a divestment ritual. What personal meanings did you remove through the ritual?

Additional Reading

For a classic paper that discusses the symbolic, cultural meanings in products, see:
Sidney J. Levy, 'Symbols of Sale', *Harvard Business Review*, July–August 1959, pp. 117–124.

For a well-written discussion of how consumers can use products to create a desirable self-concept, see:
Russell W. Belk, 'Possessions and the Extended Self', *Journal of Consumer Research*, September 1988, pp. 139–168.

For an advanced treatment of the concept of culture in a postmodern context, see:
Dominique Bouchet, 'Rails Without Ties – The Social Imaginary and Postmodern Culture', *International Journal of Research in Marketing*, 11, no. 4, 1994, pp. 405–421.

For a thorough treatment of the measurement of values in a cross-cultural context, see:
Shalom H. Schwartz, 'Universals in the Content and Structure of Values: Theoretical Advances and Empirical Tests in 20 Countries', in *Advances in Experimental Social Psychology*, ed. Mark P. Zanna (San Diego, CA: Academic Press, 1992), pp. 1–65.

For an example of relating values to consumer behaviour, see:
Suzanne C. Grunert and Hans Jørn Juhl, 'Values, Environmental Attitudes, and Buying Organic Foods', *Journal of Economic Psychology*, no. 1, 1995, pp. 39–62.

For three discussions of the problems (and opportunities) of developing global marketing strategies, see:
Teresa Domzal and Lynette Unger, 'Emerging Positioning Strategies in Global Marketing', *The Journal of Consumer Marketing*, Fall 1987, pp. 23–40.
Subhash Jain, 'Standardization of International Marketing Strategy: Some Research Hypotheses', *Journal of Marketing*, January 1989, pp. 70–79.
Robert O. Jordan 'Going Global: How to Join the Second Major Revolution in Advertising', *The Journal of Consumer Marketing*, Winter 1988, pp. 39–44.

MARKETING STRATEGY IN ACTION

When East Germany joined West Germany

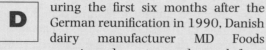

During the first six months after the German reunification in 1990, Danish dairy manufacturer MD Foods experienced a strong demand from East German retailers for their top-of-the-line products – e.g. cream cheese pies, the Garli flavoured cream cheese, etc. – expensive, luxury-type products. After six months, however, this demand has levelled off. It was replaced by a growing demand for low-price, self-service items. The trade marketing director Jens Refslund of MD Foods suspected that the reason for the short boom and subsequent decline of the premium products in East Germany was that, after a first trial, consumers may have found out that this type of product did not really match their consumption patterns. The simple products may have fitted the East German needs better.

Up to 1 October 1990, East Germany was an independent state, the German Democratic Republic, with an economic system based on a socialist, planned economy. In the food sector, just as in all other sectors, the needs of the population were assessed and turned into a production plan for the whole economy. This production plan specified in detail who had to produce what, in which quantities, and with which inputs. The goods were then distributed to the population by a system of wholesalers and retail outlets, most of which were also government owned.

The assessment of needs was partly based on desk research, but market research was carried out, too. The Institut für Marktforschung in Leipzig conducted surveys measuring consumer needs, the results of which served as input to the overall planning process. The employees of the institute (which has survived as a private institution, doing market research under the conditions of a market economy now) felt, however, that their work hardly had any noticeable impact on the plan. The central planning system led to a food supply which, in quantitative terms, was widely regarded as satisfactory. In comparison to the food supply in a typical Western

economy, however, four main differences can be noted.

1. Variety was very limited. Because competition of brands of products of the same kind was officially regarded as a waste of resources, there was usually only one brand available. Therefore for the consumer there was usually no need to make brand choices. Indeed, because brands as a means of identification and differentiation were superfluous, there was little branding and comparatively many generic products. Also, because packaging did not have to be used as a means of differentiation, most packaging was, by Western standards, dull and simple.

2. There was usually only one level of quality, i.e. there was neither horizontal nor vertical differentiation. The system did not encourage quality improvements. The Amt für Standardisierung und Meßwesen had to certify all products before they were sold in the shops. Their certification system was some kind of quality grading, in which a certain threshold value had to be surpassed before a product was allowed to be sold. Production was thus geared to meeting this threshold, but, because quality above the threshold was not rewarded – and possibly punished, when it led to an output which was quantitatively less – products were generally of a low-to-medium quality.

3. Prices differed considerably from prices in the West. First of all, there was no price variation at all – a given product would be sold at identical prices in all shops. Basic food products were heavily subsidized, and were correspondingly cheap. Items which were regarded as luxury items, e.g. coffee and chocolate, were, by Western standards, vastly overpriced. Some East German top products, which went mostly into export, and some products imported from the West could be bought in the Delikat speciality shops at prices about two to three times the average level. In addition, Western products could

be bought for Western currency in the Intershops. However, only those with relatives in the West typically had access to Western currency, and only in limited quantities. There was some possibility for exchange on the black market, but at an unfavourable rate.

4. A few product categories, like tropical fruits, were usually in short supply.

Hence, in the food sector, it was not so much the quantity as the quality and variety which could give concern. In other product categories supply was considerably more scarce. This, together with the facts that basic living was relatively cheap and that most households had two incomes, resulted in considerable excess purchasing power and a high saving rate of, on average, 20 per cent. There was no shortage of income in the GDR. The problem was spending. Some products were either unavailable or so prohibitively priced that only long-term saving made purchase possible, especially since consumer credit was unknown.

Consumer behaviour in this socialist economy differed considerably from consumer behaviour in the West. In the West, consumers have to make a large number of choices during shopping, and marketers are interested in understanding consumer decision making, i.e. which product alternatives consumers are aware of, how their choices are affected by advertising, which product attributes have an impact on their decision making, and so on. When there are not usually alternative products to choose from, and when some products may be scarce, consumers develop skills in a different direction.

After decades with no variety of brands to choose from, the monetary union and subsequent reunification with West Germany resulted in the East Germans being suddenly confronted with the problem of having to make choices. The Institut für Marktforschung in Leipzig has monitored consumer behaviour after the monetary union closely. 'Immediately after the monetary union came into being, there was an extended trial phase, during which people bought all kinds of products, also expensive ones – there was no real shortage of funds, on average people had savings of about DM4000, and the fact that they now had Western currency led to a

feeling of affluence', says Petra Knötzsch, one of the researchers at the Institut für Marktforschung. Suddenly it was possible to buy all those goods which previously were available only in the Intershops. These products were associated with high quality, and quite a number of consumers were actually disillusioned about the quality after they had tried the products. After this initial trial period, consumer demand was homing in on certain price categories, and brand preferences were slowly beginning to develop.

In the initial phase after reunification, consumer decision times in the supermarket were considerably longer in the East than in the West. Western consumers are said to take an average of 20 seconds to make a buying decision in a supermarket. East German consumers definitely took more time. A lot of discussions took place in supermarkets, and people handled products, read labels, and compared prices, some with pocket calculators. Many products were new and unknown, and their uses had to be learned first.

Most East German companies have had a hard time since the reunification, and many have closed down. Immediately after the monetary union came into effect, Eastern products basically disappeared from the shelves and were replaced by Western products. The official policy of producing more goods with less raw materials had ruined the image of Eastern products long before the political changes. The fact that Eastern products were sold at low bargain prices just before the monetary union, in order to free shelf space for Western products, did not help either. However, some East German products are now on their way back to the consumer. After the trial phase, it turned out that many consumers were conservative. For example, the attempt of the (Eastern) cigarette brand Kabinett to launch a new, lighter Kabinett, in accordance with Western trends towards lighter cigarettes, turned out to be a flop.

During the first years, there seemed to be a considerable East–West difference concerning consumers' attitude towards and expectations about advertising. The attitude towards advertising was more positive in the East than in the West. People were not yet as overloaded with advertising as Western consumers typically are. The higher degree of problem-solving behaviour in the East, and the lack of product experience, brand loyalty, and product knowledge, resulted in it being easier for advertisers to attract attention to their message in the East than in the West, moreover, the expectations with regard to message content were different. Actual advertising, however, did not seem to reflect these differences. Most manufacturers used the same advertising in the East as in the West.

Discussion Questions

1. Discuss the cultural meanings of consumer products for East and West German consumers before and after the reunification. How do these meanings affect consumers' cognitive and affective reactions to marketing strategies?

2. Most Western companies entering the East German market after the reunification used the same marketing strategy as in the West. Discuss the pros and cons of this approach as compared to a local adaptation approach.

3. How do you think the cultural meanings of consumer products have developed in the Eastern parts of Germany in the years since 1990 up to the present?

Source: Adapted from Klaus G. Grunert, *Food Products in East Germany* (Aarhus: SMR, 1993).

Subculture and Social Class

Older and Wiser

Beiersdorf, Procter & Gamble, and L'Oréal are playing it by the numbers in a race to introduce new facial-care lines in Europe and beyond for women over the age of 45.

Eyeing a potential bonanza of 60 million women aged 50-plus in Western Europe alone, beauty marketers are expanding away from their obsession with the young. Beiersdorf, which kicked off the trend with the introduction of Nivea Vital in Switzerland, has been expanding that successful franchise into Germany, France, the Benelux countries, and Austria as a prelude to a full Western European roll-out. And the company might have global ambitions for the line: a spokeswoman said the company has applied for a worldwide patent.

Hot on Beiersdorf's heels is L'Oréal, which has introduced Revitalise skin care. The five-product line, aimed at women aged 45–50 – a slightly younger target than Nivea Visage – hit French stores in 1995 supported with a TV campaign. A huge sampling effort also put six to seven million samples into French women's hands.

'This is a frontal assault', said a L'Oréal official. 'We're not bothering with testing or measuring response in one market before launching into others. This is more or less a global roll-out in three successive waves.'

Not to be left behind, P&G has introduced Pro Vital, a three-product facial-care line under the Oil of Ulay name.

'Everyone is going after the senior sector', said the L'Oréal executive. 'We had to get a product positioned towards that [age group].'

Aware of the onrushing competition, Beiersdorf pushed up its effort for Nivea Vital. Beiersdorf is continuing to use 53-year-old model Susanne Schönborn in its German language commercials.

When tested on the Swiss market, Nivea Vital's share of the ECU64 million facial-care category rose from zero to 6.2 per cent within seven months, while managing not to cannibalize Nivea Visage, which grew from 32.5 per cent of the facial-care category to 32.9 per cent during the same period.

Beiersdorf said that given that runaway success, competition was inevitable. 'We noticed that our competitors at P&G and L'Oréal, are acting very fast now', said Beiersdorf's Swiss General Manager Daniel N. Tobler.

He added that Beiersdorf's line is the most comprehensive of the three, including a night cream, day cream, tinted day cream, facial wash and concentrated liquid anti-ageing capsules. The product claims to improve older skin by improving metabolism that enables younger skin cells to grow.

L'Oréal denies its product is a knock-off. 'Nivea may have been ahead of us in creating products for seniors, but we feel that with Revitalise we've created a single cream that is more effective for older women than the five Nivea products combined,' said the official.

Even without the older women's line, Nivea has already cut a wide swathe across the ECU2.07 billion European facial-care category. In 1994, its Visage line climbed from an 11 per cent share of the category to 15 per cent in Western Europe, while Oil of Ulay fell from 11 per cent to 10 per cent L'Oréal's Plenitude slid from 13 per cent to 12 per cent.

Source: Adapted from Dagmar Mussey and Bruce Crumley, 'Older and Wiser: P&G, Beiersdorf and L'Oréal', reprinted with permission from the 17 April 1995 issue of *Advertising Age*. Copyright, Crain Communications, Inc 1995.

This example illustrates the marketing importance of a major subculture and how changing demographic characteristics can be important to marketers. In this chapter we discuss two aspects of the macro social environment – subcultures and social class. In Chapter 12 you learned that culture, subculture, and social class are three ways of dissecting the macro social environment. Culture is usually analysed at the level of a country or an entire society; subcultures are segments of the society. Social class can be considered a special subculture defined in terms of social status. Subcultures and social classes are cultural groups in that their members share common cultural meanings; however, both are part of the larger society and thus are influenced by the overall culture. Thus, we do not necessarily expect middle-class Germans to have the same meanings, behaviours, and lifestyles as middle-class Frenchmen. Social class and subcultures are useful for segmenting markets, understanding the shared cultural meanings of large groups of consumers, and developing targeted marketing strategies.

We begin the chapter by discussing the concept of subcultures. Next we describe several types of subcultures which are commonly distinguished. Then we discuss the concept of social class.

Subcultures

Subcultures are *distinctive groups of people in a society that share common cultural meanings* for affective and cognitive responses (emotional reactions, beliefs, values, goals), behaviours (customs, scripts and rituals, behavioural norms), and environmental factors (living conditions, geographic location, important objects). Although most subcultures share some cultural meanings with the overall society and/or other subcultures, some of a subculture's meanings must be unique and distinctive. Highlight 14.1 gives an example of marketing to a very distinctive subculture.

The analysis of subcultures is more important than ever. Demographic changes such as ageing populations increase the importance of age-related subcultures. Also, many societies are becoming more culturally diverse through immigration of people from other cultures. We also see an increasing degree of subcultures at the regional level which cross the borders of nations. To understand this diversity, marketers identify subcultures and try to develop marketing strategies to address their needs.

Marketers have used a variety of mostly demographic characteristics to identify subcultures. Exhibit 14.1 lists several demographic characteristics used to classify people into subgroups and gives examples of subcultures. These subcultures are not mutually exclusive – a person can simultaneously be male, reside in a particular region, be an immigrant, and be in the older age bracket. Marketers can combine demographic distinctions to identify smaller and more narrowly defined subcultures.

HIGHLIGHT 14.1

Mongol Dolls for Mongol Children

T he diagnosis of the doll is clear: Mongolism. Skew eyes, slightly protruding tongue, and low-sitting ears. And it is like dolls should be: soft and to be hugged.

The dolls are intended for children and adults born with Down's syndrome, also known as 'mongolism'. These dolls are designed and developed in Sweden and produced in Germany, and they are being exported to various European countries.

The typical Down's syndrome characteristics are common for all versions of the doll. They come in two basic versions – one with the tongue protruding from the mouth, and one with the mouth shut, and they come as boys and girls. In addition to that, there are many variations: light or dark skin colour, blue or brown eyes, short or long hair. All faces are hand-painted. The body is filled with cotton, which make the dolls washable, and the clothing has velcro sealings, which makes it easy to take off.

Before these dolls appeared on the market, mongol children never saw dolls which resembled themselves. And since people with Down's syndrome emotionally remain children throughout their lives, the dolls can follow them all their life.

Handicapped people form subcultures which many marketers find difficult to address, because it is regarded as ethically and socially problematic to remind people of their handicap. On the other hand, ignoring the fact that people are different – and in this case look different – can also be a way of expressing a lack of acceptance of the handicap.

Source: Adapted from Jette Aaes, 'Mongoldukker til mongolbørn,'
Morgenavisen Jyllands-Posten, 19 June 1997, p. 5.

Careful research and thoughtful analysis are necessary to develop a clear understanding of subcultures. Consider, for instance, the confusion about the so-called yuppies (young urban professionals). Originally a narrow subculture group, yuppies gradually came to mean rich, selfish youths and, due to intense media attention through the 1980s, became virtually synonymous with the baby boomer generation.

Subculture analysis can follow the same approach as cultural analysis discussed in Chapter 13. Typically, marketers examine the *content of the subculture* by describing the cultural meanings members of the subculture share (especially their values and lifestyles). It is much less common for marketers to examine the *cultural processes* by which cultural meanings are moved from the external world of the subculture to products and services and on to the people in the subculture.

In the following, we will discuss some major types of subcultures which are analysed in a consumer behaviour context: geographic, age, ethnic, and gender subcultures.

Geographic Subcultures

As we discussed in the previous chapter, national boundaries are often used to define units of analysis when looking at cultural differences. However, national boundaries are a result of a host of factors, including topographical, climatic, historical, political and economic factors. All of these factors are at work also at levels both above and below the national level.

EXHIBIT 14.1

Types of Subcultures

Demographic Characteristic	Examples of Subcultures
Age	Adolescents, young adults, middle-aged, elderly
Religion	Protestant, Catholic, Jewish, Muslim
Ethnic background	White, Black Caribbean, Black African, Indian, Chinese
Income level	Affluent, middle income, poor, destitute
Gender	Female, male
Family type	Single parent, divorced/no kids, two parents/kids
Occupation	Mechanic, accountant, priest, professor, clerk
Community	Rural, small town, suburban, city

At the subnational level, regions within countries are commonly known to differ in terms of various aspects of consumer behaviour and can therefore be treated as subcultures. These regional differences have many causes. Population density and degree of urbanization is one factor: sparsely populated areas, such as northern Norway, parts of Scotland or the Danish west coast, meant historically less impact from other parts of the world and more perseverance of old customs, a tendency which only very recently started to abate. Climatic differences have had an impact on the type of housing and the type of regional products produced, and these differences still have an impact on consumer behaviour even though modern transport facilities have removed the objective barriers. Thus, wine consumption in southern Germany (where wine is produced) is still considerably higher than in northern Germany (where climatic conditions prevent the production of wine).

Such environmental differences form the background for regions' differences in people's cognitions, affect, and behaviour. Sometimes they also have a political/historical background. Germany, which became a nation state relatively late, carries on some of its former political units like Bavaria and Saxonia as subcultures. Other countries such as England and Denmark, which have a long history of national unity, nevertheless have a heritage of distinct regions, e.g. the Midlands and the North in England. Some of these regions are closely related to the joint organization of economic activities in the region, such as the German Ruhr area.

Given that national boundaries are to some extent accidental, some regions which form distinct subcultures cross these boundaries. The region of Schleswig, north and south of the Danish/German border, has in the course of history changed hands between Denmark and Germany several times and has people with both Danish and German as native languages on both sides of the border, along with the corresponding societal infrastructure – newspapers, schools etc. In the borderland area between Alsace in France, Baden in Germany and the German speaking part of Switzerland, common roots are mirrored in similarities in dialects, eating habits, and festivities. New developments in communication and infrastructure can also lead to cross-border regions emerging or becoming strengthened – it is commonly expected that the Øresund region

EXHIBIT 14.2

**Territorial States and 5 Transnational Regions in a 12-Cluster Portrait
of the Food Cultures of 16 European Countries**

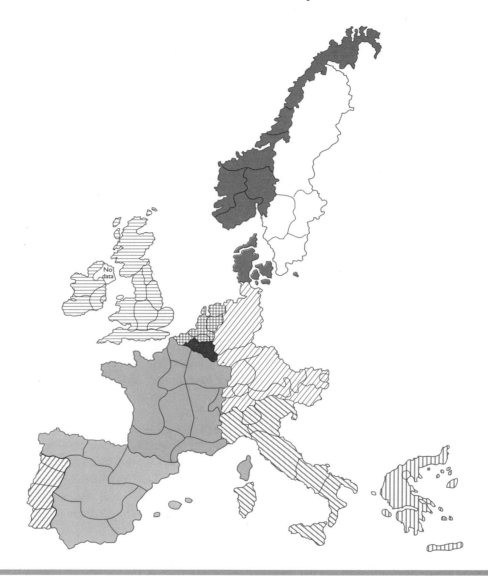

in Denmark/Sweden will become strengthened when the building of a bridge connecting Danish Copenhagen and Swedish Malmö will be completed.

Some people believe that the formation of cross-border regions is a trend, and that with increasing European integration regions will eventually become a more important unit of analysis also for marketers than nation states.[1] An interesting analysis carried out by Askegaard and Madsen[2] has looked at whether regions have become more important than nation states when looking at consumer behaviour regarding a particular product category, namely food. They used data on 138 food-related aspects of consumer behaviour in 79 European regions, and put them through a cluster analysis which grouped the regions into larger clusters based on the similarity in terms of consumer behaviour in the food area. They arrived at a 12-cluster solution, which is shown graphically in Exhibit 14.2. It includes seven nation states, namely Denmark, Norway, Sweden, Portugal, Spain, Italy, and Greece. Also included are four transnational regions, namely the British Isles, The Netherlands and Flanders, France and the French speaking part of Switzerland, and finally the 'Germanic area' of Germany, Austria, and the rest of Switzerland. The last cluster consists of Brussels, Wallonia, and Luxembourg, so this region is also fundamentally transnational. It is evident that the 'peripheral countries' of the analysis tend to form individual clusters whereas the heart of the European continent sees the formation of clusters across nation states.

The use of cross-border regions in marketing has not been very common. On the other hand, the analysis of regions within countries is quite institutionalized, at least in some countries. In Germany, for example, Nielsen Marketing Research has divided Germany into seven regions, which are widely used in market research in Germany.

Age Subcultures

Age groups can also be analysed as subcultures because they often have distinctive values and behaviours. However, marketers must be cautious about segmenting consumers based on their actual age. Many adult consumers think of themselves as younger than they really are. Thus, their behaviour, affect, and cognitions are more related to their psychological age than their chronological age. Consider this statement from an 89-year-old woman: 'I might be 89 years old. I feel good. I feel like I could fly the coop. I do. I feel younger, like I'm 45 or 50. I want to doll up, and I like to fuss. . . . I don't know I'm old. I feel like I'm going to live a long time.' This suggests marketers should analyse subjective or 'cognitive age' (the age one thinks of oneself as being) rather than chronological or actual age. Many different **age subcultures** can be identified and analysed, but we will discuss only three here: teens, baby boomers, and the grey market.

The Teen Market

The European teenage population has been gaining affluence and fluctuating in size. In the mid-1980s there were about 30 million people in Europe aged 14 to 19. This number decreased to about 25 million in the mid-1990s and will increase to about 27 million by the year 2000. (See Highlight 14.2 for more information about the fickle teen market.) Teens are important not only because they have a major influence on household purchases, but also because of their own discretionary purchasing power. Studies have found that teenagers do a large portion of the grocery shopping for the family: one study estimated that 59 per cent of 14–15-year-old schoolgirls and 44 per cent of 14–15-year-old boys participate in this task at least once a week. In addition, about 50 per cent of 14–15-year-olds think that they influence their parents' choice of convenience food brands.

However, marketers regard teenagers as a difficult target group. 'The youth market is volatile. Their behaviour can vary in a single country, but you'll find similarities in different countries. All of them are very selective. They will not listen to a marketer's message again if you do not get their attention first time around', as PepsiCo

HIGHLIGHT 14.2

The Teen Market

M arketing for the teen market is a complicated matter. Teenagers are extremely brand loyal consumers – until they suddenly change their brand preference. This was the conclusion from a project called ZapAttack whose mission was to get a grasp of the fickle age subculture of young consumers between 13 and 20. The name of the project refers to young people's merciless judgement on bad commercials. They zap immediately if they do not like what they see.

This generation has grown up in a society dominated by communication. More than any other age subculture they are familiar with commercials. They know a lot about movies and picture manipulation, and they are perfectly aware that they are being manipulated. They do not mind though – as long as it is done professionally. When communicating to them, things shouldn't be spelled out – teens want to be challenged. The story does not need to be chronologically structured for them to get the message. Thus, marketers must be advanced in their communication.

The study describes teens as individualistic herd members who change attitudes as soon as the marketer is about to get hold of the existing one. They are paradoxical, independent, anarchistic, and revolutionary. They change attitudes so rapidly that it is impossible to go further than to give a snapshot image of them. The teen target groups go exclusively for the latest craze. Therefore producers who have this group as their target must constantly be in the forefront of what is going on – otherwise their marketing will not appeal to them.

Crisp and snack producer Estrella was aware of the need to stand out from the crowd to catch the attention of the teens. Subsequently, Estrella formed an untraditional partnership with Scandinavian UFO Information which analyses observations of UFOs. Existing recordings of these observations are usually not accessible to the public, but due to this partnership they will now be accessible in connection with Estrella's promotion activity. When the consumer has collected and hands in four Estrella logos, for about £4 authentic recordings of the observations of UFOs will be available on videotape.

These are quite extraordinary steps that Estrella has taken in an attempt to catch the attention of the teen subculture. Both the occult and science fiction are subjects popular with teenagers' at present. Cult programmes like *X-Files*, as well as the revival of *Star Wars*, are examples of this trend.

Source: Mark Patterson, 'Generation Y – De individualistiske flokdyr', *Markedsføring*, 17, 1995, p. 14; Mark Patterson 'Nærkontakt af sprødeste grad', *Markedsføring*, 20, 1996, p. 2.

International's marketing director expresses it.[3] This has given rise to a host of specialist communication channels aimed at the teenage market – MTV and local music TV channels and a wide range of magazines specializing in different age brackets of male and female teenagers.[4]

Baby Boomers

Baby boomers are the people born between 1946 and 1964. There are about 130 million people in this group. This group is in its mid-30s to early 50s and in its prime earning and spending years. The baby-boomer market is the largest and most affluent in history and will have a major economic impact for the next 45 years.[5]

Baby boomers have a strong impact on markets for housing, cars, food, clothing and cosmetics, and financial services. For instance, many baby boomers are single, creating strong markets for vacations and convenience packaged goods. In addition, although they are having fewer children per household, the sheer size of the boomer group led to an increase in births in the early 1990s – a 'baby boom echo'. Boomers who are new parents are especially attractive to marketers. Given the large incomes and small family sizes of this group, spending per child is likely to be the largest in history. Markets for children's products have expanded accordingly. Toy sales, for example, are expected to increase more than twice as fast as the population of children for whom they are intended. Other markets, such as child care services and computer software for tots, may double in the next few years.

The baby boomer market, then, is the most lucrative and challenging marketers have ever seen. Many firms have designed new products and redesigned and repositioned old ones for this market. For example, commercials for Snickers chocolate bars show adults rather than children eating them. Crest and other brands have introduced toothpaste formulas to fight plaque, an adult problem. Levi Strauss has redesigned its jeans to give a little extra room in the seat to accommodate 'booming boomer bodies'. Even Clearasil, traditionally an antiacne medication for teenagers, has developed Clearasil Adult Care to appeal to the growing number of baby boomer adults with skin problems.

The Grey Market

As Europe ages (along with other industrialized countries such as Japan and the USA), marketers are recognizing the economic importance of the **grey market**, defined as consumers over the age of 50.[6] Regarded as the exclusive preserve of walking frame and chair lift manufacturers until just a few years ago, the area has begun to awaken the interest of many a marketer.[7] The grey market is one of the most rapidly growing subcultures in Europe, which has one of the highest proportions of older people in the world. Dramatic increases in life expectancy and declining birth rates mean that 23 per cent of the population will be over 60 by the year 2010. Estimates are that in 2005 there will be between 63 and 85 million consumers over 65, up from 56 million in the mid 1990s. At present about one in three Europeans is older than 50; by 2020 it will be about 40 per cent. Between now and 2020 the number of people aged 50 or older will increase by 40 per cent (as baby boomers continue to age), while the number under age 50 will decrease by 10 per cent. In 2020 there could be as many as 85 million elderly (over 65) or 74 million, according to Eurostat. The exact number of older Europeans expected in 2020 is hard to predict; it all depends on the mortality rate, especially gains made against specific diseases such as heart ailments, cancer, and stroke.

The next century will see huge increases in the demand for products and services for older consumers, including adult day care, home health care, prescriptions and over-the-counter drugs, medical care of all types, and foods low in cholesterol, sugar, salt, and calories. Other nonhealth-related products include planned holiday travel, restaurants, recreational vehicles, and hotels. Older people will be better educated than previous generations, which will create increased demand for educational programmes, books, and news. The grey market is already using its leisure time for self-development instead of seeing it as a gloomy period at the end of their lives.[8] Saga Services confirm that their range of special interest holidays, such as PC training, books out very quickly.

For years, marketing to the over 50s was limited to selling support tights and retirement homes to people that were often well over 60. But now marketers are starting to understand that not only is the whole 50-plus age group a potential goldmine, it is far too big to consider simply as one market. The market is quite diverse and marketers might benefit from considering smaller subculture groups based on narrower age ranges, such as for example older (55–64), elderly (65–74), aged (75–84), and very old (85 and over).

Perhaps marketers have traditionally ignored the grey market because it was assumed to have low purchasing power. However, in addition to its sheer size, the economic character of this market deserves careful consideration. While many of the members of this group no longer work, they often have considerable discretionary income. Many have shaken off mortgage and family responsibilities and are living in relative comfort, thanks to private pensions. In the United Kingdom, studies have shown that this sector, which represents around a third of the population, is the most affluent of any age group with 36 per cent of over 55s having a gross income of more than £19 500.[9] There is, however, a marked polarization of wealth within this age group.

Finally, because many people in the grey market subculture are retired, they have more time to enjoy entertainment and leisure activities. A UK survey found that 75 per cent of the over-50s said that holidays are their greatest annual expense.[10] Some old people have taken up university studies and other forms of higher education, now that they have the time and leisure to do so.[11] Although this market has historically spent more money on food for home consumption than away-from-home consumption, restaurants now cater for them with special discounts, early-bird dinners, and menus designed for the tastes and requirements of older people.

The elderly represent a significant market for skin-care products, vitamins and minerals, health and beauty aids, and medication that eases pain and promotes the performance of everyday activities. In addition, they are a significant market for apartments, particularly on the Spanish coast, time-share arrangements, travel and holidays, cultural activities, and luxury items given as gifts to their children and grandchildren. Overall, then, the grey market subculture represents an excellent marketing opportunity that will become even better in the future.

Developing marketing strategies that appeal to consumers in the grey market is more difficult than it looks. Few companies are experts at it and the media and marketing sector is inclined to ignore this market. There is an assumption that during the 50s you pull out your knitting and settle down for three decades of impoverished senility. Those that acknowledge the over-50s tend to overcompensate by depicting them as skydiving, tanned demigods with unlimited disposable income. Between these two myths lies the truth. Studies show that older people are time-rich with the income to enjoy themselves.[12] They are staying healthy and active much later into their lives than ever before.

Some ads are beginning to use themes and models that older consumers can identify with. No longer depicted as weak and doddery, older people are shown doing the things they do in real life: working, playing tennis, falling in love, and buying cars. The third age welcome light-hearted role models such as Joanna Lumley in the Müller yoghurt TV ads.

Ethnic Subcultures

Marketing to **ethnic subcultures** is quite common in the United States, but has been developing only slowly in Europe. One reason is that ethnic minorities account for a much smaller part of the population in European countries compared to the United States – usually not more than 5 per cent of the population. Also, it is sometimes claimed that ethnic minorities are more integrated into society in Europe, making it unnecessary to treat them as separate groups from a marketing viewpoint.

However, this view may be changing. Due to immigration for economic and political reasons, ethnic minorities have become more visible in some European countries, and because some of them tend to be younger and have more children than their fellow citizens, their size is expected to grow – like from 3 million to 6 million during the next 30 years in the United Kingdom.[13] Also, marketers have begun to realize that these people have considerable purchasing power – estimated at £10 billion per year in the United Kingdom.

The question on how these groups should be addressed by marketers is therefore being discussed to an increasing extent. With regard to some product categories some ethnic subcultures have special needs which are relatively obvious – such as ethnic food, food living up to certain religious criteria, or nonChristian greeting cards. At the same time, research has shown that ethnic subcultures may be highly attracted to mainstream brands, as an expression of a desire for integration.[14] Where the need for differentiated treatment perhaps becomes most obvious – and has spurred most discussion – is in market communication. Advertising largely ignores ethnic minorities, and some advertising is actually regarded as offensive. For example, a commercial for detergent Persil showing a Dalmatian shaking off its black spots was reportedly regarded as offensive by some black consumers in the United Kingdom. And ads which explicitly try to address ethnic minorities may blunder, as did the British Homepride commercial which showed a Sikh family in Liverpool, where the husband did not have a beard.[15]

What is regarded as offensive depends, of course, on the cognitive and affective reactions of consumers, and will therefore vary between consumers. In a survey asking consumers to remember ethnically sensitive and ethnically insensitive advertising, the famous Benetton ads were named in both categories – some consumers lauded them for showing ethnically diverse images, whereas others accused them of cynical use of ethnic images.[16]

The degree to which ethnic minorities differ in their consumer behaviour from the society of which they are part will depend on their degree of acculturation. A process of acculturation begins when a person from one culture moves to a different culture or subculture to live and work. **Acculturation** refers to how people in one culture or subculture understand and adapt to the meanings (values, beliefs, behaviours, rituals, lifestyles) of another culture or subculture.[17] **Consumer acculturation** refers to how people acquire the ability and cultural knowledge to be a skilled consumer in a different culture or subculture.[18]

Acculturation processes are important in the modern world. Many societies face the problem of assimilating large numbers of immigrants from rather different cultural backgrounds into the host culture. The degree to which immigrants become acculturated into a new culture or subculture depends on their level of **cultural interpenetration** – the amount and type of social interactions they have with people in the host culture.[19] Social contact with people in other subcultures can occur through direct, personal experience at work, while shopping, or in living arrangements.

When people come into contact with a new culture or subculture, they may go through four stages of acculturation corresponding to four levels of cultural interpenetration.[20] In the honeymoon stage people are fascinated by the foreign culture or subculture. Because cultural interpenetration is shallow and superficial, little acculturation occurs. Tourists travelling to foreign countries for short periods may experience this stage. If cultural interpenetration increases, people may enter a rejection stage, where they recognize that many of their old behaviours and meanings may be inadequate for acting in the new subculture. Some people may develop hostile attitudes towards the new subculture and reject its key values and meanings. Cultural conflicts are maximal in this stage. If cultural interpenetration continues and deepens, people may reach the tolerance stage. As people learn more cultural meanings and behaviours, they may begin to appreciate the new subculture, and cultural conflict will decrease. Finally, in the integration stage, adjustment to the subculture is adequate, although acculturation need not be complete or total. At this stage people are able to function satisfactorily in the new culture or subculture, which is viewed as an alternative way of life and is valued for its good qualities.

Gender as a Subculture

Despite the modern tendency to downplay differences between men and women, there is ample evidence that men and women differ in important respects (not only physically). For instance, women may process information differently from men and seem to be more 'generous, more nurturing, and less dominating than men'.[21] For some marketing purposes, gender differences may be significant enough to consider the two sexes as separate subcultures. For instance, research has found that women treat possessions differently than men do. Ownership and possession of products is seen by some men as a way to dominate and exert power over others, discriminate themselves from others (status differentiation), and even engage in subtle forms of aggression over others. Women, in contrast, tend to value possessions that can enhance personal and social relationships. Compared to most men, most women seem to value caring to controlling, sharing to selfishness, and cooperating to dominating. Many marketers may find it useful to develop different marketing strategies for the male and female subcultures.

However, marketers should be careful not to base their marketing towards the female subculture on outdated stereotypes. There is ample evidence that the type of role models portrayed in advertising has been lagging behind the development of the role of women in society. This is expressed in the type of products which are advertised to males and females – many ads aimed at women are still in the traditional housewife categories such as cleaning products and food, whereas high-price technical items such as cars are advertised with men in mind. It is also expressed by the situations in which women are portrayed, and by the type of speech by which they are addressed. Some of the most successful advertising targeted at women segments actually did not show any women at all.[22]

Social Class

Social class is a pervasively used concept, both in social science, in marketing, and in everyday language. Still, many people are uneasy about the concept. The very notion of social inequality which social class implies is not liked by many. Also, the usefulness of the concept for explaining human behaviour is believed to be declining, at least in Europe. The change is most pronounced in the Scandinavian countries, where one of the major ingredients of social class – income – has to an extent been redistributed through heavy taxation and considerable social welfare. Social class still exists in the minds of some people in these countries, but the concept is now much more complex.

An expert in social class research has made the following observations:

> There are no two ways about it: Social class is a difficult idea. Sociologists, in whose discipline the concept emerged, are not of one mind about its value and validity. Consumer researchers, to whose field its use has spread, display confusion about when and how to apply it. . . . All who try to measure it have trouble. Studying it rigorously and imaginatively can be monstrously expensive. Yet, all these difficulties notwithstanding, the proposition still holds: Social class is worth troubling over for the insights it offers on the marketplace behaviour of the nation's consumers.[23]

We agree with these observations concerning both the problems and the value of social class analysis. For our purposes in this text, **social class** refers to a national status hierarchy by which groups and individuals are distinguished in terms of esteem and prestige. Identification with each social class is influenced most strongly by one's level of education and occupation (including income as a measure of work success). But social class is also affected by inherited wealth, societal power, social skills, status aspirations, community participation, family history, cultural level, recreational habits, physical appearance, and social acceptance by a particular class.[24] Thus, social class is a composite of many personal and social attributes rather than a single characteristic such as income or education. The social classes can be considered as large subcultures because their members share many cultural meanings and behaviours.

There are two basic ways in which social class can be measured: subjective measures, in which consumers are asked to self-assign themselves to social classes, and objective measures, where social class is inferred based on a number of objective criteria. The latter are far more widespread in marketing research. Occupation, income, and education are the main indicators used. Often, social class is actually measured by only one indicator, namely occupation. Exhibit 14.3 shows an occupation-based classification commonly used in the United Kingdom. Other European countries have similar classifications.

Social class is of interest to marketers to the extent it is related to consumers' beliefs, values, and behaviours.[25] The basic assumption is that people have a higher probability of interacting with people from the same social class than with people from another social class. Family, peer groups, and friends at work, school, and in the neighbourhood are more likely to be of the same social class as of a different one, although the degree of class segregation varies widely. At a conceptual level, social classes are useful for investigating the process by which consumers develop different beliefs, values, and

EXHIBIT 14.3

UK Social Class Classification Based on Occupation

Grade 'A' households – upper middle class

Examples: professional and semiprofessional such as physician, surgeon, architect, chartered accountant, senior civil servant, professor, newspaper editor, commercial airline pilot, chief local government officer, headmaster. Business and industry such as senior buyer, director, insurance underwriter. Police and fire such as superintendent, chief fire officer. Armed forces such as lieutenant colonel and above; naval commander and above; wing commander and above.

Grade 'B' households – middle class

Examples: professional and semiprofessional such as higher and senior civil servant, lecturer, qualified pharmacist, qualified accountant, newly qualified professional. Business and industry such as manager of large firms, qualified insurance clerk, general foreman, clerk of works, chief buyer. Police and fire such as chief inspector, divisional officer. Armed forces: captain, major, lieutenant, squadron leader.

Grade 'C1' households – lower middle class

Examples: professional and semiprofessional such as teacher, student nurse, insurance agent, articled clerk, library assistant (not fully qualified). Business and industry such as self-employed farmer with one employee, telephonist, buyer, technician, draughtsman. Police and fire: station sergeant, leading fireman. Armed forces: sergeant, petty officer, flight sergeant.

Grade 'C2' households – skilled working class

Examples: foreman, bricklayer, carpenter, plasterer, glazier, plumber, painter, welder, minder, electrician, linotype operator, ambulance driver, maltster, officer, police constable, fireman, coach builder, lance corporal, leading seaman, aircraftsman.

Grade 'D' households – unskilled working class

Examples: labourer, mate of occupations listed in C2 grade, fisherman, gardener, bottler, opener, cleaner, traffic warden, bus conductor, porter.

Grade 'E' households – those at lowest level of subsistence

Examples: casual labourer, part-time worker, old age pensioner.

(All occupations refer to work of the household head.)

Source: Gordon R. Foxall, *Consumer Behaviour: A Practical Guide*
(London: Croom Helm, 1980), p. 146.

behaviour patterns. For example, an upper class person may well be socially secure and not find it necessary or desirable to purchase the most expensive brands to impress other people. Middle-class people, on the other hand, often engage in such conspicuous consumption.

**Back to . . .
Older and
Wiser**

The older and wiser example relates to an important change occurring in the subcultural social environment of Europe: the growing number and changing characteristics of consumers in the 50-plus age bracket. The example also shows how paying attention to such changes can be profitable.

Consumers in different age categories (such as 50–65) are likely to have somewhat different values, cultural meanings, and behaviour patterns. However, it should be recognized that these broad subculture segments can be quite diverse. Therefore, marketers may have to use other variables to identify narrower and more precise segments. For example, the age categories could be further broken down into geographic subgroups, and they could be related to social class. It is quite likely, for instance, that the cultural values and behavioural norms of 50-plus upper class rural consumers are different from those of 50-plus middle class urban consumers.

These different social groups may require different marketing strategies. This holds for all marketing parameters – advertising, product development, pricing, and distribution.

Summary

This chapter discussed two macro social influences on consumers' behaviours, cognitions, and affective responses – subculture and social class. These social factors influence how people think, feel, and behave relative to their physical, social, and marketing environments. We discussed subcultural influences in terms of geographic area, age, ethnic groups, and gender. Social class influences were discussed in terms of their role in explaining consumer behaviour.

Key Terms and Concepts

acculturation   299
age subcultures   295
baby boomers   296
consumer acculturation   299
cultural interpenetration   299
ethnic subcultures   299
geographic subcultures   292
grey market   297
social class   301
subcultures   291

Review and Discussion Questions

1. Discuss how subcultures (and social class) influence the way consumers learn cultural meanings (values, behaviours, lifestyles). Give a specific example.
2. Discuss how marketing strategies can affect a subculture (or social class). Give a concrete example to illustrate your point.
3. What ethical factors should a marketer consider in developing marketing strategies targeted at particular ethnic subcultures?

4. Are business school students a subculture? Why or why not? How could a marketer use knowledge about this group to develop marketing strategy?

5. Identify the age subcultures among members of your own family (or neighbourhood). How do these cultural differences affect the consumption behaviours of these people for foods, personal care products, and clothing?

6. Define the concept of social class. What are the major social class groups in your home country?

7. Select two product classes (perhaps foods, beverages, clothing, cars, furniture). How might each of the social classes you have identified in Question 6 respond to marketing strategies for these products?

8. Think of two subcultures not discussed in the text and briefly describe them. Discuss marketing implications for each one. What product categories would be most relevant?

9. Discuss the concept of cultural interpenetration in terms of the acculturation of immigrant populations in your country. What marketing opportunities do you see in this situation?

Additional Reading

For a discussion of the grey consumer segment, see:

H. Meyer-Hentschel and G. Meyer-Hentschel, *Das goldene Marktsegment – Produkt- und Laden-gestaltung für den Seniorenmarkt* (Frankfurt: Lang, 1991).

For a discussion of women as a target group, see:

Rena Bartos, *Marketing to Women: A Global Perspective* (Oxford: Heinemann, 1989).

For a discussion of how advertising affects consumer acculturation, see:

Thomas C. O'Guinn and Ronald J. Faber, 'Advertising and Subculture: The Role of Ethnicity and Acculturation in Market Segmentation', in *Current Issues and Research in Advertising* (Ann Arbor, MI: University of Michigan, 1986).

For discussions of social class and consumer behaviour, see:

Kjell Grønhaug and Paul S. Trapp, 'Perceived Social Class Appeals of Branded Goods and Services', *The Journal of Consumer Marketing*, Winter 1989, pp. 13–18.

James E. Fisher, 'Social Class and Consumer Behaviour: The Relevance of Class and Status', in *Advances in Consumer Research*, vol. 14, eds. Melanie Wallendorf and Paul Anderson (Provo, UT: Association for Consumer Research, 1987), pp. 492–496.

MARKETING STRATEGY IN ACTION
Slikies and Slinkies

S ingle women – particularly single women with children – are overlooked by many advertisers, according to analysis which contradicts traditional perceptions of one-parent, low-priority consumers.

The findings, from London media specialist Media Solutions, show that significant numbers of single women have above average income and suggest that many brand owners are ignoring up to 15 per cent of UK households.

Media Solutions analysed population and lifestyle data across several consumer groups. It identified two previously unrecognized female groups: 'slikies' and 'slinkies'.

Slikies are single ladies on high income – defined as £25 000 a year or more – with kids up to 15. The company identified 995 000 of them, accounting for 5 per cent of all households.

Slinkies are also single ladies on high income, but who have no kids. There are 2.2 m in the UK, about 10 per cent of households. 'These are women who are not married. Some may be widowed, others divorced, but the point is none rely on a partner financially', Media Solutions' managing partner John Carter explains.

'Slikies are classically time-poor, money-rich consumers although theirs is, undoubtedly, an expensive lifestyle with childcare and other associated costs. Slinkies are clever, ambitious, and status-conscious. Advertisers ignore these women at their peril.'

Yet, Carter insists, many do: 'The traditional nonworking housewife is still a currency used to buy many media campaigns', he says.

Companies aiming at mothers with young children and upmarket consumers with family-oriented or premium products – such as household goods, car or hi-fi brands – are among those losing out, he believes.

For example, most ads for household products appear on daytime television – when slikies and slinkies are at work.

Increasingly, advertisers recognize the advantages of targeting consumers by attitude and lifestyle, but they buy media for their campaigns according to basic demographics such as age, occupation, and sex.

These are based on traditional social classifications by professional status, ranging from A (higher managerial, administrative or professional) through B to C2 (skilled working class) and D (unskilled working class).

The rise of the service sector and decline of traditional manufacturing have led to a shift in the workforce with a perceived shift upmarket – i.e. more ABC1s and fewer C2DEs, Carter says. That does not, however, take into account either consumer attitudes or disposable income.

'Demographics clusters have lost their usefulness', Carter claims. 'Although this is being taken into account at the planning stage, it is not taken into account when media is bought. We think it's about time it was.'

Discussion Questions

1. Discuss how the slikies and slinkies target markets have been defined. Would you regard them as distinct subcultures? Why or why not?
2. Select a product category which you think is relevant for slikies and slinkies, and analyse the behaviours, affective responses, and cognitions most important in shopping for, purchasing, and using the product. Based on this, come up with proposals for a marketing strategy.
3. Do you think slikies and slinkies are a UK phenomenon, or do you think it is a cross-border subculture? Try to find some indicators for the existence of slikies and slinkies in another European country.

Source: Meg Carter, 'Slikies and Slinkies Deserve Attention', *Financial Times*, 23 June 1997, p. 10.

CHAPTER 15

Reference Groups and Family

Family Shopping at Meadowhall

 very Saturday the Keegan family goes shopping at the Meadowhall Shopping Centre. Meadowhall has been voted Retailer's No. 1 Shopping Centre in the United Kingdom three years in succession, and with its impressive 280 shops and restaurants spread on an area of around 140 000 square metres, Meadowhall receives more than 30 million visitors a year.

The Keegan family do practically all their shopping on Saturdays at Meadowhall and try to avoid shopping during the week – except for the daily necessities. Being both hard-working and parents of Adam, Monica, and Nick, aged 4, 8, and 14, Alice and James Keegan don't have much time during the week to spend on shopping activities.

The entire family looks forward to and enjoys their weekly shopping, as there are options appealing to visitors of any age. They usually spend about six hours at Meadowhall. A typical Saturday at the shopping centre starts with Alice and James leaving little Adam at the Typhoo Creche, which is run by professionally trained staff. The children are both entertained and educated at the creche which offers loads of facilities, such as a slide, climbing frame, interactive video system, painting, story telling, singing, and lots of toys. It costs between £2.25 and £4.50 to keep a child in the creche, but if the child has not settled in 15 minutes, the money is returned. Adam, however, enjoys the playtime there, and Alice and James enjoy being able to shop with peace of mind.

Monica, on the other hand, prefers playing in the open play areas in the mall and outdoors. Meanwhile Nick meets with some friends at the Coca-Cola Oasis – a spectacular recreation of a Mediterranean resort, housing over 20 different eating places and providing over 1200 seats in its central court. The Oasis is the focus for events and entertainment and there Meadowhall Television broadcasts on the giant 49 screen Vidiwall. Nick and his friends hang out in this area, fooling around with the girls and watching the latest music videos on the huge screens.

One thing is as sure as their Saturday shopping: the five of them always meet for lunch. As Meadowhall offers more than 25 places to eat, they take turns deciding on where to eat. They either go to one of the themed table service restaurants upstairs or to one of the fast food restaurants at the Oasis, depending on whether Alice and James or the children are the ones to decide.

Sometimes, Monica and Nick succeed in talking their parents into letting them go to the Warner Bros cinema next to the Oasis. Even though the cinema is open from 10 am to 10 pm, they tend to go there only in the afternoons. They may go to watch the same film, but more commonly Nick doesn't bother to watch Monica's beloved Disney films and prefers to watch an action film with some of his friends instead. With Meadowhall's 11-screen cinema it is not a problem though.

Every now and then, they bring Alice's old granny. Despite the fact that she is restricted to a wheelchair, she is hale and hearty and needs taking out of herself. They don't have to push Granny around the entire day. She is quite happy being left at one of the coffee shops, spending several hours sipping coffee and watching people. Whenever she comes along, the kids always get a treat as she loves to spoil them. As Meadowhall is constructed with great consideration to the disabled, it is no problem whatsoever to bring the old lady. All areas of the centre are accessible by wheelchair with lifts providing transport between floors as well as toilets for disabled customers. It is even possible to request accompanied shopping, although Granny does not need that kind of service as she has the entire family with her.

This example shows that shopping is often a family matter. In making purchase decisions, husbands and wives (mothers and fathers) influence each other's affective responses, cognitions, and behaviours, and both of them are influenced by their children and possibly other family members. The family is the major purchasing influence within the micro social environment in which consumer behaviour takes place. Another major influence in the micro social environment are reference groups. In this chapter we discuss the influences of families and reference groups on consumer behaviour.

Social interactions with reference groups and family are often direct and face to face, which can have immediate influences on consumers' cognitive, affective, and behavioural responses to marketing strategies.[1] For instance, the social environment created when two friends shop together can influence each person's shopping experience, decision processes, and overall satisfaction with a purchase. As you learned in Chapter 12 (see Exhibit 12.1), reference groups and family are important in transmitting (moving) cultural meanings in the overall society, subcultures, and social class to individual consumers. For all these reasons, reference groups and family have significant implications for marketing strategies.

Reference Groups

Individuals may be involved in many different types of groups. A **group** consists of *two or more people who interact with each other to accomplish some goal.* Important groups include families, close personal friends, coworkers, formal social groups (clubs, professional associations), leisure or hobby groups (a football team), and neighbours. Some of these groups may become reference groups.

A **reference group** involves *one or more people that someone uses as a basis for comparison or point of reference in forming affective and cognitive responses and performing behaviours.* Reference groups can be of any size (from one person to hundreds of people) and may be tangible (actual people) or intangible and symbolic (successful business executives or sports heroes). People's reference groups (and single referent persons) may be from the same or other social classes, subcultures, and even cultures. Exhibit 15.1 lists several types of reference group and their key distinguishing characteristics. These distinctions can be combined to better describe specific groups. For example, your immediate coworkers constitute a formal, primary, membership group. While these

EXHIBIT 15.1

Types of Reference Group

Type of Reference Group	Key Distinctions and Characteristics
Formal/informal	Formal reference groups have a clearly specified structure; informal groups do not.
Primary/secondary	Primary reference groups involve direct, face-to-face interactions; secondary groups do not.
Membership	People become formal members of membership reference groups.
Aspirational	People aspire to join or emulate aspirational reference groups.
Dissociative	People seek to avoid or reject dissociative reference groups.

distinctions can be useful, most consumer research has focused on two primary, informal groups – peers and family. Issues of major importance to marketing concerning reference group influence include the following:

1. What types of influence do reference groups exert on individuals?
2. How does reference group influence vary across products and brands?
3. How can marketers use the concept of reference groups to develop effective marketing strategies?

Analysing Reference Groups

Reference groups are cultural groups in that members share certain common cultural meanings. For instance, peer groups of students may develop specific meanings and behaviour norms about appropriate clothing, and peer groups of teenage boys may share meanings about what types of shoe, drink, or car are hot. These reference groups can influence the affective and cognitive responses of consumers as well as their purchase and consumption behaviour ('What should I wear today?').

Marketers try to determine the content of the shared meanings of various reference groups (the common values, beliefs, behavioural norms, and so on). Then they select certain reference groups to associate with or promote their products. But marketers seldom examine the social processes by which reference groups move cultural meaning to products and from products to the consumer.

Reference groups can have both positive and negative effects on consumers. Many social groups incorporate desirable, positive cultural meanings and become associative reference groups that consumers want to emulate or be affiliated with. Other social groups embody unfavourable or distasteful meanings and serve as a negative point of reference that people want to avoid; they become dissociative reference groups.

Types of Reference Group Influence

Most people are members of several primary informal groups and a few formal, membership groups (church, civic, and professional associations). In addition, people are aware of many secondary groups, both formal and informal. Why do people use some of these groups as a reference group and not others? And how do these reference groups influence consumers' affect, cognitions, and behaviours? Basically, people identify and affiliate with particular reference groups for three reasons: to gain useful knowledge, to obtain rewards or avoid punishments, and to acquire meanings for constructing, modifying, or maintaining their self-concepts. These goals reflect three types of reference group influence – informational, utilitarian, and value-expressive.

Informational reference group influence transmits useful information to consumers about themselves, other people, or aspects of the physical environment such as products, services, and stores. This information may be conveyed directly – either verbally or by direct demonstration. For instance, a consumer trying to decide on a purchase of a tennis racquet or stereo equipment might seek the advice of friends who are knowledgeable about those categories. A person who is trying to learn to play tennis might ask friends to demonstrate how to serve or hit a backhand shot.

Consumers tend to be more influenced by reference groups if the information is perceived as reliable and relevant to the problem at hand and the information source is perceived to be trustworthy.[2] Thus, some marketers hire recognized experts to endorse their product and tell consumers why it is good.

Information can also be obtained indirectly through vicarious observation. For instance, an avid fisherman may carefully note the types of equipment famous bass fishermen are using in a fishing tournament. This is common behaviour; many golfers, skiers, mountain climbers, and other sports enthusiasts engage in similar vicarious observations of products used by their reference group.

Information can be transmitted from reference groups to consumers in three ways. Sometimes informational influence is intentionally sought by consumers to reduce the perceived risk of making a decision or to help them learn how to perform certain behaviours. Thus, most novice sky divers listen very carefully to their new reference group of experienced sky-diving instructors as they present information about how to pack a parachute or how to land correctly. Consumers who buy a new computer may seek information provided by a reference group of more experienced users who can help them learn how to use the product effectively. In other cases information is accidentally transmitted, as when someone overhears reference group members talking about a product or observes members of a reference group using the product. A third way that information may be transferred to the consumer is when reference group members initiate the process. This can occur with enthusiastic reference group members who seek to advocate an activity and gain new members. For example, skateboard users might try to persuade others to take up the sport. Marketers might use a strategy of getting current customers to create new customers (bring along a friend for dinner and get your meal for half the price).

Utilitarian reference group influence on consumers' behaviours (and affect and cognitions) occurs when the reference group controls important rewards and punishments. Consumers usually will comply with the desires of a reference group if (1) they believe the group can control rewards and punishments, (2) the behaviour is visible or known to the group, and (3) they are motivated to obtain rewards or avoid punishments.

In some work groups (a formal, membership reference group), people are expected to wear formal business attire, while other work groups encourage very casual dress. Rewards and punishments may be tangible (rises, bonuses, being fired), or psychological and social consequences may occur (admiring looks or snide remarks behind your back). Peer groups often administer such psychosocial rewards and punishments for adherence to and violations of the reference group code. Marketers use these factors by showing such sanctions in TV commercials (people recoiling from offensive body odour, bad breath, or the dandruff flakes on someone's shoulder).

Value-expressive reference group influence can affect people's self-concepts. As cultural units, reference groups both contain and create cultural meanings (beliefs, values, goals, behavioural norms, lifestyles). As you learned in Chapter 13, people are constantly seeking desirable cultural meanings to use in constructing, enhancing, or maintaining their self-concepts. By identifying and affiliating with certain reference groups that express these desired meanings, consumers can draw out some of these meanings and use them in their own self-construction project.

One group of people who buy Harley-Davidson motorcycles and associated products consists of middle- and upper-middle-class professional people (including doctors, dentists, lawyers, and professors). Derisively called RUBS (rich urban bikers) or weekend warriors by the hard-core Harley owners (the tattooed and bearded outlaws or pseudo outlaws), many of these consumers treat the radical, hard-core Harley owners as an aspirational reference group (very few RUBS will ever become hard-core bikers).[3]

The hard-core Harley bikers express several desirable meanings and values for the RUBS (and probably convey negative meanings to nonbikers). By identifying to some extent with the hard-core biker as an aspirational reference group, RUBS can gain some of these important meanings, including feelings of freedom (from work and family), freedom of spirit, radical independence, and a feeling of belonging to a special, unique group. Perhaps some RUBS are also able to inspire a bit of the fear and awe (among nonbikers or owners of other brands) that the hard-core bikers relish.

These reference group meanings can influence affect, cognitions, and behaviour, including purchases of biker clothing and bike accessories. Harley-Davidson recognizes these value-expressive desires and needs and markets (often through licensing) a variety of products to satisfy them, including black leather jackets, 'colours' (clothing with insignias and biker logos), and many biking accessories.

In summary, all three types of reference group influence can be accomplished by a single reference group. For instance, as a reference group for the weekend biker, the hard-core Harley-Davidson bikers can be a source of information (through magazines and observation), rewards and punishments (waving back or haughtily ignoring the RUBS on the road), and subcultural meanings that express one's values.

Reference Group Influence on Products and Brands

Reference groups do not influence all product and brand purchases to the same degree. Based on research, reference group influence on product and brand decisions is thought to vary on at least two dimensions.[4] The first dimension concerns the degree to which the product or brand is a necessity or a luxury. A *necessity* is owned by virtually every-one (a refrigerator), whereas a *luxury* is owned only by consumers in particular groups (a sailboat). The second dimension is the degree to which the object in question is conspicuous or known by other people.[5] A *public good* is one that other people are aware an individual owns and uses, one for which they can identify the brand with little or no difficulty (a car). A *private good* is used at home or in private so that other people (outside the immediate family) would be unaware of its possession or use (a hair dryer).

EXHIBIT 15.2

Effects of Public–Private and Luxury–Necessity Dimensions on Reference Group Influence for Product and Brand Choice

	Necessity	**Luxury**
PUBLIC	PUBLIC NECESSITIES Reference group influence • product: weak • brand: strong • examples: watch, car, man's suit	PUBLIC LUXURIES Reference group influence • product: strong • brand: strong • examples: golf clubs, sailboat, mobile phones
PRIVATE	PRIVATE NECESSITIES Reference group influence • product: weak • brand: weak • examples: mattress, refrigerator, washing machine	PRIVATE LUXURIES Reference group influence • product: strong • brand: weak • examples: espresso machine, electric barbecue, floor heating

Source: Adapted from William O. Bearden and Michael J. Etzel, 'Reference Group Influences on Product and Brand Purchase Decisions', *Journal of Consumer Research*, September 1982, p. 185.

Combining these two dimensions produces the matrix shown in Exhibit 15.2. This figure suggests reference group influence will vary depending on whether the products and brands are public necessities, private necessities, public luxuries, or private luxuries. Consider wristwatches, which are public necessities. Because everyone can see whether a person is wearing a wristwatch, the *brand* may be susceptible to reference group influence. However, because the product class is owned and used by most people, there is likely to be little reference group influence on whether one should be purchased.[6]

Reference Groups and Marketing Strategy

We have seen that reference groups are an important influence on consumers. Not only do members of primary informal groups affect consumer knowledge, attitudes, and values, but they also affect the purchase of specific products and brands and the selection of stores in which purchases are made. In some cases an analysis of primary informal group influences can be used to develop marketing strategies. For example, in industrial marketing, a careful analysis of the group influence dynamics among the various people who have a role in a purchase decision may be useful for determining appropriate marketing approaches.[7] Similarly, peer group influence is a major asset of firms that sell in-home to groups, as in the case of Tupperware parties. In such instances many individuals conform to the norms of the group by purchasing a few items. Occasionally marketers may try to stimulate reference group influence – a health club might offer you two months' service free if you get a friend to sign up for a one-year membership.

Salespeople may attempt to create a reference group influence by describing how a customer is similar to previous purchasers of the product: 'There was a couple in here last week much like you. They bought the JVC speakers.' Salespeople could describe themselves as a reference group: 'Oh, your two children go to Eastwood School? My children go there, too. We bought them an IBM PC to help them in their science projects.'

Finally, soliciting experts to aid in the direct sale of products can be a successful strategy for some firms. For example, a consumer's dentist is likely to be a highly influential reference individual, particularly for products related to dental care.[8] Thus, a manufacturer of electric tooth brushes might offer gifts to dentists for encouraging patients to use the product. The company could keep track of a dentist's sales by asking consumers to identify their dentist on the warranty card for the product. Of course, experts can also have a negative impact on the sales of a new product if they convey negative information.[9]

For most mass-marketed products, a detailed analysis of the interactions of specific primary informal groups is impractical. Instead, marketers tend to portray both primary informal and aspirational groups in advertising:

> Reference group concepts have been used by advertisers in their efforts to persuade consumers to purchase products and brands. Portraying products being consumed in socially pleasant situations, the use of prominent/attractive people endorsing products, and the use of obvious group members as spokespersons in advertising are all evidence that marketers and advertisers make substantial use of potential reference group influence on consumer behaviour in the development of their communications. Alluding to reference groups in persuasive attempts to market products and brands demonstrates the belief that reference groups expose people to behaviour and lifestyles, influence self-concept develop- ment, contribute to the formation of values and attitudes, and generate pressure for conformity to group norms.[10]

There are many examples of the use of reference group concepts in advertising. This may involve celebrities endorsing products because of their expert status, such as famous sports people endorsing tennis equipment or running shoes, or it may involve celebrities unrelated to the product but which the target group for the product is expected to identify with such as a pop star advocating soft drinks. It may also involve relating the product to a stereotypic person, such as the friendly grandmother, or to a group of people assumed to be meaningful to the target group, such as colleagues at work, globetrotters, intellectuals, or business executives.

Family

Most consumer behaviour research takes the individual consumer as the unit of analysis. The usual goal is to describe and understand how individuals make purchase decisions so that marketing strategies can be developed to more effectively influence this process. The area of family research is an exception: It views the family as the unit of analysis.[11]

Actually, marketers are interested in both families and households. The distinction between a family and a household is important. The European Community Household Panel (ECHP) defines a **household** as comprising either one person living alone or a group of persons, not necessarily related, living at the same address with a common household, i.e. sharing a meal on most days or sharing a living or sitting room. In

Europe 99 per cent of people live in households involving many different living arrangements such as houses, townhouses, apartments, flats, residence halls, communes, military barracks, and nursing homes. Each household has a *householder* – the person who rents or owns the household. Households are categorized into types based on the relationship of the residents in the household to the householder. Marketers are concerned with two main types of households – families and nonfamilies.

Nonfamily households include unrelated people living together such as students in a hall of residence or unmarried couples of the opposite or same sex. In 1995 3 per cent of European households were nonfamilies. In contrast, a **family** has at least two people – the householder and someone who is related to the householder by blood, marriage, or adoption. About 70 per cent of European households are families. The difference between nuclear and extended families is an important distinction. The nuclear family includes one or more parents and one or more never-married children living together in a household. The extended family is a nuclear family plus other relatives, usually grandparents, living in one household. Extended families are more common in Mediterranean countries and Ireland than in northern countries.

Family Decision Making

Marketers are highly interested in **family decision making** – how family members interact and influence each other when making purchase choices for the household.[12] Research has shown that different people in the family may take on different social roles and perform different behaviours during decision making and consumption.[13] For example, the person who purchases cheese and sausages for lunchtime sandwiches (the husband) may not be the same person who prepares the sandwiches (the mother) or eats them (the children). To fully understand family decision making, marketers need to identify which family members take on which roles. Included among these decision-making roles are the following (see also Exhibit 15.3):[14]

- *Initiator*. Somebody who suggests that one should buy a new product or service such as a new TV set.
- *Internal advocate*. Other members of the family who share an interest in the product or service being bought – the children who like to watch TV.
- *Budget allocator*. The person or persons making decisions on the use of family funds, and who will evaluate whether the family budget can bear a new TV.
- *Decision maker*. The person or persons who make the decision on whether to buy the product or service or not.
- *Product expert*. Somebody who is knowledgeable about the product in question, due to previous experience, his/her work or personal interest.
- *Information seeker*. Family member(s) obtaining information on possible purchase alternatives, their prices and features.
- *Brand chooser*. Those family members choosing the brand to be purchased, given that the product is to be purchased and given the expertise and information available.
- *Purchaser*. The person physically making the purchase.
- *User*. All family members actually using the product once bought.

Clearly, every family member can have several of these roles, and the same role can be shared by several family members. The important point here is that various aspects of the overall purchasing process may be distributed over and/or shared by various

EXHIBIT 15.3

Roles in Family Decision Making

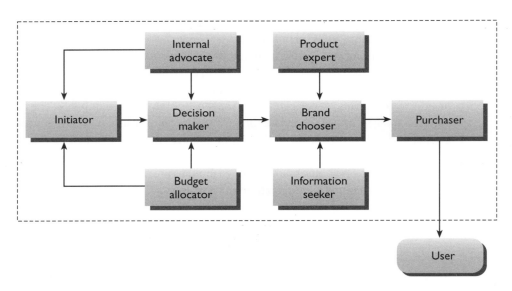

Source: Adapted from Jan Møller Jensen, 'Familiens Købsbeslutninger – et "købscenter" perspektiv',
Ledelse & Erhvervsøkonomi, April 1990, p. 86.

members of the family. Thus, studying family decision making requires that marketers study the social interactions between family members and the resulting patterns of reciprocal influence. This can be a difficult research challenge.

Developing successful marketing strategies for products purchased by families requires attention to questions such as these:

1. Is the product likely to be purchased for individual or joint family use?
2. Is the product likely to be purchased with individual or family funds?
3. Is the product so expensive that its purchase involves an important trade-off in purchasing other products for the family?
4. Are family members likely to disagree about the value of the product? If so, what can be done to reduce the conflict?
5. Is the product likely to be used by more than one family member? If so, are product modifications necessary to accommodate different people?
6. Which family members will influence the purchase and what media and messages should be used to appeal to each?
7. Are particular stores preferred by various family members or by various families in the target market?

Answers to these questions influence the appropriate marketing strategy. For example, if a TV is being purchased by a family for a teenager to use in his or her own room, the type of product, price, and appropriate promotion message and media should vary from those involved with the family's purchase of a TV that is being used by the adults in the main living room.

Influences on Family Decision Making

Among the areas explored in research on family decision making are the following: (1) differences in product class and their relationship to family decision making, (2) the structure of husband/wife roles, and (3) the determinants of joint decision making.[15] However, relatively few generalizations for consumer analysis can be offered about family decision making. In fact, several years ago a review of the subject concluded that

1. Husband/wife involvement varies widely by product class.
2. Husband/wife involvement within any product class varies by specific decision and decision stages.
3. Husband/wife involvement for any consumer decision is likely to vary considerably among families.[16]

Essentially, we should expect considerable variance both in the persons involved at each stage of the decision-making process and in the extent to which they are involved.[17] For any given marketing problem, researchers must determine the dynamics of family decision making, which family members are involved, what roles they play, and who has the major influence. This analysis will help them develop effective marketing strategies targeted at the appropriate person.

Children and Family Decision Making

The children's market is large and important. In Germany, children between 6 and 17 years of age are estimated to have a purchasing power of DM19 billion per year.[18] And in addition to that, children – both younger kids and teenagers – can have a major influence on the budget allocation decisions and purchase choices made by the family. In a German study, it was found that children aged 7–15 have both considerable brand awareness and considerable faith that they will be able to get the brand they want, either by buying it themselves or by influencing their parents. The perceived influence on family purchase decisions did vary by product category, though. It was highest for child-related products like toys and somewhat lower for food products.[19] In addition to the type of product, it seems that children's influence on buying decisions also depends on their age and the number of siblings in the family.[20] These differences across age and product category may in turn be explained by a number of other factors. For example, it has been shown that perceived competence of the child for the product in question and perceived communication ability affect the degree of influence.[21] Both can be expected to increase with age, and the former can be expected to be related to product category.

Conflict in Family Decision Making

When more than one person in a family is involved in making a purchase decision, conflict may occur.[22] **Decision conflict** arises when family members disagree about some aspect of the purchase decision. The means–end chain model provides a useful framework for analysing decision conflict.[23] Family members might disagree about the desired end goals of a purchase. For instance, in choosing a family holiday, the husband might want to go somewhere for lazy relaxation, the wife might want good shopping and nightlife, and the kids would probably want adventure and excitement. Differences in end goals often create major conflict because very different choice alternatives are likely to be related to these incompatible ends. Serious negotiations may be required to resolve the conflict.

In other cases family members might agree on the desired end goal yet disagree about the best means to achieve it. For instance, everyone might want to go out to eat or see a film, but the kids think a fast-food restaurant or action film is the best choice, while the parents prefer a gourmet restaurant or a dramatic film. Again, some means of resolving the conflict is necessary. Often a different alternative (a new means to the end) is purchased as a compromise (everyone goes out for pizza or to a comedy film). Finally, when either the ends or the means are in conflict, family members are also likely to disagree about the choice criteria for evaluating the choice alternatives (for a new car, what is the appropriate price range, what options are necessary, what is the best colour?).

Clearly, there are times when family members disagree about such factors in a purchase situation, and occasionally the conflict may be severe.[24] When this happens, family members can do several things. Some consumers might procrastinate, ignoring the problem and hoping the situation will improve by itself. Others might try to get their way in the purchase decision process by trying to influence other family members. Exhibit 15.4 describes 15 different influencing tactics that have been identified in family research.[25] Depending on the product being considered, the family members involved in the decision, the social class and subculture of the family, and the situational environment, a family member might use any of these tactics to influence other members of the family.

Although serious conflicts can occur in family decision making, many family purchases probably do not involve major conflicts. For one thing, many family purchases are recurring in that many products and brands are bought repeatedly over a long period. So even though conflict might have been present in the past, it usually will have been resolved. To minimize continuous friction, families may develop choice plans to minimize or avoid potential conflict. For instance, a family with two children might allow one to choose the breakfast cereal or ice cream flavour one week and the other to choose the next week.

Another reason decision why conflict among family members concerning purchase and consumption decisions is not often serious is that many purchases in a household are made by individuals to meet their own personal needs or those of other family members. To the degree that such purchases are reasonably consistent with family values and do not place an undue burden on family resources there is likely to be little conflict. For instance, we would expect that purchases of books, personal care items, and many food products do not involve much family conflict.

The way husband and wife influence each other will depend on the type of relationship they have. Exhibit 15.5 shows a classification of interaction principles between partners resulting from two dimensions characterizing their relationship: degree of harmony and degree of dominance of one partner over the other.[26] In a harmonious relationship, partners act according to the 'love principle': they try to optimize the mutual good, feel responsible for each other's needs and generally act altruistically regarding the partner. In a less harmonious relationship, the love principle changes to the 'credit principle': partners still show consideration towards each other, but they

---

EXHIBIT 15.4

Types of Family Influence Tactics

Tactics:

1. Positive emotions (to flatter, smile happily at, be witty, act seductively)
2. Negative emotions (to threaten, scream, be cynical, make fun of)
3. Helplessness (to cry, show weakness, act sick)
4. Physical force (to force, hurt, be violent, be aggressive)
5. Offering resources (to offer services, show attention to)
6. Withdrawing (withdraw financial resources, punish by no longer doing something)
7. Insisting (to complain, bring up the topic repeatedly, exhaust the other person)
8. Leaving the scene (to refuse any responsibility in the matter, go away, leave the scene)
9. Overt information (to make suggestions, ask the other to yield, talk about needs, subjective importance, talk openly about one's interest)
10. Distorted information (to suppress relevant information, distort information)
11. Indirect coalition (to refer to others, emphasize benefits the decision has brought to others)
12. Direct coalition (to discuss something in the presence of others, hoping for their support)
13. Trade-offs (to engage in bookkeeping, remind the other of past favours)
14. Integrative bargaining (to search for optimum solution for all parties)
15. Reason (to present objective arguments, argue logically)

Reprinted from *Journal of Economic Psychology*, 11, 1990, pp. 101–118: Erich Kirchler, 'Spouses' Influence Strategies In Purchase Decisions As Dependent On Conflict Type And Relationship Characteristics', with kind permission from Elsevier Science, NL, Sara Burgerhartstraat 25, 1055 KV Amsterdam, The Netherlands.

---

expect this consideration to be reciprocated and keep mental accounts on how much the partner owes due to previous considerations shown to him or her.[27] When the quality of the relationship falls still further, the 'equity principle' applies: partners act like business partners engaging in negotiations. The less harmonious the relationship, the more important power differences between the partners become. In a disharmonious relationship, a partner will have a higher tendency to exploit a power advantage, which means that the equity principle changes to an egoism principle.

Consumer Socialization

Through socialization processes, families transmit the cultural meanings of society, subcultures, and social class to their children and thereby influence their children's affect, cognitions, and behaviours.[28] **Consumer socialization** refers to how children acquire knowledge about products and services and various consumption-related skills, such as how to compare products and how to search for bargains.[29]

The consumer knowledge formed in childhood can influence people in later years. Some adults still use the same brands of products their parents purchased for them as children. Developing early brand awareness and loyalty is therefore an important marketing strategy for many companies. From a more general perspective, though, the

EXHIBIT 15.5

Family Interaction Principles as Dependent on the Structure of the Relationship between Parties

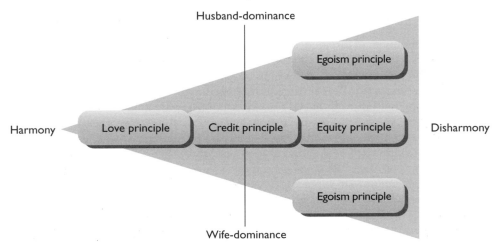

Source: Reprinted from *Journal of Economic Psychology*, 16(3), 1995, p. 396: Erich Kirchler, 'Studying Economic Decisions Within Private Households: A Critical Review and Design for a "Couple Experiences Diary" ', with kind permission from Elsevier Science, NL, Sara Burgerhartstraat 25, 1055 KV Amsterdam, The Netherlands.

consumer skills learned during the early phases of socialization are most important. The whole functioning of market economies requires that people learn that resources are scarce, and learn the principles of exchange, and the roles of buyer and seller. Also, socialization is expected to have a role with regard to the degree to which consumers learn to make decisions in an autonomous way.[30]

Younger children acquire much of their consumer knowledge and skills from their parents, but adolescents also learn from their peers. Both younger and older children learn consumer knowledge and skills from social institutions such as the media (TV, magazines, cinema) and advertising.[31]

Socialization can be analysed both in terms of cognitive learning and in terms of behavioural analysis, corresponding to the two major approaches towards analysing consumer behaviour adopted in this book.[32] The cognitive learning approach looks at how children learn concepts, like that of a product, a payment, or a commercial, and relates this to the overall cognitive development of children, as analysed, e.g. by the French psychologist Piaget.[33] Cognitive learning is mostly related to direct teaching by parents, like when parents intentionally try to teach their children consumer skills such as how to search for products, find the best price, return products to the store for a refund, and dispose of products (recycling, hold a garage sale).[34] But cognitive learning also occurs by being confronted with information from media such as TV.

In terms of behavioural analysis, consumer socialization has been analysed from the viewpoint of social interaction theory, which was discussed at length in Chapter 10.

Parents and peers serve as models for their children, for example when parents talk about products and brands or take their children on shopping trips. Parents and peers also influence socialization by providing reinforcement when their children/friends imitate their behaviours.

Some parents also try to teach their children to be critical towards advertising. This relates to a widespread discussion on the fact that advertising, and especially TV advertising, may have a negative influence on children's consumer socialization, for example by emphasizing that enjoyment and problem solving is obtained by purchasing products and not by human interaction.[35]

Household Size and Family Life Cycle

Household sizes are decreasing throughout Europe.[36] This is due to the fact that people have fewer children, young children leaving home, older people remaining single after divorce, more solitary survivors, and more people living on their own. The EU average household size is at present 2.7 persons, with the smallest average households to be found in Denmark (2.0 persons) and the largest in Spain (3.6 persons). The trend towards smaller households is stronger in northern Europe, with the exception of Ireland, than in southern Europe.

These changes in household size affect the type and quantity of goods demanded. There is a tendency towards demanding some products, such as certain food items, in smaller quantities or smaller packages. Also appliances such as washing machines, deep freezers and dish washers will be demanded in smaller sizes, whereas the demand in terms of numbers will go up. In addition, the decreasing household size will have an effect on family decision making, as the number of household members potentially involved in a decision decreases.

The changes in household size can be related to changes in the family life cycle. The family life cycle describes the changes of family composition throughout the human life span. Traditionally, the family life cycle covers the following phases: people get married, have children, stay married, raise their children and send them on their way, grow old, retire, and eventually die. The traditional family life cycle identified these typical stages as a linear sequence of family types delineated by major life events (marriage, birth of children, ageing, departure of children, retirement, death).[37] These major life events create different social environments (consider the birth of a baby) that influence consumers' affective reactions, cognitions, and consumption behaviours. For instance, the highest purchase rate for home appliances is that of newly married couples.

Recent cultural changes such as delayed marriages, childless marriages, working women, and increased divorce rates have rendered the traditional family life cycle somewhat inadequate, however. Exhibit 15.6 presents a **modern family life cycle** that incorporates the traditional family life cycle, but adds several other family types to account for the more diverse family structures of the 1990s.[38] The modern family life cycle can account for most types of families in modern European societies, including childless couples, divorced parents, and single parents with children.

Exhibit 15.7 shows data on the occurrence of several types of households in Denmark, Germany, and the United Kingdom. Although the data are not strictly comparable, they do show some common tendencies. The number of young single person households is increasing in all three countries, although the percentage of all households they account for, varies considerably. Also the number of 'old singles' is

EXHIBIT 15.6

A Modern Family Life Cycle

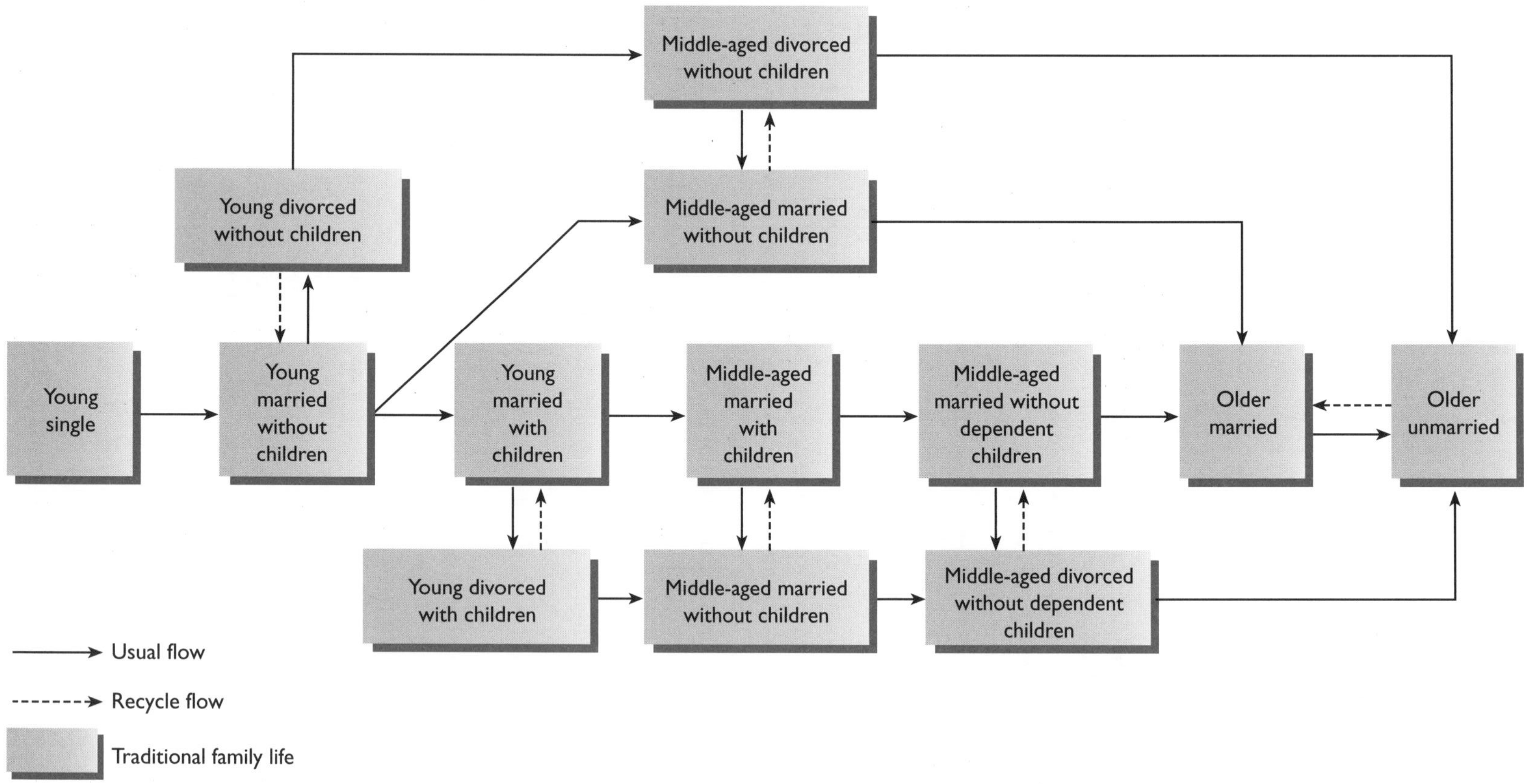

Source: Reprinted with permission from Patrick E. Murphy and William A. Staples, 'A Modernized Family Life Cycle', *Journal of Consumer Research*, June 1979, pp. 12–22.

EXHIBIT 15.7

Household Types and Family Life Cycles in Three European Countries

Households by Type in Denmark

Group	1983	1985	1990
Young singles (> 35 years) (%)	20.9	21.8	23.0
Families without children (Wife < 35 years) (%)	1.3	1.3	1.3
Families with children (%)	31.8	30.6	28.2
Families without children (Wife > 35 years) (%)	16.9	16.8	16.8
Older singles (> 35 years)	29.1	29.5	30.7
Average number of children/family	1.76	1.72	1.67
Total number of families (in 1000)	2563	2618	2742

Households by Type (millions) in Germany (West only)

Group	1975	1982	1986	1990
Younger singles (< 45 years)	1.69	2.56	3.40	3.89
Households without children	n.a.	n.a.	n.a.	7.47
Households with children	8.67	8.15	7.24	10.61
Older singles (> 45 years)	4.86	5.37	5.81	5.96
Total number of households	23.72	25.34	26.74	28.18

Households by Type (%) in the UK

Group	1961	1971	1981	1991
One person households:				
Under pensionable age	4	6	8	10
Over pensionable age	7	12	14	15
Two or more unrelated adults	5	4	5	3
One family households:				
Married couple, no children	26	27	26	28
1–2 dependent children	30	26	25	20
3 or more dependent children	8	9	6	5
Nondependent children only	10	8	8	8
Lone parent with dependent children	2	3	5	6
Nondependent children only	4	4	4	4
Two or more families	3	1	1	1
All households	100	100	100	100

Sources: Klaus G. Grunert, Suzanne C. Grunert, Wolfgang Glatzer, and Heiner Imkamp, 'The Changing Consumer in Germany', *International Journal of Research in Marketing*, 12, 1995, p. 421; Ole Stenvinkel Nilsson and Hans Stubbe Solgaard, 'The Changing Consumer in Denmark', *International Journal of Research in Marketing*, December 1995, p. 407; John Saunders and Jim Saker, 'The Changing Consumer in the UK', *International Journal of Research in Marketing*, December 1994, p. 480.

HIGHLIGHT 15.1

Eating Out with Children

E | ating out with children is not always a pleasant experience for either parents or children. Parents find that some restaurants have a negative or even hostile attitude towards children. Families with children are placed at out-of-the-way tables, are instructed that screaming and running are now allowed, or are barred from the restaurant altogether. For the children, having to sit down for a long period waiting for meals and then waiting for the parents to finish is boring, and the many rules that have to be adhered to do not add to the pleasure. As a result, eating out with children often means ending up in a fast-food place, where nobody sends angry looks at the parents, and the children perceive no pressure.

But some restaurants have now spotted families with under-teenage children as a major target group, and have started to adapt their offerings to this group's special needs. Children may be greeted with balloons or other gimmicks upon entering. Some give playing material to the children to keep them busy while waiting, such as a booklet with pictures or small tasks and a set of colour pens. Others have introduced real playing space in the restaurant, such as a ball landscape, where children can amuse themselves while the parents finish their meal. Often this is combined with special menus which make eating out easier: children have different tastes than adults and have their own favourites, which may not be on an adult menu. There may also be special price deals, such as the possibility of ordering all adult dishes as children's dishes at half price or a free children's menu when the family arrives before 6.30.

Source: Adapted from Marianne Gram, 'Her er ungerne velkomne',
JP-Hovedstaden, 3 August 1995, p. 22.

increasing. At the same time, the percentage of households consisting of families with children has been dropping, although there seems to be a recent reversal of that tendency in Germany. The UK data also show a rise in the number of single parents with dependent children, which accounted for 6 per cent of all households in 1991.[39]

Marketers use the family life cycle to segment the market, analyse market potential, identify target markets, and develop more effective marketing strategies (see Highlight 15.1 for an example). But the family segments identified by the family life cycle are not entirely homogeneous. In fact, each family type is variable and contains highly diverse types of people. For instance, the category of families with children includes two important subcategories: (1) dual-earner couples and (2) other married couples (usually a working husband and a homemaker wife). The distinction is important for two reasons: average household income is higher in the former, and lifestyles differ considerably in these households. Life in the dual-earner households is usually more hectic, and the parents are more harassed than in other married-couple households. As another example, consider the young-single stage of the family life cycle. There were 3.9 million of such households in Germany in 1990, up from 1.7 million in 1975. Much of this growth is due to the 'new' bachelors created by divorce. 'Real' male bachelors are interested in different products than 'new' male bachelors – the former, usually younger, are prime target markets for walkmans, fancy drinks, and hot cars. But the somewhat older divorced 'bachelors' may be more interested in toys for their kids, living room furniture, and relaxing holidays. With this type of diversity, developing marketing strategies for the bachelor segment is a challenge for marketers.

Another point to recognize is that some stages in the family life cycle are more important markets than others. For instance, households headed by people aged 35–54 spend more on every product category (except health care) than other types of families.[40]

The family life cycle can help marketers understand how important cultural trends affect family structures and consumption behaviour. For example, consider the 'time-starved' families.[41] Time has become more precious to many people as the pace of family life gets more hectic and as more families have two wage earners or are headed by single parents. Millions of people are stressed about time, believe they don't have enough of it, and are striving to save it. They are prime candidates for convenience products of all types that can save time, which then can be used for more enjoyable or profitable purposes.

Many of these people see shopping as a stressful chore that interferes with their leisure. Many consumers have developed time-saving shopping strategies. For instance, some people shop for clothes only two or three times a year. Some shoppers follow a certain path through the store to eliminate duplication of effort. In one extreme case a consumer followed a regimented strategy by shopping for groceries each Tuesday from 4.45 to 5.15 pm. As she sprinted through the store in a virtual trance, it would be very difficult to catch her attention with a new marketing strategy. One executive bought a car at a dealer located near the airport so he could have the car serviced during business trips.

Relatively few marketers have done much to reduce shopping time and stress, but there are many opportunities to appeal to the time-stressed shopper. These need not be highly sophisticated strategies. The following are several ideas for doing so.

- *Provide information*: marketers that provide useful information to help consumers make the right choices will save their customers time and reduce shopping stress. For instance, Blockbuster Video has a computerized database to help customers find films made by a certain director or starring a particular actor. Computer technology could be used to help consumers make the right choices of colour, size, styles for clothing, cars, and home furnishings. Coordinated displays of related products, such as showing entire ensembles, can serve the same purpose.
- *Assist in planning*: people often try to cope with time stress by carefully planning their shopping excursions. Marketers that help consumers form purchase plans will help them reduce stress. High-quality sales assistance in the clothing store or appliance showroom can help a time-stressed customer develop a decision plan. Marketers might suggest alternatives when a product is unavailable.
- *Develop out-of-store selling*: although shopping was once a pleasant and desirable experience, today many consumers would rather be relaxing at home. This trend creates problems for retailers, but also creates new opportunities for selling in the home or at the workplace. Internet shopping may be a way for people who are short of time to shop.
- *Improve delivery*: nothing upsets a time-stressed consumer more than having to wait all day at home for a service person to come to fix the washing machine. Repair and other service providers could improve their logistics to offer precise appointments for their service calls, or offer such services in the evenings or during weekends.

**Back to . . .
Family
Shopping at
Meadowhall**

The opening example illustrates several of the concepts discussed in this chapter. It illustrates vividly that shopping can be a family matter, with, in this case, up to six people involved. It shows how the success of a shopping centre depends on its ability to cater for the different needs of the various members of the family. It shows a number of examples of family conflict resolution as well: the family takes turns deciding where to eat, so that over time everybody gets his or her way at some time. Another potential conflict, namely which film to see (action versus Disney), is avoided because it is possible for Nick and Monica to go to see different films in the same cinema. This shows how the design of a service can actually capitalize on helping families to avoid possible conflicts by providing different options simultaneously. Finally, one could speculate whether Meadowhall appeals mostly to the type of household described in the example, and how, for example, single households are catered for in this type of shopping environment.

Summary

This chapter has described two aspects of the micro social environment: reference groups and family. After defining groups and reference groups, we discussed three types of reference group influence: informational, utilitarian, and value-expressive. Then we discussed how reference groups could influence choice decisions about products and brands, and we offered ideas for using reference groups in marketing strategies.

We discussed decision making by families, considering the different decision-making roles taken by family members, including children. We discussed conflict in family choices and described several ways family members might try to resolve the decision conflict and influence each other. We also discussed consumer socialization – how consumers learn knowledge about products and consumer skills. Next we mentioned changes in household size and in the stages of the family life cycle and showed how marketers could use the family life cycle to analyse markets and develop marketing strategies.

Key Terms and Concepts

consumer socialization   317
decision conflict   315
family   313
family decision making   313
group   307
household   312
informational reference group influence   309
modern family life cycle   319
reference group   307
utilitarian reference group influence   309
value-expressive reference group influence   310

Review and Discussion Questions

1. Identify two reference groups that influence your consumption behaviour. Describe each according to the types listed in the text and describe what categories of purchases each influences.
2. From a marketing manager's viewpoint, what are some advantages and problems associated with each type of reference group influence?
3. Describe how public visibility and the distinction between luxury and necessity goods affect reference group influence on choice at the product and brand levels.
4. What is the family life cycle? Discuss how it can be used to develop effective marketing strategies.
5. Identify three different family purchases in which you have played a role in the decision process. What role did you play? Discuss the interpersonal interactions involved in these decisions.
6. Suggest two ways in which marketing strategies could influence the decision process in your family or household. How are these different from strategies that might be used to influence individual decisions?
7. Offer examples of conflict in family household decision making that you have experienced or observed. What types of marketing strategies could help reduce such conflict?
8. How are family influence strategies similar to or different from other reference group influences? What marketing implications are related to these distinctions?
9. Identify two different household or family compositions. Assume each unit has the same level of income and discuss how the decision processes and conflicts might vary for a product such as an automobile, a vacation, or a stereo system.

Additional Reading

For a discussion of the influence of referent others, see:

Jacqueline Johnson Brown and Peter H. Reingen, 'Social Ties and Word-of-Mouth Referral Behaviour', *Journal of Consumer Research*, December 1987, pp. 350–362.

For a discussion of how consumers make decisions in group situations, see:

James C. Ward and Peter H. Reingen, 'Sociocognitive Analysis of Group Decision Making among Consumers', *Journal of Consumer Research*, December 1990, pp. 245–262.

For a discussion of husband–wife interaction in decision making, see:

Erich Kirchler, 'Studying Economic Decisions Within Private Households: A Critical Review and Design for a "Couple Experiences Diary"', *Journal of Economic Psychology*, 3, 1995, pp. 393–420.

For an example of a study on the influence of children, see:

Franz Böcker and Lutz Thomas, 'Der Einfluß von Kindern auf die Produktpräferenzen ihrer Mütter', *Marketing-ZFP*, 4, no. 4, 1983, pp. 245–252.

For a discussion of consumer socialization, see:

Eberhard Kuhlmann, 'Consumer Socialization of Children and Adolescents: A Review of Current Approaches', *Journal of Consumer Policy*, 6, no. 4, 1983, pp. 397–418.

For an overview of demographic and related changes among European consumers, see:

Peter S. H. Leeflang and W. Fred van Raaij, 'The Changing Consumer in the European Union: A "Meta-Analysis" ', *International Journal of Research in Marketing*, 12, no. 5, 1995, pp. 373–387.

For a discussion of spending differences in one- and dual-earner households, see:

Rose M. Rubin, Bobye J. Riney, and David J. Molina, 'Expenditure Pattern Differentials between One-Earner and Dual-Earner Households: 1972–1973 and 1984', *Journal of Consumer Research*, June 1990, pp. 43–52.

For a discussion of how women use time, see:

W. Thomas Anderson, Jr., Linda L. Golden, William A. Weeks, and U. M. Umesh, 'The Five Faces of Eve: Women's Timetable Typologies', in *Advances in Consumer Research*, vol. 16, ed. Thomas K. Srull (Provo, UT: Association for Consumer Research, 1989), pp. 346–353.

MARKETING STRATEGY IN ACTION
Supermodels at Hennes & Mauritz

 ennes & Mauritz deliberately exploits the effects of reference group influence. The Swedish clothing company has devoted itself to using supermodels to promote its products.

The first in the row of supermodels was black goddess Iman, who showed parts of the new collection to the press in Stockholm in 1988. Then Cindy Crawford campaigned for lingerie, just before marrying Richard Gere, and later Karen Mulder, Christy Turlington, Naomi Campbell, Helena Christensen, and many others followed, modelling for lingerie, swimwear, and beautiful dresses.

The strategy to stake the promotion budget exclusively on top models with soaring fees is quite unorthodox, taking Hennes & Mauritz' low-priced products into account. It is, however, not a sign of misjudgement of the product profile on behalf of the company, but a well thought-out way to communicate that clothes need only to cost a penny and still look like a million.

By means of the best models and photographers, Hennes & Mauritz shows how to get dressed on a budget. The supermodels represent quality – a quality which rubs off on the clothes – unconsciously people connect the image of the models with the Hennes & Mauritz clothes. Therefore, 53-year-old actress Lauren Hutton was used to communicate that the company sells clothes for women above 35 years, and, later, 31-year-old Linda Evangelista promoted the 'Woman' collection.

For a short period of time extraordinarily skinny models were used, such as Trish Goff and Amber Valetta, who later created a stir amid accusations of stimulating anorexia. Thereafter, Hennes & Mauritz decided that their preferred models were those who express femininity and *joie de vivre*.

The contrast between the exclusive models and the low prices is exciting and Hennes & Mauritz is convinced that, in a world of advertising, the only way to catch people's attention is to do things differently. These models have great personality. Their power, drive, and sensuality mean that the posters do not skip the attention of the passers-by.

In Norway, sumptuous Anna-Nicole Smith was even considered dangerous to road safety as her attractive appearance on billboards made the Norwegian drivers forget to concentrate on the traffic. The posters have been such a success that it has caused unforeseen problems: to an increasing extent, people would tear off the posters to use them to decorate their rooms. One 18-year-old said that he and his friends keep the Hennes & Mauritz posters as collectors' items.

Apparently, this enthusiasm is widespread, because Transmedia, the company responsible for the posters, demanded that Hennes & Mauritz take action to avoid the pillage if they wanted to remain customers, so Hennes & Mauritz started to offer posters and postcards for free from the shops.

The promotion, however, has not solely been the object of admiration. In particular, the poster featuring Pamela Anderson crawling on all fours with pout and high-heeled shoes, promoting the Hennes & Mauritz 1994 swimwear, caused an uproar. Feminists in both Norway and Sweden protested against the sexualization of the female body in public, and older people complained about how uncomfortable they felt when they were walking with their grandchildren and had to look at the sexy, scantily dressed model on the billboards all around town.

Discussion Questions

1. Analyse the potential effect of the H&M ads in terms of the three types of reference group influence discussed in this chapter.
2. Do you think the ads appeal to all types of consumers in the same way? Try to distinguish various groups of consumers in terms of the effect of these ads.
3. Do you think the purchase of H&M clothing is mostly individual or family decision making?

4. Will changes in household composition and family life cycle have an influence on H&M's business? How?

Source: Lotte Freddie, 'Supermodeller Sælger', *Berlingske Tidende*, 22 September, magasin 3, 1996; Harriet Bjerrum Nielsen, 'Mellem puritanske nordmænd og usexede danskere', *Forum: Tidsskrift for køn og kultur*, no. 4, 1995, pp. 6–8.

Market Segmentation and Product Positioning

Whose Beer?

F

rom Alaska to China virtually every country outside the Muslim world produces beer. Since 40–50 per cent of the heavy drinkers are men, beer has traditionally been marketed to the male population.

In their search for new customers in mature markets, brewers are increasingly targeting females. Television advertising in Ireland for Guinness has shown clear signs of this: the young people seen flirting amid stylish pub interiors are not men, but women. The scenes are intercut with modern Irish music from a female-led band. The whole image is less T-shirt and tattoos than short leather skirt. Women are not keen drinkers of stout, but by promoting youthful images and improving the ambience of the pub, Guinness has managed to raise the percentage of female stout drinkers from 8 to 14 per cent in 10 years.

Caffrey's, a highly successful Irish beer launched by Bass in Britain, has also placed advertisements starring females in women's magazines such as *Marie Claire* and *Elle*.

Instead of being bitter, 'female-friendly' beverages need to be fizzier and sweeter. In the light of this, Tuborg, a Danish brewery, has recently launched the 'Tuborg Porter Citron'; a mix of stout and fizzy lemonade. Although the product is not entirely directed towards women, they form 30 per cent of non-users, the group which the company is targeting with this new product. In the ads for the product the brewery attempts to attract women without alienating men.

Source: David Brierley, 'A Woman's Place Is in The Pub, Smoking', *The European*, 20–26 June 1996, Tuborg Bryggerier A/S.

What is it, that these breweries are doing? They develop products targeted at specific segments of their overall market. Market segmentation is one of the most important concepts in the consumer behaviour and marketing literature.[1] A primary reason for studying consumer behaviour is to identify bases for effective segmentation, and a large portion of consumer research is concerned with segmentation. From a marketing strategy view, selection of the appropriate target market is paramount to developing successful marketing programmes.

The logic of market segmentation is quite simple: It is based on the idea that a single product usually will not appeal to *all* consumers. Consumers' purchase goals, product knowledge, involvement, and purchase behaviour vary; and successful marketers often adapt their marketing strategies to appeal to specific consumer groups. Even a simple product such as chewing gum comes in multiple flavours and package sizes, and varies

HIGHLIGHT 16.1

Segmenting the Gum Chewers

 arketers often use a variety of segmentation dimensions to understand and describe their target market. Below is a short description of the most likely buyers of Dandy's chewing gum products.

Stimorol is primarily targeted towards the 13–24-year-olds who typically watch MTV and whose favourite leisure activity is rollerblading. Advertising for Stimorol focuses on the American image as in the TV ad for Mega Bite, which resembles a trailer for an action film. TV ads for the two new Stimorol flavours Black'n'Blue and Rose Berry are cut in short sequences, typical of music videos.

V6 is targeted towards 18–40-year-olds – women more than men – with a healthy, active and modern lifestyle. Ads for V6 stress the dental benefits of chewing V6 typically showing a professional woman in a restaurant, using V6 after her lunch.

Dandy's **Bubble gum** is targeted towards the 5–12-year-olds, and for this product marketing is down to securing extensive distribution so that the kids can be tempted by the displays in the shops.

in sugar content, calories, consistency (e.g. liquid centres), and colours to appeal to different consumers. While a single product seldom will appeal to all consumers, it can almost always serve more than one consumer. Thus, there are usually *groups of consumers* who can be served well by a single item. If a particular group can be served profitably by a firm, then it comprises a viable market segment. A marketer should then develop a marketing mix to serve that group.

In the past, many marketers have focused on target markets in a general, nonpersonal way. While they may have had some idea of the general characteristics of their target market, they could not identify individual consumers who actually purchased and used their products. However, by employing modern market research techniques and by using some of the concepts covered in this text, marketers can define and target consumer segments in a much more sophisticated way. Highlight 16.1 gives a number of examples on effective segmentation.

In this chapter we consider market segmentation. We define **market segmentation** as the process of dividing a market into groups of consumers that are similar in the way they react to elements of the marketing mix, and selecting the most appropriate group(s) for the firm to serve. We can break down the process of market segmentation into five tasks, as shown in Exhibit 16.1. In the remainder of this chapter, we discuss each of the market segmentation tasks shown in the exhibit. While we recognize that these tasks are strongly interrelated and that their order may vary (depending on the firm and the situation), market segmentation analysis can seldom (if ever) be ignored. Even if the final decision is to mass market and not to segment at all, this decision should be reached only *after* a market segmentation analysis has been conducted. Thus, market segmentation analysis is critical for sound marketing strategy development.

EXHIBIT 16.1

Tasks Involved in Market Segmentation

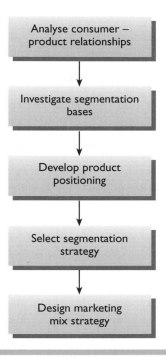

Analyse consumer – product relationships

↓

Investigate segmentation bases

↓

Develop product positioning

↓

Select segmentation strategy

↓

Design marketing mix strategy

Analyse Consumer–Product Relationships

The first task involved in segmenting markets is analysing consumer–product relationships. This entails analysis of the affect and cognitions, behaviours, and environments involved in the purchase–consumption process for the particular product.

There are three relevant sources of knowledge for this task. First, there is the experience and knowledge within the company, which may be put to use by marketing managers and other relevant members of the company brainstorming the product concept and considering what types of consumers are likely to purchase and use the product and how they differ from those less likely to buy. Second, publicly available information sources, such as official statistics, media reports, and multiclient reports available from market research and advertising agencies, may be used to investigate differences in potential target markets, determine the relative sizes of these markets, and develop a better understanding of consumers of this or similar products. Third, the company can commission market research (collection of primary data) for looking at how consumers differ in the attributes they desire, how these are linked to consequences and values, and how these are related to their shopping behaviour. Many of the types of analyses discussed in the other chapters of this book, such as laddering, survey research, and behavioural analysis, are useful for this purpose. For some product categories such as cars, toothpaste, and food products, some ways of segmenting markets have become widely accepted. For example, the category of car buyers is often divided into luxury, sports, family, mini and supermini car buyers. Within each of these markets further analysis may offer insights into market opportunities, and it is essential to keep track of developments in the different markets. A European motor analyst forecasts that by 1998 the mini and supermini segments would increase their combined share of the market from 31.8 per cent in 1994 to 34.3 per cent, while the upper-medium and luxury segments would decline from 31.3 per cent to 29.2 per cent. The percentages may seem small, but they represent hundreds of thousands of cars.[2]

However, such divisions, when used without detailed analysis, can be misleading and can give advantages to competitors who ignore them and develop products which appeal to groups of consumers across the established segments, as happened when Japanese car manufacturers began to promote off-road vehicles as family-friendly leisure and fun cars. European car manufacturers were late in picking up on this trend, because the new products did not fit into existing categorizations of buyers.

A common initial breakdown in markets is between the prestige and mass markets.[3] The prestige market seeks the highest-quality (and often the highest-priced) product available. Often particular products for consumers in this market have very important meanings, such as expressions of good taste, expertise, and status. Brands such as Rolex watches, Moët & Chandon champagne, Mercedes-Benz cars, Louis Vuitton luggage, and Gucci handbags are targeted to these consumers. The marketing strategies for these products generally involve selling them in exclusive stores at high prices and promoting them in prestige media. For consumers in this market, affect and cognitions (feelings about and meaning of the product), behaviours (shopping activities), and environments (information and store contact) differ from those of consumers in the mass market. Thus, the initial analysis of consumer–product relationships has important implications for all of the tasks involved in market segmentation and strategy development.

Analysing these differences in consumers is also important when market conditions change. For example, in 1986 the United States was BMW's largest market outside Germany reaching record sales of 96 800 cars. By 1991 sales had fallen by 45 per cent to 53 000 cars. The 1987 stock market crash had a dual impact on the luxury car market, taking money out of the pockets of potential BMW buyers and putting a psychological end to the high-flying consumption of the 1980s. The ultimate status symbol of the yuppie generation – a BMW – became outmoded and even buyers at the high end of the market became 'value oriented'. The prestige the company had sought through advertising with polo ponies and elegant parties tagged them as having outrageous prices. The company desperately needed to rethink their strategy. They came up with a redefinition of the brand and product. 'Performance' was defined to encompass three aspects: quality, safety, and social responsibility. Lower priced models available in Germany, but previously not exported to the United States, were brought to the US market to put the BMW vehicles at a lower price point. The incremental sales impact of this move went well beyond the sales of these vehicles. It also helped develop the BMW image in the direction of better value. New models were introduced to the market both at aggressive prices and to rave reviews. The new strategy also necessitated a change in advertising and the new programme shifted to a key benefit sought by drivers – safety.[4]

This example demonstrates how the analysis of consumer–product relationships led to a successful marketing strategy for BMW. However, a number of other tasks occur after the initial analysis of those relationships and before marketing strategies are finalized. A logical next step is to investigate various bases on which markets could be segmented.

Investigate Segmentation Bases

Investigation of segmentation bases involves defining criteria which are used for classifying consumers into segments. Numerous variables have been proposed and used for that purpose. In selecting an appropriate segmentation base, we should keep the basic purpose of segmentation in mind: to group consumers in such a way that, within groups, they react to marketing mix elements in a relatively homogeneous way. The major criterion for selecting segmentation variables should therefore be to what extent they are expected or documented to be related to consumers' cognitive, affective, and behavioural reactions to elements of the marketing mix – i.e. to products, prices, promotion, and distribution channels.

Exhibit 16.2 shows a classification of commonly used segmentation variables. Some are general and can be used for many different types of products, others are product-specific. Some refer to manifest, observable characteristics, and others require more elaborate measurement requirements like questionnaires. Highlight 16.2 mentions a somewhat more unusual segmentation base.

Demographic and Geographic Criteria

Demographic and geographic criteria are widely used for segmentation, because information on them is usually readily available from official statistics. It is easily determined how many consumers are in a certain age group or educational group or live in a certain region, and also more narrowly defined segments based on combinations of these criteria can usually be traced in official statistics. Their usefulness, on the other hand, has been subject to some debate. Just as all other segmentation criteria, they are useful only to the extent they are demonstrably related to consumers cognitive, affective, and behavioural reactions to marketing stimuli. As we discussed in Chapter 14 on subcultures, we find many examples where subcultures are formed related to geographic or demographic criteria, and where consumer behaviour within the subculture is different from that outside the subculture. However, grouping consumers by demographic and geographic criteria does not automatically result in a classification according to subcultures: this first becomes evident after closer inspection along the lines described in Chapter 14.

More recently, however, geodemographic segmentation has become popular again with the advent of geographical information systems (GIS), which are large-scale databases that consist of a mass of detailed information about households in certain

EXHIBIT 16.2

Useful Segmentation Bases for Consumer Markets

	General	Product-Specific
Manifest	Demographic, geographic criteria	Purchase- and usage-related criteria
Inferred	Psychographic criteria	Attitudes, benefits sought, involvement

HIGHLIGHT 16.2

Look for the Stars

ew research in a study that came from the Manchester School of Management indicates that astrology could prove a valuable consumer profiling tool by combining the measurement advantages of demographics with the psychological insights of psychographics.

The analysis showed that astrology 'does have a significant effect, and sometimes predictable effect on behaviour in the leisure, tobacco, and drinks markets'. For example, Cancerians – believed to be sensitive, pessimistic, insecure worriers – are less likely to have smoked, while the 'self-confident, independent and assertive' Areans were much more likely to be smokers. The hyperactive Virgoans apparently have no time for gardening, TV, or listening to music; the 'inventive, intelligent and eccentric' Aquarians shun mainstream activities preferring more solitary pursuits like do-it-yourself; while Sagittarians – solitary, tactless, and impulsive – prefer outdoor activities and like diversity.

The author of the study argues that astrology could be the perfect answer to today's ever-changing consumer, whose lifestyle appears to shift during the course of a single day rather than over a matter of decades.

Source: Adapted from Robert Dwek, 'Star Struck', *Marketing Business*, July/August 1997, pp. 10–13.

geographical areas. The idea is to create classifications of actual, addressable, mapable neighbourhoods where consumers live and shop, and that this is possible because, once one gets down into very small geographical segments, the neighbourhood where people live actually says quite a lot about their consumption habits. For example, UK-based Kormoran Marketing and Communications groups people into 52 types within 12 major groups, called high-income families, suburban semis, blue-collar owners, low-rise council, council flats, Victorian low status, town houses and flats, stylish singles, independent elders, mortgaged families, country dwellers, and institutional areas. These groups come about by using GIS data, and they can be related to purchasing data, showing which of the groups has an above-average probability of buying a certain product.

Psychographic Criteria

Psychographic segmentation divides markets on differences in consumer lifestyles.[5] Generally, psychographic segmentation follows a *post hoc* model. That is, consumers are first asked a variety of questions about their lifestyles and are then grouped on the basis of the similarity of their responses. **Lifestyles** have traditionally been measured by asking consumers about their activities (work, hobbies, vacations), interests (family, job, community) and opinions (about social issues, politics, business). The activity, interest, and opinion (**AIO**) questions in some studies are very general. In others, at least some of the questions are related to specific products.

Psychographic segmentation studies often include hundreds of questions and provide a tremendous amount of information about consumers. Thus, psychographic segmentation is based on the idea that 'the more you know and understand about consumers, the more effectively you can communicate and market to them'.[6] However, this approach has also been criticized.[7] It has been argued that, instead of asking consumers hundreds of questions about all kinds of things not necessarily related to their buying behaviour, and then hoping for some relationships to emerge in the analysis, consumer behaviour theory should be used to delineate those variables which on theoretical grounds one believes to be part of the lifestyle.

One of the issues about which there is no agreement in lifestyle research is whether lifestyle refers to consumers' manifest behaviours or to consumers' cognition and affect.[8] When analysing lifestyle as manifested in consumers' actual purchases, one way of segmenting consumers is to group them according to how they allocate their total income to various groups of expenditures.[9] However, this approach is tedious and has only occasionally been used in segmentation studies. It is more common to measure lifestyle by questionnaire-based devices and group consumers into segments based on their cognitions and affective reactions.

All major market research companies and many advertising agencies have developed a **lifestyle segmentation** which they offer their customers. Although details differ, all of these are based on survey data using AIO-items of the type discussed above. Usually, statistical analysis is used to derive a few, often only two, major dimensions which can be used to classify consumers into lifestyle segments. Being critical/uncritical and being modern/traditional are two dimensions often used in lifestyle segmentation.

While most of these lifestyle segmentation instruments are general, not product specific, there have also been attempts to segment consumers according to their lifestyle with regard to certain product categories, such as food, travel, or housing. Exhibit 16.3 shows an example of a lifestyle segmentation which is done specifically with regard to the food category.[10] It is based on a means–end approach: it attempts to classify consumers according to how they use food products to attain basic life values, and how this is mirrored in the type of attribute they look for in food products, how they shop for food, how they prepare meals, and how they eat. The classification is based on consumers' responses to 69 items, measuring 23 dimensions of what is called a food-related lifestyle. Exhibit 16.4 shows the distribution of segments derived using this instrument in Germany and Great Britain.[11]

Attitudes, Benefits Sought, and Involvement

While psychographic segmentation using the lifestyle concept is either general or applies to a relatively broad product class, a variety of product-specific psychological variables have also been used for segmentation. Attitudes towards the product in question can be used for segmentation, distinguishing between consumers with a positive, negative, or neutral attitude. A marketing strategy may then be devised to tackle specifically the segment consisting of consumers with a neutral attitude, because they may be susceptible to influence, to make the attitude more positive. Classifying consumers according to their degree of involvement is a rather powerful way of arriving at a meaningful segmentation base. Imagine the market for wine. For some consumers, wine is a relatively low-involvement product, and these consumers will look for moderately priced wines in supermarkets with a tendency to routine purchases. Other consumers are wine lovers who make choices carefully, shop in specialist shops,

EXHIBIT 16.3

Food-Related Lifestyle Segments

Segment Name	Segment Characteristics	Marketing Implications
The uninvolved food consumer	Uninterested in most aspects of food Not interested in quality Do not read product information Convenience important Heavy snacking Little planning Food not a family matter	Unstable shopping behaviour Little brand loyalty Few perceived differences between different food products Price as the major parameter
The careless food consumer	Resembles the uninvolved food consumer Is interested in novel products if they are convenient Buys spontaneously	Possibility for product differentiation by novelty New products should not be demanding Not likely to develop any great loyalty Constant stream of short-lived product variations probably best strategy
The conservative food consumer	Plans shopping and cooking No interest in new products or recipes Freshness and taste important Convenience not important Take time for cooking Little snacking Food is a woman's task Security by traditional food major purchase motive	Interested in shopping for food Want predictability and want to avoid change Strong preferences for products and shops, difficult to overcome through new products Maintain traditional products
The rational food consumer	High use of product information and speciality shops High degree of planning All quality aspects very important Heavy use of organic food	Most receptive to better-quality food products Easy to inform them about product improvements Quality in relation to price Highly critical consumers
The adventurous food consumer	Novelty and looking for new ways very important High involvement with cooking Convenience not important, Cooking is a task for the whole family Self-fulfilment and social aspects of food more important than security	Needs to be stimulated to creativity Must encourage self-expression, creativity, and social togetherness Possibility for experimenting in cooking important Interested in exotic food products, but not exotic precooked meals

Source: Adapted from Klaus G. Grunert, Hanne Hartvig Larsen, Tage Koed Madsen, and Allan Baadsgaard, *Market Orientation in Food and Agriculture* (Boston, MA: Kluwer, 1996), pp. 53–72.

EXHIBIT 16.4

Food-Related Lifestyle Segment Sizes in Two European Countries

Segment	Germany (%)	Great Britain (%)
The uninvolved food consumer	21	9
The careless food consumer	11	27
The conservative food consumer	18	19
The rational food consumer	26	33
The adventurous food consumer	24	12

Source: Adapted from Klaus G. Grunert, Hanne Hartvig Larsen, Tage Koed Madsen, and Allan Baadsgaard, *Market Orientation in Food and Agriculture* (Boston, MA: Kluwer, 1996), pp. 53–72.

and will be attracted by offerings which enable them to demonstrate their knowledge, such as wine tastings and wine clubs.

The most popular way of segmenting based on product-specific psychological variables is **benefit segmentation**. The belief underlying the benefit segmentation approach is that the benefits people are seeking in consuming a given product are the basic reasons for the existence of true market segments.[12] This approach thus attempts to measure consumer value systems and consumers' perceptions of various brands in a product class. The classic example of a benefit segmentation, provided by Russell Haley, concerned the toothpaste market. Haley identified four basic segments – sensory, sociable, worrier, and independent – as presented in Exhibit 16.5. Haley argued this segmentation could be very useful for selecting advertising copy, media, commercial length, packaging, and new-product design. For example, colourful packages might be appropriate for the sensory segment, perhaps aqua packages (to indicate fluoride) for the worrier group, and gleaming white packages for the sociable segment because of their interest in white teeth.[13]

Purchase and Usage-Related Criteria

Just as consumers can be grouped according to the kind of attitude they have towards the product, they can also be grouped according to their degree of usage, for example the distinction between nonusers, light users, and heavy users, each of which may require a different kind of marketing strategy. Heavy users of washing machines, such as families with several small children, will have other requirements with regard to the product and be attracted by other advertising appeals than would light users in single households. However, the example also shows another thing – that the degree of usage is not very informative unless supplemented with other information on the reasons for the low or high degree of usage.

Markets can often be divided on the basis of the usage situation in conjunction with individual differences of consumers.[14] This is known as **person/situation segmentation**. For example, the clothing and footwear markets are divided not only on the basis of the consumer's sex and size, but also on usage situation dimensions such as weather

EXHIBIT 16.5

Toothpaste Market Benefit Segments

	Sensory Segment	Sociable Segment	Worrier Segment	Independent Segment
Principal benefit sought	Flavour, product appearance	Brightness of teeth	Decay prevention	Price
Demographic strengths	Children	Teens, young people	Large families	Men
Special behavioural characteristics	Uses of spearmint-flavoured toothpaste	Smokers	Heavy users	Heavy users
Brands disproportionately favoured	Colgate	Ultra Brite	Crest	Cheapest brand
Lifestyle characteristics	Hedonistic	Active	Conservative	Value oriented

Source: Adapted from Russell I. Haley, 'Benefit Segmentation: A Decision-Oriented Research Tool,' *Journal of Marketing*, 32, July 1968, pp. 30–35. Published by the American Marketing Association.

conditions, physical activities, and social events.[15] As another example, expensive china like Rosenthal or Royal Copenhagen is designed for special occasions; IKEA dinnerware is designed for everyday family use. Dickson argues: 'In practice the product whose unique selling proposition (quality, features, image, packaging, or merchandising) is not targeted for particular people in particular usage situations is probably the exception rather than the rule.'[16] Thus, Dickson suggests the approach to segmentation outlined in Exhibit 16.6. This approach combines not only the person and the situation, but also other important segmentation bases: benefits sought, product and attribute perceptions, and marketplace behaviour.

Operationally, Dickson suggests this segmentation approach involves the following steps:

- *Step 1*. Use observational studies, focus group discussions, and secondary data to discover whether different usage situations exist and whether they are determinant, in the sense that they appear to affect the importance of various product characteristics.
- *Step 2*. If step 1 produces promising results, undertake a benefit, product perception, and reported market behaviour segmentation survey of consumers. Measure benefits and perceptions by usage situation as well as by individual difference characteristics. Assess situation usage frequency by recall estimates or usage-situation diaries.
- *Step 3*. Construct a person/situation segmentation matrix. The rows are the major

EXHIBIT 16.6

Person/Situation Segmentation

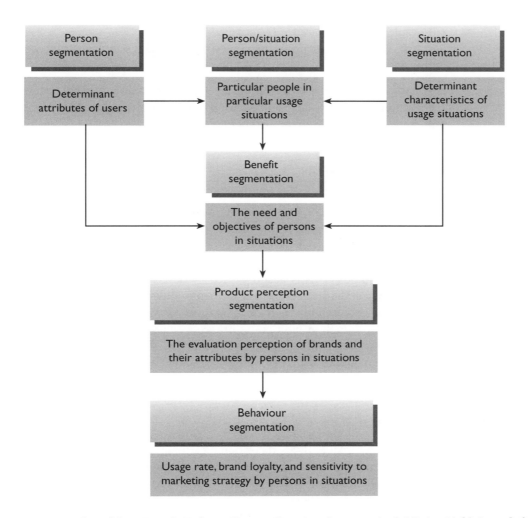

Source: Adapted from Peter R. Dickson, 'Person–Situation: Segmentation's Missing Link', *Journal of Marketing*, 46, Fall 1982, pp. 55–64. Published by the American Marketing Association.

usage situations and the columns are groups of users identified by a single character-istic or combination of characteristics.

- *Step 4.* Rank the cells in the matrix in terms of their submarket sales volume. The person/situation combination that results in the greatest consumption of the generic product would be ranked first.
- *Step 5.* State the major benefits sought, important product dimensions, and unique market behaviour for each nonempty cell of the matrix. (Some types of people will never consume the product in certain usage situations.)

- *Step 6*. Position your competitors' offerings within the matrix. The person/situation segments they currently serve can be determined by the product feature they promote and other marketing strategies.
- *Step 7*. Position your offering within the matrix on the same criteria.
- *Step 8*. Assess how well your current offering and marketing strategy meet the needs of the submarket compared to the competitions' offering.
- *Step 9*. Identify market opportunities based on submarket size, needs, and competitive advantage.[17]

This approach incorporates all four of the major factors discussed in our text – affect and cognition, behaviour, environment, and marketing strategy. It thus offers a more comprehensive analysis than many other approaches.

Develop Product Positioning

Product positioning relates to the way in which one attempts to position a product relative to competing products in the minds of consumers.[18] A recent example is Scholl, a European shoe manufacturer and retailer which is repositioning its stores as 'total footcare centres'.

The key objective of positioning strategy is to form a particular brand image in consumers' minds. This is accomplished by developing a coherent strategy that may involve all of the marketing mix elements. Building on the means–end model which we have employed in this book to analyse the way consumers perceive brands, it seems natural to look at positioning in terms of product attributes, consequences of product use, and values attained by product use. However, other forms of positioning are popular, like positioning by product user, by product class, and by competitors.

Positioning by Attribute

Probably the most frequently used positioning strategy is **positioning by attribute** – associating a product with an attribute or a product feature, or a customer benefit. Consider Unilever (Elida Fabergé) which has had great success with the introduction of the Organics shampoo stressing the 'root-nourishing nutrients' of their shampoo.

A new product can also be positioned with respect to an attribute that has not previously been emphasized. For example in ads for NIVEA's roll-on deodorant, where the soft and mild nature of the roll-on is emphasized instead of the anti-perspirant effect.

Sometimes a product can be positioned in terms of two or more attributes simultaneously. Dove has marketed its 'cream bar' as a soap which contains body lotion and therefore also leaves the skin softer.

The price/quality attribute dimension is commonly used for positioning products as well as stores. In many product categories, some brands offer more in terms of service, features, or performance – and a higher price is one signal to the customer of this higher quality. For example, Bang & Olufsen TVs are positioned as high-priced, high-quality products. Conversely, other brands emphasize low price and good quality. Samsung TVs, for example, are positioned as such.

Netto, the Danish discount chain, has used the price/quality attribute dimension in a distinct way by positioning Netto stores as the discount store with low prices on well known brand names. One of their TV ads proclaims that 'Real women shop in Netto'.

Positioning by Consequence or Value

While we would maintain that successful positioning requires not only positioning in terms of attributes, but also **positioning by consequences or values**, in practice often either one or the other is dominant. Banks and insurance companies are especially prone to position themselves in terms of consequences or values – some emphasize safety and reassuredness, and family values, whereas others emphasize thriftiness or even fun and enjoyment. Another strategy is positioning by use or application. The Danish State Railways (DSB) has positioned train travel by particular uses. For example, ads for the 'Super Red Ticket' positions train travel as a method of getting to see loved ones.

Positioning by Product User

Another approach is **positioning by product user** or a class of users. This can be done to exploit the effect which subcultures and reference groups have on consumer behaviour. For example the TV ad shown in France, Belgium, and the Netherlands for Unilever's ice-tea brand, Liptonice, starring Eric Cantona, who can only concentrate on a game of golf after a can of Liptonice.

Positioning by Product Class

For innovative products, **positioning by product class** is an important aspect of product introduction. Consumers tend to categorize new products into product categories they know, and when the new product is very innovative and the categorization therefore unclear, the way the manufacturer positions the product in terms of product class may have a considerable effect on the way consumers perceive the product and what they expect from it.

For example, a maker of dried milk introduced an instant breakfast drink positioned as a breakfast substitute and a virtually identical product positioned as a meal substitute for those on a diet. Frozen yoghurt has been repositioned as light ice cream, because consumers in Europe did not know what to expect from frozen yoghurt.

Positioning by Competitors

In most positioning strategies, an explicit or implicit frame of reference is the competition (**positioning by competitor**). Often, the major purpose of this type of positioning is to convince consumers that a brand is better than the market leader (or another well-accepted brand) on important attributes. Positioning with respect to a competitor can be done directly by naming a competitor in advertisements, but such a strategy is illegal in many European countries unless it contains actual facts about the competitor. For example in their ads Tele2, a new operator on the Danish telecommunications market, compare their prices for overseas telephone calls with TeleDanmark's.

Positioning by competitors can also be done in more subtle ways. For example, Danish State Railway's ad for the quicker trip through the new tunnel under the Great Belt refers to 'those who fly' showing dead flies on the windscreen of the train.

Positioning Maps

A useful instrument for positioning products, especially *vis-à-vis* competitors, is a positioning map. A **positioning map** is a visual depiction of consumers' perceptions of competitive products, brands, or models. It is constructed by surveying consumers about various product attributes and developing dimensions and a graph indicating the relative position of competitors.

Exhibit 16.7 shows an example of a positioning map. It shows how consumers perceived a newly launched yoghurt product ('Petit Deli'), consisting of a sweetened yoghurt and a fruit syrup, in comparison to a number of products which the manufacturer believed could be potential competitors: other yoghurts, other types of snack, other types of dessert. The map shows that consumers' perception of this set of products can be explained by two dimensions: a health dimension and a situation dimension. The

EXHIBIT 16.8

Positioning Map for a Yoghurt Product

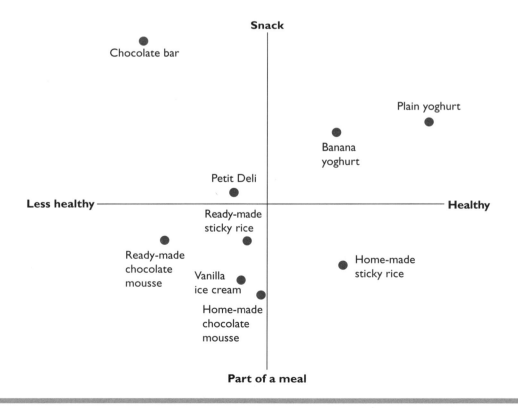

Petit Deli product seems to have an unclear positioning in the minds of the consumer, because it is placed half-way between the traditional yoghurt products and the dessert products. Such information can be used to sharpen the positioning of the product – for example, the product could be positioned more clearly as a dessert product by emphasizing this usage occasion on the packaging and in advertising.

Select Segmentation Strategy

After the analysis in the previous stages is completed, the appropriate **segmentation strategy** can be considered.[19] There are four basic alternatives. First, the firm may decide not to enter the market. Analysis to this stage may reveal that there is no viable market niche for the product, brand, or model. Second, the firm may decide not to segment, but to be a mass marketer. This may be the appropriate strategy in at least three situations:

1. When the market is so small that marketing to a portion of it is not profitable.
2. When heavy users make up such a large proportion of the sales volume that they are the only relevant target.
3. When the brand is dominant in the market and targeting to a few segments would not benefit sales and profits.[20]

Third, the firm may decide to market to only one segment. Fourth, the firm may decide to market to more than one segment and design a separate marketing mix for each.

In any case, marketers must have some criteria on which to base segmentation strategy decisions. Three important criteria are that a viable segment must be measurable, meaningful, and marketable:

1. *Measurable*. For a segment to be selected, marketers must be able to measure its size and characteristics. For example, one of the difficulties of segmenting on the basis of social class is that the concept and its divisions are not clearly defined and measured. Alternatively, income is much easier to measure.
2. *Meaningful*. A meaningful segment is one that is large enough to have sufficient sales and growth potentials to offer long-term profits.
3. *Marketable*. A marketable segment is one that can be reached and served profitably.

Segments that meet these criteria are variable markets for the product. The marketer must now give further attention to the marketing mix.

Design Marketing Mix Strategy

The firm is now in a position to complete its marketing strategy by finalizing the marketing mix for each segment. Selecting the target market and designing the marketing mix go hand in hand, and thus many marketing mix decisions should already have been carefully considered. For example, if the target market selected is price sensitive, some consideration has already been given to price levels. Product positioning also has many implications for selecting appropriate promotions and channels. Thus, many marketing mix decisions are made in conjunction with (rather than after) target market selection. In the remaining chapters of this section, consumer behaviour and marketing mix strategies will be discussed in more detail.

Back to . . . Whose Beer?

The breweries in the opening example had found that their market can fruitfully be divided into several segments, which differ in the types of product and the type of communication by which each segment is attracted. Gender is used as a first segmentation criterion, but the gender differentiation is supplemented by lifestyle characteristics which go with the segment of female drinkers. Based on this understanding of the market, the breweries have developed new products and/or new market communication specifically for this segment, and positioned it by attribute, user and/or product class.

Summary

This chapter provided an overview of market segmentation analysis. Market segmentation was defined as the process of dividing a market into groups of similar consumers and selecting the most appropriate group(s) for the firm to serve. Market segmentation was analysed in terms of five interrelated tasks: (1) analyse consumer–product relationships; (2) investigate segmentation bases; (3) develop product positioning; (4) select segmentation strategy; and (5) design marketing mix strategy. Market segmentation analysis is a cornerstone of sound marketing strategy development and is one of the major bridges between the literature dealing with consumer behaviour and that dealing with marketing strategy.

Key Terms and Concepts

AIO   336
benefit segmentation   339
lifestyle   336
lifestyle segmentation   337
market segmentation   332
person/situation segmentation   339
positioning by attribute   342
positioning by consequence/value   343
positioning by competitor   343
positioning map   344
positioning by product class   343
positioning by use   343
positioning by product user   343
product positioning   342
psychographic segmentation   336
segmentation strategy   345

Review and Discussion Questions

1. Define market segmentation and describe the management tasks involved in applying the concept.
2. Select a product (other than toothpaste) about which you are fairly knowledgeable and develop a preliminary description of possible benefit segments following the structure presented in Exhibit 16.5.

3. Identify potential advantages and problems associated with marketing to benefit segments.

4. Use the food-related lifestyle categories to suggest marketing strategies for psychographic segments of buyers of frozen Thai meals.

5. Consider person/situation segmentation as a way of viewing the hotel market. State the needs and objectives of persons in situations for at least three segments that you identify.

6. Explain each of the five approaches to product positioning and offer an example (not in the text) for each approach.

7. How does the concept of segmentation relate to positioning strategies?

8. What options are available to the organization after it identifies segments in the market? When would each of these options represent a reasonable choice?

9. How would segmentation and positioning decisions be different for a small business entrepreneur than for a large corporation?

Additional Reading

For conceptual discussions on the nature of marketing segmentation, see:

Peter R. Dickson and James L. Ginter, 'Market Segmentation, Product Differentiation, and Marketing Strategy', *Journal of Marketing*, April 1987, pp. 1–10.

Janet Hoek, Philip Gendall, and Don Esslemont, 'Market Segmentation: A Search for the Holy Grail?' *Journal of Marketing Practice: Applied Marketing Science*, no. 1, 1996, pp. 25–34.

For development of empirical procedures for use in segmentation and positioning, see:

Rajiv Grover and V. Srinivasan. 'A Simultaneous Approach to Market Segmentation and Market Structuring', *Journal of Marketing Research*, May 1987, pp. 139–153.

Wagner A. Kamakura, 'A Least Squares Procedure for Benefit Segmentation with Conjoint Experiments', *Journal of Marketing Research*, May 1988, pp. 157–167.

Steven M. Shugan, 'Estimating Brand Positioning Maps Using Supermarket Scanning Data', *Journal of Marketing Research*, February 1987, pp. 1–18.

Bruno Stegmüller and Petra Hempel, 'Empirischer Vergleich unterschiedlicher Marktsegmentierungsansätze über die Segmentpopulationen', *Marketing-ZFP*, no. 1, 1996, pp. 25–32.

Michel Wedel and Cor Kistemaker, 'Consumer Benefit Segmentation Using Clusterwise Linear Regression', *International Journal of Research in Marketing*, no. 1, 1989, pp. 45–59.

For further research evaluating various aspects of the validity of lifestyle segmentation, see:

John L. Lastovicka, John P. Murry, Jr., and Erich A. Joachimsthaler, 'Evaluating the Measurement Validity of Lifestyle Typologies with Qualitative Measures and Multiplicative Factoring', *Journal of Marketing Research*, February 1990, pp. 11–23.

Pierre Valette-Florence, *A Causal Analysis of the Predictive Power of Selected Lifestyle Indicators* (Paper presented the 1st EIASM Workshop on Value and Lifestyle Research in Marketing, Brussels, 1991).

For an example on the development of a lifestyle instrument for international use, see:

Klaus G. Grunert, Karen Brunsø, and Søren Bisp, 'Food-Related Life Style: Development of a Cross-Culturally Valid Instrument for Market Surveillance', in *Values, Lifestyles, and Psychographics*, eds. Lynn Kahle and Larry Chiagouris (Hillsdale, NJ: Erlbaum, 1997), pp. 337–354.

For an example of the use of benefit segmentation in the services industry, see:

Hans Mühlbacher and Günther Botschen, 'Benefit-Segmentierung von Dienstleistungsmärkten', *Marketing-ZFP*, no. 3, 1990, pp. 159–168.

MARKETING STRATEGY IN ACTION
Brioche Pasquier

rioche Pasquier is a family-owned company producing prepacked pastry, primarily brioches: a typical French bakery product which is very soft, mellow, rather rich, and with a slightly sweet taste. In 1974, Brioche Pasquier was a small bakery; in 1995 it was the leading company in the prepacked pastry market with more than 1300 employees and a turnover exceeding ECU180 million.

The growth in consumption of brioches has risen because of changes in lifestyle. Brioches are now not only eaten on Sundays, but also on weekdays, and it is a perfect product for the growing number of customers who snack during the day.

Usually, brioches are sold in an eight-pack plastic bag, but Pitch is a pocket-size brioche with either jam or chocolate filling especially made for school children. For hygiene reasons, they are packed individually. The Pitch brioche was launched in 1985, and the development of Pitch was based on close observation of the habits of families with children under the age of 12. The growth in female labour force participation opened new needs and expectations in terms of products for breakfast and for snacks at four or five o'clock when school ends, and children need something easy to snack by themselves. Because brioches contain flour, milk, and eggs they are perceived as healthy, compared with confectionery products.

As school children are the company's most important and targeted customers, Brioche Pasquier tries to get in contact with the school children directly. The company sponsors a first-league basketball team and more than 20 sports tournaments at schools every year. All teams are provided with T-shirts. This is a good opportunity for acquainting the most important customer groups with the Pasquier products since the spectators of these games are mostly children and their mothers. It is important for Brioche Pasquier to target mothers, given that they are believed to determine children's early taste for food.

On the packages of the brioches and Pitch, there are vouchers which offer a discount on sports items, breakfast dishes, T-shirts, etc., that can be bought from Brioche Pasquier. The system for Pitch is like a lottery, because the management feels that children want to win immediately. Prizes are basketball equipment, and the company receives between 1500 and 2000 letters per week. The addresses collected from the consumers' letters are used for further promotional activities and to obtain information on the characteristics of its customers.

Brioche Pasquier's objective is to get in contact with consumers directly, not through advertisements on TV and in magazines.

Discussion Questions

1. What are the advantages of targeting prepacked pastry to adults as well as to children?
2. Does targeting adults require a change in marketing for prepacked pastry?
3. Describe your most recent purchase of a bakery product in terms of relevant affect and cognitions, behaviours, and environments.

Source: Adapted from Francis Declerck and Tom Ottowitz, 'Brioche Pasquier SA: Industrializing Traditional French Baking', in *Product and Process Innovation in the Food Industry*, eds. Bruce Traill and Klaus G. Grunert (London: Chapman & Hall, 1997).

Consumer Behaviour and Product Strategy

Quality Experience in the Caledonian Sleeper

Simon is visiting a business associate in Glasgow and is going to travel by rail. On an earlier occasion he made the trip by car, but it was an awfully long drive and he arrived tired at his Glasgow meeting, not to speak of when he arrived back in London. This time he decided to take the train – the Caledonian sleeper. It leaves London Euston station at 23.30 and arrives at Glasgow Central at 06.56 the next morning. This way it is possible to get a good night's sleep and arrive rested at the meeting – so Simon hoped.

Back at his London office, one of his colleagues wants to know what Simon thought about the Caledonian sleeper, because he will be embarking on a similar trip next month and wants to know whether Simon can recommend it.

Simon willingly related his train travel experiences. He described the sleeper lounge at Euston station, com-plete with TV, fax and free coffee, and the brightly garbed hosts in the lounge, which are a welcome sight on Euston station late at night. Simon also admitted, however, that the Glaswegian twang of some of the staff took some adjusting to. On reaching his cabin, Simon discovered some unexpected perks – a toiletries bag, an 'in-flight' magazine, and free newspaper. There was even a room service menu and options for breakfast in bed.

Even so, he thought the cabin was looking a little frayed at the edges and was probably due for a face-lift. Simon also admitted he did not sleep very well after all. Maybe he was just unlucky, or perhaps as a Caledonian sleeper virgin he was overly sensitive to its quirky ways . . .

Source: Adapted from Robert Dwek, 'Making Tracks', *Marketing Business*, no. 52, September 1996, pp. 20–24.

Many experts consider the product area to be the most important element of the marketing mix. While distribution, price, and communication all add to the total value consumers perceive in an offering, the product itself plays a core role – if the product cannot fulfil those expectations which the other marketing parameters have contributed to shape, it is doomed to failure.

Of course, a key element in product planning is the matching of products with consumer markets. The exchange of consumer assets for products is the acid test that determines whether products will succeed or fail.

In this chapter we focus on product strategy, whereas we will deal with the other major marketing parameters in the subsequent chapters. This and the following chapters adopt a common framework, which is taken directly from the Wheel of

EXHIBIT 17.1

The Wheel of Consumer Analysis: Product Strategy Issues

Consumer analysis used throughout the book. In this chapter, we deal with consumers' affects, cognitions, and behaviours with regard to products. We look at products as part of the environment in which consumer behaviour occurs. Finally, we discuss aspects of product strategy.

Product Affect and Cognitions: Quality Perception and Satisfaction

Much of our discussion of affect and cognition in Section 2 of this text focused on products and how consumers feel about, interpret, and integrate information about them. Here we will draw on this discussion and focus on two aspects which are central in developing product strategy: consumers' quality perception and consumers' satisfaction with a product.

Consumer satisfaction is a critical concept in marketing thought and consumer research. It is generally argued that if consumers are satisfied with a product or brand, they will be more likely to continue to purchase and use it and to tell others of their favourable experiences with it. If they are dissatisfied, they will be more likely to switch brands and complain to manufacturers, retailers, and other consumers.

Given its importance to marketing, satisfaction has been the subject of considerable consumer research.[1] Most approaches regard satisfaction as a result of confirmed or disconfirmed expectations. We can understand this better by relating it to the concept of product quality.

Product quality can be defined in many ways.[2] Engineers and production people

The cultural meaning of the Union Jack is employed in this ad for the Mini.
Courtesy: Rover Group Ltd.

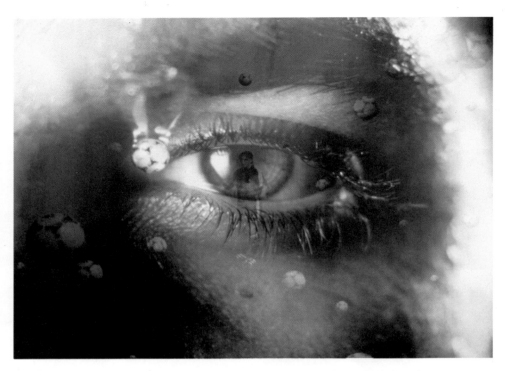

Adidas uses these football World Cup players as a credible reference group for product information.
Courtesy: Adidas and Leagas Delaney.

Med det rod der

er i min

HVERDAG

er det rart med

rene **LINIER**.

IKEA PS ER ET FORUM FOR MODERNE SKANDINAVISK DESIGN MED MØBLER, LAMPER, TEKSTILER OG BESTIK.

IKEA PS GULVLAMPE, DESIGN MIKAEL VARHELYI 498.-

This ad by IKEA appeals to the needs of the family unit.
Courtesy: © Inter IKEA Systems B.V. 1995.

The ad for sugar using celebrities, Mel Smith and Griff Rhys Jones, emphazises peripheral cues, whereas the Klippan ad (opposite) assumes that consumers will be motivated for control processing.
Courtesy: Mejeriforeningen and Klippan.

usually equate product quality with objective product characteristics, such as the durability, expected lifetime, or spinning speed of a washing machine. From a consumer behaviour perspective, we argue that product quality is related to a product's perceived ability to lead to self-relevant consequences, as analysed by the means–end chains concept.[3] Self-relevant consequences of a washing machine are, e.g. clean clothes for the family, less household stress due to easy and convenient handling, and thriftiness due to economical use of water and electricity and a long lifetime without repairs.

For most products, consumers are not able to tell with certainty at the time of purchase whether the product will lead to the desired consequences. They form a quality expectation, which they know will usually not be a perfect predictor of the quality experienced later on. Quality expectations are based on all kinds of input, which we may call quality cues – extrinsic quality cues such as information received from advertising or a salesperson, information on the product itself or its packaging, or the brand name, and intrinsic quality cues, namely the visible features of the product, i.e. the characteristics of the product which are visible at the time of purchase. In the washing machine case this may be such features as the finish of the body, the design of the knobs, and the mechanism for locking the door. For marketers, it is important to find out how consumers form their quality expectations, because it is these expectations the product has to live up to later on.

Once the product has been bought and consumers use or consume it, they tend to find out whether the product has the desired self-relevant consequences. They have a quality experience, which may deviate from the quality expectation. To the extent the experienced quality lives up to or surpasses the expected quality, consumers tend to be satisfied with the product. To the extent the experienced quality falls short of the expected quality, consumers tend to be dissatisfied. The process is visualized in the model in Exhibit 17.2.[4]

Since consumer satisfaction or dissatisfaction is important for consumers' intentions to buy the product again, it is important for marketers to understand both how consumers form quality expectations and how they experience quality. To a large degree experienced quality depends on the product itself, but other factors clearly play a role – for example how consumers use the product, whether they use it correctly, how frequently they use it, etc. Highlight 17.1 gives another example of the development of satisfaction based on shaping, disconfirming, and finally reconfirming expectations.

Consumers who are dissatisfied with products may complain to manufacturers, retailers, and other consumers. **Consumer complaint behaviour** has been the topic of considerable research.

Several generalizations have been offered about consumer complaint behaviour:

1. Those who complain when dissatisfied tend to be members of more upmarket socio-economic groups than those who do not complain.
2. Personality characteristics, including dogmatism, locus of control, and self-confidence, are only weakly related to complaint behaviour, if at all.
3. The severity of dissatisfaction or problems caused by the dissatisfaction are positively related to complaint behaviour.
4. The greater the blame for the dissatisfaction placed on someone other than the one dissatisfied, the greater the likelihood of a complaint.
5. The more positive the perception of retailer responsiveness to consumer complaints, the greater the likelihood of a complaint.[5]

EXHIBIT 17.2

Consumer Quality Perception and Satisfaction

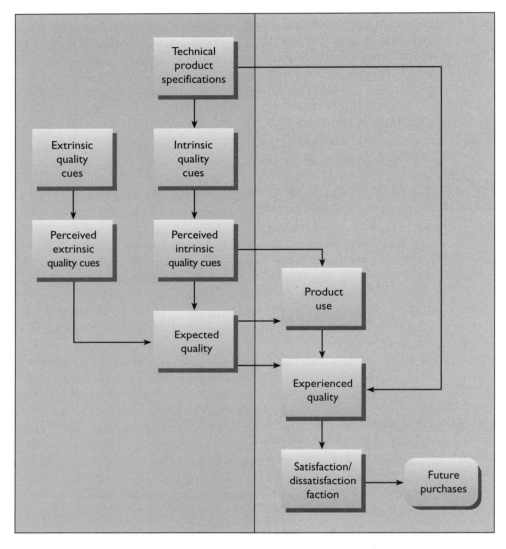

Before purchase   After purchase

Most people, and also most companies, do not like complaints, but actually they are an important source of information for marketers. Complaints inform the manufacturer about consumer dissatisfaction and why it occurs, so that the former can do something about the problem.[6] Consumers who are dissatisfied, but do not complain pose a much greater problem, because they will simply refrain from buying the product again, and the manufacturer will have to commission expensive market research to find

HIGHLIGHT 17.1

Waiting for Mickey Mouse

 hen Helle and Kurt and their two children checked in at the magnificent pink hotel which is the landmark of Disneyland Paris, they were pleasantly surprised to learn that every guest received a voucher for a free gift. The children got vouchers for a toy, and the two adults each got a voucher for a Mickey Mouse watch. The vouchers could be exchanged for the gift in the hotel's gift shop.

When they went to the gift shop a day later to exchange their vouchers, the pleasant surprise turned into disappointment, however. The children did get their toys, but the watches were out of stock. All the assistant in the gift shop could do was to take down their names and addresses and promise to send the watches to them as soon as they arrived.

For the first few weeks after returning home from the trip, Helle and Kurt occasionally thought about the watches, but when they finally arrived four months after their stay at the hotel, they had completely forgotten about them. They also found they had some mixed feelings – they were nice watches and they were happy to receive them, but in a way they also felt badly treated by the EuroDisney company.

out about the causes. Some manufacturers therefore try to encourage consumers to complain if they are not satisfied, by providing postage-paid return forms or consumer hotlines.

Product Behaviours: Brand Loyalty

From a marketing strategy viewpoint, **brand loyalty** is a very important concept. Particularly in today's low-growth and highly competitive marketplace, retaining brand-loyal customers is critical for survival; and it is often a more efficient strategy than attracting new customers. It is estimated that it costs the average company six times more to attract a new customer than to hold a current one.[7]

Much research has been conducted on brand loyalty, but a comprehensive review of the literature by Jacoby and Chestnut found few generalizations to offer.[8] In fact, few conclusions could be drawn despite the fact that over 300 articles had been published on the topic.

The study of brand loyalty has been plagued by whether it is better to conceptualize this variable as a cognitive or a behaviour phenomenon. As a cognitive phenomenon, brand loyalty is often thought of as an internal commitment to purchase and repurchase a particular brand. As a behaviour phenomenon, brand loyalty is simply repeat purchase behaviour.

Consistent with the theme of our book, we believe both cognitive and behaviour approaches to studying brand loyalty have value. From the behaviour perspective, we can analyse the pattern of consumers' actual brand choices, as shown in Exhibit 17.3:

* *Undivided brand loyalty* is an ideal. In some cases, consumers may purchase only a single brand and forego purchase if it is not available. Brand loyalty with an occasional switch is likely to be more common, though. Consumers may switch occasionally for

EXHIBIT 17.3

Examples of Purchase Pattern Categories and Brand Purchase Sequences

Purchase Pattern Category	Brand Purchase Sequence
Undivided brand loyalty	A A A A A A A A A A
Brand loyalty/occasional switch	A A A B A A C A A D
Brand loyalty/switch	A A A A A B B B B B
Divided brand loyalty	A A B A B B A A B B
Brand indifference	A B C D E F G H I J

a variety of reasons: their usual brand may be out of stock, a new brand may come on the market and be tried once, a competitive brand may be offered at a special low price, or a different brand may be purchased for a special occasion.

- *Brand-loyalty switches* are a competitive goal in low-growth or declining markets. As an example, competitors in the blue jeans market or the distilled spirits industry must obtain brand switches for long-term growth. However, switching loyalty from one to another of the brands of the same firm can be advantageous. For example, Douwe Egberts sells both conventional and luxury coffee. A switch to luxury coffee might be advantageous to Douwe Egberts in that it is more expensive and may have a higher profit margin.

- *Divided brand loyalty* refers to consistent purchase of two or more brands. For example, the shampoo market has a low level of brand loyalty. One reason for this might be that households purchase a variety of shampoos for different family members or for different purposes. Little L'Oréal shampoo for kids may be used by both youngsters as well as by those who use shampoo frequently. Other household members may have dandruff problems and use Pantene ProV's dandruff shampoo. Thus, this household would have loyalty divided between the two brands.

- *Brand indifference* refers to purchases with no apparent repurchase pattern. This is the opposite extreme from undivided brand loyalty. While we suspect total brand indifference is not common, some consumers of some products may exhibit this pattern. For example, a consumer may make weekly purchases of whatever bread is on sale, regardless of the brand.

In many ways, these loyalty categories are somewhat arbitrary. The point is that there are various degrees of brand loyalty. The degree of brand loyalty can be viewed as a continuum, and various quantitative indexes can be developed to categorize individuals or households in terms of particular products.[9]

The cognitive perspective can add to this behaviour perspective of brand loyalty by looking at the relationship between observed brand loyalty and brand involvement or **brand commitment**.[10] When consumers are involved with the purchase of a particular product category, we may expect that being brand loyal is based on a conviction that the brand is the best in the market, and the involvement with the purchase will lead to

EXHIBIT 17.4

Brand Commitment and Brand Loyalty

		Brand commitment	
		Low	High
Brand Loyalty	**Low**	Switchers	Variety seekers
	High	Habituals	Loyals

Source: Adapted from David Walker and Simon Knox, 'New Empirical Perspectives on Brand Loyalty: Implications for Market Segmentation and Equity Management', in *Marketing: Progress, Prospects, Perspectives*, eds. David Arnott *et al.* (Proceedings of the 26th Annual Conference of the European Marketing Academy, Warwick: University of Warwick, 1997), pp. 1313–1328.

a strong degree of brand commitment. Brand loyalty based on strong brand commitment will be stable and hard to break. It is the type of commitment which we can explain by cognitive learning leading to attitude formation. When consumers are not involved in the purchase of a product category, on the other hand, their manifest brand loyalty may have other reasons. One prominent reason is that being brand loyal is a way of simplifying purchases: when buying a product one is not enthusiastic about, but which is necessary, like toilet tissue, kitchen paper, or mineral water, one way of getting it done with least effort is to keep on buying the same product as long as it fulfils its purpose in a satisfactory way. This type of loyalty, which we have earlier explained by behavioural learning, will be less stable and easier to break. Some authors actually suggest that we should not call this phenomenon brand loyalty at all; Assael,[11] for example, suggests calling it inertia.

Is it also possible to have a high degree of brand commitment, but not be brand loyal? The answer is yes. Consumers may believe that one or several brands are excellent and have a positive attitude towards them, but at the same time they enjoy variety[12] and systematically experiment with new products and brands. We can thus look at all systematic combinations of brand commitment and brand loyalty, as depicted in Exhibit 17.4. Highlight 17.2 gives an example of how manufacturers can take care of some consumers' tendency towards variety seeking.

The Product Environment

The *product environment* refers to product-related stimuli that are attended to and comprehended by consumers. In general, the majority of these stimuli are received through the sense of sight, although there are many exceptions. For example, the way a stereo sounds or how a silk shirt feels also influences consumer affects, cognitions, and behaviours.

The way the product itself affects consumers can be analysed in terms of the product's attributes. Product attributes may be evaluated by consumers in terms of their own values, beliefs, and past experience. Marketing and other information also

HIGHLIGHT 17.2

Always the Right Perfume

ost women love perfume, some so much that they not only have different ones for daytime and nighttime, but also for summer and winter, workdays and weekends. This means that manufacturers have to have a range of perfumes in order to meet the wishes of these women. Christian Dior, the famous French couturier, has a number of different fragrances carrying his name. Dune and Miss Dior are for everyday and summer, as is Eau Savage, an elegant perfume with a hint of lemon. Dolce Vita and Poison are warm and are more useful for chilly winter nights. This means that women can have variety while still staying committed to Christian Dior.

influence whether purchase and use of the product is likely to be rewarding. For example, the product attributes of a new shirt might include colour, material, sleeve length, type and number of buttons, and type of collar. By investigating these attributes and by trying the shirt on, a consumer might conclude, 'This shirt is well made and I look good in it', 'This shirt is for nerds', or 'This shirt is well made but just isn't for me'.

It is unlikely that many consumers would purchase a shirt based on these product attributes alone, however. The price of the shirt would most likely be important; the shop selling the shirt (and the shop's image) might be considered. In addition, the packaging, brand name, and brand identification would very probably be factors. In fact, for many purchases, the image of the brand created through the nonproduct variables of price, promotion, and channels of distribution may be the most critical determinant of purchase.

Packaging is sometimes considered a product attribute and sometimes a marketing parameter of its own. There is no doubt that packaging has a major influence on consumer behaviour. Packaging can be analysed in terms of its function and in terms of its communication effects; recently, it has also been analysed in terms of its environmental effects.[13] Functions relevant to the consumer include storing the product and keeping it fresh. Functions can include added features, for example Duracell uses a package with a built-in tester to allow consumers to ensure the batteries they buy are fresh. MD Foods, the largest Danish dairy producer, has recently introduced a new packaging for cheese without rind. It is cheese on a tray with a reusable cover, which can be taken directly from the refrigerator and placed on the table – so that you won't get 'cheese fingers'.

Packaging's communication effects refers to the brand identification and label information on the package. Brand identification in many cases simplifies purchase for the consumer and makes the loyalty development process possible. As we noted previously, brand names, such as Lancôme, Jaguar, or Omega, may well be discriminative stimuli for consumers.

Label information includes instructions for use, contents, lists of ingredients or raw materials, warnings for use and care of the product, and the like. For some products, this information can strongly influence purchase. For example, consumers often carefully examine label information on over-the-counter drugs such as cold remedies, while

Consumers' Perceptions of Attributes of Cream Cheese Packaging

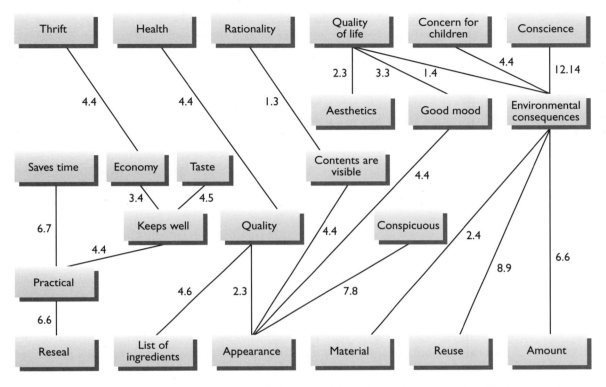

Source: Tino Bech-Larsen, 'Danish Consumers' Attitudes to the Functional and Environmental Characteristics of Food Packaging', *Journal of Consumer Policy*, 1996, pp. 339–363.

health-conscious consumers frequently consult package information to determine whether food products contain additives, or to determine fat content.

Recently, the environmental aspects of packaging have received considerable attention.[14] People have been critical about unnecessary waste and use of resources due to packaging. Germany has enacted legislation which encourages producers to recycle their packaging.[15] Many producers have adapted to this trend by redesigning their packaging so that fewer resources are used and/or by using packaging materials which are considered less harmful to the environment. Highlight 17.3 shows consumers' perception of packaging attributes for cream cheese, as uncovered by a laddering study.

Product Strategy

Product strategies are designed to influence consumers in both the short and the long run. In the short run, new-product strategies are designed to influence consumers to try the product; in the long run, product strategies are designed to develop brand loyalty and obtain large market shares. We will discuss two aspects in this section: new product development, and new product adoption.

New Product Development

Developing new consumer products is a difficult task. Most new products fail – they do not become profitable, do not attain the market shares envisaged, and disappear from the market again within a short period. What makes some new products a success and others a failure? A large body of empirical research during the last decades has focused on identifying the success factors of product innovation.[16] Despite considerable differences in the way these studies have been conducted and which types of products/ markets have been analysed, there is considerable agreement on the major groups of factors which help new products to become a success. These factors are market focus, organization of product development, and product development strategy.

Market focus means that understanding customers' needs and wants is crucial to the chances of success for a new product. Examples of factors which can be grouped under market focus which have been shown to contribute to new product success include:[17]

- The degree of product superiority from the consumer's point of view.
- The degree of contact with the consumer during new product development.
- The degree of up-front marketing activities, such as the representation of the marketing function in the early stages of the new product development process.
- The use of advanced market research techniques.

As these examples show, market focus implies not only generating information about consumers, but also integrating it into the product development process in such a way that the information becomes useful. Market focus is therefore related to the second group of success factors, organization of the product development process. Specific points which have been shown to have a positive impact on new product success include the following:[18]

- Cooperation between product development and marketing.
- Product development as a learning process, where new product ideas, concepts and prototypes are confronted with consumer reactions throughout the product development process.
- An emphasis on up-front activities (initial screening of ideas according to consumer demands, initial consumer market assessment).

Product development strategy refers to the importance of a purposeful and goal-oriented approach to product development. It is not specifically related to the understanding of consumer behaviour, but it also emphasizes the importance of balancing technological and consumer-related aspects as well as focusing on synergies with existing activities.

New Product Adoption

In analysing product strategy, it is important to recognize that consumers vary in their willingness to try new products. Different types of consumers may adopt a new product at different times in the product's life cycle. Exhibit 17.5 presents the classic adoption

EXHIBIT 17.5

The Adoption Curve

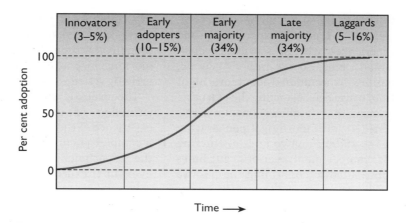

curve and five categories of adopters. The **adoption curve** represents the cumulative percentage of purchasers of a product across time.

Traditionally, the five adopter groups are characterized as follows: **innovators** are venturesome and willing to take risks; **early adopters** are respectable and often influence the early majority; the **early majority** avoids risks and are deliberate in their purchases; the **late majority** are sceptical and cautious about new ideas; **laggards** are very traditional and set in their ways.

Designers of product strategies find innovators particularly important because they may influence early adopters, who in turn may influence the early majority to purchase. Thus, a new product's chances of success are increased once innovators purchase the product and tell others about it. Also, early adopters and others can learn vicariously about the product by seeing innovators using it.

A major focus of consumer research has been to identify the characteristics of innovators and their differences from other consumers. A review of this research found that innovators tend to be more highly educated and younger and to have greater social mobility, more favourable attitudes towards risk (more venturesome), greater social participation, and higher opinion leadership than other consumers.[19] Innovators also tend to be heavy users of other products within a product class. For example, it has been found that adopters of home computers had greater experience with other technical products – such as programmable pocket calculators and video television games – than did nonadopters.[20] Innovators may have better developed knowledge structures for particular product categories. This may enable them to understand and evaluate new products more rapidly and thus adopt earlier than other consumers.[21]

Finally, it should be noted that the five adopter categories and the percentages in Exhibit 17.5 are somewhat arbitrary. These categories were developed in research in rural sociology that dealt with major farming innovations. Their validity has not been fully supported in consumer research, particularly for low-involvement products.[22]

However, the idea that different types of consumers purchase products in different stages of the products' life cycles does have important implications for product strategy. Namely, product strategy (and other elements of marketing strategy) must change across time to appeal to different types of consumers.

Back to . . .
The
Caledonian
Sleeper

Our opening story shows the complexity of creating expectations and experiences with a service product. Simon had some rather general, positive expectations about overnight train travel before starting the journey – namely that it allows one to arrive rested the next morning. Upon arriving at the station lounge and on entering his compartment, various attributes contributed to confirming the positive expectations – the friendly lounge, the unexpected perks in the cabin. However, upon arriving in Glasgow the next morning, his core expectation – namely, arriving rested – was not confirmed.

The example shows that both the formation of expectations and the experience of the quality of a product is a complex phenomenon. It also shows the importance of the core product living up to expectations.

Summary

This chapter investigated some product-related affect, cognitions, behaviours, and environmental factors as well as aspects of product strategy. Initially, product affect and cognitions were discussed in terms of consumer quality perception and satisfaction. Developing satisfied consumers is clearly a key to successful marketing. The analysis of behaviour looked at brand loyalty and emphasized various ways in which brand loyalty can be related to brand commitment. Product attributes and packaging were among the environmental factors examined. Finally, the product strategy discussion focused on how to integrate consumer research into the product development process and on the adoption of new products by consumers.

Key Terms and Concepts

adoption curve   359
brand commitment   354
brand loyalty   353
consumer complaint behaviour   351
consumer satisfaction   350
early adopters   359
early majority   359
expected quality
experienced quality
habituals
innovators   359
laggards   359
late majority   359
loyals
switchers
variety seekers

Review and Discussion Questions

1. Describe the process by which the consumer comes to experience satisfaction or dissatisfaction. Illustrate each result with an experience of your own.
2. Gather several consumer complaints from friends or classmates and make recommendations for marketing strategies to prevent similar problems.
3. Define brand loyalty as a cognitive phenomenon and as a behavioural phenomenon. Extend each of these definitions to the purchase pattern categories illustrated in Exhibit 17.3.
4. Choose a product example and recommend marketing strategies for habituals, switchers, loyals and variety seekers.
5. Identify the key stimuli in the product environment that influence your purchasing behaviour for (*a*) soft drinks, (*b*) pastry, (*c*) shampoo, and (*d*) jeans.
6. To which adopter category do you belong in general? Explain.
7. Discuss the problems and advantages that could be associated with appealing to innovators when marketing a new consumer packaged good.

Additional Reading

For a discussion of various views on quality, see:

David A. Garvin, 'What Does "Product Quality" Really Mean?,' *Sloan Management Review*, 1, 1984, pp. 25–43.

For a treatment of quality from a means–end perspective, see:

Valarie A. Zeithaml, 'Consumer Perceptions of Price, Quality, and Value: A Means–End Model and Synthesis of Evidence', *Journal of Marketing*, 3, 1988, pp. 2–22.

For approaches to analyse how extrinsic and intrinsic quality cues affect quality perception, see:

Carsten Stig Poulsen, Hans Jørn Juhl, Kai Kristensen, Anne C. Bech, and Erling Engelund, 'Quality Guidance and Quality Formation', *Food Quality and Preference*, 2, 1996, pp. 127–135.

Jan-Benedict E. M. Steenkamp and Hans C. M. van Trijp, 'Quality Guidance: A Consumer-Based Approach to Food Quality Improvement Using Partial Least Squares', *European Review of Agricultural Economics*, 23, 1996, pp. 195–215.

For discussion of satisfaction and complaint behaviour, see:

Dick A. Francken, 'Postpurchase Consumer Evaluations, Complaint Actions and Repurchase Behaviour', *Journal of Economic Psychology*, 4, no. 3, 1983, pp. 273–290.

Hans Kasper, 'On Problem Perception, Dissatisfaction, and Brand Loyalty', *Journal of Economic Psychology*, 3, 1988, pp. 387–397.

For a discussion of the role of packaging, see:

Ursula Hansen, 'Verpackung und Konsumentenverhalten', *Marketing-ZFP*, 8, no. 1, 1986, pp. 5–12.

For a general discussion of success factors in product development, see:

Angie Craig and Susan Hart, 'Where to Now In New Product Development?' *European Journal of Marketing*, 11, 1992, pp. 1–50.

For a discussion of some problems in increasing consumer orientation in product development, see:

Wim Biemans and Hanne Harmsen, 'Overcoming the Barriers to Market-Oriented Product Development', *Journal of Marketing Practice*, 2, 1995, pp. 7–25.

MARKETING STRATEGY IN ACTION
NIVEA

In the late 1960s and early '70s, Beiersdorf's range of NIVEA products was facing problems after surviving half a century and two world wars, with the creme as the only really successful product. New financially strong manufacturers were launching products in direct competition with NIVEA; the market was changing towards differentiated products such as personal-care series and speciality cremes, there was a shift in the retail business from traditional speciality stores to self-service outlets, and a study showed that the brand name was considered old-fashioned and had lost its attraction. The situation for NIVEA in the early 1970s was all but rosy.

There seemed to be an urgent need for a new strategy, and a study revealed the nature of NIVEA's position and possibilities in the market. Although the brand was considered old-fashioned and unattractive, NIVEA still enjoyed a high degree of goodwill and trust among customers, and the brand represented honesty and quality in the consumer's and the retailer's mind. Surprisingly, the study also revealed a potential for the introduction of new products under the existing brand, as long as the products were faithful to the NIVEA creme image of honest, value-for-money products of good quality.

There was to be no break with the core brand in the new strategy, but a step-by-step extension of the product range, sustaining the heart of the product – the NIVEA creme – but modernizing the brand, increasing its actuality and attraction. The strategy included extending distribution to supermarkets and increasing activity with the retailers. After less than two years NIVEA creme had regained its market share of more than 30 per cent and its position as the market leader.

Today the range of products has grown to include a number of different products; sun lotion, soap, foam, deodorant, shampoo, and facial-care products for men and women. With nine new product ranges and almost 50 products in skin and body care, NIVEA has long ago surpassed the DM billion threshold. The products are sold in 148 countries and NIVEA is now the best-selling body-care brand in the world.

Discussion Questions
1. Try to explain the development where consumers seemed to stay committed to the NIVEA brand while trying to buy and use other products at the same time.
2. How did NIVEA try to turn the development around?
3. Try to develop some criteria for launching a new product by Beiersdorf under its traditional NIVEA brand or under another brand.
4. What threats do you think NIVEA faces in the next 10 years?

Source: Hans-Jürgen Prick, 'NIVEA – Markentransfer, Von der Marke für Hauptcreme zur Dachmarke für Hauptpflege', *Markenartikel*, 51, no. 10, 12 September 1989, pp. 504–509.

CHAPTER 18

Consumer Behaviour and Communication Strategy

**Talking
Bus Stops**

In the United Kingdom, bus stop advertising is being used as never before. Scented bus stops or bus stops that bark or play music are a reality there, where 'street furniture' is one of the fastest growing media. Simple posters that are illuminated are not sufficient in the struggle to be noticed by the thousands of Britons who queue up for the bus every day. In London, Virgin Radio has fitted special bus stops with loudspeakers to entertain the waiting bus passengers. When Del Monte launched a new soft drink they used a bus stop which sent out a scent of lemon, and Disney has used 101 barking bus stops throughout Britain to promote the 101 Dalmatians video. All three use infrared sensors which activate sound or smell when they sense someone in the bus stop. Wonderbra has also used a trick photo of the Czech supermodel Eva Herzegovia who, for passers-by, looked as if she was waiting for the bus. Guinness has an ad where the beer glass is full at night and empty during the day.

Ads on the roof of the bus stops, for the benefit of those on the top floor of the double-deckers, have also been introduced, and the industry is now talking of introducing bus stops with television, where a number of commercials can be transmitted during the day. It will then be possible to sell the space to a newspaper in the morning, a chocolate brand in the afternoon, and a brewery at night. Bus stop advertising is so profitable that Adshel, the company that operates 30 000 panels mostly on bus stops, offers the bus stops and their maintenance to the local authorities for free in return for the right to sell the advertising space. The company has 200 cars on the street to avoid vandalism, although on one occasion theft was the main problem. Posters of the American Baywatch babe Pamela Anderson in black leather were too much of a temptation for passers-by and were stripped from the bus stops on a large scale.

Source: Heidi Amsinck, 'Bus stop with Pamela Anderson', *Børsen*, 16 September 1996, p. 1.

Marketers employ various means for communicating with consumers. We distinguish three types of market communication in this chapter: *Advertising*, *personal selling*, and *publicity* and *sponsoring*. Like all marketing strategies, consumers experience market communication as social and physical aspects of the environment that may influence consumers' affective and cognitive responses as well as their overt behaviours. From the view of marketing management, market communication is of utmost importance.

EXHIBIT 18.1

**The Wheel of Consumer Analysis:
Market Communication Strategy Issue**

Because they are so highly visible, market communication strategies, and especially advertising, are often the target of marketing critics. Some critics claim that market communication expenses add nothing to the value of products, but increase their cost to the consumer. Supporters, on the other hand, argue that market communication informs consumers about product attributes and consequences, prices, and places where products are available. This information may save consumers both time and money by reducing the costs of search, and it may increase competition and thus result in more efficient production and, eventually, lower prices.[1]

In this chapter we discuss how market communication strategies affect consumers' affective and cognitive responses and their overt behaviours. We begin by briefly describing the three types of market communication. Then we discuss the communication process. Next we examine selected aspects of the communication environment, consumers' affective and cognitive responses to market communication, and communication-related behaviours. These topics are shown in the Wheel of Consumer Analysis in Exhibit 18.1. We conclude by detailing how marketing managers can use their understanding of consumers to manage market communication strategies.

Types of Market Communication

The three types of **market communication** – advertising, personal selling, and publicity and sponsoring – together constitute a market communication mix that marketers try to manage strategically to achieve organizational objectives. Perhaps the most obvious type of market communication is advertising.

Communicating through the Internet

 ore and more companies are becoming aware of the Internet as an effective media for communication and as a route to gaining higher market shares. The number of companies with commercial interests on the Internet rose from 20 000 to 220 000 between 1995 and 1997.

Liva, a Swedish insurance company, had been selling part of its insurance through local post offices when, in 1996, its agreement with the Swedish post offices ended. Despite losing half its sales channels Liva increased its turnover from SEK6 to SEK7 million in 1996 by selling through the Internet. They designed a pension scheme especially directed towards the younger population with above average income – many of whom are frequent users of the Internet. Liva created a homepage that presents to the visitor the difference between their present income and their income as a pensioner, with different pension schemes. When the most suitable agreement has been decided upon, payment can – with a click on the mouse – take place through an Internet banking system.

Source: Peter Henrik Pedersen, 'Danske virksomheder er sakket bagud på Internettet',
Børsen, 13 May 1997, pp. 12–13.

Advertising

Advertising is any paid, nonpersonal presentation of information about a product, brand, company, or store.[2] It usually has an identified sponsor. Advertising is intended to influence consumers' affect and cognitions – their evaluations, feelings, knowledge, meanings, beliefs, attitudes, and images concerning products and brands. In fact, advertising has been characterized as *image management* – creating and maintaining images and meanings in consumers' minds.[3] Even though ads first impact affect and cognition, the ultimate goal is to influence consumers' purchase behaviour.

Advertisements may be conveyed via a variety of media – TV, radio, print (magazines, newspapers, brochures, leaflets), direct mail, billboards, signs, and miscellaneous media such as hot-air balloons or T-shirt decals. A new way of advertising that is of increasing importance is using interactive media such as the Internet, a type of media also receiving increasing attention at the point of sale (see Highlight 18.1).[4] For many fast-moving consumer goods, a lot of advertising is taking place at the point of purchase by means of signs, displays, leaflets, and the like.

With most forms of advertising, the seller is active in trying to bring the message to the consumer. Although the typical consumer is exposed to hundreds of ads daily, the vast majority of these messages receive low levels of attention and comprehension. Thus, it is a major challenge for marketers to develop ad messages and select media that expose consumers, capture their attention, and generate appropriate comprehension. In other cases, however, consumers are involved enough with the purchase to search for information on their own initiative. Thus, they may pick up a leaflet, write for a catalogue, or drive to a dealer to get a brochure. Finding out whether consumers are motivated to get information on their own initiative or whether the seller has to bring the information to the consumer is an important task in designing a communication strategy.[5]

Personal Selling

Personal selling involves direct personal interaction between a potential buyer and a salesperson. Personal selling can be a powerful market communication method for at least two reasons. First, the personal communication with the salesperson may increase consumers' involvement with the product and/or the decision process. Thus, consumers may be more motivated to attend to and comprehend the information the salesperson presents about the product. Second, the interactive communication situation allows salespeople to adapt their sales presentations to fit the informational needs of each potential buyer.

Certain consumer products are traditionally promoted through personal selling, such as life insurance, cars, and houses. In retailing, personal selling has decreased over the past 20 years as self-service has become more popular. However, there are considerable differences both between product classes and between segments. Upmarket clothing retailers emphasize personal advice and extended service – buying a suit at an Armani shop will involve being guided by a fashion adviser through your choice of clothing, after which you are handed over to a tailor who will discuss with you the adaptations that have to be made to the suit you bought to make it fit perfectly. Most perfume shops emphasize personal selling, and department stores mainly based on the self-service principle tend to have sales personnel in their perfume and cosmetics sections.

Personal selling by telephone is restricted or prohibited in many countries when it is seller-initiated, but is an important channel of the **buyer-initiated market communication**.[6] Many consumers pick up the phone and call shops or producers to enquire about products and services. Having personnel able and willing to take up these requests and answer them in a courteous way is an often overlooked aspect of market communication strategy.

Publicity and Sponsoring

Publicity is any unpaid form of communication about the marketer's company, products, or brands. For instance, an article in *PC World* comparing various brands of word processing software provides useful product information to consumers at no cost to the marketers of the software. Similarly, articles or tests about new cars in car magazines, descriptions of food products or appliances in gourmet magazines or TV cooking shows, or descriptions of fashion trends showing examples of branded pieces of clothing provide product information to consumers.

Publicity can be either positive or negative. When clothing manufacturer Benetton started their controversial advertising campaigns including elements like race discrimination, disease, and war, it received wide publicity in the media, ranging from high praise to very critical comments. Major product introductions like the opening of the tunnel linking Britain with the Continent resulted in considerable, mostly positive publicity, but this media attention can backfire when something goes wrong (i.e. a fire in the tunnel) which gets an equally wide coverage in the media. Sometimes, ill-founded rumours get such widespread publicity that serious damage results to the producing company. For example, some years ago Procter & Gamble had to fight a rumour in

Bäst i test!

DuoFlex Comfort och DuoFlex Basic*

DuoFlex Comfort

AKTASTOLAR VANN TEST!

I Vi Föräldrars test av bilbarnstolar juli 1998 kom två stolar ut i särklass. DuoFlex Comfort och DuoFlex Basic. Båda blev "Bäst i test" med högsta betyg 5 och Basic fick dessutom som enda stol omdömet "Mest Prisvärd".

Så nu kan du tryggt välja DuoFlex som också har flest godkännanden på marknaden. Du får en stol som är godkänd för placering på samtliga passagerarplatser i bilen.

Akta DuoFlex är godkänd från nyfödd upp till 25 kg. Den är försedd med fempunktsbälte och enhandssträckare. DuoFlex Comfort har dessutom lutningsindikator och lutningsbygel för högsta säkerhet.

Välkommen till närmaste barnfackbutik.

DuoFlex Basic
Även "Mest Prisvärd" i Vi Föräldrars test.

Nyhet!

CarryOne Plus

Akta
varandra

AKTA®
SVENSK AUKTORITET PÅ BARNSÄKERHET

För närmaste återförsäljare kontakta kundtjänst: 0418-44 90 49
www.akta.se

* Båda erhöll som enda stolar "Bäst i test" och högsta betyg 5 i Vi Föräldrars test av Bilbarnstolar juli 1998.

VOLVO

Just a small reminder that we are unveiling the new Volvo S80 in Gothenburg this Thursday. In other words, the world première for the world's safest Volvo. Stay tuned.

THE NEW VOLVO S80. WORLD PREMIÈRE - 28 MAY.

Positioning by safety.
Courtesy: Volvo Car Ltd.

Ads for feel products like perfume tend to use strong visual images that connote sensory and emotional meanings, whereas ads for think products like telephones tend to concentrate on technical product attributes having important functional consequences.
Courtesy: Golden Ltd and Siemens Nixdorf Ltd.

These two examples of vegetable sections in grocery stores convey quite different signal to the consumers. Courtesy: Tino Bech-Larsen.

Denmark that their shampoo/conditioner Wash & Go made people lose their hair. The rumour was so persistent that their market share dropped considerably and the company had to invest in an expensive series of counter argument ads.

Sometimes publicity can be more effective than advertising because consumers may not screen out the messages so readily. In addition, publicity communications may be considered more credible because they are not presented by the marketing organization. Publicity is difficult to manage, however, and marketers sometimes stage 'media events' in hopes of garnering free publicity.[7]

Sponsoring is a hybrid of advertising and publicity.[8] Some sponsoring is pure charity and does not have a market communication objective, but most forms of it involve explicitly or implicitly some kind of deal that a producer is financially or otherwise supporting an activity and, in turn, has its name or its products mentioned in the publicity about the activity. Common forms of sponsoring include the sponsoring of sports activities, for example sponsoring certain events like the European soccer championship or the Olympic Games, or sponsoring individual sports persons (Opel sponsoring Steffi Graf) or teams. Sponsoring of cultural events is also very common.

Sponsoring and publicity share the feature that the effects are difficult to predict, and there is considerable uncertainty about the kinds of effects that can occur. Sponsoring can result in some of the attention being caught by the event or the person being carried over to the product or brand. It can also result in consumers associating the product or brand with values or lifestyles related to the event or the person(s) sponsored, but little is known about the occurrence of such effects.[9]

The borderline between sponsoring and publicity is quite fluid. Product placement in films, described in Highlight 18.3, is a popular borderline case.

The Market Communication Mix

Ideally, marketing managers should develop a coherent overall market communication strategy that integrates the three types of market communication into an effective market communication mix. However, there is a considerable lack of knowledge on the cumulative effect of the various elements of the communication mix. Most research has addressed traditional mass media advertising, but many believe that the importance of this type of advertising will decline, among other things because of consumers' satiation with ads. More knowledge on how mass media advertising can enhance the effectiveness of communication at the point of sale would help communicators in developing much more efficient communication mixes.

The market communication mix of the future is likely to be more eclectic with many elements, including sponsoring, direct marketing, and public relations (see also Highlights 18.2 and 18.3).

A Communication Perspective

Market communication is information about market offerings, i.e. about products and services. How does market communication interact with the product itself in affecting consumers? This is the first question we address in this section.

Market communication is experienced by consumers as information in the environment. Thus, the cognitive processing model of decision making (see Exhibit 3.4) is relevant for understanding its effects on consumers. In the second part of this section,

HIGHLIGHT 18.2

Market Communication through Event Sponsorship

More companies have been seeking alternatives to advertising to promote their brands, including sponsoring various events such as rock concerts, boat races, and tennis tournaments. Nestlé found that the younger generation is increasingly attracted to soft drinks, and felt that more should be done to make its products more popular with children. The company therefore signed a contract with the Walt Disney Group for long-term cooperation in Europe. Nestlé is the exclusive partner for food in Disneyland's park in Paris, and Nestlé brands will be featured in the restaurants and shops of the park, which had 11.3 million visitors in 1995/96. Nestlé and Euro Disneyland have jointly developed marketing programmes extending throughout Europe, North America, and the Middle East. Nestlé is also the only company in Europe authorized to sell food products using the Walt Disney characters in the shape of their products or in their packaging or advertising.

Source: Adapted from Rein Rijkens, *European Advertising Strategies* (London: Cassell, 1992), pp. 159–172.

HIGHLIGHT 18.3

Product Placement

'**T**he name is Bond, James Bond' – the famous words spoken by 007 as we all know them. Product positioning in James Bond films is a fine way of introducing a new product with an exclusive image. In the most recent film, *Golden Eye*, Pierce Brosnan is seen driving BMW's new Z3 Roadster – *the perfect vehicle for a secret agent who experiences adventure, romance, and excitement in larger-than-life proportions.* In addition to the new BMW, Bond is also wearing the Omega Seamaster Professional Diver, which for the occasion is equipped by 'Q' with a high-performing laser. BMW reassures us that while the villain-eluding performance and passenger-pleasing luxury definitely will be carried over into the production models, customers shouldn't expect rocket launchers or ejection seats to be offered, at any price.

we look in more detail at the communication process. Based on this, we will then discuss goals of market communication.

Communication and Product

There has been some discussion in the marketing literature on the differential effect of market communication on consumer behaviour, as compared to the effect of the product itself. While everybody agrees that market communication fulfils the function of inducing consumers to buy a product, opinions differ on whether market communication can also contribute to the degree of satisfaction that consumers experience after having bought the product. The difference is important with regard to repeat purchases: when market communication only induces trial purchase, repeat purchases will be determined mainly by the product itself and not so much by market communication.

EXHIBIT 18.2

Market Offering and Market Communication

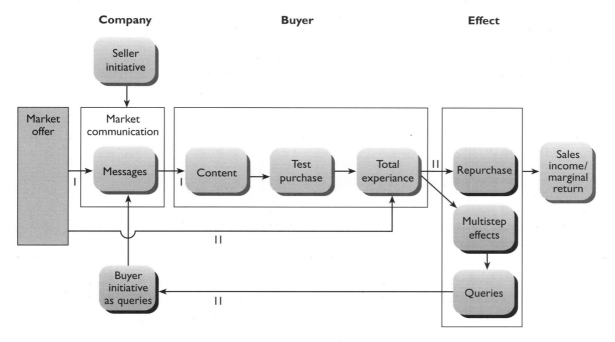

Source: Adapted from Otto Ottesen, *Markedskommunikasjon*
(Copenhagen: Handelshøjskolens Forlag, 1997), p. 44.

When market communication itself, independently of the physical product, contributes to consumer satisfaction, it will also affect repeat purchases.

It seems safe to say that market communication creates expectations about the product (see Chapter 17), and that even very good market communication cannot compensate for consumer experience where expectations are not met. An airline promising top class service in its market communication, but where passengers are met by bossy stewardesses, ugly plastic cups and delayed planes will not be able to create consumer satisfaction just by changing its advertising. On the other hand, many product expectations which market communication forms are difficult to experience. Promising safe air travel is a safe bet for most airlines, because air travel, statistically speaking, is very safe, and the chances that passengers may actually experience any disruption are tiny. But passengers may not realize this and may actually feel comforted by the promise of safe travel, creating additional consumer satisfaction.

Exhibit 18.2 shows a model of the relationship between market communication and market offering. It shows that market communication depends on the market offering, i.e. the message to be transmitted depends on the type of product or service being promoted. If the communication is successful and the consumer buys, much of his or her satisfaction will depend on the product or service, which, in turn, determines the

EXHIBIT 18.3

A General Model of the Communication Process for Promotions

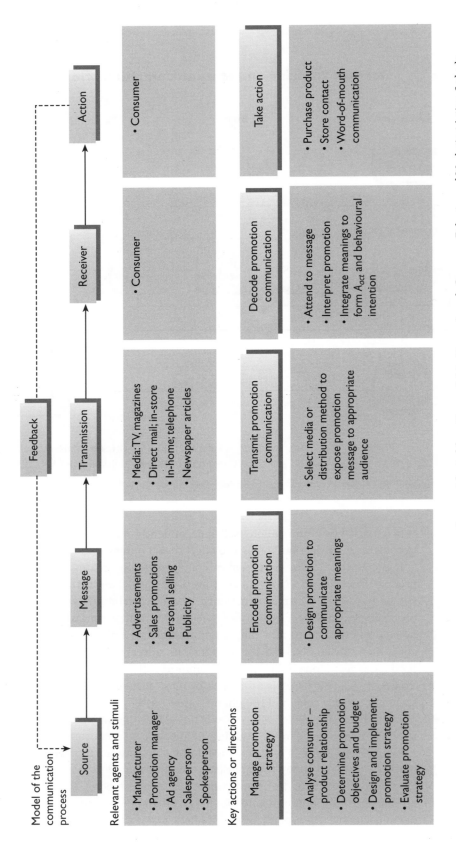

Model of the communication process

| Source | Message | Feedback | Transmission | Receiver | Action |

Relevant agents and stimuli

Source
- Manufacturer
- Promotion manager
- Ad agency
- Salesperson
- Spokesperson

Message
- Advertisements
- Sales promotions
- Personal selling
- Publicity

Transmission
- Media: TV, magazines
- Direct mail; in-store
- In-home; telephone
- Newspaper articles

Receiver
- Consumer

Action
- Consumer

Key actions or directions

Manage promotion strategy
- Analyse consumer – product relationship
- Determine promotion objectives and budget
- Design and implement promotion strategy
- Evaluate promotion strategy

Encode promotion communication
- Design promotion to communicate appropriate meanings

Transmit promotion communication
- Select media or distribution method to expose promotion message to appropriate audience

Decode promotion communication
- Attend to message
- Interpret promotion
- Integrate meanings to form A_{act} and behavioural intention

Take action
- Purchase product
- Store contact
- Word-of-mouth communication

Source: Adapted from Figure 8.1 in Henry Assael, *Consumer Behavior and Marketing Action*, 3rd edn. (Boston: PSW-KENT Publishing Company, 1987), p. 210. © by Wadsworth, Inc. Used by permission of PSW-KENT Publishing Company, a division of Wadsworth, Inc.

probability of repeat buying. But consumer experience can also lead to consumer-initiated market communication, like reordering the product, asking for information about additional products (extras for a car), or complaining.

The Communication Process

Exhibit 18.3 presents a simple model that identifies the key factors in the market **communication process**. The process begins when the *source* of the market communication determines which information is to be communicated and *encodes* the message in the form of appropriate symbols (using words, pictures, actions). Then the message is *transmitted* to a receiver over some medium such as television, direct mail, signs, a magazine, or personal conversation. The *receiver* or consumer, if exposed to the market communication, must *decode* it or interpret its meaning. Then, the consumer might take *action*, which could include going to a shop or making a purchase. Marketing managers are usually the sources of market communication, and managing the market communication mix is their responsibility. As the target of market communication, consumers may be influenced by it. But as noted above, market communication also works the other way round, when consumers are the source and sellers or producers the target.

Two stages of the communication model are particularly important to the success of market communication strategies. The first occurs when the marketer creates the market communication to encode a particular meaning. As you learned in Chapter 13, the marketer selects cultural meanings from the environment to create a message that will convey the intended meaning about the product to the consumer.[10] The other critical stage is decoding, when consumers attend to and comprehend the information in the market communication and construct their personal interpretation of its meaning. Consumers' interpretations, of course, may not be the same meaning as that intended by the marketer.

Goals of Market Communication

Traditionally, goals of market communication have been discussed in terms of a sequence of communication effects, also called the **effects hierarchy**. We discuss this hierarchy next. However, there are also communication settings where the classical hierarchy may not be the best way of thinking about communication goals. We briefly address these later.

The Classical Effects Hierarchy

Researchers have identified five types of effects that market communication may have on consumers.[11] They can be ordered in a hierarchical sequence of effects:

- Consumers *recognize need* for the product category or product form.
- Consumers become *aware* of the brand.
- Consumers develop a *favourable brand attitude*.
- Consumers develop an *intention to purchase* the brand.
- Consumers *perform various behaviours* to purchase the brand (such as travel to the store, find the brand in the store, talk to salespeople).

Stimulate category need. When consumers recognize the self-relevance of the product and have formed a general intention to purchase it, they are considered to be in the market for the product. To stimulate a category need, marketers need to create beliefs about the positive consequences of buying and using the product category or form.

Stimulating category need is most important for products with a high degree of novelty. When video recorders or home computers were first introduced, nobody had a category need for them, and marketers first had to communicate the self-relevant consequences of owning and using these products. When consumers in the target market already recognize a category need, marketers can concentrate market communication strategies on other goals. However, at any given time, relatively few consumers are likely to have a general intention to buy a product. For instance, perhaps 20 per cent of consumers might intend to buy laundry detergent at any time, compared to 1 per cent who intend to buy a new car. Moreover, it can be difficult to distinguish the consumers who have formed such an intention from those not in the market.

Marketers usually use advertising to stimulate category need among additional consumers, although publicity and personal selling also can influence category need to some extent. These strategies should be designed to convince consumers that the product category or form is associated with important end goals and values. Essentially, stimulating product need involves creating positive means–end chains at the product category or product form level.

Brand awareness. Brand awareness is a general communication goal for most market communication strategies. By creating brand awareness, the marketer hopes that whenever the category need arises, the brand will be activated from memory for inclusion in the consideration set of choice alternatives for the decision. Advertising, including advertising at the point of purchase, probably has the greatest influence on brand awareness,[12] although publicity and personal selling also can have an effect.

Sales personnel in the store can generate brand awareness by bringing certain brands to consumers' attention. Various sales market communication strategies, such as colourful price discount signs and end-of-aisle displays (a large stack of brand packages at the end of the supermarket aisle), draw consumers' attention to brands. Also shelf position and brand placement within the store can influence brand awareness. Finally, prominent brand-name signs (buses and billboards) also remind consumers of the brand name and maintain brand awareness.

The level of consumers' brand awareness necessary for purchase varies depending on how and where they make their purchase decisions for that product category or form, and it depends on their level of involvement with the product category. Many choice decisions about grocery and personal-care products, clothing items, appliances, and electronic products are made in the store. Consumers do not need to remember a brand name; they need only be able to quickly recognize familiar brands (often based on package cues), which then activate their relevant brand knowledge in memory. Thus, one strategic implication is to show the brand package in the advertising so consumers can more easily recognize the brand in the store.[13]

In other decision situations, a higher level of brand awareness is necessary to influence brand choice. If the purchase decision is made at home or in another environment where few brand-related cues are available, the brand must be recalled from memory for it to enter the consideration set. Restaurant choices tend to be like this. In such cases knowledge in memory may be more important than environmental factors. Unless consumers are able to recall the brand name (activate it from memory), the brand is not likely to be considered or purchased. Marketers can measure the level of consumers' brand awareness by asking them to state the brand names they can remember (with no hints – unaided recall) or by seeing which brands consumers recognize as familiar. Whether brand recall or recognition is suitable depends on where and when the purchase decision is made.[14]

Appropriate brand awareness strategies depend on how well known the brands are. Sometimes the marketing goal is to maintain already high levels of brand awareness. Much of the advertising for well-known brands such as Coca-Cola, Philips, and Aspirin serves as a reminder function that keeps the brand name at a high level of awareness.[15] This makes brand activation more likely in a decision-making situation. Managers of less familiar brands have a more difficult task in creating brand awareness and may rely more on in-store displays and good shelf positioning.

Brand attitude. Each market communication strategy can influence consumers' brand attitudes, but the specific communication objective depends on consumers' current attitudes towards the brand. More specifically, for a new or unfamiliar brand, the goal might be to *create* a brand attitude. For an already popular brand, marketers may be content to *maintain* existing favourable brand attitudes. For brands with neutral or slightly unfavourable attitudes, marketers may wish to *increase* the existing attitude. In each case the general market communication strategy will be to create more favourable beliefs about the consequences of salient brand attributes.[16]

Marketers make a big mistake if they analyse consumers' brand attitudes in an absolute or very general sense without specifying the situational context. Usually, the salient beliefs about important attributes, consequences, and end goals will vary across situations and contexts. Therefore, brand attitudes are likely to vary from one decision context to another. As you learned in Chapter 4, the meanings of beliefs about brand consequences depend on the ends to which they are related. For instance, a functional consequence for toothpaste, such as 'makes my mouth feel fresh', can lead to several different ends, including 'sensory enjoyment, eliminate bad breath, avoid offending others, feel more alive'. In general, the overall communication goal is to create means–end knowledge structures that link the brand to important consequences and values.

Brand purchase intention. Most market communication strategies are intended by marketers to increase (or maintain) the probability that consumers will buy the brand. Behavioural intentions (*BI*) may be activated from memory as stored decision plans (When I run low on beer, I will buy Carlsberg). Alternatively, *BI* can be constructed through integration processes at the time of the decision choice, usually in the store (I'll buy this Tyson T-shirt). As discussed in Chapter 6, an intention to buy a brand can be related to a consumer's attitude towards buying the brand (A_{act}), the influence of social norms (*SN*) about what other people expect, and the perceived difficulty in buying the brand (*PC*). A_{act} is based on means–end chains of beliefs about the consequences and values associated with the acts of buying or using the brand.

To develop effective market communication strategies directed at brand purchase intentions, it is helpful to know when *BI* are formed by most of the target consumers. Consumers do not necessarily form an intention to buy immediately on exposure to advertising information about the brand. Only consumers who recognize the category need and are actively in the market for the product (they have a general intention to buy the product) are likely to form a brand purchase intention at the time of exposure to an ad.[17]

More typically, formation of a *BI* is delayed until well after exposure to advertising, when the consumer is in a purchase context such as a shop. This situation is more likely for brands that are not high in intrinsic self-relevance (chocolate bars), which are more likely to be purchased on impulse (that is, environmental cues tend to trigger purchase). About 85 per cent of sweets purchases, 83 per cent of snack purchases, and 45 per cent of soft drinks are based on impulse where the *BI* to purchase is formed in the store.[18]

In contrast, personal selling and in-store communication usually is designed to influence purchase intentions at the time of exposure to the communication.[19] The goal is for consumers to immediately form a connection between the brand and important consequences and values. For example, communication about a lower price might be seen as leading to 'saving money' and 'having more money to spend for other things', which in turn is linked to the values of 'being a careful consumer' and 'self-esteem'. Thus, consumers might form a positive A_{act} and *BI* on the spot.

Facilitate other behaviours. Finally, some market communication strategies are designed to facilitate behaviours other than purchase. As you learned in Chapter 11, often consumers must perform several other behaviours to make a brand purchase. For instance, buying certain brands of clothing requires consumers to enter the shops that carry such brands. In-store communication and publicity are not likely to have much influence on these other behaviours. Some advertising and personal selling strategies are intended to increase the probability of these other behaviours. For instance, an ad might be directed at encouraging consumers to come to the dealership to test-drive a new car. Salespeople might encourage consumers to operate the controls of an appliance or audio equipment, which increases the probability of making a purchase. Other advertising strategies might encourage consumers to engage in positive word-of-mouth communication by telling other people about a brand.

Communication Goals For Low-Involvement Products

While we basically believe that all purchases can be regarded as being preceded by the formation of an attitude and a purchase intention, it is quite clear that there are many purchases where attitudes are very limited or rudimentary, and/or the intention to buy is formed only seconds before the purchase takes place. Purchases of many low-involvement products take place in this way. In these cases, the importance of the various communication subgoals discussed in the preceding section may be quite different. Notably, it may be quite difficult to shape positive attitudes towards the brand or the purchase by market communication, and the major communication goals may instead be to create brand awareness and to induce trial purchases. Attitudes may then be formed during consumption of the product and may influence future purchases.[20]

Being Ready to Communicate

The communication goals in the preceding two sections assumed that the marketer or seller is the one taking the initiative to the communication process. As we mentioned earlier, this is not always the case. Consumers initiate market communication as well, and address on their own initiative sellers for obtaining information, ordering products, complaining, or expressing satisfaction. While often neglected, these forms of communication should also be part of the formulation of communication goals. One could even argue that these forms of communication are especially important, since they deal with consumers who already have an interest in the product, whereas many other forms of seller-initiated communication are directed at consumers basically uninterested in both the message and the product.

Goals with regard to buyer-initiated market communication refer to both the means of communication and the content of the communication. A basic prerequisite for buyer-initiated communication is that the seller provides a means of communication. If a consumer gets interested, how will he know where to go, phone, or write? If he phones, how many times will he be put through before somebody can answer his query? Does the seller have human resources for answering such queries? Once the means has been established, can the seller anticipate the nature of the consumer request and handle it appropriately?

The Market Communication Environment: Clutter and Increasing Competitive Pressure

The *market communication environment* includes all the stimuli associated with the physical and social environment in which consumers experience market communication strategies. Many of these factors can affect the success of a market communication. In this section we discuss two environmental factors that can influence advertising and other market communication strategies – *market communication clutter* and level of competition.

A key market communication objective is to increase the probability that consumers come into contact with, attend to, and comprehend the market communication message. In recent years, however, the amount of market communication has so increased that the effectiveness of any given market communication strategy may be impaired by market communication clutter.[21]

This is especially true for TV advertising. Two trends are responsible for this.[22] First, the amount of TV advertising has increased dramatically in Europe in the past 15 years. At that time most countries only had state-controlled TV with very limited advertising or none at all. Now, there is a multitude of TV channels available to most consumers, most of them containing a considerable amount of advertising. At the same time, consumers have become more adept at avoiding commercials. They can use the remote control to switch to other channels as soon as the commercials start, or they may video-record what they want to see and delete the commercials. All this in addition to the 'classic' ways of avoiding commercials – leaving the room or being 'mentally absent.'

The development in the United States, which has had a massive amount of TV advertising for a long time, shows that European advertisers have reason to worry as well. A US study showed that the average proportion of consumers able to recall an ad seen 24 hours earlier fell from 24 per cent in 1979 to 21 per cent in 1984. A 1994 survey of 20 000 consumers found that a surprising 40 per cent could not identify a single 'outstanding' commercial. These consumers could not remember enough details of an ad to establish that they actually recalled it.[23]

The *level of competition* for a product category is a key aspect of the market communication environment. As competition heats up, marketers' use of market communication usually increases. We see this, for example, in the airline and tele-communications industries, which are currently being deregulated in Europe, creating a more competitive environment. Moreover, the types of market communication strategies change as competitive pressures increase. Sometimes miniature 'wars' are fought through the advertising media. When the tunnel under the Great Belt was opened in Denmark in 1997, bringing train travel time between Aarhus and Copenhagen down from more than four hours to under three hours, the Danish State Railways launched a massive campaign claiming that total travelling time between the two cities by train now was shorter than by flying. Scandinavian Airlines System retaliated with large ads emphasizing that travel time by plane (from airport to airport, that is) between Aarhus and Copenhagen is only 35 minutes. Slogans with this message even appeared on the airport bus in Aarhus, which takes 45 minutes from the airport to the city.

Affect and Cognition in Market Communication

All of the affective and cognitive responses we discussed in Section 2 are relevant in understanding market communication. Interpretation of market communication (attention and comprehension) and integration processes (forming attitudes and intentions) are extremely important. But some researchers claim ad information can influence consumers without any affective or cognitive responses (see Highlight 18.4).

As we discussed in Chapter 5, consumers' comprehension processes vary in depth and elaboration, depending on their levels of knowledge and involvement.[24] Thus, exposure to market communication – whether an ad, an in-store display, or a sales presentation – may produce meanings that vary in number (elaboration), level (deep versus shallow), and interconnectedness. Consumers may also form inferences about product attributes or consequences or the marketer's motivation.[25] In this section we examine two concepts relevant to understanding the effects of advertising: consumers' attitudes towards advertising and persuasion processes.

Attitude Towards the Ad

Advertisers have long been interested in measuring consumers' evaluations of advertisements.[26] Researchers have established that consumers' **attitude towards the ad** (A_{ad}) – their affective evaluations of the ad itself – can influence their attitudes towards the advertised product or brand.[27] That is, ads that consumers like seem to create more positive brand attitudes and purchase intentions than ads they don't like. The mechanism that accounts for the liking effect on brand attitude is not known. It may be that liking ads influences attention (people pay more attention to ads they like)[28] and comprehension (consumers devote more effort to elaborating the information in likeable ads).

Currently a number of other issues remain to be resolved, including what aspects of the ads (perhaps the visual material in print ads) have the greatest influence on ad attitudes and whether consumers' evaluative reactions to the ads make purchase more likely.[29] Apparently a positive attitude towards an ad may not always lead to increased purchase of the brand.

HIGHLIGHT 18.4

Subliminal Advertising

 lthough most advertisers pay little or no attention to the topic, the discussion of subliminal persuasion in advertising just won't go away. Writers like Wilson Key keep turning out widely read books that claim subliminal advertising is all around us. Key claims marketers intentionally embed subliminal stimuli — usually sexual objects, symbols, or words — in advertisements. Moreover, he claims these hidden, subliminal stimuli affect us in powerful ways of which we are unaware.

What do we know about the effects of subliminal stimulation? First, it is clear that stimulation below the level of a person's conscious awareness can be shown to have measurable effects upon some aspects of that person's behaviour. That is, people can respond to stimuli without being consciously aware of the stimuli. But these stimuli are not necessarily subliminal — that is, they are not necessarily presented at intensities below our perceptual threshold. They just tend not to be consciously noticed as consumers go about their business. As we have seen throughout this text, a great deal of cognitive activity occurs automatically. Thus, consumers are often not able to report the existence of a stimulus or an awareness that some cognitive process has occurred.

With regard to Key's claims about sexual embedding, two issues are in question. First, is subliminal embedding being made in advertisements as a matter of course, as Key claims? Virtually no evidence exists that this is so. Certainly, overtly sexual stimuli are found in a great many advertisements, but these are not subliminally embedded. Second, can subliminal stimuli affect goal-directed behaviours like purchase choices?

Most stimuli have little or no influence on our cognitions or behaviours when presented at a recognizable level. Why, then, should they suddenly have a strong impact when presented subliminally? Key claims that humans have two processing systems, one of which operates on a completely unconscious level and immediately picks up on the alleged subliminally embedded information. However, no psychological theories or data support such a system of cognition.

A central finding in cognitive psychology that we have emphasized throughout this text is that the meaning of a stimulus is not inherent in the stimulus itself. Rather, meanings are constructed by consumers in active and sometimes complex ways as they come into contact with the stimulus.

None of this is to say that ads may not have effects on consumers' meanings at a subconscious level — but the stimuli don't have to be subliminal for that to occur.

Source: Jack Haberstroh, 'Can't Ignore Subliminal Ad Charges', *Advertising Age*,
17 September 1984, pp. 3, 42; and Timothy E. Moore, 'Subliminal Advertising:
What You See Is What You Get', *Journal of Marketing*, Spring 1982, pp. 38–47.

The Persuasion Process

Persuasion refers to changes in beliefs, attitudes, and behavioural intentions caused by market communication. For the most part, marketing researchers have studied the persuasive effects of advertising communication, but in-store communication, personal selling, and publicity can also persuade consumers.

The **Elaboration Likelihood Model (ELM)** is a popular approach to analysing the communication process. It identifies two cognitive processes by which market communication such as advertising can persuade consumers – the central and peripheral routes to persuasion.[30] Exhibit 18.4 shows how these two processes work. Which persuasion process occurs is determined by consumers' level of involvement with the product message.[31] The central route to persuasion is more likely when consumers' involvement is higher; the peripheral route to persuasion is more likely when involvement is lower. The ELM also distinguishes between two types of information in the market communication. Specific claims about product attributes or demonstrations of functional and psychosocial consequences, along with supporting evidence, are central information; information about anything other than the product is peripheral.

In the *central route to persuasion*, consumers who experience higher levels of involvement are motivated to pay attention to the central, product-related information and comprehend it at deeper and more elaborate levels.[32] Consumers' comprehension of the product-related information is indicated by the types of cognitive responses they have to the market communication message.[33] *Support arguments* are positive thoughts about product attributes and the self-relevant consequences of product use (Listerine does seem like an effective mouth wash). Support arguments enhance persuasion by leading to favourable product beliefs, positive brand attitudes, and stronger intentions to buy the product. During comprehension, consumers might produce unfavourable thoughts about the product called *counterarguments* (I don't think that taking this vitamin every day will make a difference to my health). Counterarguing reduces persuasion by leading to unfavourable product beliefs, negative brand attitudes, and weaker intentions or no intention to buy the product.

The *peripheral route to persuasion* is quite different. Consumers who have low involvement with the product message (they are not in the market for the product or they buy the product but have little interest) have little motivation to attend to and comprehend the central product information in the ad. Therefore, direct persuasion is low because these consumers form few brand beliefs and are unlikely to form brand attitudes or purchase intentions. However, these consumers might pay attention to the peripheral (nonproduct) aspects of the market communication such as the pictures in a print ad or the scenery or actors in a TV commercial, perhaps for their entertainment value. For instance, ads featuring entertainers or sports celebrities might attract such attention. Consumers' affective and cognitive responses to these peripheral features might be integrated to form an attitude towards the ad (This is a great ad). Later, if consumers need to evaluate a brand during decision making, these ad-related meanings could be activated and used to form a brand attitude or a purchase intention.[34] In this way the peripheral route to persuasion can also persuade consumers to buy, but in an indirect way. Many empirical results on low involvement effects of advertising can be interpreted within this framework.[35]

At any given time relatively few consumers are in the market for a particular product, so much of the advertising consumers are exposed to every day is not particularly relevant to their end goals and values. These typically low levels of involvement suggest that most mass media advertising receives peripheral processing. Certainly, the low levels of day-after recall for most ads (about 20 per cent on average) suggest this is the case. In some cases, however, marketers might want consumers to engage in peripheral route processing. If a brand is similar to competing brands (soft drinks, beer, and cigarettes are examples), marketers may not be able to make credible claims about

EXHIBIT 18.4

Two Routes to Persuasion in the ELM

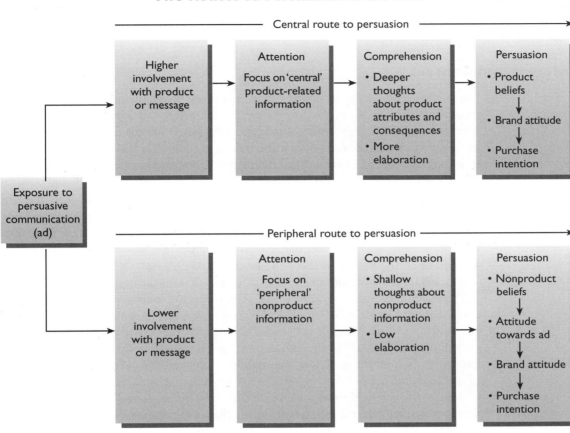

unique product attributes or consequences. Market communication strategies will therefore tend to focus on image advertising for which peripheral processing is appropriate.

In situations where a brand does have a distinctive advantage, marketers may want to encourage consumers to engage in central route processing by increasing their involvement with the ad message and the product or brand.[36] For instance, sending market communication messages directly to consumers who are in the market for the product category or product form ensures some level of motivation in the brand information.

Market Communication Behaviours

Ultimately, market communication strategies must affect not only consumers' cognitions, but also their behaviours. A firm's sales, profits, and market-share objectives can be accomplished only if consumers perform a variety of behaviours, including purchase of its product. Different types of market communication can be used to influence the various behaviours in the purchase–consumption sequence. Because we have already discussed purchase behaviour in this chapter and throughout the book, we focus here on two other behaviours that are critical to the success of market communication strategies: information contact and word-of-mouth communication with other consumers.

Information Contact

Consumers must come in contact with a market communication medium for the communication to be successful. As mentioned before, *information contact* may be *intentional* (as when consumers search the newspapers for ads on evening entertainment) or *incidental* (the consumer just happens to come into contact with an ad when engaging in some other behaviour). Sometimes information contact can even trigger the purchase decision process, as might occur when the consumer accidentally comes across a sale or other incentive market communication. As a practical matter, the marketer must place the market communication message in the target consumers' physical environment to maximize chances for exposure and must design the market communication so it will be noticed (attended to). For advertising, this requires knowledge of the media habits of the target market – what TV programmes do they watch, what radio programmes do they listen to, what magazines do they read?

Placing information in consumers' environments may be easy when target consumers can be identified accurately. For example, catalogue marketers can buy lists of consumers who have made mail-order purchases in the past year. Then they can send communication materials directly to these target consumers. Of course, sending a catalogue through the mail does not guarantee consumers will open the envelope and read its contents.

Contact for personal selling is often achieved by referrals and leads (or consumers who initiate contact with salespeople during the search process). Marketers sometimes encourage referrals by offering gifts in return for the names of potential customers.

Exposure to market communication messages is not enough, however. Consumers must also attend to the messages. How well the market communication interacts with such consumer characteristics as intrinsic self-relevance and existing knowledge affects the level of attention.

Word-of-Mouth Communication

Marketers may want to encourage consumers' **word-of-mouth communication** about a product or service. This helps spread awareness beyond those consumers who come into direct contact with the market communication.[37] Consumers may share information with friends about new products, good deals, and interesting advertising messages. For example, a consumer may phone a friend who is looking for an evening dress to say that a certain shop is having a great sale. Consumers sometimes recommend that their friends see a particular salesperson who is especially pleasant or well informed or who offers good deals on merchandise. Consumers often pass on impressions of a new restaurant, retail store, or film to their friends.

As these examples illustrate, by simply placing market communication in a consumer's environment, marketers can increase the probability that the information will be communicated to other consumers. And because personal communication from friends and relevant others is a powerful form of communication, marketers may try to design market communications that encourage word-of-mouth communication (get a friend to join the health club and you will get two months' membership free).

Managing Market Communication Strategies

Developing and implementing effective market communication strategies is a complex, difficult task. There are four key activities in managing market communication strategies: (1) analyse consumer–product relationships, (2) determine the market communication objectives and budget, (3) design and implement a market communication strategy, and (4) evaluate the effects of the market communication strategy.

Analyse Consumer–Product Relationships

Developing effective market communication strategies begins with an analysis of the relationships between consumers and the products or brands of interest. This requires identifying the appropriate target markets for the product. Then marketers must identify consumers' needs, goals, and values, their levels of product and brand knowledge and involvement, and their current attitudes and behaviour patterns. In short, marketers must strive to understand the relationship between their target consumers and the product or brand of interest.

Developing a market communication strategy for a new product is therefore intimately linked to the product development process. Research conducted during the product development process to make sure the product conforms to consumers' needs will also be valuable in designing market communication, and can be supplemented by additional research if necessary. This research could include interviews to identify the dominant means–end chains that reveal how consumers perceive the relationships between the product or brand and their own self-concepts. Other methods might include focus group interviews, concept tests, attitude and use surveys, and test marketing.

For existing products and brands, marketers may already know a great deal about consumer–product relationships. Perhaps only follow-up research would be necessary.

Exhibit 18.5 presents a simple grid model used by Foote, Cone & Belding, a major advertising agency, to analyse consumer–product relationships.[38] The figure also shows the typical locations of several different products, based on extensive consumer research conducted around the world. The **Foote, Cone & Belding (FCB) grid** is based on two concepts you studied in earlier chapters: consumers' involvement and their salient knowledge, meanings, and beliefs about the product.

Consumers have varying degrees of involvement with a product or brand due to intrinsic and situational sources of self-relevance. Moreover, various types of knowledge, meanings, and beliefs may be activated when consumers evaluate and choose among alternative products or brands. Some products are considered primarily in terms of rational meanings, such as the functional consequences of using the product.[39] These are termed *think products* in the grid model. Included in this category are such products as investments, cameras, and car batteries – all products purchased primarily for their functional consequences.

EXHIBIT 18.5

The Foote, Cone & Belding Grid for Analysing Consumer–Product Relationships

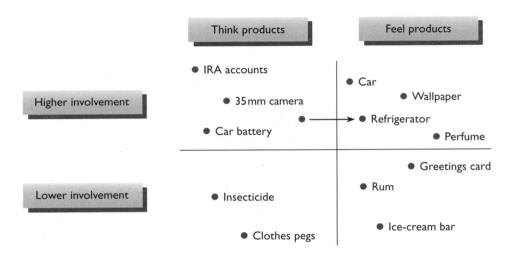

Source: David Berger, 'Theory into Practice: The FCB Grid', *European Research*, January 1986, p. 35.

In contrast, *feel products* are considered by consumers primarily in terms of nonverbal images (visual or other types of sensory images) and emotional factors, such as psychosocial consequences and values.[40] For instance, products purchased primarily for their sensory qualities – ice cream, soft drinks, perfume – as well as products for which emotional consequences are dominant – flowers or jewellery – are feel products in the FCB grid.[41]

Because the consumer–product relationships are quite different in the four quadrants of the grid, the FCB grid also has implications for developing creative advertising strategies, measuring advertising effects, and selecting media in which to place ads.

The appropriate market communication strategy depends on the product's position in the grid. Sometimes a product can be moved within the grid, like the refrigerator in Exhibit 18.5, which was shifted from a think to a feel product by the following strategy. A South American client of FCB once had a problem: 5000 ugly green refrigerators in inventory were not selling, while competing brands offered desirable product features such as ice makers. High-involvement products such as refrigerators tend to be sold in terms of functional consequences, but in this case there was no rational benefit to promote. So FCB designed a market communication strategy to move refrigerators from the think quadrant to the feel quadrant. The agency created ads that featured Venezuelan international beauty queens and termed the refrigerators 'another Venezuelan beauty'. The 5000 refrigerators sold out in 90 days. While this example may not generalize, FCB claims that traditional *think* products can often be marketed successfully using *feel* advertising market communication strategies. In sum, the FCB grid model helps marketers analyse consumer–product relationships to develop more effective market communications.

Determine Market Communication Objectives and Budget

As described in some detail above, market communication can affect consumers' affect, cognitions, and behaviours.[42] Thus, market communication strategies may be designed to meet one or more of the following objectives:

- *To influence behaviours.* Change or maintain consumers' specific behaviours concerning the product or brand – usually purchase behaviours.
- *To inform.* Create new knowledge, meanings, or beliefs about the product or brand in consumers' memories.
- *To persuade.* Change consumers' beliefs, attitudes, and intentions towards the product or brand.
- *To transform affective responses.* Modify the images, feelings, and emotions that are activated when consumers consider the product or brand.
- *To remind.* Increase the activation potential of the brand name or some other product meaning in consumers' memories.

Before designing a market communication strategy, marketers should determine their specific market communication objectives and the budget available to support them. Often market communication has multiple objectives. For example, market communication may be designed to first influence consumers' cognitions in anticipation of a later influence on their overt behaviours. When a new product or brand is introduced, a primary objective for advertising may be to create awareness of the product and some simple beliefs about it. Marketers also try to generate publicity for new products for these reasons, as well as to create a favourable brand attitude. These cognitions are intended to influence purchase intentions and sales behaviours later.

Design and Implement Market Communication Strategy

Designing alternative market communication strategies and selecting one to meet the market communication objectives are based largely on the consumer–product relationships that have been identified through marketing research. Implementing the market communication strategy may include creating ads and placing them in various media, designing and distributing in-store communication material, putting salespeople to work, and developing publicity events. Many of these tasks may be done with the aid of an advertising agency or a market communication consultant.

Developing Advertising Strategy

Marketers should specify advertising strategy in terms of how the product will be related to the consumer. Then ads should be created to communicate the appropriate means–end connections between the product attributes and consumers' goals and values.[43] The MECCAS model shown in Exhibit 18.6 can help marketers understand the key aspects of ad strategy and make better strategic decisions.[44] The **MECCAS model**

EXHIBIT 18.6

The MECCAS Model

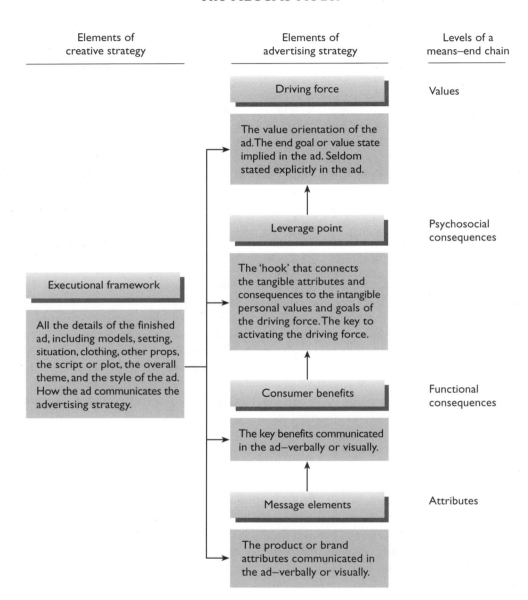

Source: Adapted from Jerry C. Olson and Thomas J. Reynolds, 'Understanding Consumers' Cognitive Structures: Implications for Advertising Strategies', in *Advertising and Consumer Psychology*, eds. Larry Percy and Arch Woodside (Lexington, MA: Lexington Books, 1983), pp. 77–90. Copyright © 1983 The New Lexington, an imprint of Jossey-Bass Inc., Publishers.

defines four elements of *advertising strategy* – the driving force, the leverage point, consumer benefits, and message elements – based on analyses of consumers' means–end chains (MECCAS stands for means–end chain conceptualization of advertising strategy). The fifth component of the MECCAS model, the executional framework, is part of the *creative strategy* that must develop the details of the actual advertisement to communicate the ad strategy.

The first step in creating an advertising strategy is to *understand the consumer–product relationship* by measuring consumers' means–end chains for the product category or product form. Then the marketer should select one means–end chain to convert into an advertising strategy. The most important means–end chain in the decision-making process is a likely candidate. Knowing which product attributes are most important for consumers helps marketers decide which information to include as *message elements* in the ad strategy. (Should the ads for Estrella crisps emphasize their flavour, their crunchiness, or their ridges?) Knowing what functional consequences are linked to these salient attributes helps marketers identify the key *consumer benefits* to be emphasized. (If Estrella crisps are for dipping, focus on the ridges. If Estrella are an accompaniment for sandwiches, emphasize flavour and crunchiness.)

The *driving force* is the basic value or end goal to be communicated by the ad. The driving force usually is communicated indirectly and in a subtle fashion; values are seldom mentioned explicitly in ads. That would be perceived as heavy-handed by most consumers, who might react negatively to being told what value they should be thinking of. Values and end goals are part of the consumer, not the product, and must be aroused or activated 'in' the consumer. Merely stating a value in an ad does not ensure that it will be activated and felt by consumers. Once activated, the emotional and motivational power of the end goals or values provides the driving force for action, including purchase of the brand.

The final component of an ad strategy is the important *leverage point* by which the relatively concrete, tangible message elements and benefits (attributes and functional consequences of the product) are linked to the abstract driving force (values of the consumer). The leverage point can be thought of as a 'hook' that 'reaches into' the consumer and attaches the product to the activated value that is the driving force of the ad strategy. In advertising, the leverage point is often portrayed as a psychosocial consequence of using the brand. Because consumers automatically perceive the values associated with most psychosocial consequences, the leverage point should activate the driving force and form a connection to it. Thus, the ad does not have to mention the value explicitly in order to communicate the ad strategy.

In sum, an advertising strategy should specify how a brand will be connected to the important ends the consumer wants. The advertising team must then create an ad that will persuasively communicate these meanings and the linkages between them. The *executional framework* refers to the various details of the creative strategy (the type of models, how they are dressed, the setting, what people are saying) that are designed to communicate the ad strategy. In general, an effective advertisement should communicate each of the four means–end levels of meaning in the ad strategy (from message elements to driving force) and the links or connections between the levels.

The MECCAS model is not a foolproof tool to create successful ads; it is a guide to developing advertising strategies and creating effective ads.[45] Marketers must still carefully analyse consumers and use creative imagination. Marketers can use the MECCAS model to translate several means–end chains into possible ad strategies, which can then be evaluated for their competitive advantages. Although any means–end chain can be translated into an advertising strategy using the MECCAS model, not every means–end chain is a viable strategy. Some strategies, for instance, may already be taken by one's competitors. Marketers also can use the MECCAS model as a framework for analysing the meanings communicated in their current advertising and for considering how these ads could be made more persuasive.[46]

Special problems arise when an advertising strategy has to be devised simultaneously for more than one market or culture. As we have explained in Chapters 12 and 13, cultural differences are an important factor in consumer behaviour, and adapting advertising strategies to the various markets and cultures therefore seems like a natural thing to do. However, marketers have been looking for ways to standardize advertising at least partly across countries and cultures. To what extent this is possible is subject to some debate,[47] but it seems to depend on the type of product, the advertising medium, and the similarity of the markets.

Developing Personal Selling Strategies

The process of developing a personal selling market communication strategy is illustrated in Exhibit 18.7.[48] This is the **ISTEA model**, which stands for impression, strategy, transmission, evaluation, and adjustment. This model suggests salespeople's influence depends on their skills at performing five basic activities: (1) developing useful *impressions* of the customer, (2) formulating selling *strategies* based on these impressions, (3) *transmitting* appropriate messages, (4) *evaluating* customer reactions to the messages, and (5) making appropriate *adjustments* in presentation should the initial approach fail.

According to this model, the personal selling process works as follows:

> In the first activity, the salesperson combines information gained through past experience with information relevant to the specific interaction to develop an impression of the customer. Salespeople can derive information about their target customers by examining past experience with this and other customers, by observing the target customer during an interaction, and by projecting themselves into the target customer's decision-making situation.
>
> In the second activity, the salesperson analyses his or her impression of the customer and develops a communication strategy that includes an objective for the strategy; a method for implementing the strategy, and specific message formats.
>
> Having formulated the strategy, the salesperson transmits the messages to the customer. As the salesperson delivers the messages, she or he evaluates their effects by observing the customer's reactions and soliciting opinions. On the basis of these evaluations, the salesperson can make adjustments by either reformulating the impression of the customer, selecting a new strategic objective, or changing the method for achieving the strategic objective, or the salesperson can continue to implement the same strategy.[49]

Although the ISTEA model was developed for industrial (business-to-business) marketing situations, it is consistent with the communication approach to consumer market communication discussed here. The model emphasizes analysis of the customer as the starting point for strategy development. Research confirms that impression formation (consumer analysis) and strategy formulation by salespeople improves their sales performance. Similarly, research on sales transactions in retail sporting goods

EXHIBIT 18.7

A Model of the Personal Selling Process

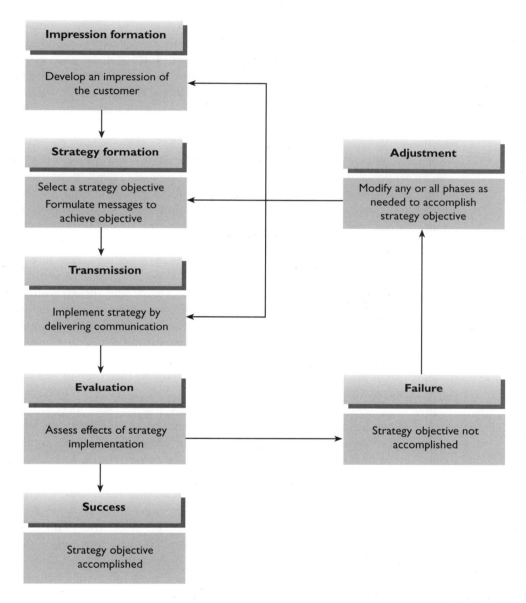

Source: Adapted from Barton A. Weitz, 'Relationship between Salesperson
Performance and Understanding Customer Decision Making', *Journal of Marketing Research*,
15 November 1978, p. 502. Published by the American Marketing Association.

shops suggests successful salespeople adapt their communication style to interact appropriately with customers.[50]

Evaluate Effects of Market Communication Strategy

Evaluating the effects of a market communication strategy involves comparing its results with the objectives. While this might seem simple, determining market communication effects can be difficult. For example, even clearly stated cognitive objectives, such as 'increase brand awareness by 25 per cent', are not easily evaluated because different methods of measuring awareness may give different results. Moreover, it is often difficult to determine whether a change in brand awareness resulted from the market communication strategy or from something else, such as word-of-mouth communication.

Similarly, market communication objectives stated in behaviour terms – 'increase sales by 10 per cent' – can be hard to evaluate. It is often difficult to determine what factors caused a sales increase. Increases in competitors' prices, opening new territories and outlets, changes in consumers' attitudes, and various other factors may be responsible for the increase in sales. Likewise, if sales decrease or remain the same during the market communication period, it is difficult to determine whether the market communication strategy was ineffective or whether other factors were responsible.[51]

Most of the effects measurement that is being done relates to advertising effects. Because the costs of advertising are so high, marketers are very interested in determining the communication effectiveness of their ads so that they can be improved. A wide variety of approaches have been taken to measuring advertising effects; these include *pretesting* (testing the effects of ads that are in rough, unfinished form before the ad is run in the natural environment) and *copy testing* (determining the meanings consumers derive from ads).[52]

Three broad criteria have been used as indicators of advertising effectiveness: sales, recall, and persuasion. Many researchers have tried to relate advertising to sales by measuring the aggregate purchase behaviour of large groups of consumers who supposedly were exposed to the ads. Linking sales to advertising has proved quite difficult because of the number of factors in addition to advertising that influence purchase behaviour. However, current technology is moving marketers closer to the day when they may be able to relate advertising exposure to purchase of the product.[53]

Another common measure of ad effectiveness is consumers' *recall* of the ad or some aspect of the ad. For example, in day-after recall studies, researchers telephone consumers the day after a TV commercial has run and ask them if they watched the TV programme the previous evening. If so, consumers are asked if they remember any ads, and what they specifically recall about the ad in question. Only viewers who can remember a visual element or a sales message are counted as having recalled the ad. Recall has been attacked for not really measuring the most important impacts of ads (such as creating product meanings or affective responses), but it can be an important objective in certain cases.[54] For ads that are intended primarily to enhance consumers' awareness of the brand, recall may be quite appropriate as a measure of effectiveness.

The third major criterion for advertising effectiveness is *persuasion*.[55] Most studies of persuasion measure whether consumers' comprehension of the ad produced changes (positive ones, preferably) in beliefs about the attributes or consequences of the product, brand attitudes (A_o), attitudes towards buying the brand (A_{act}), or purchase intentions (BI).[56] Another useful approach is to see if the ad created the desired means–end chains of product knowledge – that is, find out whether consumers formed an appropriate association between the brand and self-relevant ends.[57]

These traditional techniques of measuring advertising effects can be usefully supplemented by techniques measuring consumers' physiological reactions to advertisements.[58] Measures of skin resistance or heart rate say something about the arousing or attention-getting characteristics of advertisements, and eye movement measurements can be used to detect which elements of the ad receive attention and which do not. Such techniques are useful in the pretesting phase.

**Back to . . .
Talking
Bus Stops**

In a world of communication clutter, communication at bus stops has been found to be a means of communicating with consumers in a way that gives considerable exposure, although not necessarily attention. Attention is secured by devising highly original ways of communication, like talking or scented bus stops. This advertising medium puts heavy emphasis on peripheral cues in the communication process and seems therefore well-suited for communicating messages to consumers who are neither prepared nor interested in learning about products and services.

Summary

This chapter discussed how knowledge about consumers' affect and cognitions, behaviours, and environments can be used by marketers in developing more effective market communication strategies. We began by describing three types of market communications: advertising, personal selling, and publicity and sponsoring. Then we detailed how the basic communication model can be used for thinking about market communications and its relationship to the market offering, i.e. the product or service. Next we discussed some important aspects of the market communication environment (clutter and level of competition), affective and cognitive responses to market communications (attitude towards the ad and persuasion processes), and market-communication-related behaviours (information contact and word-of-mouth communication). Finally, we examined a managerial model for designing and executing market communication strategies. We described the various goals and objectives marketers may have for market communication strategies, and looked at two special models for developing advertising strategies and personal selling strategies. We concluded with a discussion of how to evaluate the effectiveness of market communication strategies.

Key Terms and Concepts

advertising   365
attitude towards the ad (A_{ad})   376
buyer-initiated market communication   366
communication process   371
effects hierarchy   371
Elaboration Likelihood Model (ELM)   377

Review and Discussion Questions

1. As a consumer of fast-food products, discuss the effects of market communication strategies on your decision processes.
2. Using the soft-drink industry as an example, define and illustrate each of the three major types of market communication.
3. Are the major market communication methods equally effective in influencing high- and low-involvement decisions? Explain.
4. Select a specific advertisement or in-store communication and evaluate it in terms of the elements of the communication model.
5. Describe how the two routes to persuasion differ and discuss their implications for developing effective advertising strategies.
6. Use the FCB grid model to illustrate consumer–product relationships for four products you have purchased in the last six months. How would this information be helpful to the market communication managers of these products?
7. Describe the MECCAS model for developing an effective advertising strategy. Illustrate the use of the model by suggesting a strategy for an athletic shoe market communication.
8. Do you agree with the suggestion that personal selling tends to create higher levels of involvement than other market communication strategies? How would your conclusion affect your use of the ISTEA model of personal selling (Exhibit 18.7)?
9. Identify a specific market communication strategy. Use the Wheel of Consumer Analysis model to analyse its effects on target consumers. Then suggest specific criteria that could be used to measure the effects of the market communication.

Additional Reading

For a discussion of how advertising affects consumers, see:

Rajeev Batra and Michael L. Ray, 'How Advertising Works at Contact', in *Psychological Processes and Advertising Effects: Theory, Research, and Application*, eds. Linda Alwitt and Andrew A. Mitchell (Hillsdale, NJ: Lawrence Erlbaum, 1985), pp. 129–155.

Andrew A. Mitchell, 'Theoretical and Methodological Issues in Developing an Individual-Level Model of Advertising Effects', in *Psychology and Marketing*, vol. 3, eds. Jerry Olson and Keith Sentis (New York, NY: Praeger, 1986), pp. 172–196.

For a discussion of the importance of consumer-initiated market communication, see:

Otto Ottesen, 'Buyer Initiative: Ignored, but Imperative for Marketing Management', *Tidvise Skrifter*, 15, 1995, pp. 1–46.

For a discussion of how advertising interacts with direct personal experiences, see:

John Deighton, 'The Interaction of Advertising and Evidence', *Journal of Consumer Research*, December 1984, pp. 763–770.

For a discussion of how ads influence the product meanings consumers form, see:

Roberto Friedmann and Mary R. Zimmer, 'The Role of Psychological Meaning in Advertising', *Journal of Advertising*, 1, 1988, pp. 31–40.

For a discussion of the role of affective factors in consumers' responses to advertising, see:

Morris B. Holbrook and John O'Shaughnessy, 'The Role of Emotion in Advertising', *Psychology and Marketing*, Summer 1984, pp. 45–64.

For a discussion of emotional reactions of children to advertisements, see:

Christian Derbaix and Joël Bree, 'The Impact of Children's Affective Reactions Elicited by Commercials on Attitudes Toward the Advertisement and the Brand', *International Journal of Research In Marketing*, 3, 1997, pp. 207–229.

For a discussion of the importance of brand awareness, see:

William T. Moran, 'Brand Presence and the Perceptual Frame', *Journal of Advertising Research*, October–November 1990, pp. 9–16.

For a discussion of developments in the communication environment, see:

Preben Sepstrup, 'The Electronic Dilemma of Television Advertising', in *Broadcasting Finance in Transition*, eds. Jay G. Blumler and T. J. Nossiter (Oxford: Oxford University Press, 1991), pp. 359–381.

For a discussion of how salespeople's knowledge influences their effectiveness, see:

Siew Meng Leong, Paul S. Busch, and Deborah Roedder John, 'Knowledge Bases and Salesperson Effectiveness: A Script-Theoretic Analysis', *Journal of Marketing Research*, May 1989, pp. 164–178.

For a discussion of the problems in standardizing cross-national advertising, see:

Barbara Mueller, 'Multinational Advertising: Factors Influencing the Standardised vs. Specialised Approach', *International Marketing Review*, 1, 1991, pp. 7–19.

For a discussion of some innovative methods in measuring advertising effects, see:

Stephan Buck and Alan Yates, 'Television Viewing, Consumer Purchasing and Single Source Research', *Journal of the Market Research Society*, 3, 1986, pp. 225–233.

Werner Kroeber-Riel, 'Effects of Emotional Pictorial Elements in Ads Analyzed by Means of Eye Movement Monitoring', in *Advances In Consumer Research*, vol. 11, ed. Thomas C. Kinnear (Provo, UT: Association For Consumer Research, 1984), pp. 591–596.

For a discussion of how marketers might evaluate an entire advertising campaign, see:

Julie A. Edell and Kevin Lane Keller. 'The Information Processing of Coordinated Media Campaigns', *Journal of Marketing Research*, May 1989, pp. 149–163.

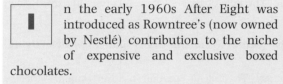

MARKETING STRATEGY IN ACTION

After Eight

I n the early 1960s After Eight was introduced as Rowntree's (now owned by Nestlé) contribution to the niche of expensive and exclusive boxed chocolates.

Consumers should perceive After Eight as a uniquely presented, wafer-thin, high-quality mint chocolate, which is enjoyed after a relaxed dinner or on comparable occasions. It should be associated with the elegance, sophistication and social status of the good hostess and of her guests. As an affordable token of friendship or appreciation, it reflects the good taste of the giver and will flatter the receiver.

Such positioning was meant to evoke the art of entertaining, the attention to detail in laying the table, the silver candelabra, the crystal brandy glasses, the black ties and cigars, all the refinements of an English country house, complete with butlers, and with the Rolls-Royce and its chauffeur waiting outside. The test launch in Scotland was initially supported by press advertising only, but the real breakthrough occurred when the first TV commercial 'Dinner Table' was put on the air on Yorkshire television in 1964. It immediately resulted in a 64 per cent sales increase, as compared to 18 per cent in other parts of the country.

Many people have wondered how Rowntree could successfully introduce a product so essentially British in character and in presentation to, for example, the French to whom the combination of chocolate and peppermint as an after-dinner treat was almost sacrilege; or to the Germans, to whom the typical English after-dinner gathering did not mean anything at all; or to the Italians, who were accustomed to purchasing big boxes of chocolates as gifts for their mothers, but who were not used to the combination of mint and chocolate, and far less to the idea of an after-dinner mint chocolate. Nestlé decided to use one international advertising agency and its subsidiaries in Europe for the task. The subtleties, the nuances, the cast and the location required by the commercials made close collaboration imperative. No risks were to be taken. But why, one might ask, could the UK commercials not simply be taken as they stood, and dubbed into the local language, thereby saving a considerable amount of money?

At the time, the answer was simple. If, in addition to introducing the new habit of having mint chocolate after dinner, the advertising had contained dinner tables or picnics unlike those to which continental consumers were accustomed, one could not have expected their audiences to identify emotionally with the situations that the commercials presented. This was all the more important because, in spite of the misgivings of many people on the Continent, management had taken the decision that the 'Englishness' of the product's concept should be maintained; the very British character of the brand, and its equally British name, were not only going to be maintained, but even highlighted.

Discussion Questions

1. Analyse the effect of the advertising for After Eight in your own country. Do this by specifying those communication goals which you think were necessary for the brand to be successful in your country.
2. Analyse the cross-cultural differences that make it necessary to adapt the advertising execution in the United Kingdom, France, and Germany.
3. Discuss the pros and cons of having the same basic advertising strategy in several countries.
4. Place the After Eight product into the FCB grid. Based on your analysis, do you think the advertising strategy was correctly chosen? Why or why not?

Source: Adapted from 'After Eight – Wafer-Thin Chocolate Mints', in Rein Rijkens, *European Advertising Strategies*, 1992, pp. 159–172.

Consumer Behaviour and Pricing Strategy

Beer for the Beach

F rans van Roekelen is a construction worker who makes about NLG2400 per month after taxes. While he could work overtime on Saturday making some extra money, he takes off two consecutive Saturdays to go to the beach together with some friends.

Frans likes to drink beer with his friends, and on the morning of his first Saturday off, he walks two blocks to a corner shop to purchase two six-packs for his beach trip. The price is NLG4.43 for a six-pack. Frans complains about the high price and is told by the assistant, 'I don't set the prices. Take it or leave it, Jack!' Frans is more than a little upset, but he pays the money because he's in a rush to get to the beach. He vows to himself never to get ripped off like this again. He walks home. The whole trip has taken 10 minutes.

The following Saturday, Frans again wants to buy two six-packs of beer for his beach trip. Remembering his previous experience at the corner shop, he decides to get in his car and drive six kilometres to a discount supermarket he knows. He is pleasantly surprised that his favourite brand of beer is on sale at NLG2.52 per six-pack. Although the store is a bit crowded and it takes him a while to get through the checkout, he drives home feeling good about the purchase and the money he saved. This shopping trip takes 45 minutes.

In several ways, price is the most unusual element of the marketing mix.[1] For one thing, it is the only one that involves revenues; all the other elements, as well as marketing research, involve expenditure of funds by the seller or producer. Another difference is that although price may seem tangible and concrete, it is perhaps more intangible and abstract than other elements of the marketing mix. For example, in the product area, consumers often have a tangible product to examine or at least information about a service to evaluate. In the promotion area consumers have magazine and newspaper ads and information from salespeople to see, listen to, and evaluate. In the distribution area consumers have stores to experience. However, the price variable is a rather abstract concept that, while represented as a sign or tag, has relatively little direct sensory experience connected with it.

These differences should not lead you to underestimate the importance of price to marketing and consumer behaviour. Price can have a considerable influence on consumer behaviour. It can also have a major effect on competitors, because competitors can react more easily to appeals based on price than to those based on product benefits and imagery. In this chapter we focus on some important relationships among consumer affect, cognitions, behaviours, and the environment as they relate to the price

EXHIBIT 19.1

The Wheel of Consumer Analysis: Pricing Strategy Issues

variable of the marketing mix. These variables and relationships are shown in Exhibit 19.1, which provides an overview of the topics to be discussed. We begin our discussion by offering a conceptual view of the role of price in marketing exchanges. We then discuss price affect and cognitions, behaviours, the environment, and, finally, pricing strategy.

Conceptual Issues in Pricing

From a consumer's point of view, *price* is usually defined as what the consumer must give up to purchase a product or service. This may include more than the monetary price. Exhibit 19.2 identifies four basic types of consumer costs: money, time, cognitive activity, and behaviour effort. These costs, when paired with whatever value or utility the product offers, are a convenient way to consider the meaning of price to the consumer. While we do not argue that consumers finely calculate each of these costs for every purchase, we do believe they are frequently considered in the purchase of some products.

In Exhibit 19.2 we have also divided marketing costs into the four categories of production, promotion, distribution, and marketing research. Most business costs and investments could be attributed to one or another of these categories. These costs, when paired with the desired level of profit a firm seeks, offer a convenient way to consider the marketing side of the exchange equation. Basically, the model implies products must usually cover at least variable costs and make some contribution to overheads or profits for the offering to be made to the marketplace.

EXHIBIT 19.2

The Pivotal Role of Price in Marketing Exchanges

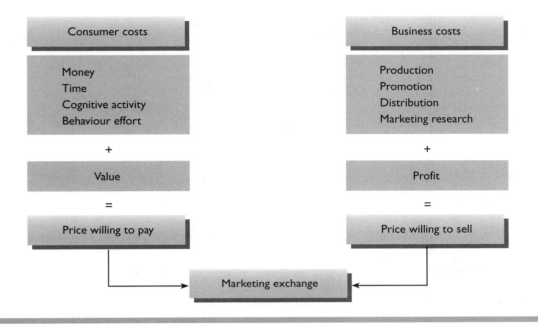

For marketing exchanges to occur, the price consumers are willing to pay must be greater than or equal to the price at which marketers are willing to sell. However, while this may seem simple enough, a number of complex relationships need to be considered when pricing is viewed from this perspective. Of major importance is the nature of consumer costs and the relationships between them. What should become clear is that the monetary price of an item may often be only a part of the total price of an exchange for the consumer.

Money

Most pricing research has focused on *money* – the amount a consumer must spend to purchase a product or service. This research has recognized that the same monetary amount may be perceived differently by different individuals and market segments, depending on income levels and other variables. However, several important aspects of the monetary cost of offerings are not always considered. One of these concerns the *source* of funds for a particular purchase. We suspect that money received as a tax rebate, gift, interest, or as gambling winnings has a different value to many consumers than money earned through work. For example, consider airline passengers whose luggage is delayed and who are therefore entitled to receive funds from their travel insurance to buy clothing. Their spending habits in such a situation may be quite different from when they buy clothing using their regular income. Consequently,

---

HIGHLIGHT 19.1

Some Short-Term Price Reduction Tactics

1. Money-off deals: 'Package price is 20p off'.
2. Special offers: 'Buy one, get one free'; 'Buy three tyres and get the fourth free'.
3. Rebates: Price reductions for repeat buyers or for consumers having the seller's charge card.
4. Increase quantity for same price: '2 extra ounces of coffee free'.
5. Free installation or service for a limited time.
6. Reduce or eliminate interest charges for a limited time: '90 days same as cash'.
7. Special sales: '25 per cent off all merchandise marked with a red tag'.

---

the price of a particular item may be perceived differently by the same individual, depending on what sources of funds are used to pay for it.

A number of methods can reduce the monetary amount spent for a particular item, although they often involve increasing other costs. For example, time, cognitive activity, and behaviour effort are required to shop at different stores seeking the lowest price, and may also involve additional monetary costs such as transportation or parking. Highlight 19.1 lists tactics marketers use to lower prices.

Time

The *time* necessary to learn about a product or service and to travel to purchase it, as well as time spent in a store, can be important costs to the consumer. Many consumers are well aware that smaller neighbourhood supermarkets may charge higher prices than hypermarkets located outside the cities. Still, many consumers do shop at the more expensive outlets. Clearly, these consumers often make a trade-off of paying more money to save time, particularly if only a few items are to be purchased. Time savings may result not only because of less travelling time, but also because less time is required in the store to locate the product and wait in line to pay for it. Given the high cost of running a car, it might even be cheaper in monetary terms to shop at stores that are closer to home, even if they have higher prices! Thus, bargain hunters who travel all over town to locate the cheapest buys of minor products may be fooling themselves if they think they are saving money.

However, we should not treat time only as a cost of purchasing. In some situations, the process of seeking product information and purchasing products is a very enjoyable experience – rather than a cost – for consumers. Many consumers enjoy Christmas shopping and spend hours at it, for instance. Some consumers enjoy window-shopping and purchasing on occasion, particularly if the opportunity cost of their time is low. Going out to shop on a Friday evening or Saturday morning may be regarded as a kind of family outing. Similarly, some consumers enjoy spending hours looking through catalogues of their favourite merchandise. Thus, while in an absolute sense consumers must spend time to shop and make purchases, in some cases this may be perceived as a benefit rather than a cost.

Cognitive Activity

One frequently overlooked cost of making purchases is the *cognitive activity* involved. Thinking and deciding what to buy can be very hard work. For example, when all of the styles, sizes, colours, and component options are considered, one Japanese manufacturer offers over 11 million variations of custom-made bicycles. Consumers would never evaluate all 11 million options, but consider the cognitive activity required to evaluate even a small fraction of them. Clearly, it would not only take a lot of time, but it would also be very taxing in terms of cognitive work.[2] Yet, if even a few comparisons are made, some cognitive effort must be expended.

In addition to all the cognitive work involved in comparing purchase alternatives, the process can also be stressful. Some consumers find it very difficult and dislike making purchase (or other types of) decisions. To some, finding parking spaces, shopping in crowded stores, waiting in long checkout queues, and viewing anxiety-producing ads can be a very unpleasant experience emotionally. Thus, the cognitive activity involved in purchasing can be a very important cost.

The cost involved in decision making is often the easiest one for consumers to reduce or eliminate. Simple decision rules or heuristics can reduce this cost considerably. By repeatedly purchasing the same brand, consumers can practically eliminate any decision making within a product class, for example. Other heuristics might be to purchase the most expensive brand, the brand on sale or display, the brand mum or dad used to buy, the brand a knowledgeable friend recommends, or the brand a selected dealer carries or recommends.

On the other hand, there are some situations in which consumers actively seek some form of cognitive involvement. Fishing enthusiasts frequently enjoy comparing the attributes of various types of equipment, judging their relative merits, and assessing the ability of different equipment to catch fish. The same goes for train buffs looking at electric train equipment, collectors comparing pieces of art, gourmet hobby cooks locating the best chateaubriand, and many others. We suspect that while consumers may enjoy periods in which they are not challenged to use much cognitive energy or ability, they may also seek purchasing problems to solve as a form of entertainment.

Behaviour Effort

Anyone who has spent several hours walking around in shopping malls can attest to the fact that purchasing involves *behaviour effort*. Perhaps the most interesting aspect of behaviour effort is the willingness of consumers to take on some marketing costs to reduce the monetary amount they spend and to make trade-offs among various types of costs. In some cases, consumers will perform part of the production process to get a lower monetary price. For example, consumers may forgo the cost of product assembly for bicycles and toys and do it themselves to save money, they buy furniture which they have to bring home and assemble themselves, or they go to fields where they can pick strawberries.

There are also cases in which consumers will take on at least part of the cost of distribution to lower the monetary price. At one time, for example, it was common to have milk delivered to the home; now an increasing number of consumers purchase it at stores. Catalogue purchases require the consumer to pay the cost of shipping directly, yet may be less expensive than store purchases. If they are not, the consumer at least saves shopping time and effort to have the product delivered to the home.

A final trade-off of interest in terms of pricing concerns the degree to which consumers participate in purchase/ownership. Consumers have several options with regard to purchase: (1) They can buy the product and enjoy its benefits as well as incur other costs such as inventory and maintenance; (2) they can rent or lease the product and enjoy its benefits but forgo ownership and often reduce some of the other costs, such as maintenance; (3) they can hire someone else to perform whatever service the product is designed to perform and forgo ownership and other postpurchase costs; or (4) they can purchase the product and hire someone else to use and maintain it for them. For many durable goods, such as cars, appliances, power tools, furniture, and lawn mowers, at least several of these options are available. Clearly, as we stated at the beginning of the chapter, price is a lot more than just money.

Value

We have discussed four aspects of price from the consumer's point of view. We have suggested that consumers can sometimes reduce one or more of these costs, but this usually requires an increase in at least one of the other costs. Purchases can be viewed in terms of which of the elements is considered a cost or a benefit and which is considered most critical for particular purchases. However, regardless of what cost trade-offs are made, it seems that whatever is being purchased must be perceived to be of greater *value* to the consumer than merely the sum of the costs. In other words, the

---

HIGHLIGHT 19.2
Increasing Prices or Increasing Service?

hen Scandinavian Airlines System announced that it would stop serving in-flight meals on some of its major routes linking the Scandinavian capitals, many passengers regarded this as a reduction in service and, since the fare remained unchanged, as a hidden price increase. The airline, however, argued that the service offered was actually being increased: instead of being served a meal in-flight, passengers can now select a wide array of light foods and drinks at the gate, before boarding the plane. For this purpose, the gates have been rebuilt to resemble a café where passengers can relax and eat. The airline says that this is to meet passenger needs, who say that being served meals on flights of about one hour is stressful. Passengers can now eat relaxed at the gate, and they are served a wider selection of drinks than before while in the air. Thus, the airline claims, the new initiative is a service increase instead of a price increase.

Not all passengers agreed. Some noted that relaxing for half an hour or so in the air over a snack and drink is the only enjoyable part of a trip by air, and that eating at the gate is quite stressful because nobody knows when boarding will start and you will have to drop your sandwich. Also, in order to really eat at ease, one has to be at the gate earlier than before, actually adding to the time of the trip. Finally, some passengers remarked that the design of the new gates resembled a Finnish sauna more than a cosy café. For them, the new initiative was perceived as a price increase rather than an increase in service.

consumer perceives that the purchase offers benefits greater than the costs and is willing to exchange to receive these benefits.

While this view of price is useful, we want to restate that consumers seldom (if ever) finely calculate each of these costs and benefits in making purchase decisions. Rather, for many types of consumer packaged goods, the amounts of money, time, cognitive activity, and behaviour effort required for a purchase are very similar. For these goods, choices between brands may be made on the basis of particular benefits or imagery, although price deals may be important.

For some purchases, all of the costs and trade-offs may be considered by consumers. Yet the major importance of our view of price is not the degree to which consumers actively analyse and compare each of the costs of a particular exchange. Instead, this view is important because it has direct implications for the design of marketing strategy, as discussed later in the chapter. Our view also has the advantage of showing that the perception of both price and value rests with the consumer. The same product change can be perceived as a price increase or a value increase by different consumers, as shown in Highlight 19.2.

Price Affect and Cognitions

As we noted, typically little sensory experience is connected with the price variable. But this makes it all the more important to understand how consumers attend to and comprehend prices, and how price consequently influences their behaviour. It is also important to understand under which circumstances consumers do not attend to price information. To make it more difficult, price information comes under many different names, as shown in Highlight 19.3.

HIGHLIGHT 19.3

Some Different Terms for Monetary Price

Alternative Terms	What Is Given in Return
Price	Most physical merchandise
Tuition	Education
Rent	A place to live or the use of equipment for a specific period
Interest	Use of money
Fee	Professional services (lawyers, doctors, consultants, etc.)
Fare	Transportation (air, taxi, bus, etc.)
Toll	Use of road or bridge
Salary	Work of employees
Wage	Work of hourly workers
Bribe	Illegal actions
Commission	Sales effort

Source: Thomas C. Kinnear and Kenneth L. Bernhardt, *Principles of Marketing*, 3rd edn., p. 576. Copyright © 1990, 1986, 1983, by Scott, Foresman and Company. Reprinted by permission of HarperCollins Publishers, Inc.

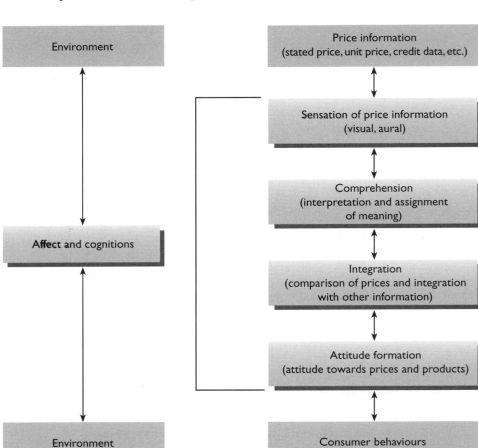

EXHIBIT 19.3

Conceptual Model of Cognitive Processing of Price Information

Several attempts have been made to summarize the research on the effects of price on consumer affect, cognitions, and behaviour, but these reviews have found few generalizations.[3] For example, for a long time it was believed that consumers perceive a strong relationship between price and the quality of products and services. Experiments typically find this relationship when consumers are given no other information about the product except price. However, when consumers are given additional information about products (which is more consistent with marketplace situations), the price–quality relationship is diminished.

In general, all of these reviews conclude that research on the behavioural effects of pricing has not been based on sound theory and that most of the studies are seriously flawed methodologically. Thus, it should not be surprising that there is little consensus on basic issues of how price affects consumer choice processes and behaviour.

The way price information affects consumers can be analysed from an information-processing perspective, as outlined in Exhibit 19.3.[4] This model illustrates an approach to describing price effects for a high-involvement product or purchase situation. Basically, it suggests price information is received through the senses of sight and hearing. The information is then comprehended, which means it is interpreted and made meaningful (i.e. consumers understand the meaning of price symbols through previous learning and experience).

In the cognitive processing of price information, consumers may make comparisons between the stated price and a price or price range they have in mind for the product. The price they have in mind for making these comparisons is called the **internal reference price**. The internal reference price may be what consumers think is a fair price, what the price has been historically, or what consumers think is a low market price or a high market price. Basically, an internal reference price serves as a guide for evaluating whether the stated price is acceptable to the consumer.[5] For example, a consumer may think 30 pence is about the right price to pay for a chocolate bar. When a vending machine offers chocolate bars at 50 pence, the internal reference price may inhibit purchase because the asking price is too high. However, the reference price may depend on the shopping environment – in the context of a fancy store, a price of 50 pence for the chocolate bar may be regarded as acceptable.[6]

The stated price for a particular brand may be considered a product attribute. This knowledge may then be compared with the prices of other brands in a product class, other attributes of the brand and other brands, and other consumer costs. Finally, an attitude is formed towards the various brand alternatives.

For a low-involvement product or purchase situation, the monetary price may have little or no impact on consumer affect and cognitions or behaviours. For many products, consumers may have an implicit price range, and as long as prices fall within it, price is not even evaluated as a purchase criterion. Similarly, some products are simply purchased without ever enquiring as to the price, but simply paying whatever is asked for at the point of purchase. Impulse items located in the checkout area of supermarkets may frequently be purchased this way, as might other products for which the consumer is highly brand loyal. In the latter cases, consumers may make purchases on the single attribute of brand name without comparing monetary price, other consumer costs, or other factors.

In other cases, price information may not be carefully analysed because consumers have a particular price image for the store they are shopping in. Discount stores such as Aldi or Netto may be generally considered low-priced outlets, and consumers may forgo comparing prices at these outlets with those at other stores.

Consumers often do not carefully store detailed price information in memory, even for products they purchase. For example, in a study of grocery shoppers, the researchers concluded:

> What is surprising is just how imperfect [price] information attention and retention are at the very point of purchase. The fact is that less than half of the shoppers could recall the price of the item they had just placed in their shopping basket, and less than half were aware they had selected an item that was selling at a reduced price. Only a small minority of those who bought a special knew both its price and the amount of the price reduction.[7]

There are good reasons why many consumers do not carefully store in memory the prices of individual products. Consumers probably do not want to exert the considerable

EXHIBIT 19.4

Price Cognitions

Type of Cognition	% of consumers able to answer				
	Average 10 products	Salt	Sugar	Ketchup	Oil
Price promotion at last buy?	92.8	100.0	100.0	86.7	96.7
Average price	84.7	90.0	83.3	80.0	83.3
Maximum price willing to pay	79.3	63.2	66.7	100.0	89.5
Frequency of price promotions	78.8	86.7	93.3	73.3	60.0
Price differences between stores	77.5	76.7	86.7	83.7	70.0
Price ranking of brands (unaided)	73.6	0	100.0	76.5	45.5
Price at last purchase	62.5	63.0	73.7	64.3	59.3
Price ranking of brands (aided)	61.7	50.0	57.1	50.0	52.6
Typical price	37.5	0	100.0	14.3	50.0
Price ranking of stores	26.2	11.1	28.6	52.6	28.6
Price of different brands	16.6	20.0	0	16.7	23.3
Price of preferred brand in different stores	9.4	30.8	0	5.0	0

Source: Adapted from Hermann Diller, 'Das Preiswissen von Konsumenten',
Marketing-ZFP, 1, 1988, pp. 17–24.

effort necessary to obtain, store, and revise prices for the many products they buy. For many purchases, consumers must pay the stated price or forgo purchase. Thus, if they choose to purchase, the price is uncontrollable by them and it may make little sense to carefully store price information when it has little impact on saving money. In sum, the cognitive activity costs, behaviour effort costs, and time costs involved in storing price information and shopping carefully are often not worth expending in relation to the potential savings.[8]

Exhibit 19.4 shows results from a survey of consumers' price cognitions in Germany. For ten different product categories, twelve different types of price knowledge were ascertained. The table in Exhibit 19.4 shows the percentage of consumers who could give an answer – independently of whether the answer was correct – for four of the products, as well as the average across the ten products. The results illustrate the point made above. The price cognitions consumers had were primarily of a kind which was general and imprecise, but also useful and easily available – like the average price and the frequency of price promotions, as compared to the price for a specific brand in different shops.[9]

Price Behaviours

Depending on the consumer, the product and its availability in various stores and other channels, and other elements of the situation, price could affect a variety of consumer behaviours. Two types of behaviours are of particular relevance to the price variable: funds access and transaction.

Funds Access

One source of embarrassment for most of us as consumers is to arrive at the point in the purchase process where we have to produce funds for an exchange and realize we do not have sufficient funds available. Not having enough money at the grocery checkout counter and having to replace several items can be embarrassing, particularly when the total amount of money needed is quite small. Similarly, it is embarrassing to bounce a cheque, to have a credit-card purchase refused, or to be refused a purchase because of a poor credit rating. For these reasons, most of us are likely to plan for funds access to ensure sufficient funds are available when we go shopping.

As we have noted previously, there are many ways consumers can access funds. First, many consumers carry a certain amount of cash to pay for small purchases. This cash supply may be replenished as needed for day-to-day activities. Second, many consumers carry charge or credit cards to handle purchases. In some countries, electronic funds transfer at the point of purchase is well developed and can also be used to obtain cash. In other countries, cheques are still widely in use.

We suspect charge-card and credit-card purchases and payments are not only convenient for the consumer, but also may make the purchase seem less expensive. This is because consumers do not see any cash flowing from their pockets; they merely need to sign their names and not even think about payment until the end of the month. In one sense, if no balance is carried over on the credit card, the purchase is 'free' for the time between the exchange and the payment. We suspect that while many consumers may keep tabs on their chequebook balances, they may be less concerned throughout the month with their credit-card balances – unless they are close to their credit limits.

Charge and credit cards also facilitate purchasing because little effort is required to access funds. Even going to a bank or to an automatic teller machine before shopping to obtain cash requires more effort than using a charge or credit card. Thus, overall, the use of charge and credit cards may reduce consumers' time, cognitive activity, and behaviour effort costs.

Transaction

The exchange of funds for products and services is typically a relatively simple transaction. It usually involves handing over cash, pushing buttons in a funds transfer device, signing a credit slip, or signing a credit contract and following up by making regular payments.

However, as we have emphasized throughout this chapter, consumers exchange much more than simply money for goods and services. They also exchange their time, cognitive activity, and behaviour effort – not only to earn money, but also to shop and make purchases. Thus, analysis of these elements, and of the value consumers receive in purchase and consumption, may provide better insights into the effects of price on consumer behaviour.

Price Environment

As we stated at the beginning of the chapter, price is perhaps the most intangible element of the marketing mix. From an environmental perspective, this means the price variable typically offers very little for the consumer to experience at the sensory level, although it may generate considerable cognitive activity and behaviour effort. In the environment, price is usually a sign, a tag, a few symbols on a package, or a few words spoken on TV, on radio, or by a salesperson in a store or on the phone. The price variable also includes purchase contracts and credit-term information.

The price variable may also include an **external reference price**. An external reference price is an explicit comparison of the stated price with another price in advertising, catalogue listings, price guides, on shopping tags and store displays, or in sales presentations. Most commonly, the stated price may be compared with the seller's former price ('£11.95, marked down from £15.00'), or with prices at competing stores ('£54.95, lowest price in town'). External reference prices are used to enhance the attractiveness of the stated price.[10]

How price information is communicated also has an effect. For example, the advent of scanner checkout systems has reduced price information in the environment for many grocery products because prices are no longer stamped on each package or can. A study by Zeithaml found that having each item marked increased consumers' certainty of price recall and decreased errors in both exact-price and unit-price recall.[11] Often prices for grocery products are stated not only as the price per package, but in addition a standard **unit price** is stated. The idea is that this makes it easier for consumers to compare prices. For example, vegetable oil comes in bottles of various sizes, and consumers may find it hard to compare their prices unless they are also stated in terms of a common unit, like the price per litre.[12] These examples support the idea that not only the price itself, but also the method by which price information is communicated influences consumer affect, cognitions, and behaviours.

Pricing Strategy

Pricing strategy is of concern in three general situations: (1) when a price is being set for a new product, (2) when a long-term change is being considered for an established product, and (3) when a short-term price change is being considered. Marketers may change prices for a variety of reasons, such as an increase in costs, a change in the price of competitive products, or a change in distribution channels.

Many models have been offered to guide marketers in designing pricing strategies.[13] Most of these models contain very similar recommendations and differ primarily in terms of how detailed the assumptions are, how many steps the pricing process is divided into, and in what sequence pricing tasks are recommended. For our purposes, we have developed a six-stage model, which is shown in Exhibit 19.5. Our model differs from traditional approaches primarily in that greater emphasis is placed on consumer analysis and greater attention is given to the four types of consumer costs in developing pricing and marketing strategies.

The six stages in our strategic approach to pricing are discussed next. Although consumer analysis is not the major focus in all of them, our discussion is intended to clarify the role of consumer analysis in pricing and to offer a useful overview of the pricing process.

Analyse Consumer–Product Relationships

Pricing strategy for a new product generally starts with at least one given: the firm has a product concept or several variations of a product concept in mind. When a price

EXHIBIT 19.5

A Strategic Approach to Pricing

1. Analyse consumer–product relationships

2. Analyse the environmental situation

3. Determine the role of price in marketing strategy

4. Estimate relevant production and marketing costs

5. Set pricing objectives

6. Develop pricing strategy and set prices

change for an existing product is being considered, typically much more information is available, including sales and cost data.

Whether the pricing strategy is being developed for a new or existing product, a useful first stage in the process is to analyse the consumer–product relationships. Answers must be found for questions such as: How does the product benefit consumers? What does it mean to them? In what situations do they use it? Does it have any special psychological or social significance to them? Of course, the answers to these questions depend on which current or potential target markets are under consideration.

A key question that must be answered is whether the product itself has a clear differential advantage that consumers would be willing to pay for, or whether a differential advantage must be created on the basis of other marketing mix variables. This question has important implications for determining which of the four areas of consumer costs (time, money, cognitive activity, or behaviour effort) can be appealed to most effectively.

Suppose a firm is considering marketing pizza for home consumption and is analysing consumer–product relationships. The firm is considering three forms of pizza and, after

EXHIBIT 19.6

Relative Consumer Costs for Various Pizza Product Forms

Cost	Frozen Pizza	Pizzeria Pizza	Home Delivery
Money	Low	High	High
Time	High	Middle	Low
Cognitive activity	High	Middle	Low
Behaviour effort	Middle	High	Low
Value:			
Taste	Worst	Best	Middle

considerable research, has developed the data presented in Exhibit 19.6. This type of analysis illustrates several important concepts. First, it is clear that consumers of the three types of pizza make trade-offs in the costs they are willing to incur. Consumers of frozen pizza are willing to spend time, cognitive activity, and behaviour effort on preparation, and they may get a poorer tasting pizza, which indicates that they are probably not willing to incur high monetary costs. Consumers eating pizza in the restaurant get a top-quality pizza, for which they incur other types of time and behavioural costs, plus higher monetary costs. Consumers eating home-delivery pizza trade lower behavioural and time costs for higher monetary costs and possibly some deterioration in taste.

Second, this analysis has clear implications for segmentation. It is important to determine the size of the markets for the different forms, their demographic profiles, and the degree of market overlap. That is, are these different consumer groups or are they the same consumers who eat different types of pizza in different situations?

Third, while this analysis has a number of implications for all facets of marketing strategy, our focus is on the implications for pricing. The question of what pizza means to consumers is critical for determining appropriate pricing strategies. For example, the frozen pizza market is apparently price sensitive. Thus, while a reduction of the other types of consumer costs or an increase in value (taste) may offer market opportunities, the monetary price of the pizza would probably have to remain low.

This brief example illustrates an approach to evaluating the relationships between consumers and products. One of the important outcomes of this analysis is an estimate of how sensitive consumers are to various monetary prices, other costs being relatively the same. Once the firm has a clear idea of these relationships and opportunities, it can then focus attention on other aspects of the environment.

Analyse the Environmental Situation

There is no question that a firm must consider elements of the environment – economic trends, political views, social changes, and legal constraints – when developing pricing strategies. These elements should be considered early in the process of formulating any part of marketing strategy and should be monitored continually. By the time a firm is making pricing decisions, many of these issues have already been considered. While this may also be true for competitive analysis, consideration of competition at this point is critical for developing pricing strategies.

In setting or changing prices, the firm must consider its competition and how that competition will react to the price of the product. Initially, consideration should be given to such factors as

- Number of competitors
- Market share of competitors
- Location of competitors
- Conditions of entry into the industry
- Degree of vertical integration of competitors
- Financial strength of competitors
- Number of products and brands sold by each competitor
- Cost structure of competitors
- Historical reaction of competitors to price changes

Analysis of these factors helps determine whether the monetary price should be at, below, or above competitors' prices. However, this analysis should also consider other consumer costs relative to competitive offerings. Consumers often pay higher monetary prices to save time and effort.

Determine the Role of Price in Marketing Strategy

This step is concerned with determining whether the monetary price is to be a key aspect of positioning the product or whether it is to play a different role. If a firm is attempting to position a brand as a bargain product, then setting a lower monetary price is clearly an important part of this strategy. Vizir washing powder positions itself as just as good only cheaper than the other brands, for example. Similarly, if a firm is attempting to position a brand as a prestige, top-of-the-line item, then a higher monetary price is a common cue to indicate this position. Chivas Regal scotch has used this approach for a long time, for example. Sometimes a seller would like to compete in several price segments, which raises the questions of whether this requires different brands or whether the same brand can serve different price segments.[14]

In many situations, monetary price may not play a particularly important positioning role other than in terms of pricing competitively. If consumers enjoy greater convenience in purchasing (e.g. free delivery), or if the product has a clear differential advantage, the price may be set at or above those of the competition but not highlighted in positioning strategy. In other cases, when the price of a product is higher than that of the competition but there is no clear differential advantage, the price may not be explicitly used in positioning. For example, premium-priced beers do not highlight price as part of their appeal. Consumers' price elasticity, i.e. to what extent they will react to price changes by changing their choice behaviour, can be analysed by employing a range of market research techniques.[15]

Estimate Relevant Production and Marketing Costs

The costs of producing and marketing a product effectively provide a useful benchmark for making pricing decisions. The variable costs of production and marketing usually provide the lowest monetary price a firm must charge to make an offering in the market. However, there are some exceptions to this rule. These exceptions typically involve inter-relationships among products. For example, a firm may sell its cameras below cost to sell a greater volume of film, or a grocery store may sell an item below cost (i.e. a loss leader) to build traffic and increase sales of other items.

Set Pricing Objectives

Pricing objectives should be derived from overall marketing objectives, which, in turn, should be derived from corporate objectives. In practice, the most common objective is to achieve a target return on investment. This objective has the advantage of being quantifiable, and it also offers a useful basis for making not only pricing decisions but also decisions on whether to enter or remain in specific markets. For example, if a firm demands a 20 per cent return on investment, and the best estimates of sales at various prices indicate a product would have to be priced too high to generate demand, then the decision may be to forgo market entry. However, marketers should be aware of the sensitivity of profits to small differences in the price they receive for their products and services, as discussed in Highlight 19.4.

Develop Pricing Strategy and Set Prices

A thorough analysis in the preceding stages should provide the information necessary to develop pricing strategies and set prices. Basically, the meaning of the product to the consumer and consumer costs have been analysed. The environment has been analysed, particularly competition. The role of pricing marketing strategy has been determined. Production and marketing costs have been estimated. Pricing objectives have been set. The pricing task now is to determine a pricing strategy and specific prices that are (1) sufficiently above costs to generate the desired level of profit and achieve stated objectives, (2) related to competitive prices in a manner consistent with the overall marketing and positioning strategy, and (3) designed to generate consumer demand based on consumer cost trade-offs and values.

In some cases, prices may be developed with a long-run strategy in mind. For example, a **penetration price policy** may include a long-run plan to sequentially raise prices after introduction at a relatively low price, or a **skimming price policy** may include a long-run plan to systematically lower prices after a high-price introduction.

However, most price changes occur as a result of changes in consumers, the environment, competition, costs, strategies, and objectives. An example of the relationships among these variables can be found in the pricing of airfares.

Before the current deregulation, prices were set by IATA jointly for all airlines serving a given route. Thus, price was not a very important competitive weapon, as all carriers charged the same fare for the same route. In the course of deregulation, airlines have started to use price much more as a competitive weapon, by developing all kinds of fare reductions and differentiated fare structures, usually linked to certain reductions in the service provided, like booking a certain number of days and weeks in advance, being away a certain number of days, possibilities of changing the ticket, etc. Consumers now have a choice of attempting to minimize monetary cost by spending more time shopping for low prices, forgoing some flexibility in departure times and dates, and giving up some additional services versus paying full fare and getting these benefits. Business travellers

HIGHLIGHT 19.4

Effects on Profitability for Small Changes in Price

S mall changes in the price received by marketers can lead to large differences in net income. For example, at Coca-Cola, a 1 per cent improvement in the price received for its products would result in a net income boost of 6.4 per cent; at Fuji Photo, 16.7 per cent; at Nestlé, 17.5 per cent; at Ford, 26 per cent; and at Philips, 28.7 per cent. In some companies, a 1 per cent improvement in the price received would be the difference between a profit and a significant loss. Given the cost structure of large corporations, a 1 per cent boost in realized price yields an average net income gain of 12 per cent. In short, when setting pricing objectives and developing pricing strategies, it's worth the effort to do pricing research to see what prices consumers are willing to pay and still feel they are receiving good value.

Source: Based on Robert J. Dolan and Hermann Simon, *Power Pricing: How Managing Price Transforms the Bottom Line* (New York, NY: The Free Press, 1996), p. 4.

often pay the higher full-fare price, while leisure travellers spend the time and effort necessary to get cheaper fares.

This example illustrates how a change in the environment (deregulation) leads to a change in competition, which leads to a change in pricing strategies (price cuts for some seats but overall attempts to maximize revenues per flight) and cost-cutting efforts. Many consumers also change as they become more involved in the purchase of airline tickets and perhaps even travel more by plane as monetary prices fall, at least in the short run.

Back to . . . Beer for the Beach

When considering only the money cost of the six-packs, at first glance it may appear that the supermarket price is better: NLG2.52 for a six-pack versus the corner shop price of NLG4.43.

Now let's consider the cost of operating Frans' car. Assume it costs NLG0.40 per kilometre; driving 12 kilometres thus equals NLG4.80. The supermarket purchase now costs Frans 2 X NLG2.52 plus NLG4.80, which equals NLG9.84 – slightly more than the corner store price of 2 X NLG4.43 = NLG8.86.

Next, it seems reasonable to estimate the cost of Frans' time. Several rates could be considered. Let us assume that the market value for his time on a Saturday is approximately NLG18.50 per hour. The corner shop trip had a time cost of 10 minutes at NLG18.50 per hour, which equals NLG3.08, for a total of NLG8.86 plus NLG3.08, which equals NLG11.94. The supermarket trip had a time cost of 45 minutes at NLG18.50 per hour, which equals NLG13.88, for a total of NLG9.84 plus NLG13.88, which equals NLG23.72. The corner shop trip now appears to be a real bargain.

Finally, let's consider how Frans felt about the two trips and what he experienced. In terms of cognitive activity, the corner shop trip was clearly stressful and unpleasant and probably required more behaviour effort than the trip to the supermarket. However, the exercise may have been good for him physically. On the other hand, the supermarket trip was pleasant, and Frans felt very good about the purchase.

So which was the better trip? To Frans, it was the price paid at the supermarket, for he ignored other costs. However, if one accepts the economic assumptions involved in valuing Frans' car operating costs and time, an outside observer might conclude the corner shop price was a better buy. Depending on how the cognitive activity and behaviour effort are evaluated, either of the two may be considered to be the better purchase.

Which was the better price? It depends on whether we consider the question from Frans' point of view or from that of an outside observer with perfect information. In addition, it depends on whether we analyse only the guilder price of the item or also consider the other monetary costs, time, cognitive activity, and behaviour effort involved

Summary

This chapter presented an overview of pricing decisions and consumer behaviour. Initially the chapter focused on developing a conceptual framework for considering pricing decisions that included discussion of four types of consumer costs – money, time, cognitive activity, and behaviour effort. These elements, when coupled with value, provide a framework for examining price from the consumer's point of view. Next affect and cognitions, behaviours, and environmental factors relative to price were discussed. The cognitive factors examined included price perceptions and attitudes, and the behaviours described included funds access and transactions. The discussion of the environment focused on price information. Finally, a pricing strategy model was developed for use in pricing new products or for making price-change decisions.

Key Terms and Concepts

external reference price   404
internal reference price   401
penetration price policy   408
skimming price policy   408
unit price   404

Review and Discussion Questions

1. Define price and explain the differences between price strategy and other elements of the marketing mix.
2. In what situations are consumers willing to pay a higher monetary cost to save time, cognitive activity, and behaviour effort?
3. Use the Wheel of Consumer Analysis to identify the interactions associated with consumer response to a credit-card pricing strategy.
4. How can price be used to position a product like T-shirts or luggage?
5. Explain how consumers determine that a particular price is too high. Use

the conceptual model of cognitive processing (Exhibit 19.3) to structure your answer.

6. Offer alternative behaviour views of consumer response that could explain the response to price in Question 5 above.

7. Could a marketing manager change price perceptions with strategies aimed at funds access and transaction behaviours? Explain and give examples.

8. Analyse consumer costs associated with the purchase of car insurance or airline tickets. What are some of the strategy implications suggested by your analysis?

Additional Reading

For a thorough treatment of price behaviour and pricing strategy, see:

Hermann Simon, *Price Strategy and Price Management* (New York, NY: Wiley, 1989).

For a review of research on pricing, see:

Els Gijsbrechts, 'Prices and Pricing Research in Consumer Marketing: Some Recent Developments', *International Journal of Research in Marketing*, 2, 1993, pp. 115–153.

For a study on the extent of consumer price knowledge, see:

Siegfried Müller and Joachim Hoenig, 'Die Preisbeachtung in einer realen Kaufsituation', *Jahrbuch der Absatz- und Verbrauchsforschung*, 20, no. 4, 1983, pp. 321–343.

For research on price elasticity, see:

Albert C. Bemmaor and Dominique Mouchoux, 'Measuring the Short-Term Effect of In-Store Promotion and Retail Advertising on Brand Sales: A Factorial Experiment', *Journal of Marketing Research*, May 1991, pp. 202–214.

Philip M. Parker, 'Price Elasticity Dynamics over the Adoption Life Cycle', *Journal of Marketing Research*, August 1992, pp. 358–367.

Raj Sethuraman and Gerard J. Tellis, 'An Analysis of the Tradeoff between Advertising and Price Discounting', *Journal of Marketing Research*, May 1991, pp. 160–174.

For additional discussion and research on reference prices, see:

Dhruv Grewal and Julie Baker, 'Do Retail Store Environment Factors Affect Consumers' Price Acceptability? An Empirical Examination', *International Journal of Research in Marketing*, 2, 1994, pp. 107–117.

Manohar U. Kalwani, Chi Kin Yim, Heikki J. Rinne, and Yoshi Sugita, 'A Price Expectations Model of Customer Brand Choice', *Journal of Marketing Research*, August 1990, pp. 251–262.

Donald R. Lichtenstein and William O. Bearden, 'Contextual Influences on Perceptions of Merchant-Supplied Reference Prices', *Journal of Consumer Research*, June 1989, pp. 55–66.

K. N. Rajendran and Gerard J. Tellis, 'Contextual and Temporal Components of Reference Price', *Journal of Marketing*, January 1994, pp. 22–34.

Joel E. Urbay and Peter R. Dickson, 'Consumer Normal Price Estimation: Market versus Personal Standards', *Journal of Consumer Research*, June 1991, pp. 45–51.

For research and discussion of price/quality relationships, see:

Donald R. Lichtenstein and Scot Burton, 'The Relationship between Perceived and Objective Price-Quality', *Journal of Marketing Research*, November 1989, pp. 429–443.

Akshay R. Rao and Kent B. Monroe, 'The Effect of Price, Brand Name, and Store Name on Buyer's Perceptions of Product Quality: An Integrative Review', *Journal of Marketing Research*, August 1989, pp. 351–357.

Akshay R. Rao and Mark E. Bergen, 'Price Premium Variations as a Consequence of Buyers' Lack of Information', *Journal of Consumer Research*, December 1992, pp. 412–423.

Gerard J. Tellis and Gary J. Gaeth, 'Best Value, Price-Seeking, and Price Aversion: The Impact of Information and Learning on Consumer Choices', *Journal of Marketing*, April 1990, pp. 34–45.

For a discussion of consumer price awareness from a public policy viewpoint, see:

Klaus G. Grunert, 'Price Transparency, Competition and the Consumer Interest. Economic Reasoning and Behavioral Evidence', in *Price Information and Public Price Controls, Consumers and Market Performance*, ed. Monique Goyens (Brussels: E. Story-Scientia, 1986), pp. 23–48.

MARKETING STRATEGY IN ACTION
Lunch at Cave

ituated in one of London's poshest areas, on the corner of Piccadilly and St James Street, Cave is an exclusive restaurant and caviar bar. It is owned and managed by the same team operating Caviar House, a successful chain of shops selling caviar and other gourmet foods in airports. The restaurant, with its blue and golden/beige colours, has recently been redecorated at a cost of £2.5 million. Shells, conchs, pebbles, and tiles emphasize the soft maritime look, and one wall in the shop is decorated with a mosaic of a sturgeon, the origin of the expensive caviar eggs. The design and surroundings mean a great deal, the owner admits, but not without good-quality food, the hallmark of Cave. Although a two-course lunch can cost you less than £20 at Cave, a couple recently came in from the street and spent £1000 on lunch in the restaurant and afterwards the same amount on the most expensive caviar in the shop: Almas, an albino caviar of which only 10–12 pounds is fished a year and which is priced at £7500 per pound.

Celebrities such as Rod Stewart, Dennis Hopper, Steven Spielberg, and well-known faces from the media and fashion world often visit the restaurant. Even members of the British royal family visit the restaurant – all are people who attract more customers.

Discussion Questions

1. Why do some customers pay up to £1000 for lunch at Cave when they could have lunch much more cheaply?
2. Analyse consumers' motives for having lunch at Cave in terms of overall costs and overall benefits (value).
3. Which role does price pay in Cave's marketing strategy? Analyse how price interacts with the other marketing parameters in Cave's strategy.

Source: Adapted from Poul Arnedal 'Det er dansk og det er typisk London', *Indenrigsmagasinet*, 6, 1997, pp. 24–27.

CHAPTER 20

Consumer Behaviour
and Channel Strategy

**Easy
Shopping**

amily structures have changed, both parents are working full time and it is difficult to find time for all the domestic practicalities – shopping, cooking, cleaning – and still have a few hours left for the family to be together. Supermarkets have generally increased in size and are located in shopping centres on the outskirts of towns, which means that shopping takes a much longer time. If the family only needs a litre of milk and some bread, they feel they waste a lot of time going to the supermarket. Petrol companies have spotted this development and are using their petrol stations for retailing convenience goods. The stations have long opening hours, which means families rushing home or young people who often don't plan their shopping can buy convenience goods at almost any time during the day.

Shell is introducing Select Shops in many of its petrol stations. The shops carry more than 2000 different convenience goods, ranging from fresh dairy products and freshly baked bread and pastry all day to deep-frozen goods. It has always been more expensive to buy convenience goods in the petrol station shops. But now Statoil argues that its prices for convenience goods are the same as supermarket prices. Advertising for the new 'convenience shops' primarily emphasizes the increased range of products and the time saved.

Source: Homepages, www.shell.dk;
www.statoil.dk

From an economic perspective, channels of distribution are thought of as providing form, time, place, and possession utilities for consumers. **Form utility** means channels convert raw materials into finished goods and services in forms the consumer seeks to purchase. **Time utility** means channels make goods and services available when the consumer wants to purchase them. **Place utility** means goods and services are made available *where* the consumer wants to purchase them. **Possession utility** means channels facilitate the transfer of ownership of goods to the consumer.

While this view of channels is useful, it perhaps understates their role in our society. For most manufacturers of consumer goods, retailers, not consumers, are their main customers. Manufacturers first have to convince retailers that their products are worth carrying, before consumers get a chance to try them. And for many manufacturers, retailers are not only customers and channels of distribution, but also partners in developing products that will appeal to consumers. Many retailers have their own

EXHIBIT 20.1

The Wheel of Consumer Analysis: Channel Strategy Issues

brands these days, and retailers actively approach manufacturers with a view to developing the kinds of products they would like to have.

From the consumer's point of view, the choice of store is often the more consequential decision than the choice of a product. Since consumers buy many products and therefore have to bundle purchases, the choice of the right store will often be a major constraint for the type of product choices which can be made. We can think of many cases where the choice of store is a much more involving decision for consumers than choice of a product.

In this chapter, we focus on the relationships among consumer affect, cognitions, behaviours, and environments at the retail level. We concentrate on store retailing, although other forms of retailing like mail-order sales and shopping by the Internet will also be mentioned.

Exhibit 20.1 provides a model of the issues addressed in this chapter. We begin by discussing store-related cues in the consumer environment, then discuss store-related affect, cognitions, and behaviours, and then turn to issues in channel strategy development.

Store Environment

As we noted previously, retail stores are relatively closed environments that can exert a significant impact on consumer affect, cognitions, and behaviour. In this section, we consider three major decision areas in designing effective store environments: store location, store layout, and in-store stimuli.

Store Location

Although not part of the internal environment of a store, **store location** is a critical aspect of channel strategy. Good locations allow ready access, can attract large numbers of consumers, and can significantly alter consumer shopping and purchasing patterns. As retail outlets with very similar product offerings proliferate, even slight differences in location can have a significant impact on market share and profitability. In addition, store location decisions represent long-term financial commitments, and changing poor locations can be difficult and costly.

Research on retail location has been dominated by a regional urban economics approach rather than a behavioural approach. Thus, many of the assumptions on which the models are based offer poor descriptions of consumer behaviour. For example, these approaches generally assume that consumers make single-purpose shopping trips from a fixed origin. Considerable behavioural research suggests, however, that 50–60 per cent of all shopping trips are multipurpose, and that consumers combine shopping trips with other purposes, like travelling to and from work or collecting children from school or from kindergarten.[1] Also, we know from the discussion in the previous chapter that time used for transportation may or may not be a cost; at least driving to a shop during rush hour is probably more of a time cost to the consumer than driving to a factory outlet on a sunny Saturday morning.

The regional models also assume consumers have equal levels of knowledge about different stores, and they often ignore the impact of store advertising and promotion on consumers. Although recent work has begun to integrate behavioural variables such as store image into location models, the models still place primary emphasis on economic variables and assumptions and on predicting rather than describing consumer behaviour. Consumers are considered primarily in terms of demographic and socio-economic variables and in terms of traffic patterns and distances to various locations. Despite these criticisms, many retail location models are quite sophisticated and can deal with a variety of criteria.[2]

Store Layout

Store layout can have important effects on consumers. At a basic level the layout influences such factors as how long the consumer stays in the store, how many products the consumer comes into visual contact with, and what routes the consumer travels within the store. Such factors may affect what and how many purchases are made. There are many types and variations of store layouts; two basic types are grid and free-flow.

Exhibit 20.2 presents an example of a **grid layout** common in many grocery stores.[3] In a grid, all counters and fixtures are at right angles to each other and resemble a maze, with merchandise counters acting as barriers to traffic flow. The grid layout in a supermarket forces customers to the sides and back of the store where items such as produce, meat, and dairy products are located. In fact, 80–90 per cent of all consumers shopping in supermarkets pass these three counters.

In a supermarket, such a layout is designed to increase the number of products a consumer comes into visual contact with, thus increasing the probability of purchase. In addition, because produce, meat, and dairy products are typically high-margin items, the grid design can help channel consumers towards these more profitable products.

EXHIBIT 20.2

Basic Store Layout

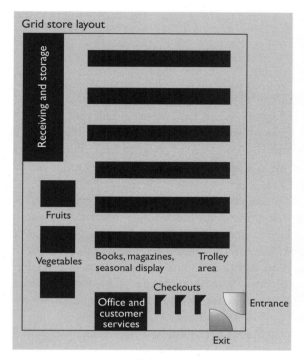
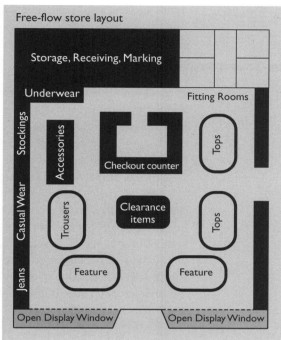

Source: Reprinted from Michael Levy and Barton A. Weitz, *Retailing Management*, 3rd edn., 1998, Irwin/McGraw-Hill, pp. 545, 547. Reproduced with permission of The McGraw-Hill Companies, Inc.

Similarly, the location of frequently purchased items towards the back of the store requires consumers, who may be shopping only for these items, to pass many other items. Because the probability of purchasing other items is increased once the consumer is in visual contact with them, the grid layout can be very effective in increasing the number of items purchased.

The grid layout is sometimes also used in department and speciality stores to direct customer traffic down the main aisles. Typically, these retailers put highly sought merchandise along the walls to pull customers past other slow-moving merchandise areas. For example, sale merchandise may be placed along the walls not only to draw consumers to these areas, but also to reward consumers for spending more time in the store and shopping carefully. This may increase the probability of consumers returning to the store and following similar traffic patterns on repeat visits. Expensive items can be placed along the main aisles to facilitate purchases by less price-sensitive consumers.

Exhibit 20.2 also presents an example of a **free-flow layout**. The merchandise and fixtures are grouped into patterns that allow unstructured flow of customer traffic. Merchandise is divided on the basis of fixtures and signs, and customers can come into visual contact with all departments from any point in the store. A free-flow arrangement is often used in speciality stores, boutiques, and clothing stores. This arrangement is particularly useful for encouraging relaxed shopping and impulse purchases.

It may also be useful for helping store salespeople to move consumers to several different types of merchandise. For example, it may aid in selling a collection of different items, such as a suit, shirt, tie, and shoes in a clothing store, thus increasing the total sale.

In-Store Stimuli

In most environments an endless number of stimuli can influence affect, cognitions, and behaviour. A retail store is no exception. Stores have many stimuli that influence consumers: the characteristics of other shoppers and salespeople, lighting, noises, smells, temperature, shelf space and displays, signs, colours, and merchandise. Highlight 20.1 gives an example of an in-store stimulus that takes advantage of the time the consumer spends queuing.

Although the effects of some in-store stimuli have been studied extensively, much of this research is proprietary, and is not available in the marketing or consumer research literature because it has been conducted by firms seeking a differential advantage over competitors. Much of the research available in the literature is dated and of questionable validity in today's marketplace. In addition, in the research that is available, the results are seldom consistent. Differences in findings are often attributable to methodological issues, but we believe effects are highly situation specific and no single in-store tactic should be expected to be effective in all cases.

With these caveats, we turn to some of the research findings concerning the effects of in-store stimuli on consumer affect, cognitions, and behaviour.

In-store signs are useful for directing consumers to particular merchandise and for offering product benefit and price information. McKinnon, Kelly, and Robison conducted an experiment that investigated the use of signs, the type of message included on the sign (price-only or product-benefit statements), and the effects of a regular versus a sale price being included on the sign.[4] Based on statistical analysis of these sales differences, the following conclusions were drawn:

HIGHLIGHT 20.1

In-Store TV

O ne of Denmark's large retail chains has only recently started using television as an in-store medium. The advantage for advertisers is that consumers are influenced by the programme on the screen while queuing, the programme being a mixture of still pictures and news spots – e.g. during the summer, from the Tour de France. The space can be sold to 23–24 companies who buy 7 seconds that are shown 18 times an hour. The commercials are sent via modem to the stores and can therefore be updated continuously which means a newspaper can change its message every day, corresponding to a new front page.

Source: Per Raahauge, 'Stor fremgang for nyt butiksmedie', *Markedsføring*, 15, 1997, p. 30.

1. Price influences sales more than sign type.
2. At regular prices, the addition of a price sign will not increase sales, but when the item is on sale, a price sign will increase sales.
3. Benefit signs increase sales at both regular and sale prices, but at a greater rate when the item is on sale.
4. A benefit sign is more effective than a price-only sign at both a regular and a sale price.

Overall, these results suggest that at regular prices, a benefit sign should be the only type of sign used, while at a sale price, both a price-only and a benefit sign will increase sales over a no-sign condition, with a benefit sign being the most effective. Thus, these results support the idea that signs affect consumer cognitions (consumers apparently processed different sign information) and consumer behaviour (sales increased with the use of certain types of signs).

Colour has been shown to have a variety of physical and psychological effects on both humans and animals. Bellizzi, Crowley, and Hasty examined the effects of colour on consumer perceptions of retail store environments in a laboratory experiment.[5] An interesting finding was that consumers were drawn to warm colours (red and yellow), but felt that warm-colour environments were generally unpleasant; cool colours (blue and green) did not draw consumers, but were rated as pleasant. The authors concluded that warm-colour environments are appropriate for store windows and entrances, as well as for buying situations associated with unplanned impulse purchases. Cool colours may be appropriate where customer deliberations over the purchase decision are necessary. Warm, tense colours in situations where deliberations are common may make shopping unpleasant for consumers and may result in premature termination of the shopping trip. On the other hand, warm colours may produce a quick decision to purchase in cases where lengthy deliberations are not necessary and impulse purchases are common.

Research generally supports the idea that more shelf space and in-store displays increase sales. Wilkinson, Mason, and Paksoy examined the impact of these two variables on sales of four grocery products in an in-store experiment.[6] Comparisons were made between normal display (regular shelf space), expanded display (double the regular shelf space allocation), and special display (regular shelf space plus special end-of-aisle or within-aisle product arrangement). While the percentage increases varied by product, as would be expected, both extended and special displays consistently increased sales for all of the products. Further, special displays consistently outperformed expanded shelf spaces. These results support the idea that the presentation of merchandise in the store has an important impact on consumer behaviour. Highlight 20.2 mentions some additional aspects of shelf space.

Considerable research supports the idea that music played in the background while other activities are being performed affects attitudes and behaviour. Music is played in many retail stores, but relatively little basic research has been conducted on its effects on consumer behaviour. Milliman examined the effects of one aspect of music – tempo – on the behaviour of supermarket shoppers.[7] Three treatments were used: no music, slow music, and fast music. The basic hypotheses investigated were that these treatments would differentially affect (1) the pace of in-store traffic flow of supermarket shoppers, (2) the daily gross volume of customer purchases, and (3) the number of supermarket shoppers expressing an awareness of the background music after they left the store.

HIGHLIGHT 20.2

The Shelf Space Battle

I t makes a difference whether a particular product is placed at eye or knee level. The goods shelved correctly are easily seen and are often the most purchased. Shelving is so important that manufacturers are willing to 'pay' quite a lot for the right space. They 'pay' by advertising in the retailer's circular, supplying the retailer with store decoration, and running expensive campaigns for the retailer. New products and small manufacturers are having a hard time getting a foot in the door, as retailers only have limited shelf space. Competition is so fierce that producers who cannot afford to 'buy' shelf space end up as the losers in the battle, while the large brands and the supermarkets' own label products are the victorious.

Source: Lise K. Lauridsen, 'Kampen om hyldepladsen', *Berlingske Tidende*, 17 September 1997.

The findings supported the idea that the tempo of background music affects consumer behaviour. The pace of in-store traffic flow was slowest under the slow-tempo treatment and fastest under the fast-tempo treatment. Further, the slow-tempo musical selections led to higher sales volumes, because consumers spent more time and money under this condition. On average, sales were 38.2 per cent greater under the slow-tempo condition than under the fast-tempo condition. Interestingly, when questioned after shopping, consumers showed little awareness of the music that had been playing in the supermarket. Thus, it seems likely that music affected behaviour without consumers being totally conscious of it.

Scents can also influence consumer cognition, affect, and behaviour in stores. For example, the smell of particular products, such as leather goods, perfume, chocolate, coffee, or flowers could attract consumers to come into contact and purchase these products. In addition, *ambient scent* – scent that is not emanating from a particular product but is present in the store environment – can influence store and product evaluations and shopping behaviour.[8] Ambient scent can influence feelings about stores and the products in them, including products that are difficult to scent such as office supplies and furniture. Scents vary in terms of how pleasant they are perceived to be, how likely they are to evoke physiological responses, and how strong they are. Neutral and pleasant scent categories, such as florals, spices, woods, citrus, and mints, can be diffused in a store to influence consumers.

A study by Spangenberg, Crowley, and Henderson found that in a simulated store environment, lavender, ginger, spearmint, and orange scents influence the evaluations of both the store and the products in it and shopping behaviours compared to a no-scent environment. The differences were observed even though there were no other changes in the environment and none of the participants mentioned the presence of a scent. The authors recommend that marketers use distinctive scents in their stores to differentiate them from competitors. In addition, stores should be scented so that the odour is not specific to any single product category. Finally, the authors point out that since many commercially available scenting oils are prohibitively expensive, marketers could use less costly scents that can be spread by a diffuser or through the heating and ventilation systems.

Store-Related Affect and Cognitions

We will deal with three elements of store-related affect and cognition: *store image*, *store atmosphere*, and *shopping motives*.

Store Image

For our purposes, we will treat **store image** as consumers' *cognitive structure* concerning a particular store, and the attitudes towards the store they derive from that. Operationally, store image is commonly assessed by asking consumers how good or how important various aspects of a retail store's operation are. Commonly studied dimensions of store image are such things as merchandise, service, clientele, physical facilities, and convenience. Often store atmosphere is also included as part of store image. Store image research then involves polling consumers concerning their perceptions of and attitudes about particular store dimensions. Typically, these dimensions are broken into a number of store attributes. For example, the merchandise dimension might be studied in terms of quality, assortment, fashion, guarantees, and pricing. The service dimension might be studied in terms of general service, sales staff service, degree of self-service, ease of merchandise return, and delivery and credit services. Often the same attributes will be studied for competitive stores to compare the strengths and weaknesses of a particular store's image with that of its closest competitors. Based on this research, store management may then change certain attributes of the store to develop a more favourable image.

   Much of the theory about consumers' cognitive structures and attitude formation processes discussed in earlier chapters in this text could be employed to develop a better understanding of consumers' store image, although only few attempts have been reported in the literature. As one example, Thelen and Woodside have investigated the associations between store names and store attributes which consumers automatically generate when prompted to think about a typical shopping situation.[9] They found that their most preferred store choice was related to associating this store to attributes such as closest to home, lowest prices, best quality of meat, friendliest personnel, largest parking area, etc. Measuring consumers' associations with stores in this way gives insight into the relative positioning of stores in the consumer mind.

Store Atmosphere

The way in which **store atmosphere** affects consumers' affective and behavioural responses is often analysed in terms of the environmental psychology model depicted in Exhibit 20.3.[10] The store environment is characterized by two dimensions: sense modality variables, which deal with elements like colour and temperature, and information rate. **Information rate** characterizes the quantity of information drawn from the store environment per unit of time. Thus, the more varied, novel, surprising, and lively the shopping environment, the higher the information rate. The information rate can therefore be used as a summary measure of various elements of the store

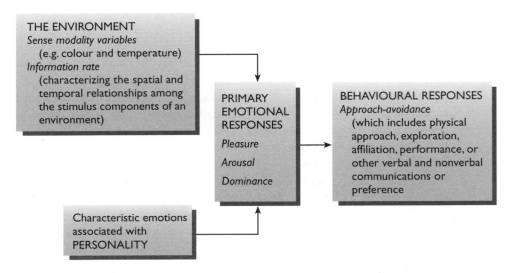

EXHIBIT 20.3

The Environmental Psychology Approach to Analysing Store Atmosphere

Source: A. Mehrabian and J.A. Russell, *An Approach to Environmental Psychology*
(Cambridge, MA: MIT Press, 1974), p. 8.

environment. Consumer reactions to the store environment depend on the consumers' personality, which is characterized on three dimensions:

1. Hedonistic or pleasure oriented.
2. Dominant as opposed to servile or obsequious.
3. Receptive to environmental stimuli.

Store environment and personality together determine the consumers' emotional responses to the store environment, which can be described in terms of pleasure, arousal, and dominance. Pleasure refers to the degree to which the consumer feels good, joyful, happy, or satisfied in the store; arousal refers to the degree to which the consumer feels excited, stimulated, alert, or active in the store; and dominance refers to the extent to which the consumer feels in control of or free to act in the store. Finally, the emotional responses lead to behavioural responses analysed as approach and avoidance behaviours. *Approach behaviours* refer to moving towards and *avoidance behaviours* refer to moving away from various environments and stimuli. Four types of approach or avoidance behaviours are related to retail stores:

1. *Physical* approach and avoidance, which can be related to store patronage intentions at a basic level.
2. *Exploratory* approach and avoidance, which can be related to in-store search and exposure to a broad or narrow range of offerings.

3. *Communication* approach and avoidance, which can be related to interactions with sales personnel and floor staff.

4. *Performance and satisfaction* approach and avoidance, which can be related to frequency of repeat shopping as well as reinforcement of time and money expenditures in the store.

Several studies have been reported employing this general framework. Donovan and Rossiter investigated the relationships between the three types of emotional responses (pleasure, arousal, and dominance) and stated intentions to perform certain store-related behaviours.[11] The study was conducted in 11 different types of retail outlet, including department, clothing, shoe, hardware, and sporting goods stores. They found that store-induced *pleasure* is a very powerful determinant of approach-avoidance behaviours within the store, including spending behaviour. Further, their research suggests *arousal*, or store-induced feelings of alertness or excitement, can increase time spent in the store as well as willingness to interact with sales personnel. However, the inducement of arousal works positively only in store environments that are already pleasant; arousal may have no influence, or even a negative influence, in unpleasant store environments. Overall, pleasure and arousal influenced consumers' stated (1) enjoyment of shopping in the store, (2) time spent browsing and exploring the store's offerings, (3) willingness to talk to sales personnel, (4) tendency to spend more money than originally planned, and (5) likelihood of returning to the store. The third emotional dimension, *dominance*, or the extent to which consumers feel in control of or free to act in the store, was found to have little effect on consumer behaviours in the retail environment.

Similar effects have been found in other studies. In a study of German self-service department stores Bost[12] found that a positive emotional response leads to more unplanned purchases, faster buying decisions, and more money spent. In a study comparing two IKEA stores in Germany, Spies *et al.*[13] found that positive emotional response leads to more satisfaction with the shopping trip, more time spent in the shop, and more money spent on spontaneous purchases, even though the overall amount spent was not affected.

Gröppel and Bloch[14] argue that based on the personality variables in Exhibit 20.3, one can distinguish a segment of sensualistic consumers, who score high on pleasure orientation and receptiveness. These consumers would be those who respond more favourably to store environments with high information rates. They grouped fashion shoppers into three clusters based on a number of lifestyle and shopping behaviour dimensions and found that one of the groups obtained corresponded well to the notion of a sensualist consumer. The two other groups they named the 'indolent buyers' and the 'young extremists.' The indolent buyers have basically no interest in shopping and are more inward oriented in their leisure activities. The young extremists have a more selective approach to shopping; they seem to enjoy certain elements of shopping, but, for example, they strongly reject being approached by a salesperson.

In their study, Gröppel and Bloch found that the group of sensualist consumers perceive the information rate of the store to be higher, and they also evaluate the store more favourably with regard to emotional characteristics, merchandise, and value for money than the two other groups. The authors stress the importance of creating stores which are full of life and surprises when catering for the sensualist consumer.

A positive impact of the information rate on consumers' emotional responses in a

EXHIBIT 20.4

Shopping Motives and Evaluation of Furniture Retail Categories

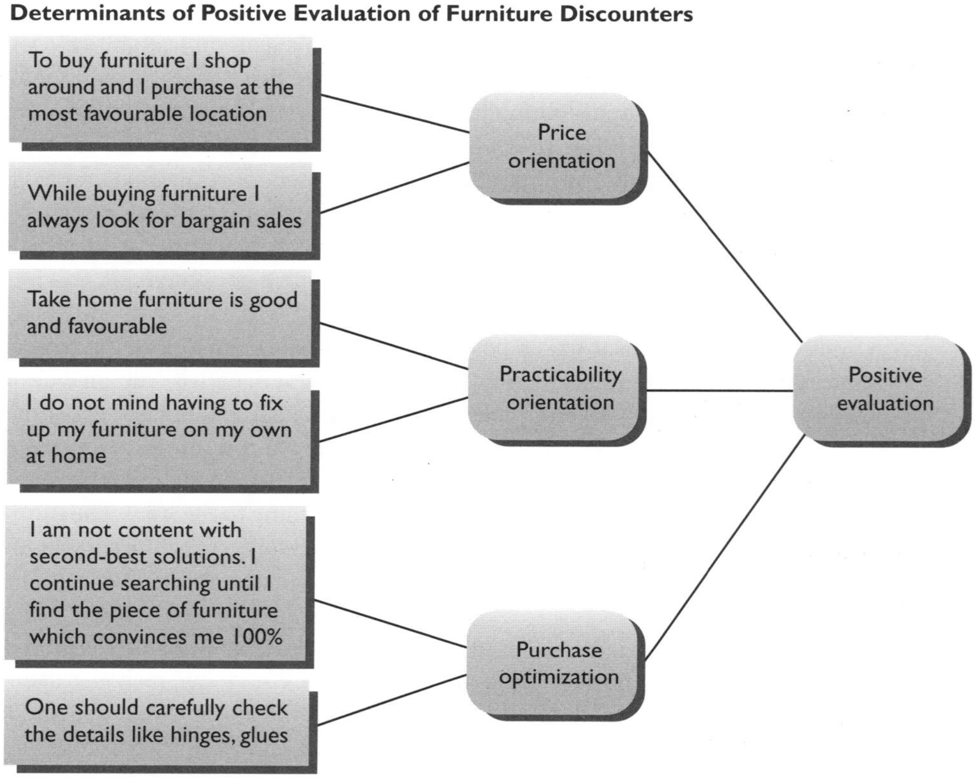

Determinants of Positive Evaluation of Furniture Discounters

To buy furniture I shop around and I purchase at the most favourable location		
While buying furniture I always look for bargain sales	Price orientation	
Take home furniture is good and favourable		Positive evaluation
I do not mind having to fix up my furniture on my own at home	Practicability orientation	
I am not content with second-best solutions. I continue searching until I find the piece of furniture which convinces me 100%		
One should carefully check the details like hinges, glues	Purchase optimization	

shopping environment has also been documented in other studies. Studies by Bost[15] and Spies *et al.*[16] have also added other dimensions to the variables characterizing the store environment, notably ease of orientation, i.e. a clear and easy to understand structuring of the store. This also had a positive impact on consumers' emotional responses. The result is interesting, because it shows that attempts to raise the information rate – by novel and unusual store environments – should preferably not be at the expense of ease of orientation in the shop.

Shopping Motives

Just as different products are chosen by consumers because they believe that their attributes will lead to different self-relevant consequences and ultimately values, different retail categories can be assumed to be chosen by consumers because of different **shopping motives**. In the previous section we linked consumers' liking or nonliking of experience-oriented stores to basic personality variables such as

EXHIBIT 20.4 (cont.)

Determinants of Positive Evaluation of Specialist Furniture Retailer

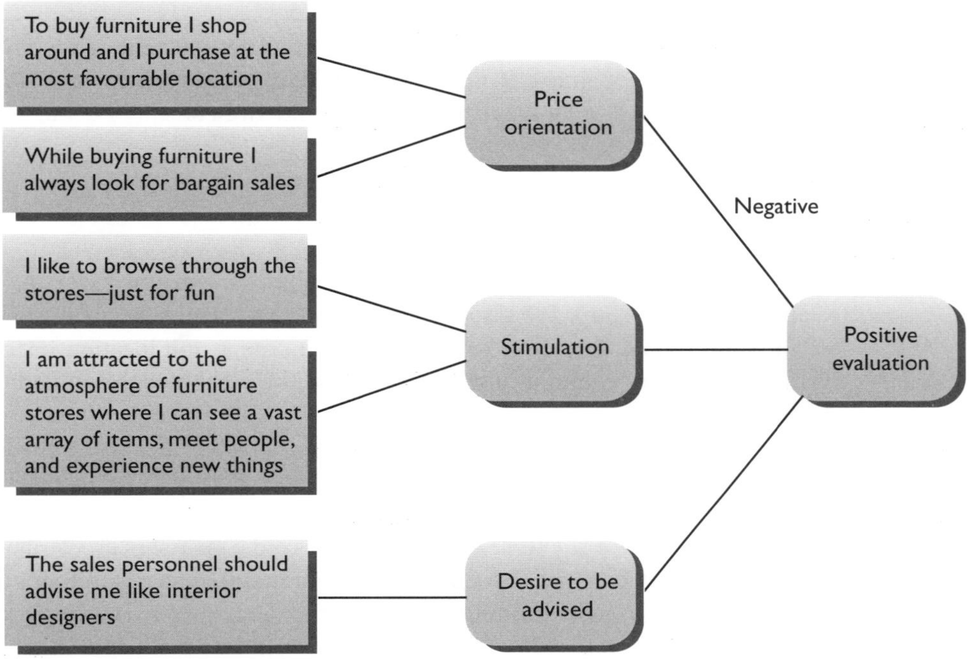

Source: Adapted from Andrea Gröppel, 'Evolution of Retail Categories – An Explanation
from Consumers' Point of View', in *European Advances in Consumer Research*, vol. 2,
ed. Flemming Hansen (Provo, UT: Association for Consumer Research, 1995), p. 242.

receptiveness or hedonistic orientation, but it makes just as much sense to assume that the same consumer will be attracted by different types of shops depending on the motives associated with the purchase.

For example, when consumers are not involved with a purchase, because the product has low self-relevance, there are few perceived quality differences, and the price is not high, we can expect that consumers will be mostly interested in getting the purchase made in an efficient way, and will be attracted by shops with easy access, possibility for one-stop shopping, good parking facilities, and easy-to-understand layout. On the other hand, when the purchase is of high personal relevance and there is considerable uncertainty and monetary outlays are high, consumers may be more attracted by outlets which provide information and products in a stimulating, arousing way.

Such differences can be observed even within the same product category. Exhibit 20.4 shows results from a study of German furniture shoppers.[17] It shows that the positive evaluation of furniture discounters as compared to specialist furniture retailers is guided by different shopping motives – specialist shops are attractive when consumers emphasize stimulation and desire to be advised, discount stores when consumers have a practical orientation and emphasize purchase optimization. In both cases price orientation plays a role, but the effect is opposite: being price-oriented favours discounters and disfavours specialist stores.

Store-Related Behaviours

Marketing managers want to encourage many behaviours in the retail environment. Two basic types of behaviour are discussed here: store contact and store loyalty. Highlight 20.3 lists several tactics designed to influence consumer behaviour in retail stores.

Store Contact

As we mentioned in Chapter 11, *store contact* involves the consumer locating, travelling to, and entering a store. We also noted that putting carnivals in car parks, having fashion shows in department stores, and printing maps and location instructions in the *Yellow Pages* are common tactics to increase these behaviours. In addition, other commonly used tactics include promotions and local advertising.

A number of the variables discussed in this chapter are also concerned with obtaining store contacts. For example, store location decisions are strongly influenced by heavy traffic and pedestrian patterns, which facilitate store contact.

Also, the visibility of the store and its distance from consumers are variables used to select locations that can increase store contact. For many small retail chains and stores, selecting locations in the central shopping district of a town or in a shopping centre may greatly increase the probability of consumers coming into contact with them. In fact, one of the major advantages of locating in such areas is the store contact available from

HIGHLIGHT 20.3

Examples of Retail Tactics Used to Influence Consumer Behaviour

Retail Design Element	Specific Example	Intermediate Behaviour	Final Desired Behaviour
Store layout	End of escalator, end of aisle, other displays	Bring customer into visual contact with product	Product purchase
Purchase locations	Purchase possible from home, store location	Product or store contact	Product purchase
In-store mobility	In-store product directories, information booths	Bring consumer into visual contact with product	Product purchase
Noise, odours, lights	Flashing lights in window	Bring consumer into visual or other sensory contact with store or product	Product purchase

pedestrians passing by on their way to another store. From the consumers' viewpoint, such locations can reduce shopping time and effort by allowing a form of one-stop shopping.

Store Loyalty

Most retailers do not want consumers to come to their stores once and never return; rather, repeat patronage is usually desired. **Store loyalty** (repeat patronage intentions and behaviour) can be strongly influenced by the arrangement of the environment, particularly the reinforcing properties of the retail store. For example, the in-store stimuli and the attributes discussed in this chapter in terms of store image and store atmosphere are the primary variables used to influence store loyalty.

Consider one further example of a tactic that may be used to develop store loyalty – in-store unadvertised specials. These specials are often marked with an attention-getting sign. Typically, consumers go to a store to shop for a particular product or just to go shopping. While going through the store, a favourite brand or long-sought-after product the consumer could not afford is found to be an unadvertised special. This could be quite reinforcing and strongly influence the probability of the consumer returning to the same store, perhaps seeking other unadvertised specials. It is quite likely that the consumer would not have to find a suitable unadvertised special on every trip to the store; a variable ratio schedule might well be powerful enough to generate a high degree of store loyalty.

These additional trips to the store allow the consumer to experience other reinforcing properties, such as fast checkout, a pleasant and arousing shop atmosphere, or high-quality merchandise at competitive prices. In sum, reinforcing tactics and positive attributes of the store are used to develop store loyalty.[18]

Nonstore Consumer Behaviour

Over 90 per cent of all consumer purchases are from retail stores. However, there is a variety of other ways consumers shop for and purchase products. These include catalogues and direct mail, vending machines, direct purchases, and electronic exchanges, such as purchasing on the Internet. We refer to the method a consumer uses to shop and purchase from store or nonstore alternatives as the **consumer purchase mode**.

Choices made among the various consumer purchase modes are influenced by many factors. Each may involve different environmental influences and different amounts and types of cognition, affect, and behaviour. Stores have dominated consumer purchases because they allow consumers to shop efficiently, compare product offerings and experience them directly, create affect in-store, and often have lower prices. However, each of the other purchase mode alternatives have advantages in some situations. We will briefly discuss each of the nonstore purchase modes and compare them with store consumer behaviour.

Catalogue and Direct-Mail Purchases

Most consumers are familiar with catalogues and other direct-mail letters and brochures sent to their homes to present merchandise and solicit orders. With the increase in dual-income families and the general need for consumers to save time, catalogues and direct mail have grown dramatically. In addition to offering consumers convenient in-home shopping, many consumers enjoy browsing through catalogues searching for unique items. For example, Paul Schrader, a German mail-order house originally specializing in tea and coffee, has expanded its product line to include items like speciality foods and spirits, silk clothing, exotic tableware, furniture items like a personal bar, and speciality appliances like a tea-brewing alarm clock.

Catalogues, however, have some disadvantages for consumers. First, prices in catalogues are often higher than comparable products in shops and consumers have to pay additional shipping charges. Second, while catalogues can describe merchandise and show pictures of it, this does not allow consumers to experience the feel, fit, or other sensory stimuli directly. Third, while consumers save shopping time using catalogues, they must wait to receive the merchandise until it is shipped and received. When purchasing in shops, consumers can usually take home the products and use them immediately. Finally, if a catalogue purchase is made and found to be unsatisfactory, consumers must repackage the product and return it, often at their own expense.

Vending Machine Purchases

Most vending machine purchases made by consumers are for hot and cold beverages, food, and sweets. Vending machine sales have experienced little growth in recent years. By no means all vending machines take bank notes and few accept credit cards. The primary advantage of vending machines for consumers is that they provide merchandise in convenient locations and are often available for purchases round the clock. However, products in vending machines typically are priced higher than the same merchandise in a shop. Also, when vending machines fail to supply the merchandise, consumers often cannot recover their money. Thus, typically consumers use vending machines rather than shops only for occasional purchases of convenience goods.

Direct-Sales Purchases

Direct-sales purchases are made by consumers in their homes or at work from salespeople in a face-to-face or telephone transaction. The most common products purchased in this way are cosmetics, perfumes, decorative accessories, vacuum cleaners, home appliances, cooking and kitchenware, jewellery, food and nutritional products, and books and educational materials. Consumers can benefit from direct-sales purchases because salespeople can provide in-depth product usage information. For example, Avon salespeople can demonstrate the various uses and shades of cosmetics and match them to the consumer's complexion and facial features. Tupperware salespeople can show how to use various storage containers and kitchen gadgets. Thus, direct-sales purchases benefit consumers when buying products that need demonstration. However, direct-sales merchandise is often higher priced than similar merchandise in stores. Also, consumers often have to spend a good deal of time watching the demonstration and discussing products. Finally, consumers sometimes feel pressured by overzealous salespeople to purchase products they don't really need.

Electronic Exchanges

Electronic exchanges involve consumers collecting information, shopping, and purchasing from web sites on the Internet. It is a fast-growing purchase mode. Many companies are unsure whether electronic commerce will flourish, but want to be on the Internet with an effective web site in case it does. Highlight 20.4 offers recommendations for developing such web sites.

Electronic exchanges offer several advantages for consumers. They allow consumers to purchase from their home or office with minimal behavioural effort. Web sites offer a variety of merchandise, some of which are unique and hard to find. They also offer abundant information for purchasing and can save consumers shopping time relative to comparing products in stores, and as a new purchase mode, they give consumers a chance to demonstrate their innovativeness. However, electronic exchanges do have limitations for consumers. First, the consumers must have access to computers to make

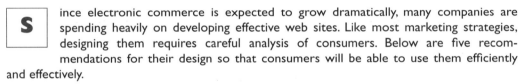

HIGHLIGHT 20.4

Recommendations for Developing Successful Commercial Web Sites

Since electronic commerce is expected to grow dramatically, many companies are spending heavily on developing effective web sites. Like most marketing strategies, designing them requires careful analysis of consumers. Below are five recommendations for their design so that consumers will be able to use them efficiently and effectively.

1. Make sure the site has contact information that is accurate and complete. Many web sites lack basics such as postal address, phone and fax numbers, and e-mail address. Don't hide this stuff five levels deep in a back corner; make it easy to find.
2. Make factual information, such as product updates and prices, easy to find. Someone other than the Webmaster should be responsible for tracking this information and keeping it up to date.
3. Make sure users can find the site with straightforward keywords. Make it simple to find the site via the various search engines. Work on improving the search function on the site itself.
4. Make it just as easy for consumers to exit the site as it is for them to find and use it. The layout and design of the site should be fairly obvious to viewers no matter where they land inside it.
5. Create a good table of contents and index. Most consumers do not want to start at the front door and proceed in an orderly fashion through the entire site. Keep the number of screens and subscreens for contents and site organization down to a bare minimum. Put links both to the table of contents and to an index on the front page so that consumer can find them quickly.

To find more information about site usability, see the *Alertbox* written by Jakob Nielsen of SunSoft (www.useit.com/alertbox) or read *Understanding Electronic Commerce* by David Koisur available through www.Amazon.com.

Sources: Mark Halper, 'So Does Your Web Site Pay?' *Forbes ASASP*, 25 August 1997, pp. 117–118;
David Strom, 'Five Steps for Site Success', *Forbes ASASP*, 25 August 1997, p. 118.

them. Second, consumers need the skills to use computers, access web sites, and make purchases effectively. Third, many consumers are reluctant to make purchases on the Internet because of a fear that their credit-card number will be accessed by hackers, and that the Internet vendor may be unscrupulous. Fourth, while the Internet can provide abundant information, pictures of products are usually of lower quality than catalogues and, of course, it is less appealing than buying from shops. Fifth, consumers have to pay shipping charges and have the hassle of mailing back merchandise that is unwanted or defective.

EXHIBIT 20.5

A Comparison of Five Consumer Purchase Modes

Criteria	Stores	Catalogues/ Direct Mail	Vending Machines	Direct Sales	Electronic Exchanges
Types of products available	All types	Shopping speciality	Convenience	Shopping speciality	All types
Number of products and brands available	Almost all	Some	Few	Few	Many
Potential for status for purchasing from this mode	High	High	None	Moderate	Moderate
Potential for fun	High	Some	Low	Moderate	Moderate
Price level	Mixed	Mixed	High	High	Mixed
Additional shipping/ delivery charges	Seldom	Usually	No	Often	Usually
Return effort	Little	Some	NA	Some	Some
Purchase time required	Moderate	Low	Low	High	Low
Shopping effort	High	Low	Low	Moderate	Low
Wait for delivery	Seldom	Yes	No	Usually	Yes

Source: A. Mehrabian and J. A. Russell, *An Approach to Environmental Psychology* (Cambridge, MA: MIT Press, 1974), p. 8. Copyright: MIT Press, 1974.

A Comparison of Consumer Purchase Modes

Exhibit 20.5 presents a comparison of five consumer purchase modes that can partially account for the relative use of each. Shops dominate consumer purchases because they offer the deepest and widest product assortment. In addition, they offer the greatest potential for fun and status. For example, many consumers enjoy shopping in shops on some occasions. Shops also have the broadest range of prices for most types of merchandise, which gives this purchase mode a selection advantage over nonstore modes. Thus, even though purchasing from stores may take more effort and time in some cases, they continue to dominate consumer retail purchasing.

Catalogues provide consumers with the convenience of shopping from home or work and offer some products and brands not available in shops. However, many products are not available in catalogues.

Vending machines are highly limited in the products offered, but provide consumers with time and place utility for convenience goods. Direct sales offer consumers only a limited number of products, although some are highly respected, such as Tupperware storage containers and Avon cosmetics. However, such purchases often require a good deal of consumers' time, and the same quality goods are available at lower prices from shops.

The growth potential for sales from electronic exchangers could increase as these modes become more interactive. In fact, several experts have argued for interactive shopping systems that have the following characteristics:

1. Faithful reproduction of descriptive and experiential product information.
2. A greatly expanded universe of offerings relative to what can be accessed now through local or catalogue shopping.
3. An efficient means of screening the offerings to find the most appealing options for more detailed considerations.
4. Unimpeded search across shops and brands.
5. Memory for past selections, which simplifies information search and purchase decisions.[19]

While such systems are not currently available, they clearly could give consumers greater convenience and selection than many other purchase modes. As more consumers become familiar with electronic commerce and security problems are solved, interactive home shopping could become a more prominent consumer purchase mode.

Channel Strategy Issues

Marketing managers have many decisions to make in designing effective channels of distribution. For example, decisions must be made as to whether to market directly to the consumer through company-owned or franchised stores or indirectly through combinations of intermediaries such as independent retailers, wholesalers, and agents. Decisions must be made as to whether to use store retailing or nonstore retailing or some combination of the two. Decisions must be made about plant and warehouse locations, how products will be delivered to consumers, and who will perform what marketing functions within the channel.

In some cases, manufacturers market products in their own shops. Many luxury brand manufacturers like Gucci, Armani, Vuitton, or Bang & Olufsen own their own shops, while they also distribute through independent retailers. Other well-known brand names distribute through franchised retail outlets, for example Benetton and McDonald's. However, most manufacturers sell through independent retailers and retail chains.

Selling through independent retailers can lead to a conflict in objectives for the two types of marketing institutions. That is, while manufacturers are concerned with developing consumer brand loyalty (repeated purchase of their brand), retailers are concerned with developing consumer store loyalty (repeated patronage of their stores). For instance, retailers may not be highly concerned with which brand of coffee the consumer buys, as long as it is purchased in their particular stores. This situation has led many manufacturers to put a large portion of their marketing budgets into trade promotions directed at retailers (e.g. 1 case free for every 10 purchased by the retailer). Trade promotions may influence retailers to put up special displays, give more shelf space to a brand, lower prices to consumers, and sponsor local advertising of the brand for the manufacturer. More recently, manufacturers and retailers have also started various forms of cooperation in order to minimize this sort of conflict, for example by joint product development.

Our discussion highlights the fact that different members of a distribution channel may be primarily concerned with influencing different consumer behaviours. Retailers affect consumers most directly, and perhaps most influentially, for many types of products and most services. As a result, in this part of the chapter we view channel strategy from the manufacturer's perspective and consider criteria for selecting channel members, particularly retailers.

As with the other elements of the marketing mix, the starting point for designing effective channels is an analysis of consumer–product relationships. At least six basic questions must be considered:

1. What is the potential annual market demand? That is, given a particular marketing strategy, how many consumers are likely to purchase the product and how often?
2. What is the long-term growth potential of the market?
3. What is the geographic dispersion of the market?
4. What are the most promising geographic markets to enter?
5. Where and how do consumers purchase this and similar types of products?
6. What is the likely impact of a particular channel system on consumers? That is, will the system influence consumer affect, cognitions, and behaviours sufficiently to achieve marketing objectives?

While these questions emphasize that consumers are the focal point in channel design, the answers require an analysis of a variety of other factors. As suggested in Exhibit 20.6, these factors must be analysed both in terms of their relationships with and impact on the consumer and in terms of their relationships with the other variables. We briefly discuss each of these factors, starting with commodity.

Commodity

By *commodity* we mean the nature of the product or service offered to the consumer. Different products and services vary in their tangibility, perishability, bulkiness, degree

EXHIBIT 20.6

Channel Design Criteria

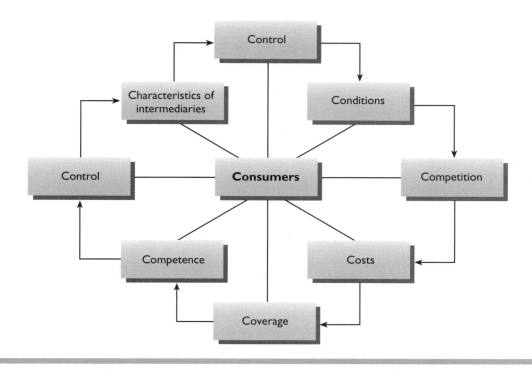

of standardization, amount of service required, and unit value. These factors influence whether it is effective to market the commodity directly to consumers (as with hair-styling services) or indirectly through a number of intermediaries (as with designer jeans).

Key consumer-related questions in considering the nature of the product or service are (1) what consequences or values the product or service provides the target market, (2) how much time and effort target-market consumers are willing to expend to shop for, locate, and purchase the product, and (3) how often target-market consumers purchase the product. Thus, it is the *relationships* among consumers, the commodity, and the channel that are critical, rather than analysis of these factors in isolation.

Conditions

Conditions refer to the current state of and expected changes in the economic, social, political, and legal environments in which the firm operates. This information is critical in channel design because channels typically involve long-term commitments by the firm that may be difficult to change. For example, in many countries regulations limit the proliferation of large hypermarkets outside the cities, based on a political desire to keep the inner cities intact. When firms react to this and invest in inner-city sites, the policy of limiting hypermarkets may change and the investments outside the cities will be devalued.

Competition

The size, financial and marketing strengths, and market share of a firm's competitors are major concerns in designing effective marketing strategies. For channel decisions, a key issue concerns how major competitors distribute products and how their distribution system affects consumers. In some cases, emulating the channels of major competitors in the industry is the only feasible alternative. For example, many convenience goods require intensive distribution to all available retailers.

In other cases, a differential advantage can be obtained by selecting nontraditional channels. For example, one reason for the success of companies such as Tupperware is that they sell their products in homes rather than in traditional retail outlets.

Costs

While channel strategies seek to provide form, time, place, and possession utilities to influence consumer affect, cognitions, and behaviour, these strategies are constrained by the cost of distribution. In general, a basic goal is to design a distribution system that facilitates exchanges between the firm and consumers, but does so in a cost-efficient manner. Distribution costs include transportation, order processing, cost of lost business, inventory carrying costs, and materials handling. Thus, costs can be viewed as a constraint on the firm's ability to distribute products and services and to serve and influence consumers. In general, firms seek distribution systems that minimize total distribution costs at a particular level of customer service.

Coverage

The term *coverage* has two separate meanings in channel strategy. First, there is the idea that seldom can every member of a selected target market receive sufficient marketing coverage to bring about an exchange. Because of cost considerations, even major consumer goods companies often cannot afford to distribute their products in outlets that do not serve a relatively large population.

Second, coverage also refers to the number of outlets in a particular geographic area in which the product or service will be sold. Distribution coverage can be viewed along a continuum ranging from intensive through selective to exclusive distribution. Intensive distribution involves marketing the product in as many outlets as possible, while selective distribution involves a more limited number and exclusive distribution involves only one outlet in an area.

Competence

A frequently overlooked criterion in designing channels is the firm's *competence* to administer the channels and to perform channel tasks at all levels to ensure effective distribution to the consumer. Both financial strength and marketing skills are crucial, but many production-oriented firms seriously underestimate the importance of marketing and overestimate their marketing abilities. Further, many manufacturers do not have a sufficiently large product line to develop their own retail stores. These firms opt for intermediaries such as large department stores.

Critics of marketing frequently point out that marketing intermediaries increase the cost of products because the profits these wholesalers and retailers make add to the cost of the product to the consumer. These critics generally do not understand that intermediaries are used because they can perform some marketing functions more efficiently and cheaply than the manufacturer can.

Control

An important managerial criterion in designing channels is the *degree of control* desired for effective marketing of the product to the consumer. In general, there is greater control in direct channels because no intermediaries are involved. Franchised channels also involve greater control than indirect channels because the franchiser typically places strong contractual constraints on the operations of the franchisee. This control is the more important in delivering the major benefit of the product to the consumer the more the product requires explanation, advice, adaptation to individual needs, and after-sales service.

Characteristics of Intermediaries

A final, but extremely important, consideration in designing channels concerns the characteristics of the intermediaries that are available and willing to handle the manufacturer's product. If no acceptable agents are available, then the firm must either market directly, encourage the development of intermediaries, or forgo entering a particular market.

In addition to such factors as the size, financial strength, and marketing skills of intermediaries, *consumer perceptions* of intermediaries can be crucial in channel strategy. For example, many consumers view discount stores as places to purchase good-quality merchandise, but not necessarily prestige items. Manufacturers of prestige products (such as shirts by Dior) may lower the image of their products by selling them in discount stores. Thus, manufacturers (and retailers) must consider the consumer–store relationships – the relationships among the store environment, consumer affect and cognitions, and consumer behaviours.

**Back to . . .
Easy
Shopping**

Retailing of convenience goods at petrol stations takes advantage of the location and the opening hours of petrol stations and combines it with knowledge about consumer time-use patterns. The range of products carried is the type of con-venience goods many consumers don't enjoy shopping, the type of goods where consumers are not particularly sensualistic, but appreciate least effort solutions.

Summary

This chapter presented an overview of consumer behaviour and channel strategy. An examination of store environment emphasized store location, store layout, and in-store stimuli. Then, consumer store-related affect and cognitions and behaviours were emphasized. The three most critical store-related affect and cognitions for channel strategy are store image, store atmosphere, and shopping motives. The store-related behaviours discussed in this chapter included store contact and store loyalty, both of which are primary objectives of retail channel strategy. We also discussed a variety of consumer purchase modes, with an emphasis on nonstore modes. The final part of this chapter delineated several criteria relevant for designing effective channels. This part of the chapter emphasized that it is the consumer and the relationships the consumer has with the other criteria that determine appropriate channel strategy.

Key Terms and Concepts

consumer purchase mode **427**
form utility **414**
free-flow layout **417**
grid layout **416**
information rate **421**
place utility **414**
possession utility **414**
shopping motives **424**
store atmosphere **421**
store image **421**
store layout **416**
store location **416**
store loyalty **427**
time utility **414**

Review and Discussion Questions

1. Offer examples of situations in which you have experienced each of the four types of approach or avoidance responses to retail store environments.
2. What specific environmental factors account for the difference in atmosphere between eating at a fast food outlet versus eating at a gourmet restaurant?
3. Describe a few shopping situations in which you would prefer a low or a high information rate.
4. Relate the concept of shaping to the store contact and store loyalty concerns in this chapter. Make a series of strategy recommendations to achieve the desired ends.
5. Why do many retailers put impulse goods near the front of the store?
6. Research suggests many consumers make over 80 per cent of their grocery purchase decisions while in the store. What do you think are the most important in-store influences on these purchases? (Examples such as biscuits, apples, yoghurt, or frozen meals could be used to focus your answer.)
7. What are the advantages and disadvantages to the consumer in purchasing from the Internet rather than from a retail store?
8. Identify some of the circumstances in which the desired consumer response guiding channel strategy development would be different for the retailer than for the manufacturer.

Additional Reading

For a thorough study on how various objective characteristics of a shop affect mood and shopping behaviour, see:

Kordelia Spies, Friedrich Hesse, and Kerstin Loesch, 'Store Atmosphere, Mood and Purchasing Behaviour', *International Journal of Research in Marketing*, 1, 1997, pp. 1–18.

For a summary of several studies on store atmosphere, see:

Andrea Gröppel, 'Store Design and Experience-Orientated Consumers in Retailing: A Comparison Between the United States and Germany', in *European Advances in Consumer Research*, vol. 1, eds. Gary J. Bamossy and Fred van Raaij (Provo, UT: Association for Consumer Research, 1993), pp. 99–109.

For further discussion of the effects of several cognitive factors on shopping intentions, see:

William R. Swinyard, 'The Effects of Mood, Involvement, and Quality of Store Experience on Shopping Intentions', *Journal of Consumer Research*, September 1993, pp. 271–280.

For further discussion of retail location strategy, see:

Avijit Ghosh and C. Samuel Craig, 'Formulating Retail Location Strategy in a Changing Environment', *Journal of Marketing*, Summer 1983, pp. 56–68.

For a key success factor approach to the study of consumer satisfaction with retailers, see:

Lutz Hildebrandt, 'Store Image and the Prediction of Performance in Retailing', *Journal of Business Research*, 1988, pp. 91–100.

For further discussion of the effects of environmental factors on consumer shopping, see:

Easwar S. Iyer, 'Unplanned Purchasing: Knowledge of Shopping Environment and Time Pressure', *Journal of Retailing*, Spring 1989, pp. 40–57.

C. Whan Park, Easwar S. Iyer, and Daniel C. Smith, 'The Effects of Situational Factors on In-Store Grocery Shopping Behaviour: The Role of Store Environment and Time Available for Shopping', *Journal of Consumer Research*, March 1989, pp. 422–433.

MARKETING STRATEGY IN ACTION

Netto

iscount stores have been a common sight in most European countries for more than a decade. They abandoned interior decoration of the stores and personal service in favour of low prices – between 15 and 20 per cent lower than prices in conventional supermarkets. Goods are placed on the shelves in the packaging they are delivered in, and tags on the shelves show the prices, which means that no time is spent pricing the goods individually. Discount stores primarily aim at retailing ordinary consumer goods that are sold in large quantities and therefore have high inventory turnover.

Netto, a Danish chain of discount stores also found in Germany and the United Kingdom, has developed a distinct kind of discount store where in addition to the range of low-priced regular products they have a number of products which are 'this week's specials'. These products are advertised in a weekly full-colour advertising circular sent out to 2.2 million households in Denmark. The circulars are built up around a theme: e.g. Italian, Mexican, or Asian week, where a majority of a week's products has something to do with the theme or country. They are either produced in the country or used in typical local cooking, and the circular usually contains a recipe where a number of the goods advertised are used as ingredients. Some of these weekly products are of a kind usually found in specialist shops, which gives Netto a peculiar image as a place where you can buy specialities at discount prices.

Netto is not reserved for the poor – everyone shops in Netto, even the rich. As an upper-class customer puts it in one of Netto's distinct black-and-white commercials where ordinary Netto customers explain why they shop in Netto: 'I shop in Netto, here I meet all my friends from the golf club'.

Netto has also expanded abroad. Since 1990 Netto has opened more than 100 stores in the United Kingdom and Germany, and has recently opened stores in Poland.

Discussion Questions

1. Try to adopt the perspective of a Netto manager and describe the kind of store image you would like to create.
2. Which kind of in-store stimuli would you choose to support the desired store image?
3. Netto tries to position itself as a different kind of discount shop. Discuss the potentials and dangers of such a strategy.

Source: Vibeke Vestergård, 'Mr. Discount', *Børsens Nyhedsmagasin*, 9, no. 13, 1993, pp. 68–71; Jacob Groes, 'Discount-kvælertag på supermarkeder', *Børsens Nyhedsmagasin*, 11, no. 20, 1995, pp 40–42; Finn Graversen, 'Discountkæden der ikke ville være discountkæde', *Børsen*, 20 May 1996.

Marketer Power
and Consumer Power

**Who Wants
to Eat
Modified
Genes?**

D eveloping beets that are resistant towards a specific weed-killer or potatoes that are resistant towards a virus may sound like a reasonably intelligent and desirable development. However, when the term *genetic engineering* is mentioned the mood changes – many people are fiercely against genetic modification of food products, and discussions are flying around in Europe concerning the use of the technology. What will really happen when products that are resistant to antibiotics are consumed by humans? Do we become resistant, too, and end up dying of a virus that could easily have been treated with antibiotics? Or is this situation a sign of hysteria, and are genetically modified products indeed the best way of securing sounder production where less herbicides/weed-killers are used?

In 1997, The Commission of the European Union decided that genetically modified food products can be sold in all member states. Consumer organizations have demanded that the modified products be marked, so that consumers can detect them in a purchase situation and decide not to buy them should they so wish. The European Union has therefore decided that all products which contain, or

may contain, genetically modified ingredients must be marked. There are three different markings: 'Does not contain', 'Contains' and 'May contain'. The debate continues concerning the third marking option, where consumer organizations foresee that farmers and manufacturers will use the 'May contain' mark for all their products, leaving the consumer with no actual choice.

Some of the member states – Austria, Luxembourg, and Italy – have decided to ban the selling of genetically modified products with reference to the uncertain health consequences. In Austria, 1.2 million people have supported the government's choice in a petition, and a majority of the populations in the United Kingdom, France, Italy, The Netherlands, Denmark, and Sweden are against the use of genetically modified food products.

Sources: Jacob Langvad, 'EU ønsker mere gen-mærkning', *Berlingske Tidende*, 24 July 1997; Jacob Langvad, 'Østrig tvinges til at acceptere gen-majs', *Berlingske Tidende*, 10 September 1997; Søren Funch, 'EU underkender forbud Mod génsplejset majs', *Morgenavisen Jyllands-Posten*, 11 September 1997.

In this text we have presented what we believe to be a useful description of some important relationships between consumer affect and cognitions, consumer behaviours, the environment, and marketing strategy development. One of the major underlying premises of the text is that marketing is an important and powerful force in society; properly designed and executed marketing strategies are often effective in changing consumer affect, cognitions, and behaviours to achieve organizational objectives.

We have also argued that attempts to modify and control affect, cognitions, and behaviours are part of the fabric of society. We believe the majority of social exchanges involve such attempts.

Further, we believe that decentralized economic systems involving market transactions offer the best and most effective system of exchange that has been developed. Where it has been applied, it has generally led to increasing economic prosperity. However, market economies pose informational problems for every actor who is part of the market, and marketing is one way of trying to solve this problem from the producer or seller's point of view. Producers and sellers have to make decisions all the time on how to allocate resources – which products to develop, how much to produce, to continue or discontinue a line of products, to invest into new distribution channels . . . . Naturally, producers and sellers would like to reduce the uncertainty involved in making such decisions, and marketing instruments, including those described in this book, can be used to do so. A better understanding of consumers helps in making decisions about which products to develop and how to distribute, price, and promote them. In this way, a better understanding of consumer behaviour helps increase the efficiency of a market economy.

However, consumers also face uncertainties and incur risks when making decisions on how to use their resources. While marketers are professionals who can study – among other things – consumer behaviour and use that knowledge to their advantage, consumers do not in general have the same possibilities for studying the behaviour of sellers and producers. There has therefore been some considerable discussion about the imbalance of power which possibly exists between sellers and buyers on consumer markets.[1]

Both marketers and consumers are granted certain rights by society, and both have a degree of power. Overall, many people believe marketers have considerably more power than consumers. A well-known American marketing researcher has summarized the rights granted to marketers in the following way:

1. Sellers have the right to introduce any product in any size, style, colour, etc., so long as it meets established health and safety requirements.
2. Sellers have the right to price the product as they please so long as they avoid discrimination that is harmful to competition.
3. Sellers have the right to promote the product using any resources, media, or message, in any amount, so long as no deception or fraud is involved.
4. Sellers have the right to introduce any buying schemes they wish, so long as they are not discriminatory.
5. Sellers have the right to alter the product offering at any time.
6. Sellers have the right to distribute the product in any reasonable manner.
7. Sellers have the right to limit the product guarantee or post-sale services.[2]

What are, in contrast to this, consumer rights, and what can or should be done to promote them? There have been varying views on this, depending on the kind of consumer view one adopts.[3]

Views of the Consumer

One view of consumers is that the *consumer is king*.[4] It is the consumer who makes the final decision about buying or not buying a product or service, and therefore all sellers are in the final analysis at the mercy of consumers. Consumers are therefore the most powerful actors in the economic system, and there is no need to be concerned about the power of marketers.

While this view occasionally still crops up in economic textbooks and political pamphlets, few would regard it as a helpful view today. The material covered in this book clearly shows that sellers have many means of influencing consumers' choice, and while it is quite correct that consumer choices are a prerequisite for the survival of a consumer goods manufacturer, it is by no means correct that sellers have to wait helplessly while the consumer is making up his or her mind.

A second view, which has been quite popular over the past decades, is that the consumer is the *potential king*, i.e. the consumer can become king if he or she is helped a little. The reasons mainly cited for why the consumer is not quite king is that being king in the sense implied requires the following:

1. The consumer should have options to choose from – but in reality the options consumers can choose from are determined by sellers, and sellers may withhold attractive options from consumers for a variety of reasons. For example, products of higher durability may not be offered because manufacturers prefer consumers to buy replacements,[5] cheaper products may not be offered because the manufacturers do not want to start a price war, or user-friendly packaging may not be introduced because retailer requirements for shelf life and logistics prevent it.
2. The consumer must be able to make informed choices – but in reality products are complex, consumers have limited knowledge about products, and advertising informs only about positive and not about negative attributes of products.
3. The consumer must be able to complain and make suggestions – but in reality consumers do not know where to go, find the effort of complaining to be too great, or do not believe their voice makes a difference.

In the United States concerns like these have led to the formulation of a Consumer Bill of Rights. First, consumers are granted the right to safety, which means the right to be protected against products and services that are hazardous to health and life. Second, consumers are granted the right to be informed, which is the right to be protected against fraudulent, deceitful, or misleading advertising or other information that could interfere with making an informed choice. Third, consumers are granted the right to choose, which is the right to have access to a variety of competitive products that are priced fairly and are of satisfactory quality. Finally, consumers are granted the right to be heard or the right to be assured that their interests will be fully and fairly considered in the formulation and administration of government policy.

This view of consumers as the potential king acknowledges an imbalance in power between consumers and sellers, and argues that this imbalance is mainly of an informational nature. By providing better means of information for consumers, the consumer actually can get quite close to being a king.

The major weakness of this view is the assumption that consumers are both capable of being and willing to be highly involved in purchase and consumption. In fact, however, as we have seen throughout this text, many consumers are neither. Young children, many elderly people, and less educated consumers often do not have the cognitive abilities to process information well enough to be protected.[6] Further, even those consumers who do have the capacity often are not willing to invest the time, money, cognitive energy, and behaviour effort to ensure their rights.

The right to choose is also predicated on the assumption that consumers are rational, autonomous, knowledgeable cognitive processors and decision makers. While we believe most consumers are capable of being so, evidence suggests consumers often do not behave this way.[7]

Considerations such as these have given rise to the third view, which adopts the opposite stance – that consumers are victims incapable of defending themselves in today's marketing world. Consumers can be influenced, conditioned, shaped: they are persuaded to buy products they don't need, pay prices which are too high, and incur risks for health and safety which they don't understand. This view leads to the need for consumer protection – consumers have to be protected at least from the worst types of attempts to persuade them by regulating products, and controlling and limiting advertising and other forms of market communication.

While there has been considerable debate over the appropriateness of any of these views, today many people agree that all have some elements of truth. In spite of everything discussed in this book, consumer choices often remain difficult to explain and predict, and sellers' competition in understanding consumers and finding new products and services which consumers will like is an effective limit to imbalances in power between sellers and consumers. In many cases consumers do make or at least want to make informed choices, and providing them with more or better information will help them. However, there are many other consumers who make choices without deliberation, and in these cases society may want to establish rules for protecting them from well-defined hazards.

Attempts to increase consumer welfare where one believes it may be endangered by seller activities are usually called *consumer policy*.[8] Consumer policy covers a variety of instruments that have been developed in reaction to the considerations sketched above regarding needs for information, protection, and uninhibited competition. They can be seen as attempts to deal with problem areas in marketing like those listed in Exhibit 21.1.

Consumer Policy and Its Instruments

Exhibit 21.2 shows a classification of the instruments of consumer policy. Their overall aim is to increase consumer welfare. This is achieved by two groups of measures: changing seller behaviour and changing consumer behaviour.

Changing Seller Behaviour

Changing seller behaviour can be achieved by legislation, usually either at the national or European level. It can also be achieved by voluntary self-control regimes of sellers. The measures taken affect all major elements of marketing strategy – communication, products, distribution, and prices.

Measures concerning communication deal mostly with preventing deception, increasing the amount of useful information available to consumers, and preventing

EXHIBIT 21.1

Some Problem Areas in Marketing

Product Issues	Promotion Issues
Unsafe products	Deceptive advertising
Poor-quality products	Advertising to children
Poor service/repair/maintenance after sale	Bait-and-switch advertising
	Anxiety-inducing advertising
Deceptive packaging and labelling practices	Deceptive personal selling tactics
Environmental impact of packaging and products	

Pricing Issues	Distribution Issues
Deceptive pricing	Sale of counterfeit products and brands
Fraudulent or misleading credit practices	Pyramid selling
Warranty refund problems	Deceptive in-store selling influence

EXHIBIT 21.2

Instruments of Consumer Policy

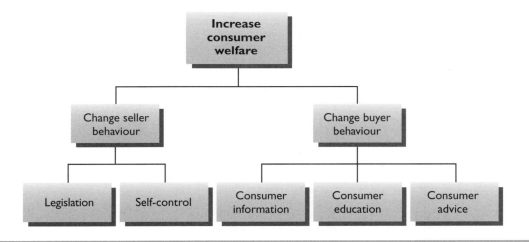

or limiting the promotion of products regarded as harmful to society (cigarettes or alcoholic beverages).

Deception is a difficult concept, and consumer researchers have done considerable work in trying to elucidate it.[9] Intuitively, a consumer has been deceived by an advertisement if he or she believes a product has a characteristic which it in fact does not have. In practice, only extreme cases are clear-cut, such as when a drug promises

EXHIBIT 21.3

Misleading Elements in Advertising Cars

 Two versions of advertising text elements were compared concerning their effect on consumer impressions of the product. Here are some examples where the differences in text did make a difference in consumers' impression.

Original Text Impression	Revised Text	Effect on Consumer
It has everything to keep fuel consumption low. For example, an aerodynamic car body, low weight, and a motor with a special carburetor which is content with 5.9 litres at 90 km/h. But has the temperament for a top speed of 150 km/h.	It has everything to keep fuel consumption low. For example, an aerodynamic car body, low weight, and a motor with a special carburetor which is content with 5.9 litres at 90 km/h, 8.3 litres at 120 km/h, and 8.2 litres in city traffic. But has the temperament for a top speed of 150 km/h.	Original text leads to better impression of fuel economy.
Now you have a six-year corrosion-protection warranty on all our models. We guarantee this to you, because we know best how well our cars are built and protected against corrosion. Even when your car has to be inspected the third time, you don't have to worry. Provided you had the car checked once a year by one of our authorized dealers.	Now you have a six-year warranty against rust holes on all our models. We guarantee this to you, because we know best how well our cars are built and protected against corrosion. Even when your car has to be inspected the third time, you don't have to worry. Provided you had the car checked once a year by one of our authorized dealers.	Original text leads to better impression concerning car's susceptibility to rust.
We have the broadest service network in Europe. More than 7500 service stations in the east and the west.	We have the broadest service network in Europe. More than 7500 service stations in the east and the west, of which 1370 are in the Federal Republic.	Original text leads to better impression about availability of a service station close to one's home.
A big German car magazine tried to find the most economical cars of the world. Six cars were tested. Winner with an average fuel consumption of 6.3 litres: Model X diesel.	A big German car magazine tried to find the most economical cars of the world. Six cars were tested (1 diesel, 5 gasoline cars). Winner with an average fuel consumption of 6.3 litres: Model X diesel.	Original text leads to better impression of fuel economy.
From the start it had an acceleration never seen before in its class of economy cars. Because no other economy car with 40 hp and 1000 ccm was sold so much in Europe in its first year.	From the start it found many new friends in its class of economy cars. Because no other economy car with 40 hp and 1000 ccm was sold so many times in Europe in its first year.	Original text leads to better impression of car's acceleration abilities.

Source: Adapted from Klaus G. Grunert and Konrad Dedler, 'Misleading Advertising: In Search of a Measurement Methodology', *Journal of Public Policy & Marketing*, 4, 1985, pp. 153–165.

that 5 kg will be lost within a week just by taking the drug, and the consumer finds out after a week that he or she did not lose weight. Such extreme cases, because they are so obvious, are rare in practice. The difficult cases are those concerned with such things as whether teenagers are deceived or misled when advertising suggests that smoking cigarettes is part of a fancy lifestyle, or when a brand of petrol is perceived by a consumer as the best, whereas the only thing that was claimed in the ad was that none is better (implying that all brands could be equally good). Self-regulatory bodies of the advertising industry, which exist in all major European countries, usually only deal with the most obvious cases, and while there is legislation preventing deceitful or misleading advertising, the courts have usually been conservative in applying it. Consumer research can help in establishing whether a particular text element in advertising is misleading, as shown in Exhibit 21.3.

Increasing the amount of information available to consumers deals mostly with information which accompanies the product, i.e. on the product itself, on the packaging, or on other media that are available at the point of purchase. Usually the rationale is that the information would not otherwise be given by sellers, or it would be given in a less useful way. The latter refers especially to the comparability of the information across products, which sellers may not always be interested in bringing about. Examples of such regulations are rules about giving information about price (especially when the price is intricate, e.g. when obtaining a loan or a mortgage), about ingredients in foods, about risks associated with drugs, and about fuel economy of cars.

Many of these measures and the information resulting from them have been criticized for ignoring insights on consumer behaviour.[10] If one wants this information to be used, one should provide it in a way that takes into account where consumers search for information, and how they perceive and process the information. Thus, lists of ingredients which consumers do not understand will not be used, and much factual information, for instance on the fuel economy of a car in litres per kilometre, becomes useful only when consumers know the market average or start comparing various offerings.

Regulation of products has traditionally dealt with ensuring minimum standards of product safety, especially in cases where the potential safety hazards are hidden and cannot be ascertained by consumers. More recently, product regulations have also dealt with products' environmental effects. For example, car exhaust emissions have been limited, and some countries have adopted regulations for limiting packaging waste.

Regulations in the distribution realm concern restraints on the contractual arrangements between seller and buyer. Consumers may be granted rights concerning warranties, and the right to abstain from a contract. The latter is related to the fact that consumers may have second thoughts, especially after signing contracts in situations where they were perceived to be under pressure.

As for prices, most countries require price information to be posted in shops. In addition, there are regulations for the type of price to be quoted, as mentioned above, and there are regulations trying to inhibit deceitful pricing, such as arguing that a price has been reduced when actually the 'full price' has never been asked.

Changing Consumer Behaviour

First of all, we should perhaps remember that the whole of this book has been concerned with understanding consumer behaviour and employing the understanding gained to influence and eventually change consumer behaviour. The difference in the current section is that the change attempts we are dealing with do not originate in the producer/seller realm; instead, they originate from government intervention and/or from nonprofit organizations. The attempts to change consumer behaviour, which we are dealing with here, are commonly categorized into consumer information, consumer education, and consumer advice.

Consumer information measures aim to make consumers use more and/or better information when choosing between products and services. The measures discussed in the preceding section on forcing sellers to make more or different information available to consumers are indirect attempts to influence consumers' use of information. In addition to that, various types of consumer organization provide information which consumers can use in their decision making. The most well-known ones are comparative product tests and information systems.

Comparative product tests compare products within a product category on a number of criteria and arrive at an overall evaluation. They are often published in consumer magazines like *Which?* in the United Kingdom, *test* in Germany, and *Råd og Resultater* in Denmark (Exhibit 21.4 shows an example from such a magazine). For certain product categories, comparative tests are also done by commercial magazines, for example for cars, photographic equipment, boats, and travel. Hotel guides, like the well-known Michelin guide, are cited by some people as the first forms of comparative quality marks awarded by an independent institution.

Consumer research indicated that this type of information does change consumer behaviour.[11] It seems that certain groups of consumers, sometimes called *information seekers*, do use this information quite extensively. In addition to that, it seems that this type of information also changes producer behaviour.[12] Exhibit 21.5 shows results from a German survey of manufacturers of product categories which are commonly subjected to comparative tests, namely compact hi-fi sets and washing machines. A total of 53 manufacturers were interviewed. The results show that producers try to anticipate the criteria used in the tests and design their products accordingly, and that they use test results in their market communication.

Consumer education is not related to specific product choices and has the aim of making consumers better and more competent partners in market transaction.[13] Consumer education can therefore be related to the concept of consumer socialization dealt with in Chapter 15. Consumer education in school can deal with topics such as understanding the concept of exchange, understanding the selling intent of advertising, training ways of comparing and evaluating products and services, understanding the harmful effects of certain products such as tobacco and alcohol, and understanding the environmental impact of consumer behaviour.

Consumer advice deals with a variety of measures designed to help consumers solve problems by personal communication.[14] It is usually carried out by or on the initiative of consumer organizations, but can also be carried out by state institutions or private organizations. It usually deals with less clearly defined problems than choosing between a set of products, and part of the advisory process therefore deals with defining the problem, thinking about one's needs, and relating it to possible solutions. Typical examples of topics dealt with by consumer advice are budgetary problems (a family cannot find out how to deal with the resources available), nutrition (a family wants to eat in a healthier way), and credit (how to finance housing). Much of the consumer advice

EXHIBIT 21.4

Example of Comparative Test Information

STIFTUNG WARENTEST test-	KOMPASS				KÜHLSCHRÄNKE test- Ausgabe 7/97			

	Mittler Preis in DM	Preis nach Markterhebung in DM	Strom-kosten für 10 Jahre in DM)	Kühlen und Ge-frieren	Kühlen und Ge-frieren	Hand-habung	test-Qualitäts-urteill
Gewichtung				55%	35%	10%	
Gerät mit Vier-Sterne-Fach							
Neckermann Lloyds Öko 160 Best.-Nr. 8073/822	699,–		655,–	+	+	o	gut
Zanussi ZFC 1604 S[2])	749,–	baugleich mit Elektrolux ER 1537 T					
Quelle Privileg 150 Luxus Best.-Nr 0137453	749, 50		552,–	+	++	+	gut
Bauknecht KVNC 1554/2	779,–	739,– bis 799,–	613,–	+	++	+	gut
Electrolux ER 1537 T[3])	799,–	749,– bis 849,–	571,–	+	++	+	gut
Siemens Öko Plus KT 15 LS 2	839,–	749,– bis 899,–	482,–	+	++	+	gut
Bosch KTL 1572 economic	849,–	768,– bis 929,–	482,–	+	++	+	gut
Gerät mit Drei-Sterne-Fach							
AEG Öko-Santo Super 1472 TK	799,–	748,– bis 899,–	501,–	++	+	+	gut
Foron Vitacool KT 1436 D[4])	829,–		725,–	++	+	+	gut
Liebherr KTe 1483-21[5])		nicht mehr im Angebot	552,–	++	+	o	gut

KÜHLGEFRIER KOMBINA-TIONEN	Mittler Preis in DM	Preis nach Markterhebung in DM	Strom-kosten für 10 Jahre in DM1)	Kühlen und Ge-frieren	Diese neuen Kühlgefrier-kombinationen mit Kaltlagerfach versprechen auch länger anhaltende Frische. Da jedoch die Beurteilung von Frische testmethodische Probleme aufwirft, beschränkte sich die Bewertung der Kühl- und Gefriereigenschaften sowie des Energiebedarfs. Ein test-Qualitätsurteil wurde nicht vergen.
Siemens KG 37 F 00	1799,–	1699,– bis 1859,–	1943,–	++	
Bosch KGF 3700	1859,–	1749,– bis 1920,–	1943,–	++	
Siemens KS 32 F 00	1889,–	1789,– bis 1959,–	1870,–	+	
Bosch KSF 3200	1949,–	1749,– bis 2019,–	1870,–	+	
Siemens KD 32 F 00	1989,–	1798,– bis 2059,–	1319,–	+	
Bosch KDF 3200 economic	2049,–	1859,– bis 2129,–	1319,–	+	

Reihenfolge der Bewertung: ++ = sehr gut, + = gut, o = zufriedenstellend,
                              – = mangelhaft, –– = sehr mangelhalt

1) Arbeitsstrompreis 0,28 DM/kWh.
2) Lt. Anbieter inzwischen Nachfolgemodell ZFT 164 RM.
3) Lt. Anbieter inzwischen Nachfolgemodell ER 6537 T.
4) Lt. Anbieter inzwischen Nachfolgemodell KT 1446 D.
5) Lt. Anbieter inzwischen ersetzt durch Vier-Sterne-Modell KTe 1464.

Sonderdrucke des ausführlichen Tests können unter Einsendung eines mit,– DM frankierten Umschlags bei der Stiftung Warentest, Postfach 30 41 41, 10724 Berlin, angeford werden.

Source: Courtesy Stiftung Warentest

EXHIBIT 21.5

Supplier Effects of Comparative Testing

Effect Reported	All Suppliers (%)	Suppliers of Products Tested (%)	Suppliers of Products Not Tested (%)
Sales force uses test results in sales talks	81.1	91.0	56.2
Test results are systematically analysed	79.2	83.8	68.7
Top management informs sales force about test results	75.5	83.8	56.2
Test criteria are used in product development	56.6	67.6	31.2
Positive test results are used in sales promotions	–	78.0	–

Source: Adapted from Wolfgang Fritz, Harald Hilger *et al.*, 'Testnutzung und Testwirkungen im Bereich der Konsumgüterindustrie', in *Warentest und Unternehmen*, eds. Hans Raffée and Günter Silberer (Frankfurt: Campus, 1984), pp. 27–114.

taking place is also related to the purchase of major appliances – which type of washing machine is right for me, what are the product characteristics I should look for, and the like.

Consumer Policy from a Marketing Perspective

Some marketers look at measures of consumer policy with suspicion, since they are motivated at least partly by criticisms of marketers and their power. However, we regard this as a basically shortsighted view. In the long-term, marketers can usually profit from effective consumer policy measures.

Many consumer policy measures deal with increasing the involvement of consumers with their purchases and helping consumers make informed choices. As has been demonstrated abundantly throughout this text, more involved and well-informed consumers are clearly in the interest of marketers. These consumers are receptive to new and better products, they are interested in listening to marketer-initiated communication, and their needs and interests can be researched in a way which makes it possible to predict purchases of future products in a reasonably reliable way. In contrast, uninvolved and uninterested consumers are more unpredictable in their purchase behaviour, are not interested in listening to messages advocating products and services, and are difficult to motivate to buy new products.

Environmental effects of consumption are a good case in point. When consumer organizations, environmentalists, and government raised issues about environmental effects, many marketers perceived this as a threat. However, for many the threat has turned into opportunity, as it became clear that the environmental dimension has opened up for new possibilities for product differentiation and has increased the involvement of at least some consumers with products which were typically low involvement, such as detergent or milk.

**Back to . . .
Who Wants
to Eat
Modified
Genes?**

Whether genetically modified food products actually entail health risks is heavily debated, and therefore there are different views on how the marketing of such products should be restrained or regulated. Providing labelling information, as the Commission of the European Union now requires, indicates that consumers must be given a choice. Consumers should by themselves make up their minds whether they want genetically modified products or not, and they should be given a chance to choose.

Such measures obviously assume that consumes are interested and willing to process such information and will make informed choices. Since many purchase decisions in the food category are low involvement and/or habitual, it remains to be seen how many consumers will make use of this information.

Summary

In the final chapter of the text, we have discussed some of the concerns which have been raised concerning the power of marketers, and some of the instruments which are being used to control this power. Application of such instruments is usually called consumer policy, and they include regulation of the various elements of marketing strategy, provision of consumer information, and consumer education and advice.

Key Terms and Concepts

comparative product test   446
consumer advice   446
consumer education   446
consumer information   446
consumer policy   442
consumer rights   440
misleading advertising   441
product safety   445

Review and Discussion Questions

1. Compare the rights of marketers and rights of consumers discussed in this chapter. Which group do you think has more power?
2. Which of the buyer and seller rights become a problem if we assume consumers are not highly involved in most purchases?
3. Select three newspaper ads that you consider to be misleading. Explain what elements of the communication are deceptive and which groups of consumers might be harmed.
4. What would you consider to be the major elements of consumer education aiming at educating consumers to make informed decisions?
5. Discuss the ethics of tobacco or liquor marketing. Could you develop a code of personal ethics to guide you as a promotion manager in these industries?

Additional Reading

For further discussions of ethical dimensions in marketing, see:

O. C. Ferrell and Steven J. Skinner. 'Ethical Behaviour and Bureaucratic Structure in Marketing Research Organizations', *Journal of Marketing Research*, February 1988, pp. 103–109.

Jerry R. Goolsby and Shelby D. Hunt. 'Cognitive Moral Development and Marketing', *Journal of Marketing*, January 1992, pp. 55–68.

For a discussion of the consumer views guiding consumer policy principles, see:

Hans Rask Jensen, 'The Relevance of Alternative Paradigms as Guidelines for Consumer Policy and Organized Consumer Action', *Journal of Consumer Policy*, 9, no. 4, 1986, pp. 389–405.

For the possibilities of applying consumer research in non-marketing contexts, see:

Folke Ölander, 'Consumer Psychology: Not Necessarily a Manipulative Science', *Applied Psychology: An International Review*, 1, 1990, pp. 105–126.

MARKETING STRATEGY IN ACTION
Consumer Boycotts

 hen France started underground nuclear bomb tests on the Muroroa Islands, many countries protested, and consumers throughout Europe stopped buying French products. French exporters lost considerable sales in the period of the tests. In Denmark, for example, the sale of French wine decreased by 20 per cent, and producers have had difficulties regaining their market share after Spanish and Italian wine took over the shelf space. Eventually the French president decided to stop the tests. Whether it was the pressure from the international community as a whole or from the consumers who boycotted French products remains uncertain. However, some consumers have clearly shown that they take their choices seriously and are willing to use them as a political tool.

In reaction to this and other incidents, a number of major European companies, Shell, IKEA, Heineken and British Telecom, have decided to incorporate softer values in their accounting system by introducing ethical and social accounts. All of them are aware of the consequences of not taking ethics into consideration. The Brent Spar incident, where Shell had to change their plan of dumping an old oil rig into deep water as a consequence of consumer boycotts and protests led by Greenpeace, has had consequences for the way Shell handles ethical issues today. The Brent Spar incident occurred despite the fact that Shell was following the recommendations of a report concluding that the dumping was the most environmentally safe solution.

Recently, Heineken, the Dutch brewery, was forced, after pressure from employees, to halt investment in the military dictatorship of Burma. Although ethical accounting is a new and not even properly defined concept it is likely that it has come to stay.

Discussion Questions
1. Discuss possible strategies of consumer goods manufacturers in dealing with consumer boycotts.
2. What are the lessons to be learned from the way Shell handled the Brent Spar crisis?
3. Analyse consumers' decision to boycott a product for political or environmental reasons using the concepts you have learned in this book.

Sources: Lisbeth Wirgowitsch, 'Bordeaux vil generobre den tabte hyldeplads', *Markedsføring*, no. 12, 1996, p. 6; Birgitte Erhardtsen, 'Globale koncerner sætter tal på etik', *Børsen*, 18 September 1997, pp. 8–9.

Notes

Chapter 1

1 Bernard J. Jaworski and Ajay K. Kohli, 'Market Orientation: Antecedents and Consequences', *Journal of Marketing*, July 1993, pp. 53–79.
2 In addition to Jaworski and Kohli, see, e.g. Robert Deshpandé, John U. Farley, and Frederick E. Webster, Jr., 'Corporate Culture, Customer Orientation And Innovativeness in Japanese Firms: A Quadrad Analysis', *Journal of Marketing*, January 1993, pp. 23–37; John C. Narver and Stanley F. Slater, 'The Effect of a Market Orientation on Business Profitability', *Journal of Marketing*, October 1990, pp. 20–35; Robert W. Ruekert, 'Developing a Market Orientation: An Organizational Strategy Perspective', *International Journal of Research in Marketing*, August 1992, pp. 225–245.
3 Peter D. Bennett, *Dictionary of Marketing Terms* (Chicago, IL: American Marketing Association, 1989), p. 40.

Chapter 2

1 The example is adapted from Albert Bandura, 'The Self System in Reciprocal Determinism', *American Psychologist*, April 1978, p. 346. Also see Albert Bandura, *Social Foundations of Thought and Action: A Social Cognitive Theory* (Englewood Cliffs, NJ: Prentice-Hall, 1986).

Chapter 3

1 C. E. Izard, 'Emotion-Cognition Relationships and Human Development', in *Emotions, Cognition and Behavior*, eds. C. E. Izard, J. Kagan, and Robert B. Zajonc (New York, NY: Cambridge University Press, 1984, pp. 17–37; Rom Harre, David Clarke, and Nicola De Carlo, *Motives and Mechanisms: An Introduction to the Psychology of Action* (London: Methuen, 1985), chap. 2, pp. 20–39; Jaak Panksepp, 'Toward a General Psychobiological Theory of Emotions. With Commentaries', *The Behavioral and Brain Sciences*, 5, 1982, pp. 407–467; and Robert Plutchik, *Emotion: A Psychoevolutionary Synthesis* (New York, NY: Harper & Row, 1980).
2 Christian Derbaix and Michel T. Pham, 'Affective reactions to consumption situations: A pilot investigation', *Journal of Economic Psychology*, 12, 1991, pp. 325–355; and Rik G. M. Pieters and W. Fred Van Raaij, 'Functions and Management of Affect: Applications to Economic Behavior', *Journal of Economic Psychology*, 9, 1988, pp. 251–282.
3 Werner Kroeber-Riel, 'Activation Research: Psychobiological Approaches in Consumer Research', *Journal of Consumer Research*, March 1979, pp. 240–250.

4 Meryl Paula Gardner, 'Mood States and Consumer Behavior: A Critical Review', *Journal of Consumer Research*, December 1985, pp. 281–300.

5 See Rom Harre, David Clarke, and Nicola De Carlo, *Motives and Mechanisms: An Introduction to the Psychology of Action* (London: Methuen, 1985), chap. 2, pp. 20–39; Robert B. Zajonc and Hazel Markus, 'Affective and Cognitive Factors in Preferences', *Journal of Consumer Research*, 9, 1982, pp. 123–131; Robert B. Zajonc, 'On the Primacy of Affect', *American Psychologist*, 39, 1984, pp. 117–123; and Richard S. Lazarus, 'On the Primacy of Cognition', *American Psychologist*, 39, 1984, pp. 124–129.

6 Michael K. Hui and John E. G. Bateson, 'Perceived Control and the Effects of Crowding and Consumer Choice on the Service Experience', *Journal of Consumer Research*, September 1991, pp. 174–184.

7 G. Meyer-Hentschel, *Aktivierungswirkung von Anzeigen* (Würzburg: Physica, 1983).

8 Werner Kroeber-Riel, 'Analysis of Non-Cognitive Behavior – Especially by Nonverbal Measurement', in *Advances in Communication and Marketing Research*, ed. Richard Bagozzi (Greenwich, CO: JAI, 1989).

9 John R. Anderson, *Cognitive Psychology and its Implications* (San Francisco, CA: W. H. Freeman, 1985).

10 Banwari Mittal, 'The Role of Affective Choice Mode in the Consumer Purchase of Expressive Products', *Journal of Economic Psychology*, 9, 1988, pp. 499–524; Yehoshua Tsal, 'On the Relationship Between Cognitive and Affective Processes: A Critique of Zajonc and Markus', *Journal of Consumer Research*, 12, 1985, pp. 358–364; Robert B. Zajonc and Hazel Markus, 'Affective and Cognitive Factors in Preferences'; and Robert B. Zajonc and Hazel Markus, 'Must All Affect Be Mediated by Cognition?' *Journal of Consumer Research*, 12, 1985, pp. 363–364.

11 S. S. Tomkins, 'Affect Theory', in *Emotion in the Human Face*, ed. P. Ekman (Cambridge: Cambridge University Press, 1983); Robert B. Zajonc, 'On the Primacy of Affect', *American Psychologist*, 39, 1984, pp. 117–123; and Richard S. Lazarus, 'On the Primacy of Cognition', *American Psychologist*, 39, 1984, pp. 124–129.

12 Richard S. Lazarus, 'On the Primacy of Cognition', *American Psychologist*, 39, 1984, pp. 124–129; Rik Pieters and Fred Van Raaij, 'Functions and Management of Affect: Applications to Economic Behavior', pp. 251–282; and Richard S. Lazarus, 'Cognition and Motivation in Emotion', *American Psychologist*, April 1991, pp. 352–367.

13 For example, see Julie A. Edell and Marian Chapman Burke, 'The Power of Feelings in Understanding Advertising Effects', *Journal of Consumer Research*, December 1987, pp. 421–433; William J. Havlena and Morris B. Holbrook, 'The Varieties of Consumption Experience: Comparing Two Typologies of Emotion in Consumer Behavior', *Journal of Consumer Research*, December 1986, pp. 394–404; Morris B. Holbrook and Rajeev Batra, 'Assessing the Role of Emotions as Mediators of Consumer Responses to Advertising', *Journal of Consumer Research*, December 1987, pp. 404–420; and Rajeev Batra and Douglas M. Stayman, 'The Role of Mood in Advertising Effectiveness', *Journal of Consumer Research*, September 1990, pp. 203–214.

14 For example, see Robert B. Zajonc and Hazel Markus, 'Affective and Cognitive Factors in Preferences', *Journal of Consumer Research*, 9, 1982, pp. 123–131.

15 Suzanne C. Grunert, *Essen und Emotionen* (Weinheim: Beltz, 1993).

16 Dawn Dobni and George M. Zinkhan, 'In Search of Brand Image: A Foundation Analysis', in *Advances in Consumer Research*, vol. 17 (Provo, UT: Association for Consumer Research, 1990), pp. 110–119; Ernest Dichter, 'What's in an Image?' *Journal of Consumer Marketing*, Winter 1985, pp. 75–81.

17 John R. Rossiter, Larry Percy, and Robert J. Donovan, 'A Better Advertising Planning Grid', *Journal of Advertising Research*, October–November 1991, pp. 11–21; and Brian Ratchford, 'New Insights about the FCB Grid', *Journal of Advertising Research*, August–September 1987, pp. 24–38.

18 Mark Maremont, 'They're All Screaming for Haagen-Dazs', *Business Week*, 14 October 1991, p. 121.

19 Kathleen Deveny, 'As Lauder's Scent Battles Calvin Klein's, Cosmetics Whiz Finds Herself on the Spot', *The Wall Street Journal*, 27 June 1991, pp. B1, B6.

20 An early complex information-processing model of consumer decision making was developed by John Howard and Jagdish Sheth, *The Theory of Buyer Behavior* (New York, NY: Wiley, 1969). Later, Bettman introduced another complex information-processing model – James R. Bettman, *An Information Processing Model of Consumer Choice* (Reading, MA: Addison-Wesley, 1979).

21 For example, see William J. McGuire, 'The Internal Psychological Factors Influencing Consumer Choice', *Journal of Consumer Research*, March 1976, pp. 302–319; and Ivan L. Preston, 'The Association Model of the Advertising Communication Process', *Journal of Advertising*, 2, 1982, pp. 3–15.

22 F. C. Bartlett, *Remembering: A Study in Experimental and Social Psychology* (Cambridge: Cambridge University Press, 1932); Klaus G. Grunert, 'Cognitive Determinants of Attribute Information Usage', *Journal of Economic Psychology*, March 1986, pp. 95–123; and Jerry C. Olson, 'Theories of Information Encoding and Storage: Implications for Consumer Research', in *The Effect of Information on Consumer and Market Behavior*, ed. Andrew A. Mitchell (Chicago, IL: American Marketing Association, 1978), pp. 49–60.

23 Alan M. Collins and Elizabeth F. Loftus, 'A Spreading Activation Theory of Semantic Memory', *Psychological Review*, 82, 1975, pp. 407–428; and Klaus G. Grunert, 'Automatic and Strategic Processes in Advertising Effects', *Journal of Marketing*, Fall 1996, pp. 88–101.

24 John R. Anderson, 'A Spreading Activation Theory of Memory', *Journal of Verbal Learning and Verbal Behavior*, 22, 1983, pp. 261–275; and Allan Collins and Elizabeth Loftus, 'A Spreading Activation Theory of Semantic Memory', pp. 407–428.

25 Allan Newell and Herbert A. Simon, *Human Problem Solving* (Englewood Cliffs, NJ: Prentice-Hall, 1972).

26 John A. Bargh, 'Automatic and Conscious Processing of Social Information', in *Handbook of Social Cognition*, vol. 3, eds. Robert S. Wyer and Thomas K. Srull (Hillsdale, NJ: Lawrence Erlbaum, 1984), pp. 1–43; and Richard M. Schiffrin and Susan T. Dumais, 'The Development of Automatism', in *Cognitive Skills and Their Development*, ed. John R. Anderson (Hillsdale, NJ: Lawrence Erlbaum, 1981), pp. 111–140.

27 Jeffrey F. Durgee and Robert W. Stuart, 'Advertising Symbols and Brand Names That Best Represent Key Product Meanings', *Journal of Advertising*, Summer 1987, pp. 15–24.

28 Wayne A. Wickelgren, 'Human Learning and Memory', in *Annual Review of Psychology*, eds. M. R. Rosenzweig and L. W. Porter (Palo Alto, CA: Annual Reviews, 1981), pp. 21–52.

29 John R. Anderson, *The Architecture of Cognition* (Cambridge, MA: Harvard University Press, 1983); and Terence R. Smith, Andrew A. Mitchell, and Robert Meyer, 'A Computational Process Model of Evaluation Based on the Cognitive Structuring of Episodic Knowledge', in *Advances in Consumer Research*, vol. 9, ed. Andrew A. Mitchell (Ann Arbor, MI: Association for Consumer Research, 1982), pp. 136–143.

30 Endel Tulving, 'Episodic and Semantic Memory', in *Organization of Memory*, ed. Endel Tulving (New York, NY: Academic Press, 1972), pp. 382–404.

31 Merrie Brucks and Andrew Mitchell, 'Knowledge Structures, Production Systems, and Decision Strategies', in *Advances in Consumer Research*, vol. 8, ed. Kent B. Monroe (Ann Arbor, MI: Association for Consumer Research, 1982).

32 Donald A. Norman, *The Psychology of Everyday Things* (New York, NY: Basic Books, 1988).

33 Bruce Nussbaum and Robert Neff, 'I Can't Work This Thing!' *Business Week*, 29 April 1991, pp. 58–66.

34 Although many types of memory structures have been proposed, most can be reduced to the more general associative network model. See James R. Bettman, 'Memory Factors in Consumer Choice: A Review', *Journal of Marketing*, 43, Spring 1979, pp. 37–53; Andrew A. Mitchell, 'Models of Memory: Implications for Measuring Knowledge Structures', in *Advances in Consumer Research*, vol. 9, ed. Andrew A. Mitchell (Ann Arbor, MI: Association for Consumer Research, 1982), pp. 45–51; and Edward Smith, 'Theories of Semantic Memory', in *Handbook of Learning and Cognitive Processes*, vol. 6, ed. William K. Estes (Hillsdale, NJ: Lawrence Erlbaum, 1978), pp. 1–56.

35 Joseph W. Alba and Lynn Hasher, 'Is Memory Schematic?', *Psychological Bulletin*, March 1983, pp. 203–231; and David E. Rumelhart and Anthony Ortony, 'The Representation of Knowledge in Memory', in *Schooling and the Acquisition of Knowledge*, eds. R. C. Anderson, R. J. Spiro, and W. E. Montague (Hillsdale, NJ: Lawrence Erlbaum, 1977), pp. 99–136. The example in Exhibit 3.5 is partly based on the dissertation work by Susan Baker, *Extending Means–End Theory Through an Investigation of the Consumer Benefit/Price Sensitivity Relationship in Two Markets* (Cranfield University, School of Management, 1996).

36 Thomas W. Leigh and Arno J. Rethans, 'Experiences with Script Elicitation within Consumer Decision-Making Contexts', in *Advances in Consumer Research*, vol. 10, eds. Richard P. Bagozzi and Alice M. Tybout (Ann Arbor, MI: Association for Consumer Research, 1983), pp. 667–672; and Roger C. Schank and Robert P. Abelson, Scripts, *Plans, Goals, and Understanding: An Inquiry into Human Knowledge Structure* (Hillsdale, NJ: Lawrence Erlbaum, 1977).

37 David E. Rumelhart and Donald A. Norman, 'Accretion, Tuning, and Restructuring: Three Modes of Learning', in *Semantic Factors in Cognition*, eds. J. W. Cotton and R. L. Klatsky (Hillsdale, NJ: Lawrence Erlbaum, 1978), pp. 37–53.

Chapter 4

1 Klaus G. Grunert, Søren Bisp, Lone Bredahl, Elin Sørensen, and Niels Asger Nielsen, *A Survey of Danish Consumers' Purchase of Seafood*, MAPP project report (Aarhus: The Aarhus School of Business, 1996).

2 For example, see Roy Lachman, Janet L. Lachman, and Earl C. Butterfield, *Cognitive Psychology and Information Processing* (Hillsdale, NJ: Lawrence Erlbaum, 1979).

3 Eleanor Rosch, Carolyn B. Mervis, Wayne D. Gray, David M. Johnson, and Penny Boyes-Braem, 'Basic Objects in Natural Categories', *Cognitive Psychology*, July 1976, pp. 382–439.

4 For examples, see Joseph W. Alba, and Amitava Chattopadhyay, 'The Effects of Context and Part-Category Cues on the Recall of Competing Brands', *Journal of Marketing Research*, August 1985, pp. 340–349; Kunal Basu, 'Consumers' Categorization Processes: An Examination with two Alternative Methodological Paradigms', *Journal of Consumer Psychology*, no. 2, 1993, pp. 97–122; Mita Sujan and Christine Dekleva, 'Product Categorization and Inference Making: Some Implications for Comparative Advertising', *Journal of Consumer Research*, September 1987, pp. 14–54; and Mita Sujan and James R. Bettman, 'The Effects of Brand Positioning Strategies on Consumers' Brand and Category Perceptions: Some Insights from Schema Research', *Journal of Marketing Research*, November 1989, pp. 454–467.

5 Mita Sujan, 'Consumer Knowledge: Effects on Evaluation Strategies Mediating Consumer Judgments', *Journal of Consumer Research*, June 1985, pp. 31–46; Joel Cohen and Kunal Basu, 'Alternative Models of Categorization: Toward a Contingent Processing Framework', *Journal of Consumer Research*, March 1987, pp. 455–472; and Carolyn B. Mervis, 'Category Structure and the Development of Categorization', in *Theoretical Issues in Reading Comprehension*, eds. Rand Spiro *et al.* (Hillsdale, NJ: Lawrence Erlbaum, 1980), pp. 279–307.

6 Michael D. Johnson, 'The Differential Processing of Product Category and Noncomparable Choice Alternatives', *Journal of Consumer Research*, December 1989, pp. 300–309.

7 For example, Elizabeth C. Hirschman, 'Attributes of Attributes and Layers of Meaning', in *Advances in Consumer Research*, vol. 7, ed. Jerry C. Olson (Ann Arbor, MI: Association for Consumer Research, 1980), pp. 7–12.

8 Loren V. Geistfeld, George B. Sproles, and Susan B. Badenhop, 'The Concept and Measurement of a Hierarchy of Product Characteristics', in *Advances in Consumer Research*, vol. 4, ed. H. Keith Hunt (Ann Arbor, MI: Association for Consumer Research, 1977), pp. 302–307.

9 Theodore Levitt, 'Marketing Myopia', *Harvard Business Review*, July–August 1960, pp. 45–56.

10 Paul E. Green, Yoram Wind, and Arun K. Jain, 'Benefit Bundle Analysis', *Journal of Advertising Research*, April 1972, pp. 32–36.

11 Russell I. Haley, 'Benefit Segmentation: A Decision-Oriented Research Tool', *Journal of Marketing*, July 1972, pp. 30–35.

12 Lynn Coleman, 'Advertisers Put Fear into the Hearts of Their Prospects', *Marketing News*, 15 August 1988, pp. 1–2.

13 For instance, Sharon E. Beatty and Lynn R. Kahle, 'Alternative Measurement Approaches to Consumer Values: The List of Values and the Rokeach Value Survey', *Psychology & Marketing*, no. 3, 1985, pp. 181–200; Jonathan Gutman and Donald E. Vinson, 'Values Structures and Consumer Behavior', in *Advances in Consumer Research*, vol. 6, ed. William L. Wilkie (Ann Arbor, MI: Association for Consumer Research, 1979), pp. 335–339; Janice G. Hanna, 'A Typology of Consumer Needs', in *Research in Marketing*, vol. 3, ed. Jagdish N. Sheth (Greenwich, CO: JAI Press, 1980), pp. 83–104; and Lynn Kahle, 'The Values of Americans: Implications for Consumer Adaptation', in *Personal Values & Consumer Psychology*, eds. Robert E. Pitts, Jr. and Arch G. Woodside (Lexington, MA: Lexington Books, 1984), pp. 77–86.

14 Milton J. Rokeach, *The Nature of Human Values* (New York, NY: Free Press, 1973).

15 Shalom H. Schwartz, 'Universals in the Content and Structure of Values: Theoretical Advances and Empirical Tests in 20 Countries', in *Advances in Experimental Social Psychology*, ed. Mark P. Zanna (San Diego, CA: Academic Press, 1992), pp. 1–65.

16 Anthony G. Greenwald and Anthony R. Pratkanis, 'The Self', in *The Handbook of Social Cognition*, eds. Robert S. Wyer and Thomas K. Srull (Hillsdale, NJ: Lawrence Erlbaum, 1984), pp. 129–178; and Hazel Markus and Paula Nurius, 'Possible Selves', *American Psychologist*, September 1986, pp. 954–969.

17 John F. Kihlstrom and Nancy Cantor, 'Mental Representations of the Self', in *Advances in Experimental Social Psychology*, 17, 1984, pp. 1–47; Hazel Markus, 'Self-Schemata and Processing Information about the Self', *Journal of Personality and Social Psychology*, 35, 1977, pp. 63–78; and Hazel Markus and Keith Sentis, 'The Self in Social Information Processing', in *Psychological Perspective on the Self*, ed. J. Suls (Hillsdale, NJ: Lawrence Erlbaum, 1982), pp. 41–70.

18 The basic idea of means–end chains can be traced back at least to Edward C. Tolman, *Purposive Behavior in Animals and Men* (New York, NY: Century, 1932). Among the first to suggest its use in marketing was John A. Howard, *Consumer Behavior Application and Theory* (New York, NY: McGraw-Hill, 1977). More recently Jonathan Gutman, Thomas J. Reynolds,

and Jerry C. Olson have been active proponents of means–end chain models. For example, see Jonathan Gutman and Thomas J. Reynolds, 'An Investigation of the Levels of Cognitive Abstraction Utilized by Consumers in Product Differentiation', in *Attitude Research under the Sun*, ed. John Eighmey (Chicago, IL: American Marketing Association, 1979), pp. 125–150; Jonathan Gutman, 'A Means–End Chain Model Based on Consumer Categorization Processes', *Journal of Marketing*, Spring 1982, pp. 60–72; and Jerry C. Olson and Thomas J. Reynolds, 'Understanding Consumers' Cognitive Structures: Implications for Marketing Strategy', in *Advertising and Consumer Psychology*, vol. 1, eds. Larry Percy and Arch Woodside (Lexington, MA: Lexington Books, 1983), pp. 77–90. The idea has been well received in Europe as well, see for example Christel Claeys and Ann Swinnen, 'Consumers' means–end chains for "think" and "feel" products', *International Journal of Research in Marketing*, no. 2, 1995, pp. 193–208; Klaus G. Grunert, 'Food quality: A means–end perspective', *Food Quality and Preference*, no. 3, 1995, pp. 171–176; Alfred Kuß, 'Analyse von Kundenwünschen mit Hilfe von Means–End Chains', in *Kundenwünsche Realisieren*, eds. T. Tamczak and Christian Belz (St Gallen: Thexis, 1994); Rik Pieters, Hans Baumgartner, and Huib Stad, 'Diagnosing Means–End Structures: The Perception of Word-processing Software and the Adaptive-Innovative Personality of Managers', in *Proceedings of the 23rd EMAC Conference*, eds. Hans Kasper, Josée Bloemer, and Jos Lemmink (Maastricht: European Marketing Academy, 1994), pp. 749–763; and Pierre Valette-Florence and Bernard Rapacchi, 'A cross-cultural means–end chain analysis of perfume purchases', in *Proceedings of the Third Symposium on Cross-cultural Consumer and Business Studies*, eds. Nicholas E. Synodinos, Charles E. Keown, Klaus G. Grunert, T. E. Muller, and Julie H. Yu (Honolulu, HI: University of Hawaii, 1990), pp. 161–172.

19 Shirley Young and Barbara Feigen, 'Using the Benefit Chair for Improved Strategy Formulation', *Journal of Marketing*, July 1975, pp. 72–74; James H. Myers and Alan D. Schocker, 'The Nature of Product-Related Attributes', in *Research in Marketing*, ed. Jagdish N. Sheth (Greenwich, CO: JAI Press, 1981), pp. 211–236; Jonathan Gutman and Thomas J. Reynolds, 'An Investigation of the Levels of Cognitive Abstraction Utilized by Consumers in Product Differentiation', pp. 128–150; and Joel B. Cohen, 'The Structure of Product Attributes: Defining Attribute Dimensions for Planning and Evaluation', in *Analytic Approaches to Product and Marketing Planning*, ed. Alan D. Shocker (Cambridge, MA: Marketing Science Institute, 1979), pp. 54–86.

20 Jerry C. Olson and Thomas J. Reynolds, 'Understanding Consumer Cognitive Structures', pp. 77–90.

21 For a good example, see Sunil Mehrotra and John Palmer, 'Relating Product Features to Perceptions of Quality: Appliances', in *Perceived Quality*, eds. Jacob Jacoby and Jerry Olson (Lexington, MA: Lexington Books, 1985), pp. 81–96.

22 Tino Bech-Larsen, Niels Asger Nielsen, Klaus G. Grunert, and Elin Sørensen, 'Attributes of Low Involvement Products – A Comparison of Five Elicitation Techniques and a Test of Their Nomological Validity', MAPP Working Paper no. 43 (Aarhus: The Aarhus School of Business, 1997).

23 Thomas J. Reynolds and Jonathan Gutman, 'Laddering Theory, Method, Analysis, and Interpretation', *Journal of Advertising Research*, February–March 1988, pp. 11–31; Jonathan Gutman, 'Exploring the Nature of Linkages Between Consequences and Values', *Journal of Business Research*, 22, 1991, pp. 143–148; and Klaus G. Grunert and Suzanne C. Grunert, 'Measuring Subjective Meaning Structures by the Laddering Method: Theoretical Considerations and Methodological Problems', *International Journal of Research in Marketing*, no. 2, 1995, pp. 209–225.

24 For an example, see Klaus G. Grunert, 'What's in a Steak? A Cross-Cultural Study on the Quality Perception of Beef', *Food Quality and Preference*, no. 4, 1997, pp. 1–18.

25 For a good example, see Jonathan Gutman and Scott D. Alden, 'Adolescents' Cognitive Structures of Retail Stores and Fashion Consumption: A Means–End Chain Analysis of Quality', in *Perceived Quality*, eds. Jacob Jacoby and Jerry Olson (Lexington, MA: Lexington Books, 1985), pp. 99–114.

26 One of the first and most influential writers about involvement was Herbert E. Krugman. See Herbert E. Krugman, 'The Impact of Television Advertising: Learning Without Involvement', *Public Opinion Quarterly*, 29, 1965, pp. 349–356; and Herbert E. Krugman, 'The Measurement of Advertising Involvement', *Public Opinion Quarterly*, 30, 1967, pp. 583–596.

27 For instance, see John H. Antil, 'Conceptualization and Operationalization of Involvement', in *Advances in Consumer Research*, vol. 11, ed. Thomas C. Kinnear (Ann Arbor, MI: Association for Consumer Research, 1984), pp. 203–209; Andrew A. Mitchell, 'Involvement: A Potentially Important Mediator of Consumer Behavior', in *Advances in Consumer Research*, vol. 6, ed. William Wilkie (Ann Arbor, MI: Association for Consumer Research, 1979), pp. 191–196; or Robert N. Stone, 'The Marketing Characteristics of Involvement', in *Advances in Consumer Research*, vol. 11, ed. Thomas C. Kinnear (Ann Arbor, MI: Association for Consumer Research, 1984), pp. 210–215. Also see Peter N. Bloch, 'An Exploration into the Scaling of Consumers' Involvement in a Product Class', in *Advances in Consumer Research*, vol. 8, ed. Kent B. Monroe (Ann Arbor, MI: Association for Consumer Research, 1981), pp. 61–65; and Judith Lynne Zaichkowsky, 'Measuring the Involvement Construct', *Journal of Consumer Research*, December 1985, pp. 341–352.

28 Joel B. Cohen, 'Involvement and You: 100 Great Ideas', in *Advances in Consumer Research*, vol. 9, ed. Andrew A. Mitchell (Ann Arbor, MI: Association for Consumer Research, 1982), pp. 324–327.

29 Richard L. Celsi and Jerry C. Olson, 'The Role of Involvement in Attention and Comprehension Processes', *Journal of Consumer Research*, September 1988, pp. 210–224; Gabi Jeck-Schlottmann, 'Anzeigenbetrachtung bei Geringem Involvement', *Marketing-ZFP*, no. 1, 1988, pp. 33–43; Andrew A. Mitchell, 'The Dimensions of Advertising Involvement', in *Advances in Consumer Research*, vol. 8, ed. Kent B. Monroe (Ann Arbor, MI: Association for Consumer Research, 1981), pp. 25–30; Gilles Laurent and Jean-Noël Kapferer, 'Measuring Consumer Involvement Profiles', *Journal of Marketing Research*, no. 1, 1985, pp. 41–53; and William L. Moore and Donald R. Lehmann, 'Individual Differences in Search Behavior for a Nondurable', *Journal of Consumer Research*, December 1980, pp. 296–307.

30 Richard L. Celsi and Jerry C. Olson, 'The Role of Involvement in Attention and Comprehension Processes', pp. 210–224.

31 Beth A. Walker and Jerry C. Olson, 'Means–End Chains: Connecting Products with Self', *Journal of Business Research*, no. 2, 1991, pp. 111–118; and Christel Claeys and Ann Swinnen, 'Consumers' means–end chains for "think" and "feel" products', *International Journal of Research in Marketing*, no. 2, 1995, pp. 193–208.

32 Richard L. Celsi and Jerry C. Olson, 'The Role of Involvement in Attention and Comprehension Processes', pp. 210–224.

33 Harold H. Kassarjian, 'Low Involvement – A Second Look', in *Advances in Consumer Research*, vol. 8, ed. Kent B. Monroe (Ann Arbor, MI: Association for Consumer Research, 1981), pp. 31–34.

34 Richard L. Celsi and Jerry C. Olson, 'The Role of Involvement in Attention and Comprehension Processes', pp. 210–224.

35 See Richard L. Celsi and Jerry C. Olson, 'The Role of Involvement in Attention and Comprehension Processes', pp. 210–224. A similar perspective is provided by Peter H. Bloch and
Marsha L. Richins, 'A Theoretical Model of the Study of Product Importance Perceptions',
Journal of Marketing, Summer 1983, pp. 69–81. Some researchers treat these two factors
as two forms of involvement – enduring and situational involvement, respectively. For
instance, see Michael J. Houston and Michael L. Rothschild, 'Conceptual and Methodological
Perspectives on Involvement', in *1978 Educators' Proceedings*, ed. S. C. Jain (Chicago, IL:
American Marketing Association, 1978), pp. 184–187. We believe it is clearer to treat these
factors as sources of involvement.

36 For a similar proposal, see Peter H. Bloch, 'Involvement Beyond the Purchase Process:
Conceptual Issues and Empirical Investigation', in *Advances in Consumer Research*, vol. 9,
ed. Andrew A. Mitchell (Ann Arbor, MI: Association for Consumer Research, 1982),
pp. 413–417. Some researchers have called this 'enduring involvement' – e.g. Michael J.
Houston and Michael L. Rothschild, 'Conceptual and Methodological Perspectives on Involvement', in *1978 Educators' Proceedings*, ed. S. C. Jain (Chicago, IL: American Marketing
Association, 1978), pp. 184–187.

37 Gilles Laurent and Jean-Noël Kapferer, 'Measuring Consumer Involvement Profiles', *Journal of
Marketing Research*, no. 1, 1985, pp. 41–53.

38 Russell W. Belk, 'Worldly Possessions: Issues and Criticisms', in *Advances in Consumer Research*,
vol. 10, eds. Richard P. Bagozzi and Alice M. Tybout (Ann Arbor, MI: Association for
Consumer Research, 1983), pp. 514–519; and Terence A. Shimp and Thomas J. Madden,
'Consumer-Object Relations: A Conceptual Framework Based Analogously on Sternberg's
Triangular Theory of Love', in *Advances in Consumer Research*, vol. 15, ed. Michael J. Houston
(Ann Arbor, MI: Association for Consumer Research, 1988), pp. 163–168.

39 For a similar idea in an advertising context, see Thomas J. Reynolds and Jonathan Gutman,
'Advertising Is Image Management', *Journal of Advertising Research*, February–March 1984,
pp. 27–37.

40 Peter Cushing and Melody Douglas-Tate, 'The Effect of People/Product Relationships on
Advertising Processing', in *Psychological Processes and Advertising Effects*, eds. Linda Alwitt
and Andrew A. Mitchell (Hillsdale, NJ: Lawrence Erlbaum, 1985), pp. 241–259.

41 Sunil Mehrotra and John Palmer, 'Relating Product Features to Perceptions of Quality:
Appliances', in *Perceived Quality*, eds. Jacob Jacoby and Jerry C. Olson (Lexington, MA:
Lexington Books, 1985), pp. 81–96.

Chapter 5

1 See Anthony A. Greenwald and Clark Leavitt, 'Audience Involvement in Advertising: Four
Levels', *Journal of Consumer Research*, June 1984, pp. 581–592.

2 For example, see William Schneider and Richard M. Shiffrin, 'Controlled and Automatic
Human Information Processing: I. Detection, Search, and Attention', *Psychological Review*,
January 1977, pp. 1–66; and Richard M. Shiffrin and William Schneider, 'Controlled and
Automatic Human Information Processing: II. Perceptual Learning, Automatic Attending,
and a General Theory', *Psychological Review*, March 1977, pp. 127–190.

3 Daniel Kahneman and Anne Treisman, 'Changing Views of Attention and Automaticity', in
Varieties of Attention, eds. R. Parasuraman and D. R. Davies (New York, NY: Academic Press,
1984), pp. 29–61; and John G. Lynch, Jr. and Thomas K. Srull, 'Memory and Attention
Factors in Consumer Choice: Concepts and Research Methods', *Journal of Consumer Research*,
September 1982, pp. 18–37.

4   Sharon E. Beatty and Scott M. Smith, 'External Search Effort: An Investigation Across Several Product Categories', *Journal of Consumer Research*, June 1987, pp. 83–95; Peter H. Bloch, Daniel Sherrell, and Nancy M. Ridgway, 'Consumer Search: An Extended Framework', *Journal of Consumer Research*, June 1986, pp. 119–126; Joseph W. Newman, 'Consumer External Search: Amount and Determinants', in *Consumer and Industrial Buying Behavior*, eds. Arch G. Woodside, Jagdish N. Sheth, and Peter D. Bennett (New York, NY: Elsevier-North Holland, 1977), pp. 79–94; and Richard R. Olshavsky and Donald H. Granbois, 'Consumer Decision Making – Fact or Fiction', *Journal of Consumer Research*, June 1979, pp. 63–70.

5   Leo Bogart, 'Executives Fear Ad Overload Will Lower Effectiveness', *Marketing News*, 25 May 1984, pp. 4–5.

6   Peter H. Bloch and Marsha L. Ritchins, 'Shopping Without Purchase: An Investigation of Consumer Browsing Behavior', in *Advances in Consumer Research*, vol. 10, eds. Richard P. Baggozi and Alice M. Tybout (Ann Arbor, MI: Association for Consumer Research, 1983), pp. 389–393.

7   Joanne Lipman, 'CNN Ads Get Extra Mileage During the War', *The Wall Street Journal*, 27 February 1991, pp. B1, B4.

8   Colin McDonald, 'Zapping and zipping', *Admap*, January 1996, pp. 13–14; Kerry Jonas, 'Does clutter matter?' *Admap*, March 1996, pp. 14–15.

9   Dennis Kneale, 'Zapping of TV Ads Appears Pervasive', *The Wall Street Journal*, 25 April 1988, p. 21.

10 Otto Ottesen, 'Buyer Initiative: Ignored, But Imperative for Marketing Management', *Tidvise Skrifter*, no. 15, 1995, pp. 1–44.

11 Joanne Lipman, 'Brand-Name Products Are Popping up in TV Shows', *The Wall Street Journal*, 19 February 1991, pp. B1, B3.

12 Bill Saporito, 'IKEA's Got 'Em Lining Up', *Fortune*, 11 March 1991, p. 72.

13 Roy Lachman, Janet L. Lachman, and Earl C. Butterfield, *Cognitive Psychology and Information Processing: An Introduction* (Hillsdale, NJ: Lawrence Erlbaum, 1979).

14 Daniel Kahneman, *Attention and Effort* (Englewood Cliffs, NJ: Prentice-Hall, 1973).

15 Anthony A. Greenwald and Clark Leavitt, 'Audience Involvement in Advertising: Four Levels', *Journal of Consumer Research*, June 1984, pp. 58–92; and Chris Janiszewski, 'The Influence of Nonattended Material on the Processing of Advertising Claims', *Journal of Marketing Research*, August 1990, pp. 263–278.

16 David W. Schumann, Jennifer Gayson, Johanna Ault, Kerri Hargrove, Lois Hollingsworth, Russell Ruelle, and Sharon Seguin, 'The Effectiveness of Shopping Cart Signage: Perceptual Measures Tell a Different Story', *Journal of Advertising Research*, February–March 1991, pp. 17–22.

17 The relationship between arousal and various aspects of information processing goes as far back as the study by R. N. Yerkes and J. D. Dodson, 'The relation of strength of stimulus to rapidity of habit formation', *Journal of Comparative Neurology and Psychology*, 1908, pp. 459–482. In a consumer behaviour context, it looks as if overarousal, which inhibits attention, takes place only on very rare occasions, so that it is usually a good communication strategy to raise arousal. See Werner Kroeber-Riel and Peter Weinberg, *Konsumenten-verhalten*, 6th edn. (Munich: Vahlen, 1996), pp. 78–100; and David M. Sanbonmatsu and Frank R. Kardes, 'The Effects of Physiological Arousal on Information Processing and Persuasion', *Journal of Consumer Research*, December 1988, pp. 379–385.

18 Meryl Paula Gardner, 'Mood States and Consumer Behavior', *Journal of Consumer Research*, December 1985, pp. 281–300; and Noel Murray, Harish Sujan, Edward R. Hirt, and Mita

Sujan, 'The Effects of Mood on Categorization: A Cognitive Flexibility Hypothesis', *Journal of Personality and Social Psychology*, September 1990, pp. 411–425.

19 Marvin E. Goldberg and Gerald J. Gorn, 'Happy and Sad TV Programs: How They Affect Reactions to Commercials', *Journal of Consumer Research*, December 1987, pp. 387–403.

20 See Richard L. Celsi and Jerry C. Olson, 'The Role of Involvement in Attention and Comprehension Processes', *Journal of Consumer Research*, September 1988, pp. 210–224; and Klaus G. Grunert, 'Automatic and Strategic Processes in Advertising Effects', *Journal of Marketing*, no. 4, 1996, pp. 88–101.

21 Both examples were taken from 'Intuition, Microstudies, Humanized Research Can Identify Emotions That Motivate Consumers', *Marketing News*, 19 March 1982, p. 11.

22 Klaus G. Grunert, 'Automatic and Strategic Processes in Advertising Effects', *Journal of Marketing*, no. 4, 1996, pp. 88–101 and Richard L. Celsi and Jerry C. Olson, 'The Role of Involvement in Attention and Comprehension Processes', *Journal of Consumer Research*, September 1988, pp. 210–224.

23 Ann L. McGill and Punam Anand, 'The Effect of Vivid Attributes on the Evaluation of Alternatives: The Role of Differential Attention and Cognitive Elaboration', *Journal of Consumer Research*, September 1989, pp. 188–196.

24 'Four More Years: The Marketing Implications', *Marketing News*, 4 January 1985, pp. 1, 50, 52.

25 Brian Davis, 'FCO's Run of Bad Luck', *Advertising Age*, 10 June 1985, p. 58.

26 Patricia Winters, 'Topsy-Turvy Look Puts a New Spin on Ad Placements', *Advertising Age*, 12 September 1988, p. 4.

27 Klaus G. Grunert, 'Automatic and Strategic Processes in Advertising Effects', *Journal of Marketing*, no. 4, 1996, pp. 88–101.

28 Klaus G. Grunert and Eduard Stupening, *Werbung – ihre gesellschaftliche und ökonomische Problematik* (Frankfurt: Campus, 1981).

29 H. H. Clark and S. E. Haviland, 'Psychological Processes in Linguistic Explanation', in *Explaining Linguistic Phenomena*, ed. D. Cohen (Washington, DC: Hemisphere, 1974), pp. 91–124.

30 Klaus G. Grunert, 'Automatic and Strategic Processes in Advertising Effects', *Journal of Marketing*, no. 4, 1996, pp. 88–101. For some very instructive basic psychological studies in automatic perception and comprehension see Walter Schneider and Richard M. Shiffrin, 'Controlled and Automatic Human Information Processing: I. Detection, Search, and Attention', *Psychological Review*, no. 1, 1977, pp. 1–66.

31 Fergus I. M. Craik and Robert S. Lockhart, 'Levels of Processing: A Framework for Memory Research', *Journal of Verbal Learning and Verbal Behavior*, 11, 1972, pp. 671–689; and Jerry C. Olson, 'Encoding Processes: Levels of Processing and Existing Knowledge Structures', in *Advances in Consumer Research*, vol. 7, ed. Jerry C. Olson (Ann Arbor, MI: Association for Consumer Research, 1980), pp. 154–159.

32 The term *depth* is being used as a metaphor, of course. Depth does not connote any physical dimension of brain storage.

33 John R. Anderson and Lynne M. Reder, 'An Elaboration Processing Explanation of Depth of Processing', in *Levels of Processing in Human Memory*, eds. Larry S. Cermak and Fergus I. M. Craik (Hillsdale, NJ: Lawrence Erlbaum, 1979), pp. 385–404; and Richard E. Petty and John T. Cacioppo, 'The Elaboration Likelihood Model of Persuasion', in *Advances in Experimental Social Psychology*, vol. 19, ed. Leonard Berkowitz (New York, NY: Academic Press, 1986), pp. 123–205.

34 John R. Anderson and Lynne M. Reder, 'An Elaboration Processing Explanation of Depth of Processing', pp. 385–404.

35 Alain d'Astous and Marc Dubuc, 'Retrieval Processes in Consumer Evaluative Judgment Making: The Role of Elaborative Processing', in *Advances in Consumer Research*, vol. 13, ed. Richard J. Lutz (Provo, UT: Association for Consumer Research, 1986), pp. 132–137; Jerry C. Olson, 'Encoding Processes: Levels of Processing and Existing Knowledge Structures', in *Advances in Consumer Research*, vol. 7, ed. Jerry C. Olson (Ann Arbor, MI: Association for Consumer Research, 1980), pp. 154–159; and Douglas M. Stayman and Rajeev Batra, 'Encoding and Retrieval of Ad Affect in Memory', *Journal of Consumer Research*, May 1991, pp. 232–239.

36 Kevin Lane Keller, 'Memory Factors in Advertising: The Effect of Advertising Retrieval Cues on Brand Evaluations', *Journal of Consumer Research*, December 1987, pp. 316–333; Joan Myers-Levy, 'Priming Effects on Product Judgments: A Hemispheric Interpretation', *Journal of Consumer Research*, 16, June 1989, pp. 76–86.

37 Gary T. Ford and Ruth Ann Smith, 'Inferential Beliefs in Consumer Evaluations: An Assessment of Alternative Processing Strategies', *Journal of Consumer Research*, December 1987, pp. 363–371; Richard J. Harris, 'Inference in Information Processing', in *The Psychology of Learning and Motivation*, vol. 15, ed. Gordon A. Bower (New York, NY: Academic Press, 1981), pp. 81–128; and Mita Sujan and Christine Dekleva, 'Product Categorization and Inference Making: Some Implications for Comparative Advertising', *Journal of Consumer Research*, December 1987, pp. 372–378.

38 Amna Kirmani, 'The Effect of Perceived Advertising Costs on Brand Perceptions', *Journal of Consumer Research*, September 1990, pp. 160–171; Amna Kirmani and Peter Wright, 'Money Talks: Perceived Advertising Expense and Expected Product Quality', *Journal of Consumer Research*, December 1989, pp. 344–353.

39 For examples of inferring means–end chains, see Valarie A. Zeithaml, 'Consumer Perceptions of Price, Quality, and Value', *Journal of Marketing*, July 1988, pp. 2–22; and Sunil Mehrotra and John Palmer, 'Relating Product Features to Perceptions of Quality: Appliances', in *Perceived Quality*, eds. Jacob Jacoby and Jerry C. Olson (Lexington, MA: Lexington Books, 1985), pp. 81–96.

40 See Joseph W. Alba and J. Wesley Hutchinson, 'Dimensions of Consumer Expertise', *Journal of Consumer Research*, March 1987, pp. 411–454; and Jerry C. Olson, 'Inferential Belief Formation in the Cue Utilization Process', in *Advances in Consumer Research*, vol. 5, ed. H. Keith Hunt (Ann Arbor, MI: Association for Consumer Research, 1978), pp. 706–713.

41 Carl Obermiller, 'When Do Consumers Infer Quality from Price?', in *Advances in Consumer Research*, vol. 15, ed. Michael J. Houston (Provo, UT: Association for Consumer Research, 1988), pp. 304–310; Jerry C. Olson, 'Price as an Informational Cue: Effects on Product Evaluations', in *Consumer and Industrial Buying Behavior*, eds. Arch G. Woodside, Jagdish N. Sheth, and Peter D. Bennett (New York, NY: North Holland, 1977), pp. 267–286; and Valarie Zeithaml, 'Consumer Perceptions of Price, Quality, and Value', pp. 2–22; and Hermann Diller, *Preispolitik* (Stuttgart: Poeschel, 1985).

42 Frank R. Kardes, 'Spontaneous Inference Processes in Advertising: The Effects of Conclusion Omission and Involvement on Persuasion', *Journal of Consumer Research*, September 1988, pp. 225–233; Richard D. Johnson and Irwin P. Levin, 'More Than Meets the Eye: The Effect of Missing Information on Purchase Evaluations', *Journal of Consumer Research*, June 1985, pp. 169–177; and Carolyn J. Simmons and John G. Lynch, Jr., 'Inference Effects with Inference Making? Effects of Missing Information on Discounting and Use of Presented Information', *Journal of Consumer Research*, March 1991, pp. 477–491.

43 Donald F. Cox, 'The Sorting-Rule Model of the Consumer Product Evaluation Process', in *Risk Taking and Information Handling in Consumer Behavior*, ed. Donald F. Cox (Boston, MA: Harvard

University, 1967), pp. 324–369; and Klaus G. Grunert, 'Cognitive Determinants of Attribute Information Usage', *Journal of Economic Psychology*, March 1986, pp. 95–124.

44 Durairaj Maheswaran and Brian Sternthal, 'The Effects of Knowledge, Motivation, and Type of Message on Ad Processing and Product Judgments', *Journal of Consumer Research*, June 1990, pp. 66–73.

45 James R. Bettman and Mita Sujan, 'Effects of Framing on Evaluation of Comparable and Noncomparable Alternatives by Expert and Novice Consumers', *Journal of Consumer Research*, September 1987, pp. 141–154; Joseph W. Alba and J. Wesley Hutchinson, 'Dimensions of Consumer Expertise', *Journal of Consumer Research*, March 1987, pp. 411–454; Eric J. Johnson and J. Edward Russo, 'Product Familiarity and Learning New Information', *Journal of Consumer Research*, June 1984, pp. 542–550; Lawrence J. Marks and Jerry C. Olson, 'Toward a Cognitive Structure Conceptualization of Product Familiarity', in *Advances in Consumer Research*, vol. 8, ed. Kent B. Monroe (Ann Arbor, MI: Association for Consumer Research, 1981), pp. 145–150; and Fred Selnes and Sigurd Villads Trøye, 'Buying Expertise, Information Search, and Problem Solving', *Journal of Economic Psychology*, no. 3, 1989, pp. 411–428.

46 Mita Sujan, 'Consumer Knowledge: Effects on Evaluation Processes Mediating Consumer Judgments', *Journal of Consumer Research*, June 1985, pp. 31–46; Klaus G. Grunert, 'Attributes, attribute values and their characteristics: A unifying approach and an example involving a complex household investment', *Journal of Economic Psychology*, no. 2, 1989, pp. 229–251.

47 Michael Oneal, 'Attack of the Bug Killers', *Business Week*, 16 May 1988, p. 81.

48 Richard E. Petty, John T. Cacioppo, and David Schumann, 'Central and Peripheral Routes to Advertising Effectiveness: The Moderating Role of Involvement', *Journal of Consumer Research*, September 1983, pp. 135–144; and Hans Mühlbacher, 'Ein situatives Modell zur Informationsaufnahme und -Verarbeitung bei Werbekontakten', *Marketing-ZFP*, 1988, pp. 85–96.

49 Peter L. Wright and Barton Weitz, 'Time Horizon Effects on Product Evaluation Strategies', *Journal of Marketing Research*, November 1977, pp. 429–443.

50 Christine Moorman, 'The Effects of Stimulus and Consumer Characteristics on the Utilization of Nutrition Information', *Journal of Consumer Research*, December 1990, pp. 362–374.

51 Deborah J. MacInnis and Linda L. Price, 'The Role of Imagery in Information Processing: Review and Extensions', *Journal of Consumer Research*, March 1987, pp. 473–491.

52 Elizabeth C. Hirschman, 'Point of View: Sacred, Secular, and Mediating Consumption Imagery in Television Commercials', *Journal of Marketing Research*, December–January 1991, pp. 38–43.

53 Ronald Alsop, 'Marketing: The Slogan's Familiar, But What's the Brand?' *The Wall Street Journal*, 8 January 1988, p. B1.

54 Tim Perfect and Sue Heatherley, 'Implicit memory in print ads', *Admap*, January 1996, pp. 41–42.

55 Jacob Jacoby and Wayne D. Hoyer, 'Viewer Miscomprehension of Televised Communications: Selected Findings', *Journal of Marketing*, Fall 1982, pp. 12–26; Jacob Jacoby and Wayne D. Hoyer, 'The Comprehension/Miscomprehension of Print Communication: Selected Findings', *Journal of Consumer Research*, March 1989, pp. 434–443; and Klaus G. Grunert and Konrad Dedler, 'Misleading advertising: In search of a measurement methodology', *Journal of Public Policy & Marketing*, 4, 1985, pp. 153–165.

56 Some researchers believe these estimates are too high due to problems in measuring miscomprehension. See Gary T. Ford and Richard Yalch, 'Viewer Miscomprehension of

Televised Communication – A Comment', *Journal of Marketing*, Fall 1982, pp. 27–31; and Richard W. Mzerski, 'Viewer Miscomprehension Findings Are Measurement Bound', *Journal of Marketing*, Fall 1982, pp. 32–34.

57 Chris Janiszewski, 'The Influence of Print Advertisement Organization on Affect Toward a Brand Name', *Journal of Consumer Research*, June 1990, pp. 53–65; James M. Munch and Jack L. Swasy, 'Rhetorical Question, Summarization Frequency, and Argument Strength Effects on Recall', *Journal of Consumer Research*, June 1988, pp. 69–76; and Thomas J. Olney, Morris B. Holbrook, and Rajeev Batra, 'Consumer Responses to Advertising: The Effects of Ad Content, Emotions, and Attitude Toward the Ad on Viewing Time', *Journal of Consumer Research*, March 1991, pp. 440–453.

58 Jacob Jacoby, Robert W. Chestnut, and William Silberman, 'Consumer Use and Comprehension of Nutrition Information', *Journal of Consumer Research*, September 1977, pp. 119–128; Joyce A. Vermeersch and Helene Swenerton, 'Interpretations of Nutrition Claims in Food Advertisements by Low-Income Consumers', *Journal of Nutrition Education*, January–March 1980, pp. 19–25; and Christine Moorman, 'The Effects of Stimulus and Consumer Characteristics on the Utilization of Nutrition Information', *Journal of Consumer Research*, December 1990, pp. 362–374.

Chapter 6

1 Anthony G. Greenwald, 'On Defining Attitude and Attitude Theory', in *Psychological Foundations of Attitudes*, eds. Anthony G. Greenwald, T. C. Brock, and Thomas M. Ostrom (New York, NY: Academic Press, 1968), pp. 361–388; William J. McGuire, 'The Vicissitudes of Attitudes and Similar Representational Constructs in Twentieth Century Psychology', *European Journal of Social Psychology*, 1986, pp. 89–130; and Günter Silberer, 'Einstellungen und Werthaltungen', in *Marktpsychologie als Sozialwissenschaft*, ed. Martin Irle (Göttingen: Hogrefe, 1981), pp. 533–625.

2 Richard P. Bagozzi, 'The Rebirth of Attitude Research in Marketing', *Journal of the Market Research Society*, 30, no. 2, 1988, pp. 163–195.

3 Many authors have defined attitudes in this way, including Russell H. Fazio, 'How Do Attitudes Guide Behavior?', in *Handbook of Motivation and Cognition: Foundations of Social Behavior*, eds. R. M. Sorrentino and E. T. Higgins (New York, NY: Guilford Press, 1986), pp. 204–243.

4 Chris T. Allen and Thomas J. Madden, 'A Closer Look at Classical Conditioning', *Journal of Consumer Research*, December 1985, pp. 301–315; Werner Kroeber-Riel and Peter Weinberg, *Konsumentenverhalten*, 6th edn. (Munich: Vahlen, 1996), especially pp. 128–140; Terence A. Shimp, Elenora W. Stuart, and Randall W. Engle, 'A Program of Classical Conditioning Experiments Testing Variations in the Conditioned Stimulus and Context', *Journal of Consumer Research*, June 1991, pp. 1–12; and Elenora W. Stuart, Terence A. Shimp, and Randall W. Engle, 'Classical Conditioning of Consumer Attitudes: Four Experiments in an Advertising Context', *Journal of Consumer Research*, December 1987, pp. 334–349.

5 Alain d'Astous and Marc Dubuc, 'Retrieval Processes in Consumer Evaluative Judgment Making: The Role of Elaborative Processing', in *Advances in Consumer Research*, vol. 13, ed. Richard J. Lutz (Provo, UT: Association for Consumer Research, 1986), pp. 132–137; and Paul W. Miniard, Thomas J. Page, April Atwood, and Randall L. Ross, 'Representing Attitude Structure Issues and Evidence', in *Advances in Consumer Research*, vol. 13, ed. Richard J. Lutz (Provo, UT: Association for Consumer Research, 1986), pp. 72–76.

6 Russell H. Fazio, Martha C. Powell, and Carol J. Williams, 'The Role of Attitude Accessibility in the Attitude-to-Behavior Process', *Journal of Consumer Research*, December 1989, pp. 280–288; and Ida E. Berger and Andrew A. Mitchell, 'The Effect of Advertising on Attitude Accessibility, Attitude Confidence, and the Attitude–Behavior Relationship', *Journal of Consumer Research*, December 1989, pp. 269–279.

7 Peter H. Farquhar, 'Managing Brand Equity', *Marketing Research*, September 1989, pp. 24–33.

8 For instance, see Joan Myers-Levy, 'Priming Effects on Product Judgments: A Hemispheric Interpretation', *Journal of Consumer Research*, June 1989, pp. 76–86.

9 Kenneth E. Miller and James L. Ginter, 'An Investigation of Situational Variation in Brand Choice Behavior and Attitude', *Journal of Marketing Research*, February 1979, pp. 111–123.

10 Patrick Barwise, 'Brand Equity: Snark or Boojum?', *International Journal of Research in Marketing*, March 1993, pp. 93–104.

11 Wagner A. Kamakura and Gary J. Russell, 'Measuring Brand Value with Scanner Data', *International Journal of Research in Marketing*, March 1993, pp. 9–22.

12 Peter H. Farquhar, 'Managing Brand Equity', *Marketing Research*, September 1989, pp. 24–33.

13 Ibid.

14 Esben Sloth Andersen, 'The Evolution of Credence Goods: A Transaction Approach to Product Specification and Quality Control', MAPP working paper no. 21 (Aarhus: The Aarhus School of Business, 1994).

15 David M. Boush and Barbara Loken, 'A Process-Tracing Study of Brand Extension Evaluation', *Journal of Marketing Research*, February 1991, pp. 16–28; Lorraine Sunde and Roderick J. Brodie, 'Consumer Evaluations of Brand Extensions: Further Empirical Results', *International Journal of Research in Marketing*, March 1993, pp. 47–53.

16 C. Whan Park, Sandra Milberg, and Robert Lawson, 'Evaluation of Brand Extensions: The Role of Product Feature Similarity and Brand Concept Consistency', *Journal of Consumer Research*, September 1991, pp. 185–193.

17 Martin Fishbein and Icek Ajzen, *Belief, Attitude, Intention, and Behavior: An Introduction to Theory and Research* (Reading, MA: Addison-Wesley, 1975); and Andrew A. Mitchell and Jerry C. Olson, 'Are Product Attributes the Only Mediators of Advertising Effects on Brand Attitude?', *Journal of Marketing Research*, 18, pp. 318–332.

18 Susan B. Hester and Mary Yuen, 'The Influence of Country of Origin on Consumer Attitudes and Buying Behavior in the United States and Canada', in *Advances in Consumer Research*, vol. 14, eds. Melanie Wallendorf and Paul Anderson (Provo, UT: Association for Consumer Research, 1987), pp. 538–542; and Sung-Tai Hong and Robert S. Wyer, 'Determinants of Product Evaluation: Effects of the Time Interval between Knowledge of a Product's Country of Origin and Information about its Specific Attributes', *Journal of Consumer Research*, December 1990, pp. 277–288.

19 William B. Dodds, Kent B. Monroe, and Dhruv Grewal, 'Effects of Price, Brand, and Store Information on Buyer's Product Evaluations', *Journal of Marketing Research*, August 1991, pp. 307–319; Meryl P. Gardner, 'Advertising Effects on Attributes Recalled and Criteria Used for Brand Evaluations', *Journal of Consumer Research*, December 1983, pp. 310–331; and Richard Paul Hinkle, 'Medals from Wine Competitions Win Sales', *Advertising Age*, 31 January 1985, p. 31.

20 Kenneth E. Miller and James L. Ginter, 'An Investigation of Situational Variation in Brand Choice Behavior and Attitude', *Journal of Marketing Research*, February 1979, pp. 111–123.

21 See William L. Wilkie and Edgar A. Pessemier, 'Issues in Marketing's Use of Multiattribute Attitude Models', *Journal of Marketing Research*, November 1973, pp. 428–441. Another influential model, particularly in the early days of marketing research on attitudes, was developed by Milton J. Rosenberg, 'Cognitive Structure and Attitudinal Affect', *Journal of Abnormal and Social Psychology*, November 1956, pp. 367–372. Although different terminology is used, the structure of Rosenberg's model is quite similar to Fishbein's.

22 Michael Fishbein and Icek Ajzen, *Belief, Attitude, Intention, and Behavior* (Reading, MA: Addison-Wesley, 1975).

23 Joel B. Cohen, Paul W. Miniard, and Peter R. Dickson, 'Information Integration: An Information Processing Perspective', in *Advances in Consumer Research*, vol. 11, ed. Thomas C. Kinnear (Ann Arbor, MI: Association for Consumer Research, 1980), pp. 161–170; and Klaus G. Grunert, 'Linear Processing in a Semantic Network: An Alternative View of Consumer Product Evaluation', *Journal of Business Research*, 1982, pp. 31–42.

24 It should be noted that the multiplication of strength and evaluation causes a number of problems in statistical analysis, because such multiplication requires ratio scales, which is an unrealistic assumption for the type of data typically available. For a discussion of the problems involved and possible solutions, see Martin G. Evans, 'The Problem of Analyzing Multiplicative Composites', *American Psychologist*, January 1991, pp. 6–15; Bernhard Orth, 'Bedeutsamkeitsanalysen Bilinearer Einstellungsmodelle', *Zeitschrift für Sozialpsychologie*, 1985, pp. 101–115.

25 See Phillip A. Dover and Jerry C. Olson, 'Dynamic Changes in an Expectancy-Value Attitude Model as a Function of Multiple Exposures to Product Information', in *Contemporary Marketing Thought*, eds. Barnett A. Greenberg and Danny N. Dellenger (Chicago, IL: American Marketing Association, 1977), pp. 455–459; Lynn Frewer, Chaya Howard, and Richard Shepherd, 'The Influence of Realistic Product Exposure on Attitudes Towards Genetic Engineering of Food', *Food Quality and Preference* (in press); Robert E. Smith and William R. Swinyard, 'Information Response Models: An Integrated Approach', *Journal of Marketing*, Winter 1982, pp. 81–93; and Russell H. Fazio and Mark P. Zanna, 'Attitudinal Qualities Relating to the Strength of the Attitude-Behavior Relationship', *Journal of Experimental Social Psychology*, vol. 14, 1987, pp. 398–408.

26 Michael Fishbein and Icek Ajzen, *Belief, Attitude, Intention, and Behavior* (Reading, MA: Addison-Wesley, 1975).

27 An example of this link of attitude theory to means–end theory can be found in Richard P. Bagozzi and Pratibha A. Dabholkar, 'Consumer Recycling Goals and Their Effects on Decisions to Recycle: A Means–End Analysis', *Psychology & Marketing*, September–October 1994, pp. 1–28. See also Richard J. Lutz, 'The Role of Attitude Theory in Marketing', in *Perspectives in Consumer Behavior*, eds. H. H. Kassarjian and Thomas S. Robertson (Glenview, IL: Scott, Foresman, 1981), pp. 233–250. An early discussion of this idea was provided by James M. Carmen, 'Values and Consumption Patterns: A Closed Loop', in *Advances in Consumer Research*, vol. 5, ed. H. Keith Hunt (Ann Arbor, MI: Association for Consumer Research, 1978), pp. 403–407; and Jonathan Gutman, 'Exploring the Nature of Linkages between Consequences and Values', *Journal of Business Research*, 22, 1991, pp. 143–148. This means–end view of belief evaluation also solves the problem of infinite regress of attitudes, see A. Upmeyer, 'Attitudes and Social Behavior', in *Cognitive Analysis of Social Behaviour*, eds. Jacques-Philippe Leyens and Jean P. Codol (The Hague: Nijhoff, 1982), pp. 51–86.

28 Jerry C. Olson and Philip A. Dover, 'Attitude Maturation: Changes in Related Belief Structures over Time', in *Advances in Consumer Research*, vol. 5, ed. H. Keith Hunt (Ann Arbor, MI: Association for Consumer Research, 1978), pp. 333–342.

29 Hermann Freter, 'Interpretation und Aussagewert mehrdimensionaler Einstellungs-modelle im Marketing', in *Konsumentenverhalten und Information*, eds. Heribert Meffert, H. Steffenhagen, and Hermann Freter (Wiesbaden: Gabler, 1979), pp. 163–184; Helmut Laberenz and Bernhard Orth, 'Multiattributive Einstellungsmodelle und die Vorhersage von Konsumentenverhalten', *Marktforschung & Management*, no. 3, 1988, pp. 83–86; and Richard J. Lutz and James R. Bettman, 'Multiattribute Models in Marketing: A Bicentennial Review', in *Consumer and Industrial Buying Behavior*, eds. Arch G. Woodside, Jagdish N. Sheth, and Peter D. Bennett (New York, NY: Elsevier-North Holland Publishing, 1977), pp. 137–150.

30 The example is from Klaus G. Grunert, Allan Baadsgaard, Hanne Hartvig Larsen, and Tage Koed Madsen, *Market Orientation in Food and Agriculture* (Boston: Kluwer, 1996), chap. 3.

31 Christopher Power, Walecia Konrad, Alice Z. Cuneo, and James B. Treece, 'Value Marketing: Quality, Service, and Fair Pricing Are the Keys to Selling in the '90s', *Business Week*, 11 November 1991, pp. 132–140.

32 Tino Bech-Larsen, Niels Asger Nielsen, Klaus G. Grunert and Elin Sørensen, 'Means–End Chains for Low Involvement Products – A Study of Danish Consumers' Cognitions Regarding Different Applications of Vegetable Oil', MAPP working paper no. 41 (Aarhus: The Aarhus School of Business, 1996).

33 Richard J. Lutz, 'Changing Brand Attitudes through Modification of Cognitive Structure', *Journal of Consumer Research*, March 1975, pp. 49–59; and Andrew A. Mitchell, 'The Effect of Verbal and Visual Components of Advertisements on Brand Attitudes and Attitude toward the Advertisement', *Journal of Consumer Research*, June 1986, pp. 12–24.

34 Ulrike Hofsähs, 'Haribo bøjer tidsånden i vingummi', *Morgenavisen Jyllands-Posten*, 6 August 1966, p. 11; 'Produktudvikling af Haribo slik', *Plus Proces*, no. 11, 1996, p. 9.

35 Sanford Grossbart, Jim Gill, and Russ Laczniak, 'Influence of Brand Commitment and Claim Strategy on Consumer Attitudes', in *Advances in Consumer Research*, vol. 14, eds. Melanie Wallendorf and Paul Anderson (Provo, UT: Association for Consumer Research, 1987), pp. 510–513.

36 Frank Rose, 'If It Feels Good, It Must Be Bad', *Fortune*, 21 October 1991, pp. 91–108.

37 Klaus G. Grunert, 'What's in a Steak? A Cross-Cultural Study of Consumers' Quality Perception of Beef', *Food Quality and Preference*, 8, 1997, pp. 157–174.

38 Kathleen Deveny, 'Seeking Sunnier Sales, Lotion Makers Play on Fears, Target Teens, and Men', *The Wall Street Journal*, 24 May 1991, pp. B1, B3.

39 R. Brannon, 'Attitudes and the Prediction of Behavior', in *Social Psychology*, eds. Bernard Seidenberg and Alvin Snadowsky (New York, NY: Free Press, 1976), pp. 145–198; H. Mayer and B. van Eimeren, 'Einstellungen als Prädiktoren von (Kauf-)Verhalten', *Jahrbuch der Absatz- und Verbrauchsforschung*, 1985, pp. 207–229; and B. Six, 'Die Relation von Einstellung und Verhalten', *Zeitschrift für Sozialpsychologie*, 6, 1975, pp. 270–296.

40 Martin Fishbein, 'An Overview of the Attitude Construct', in A *Look Back, A Look Ahead*, ed. G. B. Hafer (Chicago, IL: American Marketing Association, 1980), p. 3.

41 See Icek Ajzen and Martin Fishbein, 'Attitude–Behavior Relations: A Theoretical Analysis and Review of Empirical Research', *Psychological Bulletin*, September 1977, pp. 888–918; Klaus G. Grunert, 'Another Attitude to Multiattribute Attitude Theories', in *Understanding Economic Behaviour*, eds. Klaus G. Grunert and Folke Ölander (Dordrecht: Kluwer, 1989), pp. 213–230; and Alan W. Wicker, 'Attitudes versus Action: The Relationship of Verbal and Overt Behavioral Responses to Attitude Objects', *Journal of Social Issues*, 25, 1969, pp. 41–78, among others.

42 Icek Ajzen, 'From Intentions to Actions: A Theory of Planned Behavior', in *Action Control: From Cognition to Behavior* (Berlin: Springer, 1985), pp. 11–39; Icek Ajzen and Thomas J. Madden, 'Prediction of Goal-Directed Behavior: Attitudes, Intentions, and Perceived Behavioral Control', *Journal of Experimental Social Psychology*, 1986, pp. 453–474; and S. Taylor and P. Todd, 'Decomposition and Crossover Effects in the Theory of Planned Behavior: A Study of Consumer Adoption Intentions', *International Journal of Research in Marketing*, July 1995, pp. 137–156.

43 Michael Fishbein and Icek Ajzen, *Belief, Attitude, Intention, and Behavior* (Reading, MA: Addison-Wesley, 1975).

44 Examples of applications can be found in Icek Ajzen and B. L. Driver, 'Prediction of Leisure Participation from Behaviour, Normative, and Control Beliefs: An Application of the Theory of Planned Behavior', *Leisure Sciences*, 1991, pp. 185–204; Robert East, 'Investment Decisions and the Theory of Planned Behavior', *Journal of Economic Psychology*, June 1993, pp. 337–375; and Paul Sparks, 'Attitudes Toward Food: Applying, Assessing and Extending the Theory of Planned Behavior', in *The Social Psychology of Health and Safety*, eds. D. R. Rutter and L. Quine (Aldershot: Avebury, 1994). A related approach can be found in John Thøgersen, 'A Model of Recycling Behaviour, With Evidence from Danish Source Separation Programmes', *International Journal of Research in Marketing*, March 1994, pp. 145–165.

45 Icek Ajzen and Michael Fishbein, 'Attitude–Behavior Relations: A Theoretical Analysis and Review of Empirical Research', pp. 888–918.

46 Richard P. Bagozzi and Paul R. Warshaw, 'Trying to Consume', *Journal of Consumer Research*, September 1990, pp. 127–140.

47 Barbara Loken, 'Effects of Uniquely Purchased Information on Attitudes toward Objects and Attitudes toward Behaviors', in *Advances in Consumer Research*, vol. 10, eds. Richard P. Bagozzi and Alice M. Tybout (Ann Arbor, MI: Association for Consumer Research, 1983), pp. 88–93.

48 Pat McIntyre, Mark A. Barnett, Richard Harris, James Shanteau, John Skowronski, and Michael Klassen, 'Psychological Factors Influencing Decisions to Donate Organs', in *Advances in Consumer Research*, vol. 14, eds. Melanie Wallendorf and Paul Anderson (Provo, UT: Association for Consumer Research, 1987), pp. 331–334.

49 William O. Bearden and Randall L. Rose, 'Attention to Social Comparison Information: An Individual Difference Factor Affecting Consumer Conformity', *Journal of Consumer Research*, March 1990, pp. 461–471.

50 Cited in Kenneth A. Longman, 'Promises, Promises', in *Attitude Research on the Rocks*, eds. L. Adler and L. Crespi (Chicago, IL: American Marketing Association, 1968), pp. 28–37.

51 Michel Laroche and Jacques E. Brisoux, 'Development of a Non-Linear Model of Attitudes, Intentions and Competition', *International Journal of Research in Marketing*, 1989, pp. 159–173.

52 Kenneth A. Longman, 'Promises, Promises', in *Attitude Research on the Rocks*, eds. L. Adler and L. Crespi (Chicago, IL: American Marketing Association, 1968), pp. 28–37.

53 For an interesting discussion of this issue, see Gordon R. Foxall, 'Consumers' Intentions and Behavior: A Note on Research and a Challenge to Researchers', *Journal of Market Research Society*, 26, 1985, pp. 231–241.

Chapter 7

1 Flemming Hansen, 'Psychological Theories of Consumer Choice', *Journal of Consumer Research*, December 1976, pp. 117–142.

2 It is important to recognize that consumer decision making is actually a seamless continuous flow of cognitive processes and behavioural actions. Researchers 'divide' this flow into separate stages and subprocesses for convenience in trying to research and understand the entire process and for helping to develop market strategies.

3 Joel B. Cohen, Paul W. Miniard, and Peter Dickson, 'Information Integration: An Information Processing Perspective', in *Advances in Consumer Research*, vol. 7, ed. Jerry C. Olson (Ann Arbor, MI: Association for Consumer Research, 1980), pp. 161–170; and Jerry C. Olson, 'Theories of Information Encoding and Storage: Implications for Consumer Behavior', in *The Effect of Information on Consumer and Market Behavior*, ed. Andrew A. Mitchell (Chicago, IL: American Marketing Association, 1978), pp. 49–60.

4 Richard W. Olshavsky and Donald H. Granbois, 'Consumer Decision Making – Fact or Fiction?', *Journal of Consumer Research*, September 1979, pp. 93–100.

5 Peter H. Bloch, Daniel L. Sherrell, and Nancy M. Ridgway, 'Consumer Search: An Extended Framework', *Journal of Consumer Research*, June 1986, pp. 119–126.

6 A similar notion is presented by Girish N. Punj and David W. Stewart, 'An Interaction Framework of Consumer Decision Making', *Journal of Consumer Research*, September 1983, pp. 181–196.

7 Daniel Kahneman and Amos Tyersky, 'Choices, Values, and Frames', *American Psychologist*, 39, 1984, pp. 341–350; Christopher P. Puto, 'The Framing of Buying Decisions', *Journal of Consumer Research*, December 1987, pp. 301–315; and William J. Qualls and Christopher P. Puto, 'Organizational Climate and Decision Framing: An Integrated Approach to Analyzing Industrial Buying Decisions', *Journal of Marketing Research*, May 1989, pp. 179–192.

8 James R. Bettman and Mita Sujan, 'Effects of Framing on Evaluation of Comparable and Noncomparable Alternatives by Experts and Novice Consumers', *Journal of Consumer Research*, September 1987, pp. 141–154; Joshua L. Wiener, James W. Gentry, and Ronald K. Miller, 'The Framing of the Insurance Purchase Decision', in *Advances in Consumer Research*, vol. 13, ed. Richard J. Lutz (Provo, UT: Association for Consumer Research, 1986), pp. 257–262; and Peter Wright and Peter D. Rip, 'Product Class Advertising Effects on First-Time Buyers' Decision Strategies', *Journal of Consumer Research*, September 1980, pp. 176–188.

9 Lawrence A. Crosby and James R. Taylor, 'Effects of Consumer Information and Education in Cognition and Choice', *Journal of Consumer Research*, June 1981, pp. 43–56; John G. Lynch and Thomas K. Srull, 'Memory and Attentional Factors in Consumer Choice: Concepts and Research Methods', *Journal of Consumer Research*, June 1982, pp. 18–37; and Gabriel Biehal and Dipankar Chakravarti, 'Consumers' Use of Memory and External Information in Choice: Macro and Micro Perspectives', *Journal of Consumer Research*, March 1986, pp. 382–405.

10 Gabriel Biehal and Dipankar Chakravarti, 'Information Accessibility as a Moderator of Consumer Choice', *Journal of Consumer Research*, June 1983, pp. 1–14; and Valerie S. Folkes, 'The Availability Heuristic and Perceived Risk', *Journal of Consumer Research*, June 1988, pp. 13–23.

11 David B. Klenosky and Arno J. Rethans, 'The Formation of Consumer Choice Sets: A Longitudinal Investigation at the Product Class Level', in *Advances in Consumer Research*, vol. 15, ed. Michael J. Houston (Provo, UT: Association for Consumer Research, 1988), pp. 13–18; John R. Hauser and Birger Wernerfelt, 'An Evaluation Cost Model of Consideration Set', *Journal of Consumer Research*, March 1990, pp. 393–408; and John H. Roberts and James M. Lattin, 'Development and Testing of a Model of Consideration Set Composition', *Journal of Marketing Research*, November 1991, pp. 429–440.

12 John Howard and Jagdish N. Sheth, *The Theory of Buyer Behavior* (New York, NY: Wiley, 1969); and Prakash Nedungadi, 'Recall and Consumer Consideration Sets: Influencing Choice without Altering Brand Evaluations', *Journal of Consumer Research*, December 1990, pp. 263–276.

13 Sharon E. Beatty and Scott M. Smith, 'External Search Effort: An Investigation across Several Product Categories', *Journal of Consumer Research*, June 1987, pp. 83–95.

14 Wayne D. Hoyer and Steven P. Brown, 'Effects of Brand Awareness on Choice for a Common, Repeat-Purchase Product', *Journal of Consumer Research*, September 1990, pp. 141–148.

15 William Baker, J. Wesley Hutchinson, Danny Moore, and Prakash Nedungadi, 'Brand Familiarity and Advertising: Effects on the Evoked Set and Brand Preference', in *Advances in Consumer Research*, vol. 13, ed. Richard J. Lutz (Provo, UT: Association for Consumer Research, 1986), pp. 637–642.

16 Kristian E. Moller and Pirjo Karppinen, 'Role of Motives and Attributes in Consumer Motion Picture Choice', *Journal of Economic Psychology*, 4, 1983, pp. 239–262.

17 Joel E. Urbany, Peter R. Dickson, and William L. Wilkie, 'Buyer Uncertainty and Information Search', *Journal of Consumer Research*, September 1989, pp. 208–215.

18 Klaus G. Grunert, 'Cognitive Determinants of Attribute Information Usage', *Journal of Economic Psychology*, 7, 1986, pp. 95–124; and C. Whan Park and Daniel C. Smith, 'Product Level Choice: A Top Down or Bottom Up Process?', *Journal of Consumer Research*, December 1989, pp. 289–299.

19 Loren V. Geistfeld, George B. Sproles, and Suzanne B. Badenhop, 'The Concept and Measurement of a Hierarchy of Product Characteristics', in *Advances in Consumer Research*, vol. 4, ed. W. D. Perrault (Chicago, IL: Association For Consumer Research, 1977), pp. 302–307.

20 Some of the examples are drawn from Donald F. Cox, 'The Sorting Rule Model of the Consumer Product Evaluation Process', in *Risk Taking and Information Handling in Consumer Behaviour*, ed. Donald F. Cox (Boston, MA: Graduate School of Business Administration, Harvard University, 1967), pp. 324–369; Klaus G. Grunert, 'What's in a Steak? A Cross-Cultural Study on the Quality Perception of Beef', *Food Quality And Preference*, 8, 1997, pp. 157–174; Graham J. Hooley, David Shipley, David and Nathalie Krieger, 'A Method for Modelling Consumer Perceptions of Country of Origin', *International Marketing Review*, 3, 1988, pp. 67–76; Johnny K. Johansson, 'Determinants and Effects of the Use of "Made in" Labels', *International Marketing Review*, 1, 1989, pp. 47–58; Wai-Kwan Li and Robert S. Wyerm, 'The Role of Country of Origin in Product Evaluations: Informational and Standard-Of-Comparison Effect', 2, 1994, pp. 187–213; Carl Obermiller and E. Spangenberg, 'Exploring the Effects of Country of Origin Labels: An Information Processing Framework', in *Advances in Consumer Research*, vol. 16, ed. Thomas K. Srull (Provo, UT: Association For Consumer Research, 1989), pp. 454–459; and Hans B. Thorelli, Jeen-Su Lim, and Jongsuk Ye, 'Relative Importance of Country of Origin, Warranty and Retail Store Image on Product Evaluations', *International Marketing Review*, 1989, pp. 35–46.

21 Mark I. Alpert, 'Unresolved Issues in Identification of Determinant Attributes', in *Advances in Consumer Research*, vol. 7, ed. Jerry C. Olson (Ann Arbor, MI: Association for Consumer Research, 1980), pp. 83–88.

22 John U. Farley, Jerrold Katz, and Donald R. Lehmann, 'Impact of Different Comparison Sets on Evaluation of a New Subcompact Car Brand', *Journal of Consumer Research*, September 1978, pp. 138–142; Srinivasan Ratneshwar, Allan D. Shocker, and David W. Steward, 'Toward Understanding the Attraction Effect: The Implications of Product Stimulus Meaningfulness and Familiarity', *Journal of Consumer Research*, March 1987, pp. 520–533; Merrie Brucks and Paul H. Schurr, 'The Effects of Bargainable Attributes and Attribute Range Knowledge on

Consumer Choice Processes', *Journal of Consumer Research*, March 1990, pp. 409–419; Kim P. Corfman, 'Comparability and Comparison Levels Used in Choices among Consumer Products', *Journal of Marketing Research*, August 1991, pp. 368–374; Noreen M. Klein and Manjit S. Yadav, 'Context Effects on Effort and Accuracy in Choice: An Enquiry into Adaptive Decision Making', *Journal of Consumer Research*, March 1989, pp. 411–421; and Rashi Glazer, Barbara E. Kahn, and William L. Moore, 'The Influence of External Constraints on Brand Choice: The Lone Alternative Effect', *Journal of Consumer Research*, June 1991, pp. 119–127.

23 Valerie S. Folkes, 'The Availability Heuristic and Perceived Risk', *Journal of Consumer Research*, June 1988, pp. 13–23.

24 John W. Vann, 'A Conditional Probability View of the Role of Product Warranties in Reducing Perceived Financial Risk', in *Advances in Consumer Research*, vol. 14, eds. Melanie Wallendorf and Paul Anderson (Provo, UT: Association for Consumer Research, 1987), pp. 421–425.

25 Narasimhan Srinivasan and Brian T. Ratchford, 'An Empirical Test of a Model of External Search for Automobiles', *Journal of Consumer Research*, September 1991, pp. 233–242; and Keith B. Murray, 'A Test of Services Marketing Theory: Consumer Information Acquisition Activities', *Journal of Marketing*, January 1991, pp. 10–25.

26 Robert S. Billings and Lisa L. Scherer, 'The Effects of Response Mode and Importance on Decision Making Strategies: Judgment versus Choice', *Organizational Behavior and Human Decision Processes*, 41, 1988, pp. 1–19; Kenneth R. MacCrimmon, 'An Overview of Multiple Objective Decision Making', in *Multiple Criteria Decision Making*, eds. J. L. Cochrane and M. Zeleny (Columbia, SC: University of South Carolina Press, 1973), pp. 19–44; and Peter Wright, 'Consumer Choice Strategies: Simplifying versus Optimizing', *Journal of Marketing Research*, February 1975, pp. 60–67.

27 Robert M. Dawes and Bernard Corrigan, 'Linear Models in Decision Making', *Psychological Bulletin*, 2, 1974, pp. 95–106.

28 Hillel J. Einhorn, 'The Use of Nonlinear, Noncompensatory Models in Decision Making', *Psychological Bulletin*, vol. 6, 1970, pp. 221–230.

29 James R. Bettman and C. Whan Park, 'Effects of Prior Knowledge and Experience and Phase of the Choice Process on Consumer Decision Processes: A Protocol Analysis', *Journal of Consumer Research*, 7, 1980, pp. 234–248; Joel B. Cohen, Paul W. Miniard, and Peter Dickson, 'Information Integration: An Information Processing Perspective', in *Advances in Consumer Research*, vol. 7, ed. Jerry C. Olson (Ann Arbor, MI: Association for Consumer Research, 1980), pp. 161–170; Wayne D. Hoyer, 'An Examination of Consumer Decision Making for a Common Repeat Purchase Product', *Journal of Consumer Research*, December 1984, pp. 822–829; David J. Curry, Michael B. Menasco, and James W. Van Ark, 'Multiattribute Dyadic Choice: Models and Tests', *Journal of Marketing Research*, August 1991, pp. 259–267; and O. Svenson, 'Process Descriptions of Decision Making', *Organizational Behavior And Human Performance*, 1979, pp. 86–112.

30 James Bettman and C. Whan Park, 'Effects of Prior Knowledge and Experience and Phase of the Choice Process on Consumer Decision Processes: A Protocol Analysis', *Journal of Consumer Research*, 7, 1980, pp. 234–248; and Wayne D. Hoyer, 'An Examination of Consumer Decision Making for a Common Repeat Purchase Product', *Journal of Consumer Research*, December 1984, pp. 822–829.

31 Robert S. Billings and Stephen A. Marcus, 'Measures of Compensatory and Noncompensatory Models of Decision Behavior: Process Tracing Versus Policy Capturing', *Organizational Behavior and Human Performance*, 1983, pp. 331–352; Donald R. Lehmann and William L. Moore, 'Validity of information display boards: An assessment using longitudinal data',

Journal of Marketing Research, 1980, pp. 450–459; John A. Quelch, 'Measurement of the relative importance of product attribute information: A review of the information display approach', *Journal of Consumer Policy*, 1979, pp. 232–245; and Peter Weinberg and Helmut Schulte-Frankenfeld, 'Informations-Display-Matrizen zur Analyse der Informations-aufnahme von Konsumenten', in *Innovative Marktforschung*, ed. Forschungsgruppe Konsum und Verhalten (Würzburg: Physica, 1983), pp. 63–74.

32 James R. Bettman, 'Presidential Address: Processes of Adaptivity in Decision Making', in *Advances in Consumer Research*, vol. 15, ed. Michael J. Houston (Provo, UT: Association for Consumer Research, 1988), p. 14; Surjit Chabra and Richard W. Olshavsky, 'Some Evidence for Additional Types of Choice Strategies', in *Advances in Consumer Research*, vol. 13, ed. Richard J. Lutz (Provo, UT: Association for Consumer Research, 1986), pp. 12–16; Wayne D. Hoyer, 'Variations in Choice Strategies across Decision Contexts: An Examination of Contingent Factors', in *Advances in Consumer Research*, vol. 13, ed. Richard J. Lutz (Provo, UT: Association for Consumer Research, 1986), pp. 32–36; James R. Bettman and Michel A. Zins, 'Constructive Processes in Consumer Choice', *Journal of Consumer Research*, September 1977, pp. 75–85; and James Bettman and C. Whan Park, 'Effects of Prior Knowledge and Experience and Phase of the Choice Process on Consumer Decision Processes: A Protocol Analysis', *Journal of Consumer Research*, 7, 1980, pp. 234–248

33 Wayne D. Hoyer, 'An Examination of Consumer Decision Making for a Common Repeat Purchase Product', *Journal of Consumer Research*, December 1984, pp. 822–829; John Payne, 'Task Complexity and Contingent Processing in Decision Making', *Organizational Behavior and Human Performance*, 16, 1976, pp. 366–387; and David Grether and Louis Wilde, 'An Analysis of Conjunctive Choice: Theory and Experiments', *Journal of Consumer Research*, March 1984, pp. 373–385.

34 A. Mitra, 'Price Cue Utilization in Product Evaluations: The Moderating Role of Motivation and Attribute Information', *Journal of Business Research*, 3, 1995, pp. 187–195.

35 C. Whan Park and Richard J. Lutz, 'Decision Plans and Consumer Choice Dynamics', *Journal of Marketing Research*, February 1982, pp. 108–115.

36 This terminology is borrowed from John Howard, *Consumer Behavior: Applications of Theory* (New York, NY: McGraw-Hill, 1979).

37 Robert J. Meyer, 'The Learning of Multiattribute Judgment Policies', *Journal of Consumer Research*, September 1987, pp. 155–173.

38 James H. Myers, 'Attribute Deficiency Segmentation: Measuring Unmet Wants', in *Advances in Consumer Research*, vol. 15, ed. Michael J. Houston (Provo, UT: Association for Consumer Research, 1988), pp. 108–113.

39 Lawrence W. Barsalou and J. Wesley Hutchinson, 'Schema Based Planning of Events in Consumer Contexts', in *Advances in Consumer Research*, vol. 14, eds. Melanie Wallendorf and Paul Anderson (Provo, UT: Association for Consumer Research, 1987), pp. 114–118.

40 Fred Selnes and Sigurd V. Trøye, 'Buying Expertise, Information Search, and Problem Solving', *Journal of Economic Psychology*, 3, 1989, pp. 411–428.

41 Banwari Mittal and Myong-Soo Lee, 'A Causal Model of Consumer Involvement', *Journal of Economic Psychology*, 3, 1989, pp. 363–389.

42 See also D. L. Alden, Wayne D. Hoyer, and G. Wechasara, 'Choice Strategies and Involvement: A Cross-Cultural Analysis', in *Advances in Consumer Research*, ed. Thomas K. Srull (Provo, UT: Association For Consumer Research, 1989), pp. 119–126.

43 Hillel J. Einhorn, 'Use of Nonlinear, Noncompensatory Models as a Function of Task and Amount of Information', *Organizational Behavior and Human Performance*, vol. 6, 1971, pp. 1–27; and John W. Payne, 'Task Complexity and Contingent Processing in

Decision-Making: An Information Search and Protocol Analysis', *Organizational Behavior and Human Performance*, vol. 16, 1976, pp. 366–387.

44 This section was adapted from James R. Bettman, *An Information Processing Theory of Consumer Choice* (Reading, MA: Addison-Wesley, 1979).

45 Ronald P. Hill and Meryl P. Gardner, 'The Buying Process: Effects Of and On Consumer Mood States', in *Advances in Consumer Research*, vol. 14, eds. Melanie Wallendorf and Paul Anderson (Provo, UT: Association for Consumer Research, 1987), pp. 408–410.

46 Flemming Hansen, 'Psychological Theories of Consumer Choice', *Journal of Consumer Research*, 3, 1976, pp. 117–142; and James R. Bettman, *An Information Processing Theory of Consumer Choice* (Reading, MA: Addison-Wesley, 1979).

47 George A. Miller, Eugene Galanter, and Karl H. Pribram, *Plans and the Structure of Behavior* (New York, NY: Henry Holt, 1960).

48 Robert M. Schlinder, Michael Berbaum, and Donna R. Weinzimer, 'How an Attention Getting Device Can Affect Choice among Similar Alternatives', in *Advances in Consumer Research*, vol. 14, eds. Melanie Wallendorf and Paul Anderson (Provo, UT: Association for Consumer Research, 1987), pp. 50–59.

49 Dennis W. Rook, 'The Buying Impulse', *Journal of Consumer Research*, September 1987, pp. 189–199.

50 Kevin Lane Keller and Richard Staelin, 'Effects of Quality and Quantity of Information on Decision Effectiveness', *Journal of Consumer Research*, September 1987, pp. 200–213.

Chapter 8

1 Tom Ottowitz and Francis Declerck, 'The Case of Brioche Pasquier S.A.: Industrializing Traditional French Baking', in *Product and Process Innovation in the Food Industry*, eds. Bruce Traill and Klaus G. Grunert (London: Chapman & Hall, 1997).

2 'Stimorol til Verden', *Morgenavisen Jyllands-Posten*, 30 October 1996, p. 6; and Ole Farbøl, 'Tyggegummikongen', *Signature*, no. 1, 1997, pp. 7–11.

3 For examples of the analysis of economic behaviour of animals and comparisons with human behaviour, see Stephen E. G. Lea, 'The Psychology and Economics of Demand', *Psychological Bulletin*, 1978, pp. 441–466; and Stephen R. Hursh, 'Behavioral Economics', *Journal of the Experimental Analysis of Behavior*, 1984, pp. 219–238.

4 This and the following views are elaborated in detail in Gordon R. Foxall, 'Behavior Analysis and Consumer Psychology', *Journal of Economic Psychology*, March 1994, pp. 5–91.

5 For discussions of the mere exposure effect, see Chris Janiszewski, 'Preattentive Mere Exposure Effects', *Journal of Consumer Research*, December 1993, pp. 376–393; and Robert B. Zajonc and Hazel Markus, 'Affective and Cognitive Factors in Preferences', *Journal of Consumer Research*, 1982, pp. 123–131.

6 Werner Kroeber-Riel, 'Emotional Product Differentiation by Classical Conditioning', in *Advances in Consumer Research*, vol. 11, ed. Thomas C. Kinnear (Provo, UT: Association for Consumer Research, 1984), pp. 538–543.

7 J. H. Donnelly and J. M. Ivancevich, 'Post-Purchase Reinforcement and Back-Out Behaviour', *Journal of Marketing Research*, 1970, pp. 399–400.

8 Robert C. Blattberg and Scott A. Neslin, *Sales Promotion: Concepts, Methods, and Strategies* (Englewood Cliffs, NJ: Prentice-Hall, 1990), p. 3.

9 J. Paul Peter and James H. Donnelly, Jr., *A Preface to Marketing Management*, 6th edn. (Homewood, IL: Irwin, 1994), pp. 163–164.

10 'Study: Some Promotions Change Consumer Behavior', *Marketing News*, 15 October 1990, p. 12.

Chapter 9

1   We will use these terms throughout the chapter because they are common in the consumer behaviour literature. However, behaviourists refer to classical conditioning as 'respondent conditioning.' Operant conditioning can also be called 'instrumental conditioning.'

2   Much of the material in this chapter is based on Walter R. Nord and J. Paul Peter, 'A Behaviour Modification Perspective on Marketing', *Journal of Marketing*, Spring 1980, pp. 36–47; and J. Paul Peter and Walter R. Nord, 'A Clarification and Extension of Operant Conditioning Principles in Marketing', *Journal of Marketing*, Summer 1982, pp. 102–107.

3   Behaviourists do not consider emotions or feelings as cognitive events but rather as behaviours. For example, if someone is observed yelling and screaming and throwing books at a classmate, behaviourists would have no problem describing the person as angry. However, the idea that the person is angry is determined through observation of the behaviours. Alternatively, measures of the person's blood pressure or other physiological measures could be used. However, the behaviours of yelling, screaming, and throwing are the phenomena to be analysed; the idea that there is an internal feeling called anger is believed to be impossible to prove or study scientifically by behaviourists. Today, many behaviourists find self-report measures of cognitive events useful for providing supportive evidence in an analysis and for diagnostic purposes. However, self-reports alone of mental states and events are still considered less valuable than measures of observed behaviours.

4   For recent discussion and more cognitively oriented interpretations of this type of conditioning, see Terence A. Shimp, 'Neo-Pavlovian Conditioning and Its Implications for Consumer Theory and Research', in *Handbook of Consumer Research and Theory*, eds. Thomas Robertson and Harold Kassarjian (Englewood Cliffs, NJ: Prentice-Hall, 1991), pp. 162–187; and Robert A. Rescorla, 'Pavlovian Conditioning: It's Not What You Think', *American Psychologist*, March 1988, pp. 151–160.

5   Gerald J. Gorn, 'The Effects of Music in Advertising on Choice Behaviour: A Classical Conditioning Approach', *Journal of Marketing*, Winter 1982, pp. 94–101.

6   Werner Kroeber-Riel, 'Emotional Product Differentiation by Classical Conditioning', in *Advances in Consumer Research*, vol. 11, ed. Thomas C. Kinnear (Provo, UT: Association for Consumer Research, 1984), pp. 538–543.

7   For additional discussion and empirical research on classical conditioning, see Francis K. McSweeney and Calvin Bierley, 'Recent Developments in Classical Conditioning', *Journal of Consumer Research*, December 1985, pp. 310–315; Calvin Bierley, Francis McSweeney, and Renee Vannieuwkerk, 'Classical Conditioning of Preferences for Stimuli', *Journal of Consumer Research*, December 1985, pp. 316–323; M. Carole Macklin, 'Classical Conditioning Effects in Product/Character Pairings Presented to Children', in *Advances in Consumer Research*, vol. 13, ed. Richard J. Lutz (Provo, UT: Association for Consumer Research, 1985), pp. 198–203; Elnora W. Stuart, Terence A. Shimp, and Randall W. Engle, 'Classical Conditioning of Consumer Attitudes: Four Experiments in an Advertising Context', *Journal of Consumer Research*, December 1987, pp. 334–349; Chris T. Allen and Chris A. Janiszewski, 'Assessing the Role of Contingency Awareness in Attitudinal Conditioning with Implications for Advertising Research', *Journal of Marketing Research*, February 1989, pp. 30–43; Chris Janiszewski and Luk Warlop, 'The Influence of Classical Conditioning Procedures on Subsequent Attention to the Conditioned Brand', *Journal of Consumer Research*, September 1993, pp. 171–189; Gerold Behrens, 'Kommunikative Beeinflussung durch emotionale Werbeinhalte', in *Marktorientierte Unternehmensführung*, eds. Josef Mazanec and Fritz

Scheuch (Vienna: Fachverlag an der Wirtschaftsuniversität Wien, 1984), pp. 687–705; and U. H. Ghazizadeh, *Werbewirkungen durch emotionale Konditionierung* (Frankfurt: Lang, 1987).

8   There are also a number of other possibilities, such as punishment by the removal of a positive consequence. For complete descriptions of these processes, see Arthur W. Staats, *Social Behaviorism* (Chicago, IL: Dorsey Press, 1975).

9   J. Ronald Carey, Stephen H. Clicque, Barbara A. Leighton, and Frank Milton, 'A Test of Positive Reinforcement of Customers', *Journal of Marketing*, October 1976, pp. 98–100.

10 A. J. McSweeney, 'Effects of Response Cost on the Behaviour of a Million Persons: Charging for Directory Assistance in Cincinnati', *Journal of Applied Behavioral Analysis*, Spring 1978, pp. 47–51.

Chapter 10

1   Albert Bandura, *Principles of Behavior Modification* (New York, NY: Holt, Rinehart & Winston, 1969), p. 120. This is a classic reference in the literature of psychology.

2   This discussion of the three major types of modelling influences is based on Walter R. Nord and J. Paul Peter, 'A Behavior Modification Perspective on Marketing', *Journal of Marketing*, Spring 1980, pp. 40–41.

3   Albert Bandura, *Principles of Behavior Modification* (New York, NY: Holt, Rinehart & Winston, 1969), p. 120

4   See Joseph R. Cautela, 'The Present Status of Covert Modeling', *Journal of Behavior Therapy and Experimental Psychiatry*, December 1976, pp. 323–326.

5   Joseph R. Cautela, 'The Present Status of Covert Modeling', *Journal of Behavior Therapy and Experimental Psychiatry*, December 1976, pp. 323–326.

6   Viola Catt and Peter L. Benson, 'Effect of Verbal Modeling on Contributions to Charity', *Journal of Applied Psychology*, February 1977, pp. 81–85.

7   See Charles C. Manz and Henry P. Sims, 'Vicarious Learning: The Influence of Modeling on Organizational Behavior', *Academy of Management Review*, January 1981, pp. 105–113. For discussions of model characteristics in advertising, see Michael J. Baker and Gilbert A. Churchill, Jr., 'The Impact of Physically Attractive Models on Advertising Evaluations', *Journal of Marketing Research*, November 1977, pp. 538–555; 'Models' Clothing Speaks to Ad Market: Study', *Marketing News*, 22 November 1985, p. 16; and Lynn R. Kahle and Pamela M. Homer, 'Physical Attractiveness of the Celebrity Endorser: A Social Adaptation Perspective', *Journal of Consumer Research*, March 1985, pp. 954–961.

8   Charles C. Manz and Henry P. Sims, 'Vicarious Learning: The Influence of Modeling on Organizational Behavior', *Academy of Management Review*, January 1981, pp. 105–113.

9   Werner Kroeber-Riel and Peter Weinberg, *Konsumetenverhalten*, 6th edn. (Munich: Vahlen, 1996), pp. 617–619.

10 Albert Bandura, *Social Learning Theory* (Englewood Cliffs, NJ: Prentice-Hall, 1977), p. 89. This book discusses a number of other variables affecting the modelling process.

11 Richard I. Evans, Richard M. Rozelle, Scott E. Maxwell, Betty E. Raines, Charles A. Dill, and Tanya J. Guthrie, 'Social Modeling Films to Deter Smoking in Adolescents: Results of a Three-Year Field Investigation', *Journal of Applied Psychology*, August 1981, pp. 399–414.

12 Denise A. DeRicco and John E. Niemann, 'in Vivo Effects of Peer Modeling on Drinking Rate', *Journal of Applied Behavioral Analysis*, Spring 1980, pp. 149–152; and Barry D. Caudill and Thomas R. Lipscomb, 'Modeling Influences on Alcoholics' Rates of Alcohol Consumption', *Journal of Applied Behavioral Analysis*, Summer 1980, pp. 355–365.

13 Trevor F. Stokes and Suzanne H. Kennedy, 'Reducing Child Uncooperative Behavior during Dental Treatment through Modeling and Reinforcement', *Journal of Applied Behavioral Analysis*, Spring 1980, pp. 41–49.

14 Richard A. Winnett, Joseph W. Hatcher, T. Richard Fort, Ingrid N. Lechliter, Susan Q. Love, Anne W. Riley, and James F. Fishback, 'The Effects of Videotape Modeling and Daily Feedback on Residential Electricity Conservation, Home Temperature and Humidity, Perceived Comfort and Clothing Worn: Winter and Summer', *Journal of Applied Behavioral Analysis*, Fall 1982, pp. 381–402.

15 See Charles C. Manz and Henry P. Sims, 'Vicarious Learning: The Influence of Modeling on Organizational Behavior', *Academy of Management Review*, January 1981, pp. 105–113.

16 William J. Froming and William Chambers, 'Modeling: An Analysis in Terms of Category Accessibility', *Journal of Experimental Social Psychology*, September 1983, pp. 403–421.

17 Albert Bandura, *Social Learning Theory* (Englewood Cliffs, NJ: Prentice-Hall, 1977), pp. 24–29; also see Albert Bandura, *Social Foundations of Thought and Action: A Social Cognitive Theory* (Englewood Cliffs, NJ: Prentice-Hall, 1986).

Chapter 11

1 For example, see Merrie Brucks, 'The Effects of Product Class Knowledge on Information Search Behavior', *Journal of Consumer Research*, June 1985, pp. 1–16; and Peter H. Bloch, Daniel L. Sherrell, and Nancy M. Ridgeway, 'Consumer Search: An Extended Framework', *Journal of Consumer Research*, June 1986, pp. 119–126.

2 Hans-Georg Gemünden, 'Perceived Risk and Information Search. A Systematic Meta-analysis of the Empirical Evidence', *International Journal of Research in Marketing*, no. 2, 1985, pp. 79–100.

3 Fred Selnes and Sigurd V. Trøye, 'Buying Expertise, Information Search, and Problem Solving', *Journal of Economic Psychology*, no. 3, 1989, pp. 411–428.

4 Sharon E. Beatty and Scott M. Smith, 'External Search Effort: An Investigation across Several Product Categories', *Journal of Consumer Research*, June 1987, p. 84; and Eberhard Kuhlmann, *Das Informationsverhalten der Konsumenten* (Freiburg: Rombach, 1970).

5 For a complete discussion of these issues, see Howard Beales, Michael B. Mazis, Steven Salop, and Richard Staelin, 'Consumer Search and Public Policy', *Journal of Consumer Research*, June 1981, pp. 11–22; Konrad Dedler, Ingrid Gottschalk, Klaus G. Grunert, Margot Heiderich, and Gerhard Scherhorn, *Das Informationsdefizit der Verbraucher* (Frankfurt: Campus, 1984); and Eberhard Kuhlmann, *Verbraucherpolitik* (Munich: Vahlen, 1990).

6 See Hans Raffee and Günter Silberer, *Warentest und Unternehmen – Nutzung, Wirkungen und Beurteilung des vergleichenden Warentests in Industrie und Handel* (Frankfurt: Campus, 1984), and Hans B. Thorelli and Jack L. Engledow, 'Information Seekers and Information Systems: A Policy Perspective.' *Journal of Marketing*, Spring 1980, pp. 9–27.

7 'American Express Plays Its Trump Card', *Business Week*, 24 October 1983, p. 62; also see 'Credit Cards: The US is Taking its Time Getting "Smart",' *Business Week*, 9 February 1987, pp. 88–89.

8 See John Thøgersen, 'Facilitating Recycling. Reverse Distribution Channel Design for Participation and Support', *Social Marketing Quarterly*, 1, 1997, pp. 42–55.

9 See Dick A. Francken 'Postpurchase Consumer Evaluations, Complaint Actions and Repurchase Behavior', *Journal of Economic Psychology*, September 1983, pp. 273–290; and Ursula Hansen and Ingo Schoenheit, *Verbraucherzufriedenheit und Beschwerdeverhalten* (Frankfurt: Campus, 1983).

10 For examples of the use of scanner data in marketing research, see Wagner A. Kamakura and Gary J. Russell, 'Measuring Brand Value with Scanner Data', *International Journal of Research in Marketing*, no. 1, 1993, pp. 9–22; and Peter S. H. Leeflang and Dick R. Wittink, 'Diagnosing Competitive Reactions Using (Aggregated) Scanner Data', *International Journal of Research in Marketing*, no. 1, 1992, pp. 39–58.

11 See Henry Assael, *Consumer Behavior and Marketing Action*, 4th edn. (Boston, MA: Kent Publishing, 1992).

Chapter 12

1 Adapted for this text from Jack Block and Jeanne H. Block, 'Studying Situational Dimensions: A Grand Perspective and Some Limited Empiricism', in *Toward a Psychology of Situations: An Interactional Perspective*, ed. David Magnusson (Hillsdale, NJ: Lawrence Erlbaum, 1981), pp. 85–102.

2 See, e.g. Søren Askegaard and Tage Koed Madsen, 'European Food Cultures: An Exploratory Analysis of Food Related Preferences and Behaviour in European Regions', MAPP working paper no. 26 (Aarhus: The Aarhus School of Business, 1995).

3 See Karen Brunsø, Klaus G. Grunert and Lone Bredahl, 'An Analysis of National and Cross-National Consumer Segments Using the Food-Related Lifestyle Instrument in Denmark, France, Germany and Great Britain', MAPP working paper no. 35 (Aarhus: The Aarhus School of Business, 1996).

4 C. Whan Park, Easwar S. Iyer, and Daniel C. Smith, 'The Effects of Situational Factors on In-Store Grocery Shopping Behavior: The Role of Store Environment and Time Available for Shopping', *Journal of Consumer Research*, March 1989, pp. 422–433.

5 Adapted from William D. Crano and Lawrence A. Messe, *Social Psychology: Principles and Themes of Interpersonal Behavior* (Homewood, IL: Dorsey Press, 1982), p. 15.

6 For example, see Robert J. Graham, 'The Role of Perception of Time in Consumer Research', *Journal of Consumer Research*, March 1981, pp. 335–342; Lawrence P. Feldman and Jacob Hornik, 'The Use of Time: An Integrated Conceptual Model', *Journal of Consumer Research*, March 1981, pp. 407–419; Jacob Hornik, 'Situational Effects on the Consumption of Time', *Journal of Marketing*, Fall 1982, pp. 44–55; Jacob Hornik, 'Subjective versus Objective Time Measures: A Note on the Perception of Time in Consumer Behavior', *Journal of Consumer Research*, June 1984, pp. 615–618; and Gabriele Morello, 'The Time Dimension in Marketing', *Irish Marketing Review*, no. 1, 1989, pp. 11–20.

7 See Debra A. Michal, 'Pitching Products by the Barometer', *Business Week*, 8 July 1985, p. 45; Ronald Alsop, 'Companies Look to Weather to Find Best Climate for Ads', *The Wall Street Journal*, 19 January 1985, p. 27; and Fred Ward, 'Weather, Behavior Correlated in New Market Test', *Marketing News*, 7 June 1985, p. 9.

8 Carl P. Zeithaml and Valarie A. Zeithaml, 'Environmental Management: Revising the Marketing Perspective', *Journal of Marketing*, Spring 1985, pp. 46–53.

9 See James H. Leigh and Claude R. Martin, 'A Review of Situational Influence Paradigms and Research', in *Review of Marketing 1981*, eds. Ben M. Enis and Kenneth J. Reering (Chicago, IL: American Marketing Association, 1981), pp. 57–74; Pradeep Kakkar and Richard J. Lutz, 'Situational Influences on Consumer Behavior', in *Perspectives in Consumer Behavior*, 3rd edn., eds. Harold H. Kassarjian and Thomas S. Robertson (Glenview, IL: Scott, Foresman, 1981), pp. 204–215; and Joseph A. Cote, Jr., 'Situational Variables in Consumer Research: A Review', Working Paper (Washington State University, 1985).

10 See Russell W. Belk, 'The Objective Situation as a Determinant of Consumer Behavior', in

Advances in Consumer Research, vol. 2, ed. Mary J. Schlinger (Chicago, IL: Association for Consumer Research, 1975), pp. 427–438; and Richard J. Lutz and Pradeep K. Kakkar, 'The Psychological Situation as a Determinant of Consumer Behavior', in *Advances in Consumer Research*, vol. 2, ed. Mary J. Schlinger (Chicago, IL: Association for Consumer Research, 1975), pp. 439–454.

11 Geraldine Fennell, 'Consumers' Perceptions of the Product Use Situation', *Journal of Marketing*, April 1978, pp. 38–47.

12 Russell W. Belk, 'Situational Variables and Consumer Behavior', *Journal of Consumer Research*, December 1976, pp. 157–164; and Kenneth E. Miller and James L. Ginter, 'An Investigation of Situational Variation in Brand Choice Behavior and Attitude', *Journal of Marketing Research*, February 1979, pp. 111–123.

13 Christian Derbaix and Michel T. Pham, 'Affective Reactions to Consumption Investigations: A Pilot Investigation', *Journal of Economic Psychology*, June 1991, pp. 325–356; and Andrea Gröppel, 'Store Design and Experience-Orientated Consumers in Retailing: A Comparison Between the United States and Germany', in European *Advances in Consumer Research*, vol. 1, eds. Gary J. Bamossy and Fred van Raaij (Provo, UT: Association for Consumer Research), pp. 99–109.

14 This case is described in more detail in Klaus G. Grunert, Allan Baadsgaard, Hanne Hartvig Larsen, and Tage Koed Madsen, *Market Orientation in Food and Agriculture* (Boston, MA: Kluwer, 1996), chap. 7.

15 See Andrea Gröppel and Brian Bloch, 'An Investigation of Experience-Orientated Consumers in Retailing', *International Review of Retail, Distribution and Consumer Research*, 1, 1990, pp. 101–118.

16 Ronald E. Milliman, 'The Influence of Background Music on the Behavior of Restaurant Patrons', *Journal of Consumer Research*, September 1986, pp. 286–289.

Chapter 13

1 Over 160 definitions of culture are reported in Frederick D. Sturdivant, 'Subculture Theory: Poverty, Minorities, and Marketing', in *Consumer Behavior: Theoretical Sources*, eds. Scott Ward and Thomas S. Robertson (Englewood Cliffs, NJ: Prentice-Hall, 1973), pp. 469–520.

2 See, for example, Dominique Bouchet, 'Rails Without Ties – The Social Imaginary and Postmodern Culture', *International Journal of Research in Marketing*, September, 1994, pp. 405–421; and Grant McCracken, *Culture and Consumption: New Approaches to the Symbolic Character of Consumer Goods and Activities* (Bloomington, IN: Indiana University Press, 1988).

3 John F. Sherry, 'The Cultural Perspective in Consumer Research', in *Advances in Consumer Research*, vol. 13, ed. Richard J. Lutz (Provo, UT: Association for Consumer Research, 1986), pp. 573–575.

4 Most consumer behaviour textbooks focus on the content of culture, describing the values and lifestyles of consumers in different cultures. For example, see Leon G. Shiffman and Leslie Lazar Kanuk, *Consumer Behavior*, 4th edn. (Englewood Cliffs, NJ: Prentice-Hall, 1991); and William L. Wilkie, *Consumer Behavior*, 2nd edn. (New York, NY: Wiley, 1990).

5 Ann Swidler, 'Culture in Action: Symbols and Strategies', *American Sociological Review*, April 1986, pp. 273–286; and Grant McCracken, *Culture and Consumption: New Approaches to the Symbolic Character of Consumer Goods and Activities* (Bloomington, IN: Indiana University Press, 1988), pp. 73–74.

6 Margot Hornblower, 'Advertising Spoken Here', *Time*, 15 July 1991, pp. 71–72.

7 David Kilburn, 'Japan's Sun Rises', *Advertising Age*, 3 August 1987, p. 42.

8 Saeed Samiee and I. Jong, 'Cross-Cultural Research in Advertising: An Assessment of Methodologies', *Journal of the Academy of Marketing Science*, no. 3, 1994, pp. 205–217.

9 See, for example, M. Hui, C. Joy, and Michel Laroche, 'Differences in Lifestyle Among Four Major Subcultures in a Bi-Cultural Environment', in *Proceedings from the Third Symposium on Cross-Cultural Consumer and Business Studies*, eds. Charles F. Keown *et al.* (Honolulu, HI: University of Hawaii, 1990).

10 Sharon E. Beatty, Lynn E. Kahle, Pamela Homer, and Shekhar Misra, 'Alternative Measurement Approaches to Consumer Values: The List Of Values and The Rokeach Value Survey', *Psychology and Marketing*, no. 2, 1985, pp. 189–200; Lynn R. Kahle, Sharon E. Beatty, and Pamela Homer, 'Alternative Measurement Approaches to Consumer Values; The List Of Values (LOV) and Values And Life Style (VALS)', *Journal of Consumer Research*, 1986, pp. 405–409; and Shalom H. Schwartz, 'Universals in the Content and Structure of Values: Theoretical Advances and Empirical Tests in 20 Countries', in *Advances in Experimental Social Psychology*, ed. Mark P. Zanna (San Diego, CA: Academic Press, 1992), pp. 1–65.

11 R. Chandran and J. B. Wiley, 'Instrument Equivalence in Cross-Cultural Research', in *Proceedings from the Third Symposium on Cross-Cultural Consumer and Business Studies*, eds. Charles F. Keown *et al.* (Honolulu, HI: University of Hawaii, 1990).

12 Allan R. Buss and Joseph R. Royce, 'Detecting Cross-Cultural Commonalities and Differences: Intergroup Factor Analysis', *Psychological Bulletin*, no. 1, 1975, pp. 128–136; S. Tamer Cavusgil, 'Factor Congruence Analysis: A Methodology for Cross-Cultural Research', *Journal of the Market Research Society*, no. 2, 1985, pp. 147–155; and C. H. Hui and Harry C. Triandis, 'Measurement in Cross-Cultural Psychology', *Journal of Cross-Cultural Psychology*, no. 2, 1985, pp. 131–152.

13 As another example, the cross-cultural validity of the List of Values has been investigated in Suzanne C. Grunert, Klaus G. Grunert, and Kai Kristensen, 'Une Méthode d'Éstimation de la Validité Interculturelle des Instruments de Mesure: Le Cas de la Mesure des Valeurs des Consommateurs par la Liste des Valeurs LOV', *Recherche et Applications en Marketing*, no. 4, 1994, pp. 5–28.

14 As an example, see Pierre Valette-Florence and Bernard Rapacchi, 'A Cross-Cultural Means–End Chain Analysis of Perfume Purchases', in *Proceedings from the Third Symposium on Cross-Cultural Consumer and Business Studies*, eds. Charles F. Keown *et al.* (Honolulu, HI: University of Hawaii, 1990), pp. 161–172.

15 Harold W. Kassarjian, 'Content Analysis in Consumer Research', *Journal of Consumer Research*, June 1977, pp. 8–18; Klaus Krippendorff, *Content Analysis* (Beverly Hills, CA: Sage, 1980); R. P. Weber, 'Measurement Models for Content Analysis', *Quality and Quantity*, 17, 1983, pp. 127–149; David R. Wheeler, 'Content Analysis: An Analytical Technique for International Marketing Research', *International Marketing Review*, no. 4, 1988, pp. 34–40.

16 For examples see Susan Spiggle, 'Measuring Social Values: A Content Analysis of Sunday Comics and Underground Comix', *Journal of Consumer Research*, June 1986, pp. 100–113; Russell W. Belk, 'Material Values in the Comics: A Content Analysis of Comic Books Featuring Themes of Wealth', *Journal of Consumer Research*, June 1987, pp. 26–42; Russell W. Belk and Richard W. Pollay, 'Images of Ourselves: The Good Life in Twentieth-Century Advertising', *Journal of Consumer Research*, March 1985, p. 888; and A. Belkaoui and J. M. Belkaoui, 'A Comparative Analysis of the Roles Portrayed by Women in Print Advertisements: 1958, 1970, 1972', *Journal of Marketing Research*, 1976, pp. 168–172.

17 Clifford Geertz, 'Thick Description', in *The Interpretation of Cultures* (New York, NY: Basic Books, 1973), pp. 3–30.

18 Shalom H. Schwartz and Werner Bilsky, 'Toward a Universal Structure of Human Values', *Journal of Personality and Social Psychology*, no. 3, 1987, pp. 550–562; and Shalom H. Schwartz, 'Universals in the Content and Structure of Values: Theoretical Advances and Empirical Tests in 20 Countries', in *Advances in Experimental Social Psychology*, ed. Mark P. Zanna (San Diego, CA: Academic Press, 1992), pp. 1–65.

19 Suzanne C. Grunert and Hans Jørn Juhl, 'Values, Environmental Attitudes, and Buying Organic Foods', *Journal of Economic Psychology*, no. 1, 1995, pp. 39–62.

20 This result is from ongoing research at the Aarhus School of Business.

21 This model is an adaptation and extension of the cultural process described by Grant McCracken (*Culture and Consumption*), who focused on how cultural meanings are first transferred to products and then passed on to individuals. The following discussion elaborates McCracken's ideas and extends them into a systems model of cultural processes.

22 Grant McCracken, 'Culture and Consumption: A Theoretical Account of the Structure and Movement of the Cultural Meaning of Consumer Goods', *Journal of Consumer Research*, June 1986, pp. 71–84.

23 Grant McCracken, 'Culture and Consumption: A Theoretical Account of the Structure and Movement of the Cultural Meaning of Consumer Goods', *Journal of Consumer Research*, June 1986, p. 79.

24 Jeffrey F. Durgee and Robert W. Stuart, 'Advertising Symbols and Brand Names That Best Represent Key Product Meanings', *Journal of Advertising*, Summer 1987, pp. 15–24.

25 Elizabeth C. Hirschman, 'The Creation of Product Symbolism', in *Advances in Consumer Research*, vol. 13, ed. Richard J. Lutz (Provo, UT: Association for Consumer Research, 1986), pp. 327–331.

26 For a brief discussion of the meaning transfer aspects of the fashion system, see Grant McCracken, 'Culture and Consumption: A Theoretical Account'.

27 Grant McCracken, 'Culture and Consumption: A Theoretical Account'.

28 For example, see Dennis W. Rook, 'The Ritual Dimension of Consumer Behavior', *Journal of Consumer Research*, December 1985, pp. 251–264.

29 John F. Sherry, Jr., 'A Sociocultural Analysis of a Midwestern American Fleamarket', *Journal of Consumer Research*, June 1990, pp. 13–30.

30 Peter H. Bloch, 'Product Enthusiasm: Many Questions, a Few Answers', in *Advances in Consumer Research*, vol. 13, ed. Richard J. Lutz (Provo, UT: Association for Consumer Research, 1986), pp. 61–65.

31 Russell W. Belk, 'Gift-Giving Behavior', in *Research in Marketing*, vol. 2, ed. Jagdish Sheth (Greenwich, CO: JAI Press, 1979), pp. 95–126.

32 Thomas Reynolds and Jonathan Gutman, 'Advertising Is Image Management', *Journal of Advertising Research*, 24, 1984, pp. 27–37; and for a similar viewpoint, see C. Whan Park, Bernard J. Jaworski, and Deborah J. MacInnis, 'Strategic Brand Concept-Image Management', *Journal of Marketing*, October 1986, pp. 135–145.

33 Peter H. Farquhar, 'Managing Brand Equity', *Marketing Research*, September 1989, pp. 24–33.

34 Russell W. Belk, 'ACR Presidential Address: Happy Thought', in *Advances in Consumer Research*, vol. 14, eds. Melanie Wallendorf and Paul Anderson (Provo, UT: Association for Consumer Research, 1986), pp. 1–4.

35 Grant McCracken, 'Who Is the Celebrity Endorser? Cultural Foundations of the Endorsement Process', *Journal of Consumer Research*, December 1989, pp. 310–321.

36 Shekhar Misra and Sharon E. Beatty, 'Celebrity Spokesperson and Brand Congruence: An Assessment of Recall and Affect', *Journal of Business Research*, 1990, pp. 159–173.

37 Flemming Hansen, 'Managerial Implications of Cross-Cultural Studies on Buyer Behavior', in *Consumer and Industrial Buying Behavior*, eds. Arch G. Woodside, Jagdish E. Sheth, and Peter D. Bennett (New York, NY: Elsevier, 1977), pp. 387–395.

38 See Anne B. Fisher, 'The Ad Biz Gloms onto "Global" ', *Fortune*, 12 November 1984, pp. 77–80.

39 Theodore Levitt, 'The Globalization of Markets', *Harvard Business Review*, May–June 1983, pp. 92–102.

40 Subhash C. Jain, 'Standardization of International Marketing Strategy: Some Research Hypotheses', *Journal of Marketing*, no. 1, 1989, pp. 70–79; Saeed Samiee and Kendall Roth, 'The Influence of Global Marketing Standardization on Performance', *Journal of Marketing*, no. 2, 1992, pp. 1–17; and Yoram Wind, 'The Myth of Globalization', *Journal of Consumer Marketing*, no. 2, 1986, pp. 23–26.

41 Nick Bull and Martin Oxley, 'The Search for Focus – Brand Values Across Europe', *Marketing and Research Today*, November 1996, pp. 239–246.

42 Lars Nielsen, 'Gaio giver MD Foods mavepine', *Morgenavisen Jyllands-Posten*, 2 September 1996; and Arne Panduro, 'MD standser salg af Gaio i England', *Morgenavisen Jyllands-Posten*, 7 January 1997.

43 Neil McKendrick, John Brewer, and J. H. Plumb, *The Birth of a Consumer Society: The Commercialization of Eighteenth-Century England* (Bloomington, IN: Indiana University Press, 1982).

44 Grant McCracken's, 'Culture and Consumption: A Theoretical Account', *Journal of Consumer Research*, June 1986, argues persuasively that status was not the only important value or meaning sought by people in eighteenth-century England.

Chapter 14

1 J. Gidlund, 'Nyregionalismen Och Europas Enande', *Framtider*, no. 4, 1991, pp. 14–17.

2 Søren Askegaard and Tage Koed Madsen, 'European Food Cultures: An Exploratory Analysis of Food Related Preferences and Behaviour in European Regions', MAPP working paper no. 26 (Aarhus: The Aarhus School of Business, 1995).

3 Julians Koranteng, 'Tracking What's Trendy, Hot Before It's Old News', *Ad Age International*, May 1996, p. 130.

4 Geoff Wicken, 'Keeping Young Readers', *Admap*, April 1996, pp. 48–50.

5 This discussion is based on Geoffrey Calvin, 'What the Baby-Boomers Will Buy Next', *Fortune*, 15 October 1984, pp. 28–34.

6 Andy Fry, 'Shades of Grey', *Marketing*, 24 April 1997, pp. 23–24.

7 Claire Murphy, 'No Olds Barred', *Marketing Week*, 16 February 1996, pp. 59–63.

8 Andy Fry, 'Shades of Grey', *Marketing*, 24 April 1997, pp. 23–24.

9 Claire Murphy, 'No Olds Barred'.

10 Sharon Marshall, 'The Old Grey Matter', *Marketing*, 13 March 1997, p. 23.

11 Harriet Swain, 'Older and Wiser: The Over-60s Flock to Learn', *The Times*, 29 June 1997, p. 5.

12 Andy Fry, 'Shades of Grey', *Marketing*, 24 April 1997, pp. 23–24.

13 Alicia Clegg, 'Colour Blind', *Marketing Week*, 21 June 1996, pp. 38–40.

14 Graham Bann, 'Race for Opportunity', *New Impact Journal*, December 1996–January 1997, pp. 8–9.

15 Robert Dwek, 'Losing the Race', *Marketing Business*, March 1997, pp. 10–15.

16 Ibid.

17 Ronald J. Faber, Thomas C. O'Guinn, and John A. McCarty, 'Ethnicity, Acculturation, and the Importance of Product Attributes', *Psychology & Marketing*, Summer 1987, pp. 121–134.

18 Lisa N. Penaloza, 'Immigrant Consumer Acculturation', in *Advances in Consumer Research*, vol. 16, ed. Thomas K. Srull (Provo, UT: Association for Consumer Research, 1989), pp. 110–118, 121–134.

19 Alan R. Andreasen, 'Cultural Interpenetration: A Critical Consumer Research Issue for the 1990s', in *Advances in Consumer Research*, vol. 17, eds. Marvin E. Goldberg, Gerald Gorn, and Richard W. Pollay (Provo, UT: Association for Consumer Research, 1990), pp. 847–849.

20 Kalervo Oberg, 'Cultural Shock: Adjustment to New Cultural Environments', *Practical Anthropologist*, 7, 1960, pp. 177–182.

21 Joan Myers-Levy and Durairaj Maheswaran, 'Exploring Differences in Males' and Females' Processing Strategies', *Journal of Consumer Research*, June 1991, pp. 63–70; and Floyd W. Rudmin, 'German and Canadian Data on Motivations for Ownership: Was Pythagoras Right?', in *Advances in Consumer Research*, vol. 17, eds. Marvin E. Goldberg, Gerald Gorn, and Richard W. Pollay (Provo, UT: Association for Consumer Research, 1990), pp. 176–181.

22 Rena Bartos, 'How to Advertise to Woman', *Admap*, September 1995, pp. 17–22; and Judith Wardle, 'The Good, the Bad and the Ugly', *Admap*, September 1995, pp. 26–29.

23 Richard P. Coleman, 'The Continuing Significance of Social Class to Marketing', *Journal of Consumer Research*, December 1983, pp. 265–280.

24 See Werner Kroeber-Riel and Peter Weinberg, *Konsumentenverhalten*, 6th edn. (Munich: Vahlen, 1996), pp. 554–558.

25 James E. Fisher, 'Social Class and Consumer Behavior: The Relevance of Class and Status', in *Advances in Consumer Research*, vol. 14, eds. Melanie Wallendorf and Paul Anderson (Provo, UT: Association for Consumer Research, 1987), pp. 492–496.

Chapter 15

1 Lakshman Krishnamurthi, 'The Salience of Relevant Others and Its Effects on Individual and Joint Preferences: An Experimental Investigation', *Journal of Consumer Research*, June 1983, pp. 62–72.

2 C. Whan Park and V. Parker Lessig, 'Students and Housewives: Differences in Susceptibility to Reference Group Influences', *Journal of Consumer Research*, September 1977, pp. 102–110; and William O. Bearden, Richard G. Netemeyer, and Jesse E. Teel, 'Measurement of Consumer Susceptibility to Interpersonal Influence', *Journal of Consumer Research*, March 1989, pp. 473–481.

3 John W. Schouten and James H. Alexander, 'Hog Heaven: The Structure, Ethos, and Market Impact of a Consumption Culture', a paper presented at the Annual Conference of the Association for Consumer Research, 1992.

4 William O. Bearden and Michael J. Etzel, 'Reference Group Influences on Product and Brand Purchase Decision', *Journal of Consumer Research*, September 1982, pp. 183–194.

5 David Brinberg and Linda Plimpton, 'Self-Monitoring and Product Conspicuousness in Reference Group Influence', in *Advances in Consumer Research*, vol. 13, ed. Richard J. Lutz (Provo, UT: Association for Consumer Research, 1986), pp. 297–300.

6 For further discussion and an alternative approach to studying reference group influences, see Peter H. Reingen, Brian L. Foster, Jacqueline Johnson Brown, and Stephen B. Seidman, 'Brand Congruence in Interpersonal Relations: A Social Network Analysis', *Journal of Consumer Research*, December 1984, pp. 771–783.

7 Julia M. Bristor, 'Coalitions in Organizational Purchasing: An Application of Network Analysis', in *Advances in Consumer Research*, vol. 15, ed. Michael J. Houston (Provo, UT: Association for Consumer Research, 1988), pp. 563–568.

8 Jacqueline Johnson Brown and Peter H. Reingen, 'Social Ties and Word-of- Mouth Referral Behavior', *Journal of Consumer Research*, December 1987, pp. 350–362; and Peter H. Reingen, 'A Word-of-Mouth Network', in *Advances in Consumer Research*, vol. 14, eds. Melanie Wallendorf and Paul Anderson (Provo, UT: Association for Consumer Research, 1987), pp. 213–217.

9 Dorothy Leonard-Barton, 'Experts as Negative Opinion Leaders in the Diffusion of a Technological Innovation', *Journal of Consumer Research*, March 1985, pp. 914–926.

10 William O. Bearden and Michael J. Etzel. 'Reference Group Influences on Product and Brand Purchase Decision', *Journal of Consumer Research*, September 1982, p. 184.

11 Joel Rudd, 'The Household as a Consuming Unit', in *Advances in Consumer Research*, vol. 14, eds. Melanie Wallendorf and Paul Anderson (Provo, UT: Association for Consumer Research, 1987), pp. 451–452.

12 Sunil Gupta, Michael R. Hagerty, and John G. Myers, 'New Directions in Family Decision Making Research', in *Advances in Consumer Research*, vol. 10, eds. Richard P. Bagozzi and Alice M. Tybout (Ann Arbor, MI: Association for Consumer Research, 1983), pp. 445–450; and Jagdish N. Sheth, 'A Theory of Family Buying Decision', in *Models of Buyer Behavior: Conceptual, Quantitative, and Empirical*, ed. Jagdish N. Sheth (New York, NY: Harper and Row, 1974), pp. 17–33.

13 Dennis L. Rosen and Donald H. Granbois, 'Determinants of Role Structure in Family Financial Management', *Journal of Consumer Research*, September 1983, pp. 253–285; and Irene Raj Foster and Richard W. Olshavsky, 'An Exploratory Study of Family Decision Making Using a New Taxonomy of Family Role Structure', in *Advances in Consumer Research*, vol. 16, ed. T. K. Srull (Provo, UT: Association for Consumer Research, 1989), pp. 665–670.

14 Jan Møller Jensen, 'Family Purchase Decisions; A Buying Center Approach', in *Proceedings of the 5th Biannual International Conference of the Academy of Marketing Science*, eds. Kristina D. Frankenberg, Hanne Hartvig Larsen, Flemming Hansen, Marian Friestad, and Gerald S. Albaum (Copenhagen: CBS, 1991), pp. 332–337.

15 William J. Qualls, 'Household Decision Behavior: The Impact of Husbands' and Wives' Sex Role Orientation', *Journal of Consumer Research*, September 1987, pp. 264–279; Dennis L. Rosen and Donald H. Granbois, 'Determinants of Role Structure in Family Financial Management', *Journal of Consumer Research*, September 1983, pp. 253–285; Charles M. Schaninger, W. Christian Buss, and Rajiv Grover, 'The Effect of Sex Roles on Family Economic Handling and Decision Influence', in *Advances in Consumer Research*, vol. 9, ed. Andrew A. Mitchell (Ann Arbor, MI: Association for Consumer Research, 1982), pp. 43–47; and Daniel Seymour and Greg Lessne, 'Spousal Conflict Arousal: Scale Development', *Journal of Consumer Research*, December 1984, pp. 810–821.

16 Harry L. Davis, 'Decision Making within the Household', *Journal of Consumer Research*, March 1976, pp. 241–260.

17 George P. Moschis and Linda G. Mitchell, 'Television Advertising and Interpersonal Influences on Teenagers' Participation in Family Consumer Decisions', in *Advances in Consumer Research*, vol. 13, ed. Richard J. Lutz (Provo, UT: Association for Consumer Research, 1986), pp. 181–186.

18 Jörg Palczewski, 'Werbung für Kinder und gesellschaftliche Verantwortung', *Markenartikel*, 1, 1996, pp. 2–5.

19 Andreas Ebeling, 'Aus Kids werden Kunden', *Markenartikel*, 1, 1996, pp. 9–14.

20 Franz Böcker and Lutz Thomas, 'Der Einfluß von Kindern auf die Produktpräferenzen ihrer Mütter', *Marketing-ZFP*, 1983, pp. 245–252.

21   Walter Hubel, *Der Einfluß von Familienmitgliedern auf gemeinsame Kaufentscheidungen* (Berlin: Duncker & Humblot, 1986).

22   Alvin Burns and Donald Granbois, 'Factors Moderating the Resolution of Preference Conflict in Family Automobile Purchasing', *Journal of Marketing Research*, February 1977, pp. 68–77; Alvin C. Burns and Jo Anne Hopper, 'An Analysis of the Presence, Stability and Antecedents of Husband and Wife Purchase Decision Making Influence Assessment and Disagreement', in *Advances in Consumer Research*, vol. 13, ed. Richard J. Lutz (Provo, UT: Association for Consumer Research, 1986), pp. 175–180; and Margaret C. Nelson, 'The Resolution of Conflict in Joint Purchase Decisions by Husbands and Wives: A Review and Empirical Test', in *Advances in Consumer Research*, vol. 15, ed. Michael J. Houston (Provo, UT: Association for Consumer Research, 1988), pp. 442–448.

23   A similar approach can be found in Erich Kirchler, *Kaufentscheidungen im privaten Haushalt* (Göttingen: Hogrefe, 1989).

24   Kim P. Corfman and Donald R. Lehmann, 'Models of Cooperative Group Decision-Making and Relative Influence: An Experimental Investigation of Family Purchase Decisions', *Journal of Consumer Research*, June 1987, pp. 1–13; Alvin Burns and Donald Granbois, 'Factors Moderating the Resolution of Preference Conflict in Family Automobile Purchasing', *Journal of Marketing Research*, February 1977, pp. 68–77; and Pierre Filiatrault and J. R. Brent Ritchie, 'Joint Purchasing Decisions: A Comparison of Influence Structure in Family and Couple Decision-Making Units', *Journal of Consumer Research*, September 1980, pp. 131–140.

25   Erich Kirchler, 'Spouses' Influence Strategies in Purchase Decisions As Dependent On Conflict Type And Relationship Characteristics', *Journal of Economic Psychology*, March 1990, pp. 101–118.

26   Erich Kirchler, *Kaufentscheidungen im privaten Haushalt* (Göttingen: Hogrefe, 1989).

27   Erich Kirchler, 'Diary Reports on Daily Economic Decisions of Happy Versus Unhappy Couples', *Journal of Economic Psychology*, 3, 1988, pp. 327–357.

28   Scott Ward, Donna M. Klees, and Daniel B. Wackman, 'Consumer Socialization Research: Content Analysis of Post-1980 Studies, and Some Implications for Future Work', in *Advances in Consumer Research*, vol. 17 (Provo, UT: Association for Consumer Research, 1990), pp. 798–803.

29   George P. Moschis, 'The Role of Family Communication in Consumer Socialization of Children and Adolescents', *Journal of Consumer Research*, March 1985, pp. 898–913; and Eberhard Kuhlmann, 'Consumer Socialization of Children and Adolescents: A Review of Current Approaches', *Journal of Consumer Policy*, 6, no. 4, 1983, pp. 397–418.

30   Gerhard Scherhorn, 'The Goal of Consumer Advice: Transparency or Autonomy?', *Journal of Consumer Policy*, 1985, pp. 133–151.

31   Gilbert A. Churchill, Jr. and George P. Moschis, 'Television and Interpersonal Influences on Adolescent Consumer Learning', *Journal of Consumer Research*, June 1979, pp. 23–35.

32   Klaus G. Grunert, 'TV Advertising, Product Preferences and Consumer Socialization', in *Commercial Television and European Children*, eds. Scott Ward, Tom Robertson and Ray Brown (Aldershot: Gower, 1986), pp. 177–190.

33   Eduard Stupening, 'Detrimental Effects of Television Advertising on Consumer Socialization', *Journal of Business Research*, 10, no. 1, 1981, pp. 75–84.

34   Sanford Grossbart, Les Carlson, and Ann Walsh, 'Consumer Socialization Motives for Shopping with Children', *AMA Summer Educators' Proceedings* (Chicago, IL: American Marketing Association, 1988); Bonnie B. Reece, Sevgin Eroglu, and Nora J. Rifon, 'Parents Teaching Children to Shop: How, What, and Who?', *AMA Summer Educators' Proceedings* (Chicago, IL: American Marketing Association, 1988), pp. 274–278; and Les Carlson and

Sanford Grossbart, 'Parental Style and Consumer Socialization of Children', *Journal of Consumer Research*, June 1988, pp. 77–94.

35 For various views see Reinhold Bergler and Ulrike Six, *Psychologie des Fernsehens* (Bern: Huber, 1979); F. Bockelmann, J. Huber, and A. Middelmann, *Werbefernsehkinder* (Berlin: Spiess, 1979); Joann Paley Galst and Mary Alice White, 'The Unhealthy Persuader: The Reinforcing Value of Television and Children's Purchase-Influencing Attempts at the Supermarket', *Child Development*, 47, 1976, pp. 1089–1096; Arnold Hermanns, *Sozialisation durch Werbung* (Düsseldorf: Berterlsmann, 1972); and Brian M. Young, *Television Advertising and Children* (Oxford: Clarendon, 1990).

36 Peter S. H. Leeflang and W. Fred van Raaij, 'The Changing Consumer in the European Union: A 'Meta-Analysis" ', *International Journal of Research in Marketing*, 1995, pp. 373–387.

37 For a review of a number of these, see Patrick E. Murphy and William A. Staples, 'A Modernized Family Life Cycle', *Journal of Consumer Research*, June 1979, pp. 12–22.

38 Ibid. For other approaches and discussion, see Frederick W. Derrick and Alane K. Lehfeld, 'The Family Life Cycle: An Alternative Approach', *Journal of Consumer Research*, September 1980, pp. 214–217; Mary C. Gilly and Ben M. Enis, 'Recycling the Family Life Cycle: A Proposal for Redefinition', in *Advances in Consumer Research*, vol. 8, ed. Andrew Mitchell (Ann Arbor, MI: Association for Consumer Research, 1982), pp. 271–276; and Janet Wagner and Sherman Hanna, 'The Effectiveness of Family Life Cycle Variables in Consumer Expenditure Research', *Journal of Consumer Research*, December 1983, pp. 281–291.

39 Klaus G. Grunert, Suzanne C. Grunert, Wolfgang Glatzer, and Heiner Imkamp, 'The Changing Consumer in Germany', *International Journal of Research in Marketing*, December 1995, pp. 417–433; Ole Stenvinkel Nilsson and Hans Stubbe Solgaard, 'The Changing Consumer in Denmark', *International Journal of Research in Marketing*, 1995, pp. 405–416; John Saunders and Jim Saker, 'The Changing Consumer in the UK', *International Journal of Research in Marketing*, 1994, pp. 477–489.

40 Margaret Ambry, 'The Age of Spending', *American Demographics*, November 1990, pp. 16–23, 52.

41 This section is adapted from Eugene H. Fram, 'The Time Compressed Shopper', *Marketing Insights*, Summer 1991, pp. 34–39; and Eugene H. Fram and Joel Axelrod, 'The Distressed Shopper', *American Demographics*, October 1990, pp. 44–45.

Chapter 16

1 Johan Arndt, *Market Segmentation, Theoretical and Empirical Dimensions* (Tromsø: Universitetsforlaget, 1974); Hermann Freter, 'Strategien, Methoden und Modelle der Marktsegmentierung bei der Markterfassung und Marktbearbeitung', *DBW – die Betriebswirtschaft*, 1980, pp. 453–463; Janet Hoek, Philip Gendall, and Don Esslemont, 'Market Segmentation: A Search for the Holy Grail?', *Journal of Marketing Practice: Applied Marketing Science*, 1, 1996, pp. 25–34; and Bruno Stegmüller and Petra Hempel, 'Empirischer Vergleich unterschiedlicher Marktsegmentierungsansätze über die Segmentpopulationen', *Marketing-ZFP*, no. 1, 1996, pp. 25–32.

2 Andrew Lorenz, 'The Driving Test', *Marketing Business*, no. 54, November 1996, pp. 12–15.

3 Günther Haedrich, Frank Gussek, and Torsten Tomcza, 'Differenzierte Marktbearbeitung und Markterfolg im Reiseveranstaltermarkt der Bundesrepublik Deutschland', *Marketing-ZFP*, 1989, pp. 11–18.

4 Robert Dolan, 'Marketing Turnarounds', *European Management Journal*, 13, 1995, pp. 239–244.

5 Alfred S. Boote, 'Psychographic Segmentation in Europe', *Journal of Advertising Research*, no. 6, 1983, pp. 19–25.

6 Joseph T. Plummer, 'The Concept and Application of Life Style Segmentation', *Journal of Marketing*, January 1974, p. 33.

7 See Søren Askegaard, 'Livsstilsbegrebet: Problemer og muligheder', *Ledelse & Erhvervsøkonomi*, no. 2, 1993, pp. 91–101; Thomas E. Banning, *Lebensstilorientierte Marketing-Theorie* (Heidelberg: Physica, 1987); Tim Bowles, 'Does Classifying People by Lifestyle Really Help the Advertiser?', *European Research*, February 1988, pp. 17–24; Peter Sampson, 'People Are People the World Over: The Case for Psychological Market Segmentation', *Marketing and Research Today*, 4, 1992, pp. 236–244; Pierre Valette-Florence, 'A Causal Analysis of the Predictive Power of Selected Life-Style Indicators' (Brussels: Paper presented the 1st EIASM Workshop on Value and Lifestyle Research in Marketing, 1991); and William D. Wells, 'Psychographics: A Critical Review', *Journal of Marketing Research*, May 1975, pp. 196–213; and John L. Lastovicka, 'On the Validation of Lifestyle Traits: A Review and Illustration', *Journal of Marketing Research*, February 1982, pp. 126–138.

8 W. Thomas Anderson and Linda L. Golden, 'Life Style and Psychographics: A Critical Review and Recommendation', in *Advances in Consumer Research*, vol. 11, ed. Thomas C. Kinnear (Provo, UT: Association for Consumer Research, 1984), pp. 405–411.

9 Liisa Uusitalo, *Consumption Style and Way Of Life* (Helsinki: Helsinki School of Economics, 1979).

10 Klaus G. Grunert, Karen Brunsø, and Søren Bisp, 'Food-Related Life Style: Development of a Cross-Culturally Valid Instrument for Market Surveillance', in *Values, Lifestyles, and Psychographics*, eds. Lynn Kahle and Larry Chiagouris (Hillsdale, NJ: Erlbaum, 1997), pp. 337–354.

11 Results for Spain can be found in Lone Bredahl and Klaus G. Grunert, 'Identificacion de los Estilos de Vida Alimenticios en España', *Investigación Agraria. Economía*, 2, 1997, pp. 247–263; and results for France in Klaus G. Grunert, Allan Baadsgaard, Hanne Hartvig Larsen, and Tage Koed Madsen, *Market Orientation in Food and Agriculture* (Boston, MA: Kluwer, 1996).

12 Russell I. Haley, 'Benefit Segmentation: A Decision-Oriented Research Tool', *Journal of Marketing*, July 1968, pp. 30–35; also see Russell I. Haley, 'Beyond Benefit Segmentation', *Journal of Advertising Research*, August 1971, pp. 3–8; Russell I. Haley, 'Benefit Segmentation – 20 Years Later', *Journal of Consumer Marketing*, 2, 1983, pp. 5–13; and Hans Mühlbacher and Günther Botschen, 'Benefit-Segmentierung von Dienstleistungsmärkten', *Marketing-ZFP*, no. 3, 1990, pp. 159–168.

13 Russell I. Haley, 'Benefit Segmentation – 20 Years Later', *Journal of Consumer Marketing*, 2, 1983, pp. 5–13

14 Yvette M. Eimers, Rik G. M. Pieters, and Theo M. M. Verhallen, 'Product Evaluation as a Function of Consumer Type and Usage Situation: Towards an Alternative Segmentation Base', in *Proceedings of the IAREP/SABE Joint Annual Conference*, eds. Gerrit Antonides and W. Fred van Raaij (Rotterdam: Erasmus University, 1994), pp. 32–51.

15 Russell W. Belk, 'A Free Response Approach to Developing Product Specific Consumption Situation Taxonomies', in *Analytic Approaches to Product and Marketing Planning*, ed. Allan D. Shocker (Cambridge, MA: Marketing Science Institute, 1979).

16 Peter R. Dickson, 'Person-Situation: Segmentation's Missing Link', *Journal of Marketing*, Fall 1982, p. 57.

17 Ibid., p. 61.

18 It should be noted that the concept of 'positioning' is somewhat ambiguous in the marketing literature and is used in a number of different ways. See John P. Maggard, 'Positioning Revisited', *Journal of Marketing*, January 1976, pp. 63–73.

19 David A. Aaker and J. Gary Shansby, 'Positioning Your Product', *Business Horizons*, May–June 1982, pp. 36–62.

20 Shirley Young, Leland Ott, and Barbara Feigin, 'Some Practical Considerations in Market Segmentation', *Journal of Marketing Research*, August 1978, p. 405.

Chapter 17

1 For example, see Ursula Hansen and Ingo Schoenheit, *Verbraucherzufriedenheit und Beschwerdeverhalten* (Frankfurt: Campus, 1987); Hans Kasper, 'On Problem Perception, Dissatisfaction, and Brand Loyalty', *Journal of Economic Psychology*, 3, 1988, pp. 387–397; Richard L. Oliver, 'A Cognitive Model of the Antecedents and Consequences of Satisfaction Decisions', *Journal of Marketing Research*, November 1980, pp. 460–469; Richard L. Oliver and Wayne S. De Sarbo, 'Response Determinants in Satisfaction Judgments', *Journal of Consumer Research*, March 1988, pp. 495–507; Richard L. Oliver and John E. Swan, 'Equity and Disconfirmation Perceptions as Influences on Merchant and Product Satisfaction', *Journal of Consumer Research*, December 1989, pp. 372–383; and Robert A. Westbrook and Richard L. Oliver, 'The Dimensionality of Consumption Emotion Patterns and Consumer Satisfaction', *Journal of Consumer Research*, June 1991, pp. 84–91; and Richard L. Oliver, *Satisfaction: A Behavioral Perspective on the Consumer* (New York, NY: McGraw-Hill, 1997).

2 David A. Garvin, 'What Does 'Product Quality' Really Mean?', *Sloan Management Review*, 1, 1984, pp. 25–43.

3 Klaus G. Grunert, 'Food Quality: A Means–End Perspective', *Food Quality and Preference*, 3, 1995, pp. 171–176; Jonathan Gutman and Scott D. Alden, 'Adolescents' Cognitive Structures of Retail Stores and Fashion Consumption: A Means–End Chain Analysis of Quality', in *Perceived Quality – How Consumers View Stores and Merchandise*, eds. Jacob Jacoby and Jerry C. Olson (Lexington, MA: Lexington, 1985), pp. 99–114; and Valarie A. Zeithaml, 'Consumer Perceptions of Price, Quality, and Value: A Means–End Model and Synthesis of Evidence', *Journal of Marketing*, 3, 1988, pp. 2–22.

4 The model is based on sources like Esben Sloth Andersen, 'The Evolution of Credence Goods: A Transaction Approach to Product Specification and Quality Control', MAPP working paper no. 21 (Aarhus: The Aarhus School of Business, 1994); Jerry C. Olson and Jacob Jacoby, 'Cue Utilization in the Quality Perception Process', in *Proceedings, Third Annual Conference of the Association For Consumer Research*, ed. M. Venkatesan (Chicago, IL: Association For Consumer Research, 1972), pp. 167–169 ; Carsten Stig Poulsen, Hans Jørn Juhl, Kai Kristensen, Anne C. Bech, and Erling Engelund, 'Quality Guidance and Quality Formation', *Food Quality and Preference*, 2, 1996, pp. 127–135; Jan-Benedict E. M. Steenkamp and Hans C. M. van Trijp, 'Quality Guidance: A Consumer-Based Approach to Food Quality Improvement Using Partial Least Squares', *European Review of Agricultural Economics*, 21, 1996, pp. 195–215; Jan-Benedict E. M. Steenkamp, 'Conceptual Model of the Quality Perception Process', *Journal of Business Research*, 4, 1990, pp. 309–333.

5 Dick A. Francken and W. Fred van Raaij, 'Socio-Economic and Demographic Determinants of Consumer Problem Perception', *Journal of Consumer Policy*, 1985, pp. 303–314; Dick A. Francken, 'Postpurchase Consumer Evaluations, Complaint Actions and Repurchase Behavior', *Journal of Economic Psychology*, 1983, pp. 273–290; Ursula Hansen and Ingo Schoenheit, *Verbraucherzufriedenheit und Beschwerdeverhalten* (Frankfurt: Campus, 1987); Hans Kasper, 'On Problem Perception, Dissatisfaction, and Brand Loyalty', *Journal of Economic Psychology*, 3, 1988, pp. 387–397; Heribert Meffert and Manfred Bruhn, 'Beschwerdeverhalten und Zufriedenheit von Konsumenten', *Die Betriebswirtschaft*, 4, 1981,

pp. 597–613; Marsha L. Richens, 'Negative Word-of-Mouth by Dissatisfied Consumers: A Pilot Study', *Journal of Marketing*, Winter 1983, p. 69; Jagdip Singh, 'Consumer Complaint Intentions and Behavior: Definitional and Taxonomical Issues', *Journal of Marketing*, January 1988, pp. 93–107; Jagdip Singh, 'A Typology of Consumer Dissatisfaction Response Styles', *Journal of Retailing*, Spring 1990, pp. 57–98.

6 Ursula Hansen and Kurt Jeschke, 'Nachkaufmarketing – Ein neuer Trend im Konsumgüter-marketing?', *Marketing-ZFP*, 2, 1992, pp. 88–97.

7 See Larry J. Rosenberg and John A. Czepiel, 'A Marketing Approach to Customer Retention', *Journal of Consumer Marketing*, 2, 1983, pp. 45–51.

8 Jacob Jacoby and Robert W. Chestnut, *Brand Loyalty: Measurement and Management* (New York, NY: Wiley, 1978). Also see Terry Elrod, 'A Management Science Assessment of a Behavioral Measure of Brand Loyalty', in *Advances in Consumer Research*, vol. 15, ed. Michael J. Houston (Provo, UT: Association for Consumer Research, 1987), pp. 481–486; and Richard E. DuWors, Jr., and George H. Haines, Jr., 'Event History Analysis Measures of Brand Loyalty', *Journal of Marketing Research*, November 1990, pp. 485–493; and Rajiv Grover and V. Srinivasan, 'Evaluating the Multiple Effects of Retail Promotions on Brand Loyal and Brand Switching Segments', *Journal of Marketing Research*, February 1992, pp. 76–89.

9 For example, see John W. Keon and Judy Bayer, 'Analyzing Scanner Panel Households to Determine the Demographic Characteristics of Brand Loyal and Variety Seeking Households Using a New Brand Switching Measure', in *AMA Summer Educators' Proceedings*, eds. Russell W. Belk *et al.* (Chicago, IL: American Marketing Association, 1984), pp. 416–420; and George J. Szybillo and Jacob Jacoby, 'Intrinsic Versus Extrinsic Cues as Determinants of Perceived Product Quality', *Journal of Applied Psychology*, 1, 1974, pp. 74–78.

10 David Walker and Simon Knox, 'New Empirical Perspectives on Brand Loyalty: Implications for Market Segmentation and Equity Management', in *Marketing: Progress, Prospects, Perspectives – Proceedings of the 26th Annual Conference of the European Marketing Academy*, eds. David Arnott *et al.* (Warwick: University of Warwick, 1997), pp. 1313–1328; and Hans C. M. van Trijp, Wayne D. Hoyer, and J. Jeffrey Inman, 'Why Switch? Product Category-Level of Explanations for True Variety-Seeking Behavior', *Journal of Marketing Research*, August 1996, pp. 281–292.

11 Henry Assael, *Consumer Behavior and Marketing Action*, 4th edn. (Boston, MA: Kent, 1992).

12. Liisa Lähteenmäki and Hans C. M. van Trijp, 'Hedonic Responses, Variety-Seeking Tendency and Expressed Variety in Sandwich Choices', *Appetite*, 1995, pp. 139–152; Satya Menon and Barbara E. Kahn, 'The Impact of Context on Variety Seeking in Product Choices', *Journal of Consumer Research*, 3, 1995, pp. 285–295; Itamar Simonson, 'The Effect of Purchase Quantity and Timing on Variety-Seeking Behaviour', *Journal of Marketing Research*, 2, 1990, pp. 150–162.

13 Ursula Hansen, 'Verpackung und Konsumentenverhalten', *Marketing-ZFP*, 8, no. 1, 1986, pp. 5–12.

14 See, for example, Tino Bech-Larsen, 'Danish Consumers' Attitudes to the Functional and Environmental Characteristics of Food Packaging', *Journal of Consumer Policy*, 19, 1996, pp. 339–363, and the literature cited there.

15 Ingo Balderjahn, 'Betriebswirtschaftliche Aspekte der Verpackungsverordnung', *Die Betriebswirtschaft*, July–August 1994, pp. 481–499.

16 Wim Biemans and Hanne Harmsen, 'Overcoming the Barriers to Market-Oriented Product Development', *Journal of Marketing Practice*, 2, 1995, pp. 7–25; Angie Craig and Susan Hart, 'Where to Now in New Product Development?', *European Journal of Marketing*, 11, 1992, pp. 1–50; Hanne Harmsen, *Succesfaktorer i Produktudvikling og deres Implementering i*

Mellemstore Danske Fødevarevirksomheder (Aarhus: the Aarhus School of Business, 1995); and Gerhard Schewe, *Key Factors of Successful Innovation Management* (Kiel: Institute For Business Administration, University of Kiel, 1991).

17 Ian Barclay, 'The New Product Development Process: Past Evidence and Future Practical Application', *R&D Management*, 3, 1992, pp. 255–263; Robert G. Cooper and Elko J. Kleinschmidt, *New Products: The Key Success Factors* (Chicago, IL: American Marketing Association, 1990); and Axel Johne and Patricia Snelson, 'Successful Product Innovation in UK and US Firms', *European Journal of Marketing*, 12, 1990, pp. 7–21.

18 Gloria Barczak and David Wilemon, 'Leading the Way', *Product & Process Innovation*, 6, 1991, pp. 21–26; Robert G. Cooper and Elko J. Kleinschmidt, *New Products: The Key Success Factors* (Chicago, IL: American Marketing Association, 1990); and Axel Johne and Patricia Snelson, 'Successful Product Innovation in UK and US Firms', *European Journal of Marketing*, 12, 1990, pp. 7–21.

19 Hubert Gatignon and Thomas S. Robertson, 'A Propositional Inventory for New Diffusion Research', *Journal of Consumer Research*, March 1985, pp. 849–867; and Vijay Mahajan, Eitan Muller, and Frank M. Bass, 'New Product Diffusion Models in Marketing: A Review and Directions for Research', *Journal of Marketing*, January 1990, pp. 1–26.

20 Mary Dee Dickerson and James W. Gentry, 'Characteristics of Adopters and Non-Adopters of Home Computers', *Journal of Consumer Research*, September 1983, pp. 225–235. Also see William E. Warren, C. L. Abercrombie, and Robert L. Berl, 'Characteristics of Adopters and Nonadopters of Alternative Residential Long-Distance Telephone Services', in *Advances in Consumer Research*, vol. 15, ed. Michael J. Houston (Provo, UT: Association for Consumer Research, 1987), pp. 292–298.

21 Elizabeth C. Hirschman, 'Innovativeness, Novelty Seeking, and Consumer Creativity', *Journal of Consumer Research*, December 1980, pp. 283–295.

22 Hubert Gatignon and Thomas S. Robertson, 'A Propositional Inventory for New Diffusion Research', *Journal of Consumer Research*, March 1985, p. 861.

Chapter 18

1 See, for example, Lee Benham, 'The Effect of Advertising on The Price of Eyeglasses', *Journal of Law and Economics*, 15, 1972, pp. 337–352; and Peter Doyle, 'Economic Aspects of Advertising: A Survey', *Economic Journal*, September 1968, pp. 570–602.

2 For a good general overview see Werner Kroeber-Riel, *Strategie und Technik der Werbung* (Stuttgart: Kohlhammer, 1988).

3 C. Whan Park, Bernard J. Jaworski, and Deborah J. MacInnis, 'Strategic Brand Concept Image Management', *Journal of Marketing*, October 1986, pp. 135–145; and Thomas J. Reynolds and Jonathan Gutman, 'Advertising Is Image Management', *Journal of Advertising Research*, February–March 1984, pp. 27–37.

4 Bernhard Swoboda, 'Wirkungen interaktiver Medien am Point of Sale', *Marketing-ZFP*, 4, 1996, pp. 253–266; and Klaus Wenke, 'Direktvertrieb und Neue Medien', *Marketing-ZFP*, 4, 1981, pp. 251–258.

5 Otto Ottesen, 'Buyer Initiative: Ignored, But Imperative for Marketing Management', *Tidvise Skrifter*, 15, 1995, pp. 1–46.

6 Otto Ottesen, *Markedskommunikasjon*, 2nd edn. (Copenhagen: Handelshøjskolens Forlag, 1997).

7 Cornelia Zanger and Frank Sistenich, 'Eventmarketing', *Marketing-ZFP*, 4, 1996, pp. 233–242.

8   See the examples in Tony Meenaghan, 'Current Developments and Future Directions in Sponsorship', *International Journal of Advertising*, 1, 1998, pp. 3–28; Arnold Hermanns and Michael Püttmann, 'Internationales Musik-Sponsoring – Grundlagen und Fallbeispiele aus der Pop-Musik', *Jahrbuch der Absatz- und Verbaruchsforschung*, 3, 1989, pp. 277–291.

9   Orla Nielsen, *Sportssponsering* (Copenhagen: Civiløkonomernes Forlag, 1986).

10 Alan J. Bush and Gregory W. Boller, 'Rethinking the Role of Television Advertising during Health Crises: A Rhetorical Analysis of the Federal AIDS Campaigns', *Journal of Advertising*, 20, no. 1, 1991, pp. 28–37.

11 This section is adapted from John R. Rossiter and Larry Percy, *Advertising and Promotion Management* (New York, NY: McGraw-Hill, 1987), pp. 129–164.

12 Rao Unnava and Robert E. Burnkrant, 'Effects of Repeating Varied Ad Executions on Brand Name Memory', *Journal of Marketing Research*, November 1991, pp. 406–416.

13 Kevin Lane Keller, 'Memory and Evaluation Effects in Competitive Advertising Environments', *Journal of Consumer Research*, March 1991, pp. 463–476.

14 James R. Bettman, *An Information Processing Model of Consumer Choice* (Reading, MA: Addison Wesley, 1979).

15 Punam Anand and Brian Sternthal, 'Ease of Message Processing as a Moderator of Repetition Effects in Advertising', *Journal of Marketing Research*, August 1990, pp. 345–353.

16 Banwari Mittal, 'The Relative Roles of Brand Beliefs and Attitude toward the Ad as Mediators of Brand Attitude: A Second Look', *Journal of Marketing Research*, May 1990, pp. 209–219.

17 Cornelia Pechmann and David W. Stewart, 'The Effects of Comparative Advertising on Attention, Memory, and Purchase Intentions', *Journal of Consumer Research*, September 1990, pp. 180–191.

18 Michael Wahl, 'Eye POPping Persuasion', *Marketing Insights*, 1989, pp. 130–134.

19 Aradhna Krishna, 'Effect of Dealing Patterns on Consumer Perceptions of Deal Frequency and Willingness to Pay', *Journal of Marketing Research*, November 1991, pp. 441–451.

20 Greg Harris, 'The Implications of Low-involvement Theory for Advertising Effectiveness', *International Journal of Advertising*, 1987, pp. 207–221; and George M. Zinkhan and Claes Fornell, 'A Test of the Learning Hierarchy in High- and Low-Involvement Situations', in *Advances in Consumer Research*, vol. 16, ed. Thomas K. Srull (Provo, UT: Association for Consumer Research, 1989), pp. 152–159.

21 Michael Wahl, 'Eye POPping Persuasion', *Marketing Insights*, 1989, pp. 130–134.

22 Preben Sepstrup, 'The Electronic Dilemma of Television Advertising', in *Broadcasting Finance in Transition*, eds. Jay G. Blumler and T. J. Nossiter (Oxford: Oxford University Press, 1991), pp. 359–381.

23 Laura Bird, 'Loved the Ad. May (or May Not) Buy the Product', *The Wall Street Journal*, 7 April 1994, p. B1.

24 Richard L. Celsi and Jerry C. Olson, 'The Role of Involvement in Attention and Comprehension Processes', *Journal of Consumer Research*, September 1988, pp. 210–224; Klaus G. Grunert, 'Automatic and Strategic Processes in Advertising Effects', *Journal of Marketing*, 4, 1996, pp. 88–101; Michael J. Houston, Terry L. Childers, and Susan E. Heckler, 'Picture-Word Consistency and the Elaborative Processing of Advertisements', *Journal of Marketing Research*, November 1987, pp. 359–369; and Deborah J. MacInnis, Christine Moorman, and Bernard J. Jaworski, 'Enhancing and Measuring Consumers' Motivation, Opportunity, and Ability to Process Brand Information from Ads', *Journal of Marketing*, October 1991, pp. 32–53.

25 Alan G. Sawyer and Daniel J. Howard, 'Effects of Omitting Conclusions in Advertisements to Involved and Uninvolved Audiences', *Journal of Marketing Research*, November 1991, pp. 467–474.

26 Mary Jane Schlinger, 'A Profile of Responses to Commercials', *Journal of Advertising Research*, April 1979, pp. 37–46; and David A. Aaker and Douglas M. Stayman, 'Measuring Audience Perceptions of Commercials and Relating Them to Ad Impact', *Journal of Advertising Research*, August–September 1990, pp. 7–18.

27 Christian Derbaix and Joël Bree, 'The Impact of Children's Affective Reactions Elicited by Commercials on Attitudes toward the Advertisement and The Brand', *International Journal of Research in Marketing*, 3, 1997, pp. 207–229. See Andrew A. Mitchell and Jerry C. Olson, 'Are Product Attribute Beliefs the Only Mediator of Advertising Effects on Brand Attitude?', *Journal of Marketing Research*, August 1981, pp. 318–332; and Meryl Paula Gardner, 'Does Attitude toward the Ad Affect Brand Attitude under a Brand Evaluation Set?', *Journal of Marketing Research*, May 1985, pp. 192–198.

28 Thomas J. Olney, Morris B. Holbrook, and Rajeev Batra, 'Consumer Responses to Advertising: The Effects of Ad Content, Emotions, and Attitude toward the Ad on Viewing Time', *Journal of Consumer Research*, March 1991, pp. 440–453.

29 Scott B. MacKenzie, Richard J. Lutz, and George E. Belch, 'The Role of Attitude toward the Ad as a Mediator of Advertising Effectiveness: A Test of Competing Explanations', *Journal of Marketing Research*, May 1986, pp. 130–143; Andrew A. Mitchell, 'The Effect of Verbal and Visual Components of Advertisements on Brand Attitudes and Attitude toward the Advertisement', *Journal of Consumer Research*, June 1986, pp. 12–24; Pamela M. Homer, 'The Mediating Role of Attitude toward the Ad: Some Additional Evidence', *Journal of Marketing Research*, February 1990, pp. 78–86; and Douglas M. Stayman and Rajeev Batra, 'Encoding and Retrieval of Ad Affect in Memory', *Journal of Consumer Research*, May 1991, pp. 232–239.

30 Richard E. Petty, John T. Cacioppo, and David Schumann, 'Central and Peripheral Routes to Advertising Effectiveness: The Moderating Role of Involvement', *Journal of Consumer Research*, September 1983, pp. 135–146.

31 Richard L. Celsi and Jerry C. Olson, 'The Role of Involvement in Attention and Comprehension Processes', *Journal of Consumer Research*, September 1988, pp. 210–224; and Deborah J. MacInnis and C. Whan Park, 'The Differential Role of Characteristics of Music on High- and Low-Involvement Consumers' Processing of Ads', *Journal of Consumer Research*, September 1991, pp. 161–173.

32 Richard L. Celsi and Jerry C. Olson, 'The Role of Involvement in Attention and Comprehension Processes', *Journal of Consumer Research*, September 1988, pp. 201–224; Deborah J. MacInnis and C. Whan Park, 'The Differential Role of Characteristics of Music on High- and Low-Involvement Consumers' Processing of Ads', *Journal of Consumer Research*, September 1991, pp. 161–173; David W. Schumann, Richard E. Petty, and D. Scott Clemons, 'Predicting the Effectiveness of Different Strategies of Advertising Variation: A Test of the Repetition–Variation Hypotheses', *Journal of Consumer Research*, September 1990, pp. 192–202; and H. Rao Unnava and Robert E. Burnkrant, 'An Imagery-Processing View of the Role of Pictures in Print Advertisements', *Journal of Marketing Research*, May 1991, pp. 226–231.

33 Manoj Hastak and Jerry C. Olson, 'Assessing the Role of Brand-Related Cognitive Responses as Mediators of Communication Effects on Cognitive Structure', *Journal of Consumer Research*, March 1989, pp. 444–456; and John L. Swasy and James M. Munch, 'Examining the Target of Receiver Elaborations: Rhetorical Question Effects on Source Processing and Persuasion', *Journal of Consumer Research*, 11 March 1985, pp. 877–886.

34 Andrew A. Mitchell and Jerry C. Olson, 'Are Product Attribute Beliefs the Only Mediator of Advertising Effects on Brand Attitude?' *Journal of Marketing Research*, August 1981, pp. 318–332; Meryl Paula Gardner, 'Does Attitude toward the Ad Affect Brand Attitude

under a Brand Evaluation Set?', *Journal of Marketing Research*, May 1985, pp. 192–198; Thomas J. Olney, Morris B. Holbrook, and Rajeev Batra, 'Consumer Responses to Advertising: The Effects of Ad Content, Emotions, and Attitude toward the Ad on Viewing Time', *Journal of Consumer Research*, March 1991, pp. 440–453; Scott B. MacKenzie, Richard J. Lutz, and George E. Belch, 'The Role of Attitude toward the Ad as a Mediator of Advertising Effectiveness: A Test of Competing Explanations', *Journal of Marketing Research*, May 1986, pp. 130–143; Andrew A. Mitchell, 'The Effect of Verbal and Visual Components of Advertisements on Brand Attitudes and Attitude toward the Advertisement', *Journal of Consumer Research*, June 1986, pp. 12–24; Pamela M. Homer, 'The Mediating Role of Attitude toward the Ad: Some Additional Evidence', *Journal of Marketing Research*, February 1990, pp. 78–86; and Douglas M. Stayman and Rajeev Batra, 'Encoding and Retrieval of Ad Affect in Memory', *Journal of Consumer Research*, May 1991, pp. 232–239.

35 For example, Heribert Gierl and Tanja Nadine Ertel, 'Die Wirkung von Werbeanzeigen für unbekannte Marken von Low-involvement-Produkten', *Jahrbuch der Absatz- und Verbrauchsforschung*, 1, 1993, pp. 87–104; and Elisabeth Tolle, 'Der Einfluß ablenkender Tätigkeiten auf die Werbewirkung von Rundfunkspots', *Marketing-ZFP*, 1988, pp. 261–270.

36 Richard L. Celsi and Jerry C. Olson, 'The Role of Involvement in Attention and Comprehension Processes', *Journal of Consumer Research*, September 1988, pp. 210–224; Manoj Hastak and Jerry C. Olson, 'Assessing the Role of Brand-Related Cognitive Responses as Mediators of Communication Effects on Cognitive Structure', *Journal of Consumer Research*, March 1989, pp. 444–456; and Deborah J. MacInnis, Christine Moorman, and Bernard J. Jaworski, 'Enhancing and Measuring Consumers' Motivation, Opportunity, and Ability to Process Brand Information from Ads', *Journal of Marketing*, October 1991, pp. 32–53.

37 Barry L. Bayus, 'Word of Mouth: The Indirect Effects of Marketing Efforts', *Journal of Advertising Research*, June–July 1985, pp. 31–39.

38 See David Berger, 'Theory into Practice: The FCB Grid', *European Research*, January 1986, pp. 35–46; Richard Vaughn, 'How Advertising Works: A Planning Model', *Journal of Advertising Research*, October 1980, pp. 27–33; and Richard Vaughn, 'How Advertising Works: A Planning Model Revisited', *Journal of Advertising Research*, February–March 1986, pp. 57–66.

39 Roberto Friedman and V. Parker Lessig, 'A Framework of Psychological Meaning of Products', in *Advances in Consumer Research*, vol. 13, ed. Richard J. Lutz (Provo, UT: Association for Consumer Research, 1986), pp. 338–342.

40 Julie A. Edell, 'Nonverbal Effects in Ads: A Review and Synthesis', in *Nonverbal Communication in Advertising*, eds. David Stewart and Sidney Hecker (Lexington, MA: Lexington Books, 1988); Werner Kroeber-Riel, 'Emotional Product Differentiation by Classical Conditioning', in *Advances in Consumer Research*, vol. 11, ed. Thomas C. Kinnear (Ann Arbor, MI: Association for Consumer Research, 1984), pp. 538–543; and Marian Chapman Burke and Julie A. Edell, 'The Impact of Feelings on Ad-Based Affect and Cognition', *Journal of Marketing Research*, February 1989, pp. 69–83.

41 See the analysis of means–end chains for think and feel products in Christel Claeys, Ann Swinnen, and Piet Vanden Abeele, 'Consumers' Means–End Chains for "Think" and "Feel" Products', *International Journal of Research in Marketing*, 1995, pp. 193–208.

42 Meryl P. Gardner and Roger A. Strang, 'Consumer Response to Promotions: Some New Perspectives', in *Advances in Consumer Research*, vol. 11, ed. Thomas C. Kinnear (Ann Arbor, MI: Association for Consumer Research, 1984), pp. 420–425.

43 Thomas J. Reynolds and John P. Rochon, 'Means–End Based Advertising Research: Copy Testing Is Not Strategy Assessment', *Journal of Business Research*, 22, 1991, pp. 131–142.

44 Material for this section is derived from Jerry C. Olson and Thomas J. Reynolds, 'Understanding Consumers' Cognitive Structures: Implications for Advertising Strategies', in *Advertising and Consumer Psychology*, eds. Larry Percy and Arch Woodside (Lexington, MA: Lexington Books, 1983), pp. 77–90.

45 For instance, see Thomas J. Reynolds and Alyce Byrd Craddock, 'The Application of the MECCAS Model to the Development and Assessment of Advertising Strategy: A Case Study', *Journal of Advertising Research*, April–May 1988, pp. 43–54.

46. For example, see Thomas J. Reynolds and Charles Gengler, 'A Strategic Framework for Assessing Advertising: The Animatic vs. Finished Issue', *Journal of Advertising Research*, 31, 1991, pp. 61–72.

47 Hiroshi Kosaka, 'A Global Marketing Strategy Responding to National Cultures', *Marketing and Research Today*, 4, 1992, pp. 245–255; Barbara Mueller, 'Multinational Advertising: Factors Influencing the Standardized vs. Specialized Approach', *International Marketing Review*, 1, 1991, pp. 7–19; Ravlos Michaels, 'The Standardization Versus Adaptation Issue in International Advertising', in *Marketing Thought and Practice in the 1990's*, ed. George J. Avlonitis (Athens: European Marketing Academy, 1989), pp. 1533–1544; and Bruce Seifert and John Ford, 'Are Exporting Firms Modifying Their Product, Pricing and Promotion Policies?', *International Marketing Review*, 6, 1989, pp. 53–68.

48 Barton W. Weitz, 'Relationship between Salesperson Performance and Understanding of Customer Decision Making', *Journal of Marketing Research*, November 1978, p. 502. Also see Barton W. Weitz, 'Effectiveness in Sales Interactions: A Contingency Framework', *Journal of Marketing*, Winter 1981, pp. 85–103. For other views on salesperson effectiveness, see David M. Szymanski, 'Determinants of Selling Effectiveness: The Importance to the Personal Selling Concept', *Journal of Marketing*, January 1988, pp. 64–77; and Gilbert A. Churchill, Neil M. Ford, Steven W. Hartley, Jr., and Orville C. Walker, Jr., 'The Determinants of Salesperson Performance: A Meta-Analysis', *Journal of Marketing Research*, May 1985, pp. 103–118.

49 Barton A. Weitz, Harish Sujan, and Mita Sujan, 'Knowledge, Motivation and Adaptive Behavior: A Framework for Improving Selling Effectiveness', *Journal of Marketing Research*, October 1986, pp. 174–191.

50 Harish Sujan, 'Smarter versus Harder: An Exploratory Attributional Analysis of Salespeople's Motivations', *Journal of Marketing Research*, February 1986, pp. 41–49; Kaylene C. Williams and Rosann L. Spiro, 'Communication Style in the Salesperson-Customer Dyad', *Journal of Marketing Research*, November 1985, pp. 434–442; and Rosann L. Spiro and Barton A. Weitz, 'Adaptive Selling: Conceptualization, Measurement, and Nomological Validity', *Journal of Marketing Research*, February 1990, pp. 61–69.

51 Albert C. Bemmaor and Dominique Mouchoux, 'Measuring the Short-Term Effect of In-Store Promotion and Retail Advertising on Brand Sales: A Factorial Experiment', *Journal of Marketing Research*, May 1991, pp. 202–214.

52 For a review of various measures of advertising effectiveness, see David W. Stewart, Connie Pechmann, Srinivasan Ratneshwar, John Stroud, and Beverly Bryant, 'Advertising Evaluation: A Review of Measures', in *Marketing Communications – Theory and Research*, eds. Michael J. Houston and Richard J. Lutz (Chicago, IL: American Marketing Association, 1985), pp. 3–6. For a discussion of copy testing, see Benjamin Lipstein and James P. Neelankavil, 'Television Advertising Copy Research: A Critical Review of the State of the Art', *Journal of Advertising Research*, April–May 1984, pp. 19–25; Joseph T. Plummer, 'The Role of Copy Research in Multinational Advertising', *Journal of Advertising Research*, October–November 1986, pp. 11–15; and Harold M. Spielman, 'Copy Research: Facts and Fictions', *European Research*, November 1987, pp. 226–231.

53 Stephan Buck and Alan Yates, 'Television Viewing, Consumer Purchasing and Single Source Research', *Journal of the Market Research Society*, 3, 1986, pp. 225–233.

54 Lawrence D. Gibson, 'Not Recall', *Journal of Advertising Research*, February–March 1983, pp. 39–46; Herbert E. Krugman, 'Low Recall and High Recognition of Advertising', *Journal of Advertising Research*, February–March 1986, pp. 79–86; and Jan Stapel, 'Viva Recall: Viva Persuasion', *European Research*, November 1987, pp. 222–225.

55 Marvin E. Goldberg and Jon Hartwick, 'The Effects of Advertiser Reputation and Extremity of Advertising Claim on Advertising Effectiveness', *Journal of Consumer Research*, September 1990, pp. 172–179; and Arne Krogh Nielsen and Lorenz C. Andersen, 'Comparability in the Measurement of Advertising Persuasion', in *Effective Advertising – Can Research Help?* (Amsterdam: ESOMAR, 1983).

56 Jerry C. Olson, Daniel R. Toy, and Philip A. Dover, 'Do Cognitive Responses Mediate the Effects of Advertising Content on Cognitive Structure?', *Journal of Consumer Research*, December 1982, pp. 245–262; Arno J. Rethans, John L. Swasy, and Lawrence J. Marks, 'Effects of Television Commercial Repetition, Receiver Knowledge, and Commercial Length: A Test of the Two-Factor Model', *Journal of Marketing Research*, February 1986, pp. 50–61; and Daniel R. Toy, 'Monitoring Communication Effects: A Cognitive Structure/Cognitive Response Approach', *Journal of Consumer Research*, June 1982, pp. 66–76.

57 Jonathan Gutman and Thomas J. Reynolds, 'Coordinating Assessment to Strategy Development: An Advertising Assessment Paradigm Based on the MECCAS Approach', in *Advertising and Consumer Psychology*, vol. 3, eds. Jerry Olson and Keith Sentis (New York, NY: Praeger, 1987).

58 For example: Ulrich Bernhard, 'Das Verfahren der Blickaufzeichnung', in *Innovative Marktforschung*, ed. Forschungsgruppe Konsum und Verhalten (Würzburg: Physica, 1983), pp. 105–121; Gabi Jeck-Schlottmann, 'Anzeigenbetrachtung bei geringem Involvement', *Marketing-ZFP*, 1, 1988, pp. 33–34; Werner Kroeber-Riel, 'Effects of Emotional Pictorial Elements in Ads Analyzed by Means of Eye Movement Monitoring', in *Advances in Consumer Research*, vol. 11, ed. Thomas C. Kinnear (Provo, UT: Association for Consumer Research, 1984), pp. 591–596; Werner Kroeber-Riel, 'Activation Research: Psychobiological Approaches in Consumer Research', *Journal of Consumer Research*, 5, 1979, pp. 240–250; and Andreas Steiger, *Computergestützte Aktivierungsmessung in der Marketingforschung* (Frankfurt: Peter Lang, 1988).

Chapter 19

1 For good reviews, see Els Gijsbrechts, 'Prices and Pricing Research in Consumer Marketing: Some Recent Developments', *International Journal of Research in Marketing*, 2 1993, pp. 115–153; and Vithala R. Rao, 'Pricing Research in Marketing: The State of the Art', *Journal of Business*, January 1984, p. S39.

2 For a model and approach to measuring this cost, see Steven M. Shugan, 'The Cost of Thinking', *Journal of Consumer Research*, September 1980, pp. 99–111. Also see Howard Marmorstein, Dhruv Grewal, and Raymond P. H. Fishe, 'The Value of Time Spent in Price Comparison Shopping: Survey and Experimental Evidence', *Journal of Consumer Research*, June 1992, pp. 52–61; and France Leclerc, Bernd H. Schmitt, and Laurette Dube, 'Waiting Time and Decision Making: Is Time Like Money?', *Journal of Consumer Research*, June 1995, pp. 110–119.

3 Els Gijsbrechts, 'Prices and Pricing Research in Consumer Marketing: Some Recent Developments', *International Journal of Research in Marketing*, 2, 1993, pp. 115–153; Klaus G.

Grunert, 'Price Transparency, Competition and the Consumer Interest. Economic Reasoning and Behavioral Evidence', in *Price Information and Public Price Controls, Consumers and Market Performance*, ed. Monique Goyens (Brussels: E. Story-Scientia, 1986), pp. 23–48; Vithala R. Rao, 'Pricing Research in Marketing: The State of the Art', *Journal of Business*, January 1984, p. S39; Jerry C. Olson, 'Price as an Informational Cue: Effects on Product Evaluations', in *Consumer and Industrial Buyer Behavior*, eds. Arch G. Woodside, Jagdish N. Sheth, and Peter D. Bennett (New York, NY: Elsevier-North Holland Publishing, 1977), pp. 267–286; Valarie A. Zeithaml, 'Issues in Conceptualizing and Measuring Consumer Response to Price', in *Advances in Consumer Research*, vol. 11, ed. Thomas C. Kinnear (Provo, UT: Association for Consumer Research, 1984), pp. 612–616; and Kent B. Monroe and R. Krishman, 'A Procedure for Integrating Outcomes across Studies', in *Advances in Consumer Research*, vol. 10, eds. Richard P. Bagozzi and Alice M. Tybout (Ann Arbor, MI: Association for Consumer Research, 1983), pp. 503–508.

4 Jacob Jacoby and Jerry C. Olson, 'Consumer Response to Price: An Attitudinal, Information Processing Perspective', in *Moving Ahead with Attitude Research*, eds. Yoram Wind and Marshall Green (Chicago, IL: American Marketing Association, 1977), pp. 73–86. Also see Jerry C. Olson, 'Implications of an Information Processing Approach to Pricing Research', in *Theoretical Developments in Marketing*, eds. Charles W. Lamb, Jr. and Patrick M. Dunne (Chicago, IL: American Marketing Association, 1980), pp. 13–16.

5 Abhijit Biswas and Edward A. Blair, 'Contextual Effects of Reference Prices in Retail Advertisements', *Journal of Marketing*, July 1991, pp. 1–12; and Glenn E. Mayhew and Russell S. Winer, 'An Empirical Analysis of Internal and External Reference Prices Using Scanner Data', *Journal of Consumer Research*, June 1992, pp. 62–70.

6 Dhruv Grewal and Julie Baker, 'Do Retail Store Environment Factors Affect Consumers' Price Acceptability? An Empirical Examination', *International Journal of Research in Marketing*, 2, 1994, pp. 107–117.

7 Peter R. Dickson and Alan G. Sawyer, 'The Price Knowledge and Search of Supermarket Shoppers', *Journal of Marketing*, July 1990, p. 49.

8 Klaus G. Grunert, 'Price Transparency, Competition and the Consumer Interest. Economic Reasoning and Behavioral Evidence', in *Price Information and Public Price Controls, Consumers and Market Performance*, ed. Monique Goyens (Brussels: E. Story-Scientia, 1986), pp. 23–48.

9 Hermann Diller, 'Das Preiswissen von Konsumenten', *Marketing-ZFP*, 1, 1988, pp. 17–24.

10 Abhijit Biswas and Edward A. Blair, 'Contextual Effects of Reference Prices in Retail Advertisements', *Journal of Marketing*, July 1991, pp. 1–12.

11 Valarie A. Zeithaml, 'Consumer Response to In-Store Price Information Environments', *Journal of Consumer Research*, March 1982, pp. 357–368.

12 David A. Aaker and Gary Ford, 'Unit Pricing Ten Years Later: A Replication', *Journal of Marketing*, Winter 1983, pp. 118–122.

13 For complete works on pricing strategy, see Kent B. Monroe, *Pricing: Making Profitable Decisions*, 2nd edn. (New York, NY: McGraw-Hill, 1990); Hermann Simon, *Price Strategy and Price Management* (New York, NY: Wiley, 1989); and Robert J. Dolan and Hermann Simon, *Power Pricing* (New York, NY: Free Press, 1996).

14 Devangana Bhat and Sakina Pittalwala, 'Transporting Brand Equity Across Price Segments', *Marketing and Research Today*, 2, 1993, pp. 97–101.

15 See, for example, Ingo Balderjahn, 'Der Einsatz der Conjoint-Analyse zur empirischen Bestimmung von Preisresponsefunktionen', *Marketing-ZFP*, 1994, pp. 12–20; Hermann Simon and Eckhard Kucher, 'Die Bestimmung empirischer Preisabsatzfunktionen', *Zeitschrift für Betriebswirtschaft*, 1, 1988, pp. 171–183.

Chapter 20

1 Hans Engstrøm and Hanne Hartvig Larsen, *Husholdningernes Butiksvalg* (Copenhagen: Arnold Busck, 1987).

2 For excellent discussions of these topics, see C. Samuel Craig, Avijit Ghosh, and Sara McLafferty, 'Models of the Retail Location Process: A Review', *Journal of Retailing*, Spring 1984, pp. 5–36; and Michael Levy and Barton A. Weitz, *Retailing Management*, 3rd edn. (Boston, MA: McGraw-Hill, 1998), chap. 8.

3 The figures are from Michael Levy and Barton A. Weitz, *Retailing Management*, 3rd edn. (Boston, MA: McGraw-Hill, 1998).

4 Gary F. McKinnon, J. Patrick Kelly, and E. Doyle Robison, 'Sales Effects of Point-of-Purchase In-Store Signing', *Journal of Retailing*, Summer 1981, pp. 49–63.

5 Joseph A. Bellizzi, Ayn E. Crowley, and Ronald W. Hasty, 'The Effects of Color in Store Design', *Journal of Retailing*, Spring 1983, pp. 21–45. Also see Gerald J. Gorn, Amitava Chattopadhyay, Tracey Yi, and Darren W. Dahl, 'Effects of Color as an Executional Cue in Advertising: They're in the Shade', *Management Science* (in press) for further use of colour in marketing.

6 J. B. Wilkinson, J. Barry Mason, and Christie H. Paksoy, 'Accessing the Impact of Short-Term Supermarket Strategy Variables', *Journal of Marketing Research*, February 1982, pp. 72–86. Also see Rockney G. Walters and Scott B. MacKenzie, 'A Structural Equations Analysis of the Impact of Price Promotions on Store Performance', *Journal of Marketing Research*, February 1988, pp. 51–63; and V. Kumar and Robert P. Leone, 'Measuring the Effect of Retail Store Promotions on Brand and Store Substitution', *Journal of Marketing Research*, May 1988, pp. 178–185.

7 Ronald E. Milliman, 'Using Background Music to Affect the Behavior of Supermarket Shoppers', *Journal of Marketing*, Summer 1982, pp. 86–91. For additional support for these ideas, see Ronald E. Milliman, 'The Influence of Background Music on the Behavior of Restaurant Patrons', *Journal of Consumer Research*, September 1986, pp. 286–289. Also see Richard Yalch and Eric Spangenberg, 'Effects of Store Music on Shopping Behavior', *Journal of Consumer Marketing*, Spring 1990, pp. 55–63; and Gordon C. Bruner II, 'Music, Mood, and Marketing', *Journal of Marketing*, October 1990, pp. 94–104.

8 Information in this section is taken from Eric R. Spangenberg, Ayn E. Crowley and Pamela W. Henderson, 'Improving Store Environment: Do Olfactory Cues Affect Evaluations and Behavior?' *Journal of Marketing*, April 1966, pp. 67–80.

9 Eva Thelen and Arch G. Woodside, 'What Evokes the Brand or Store? Consumer Research on Accessibility Theory Applied to Modeling Primary Choice', *International Journal of Research in Marketing*, 2, 1997, pp. 125–145; and Arch G. Woodside and Eva M. Thelen, 'Accessing Memory and Customer Choice: Benefit-To-Store (Brand) Retrieval Models That Predict Purchase', *Marketing and Research Today*, November 1996, pp. 260–267.

10 Andrea Gröppel and Brian Bloch, 'An Investigation of Experience-Orientated Consumers in Retailing', *International Review of Retail, Distribution and Consumer Research*, 1, 1990, pp. 101–118; Eberhard Bost, *Ladenatmosphäre und Konsumentenverhalten* (Heidelberg: Physica, 1987); and Robert J. Donovan and John R. Rossiter, 'Store Atmosphere: An Environmental Psychology Approach', *Journal of Retailing*, Spring 1982, pp. 34–57.

11 Robert J. Donovan and John R. Rossiter, 'Store Atmosphere: An Environmental Psychology Approach', *Journal of Retailing*, Spring 1982, pp. 34–57.

12 Eberhard Bost, *Ladenatmosphäre und Konsumentenverhalten* (Heidelberg: Physica, 1987).

13 Kordelia Spies, Friedrich Hesse, and Kerstin Loesch, 'Store Atmosphere, Mood and Purchasing Behavior', *International Journal of Research in Marketing*, 1, 1997, pp. 1–18.

14 Andrea Gröppel and B. Bloch, 'An Investigation of Experience-Orientated Consumers in Retailing', *International Review of Retail, Distribution, and Consumer Research*, 1, 1990, pp. 101–118.

15 Eberhard Bost, *Ladenatmosphäre und Konsumentenverhalten* (Heidelberg: Physica, 1987).

16 Kordelia Spies, Friedrich Hesse, and Kerstin Loesch, 'Store Atmosphere, Mood and Purchasing Behavior', *International Journal of Research in Marketing*, 1, 1997, pp. 1–18.

17 Andrea Gröppel, 'Evolution of Retail Categories – An Explanation from Consumers' Point of View', in *European Advances in Consumer Research*, vol. 2, ed. Flemming Hansen (Provo, UT: Association For Consumer Research, 1995), pp. 237–245.

18 For further discussion of store loyalty, see Kau Ah Keng and Andrew S. C. Ehrenberg, 'Patterns of Store Choice', *Journal of Marketing Research*, November 1984, pp. 399–409. Also see Susan Spiggle and Murphy A. Sewell, 'A Choice Sets Model of Retail Selection', *Journal of Marketing*, April 1987, pp. 97–111.

19 Joseph Alba, John Lynch, Barton Weitz, Chris Janiszeski, Richard Lutz, Alan Sawyer, and Stacy Wood, 'Interactive Home Shopping: Consumer, Retailer, and Manufacturer Incentives to Participate in Electronic Marketplaces', *Journal of Marketing*, July 1997, pp. 38–53.

Chapter 21

1 Gerhard Scherhorn, 'Die Funktionsfähigkeit von Konsumgütermärkten', in *Marktpsychologie als Sozialwissenschaft*, ed. Martin Irle (Göttingen: Hogrefe, 1983), pp. 45–150; and Gerhard Scherhorn, *Verbraucherinteresse und Verbraucherpolitik* (Göttingen: Schwartz, 1975).

2 Phillip Kotler, 'What Consumerism Means for Marketers', *Harvard Business Review*, May–June 1972, pp. 48–57. Also see Joseph V. Anderson, 'Power Marketing: Its Past, Present, and Future', *Journal of Consumer Marketing*, Summer 1987, pp. 5–13.

3 Hans Rask Jensen, 'The Relevance of Alternative Paradigms as Guidelines for Consumer Policy and Organized Consumer Action', *Journal of Consumer Policy*, 9, no. 4, 1986, pp. 389–405.

4 D. Jeschke, *Konsumentensouveränität in der Marktwirtschaft – Idee, Kritik, Realität* (Berlin: Duncker & Humblot, 1975).

5 Gerhard Bodenstein and Hans Leuer, 'Obsoleszenz – Ein Synonym für die Warenproduktion in entfalteten Marktwirtschaften', *Journal of Consumer Policy*, 14, no. 1, 1981, pp. 39–50.

6 See, for example, Deborah Roedder John and Catherine A. Cole, 'Age Differences in Information Processing: Understanding Deficits in Young and Elderly Consumers', *Journal of Consumer Research*, December 1986, pp. 297–315; and Gary J. Gaeth and Timothy B. Heath, 'The Cognitive Processing of Misleading Advertising in Young and Old Adults: Assessment and Training', *Journal of Consumer Research*, March 1988, pp. 471–482.

7 For example, see Richard W. Olshavsky and Donald H. Granbois, 'Consumer Decision Making: Fact or Fiction?' *Journal of Consumer Research*, September 1979, pp. 93–100.

8 Eberhard Kuhlmann, *Verbraucherpolitik* (Munich: Vahlen, 1990).

9 See, for example, Gary J. Gaeth, and Timothy B. Heath, 'The Cognitive Processing of Misleading Advertising in Young and Old Adults: Assessment and Training', *Journal of Consumer Research*, 14, no. 1, 1987, pp. 43–54; Klaus G. Grunert and Konrad Dedler, 'Misleading Advertising: In Search of a Measurement Methodology', *Journal of Public Policy & Marketing*, 4, 1985, pp. 153–165; Pauline M. Ippolito and Alan D. Mathios, 'The Regulation of Science-Based Claims in Advertising', *Journal of Consumer Policy*, 4, 1990, pp. 413–446; Jerry C. Olson and Philip A. Dover, 'Cognitive Effects of Deceptive Advertising', *Journal of Marketing Research*, February 1978, pp. 29–38; and J. Edward Russo, Barbara L. Metcalf,

and Debra Stephens, 'Identifying Misleading Advertising', *Journal of Consumer Research*, 1981, pp. 119–131.

10 See, for example, James R. Bettman, 'Issues in Designing Consumer Information Environments', *Journal of Consumer Research*, 2, 1975, pp. 169–177; Monroe Friedman, 'Consumer Use of Informational Aids in Supermarkets', *Journal of Consumer Affairs*, 1, 1977, pp. 78–89; B. Lundgren, 'Effect of Nutritional Information on Consumer Responses', in *Criteria of Food Acceptance – How Man Chooses What He Eats*, eds. J. Solms and R. L. Hall (Zürich: Forster, 1981), pp. 27–33; and Kim R. Robertson and Roger Marshall, 'Amount of Label Information Effects on Perceived Product Quality', *International Journal of Advertising*, 6, 1987, pp. 199–205.

11 Klaus Peter Kaas and Klaus Tölle, 'Der Einfluß von Warentestinformationen auf das Informationsverhalten von Konsumenten', *Journal of Consumer Policy*, 5, no. 4, 1981, pp. 293–309; Günter Silberer, 'The Impact of Comparative Product Testing Upon Consumers: Selected Findings of a Research Project', *Journal of Consumer Policy*, 8, no. 1, 1985, pp. 1–27; and Hans B. Thorelli and Jack L. Engledow, 'Information Seekers and Information Systems: A Policy Perspective.', *Journal of Marketing*, Spring 1980, pp. 9–27.

12 Wolfgang Fritz, Harald Hilger *et al.*, 'Testnutzung und Testwirkungen im Bereich der Konsumgüterindustrie', in *Warentest und Unternehmen*, eds. Hans Raffée and Günter Silberer (Frankfurt: Campus, 1984), pp. 27–114; and Hans Raffée and Wolfgang Fritz, 'The Effects of Comparative Product Testing on Industry and Trade: Findings of a Research Project', *Journal of Consumer Policy*, 7, no. 4, 1984, pp. 423–437.

13 Heiko Steffens and Günter Rosenberger, 'The Arduous Task of Defining and Developing Consumer Education', *Journal of Consumer Policy*, 9, no. 1, 1986, pp. 65–78.

14 Gerhard Scherhorn, 'The Goal of Consumer Advice: Transparency or Autonomy?', *Journal of Consumer Policy*, 8, no. 2, 1985, pp. 133–151.

Glossary of Consumer Behaviour Terms

abstract attributes Intangible, subjective characteristics of the product, such as the quality of a blanket or the stylishness of a car.

accessibility The probability that a meaning concept will be (or can be) activated from memory. Highly related to top-of-mind awareness and salience.

accidental exposure Occurs when consumers come in contact with marketing information in the environment that they haven't deliberately sought out. Compare with **intentional exposure**.

accretion The most common type of cognitive learning. Adding new knowledge, meanings, and beliefs to an associative network.

acculturation The process by which people in one culture or subculture learn to understand and adapt to the meanings, values, lifestyles, and behaviours of another culture or subculture.

activation The essentially automatic process by which knowledge, meanings, and beliefs are retrieved from memory and made available for use in cognitive processing.

adopter categories A classification of consumers based on the time of initial purchase of a new product. Typically, five groups are considered including **innovators**, **early adopters**, **early majority**, **late majority**, and **laggards**.

adoption curve A visual representation of the cumulative percentage of persons who adopt a new product across time.

advertising Any paid, nonpersonal presentation of information about a product, brand, company, or store.

affect A basic mode of psychological response that involves a general positive/negative feeling and varying levels of activation or arousal of the physiological system that consumers experience in their bodies. Compare with **cognition**. See also **affective responses**.

affective responses Consumers can experience four types of affective responses – emotions, specific feelings, moods, and evaluations – that vary in level of intensity and arousal.

age subcultures Groups of people defined in terms of age categories (teens, elderly) with distinctive behaviours, values, beliefs, and lifestyles.

AIO An acronym standing for activities, interest, and opinions. AIO measures are the primary method for investigating consumer lifestyles and forming psychographic segments.

aspirational group A reference group an individual consumer wants to join or be similar to.

associative network An organized structure of knowledge, meanings, and beliefs about some concept such as a brand. Each meaning concept is linked to other concepts to form a network of associations.

attention The process by which consumers select information in the environment to interpret. Also the point at which consumers become conscious or aware of certain stimuli.

attitude   A person's overall evaluation of a concept. An attitude is an affective response at a low level of intensity and arousal. General feelings of favourability or liking.

attitude-change strategies   The multiattribute attitude model suggests several processes for changing attitudes, including adding a new salient belief, making a salient belief stronger, and making a salient belief more positive. See **attitude** and **multiattribute attitude models**.

attitude models   See **multiattribute attitude models**.

attitude towards objects (A_o)   Consumers' overall evaluation (like/dislike) of an object such as a product or store. May be formed in two quite different ways: a cognitive process that involves relatively controlled and conscious integration of information about the object, and a largely automatic and unconscious response of the affective system.

attitude towards the ad (A_{ad})   Consumers' affective evaluations of advertisements themselves, not the product or brand being promoted.

attitude towards the behaviour or action (A_{act})   The consumer's overall evaluation of a specific behaviour.

automatic processing   Cognitive processes tend to become more automatic – to require less conscious control and less cognitive capacity – as they become more practised and familiar.

baby boomers   The very large cohort of people born during the years after the Second World War from about 1946 until about 1964. The baby boomers constitute a huge market with tremendous spending power. See **market segmentation**.

behaviour   Overt acts or actions that can be directly observed.

behavioural approach   An approach to studying consumer behaviour that focuses on the relationship between overt behaviour and the environment.

behavioural intention (BI)   A plan to perform an action – 'I intend to go shopping this afternoon.' Intentions are produced when beliefs about the behavioural consequences of the action and social normative beliefs are considered and integrated to evaluate alternative behaviours and select among them.

behaviour change strategy   A strategy developed to change the frequency or quality of a behaviour.

behaviour effort   The effort consumers expend when making a purchase.

belief   The perceived association between two concepts. May be represented cognitively as a proposition. Beliefs about products often concern their attributes or functional consequences. For example, after trying a new brand of toothpaste, a consumer may form a belief that it has a minty taste. Beliefs are synonymous with knowledge and meaning in that each term refers to consumers' cognitive representations of important concepts.

belief evaluation (e_i)   Reflects how favourably the consumer perceives an attribute or consequence associated with a product.

belief strength (b_i)   The perceived strength of association between an object and its relevant attributes or consequences.

benefits   Desirable consequences or outcomes that consumers seek when purchasing and using products and services.

benefit segmentation   The process of grouping consumers on the basis of the benefits they seek from the product. For example, the toothpaste market may include one segment seeking cosmetic benefits such as white teeth and another seeking health benefits such as decay prevention.

brand choice   The selection of one brand from a consideration set of alternative brands.

brand commitment   The degree to which consumers are engaged/involved in the purchase of a brand.

brand equity   The value of a brand. From the consumer's perspective, brand equity is reflected by the brand attitude based on beliefs about positive product attributes and favourable consequences of brand use.

brand indifference   A purchasing pattern characterized by a low degree of brand loyalty.

brand loyalty   The degree to which a consumer consistently purchases the same brand within a product class.

brand switching   A purchasing pattern characterized by a change from one brand to another.

buyer-initiated market communication   Market communication where the buyer actively addresses the seller for information on, e.g. products and prices, or with complaints, or expressing satisfaction.

categorization   A cognitive process by which objects, events, and persons are grouped together and responded to in terms of their class membership rather than their unique characteristics.

category accessibility   The degree to which a consumer can activate a category of meaning from memory. A cognitive approach to describing modelling effects, where the process of viewing a model's behaviour involves the activation of an interpretative schema.

central route to persuasion   One of two types of cognitive processes by which persuasion occurs. In the central route, consumers focus on the product messages in the ad, interpret them, form beliefs about product attributes and consequences, and integrate these meanings to form brand attitudes and intentions. See **peripheral route to persuasion**.

choice   Choice among alternative actions or behaviours is the outcome of the integration processes involved in consumer decision making. See also **behavioural intention**.

choice alternatives   The different product classes, product forms, brands, or models available for purchase.

choice criteria   The specific product attributes or consequences used by consumers to evaluate and choose from a set of alternatives.

classical conditioning   A process through which a previously neutral stimulus, by being paired with an unconditioned stimulus, comes to elicit a response very similar to the response originally elicited by the unconditioned stimulus.

cognition   The mental processes of interpretation and integration and the thoughts and meanings they produce.

cognitive activity   The mental thought and effort involved in interpreting and integrating information, as in a purchase decision. Often considered as a cost.

cognitive approach   An approach which explains human behaviour by the intake, interpretation, storage, and use of information from the environment.

cognitive dissonance   A psychologically uncomfortable condition brought about by an imbalance in thoughts, beliefs, attitudes, or behaviour. For example, behaving in a way that is inconsistent with one's beliefs creates cognitive dissonance and a motivation to reduce the inconsistency.

cognitive learning   The processes by which knowledge structures are formed and changed as consumers interpret new information and acquire new meanings and beliefs.

cognitive processing   The mental activities (both conscious and unconscious) by which external information in the environment is transformed into meanings and combined to form evaluations of objects and choices about behaviour.

cognitive representations   The subjective meanings that reflect each person's personal interpretation of stimuli in the environment and of behaviour.

cognitive response   The thoughts one has in response to a persuasive message such as support arguments or acceptance thoughts, counterarguments, and curiosity thoughts.

cognitive structure   The organization of knowledge and experience in memory.

communication   A type of behaviour that marketers attempt to increase, involving two basic audiences: consumers who can provide the company with marketing information and consumers who can tell other potential consumers about the product and encourage them to buy it.

communication model   A simple representation of human communication processes that focuses on characteristics of the source, message, medium, and receiver.

communication process   The physical and social processes involved in transferring messages and meaning from a source to a receiver. See also **communication model**.

comparative product tests   Tests carried out by, e.g. consumer organizations, which compare products within the same product category on different criteria. They are often published in consumer magazines.

compatibility   The degree to which a product is consistent with consumers' current cognitions and behaviours.

compensatory integration processes   In decision making, the combination of all the salient beliefs about the consequences of the choice alternatives to form an overall evaluation or attitude (A_{act}) towards each behavioural alternative. See also **noncompensatory integration processes**.

compensatory rule   In evaluating alternatives, the compensatory rule suggests a consumer will select the alternative with the highest overall evaluation on a set of criteria. Criteria evaluations are done separately and combined such that positive evaluations can offset (or compensate for) negative evaluations. This term is also called compensatory process, compensatory integration procedure, and compensatory model. See also **noncompensatory integration processes**.

competitive influences   Actions of competing firms intended to affect each other and consumers.

complete environment   The total complex of physical and social stimuli in the external world that are potentially available to the consumer.

comprehension   The cognitive processes involved in interpreting and understanding concepts, events, objects, and persons in the environment.

concrete attributes   Tangible, physical characteristics of a product such as the type of fibre in a blanket or the front-seat leg room in a car.

conjunctive rule   See **noncompensatory integration processes**.

consensual environment   Those parts of the environment that are attended to and similarly interpreted by a group of people with relatively similar cultural and social backgrounds.

consideration set   A set of alternatives that the consumer evaluates in making a decision. Compare with **evoked set**.

consumer acculturation   The process by which people acquire the ability and cultural knowledge to be a skilled consumer in a different culture or subculture.

consumer advice   Consumer advice deals with a variety of measures designed to help consumers solve problems by personal communication. It is usually carried out by or on the initiative of consumer organizations, but can also be carried out by state institutions or private organizations.

consumer behaviour   (1) The dynamic interaction of affect and cognition, behaviour, and environmental events by which human beings conduct the exchange aspects of their lives; (2) a field of study concerned with (1); (3) a college course concerned with (1); and (4) the overt actions of consumers.

consumer complaints   Specific type of communication by which consumers voice their dissatisfaction with a product or service bought to the manufacturer, the store, or a third party like a government agency or a consumer organization.

consumer decision making   The cognitive processes by which consumers interpret product information and integrate that knowledge to make choices among alternatives.

consumer education   Has the aim of making consumers better and more competent partners in market transactions. Consumer education can deal with topics like understanding the concept of exchange, the selling intent of advertising, the harmful effects of certain products like tobacco and alcohol, the environmental impact of consumer behaviour, and with training ways of comparing and evaluating products and services.

consumer information processing   The cognitive processes by which consumers interpret and integrate information from the environment.

consumer information   Consumer information measures have the aim of making consumers use more and/or better information when choosing between products and services. Measures forcing sellers to make more or different information available to consumers are indirect attempts to influence consumers' use of information. In addition, various types of consumer organization provide information which consumers can use in their decision making. The most well-known ones are comparative product tests and information systems.

consumer policy   A set of policy measures trying to improve the stance of consumers facing sellers in a market economy. Its major subareas are consumer information, consumer advice, consumer education, and consumer protection.

consumer promotion   Marketing tactics, such as coupons and free samples, designed to have a direct impact on consumer purchase behaviour.

consumer purchase mode   The method a consumer uses to shop and purchase from store or nonstore alternatives.

consumer satisfaction   The degree to which a consumer's prepurchase expectations are fulfilled or surpassed by a product.

consumer socialization   How children acquire knowledge about products and services and various consumption-related skills.

consumer–product relationship   The relationship between target consumers and the product or brand of interest. How consumers perceive the product as relating to their goals and values. Important to consider in developing all phases of a marketing strategy. See also **means–end chain**.

consumption situation   The social and physical factors present in the environments where consumers actually use and consume the products and services they have obtained.

consumption   Use of a product.

content of culture   All the beliefs, attitudes, goals, and values shared by most people in a society, as well as the typical behaviours, rules, customs, and norms that most people follow, plus characteristic aspects of the physical and social environment.

continuous reinforcement schedule   A schedule of reinforcement that provides a reward after every occurrence of the desired behaviour.

continuous schedule   Reinforcement is administered after every desired behaviour. Marketers usually try to keep the quality of their products and services constant so that they will be continuously reinforcing every time they are purchased.

corrective advertising   Ads that are mandated to correct the false beliefs created by previous misleading or deceptive advertising.

covert modelling   In this type of modelling, no actual behaviours or consequences are demonstrated; instead, subjects are told to imagine observing a model behaving in various situations and receiving particular consequences.

cross-cultural differences   How the content of culture (meanings, values, norms) differs between different cultures.

cross-cultural research   Studies in which marketers seek to identify the differences and similarities in the cultural meaning systems of consumers living in different societies.

cultural interpenetration   The amount and type of social interaction between newcomers to a culture (immigrants) and people in the host culture. Influences the degree of acculturation the newcomers can attain.

cultural meanings   The shared or similar knowledge, meanings, and beliefs by which people in a social system represent significant aspects of their environments.

cultural process   The process by which cultural meaning is moved or transferred between three locations in a society – the social and physical environment, products and services, and individual consumers.

culture   The complex of learned meanings, values, and behavioural patterns that are shared by a society.

deal proneness   A consumer's general inclination to use promotional deals such as buying on sale or using coupons.

decision   A choice between two or more alternative actions or behaviours. See also **choice** and **behavioural intention**.

decision conflict   Arises when family members disagree about various aspects of the purchase decision such as goals and appropriate choice criteria.

decision making   See **consumer decision making**.

decision plan   The sequence of behavioural intentions produced when consumers engage in problem solving during the decision-making process. See also **behavioural intention**.

diffusion process   The process by which new ideas and products become accepted by a society. See also **adopter categories**.

discriminant consequences   Consequences that differ across a set of alternatives that may be used as choice criteria.

discriminative stimulus   A stimulus that by its mere presence or absence changes the probability of a behaviour. For example, a '50 per cent off' sign in a store window could be a discriminative stimulus.

disjunctive rule   See **noncompensatory integration processes**.

disposition situation   The physical and social aspects of the environments in which consumers dispose of products, as well as consumers' goals, values, beliefs, feelings, and behaviours while in those environments.

dissatisfaction   Occurs when prepurchase expectations are negatively confirmed – that is, when the product performs worse than expected.

dissociative group   A reference group that an individual does not want to join or be similar to.

early adopters   The second group of adopters of a new product.

early majority   The third group of adopters of a new product.

effects hierarchy   A hypothesized hierarchical sequence of effects that market communication may have on consumers. An example is: stimulate category need, brand awareness, brand attitude, brand purchase intention, and facilitate other behaviours.

elaboration   The extensiveness of comprehension processes. The degree of elaboration determines the amount of knowledge or the number of meanings produced during comprehension as well as the richness of the interconnections between those meanings.

Elaboration Likelihood Model (ELM)   A formal model of how consumers comprehend and elaborate information. Two processes are possible, depending on the consumer's level of involvement – the central route and peripheral route. See **elaboration**, **central route to persuasion**, and **peripheral route to persuasion**.

end goal   The most abstract or most basic consequence, need, or value a consumer wants to achieve or satisfy in a given problem-solving situation.

enduring involvement   The personal relevance of a product or activity. See also **intrinsic self-relevance**. Compare with **situational involvement**.

environment   The complex set of physical and social stimuli in consumers' external world.

environmental prominence   The marketing strategy of making certain stimuli obvious or prominent in the environment.

episodic knowledge   Cognitive representations of specific events in a person's life. Compare with **semantic knowledge**.

ethical influences   Basic values concerning right and wrong that constrain marketing practices.

ethnic subcultures   Large social groups based on consumers' ethnic background. In many European countries guest workers and immigrants have created ethnic subcultures.

ethnographic studies   Studies where consumer behaviour is studied in its natural setting by a combination of observational and questioning techniques.

evaluation   An overall judgement of favourable/unfavourable, pro/con, or like/dislike. An attitude towards an object such as a brand, an ad, or a behavioural act.

evoked set   The set of choice alternatives activated directly from memory.

expectancy theory   A possible explanation for modelling, this cognitive theory suggests models influence observer behaviour by influencing their expectations.

expected quality   The quality expected by the consumer before purchase of the product.

experienced quality   The quality experienced by the consumer after purchase and use of the product.

expertise   Occurs when consumers are quite familiar with a product category and specific brands, possessing substantial amounts of declarative and procedural knowledge organized in schemas and scripts.

exposure   Occurs when consumers come into contact with information in the environment, sometimes through their own intentional behaviours and sometimes by accident.

extensive decision making   A choice involving substantial cognitive and behavioural effort, as compared to **limited decision making** and **routinized choice behaviour**.

external reference price   Explicit comparison of the stated price with another price in advertising, catalogues, and so on.

extinction   The process of arranging the environment so that a particular response results in neutral consequences, thus diminishing the frequency of the response over time.

family   A group of at least two people formed on the basis of marriage, cohabitation, blood relationships, or adoption. Families often serve as a basis for various types of consumer analysis.

family decision making   The processes, interactions, and roles of family members involved in making decisions as a group.

family life cycle   A sociological concept that describes changes in families across time. Emphasis is placed on the effects of marriage, births, ageing, and deaths on families and the changes in income and consumption through various family stages.

fixed ratio schedule   A type of reinforcement schedule where every second, third, tenth, and so on response is reinforced.

focal attention   A controlled, conscious level of attention that focuses cognitive processes on relevant or prominent stimuli in the environment. Compare with **preconscious attention**.

Foote, Cone & Belding (FCB) grid   A two-by-two grid developed by the Foote, Cone & Belding advertising agency for analysing consumers and products. The FCB grid categorizes products based on consumers' level of involvement (high or low) and on whether consumers' dominant responses to the product are cognitive or affective (think or feel).

form utility   What occurs when channels convert raw materials into finished goods and services in forms the consumer seeks to purchase.

four stages of acculturation   Four levels of acculturation a newcomer to a culture could achieve, depending on the level of cultural interpenetration honeymoon, rejection, tolerance, and integration stages.

free-flow layout   A store layout that permits consumers to move freely rather than being constrained to movement up and down specific aisles.

functional (or perceived) environment   Those parts of the complete environment that are attended to and interpreted by a particular consumer on a particular occasion.

functional consequences   The immediate outcomes of product use that can be directly experienced by consumers. For instance, a toothpaste may whiten your teeth.

funds access   The ways consumers obtain money for their purchases. Primary marketing issues include the methods consumers use to pay for particular purchases and the marketing strategies used to increase the probability that consumers are able to access their funds for purchase.

general knowledge   The meanings that consumers construct to represent important informational stimuli they encounter in the environment. Compare with **procedural knowledge**.

geodemographic segmentation   A segmentation approach that focuses on local neighbourhood geography, demographics, and other market characteristics to classify actual, addressable, mapable neighbourhoods where consumers live and shop.

geographic subculture   Large social groups defined in geographic terms. For instance, people living in different parts of a country may exhibit cultural differences.

global marketing   An approach that argues for marketing a product in essentially the same way everywhere in the world.

goal hierarchy   The end goal and the subgoals that are involved in achieving it.

grid layout   A store layout where all counters and fixtures are at right angles to each other, with merchandise counters acting as barriers to traffic flow.

group   Two or more people who interact with each other to accomplish some goal. Examples include families, co-workers, bowling teams, and church members.

habituals   Consumers who usually purchase the same product or brand out of habit. They have high brand loyalty but low brand commitment.

heuristics   Propositions connecting an event with an action. Heuristics simplify problem solving. For example, 'buy the cheapest brand' could be a choice heuristic that would simplify purchase choice.

hierarchy of effects model   An early model that depicted consumer response to advertising as a series of stages including awareness, knowledge, liking, preference, conviction, and purchase.

hierarchy of needs   See **Maslow's need hierarchy**.

high involvement   See **involvement**.

household   The people living in a housing unit – a dwelling with its own entrance and basic facilities.

human values   The abstract, broad, general end goals that people are trying to achieve in their lives.

ideal self-concept The ideas, attitudes, and meanings people have about themselves concerning what they would be like if they were perfect or ideal. Compare with **self-concept**.

impulse purchase A purchase choice typically made quickly in-store with little decision-making effort.

inferences Meanings or beliefs that consumers construct to represent the relationships between concepts that are not based on explicit environmental information.

information acquisition situation Includes physical and social aspects of environments where consumers acquire information relevant to a problem-solving goal, such as a store choice or a decision to buy a particular brand.

information contact A common early stage in the purchase sequence that occurs when consumers come into contact with information about the product or brand. This often occurs in promotions, where such contact can be intentional (consumers search newspapers for bargains) or accidental (a consumer just happens to come into contact with a promotion while engaging in some other behaviour). See also **exposure**.

information processing See **consumer information processing**.

information rate The quantity of information drawn from the store environment per unit of time. Thus, the more varied, novel, surprising, and lively the shopping environment, the higher the information rate. The information rate can therefore be used as a summary measure of various elements of the store environment.

information search Consumers' deliberate search for relevant information in the external environment.

information-processing model Used to divide complex cognitive processes into a series of simpler subprocesses that are more easily measured and understood.

informational reference group influence Information from a group that is accepted if the consumer believes it will help achieve a goal.

innovativeness A personality trait to account for the degree to which a consumer accepts and purchases new products and services.

innovators The first group of consumers to adopt a new product.

instrumental conditioning See **operant conditioning**.

instrumental values One of two major types of values proposed by Milton Rokeach. Instrumental values represent preferred modes of conduct or preferred patterns of behaviour. See **terminal values**.

integration process The process by which consumers combine knowledge to make two types of judgement. Attitude formation concerns how different types of knowledge are combined to form overall evaluations of products or brands. Decision making concerns how knowledge is combined to make choices about what behaviours to perform.

intentional exposure Occurs when consumers are exposed to marketing information due to their own intentional, goal-directed behaviour. Compare with **accidental exposure**.

internal reference price The price consumers have in mind for a product.

interpretation processes The processes by which consumers make sense of or determine the meaning of important aspects of the physical and social environment as well as their own behaviours and internal affective states.

interrupts Stimuli that interrupt or stop the problem-solving process, such as unexpected information encountered in the environment.

intrinsic self-relevance A consumer's personal level of self-relevance for a product. Cognitively represented by the general means–end chains of product-self relationships that consumers have learned and stored in memory. Compare with **situational self-relevance**.

involvement   The degree of personal relevance a product, brand, object, or behaviour has for a consumer. Experienced as feelings of arousal or activation and interest or importance. Determined by **intrinsic** and **situational self-relevance**. A *high-involvement* product is one a consumer believes has important personal consequences or will help achieve important personal goals. A *low-involvement product* is one that is not strongly linked to important consequences or goals.

ISTEA model   A model for the process of developing a personal selling promotion strategy; stands for impression, strategy, transmission, evaluation, and adjustment.

knowledge   Cognitive representation of products, brands, and other aspects of the environment that are stored in memory. Also called meanings or beliefs.

laggards   The last group to adopt a new product.

late majority   The next-to-last group to adopt a new product.

level of comprehension   Refers to the different types of meanings that consumers construct during interpretation processes.

levels of abstraction   Consumers' product knowledge is at different levels of abstraction from concrete attributes to more abstract functional consequences to very abstract value outcomes.

levels of product knowledge   Consumers can have different levels of knowledge about products. Product knowledge can be at different levels of abstraction – attributes, functional consequences, psychosocial consequences, and values. Also, consumers have knowledge about levels of products, including product categories, product forms, brands, and models. See **knowledge**.

lexicographic rule   See **noncompensatory integration processes**.

lifestyle   The manner in which people conduct their lives, including their activities, interests, and opinions.

lifestyle segmentation   Procedure where consumers are split into groups according to their lifestyle based on, e.g. AIO items: activities, interest, and opinion.

limited capacity   The notion that the amount of knowledge that can be activated and thought about at one time is limited and quite small.

limited decision making   A choice process involving a moderate degree of cognitive and behavioural effort. See also **extensive decision making**.

low-involvement communication   When involvement is low, the formation of attitudes is very limited or rudimentary, and/or the intention to buy is formed only seconds before the purchase takes place. In these cases it may be quite difficult to shape positive attitudes towards the brand or the purchase by market communication, and the major communication goals may instead be to create brand awareness and to induce trial purchases. Attitudes may then be formed during consumption of the product and may influence future purchases.

loyals   Consumers who with some degree of consistency purchase the same product or brand and have a positive attitude towards it. They have high brand loyalty and high brand commitment.

macro environment   Large-scale environmental characteristics or features, such as the state of the economy, the political climate, or the season of the year. See **environment**.

macro social environment   The broad, pervasive aspects of the social environment that affect the entire society or at least large portions of it, including culture, subculture, and social class.

market communication   Various types of information distributed in different ways (by the seller) to the consumer. Three categories can be defined: advertising, personal selling, and publicity and sponsoring.

market orientation   The organizationwide generation of market intelligence, pertaining to current and future customer needs, dissemination of the intelligence across departments, and organizationwide responsiveness to it.

market segmentation   The process of dividing a market into groups of similar consumers and selecting the most appropriate group(s) for the firm to serve.

marketing concept   A business philosophy that argues organizations should satisfy consumer needs and wants to make profits.

marketing environment   All of the social and physical stimuli in consumers' environments that are under the control of the marketing manager.

marketing strategy   A plan designed to influence exchanges to achieve organizational objectives; a part of the environment consisting of a variety of physical and social stimuli.

Maslow's need hierarchy   A popular theory of human needs developed by Abraham Maslow. The theory suggests humans satisfy their needs in a sequential order starting with physiological needs (food, water, sex) and ranging through safety needs (protection from harm), belongingness and love needs (companionship), esteem needs (prestige, respect of others), and, finally, self-actualization needs (self-fulfilment).

materialism   A multidimensional value held by many consumers in developed countries. Materialism includes possessiveness, envy of other people's possessions, and nongenerosity.

meanings   People's personal interpretations (cognitive representations, knowledge, or beliefs) of stimuli in the environment.

means–end chain   A simple knowledge structure that links product attributes to more functional and social consequences and perhaps to high-level consumer values. Means–end chains organize consumers' product knowledge in terms of its self-relevance.

MECCAS model   Attempts to simplify the difficult task of developing effective advertising strategies by identifying five key factors; stands for means–end chain conceptualization of advertising strategy.

micro environment   Characteristics or features of the immediate, surrounding environment, such as the furnishings in the room where you are or the number of people close by you. See **environment**.

micro social environment   Important aspects of consumers' immediate social environment, especially reference groups and family.

misleading advertising   Advertising that is untruthful, fraudulent, deceitful or that in any other way misinforms the consumer.

modelling   See **vicarious learning**.

modern family life cycle   An extension of the traditional family life cycle including other stages found in modern culture such as divorce, single (never married), and single parents.

multiattribute attitude models   Models designed to predict consumers' attitudes towards objects (such as brands) or behaviours (such as buying a brand) based on their beliefs about and evaluations of associated attributes or expected consequences.

negative reinforcement   Occurs when the frequency of a given behaviour is increased by removing an aversive stimulus. See also **reinforcement**.

noncompensatory integration processes   Choice strategies in which the positive and negative consequences of the choice alternatives do not balance or compensate for each other. See also **compensatory integration processes**. In evaluating alternatives using noncompensatory rules, positive and negative consequences of alternatives do not compensate for each other. Included among the types of noncompensatory integration processes are conjunctive, disjunctive, and lexicographic. The *conjunctive rule* suggests consumers establish a minimum acceptable level for each choice criterion and accept an alternative only if it equals or exceeds the minimum cut-off level for every criterion. The *disjunctive rule* suggests consumers establish acceptable standards for each criterion and accept an alternative if it exceeds the standard on at least one criterion. The *lexicographic rule* suggests consumers rank choice criteria from most to least important and choose the best alternative on the most important criterion.

observability   The degree to which products or their effects can be sensed by other consumers.

open and closed settings   A situation with a limited number of environmental cues and a limited number of possibilities on how to behave can be called a closed setting. A consumer shopping in a supermarket with thousands of options on what to do operates in an open setting. Consumers taking part in laboratory experiments operate in a closed setting. Generalizing behavioural principles from the laboratory to the real consumer world will be easier, the more closed the setting is in which the consumer operates in the real world.

operant conditioning   The process of altering the probability of a behaviour being emitted by changing the consequences of the behaviour.

opportunity to process   The extent to which consumers have the chance to attend to and comprehend marketing information; can be affected by factors such as time pressure, consumers' affective states, and distractions.

overt modelling   The most common form of vicarious learning, this requires that consumers actually observe the model performing the behaviour.

penetration price policy   A pricing strategy that includes a plan to sequentially raise prices after introduction at a relatively low price.

perceived control   Perceived control (PC) reflects to what extent the consumer believes that he or she is actually able to perform a certain behaviour (Shopping at a certain supermarket presupposes that there is such an outlet in the neighbourhood, that one knows where it is, and that there is a means of transportation to get there and to bring the merchandise home after shopping. If some of these preconditions are not met, consumers may not form an intention of shopping there, even though both they and their family have a positive attitude.) The power (p_k) of a factor to assist the action, weighted with the degree to which the consumer believes he or she has access to that factor (c_k) are combined to form PC.

perceived risk   The expected negative consequences of performing an action such as purchasing a product.

peripheral route to persuasion   One of two types of cognitive processes by which persuasion occurs. In the peripheral route the consumer focuses not on the product message in an ad but on 'peripheral' stimuli such as an attractive, well-known celebrity or popular music. Consumers' feelings about these other stimuli may influence beliefs and attitude about the product. Compare with **central route to persuasion**.

person/situation segmentation   Occurs when markets are divided on the basis of the usage situation in conjunction with individual differences of consumers.

personal selling   Direct personal interactions between a salesperson and a potential buyer.

personality   The general, relatively consistent pattern of responses to the environment exhibited by an individual.

persuasion   Refers to the cognitive and affective processes by which consumers' beliefs and attitudes are changed by promotion communications.

physical environment   The collection of nonhuman, physical, tangible elements that comprises the field in which consumer behaviour occurs. Compare with **social environment**.

place utility   Occurs when goods and services are made available where the consumer wants to purchase them.

positioning   See **product positioning**.

positioning by attribute   Probably the most frequently used positioning strategy, this associates a product with an attribute, a product feature, or a customer benefit.

positioning by competitor   A positioning strategy where the explicit or implicit frame of reference is the competition.

positioning by consequence/value   Banks and insurance companies are especially prone to position themselves in terms of consequences or values – some emphasize safety and reassuredness, and family values, whereas others emphasize thriftiness or even fun and enjoyment.

positioning by product class   A positioning strategy involving product-class associations (for example, positioning a margarine with respect to butter).

positioning by product user   A positioning approach where a product is associated with a user or class of users.

positioning by use   A positioning strategy where the product is associated with its use or application.

positioning map   A visual depiction of consumers' perceptions of competitive products, brands, or models on selected dimensions.

positive reinforcement   Occurs when rewards are given to increase the frequency with which a given behaviour is likely to occur. See also **reinforcement**.

possession utility   Occurs when channels facilitate the transfer of ownership of goods to the consumer.

preconscious attention   The highly automatic, largely unconscious selection of certain stimuli for simple cognitive processing. More likely for familiar concepts of low importance. Further processing tends to lead to focal attention.

price elasticity   A measure of the relative change in demand for a product for a given change in monetary price.

price perceptions   Concerned with how price information is comprehended by consumers and made meaningful to them.

problem representation   Consumers' cognitive representation of the various aspects of the decision problem. Includes an end goal, a set of subgoals, relevant product knowledge, and a set of choice rules or simple heuristics by which consumers search for, evaluate, and integrate this knowledge to reach a choice.

problem solving   A general approach to understanding consumer decision making. Focuses on consumers' cognitive representation of the decision as a problem. Important aspects of the problem representation include end goals, subgoals, and relevant knowledge. Consumers construct a decision plan by integrating knowledge within the constraints of the problem representation.

procedural knowledge   Consumers' cognitive representations of how to perform behaviours. See also **script**.

product contact   Occurs when a consumer comes into physical contact with a product.

product knowledge and involvement   Two very important concepts for understanding consumer cognition and affect. Product knowledge and involvement influence how consumers interpret and integrate information during decision making. See **knowledge**, **involvement**, **consumer decision making**, **interpretation processes**, and **integration process**.

product positioning   Designing and executing a marketing strategy to form a particular mental representation of a product or brand in consumers' minds. Typically, the goal is to position the product in some favourable way relative to competitive offerings.

product safety   Product regulations have traditionally dealt with ensuring minimum standards of product safety, especially in cases where the potential safety hazards are hidden and cannot be ascertained by consumers.

product symbolism   The various meanings of a product to a consumer and what the consumer experiences in purchasing and using it.

psychographic segmentation   Dividing markets into segments on the basis of consumer lifestyles.

psychosocial consequences   This term refers to two types of outcomes or consequences of product use: psychological consequences (I feel good about myself) and social consequences (other people are making fun of me).

publicity   Any unpaid form of communication about the marketer's company, products, or brand.

pull strategies   Ways to encourage the consumer to purchase the manufacturer's brand.

punishment   A term used to describe the process of a response being followed by a noxious or aversive event, thus decreasing the frequency of the response.

purchase intention   A decision plan or intention to buy a particular product or brand. See also **behavioural intention**.

push strategies   Ways to enhance the selling efforts of retailers, such as trade discounts.

rate of usage   The rate at which a consumer uses or uses up a product.

reciprocal systems   The idea that affect and cognition, behaviour, and the environment cause and are caused by each other continuously over time.

reference group   People who influence an individual's affect, cognitions, and behaviours.

reinforcement   A consequence that occurs after a behaviour that increases the probability of future behaviour of the same type.

reinforcement schedules   The administration of positive or negative rewards of a behaviour within a specific time span. One can distinguish between a continuous, fixed ratio or variable ratio schedule.

relative advantage   Refers to the degree to which an item has a sustainable, competitive, differential advantage over other product classes, product forms, and brands.

relevant knowledge   Appropriate or useful knowledge activated from memory in the context of a decision or interpretation situation.

respondent conditioning   See **classical conditioning**.

response hierarchy   The total list of behaviours a consumer could perform at any given time arranged from most probable to least probable.

restructuring   A rare type of cognitive learning that occurs when an entire associative network of knowledge is revised, reorganizing old knowledge and creating entirely new meanings. Very complex and infrequent compared with **accretion** and **tuning**.

rights of consumers   The United States has formulated a Consumer Bill of Rights which states that consumers are granted the right to safety, the right to be informed, the right to choose, and the right to be heard.

rights of marketers   A well-known American marketing researcher has summarized the rights granted to marketers in the following way: Sellers have the right to alter the product offering at any time, to distribute the product in any reasonable manner, to introduce any buying schemes they wish, so long as they are not discriminatory, to introduce any product in any size, style, colour, etc., so long as it meets established health and safety requirements, to limit the product guarantee or post-sale services, to price the product as they please so long as they avoid discrimination that is harmful to competition, to promote the product using any resources, media, or message, in any amount, so long as no deception or fraud is involved.

rituals Actions or behaviours performed by consumers to create, affirm, evoke, revise, or obtain desired symbolic cultural meanings.

routinized choice behaviour A purchase involving little cognitive and behavioural effort and perhaps no decision. Purchase could be merely carrying out an existing decision plan. Compare with **limited decision making** and **extensive decision making**.

sales promotions Direct inducements to the consumer to make a purchase, such as price reductions.

salient beliefs The set of beliefs activated in a particular situation; may be represented as an associative network of linked meanings.

scanner data A method for monitoring consumer behaviour by taking advantage of the data generated by supermarket cashiers involving bar-code scanners.

schema An associative network of interrelated meanings that represents a person's declarative knowledge about some concept. Compare with **script**.

script A sequence of productions or mental representations of the appropriate actions associated with particular events. Consumers often form scripts to organize their knowledge about behaviours to perform in familiar situations. Compare with **schema**.

segmentation See **market segmentation**.

segmentation strategy The general approach marketers use to approach markets such as mass marketing, or marketing to one or more segments.

selective exposure A process by which people selectively come into contact with information in their environment. For instance, consumers may avoid marketing information by leaving the room while commercials are on TV.

self-concept The ideas, meanings, attitudes, and knowledge people have about themselves. See also **self-schema**.

self-schema An associative network of interrelated knowledge, meanings, and beliefs about one's self. See also **self-concept**.

semantic knowledge The general meanings and beliefs people have acquired about their world. Compare with **episodic knowledge**.

shaping A process of reinforcing successive approximations of a desired behaviour, or of other required behaviours, to increase the probability of the desired response.

shopping motive Just as different products are chosen by consumers because they believe that their attributes will lead to different self-relevant consequences and ultimately values, different retail categories can be assumed to be chosen by consumers because of different shopping motives. The assumption is that the same consumer will be attracted by different types of shops depending on the motives associated with the purchase.

shopping situation The physical and spatial characteristics of the environments where consumers shop for products and services.

simplicity The degree to which a product is easy for a consumer to understand and use.

situation The ongoing stream of reciprocal interactions between goal-directed behaviours, affective and cognitive responses, and environmental factors that occur over a defined period of time. Situations have a purpose, and a beginning, middle, and end.

situational involvement Temporary interest or concern with a product or a behaviour brought about by the situational context. For example, consumers may become situationally involved with buying a hot water heater if their old one breaks. See also **situational self-relevance**. Compare with **enduring involvement**.

situational self-relevance Temporary feelings of self-relevance due to specific external physical and social stimuli in the environment. Compare with **intrinsic self-relevance**.

skimming price policy A pricing strategy that includes a plan to systematically lower prices after a high-price introduction.

social class A status hierarchy by which groups and individuals are categorized on the basis of esteem and prestige. For example, one classification divides society into upper class, middle class, working class, and lower class.

social environment Includes all human activities in social interactions.

socialization The processes by which an individual learns the values and appropriate behaviour patterns of a group, institution, or culture. Socialization is strongly influenced by family, reference groups, and social class.

social learning theory One of a number of theories of human behaviour.

social stratification See **social class**.

speed Refers to how quickly the benefits of the product are experienced by the consumer.

sponsoring Sponsoring is a hybrid of advertising and publicity. Some sponsoring is pure charity and does not have a market communication objective, but most forms of sponsoring involve explicitly or implicitly some kind of deal that a producer is financially or otherwise supporting an activity and has its name or its products mentioned in the publicity about the activity in turn. Common forms of sponsoring include the sponsoring of sports activities, or individual sports persons or teams. Sponsoring of cultural events is another common form of sponsoring.

spreading activation Through this usually unconscious process, interrelated parts of a knowledge structure may be activated during interpretation and integration processes (or even daydreaming).

store atmosphere Affective and cognitive states that consumers experience in a store but may not be fully conscious of while shopping.

store contact An important aspect of most consumer goods purchases, this includes locating the outlet, travelling to the outlet, and entering the outlet.

store image The set of meanings consumers associate with a particular store.

store layout The basic floor plan and display of merchandise within a store. At a basic level, this influences such factors as how long the consumer stays in the store, how many products the consumer comes into visual contact with, and what routes the consumer travels within the store. Two basic types are *grid* and *free-flow layouts*.

store location Where a store is situated in a specific geographic area.

store loyalty The degree to which a consumer consistently patronizes the same store when shopping for particular types of products.

store patronage The degree to which a consumer shops at a particular store relative to competitive outlets.

subcultures Segments within a culture that share a set of distinguishing meanings, values, and patterns of behaviour that differ from those of the overall culture.

subjective or social norm (SN) Consumers' perceptions of what other people want them to do.

switchers Consumers who purchase whatever product or brand is available. They have both low brand loyalty and commitment.

symbolic meaning The set of psychological and social meanings products have for consumers. More abstract meanings than physical attributes and functional consequences.

terminal values One of two major types of values proposed by Milton Rokeach. Terminal values represent preferred end states of being or abstract, global goals that consumers are trying to achieve in their lives. Compare with **instrumental values**.